9896

Bumsted, J. M., 1938-
   The peoples of Canada : a pre-Confederation
history / J.M. Bumsted. -- Toronto : Oxford University
Press, 1992.
   xiii, 442 p. : ill.

Includes bibliographical references (p. [402]-429) and
index.
06564410   ISBN:0195406907 (pbk.)

1. Canada - History - To 1763 (New France). 2. Canada
- History - 1763-1867. I. Title

J. M. Bumsted

The
Peoples
Of
Canada

A Pre-Confederation
History

Toronto
OXFORD
UNIVERSITY
PRESS
1992

Oxford University Press, 70 Wynford Drive, Don Mills, Ontario M3C 1J9

Toronto   Oxford   New York
Delhi   Bombay   Calcutta   Madras   Karachi   Kuala Lumpur
Singapore   Hong Kong   Tokyo   Nairobi   Dar es Salaam
Cape Town   Melbourne   Auckland   Madrid

and associated companies in
Berlin   Ibadan

This book is printed on permanent (acid-free) paper ∞.

Canadian Cataloguing in Publication Data

Bumsted, J. M., 1938-
    The peoples of Canada : a pre-Confederation
history

Includes bibliographical references and index.
ISBN 0-19-540690-7

1. Canada - History - To 1763 (New France).
2. Canada - History - 1763-1867. I. Title.

FC161.B86 1992   971   C92-094547-3
F1032.B86 1992

Design by Marie Bartholomew

1 2 3 4 - 95 94 93 92

Printed in Canada by Tri-Graphic

To my children

Contents

Maps

Preface

Although the formal contract with Oxford University Press Canada for this by-now two-volume work was signed as long ago as November 1986, it has been more than twenty-five years in the making when I consider my involvement in teaching and researching Canadian history. This period of gestation and writing now appears to be virtually coterminous with the disintegration of the traditional approach to the writing of Canadian history, with its emphasis on progressive nation-building.

Over the last quarter-century the old paradigm of Canadian historical writing that concentrated on such male-dominated subjects as political, constitutional, and military issues from a centralist and élitist perspective has been reduced to tatters. But at the level of the general survey it has remained quite alive. As any current graduate student in Canadian history can explain, destroying a paradigm is much easier than creating a new one. The forces of revisionism, from the mid-1960s on, that pressed against the 'national interpretation' were many and diverse. They included the adoption by Canadian historians of social and economic modes of analysis from France, Britain, and the United States, as well as their responses to new research on hitherto neglected collectivities such as women, native peoples, and ethnic communities. Also important was a general weakening of centralism and a resurgence of regionalism. The result amounted to a new discourse that was much less concerned with the traditional concentration on nation-building, presented in a chronological narrative, than with other matters, including changes and developments at the levels of the family and society—subjects for which the writings of previous generations of Canadian historians hardly contained any context.

In responding to the new scholarship I was faced with several problems of composition and emphasis. One of the most important was the matter of providing narrative and chronology—elements that the new scholarship tends to downplay—for without some such structure many readers would likely be perplexed and bored. Other problems involved the treatment of heroes/heroines and the task of discussing Canadian history in such a way as to develop an informed citizenry. The new scholarship is likely to be highly critical of the nation's traditional leadership and its institutional structures, at the same time insisting on a new set of values and assumptions. Some scholars have also worried about employing what they consider to be anachronistic ways of interpreting Canada's past by imposing the present upon the past. Every generation, however, rewrites the past to suit its own agenda. In my case the general history I have written combines insights I have gained from a wide reading of recent scholarship on Canadian social history with essential political, military, and constitutional content. Even though the narrative is broken into many sections, I hope its flow is evident. While the chronological presentation is not usual—each main period is examined over and over again in differing contexts—it will perhaps highlight subjects that in other treatments are somewhat buried.

This work attempts to incorporate the new scholarship by embracing new perspectives and new emphases while by no means disregarding either key events in the traditional framework or the values of traditional historiography. It is mainly about the peoples of Canada (rather than the political evolution of the nation) set in a matrix in which politics is only one of many important aspects of historical development. This volume covers the First Nations before contact with the early European visitors; the explorers, and the settlement of New France along the St Lawrence; the Atlantic region; the Conquest and its aftermath; the development of British North America and its society; the agricultural, commercial, and political changes that necessitated the federation of the provinces of British North America; and the expansion of the domain of the Dominion of Canada, and its economic strength, to 1885. That year marked both the completion of the Canadian Pacific Railway and the suppression of the Northwest Rebellion, which had a far-reaching and hardening effect on French-English relations in central Canada. While this study treats the implementation of the British North America Act, on 1 July 1867, as an important and transforming event, it does not view Confederation as a crucial dividing point.

In this history—which has been structured around multiplicities, not a simple duality—women, native peoples, and other groups, including the poor, are intrinsic, as are the regional and ethnic aspects of the Canadian experience and its cultural manifestations. The task, as I have seen it, has not been to give equal amounts of attention to every collectivity, social grouping, and region, but to ensure that the reader is constantly reminded of the importance of all these elements.

It is impossible, in this post-modern era, not to be conscious of the fact that every word written makes some sort of political statement; that even inclusions, exclusions, and connections can be political. Traditional surveys of Canadian history could be relatively impervious to criticism about their references (or lack of references) to matters we treat seriously today; once one had noted the slight or non-inclusion of women, native peoples, or Atlantic Canada, for example, there was little that could be said about what was absent. But now, when these and other topics have an essential place in any discussion of Canadian history, criticism from all directions is being invited by any author who attempts to include them. Suffice it to say that while both volumes of this work cover many matters that are highly controversial, no attempt has been made to please everyone in treating them. I believe the risk of criticism is well worth running, however, in relating a history of the Canadian peoples that attempts to transcend, while never disregarding, matters that have traditionally been associated with it.

As I firmly believe that everything connects and relationships are omnipresent, the structure of this work—as conveyed in the chapter headings—offers only one way of putting things together. There are obviously others. But I hope readers will find that the way I have chosen presents the development of Canada, its people, and its affairs freshly and accurately—and that to some degree they have been illuminated.

In the years of writing this work I have been greatly helped by many people—beginning with my students, whom I thank for their continual stimulation and their demands that I think about some connections I would rather have avoided. My editor, William Toye, has been an essential part of the development of this history, challenging me constantly and attempting to keep my writing lucid. In this regard Sally Livingston, who read the proofs, was particularly helpful. My wife, Wendy Owen, has aided me in many ways, both intangibly and—in advising on the fruits of her unpublished research on Canadian imperialism that resonates through that chapter in the post-Confederation volume—most tangibly. My children have helped keep me sane. The librarians in the Government Documents section of the University of Manitoba's Dafoe Library have performed great feats of locating material; and Pat Wright and his colleagues at the St John's College Library have been invariably helpful. A number of friends and colleagues have read parts of this work in manuscript. They include Kerry Abel, Doug Cole, Barry Ferguson, Robin Fisher, John Kendle, Allan Levine, Larry McCann, Terry Murphy, John Reid, Andy Robb, John Thompson, and Paul Voisey. Their comments have resulted in great improvements to the text. But I alone am responsible for the final product, including any errors of omission or commission.

JMB
Stanhope,
Prince Edward Island
June 1992

chapter one

The People of Early North America

The place was a point at the entrance to Gaspé Harbour on the Gulf of St Lawrence. The time was the morning of 24 July 1534. On an overcast day with a heavy mist—typical summer weather on this coast—a party of French sailors, working under their captain, Jacques Cartier, had erected a large wooden cross thirty feet high. Below the cross-bar they had carefully placed a shield with three *fleurs-de-lys*, and above it a board on which they had carved in large Gothic letters VIVE LE ROY DE FRANCE. This was raised in the presence of many natives, who had arrived a few days earlier to fish for mackerel and had already received gifts of trinkets.

After the Frenchmen returned to their ships, an Indian whom the visitors took to be a chief arrived in a canoe with four others. According to the account of Cartier's voyage:

> ...pointing to the cross he made us a long harangue, making the sign of the cross with two of his fingers; and then he pointed to the land all around about, as if he wished to say that all this region belonged to him, and that we ought not to have set up this cross without his permission.[1]

The Frenchmen beckoned to the Indians to come closer; then they forced the natives to board their ship. They indicated that they wished to take away two of the young men—the text calls them '*ses filz*', the chief's sons—promising to return them eventually to the harbour. The young men were dressed in shirts and red caps and given brass chains to wear round their necks. Their 'old rags' of fur were handed to the other Indians, each of whom was sent away with a hatchet and two knives. Later that day more canoes arrived filled with Indians who had come to say good-bye to the captives and to give them gifts of fish. 'These made signs to us that they would not pull down the cross, delivering at the same time several harangues which we did not understand.' The next day the Frenchmen weighed anchor and left the harbour. They sailed back to France with the two Indians, who were greatly admired. Cartier did, however, return with them the following year.

This incident is symbolic and symptomatic of the early contact between Europeans and the native inhabitants of North America on several levels— including that of trust. But one interesting aspect is not readily apparent. Only when we read the journal of Cartier's second voyage, in 1535, do we learn that the two captives were named Taignoagny and Domagaya; the chief, the 'lord of Canada' as he is called, was Donnacona. That time was required for the Frenchmen to ascertain names is not surprising, since they could not immediately communicate with the natives in any but the most elementary terms. Nevertheless, with this incident Donnacona and his sons step out of the mists into the full light of European recorded history as the first natives in what would become Canada to have established personal identities.

While we can thus date fairly precisely the moment at which Canada's native peoples enter into the European historical record, at least as individual participants, such an event ought not to obscure the fact that thousands of years of development had preceded it. The native inhabitants of North America had only oral traditions on which to rely, and their sense of historical time and their conception of the meaning of history were unlike those of the Europeans. Improved communication would have helped very little to convey much about their ancient past. The work of countless modern specialists, chiefly linguistic scholars and archaeologists, has uncovered only the bare outlines of development in the pre-European period. The record of human settlement in North America does *not* begin with Donnacona and his sons, any more than it begins with the arrival of the Europeans. Moreover, at no point does that record cease to display change and development.

The Early Record

The native peoples of North America probably migrated there from Asia during one of the more recent ice ages, when the level of the oceans was lower and the Bering Land Bridge between Siberia and Alaska had been exposed for many centuries. Although the environment of this land bridge was itself favourable to human life, the glaciers that covered the northern part of the continent were not. The human sojourners migrated along a gap between the ice sheets, making their way into the southern part of the continent, where their presence can first be detected.[2] The earliest indisputable evidence of humankind's existence on the continent has been discovered in New Mexico, in the remains of a mammal still retaining the stone weapon that had killed it. This evidence has been dated at around 12,000 B.C. As the ice retreated and the climate changed in the northern part of the continent, more and more people moved into southern regions. Although they may have initially moved quickly, it took many years to adapt to each new climate system.

The existence of an ice age only a relatively short time ago—at least in terms of the age of this planet and even of the emergence of humankind on it several million years ago — reminds us that climatic conditions are not fixed but constantly change and shift. For our purposes the last few thousand years since the documentable human presence in North America can be divided into four periods. The first, lasting from 11,000 B.C. to 8000 B.C., was a period of rapid glacial retreat and the reoccupation of the land, previously covered with ice, by flora and fauna. From 8000 to 5000 B.C. the climate was warmer and drier, with some rapid climatic changes and movements of forests and grassland. From 5000 to 500 B.C. the continent was very warm, and the forest reached its northernmost extension around 3000 B.C.[3]

Since 500 B.C. conditions have been relatively stable, although minor shifts can be detected that could have produced substantial change along the borders between climatic zones. Thus the period between 500 B.C. and A.D. 400 was one of severe changes from winter to summer, while from 400 to 900 ameliorating conditions prevailed and the forest again extended north-wards. Between 1200 and 1500 the climate turned cooler and drier, again sending the northern forest into retreat; while from 1550 to 1850 further cold reduced the growing season and sent the forests still further south. The low point of this period was reached in 1816, the famous 'year without a summer', during which much of the northern hemisphere failed to harvest any crops. Since 1850 Canada has experienced slight warming trends within a stable climate, although conditions probably began another major shift in the 1980s.

Climatic patterns and movements of people within the continent roughly correspond, as do many early cultural changes associated with them. The early inhabitants of North America attempted less to modify their environ-ment than to adapt themselves to it. Since the environment was itself in constant flux, so were the cultures that were the products of adaptation. The record of early peoples in North America is one of continual change and adaptation. Most of the change occurred gradually over relatively long periods, but occasionally it could appear abrupt and swift, particularly for those living on the borders of climate zones and ecosystems. As might be anticipated, the patterns of native response to the ecological environment varied in accordance with that environment itself. The most important feature of any area was its available food supply.

Given the extent to which Canada's indigenous peoples used their natural environment, and the ways they related to it, the European newcomers could have learned a good deal about any given region by concentrating on how the natives had adapted to it. The prevailing relationship between the natives and their natural surroundings, which included the difficulties certain groups had in supporting themselves, ought perhaps to have foretold the ease, or lack of it, with which European settlers would be able to establish their own communities. On the whole the Europeans did not make this connection. Indian life was to a great degree environmentally determined — though

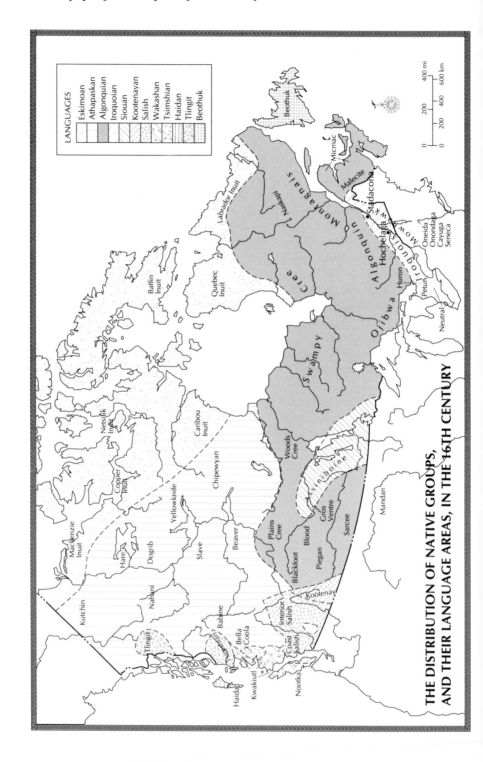

LANGUAGES

	Eskimoan
	Athapaskan
	Algonquian
	Iroquoian
	Siouan
	Kootenayan
	Salish
	Wakashan
	Tsimshian
	Haidan
	Tlingit
	Beothuk

THE DISTRIBUTION OF NATIVE GROUPS, AND THEIR LANGUAGE AREAS, IN THE 16TH CENTURY

other factors governed the establishment and movement of Indian communities besides environment. The Europeans' conviction that they could master their natural surroundings would often be proved mistaken. By the time of European intrusion into Canada, native history and native adaptations strongly suggest that the land was in most places not encouraging to agriculture, and that the climate was relatively harsh, particularly in the winter months. The new arrivals soon experienced the harshness, but did not recognize all its implications for their own strategies of survival. Europeans had to learn the realities for themselves.

When Christopher Columbus sailed to America in 1492, he thought he had reached the Indies on the east coast of Asia. He called the people he met Indians, but this word meant nothing to them. They called themselves, in their own tongue, 'the people', or by names describing the region they lived in. In northeastern North America there were two main linguistic families of Indian peoples: the Algonquian and the Iroquoian. The Algonquian, by far the most widespread, included (from east to west) the Micmac, Malecite, Montagnais-Naskapi, Algonquin, Ottawa, Ojibwa, the Wood and Plains Cree, and the Blackfoot.

The Eastern Maritime Peoples

On the eastern seaboard, the first region reached by Europeans, the native population depended on hunting in the interior in the winter and on fishing and collecting shellfish in the summer. Different groups developed their own mix of seasonal activity, particularly those living along tidal rivers, with some oriented inland and others towards the coast. Changes in the sea level, brought about by continual glacial melting, affected the inhabitants considerably; particularly in the Bay of Fundy region, such changes altered water temperatures and hence the productivity of shellfish beds. Higher levels meant colder water, despite overall warming trends, and while at one time it was possible to inhabit the coastal region of the Fundy Basin year round, in the centuries before European arrival the population had reverted to a seasonal migration inland in the winter. In most of the coastal region the population stabilized at a fairly early date, and there were few new migrations or intrusions.

The situation was different in Newfoundland, where a Dorset Eskimo population disappeared around A.D. 600, and was replaced by the Beothuk. Both peoples relied on the sea for much of the year, following the caribou migrations inland in the depths of winter.

In Newfoundland, whose people were the first contacted by Europeans—possibly by John Cabot in 1497, and certainly by the international fishing community that exploited his landfall—the Beothuk relied for food on small sea mammals and shellfish in the summer and on caribou in the winter. They were forced to retreat from the coastline as the Europeans began to spread along it, and became a fairly mysterious interior population that disappeared completely in the early nineteenth century under the pressures of European expansion—neither the first nor the only native group to become extinct in the course of European settlement. Never particularly numerous, the Beothuk succumbed to European hostility—island legend has them hunted for sport—and particularly to the introduction of disease for which they had no immunity, a more subtle form of destruction. They spoke a fairly distinctive language that was perhaps distantly related to Algonquian, suggesting their relative isolation from influences of the mainland since their arrival in Newfoundland.[4]

In the modern Maritime Provinces, and the Gaspé peninsula of Quebec, lived the Micmacs, the northernmost speakers of Eastern Algonquian. They occupied a region of heavy forests, frequently pierced by tidal rivers and coastal harbours. Winter was severe and the cultivation of domestic crops (well developed in 1500 in what is now southwestern Ontario) had not spread from south or west among the Micmac population, except for a bit of tobacco-growing. The Micmacs were hunters and fishermen who utilized the extensive river system of the region to transport themselves from interior to coast in response to the changing seasons. Sixteenth-century European observers, arriving in the summer, saw Micmacs along the coast during the time of their greatest plenty. They gathered in bands of up to 200 people at traditional locations on the water in the summer, and each band regularly hunted in the same territory during the winter. Inhabiting a rich region that offered a good many varied resources to a hunting, fishing, and gathering people, the Micmacs were fairly numerous in pre-European times, perhaps numbering as many as 50,000 before the process of decimation began. They were extremely conscious of the effect of European intrusion on their numbers, complaining in 1616 to Father Pierre Biard (*c*.1567-1622) that 'before this association and intercourse, all their countries were very populous.'[5]

A little to the west of the Micmacs lived the Malecite and Passamaquoddy peoples, the former inhabiting the drainage basin of the Saint John River and the latter the coast of the Bay of Fundy to the west, and the region around Passamaquoddy Bay. The Malecite and Passamaquoddy spoke dialects of Algonquin that were mutually understandable, but were quite distinctive from that of the Micmacs. Unlike their neighbours to the east, the Malecite had begun the cultivation of corn, reflecting the richness of the land along the Saint John River and influences from horticultural people to the south. But at the time of European contact they were still principally hunters. In contrast, the Passamaquoddy—while also hunters—concentrated on the sea mammals of the Fundy basin. European observers were generally incapable of distinguishing the Malecite-Passamaquoddy from the Micmacs, although they were politically quite separate.[6]

Hibbert Newton Binney, *Micmac Encampment, c.* 1790, possibly at Tufts Cove, Dartmouth, NS. Watercolour, pencil, and ink. This painting—of which at least six copies were made by other artists—illustrates in particular the use of birch-bark for the canoe and the tipis and the decorative clothing of the women, whose coats and high peaked caps were often trimmed with embroidery in bright colours—red, violet, and blue were favourites. Binney was a Halifax customs officer. His painting was presented to the lieutenant-governor, Lord Dalhousie, and was taken to Scotland in 1821. It remained there until 1980, when it was repatriated to Nova Scotia. Nova Scotia Museum, Halifax, 7.146/N-9410.

Micmac women wearing their typical embroidered peaked caps, drawn by Robert Petley, a lieutenant in the 50th Regiment who was stationed in Halifax from 1832 to 1836. These studies were included in his *Sketches in Nova Scotia and New Brunswick, Drawn from Nature and on Stone,* published in London in 1836.

～～～ *Northeastern Hunters*

In the northern forests and subarctic tundra of the continent, climatic and vegetation boundaries had constantly shifted throughout the time of human occupation. Hunters, gradually moving north to escape the encroaching woodlands of the southern areas, composed much of the population. Notched projectile points had spread across the entire continent from west to east, reflecting the hunting orientation of most of the population, but ceramic pottery—imported from the south into eastern Manitoba and northern Ontario—never extended widely onto the eastern seaboard.[7] In the lands above the St Lawrence River, in what is now northeastern Quebec and Labrador, lived the Montagnais and Naskapi, who were among the first to come into close contact with Europeans. The Montagnais inhabited a sprawling territory between the St Lawrence and the drainage area of

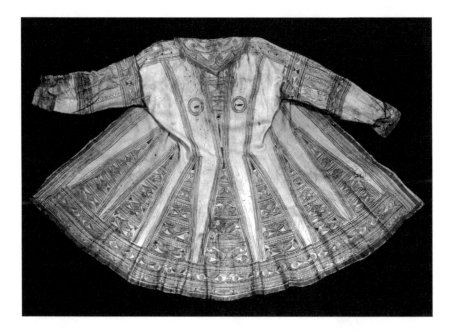

Man's painted caribou-skin coat (back). Montagnais-Naskapi, Quebec-Labrador, 1805-10. The caribou was the main source of food and clothing for these native people, and caribou-skin coats like this one—meticulously painted with a wide range of motifs—were considered by the hunters who wore them to have magical or 'holy' properties: hunting caribou was a holy occupation. This coat—its designs painted in red, ochre, and black on a light, skin-coloured ground—is unusual in having a touch of realism in the two medallions containing a stylized bird (incomplete because some of the paint has disappeared) and fish respectively. Royal Ontario Museum (36435).

James Bay. The Naskapi hunted over much of eastern Labrador. The southernmost Montagnais tended to merge into the adjacent Micmacs, while the northern Montagnais and Naskapi shared some characteristics with the Inuit of the High Arctic. Such cultural overlaps were quite common across North America. Both Montagnais and Naskapi lived in the eastern extremities of the Canadian Shield—that vast, relatively inhospitable region of pre-Cambrian rock encircling Hudson Bay. Given the infertility of the Shield and its northern climate, it was hardly surprising that the Montagnais and Naskapi lacked any familiarity with agriculture. Their life was dominated by the itinerant hunt and by the animals around which they focused their lives: the moose for the Montagnais and the caribou for the Naskapi. Neither had a highly developed political organization. Their social structure was character-ized by the small and mobile hunting band. Population density was low, the hunting territories huge. Clearly the region was inhospitable for extensive and settled human habitation.

To the west of the Montagnais lived a number of bands of scattered hunters called by the Europeans the 'Algonquins', and to their west—right across the lakes and Shield to the Prairies—were the Ojibwa or Chippewa. The inhabitants of this region were always hunters, presumably of caribou. But as

Paul Kane, *An Ojibwa Encampment near Sault Ste Marie*, showing dome-shaped lodges of matting and birch-bark, a tripod for cooking, and blankets thrown over the bushes to dry. Oil on canvas, based on a pencil sketch made in the summer of 1845. Royal Ontario Museum. 912.1.9; CR III-65.

the forest began to move north, the herds disappeared and the people were forced to adapt to a new environment of mixed hardwood forests that had covered eastern Canada between 6000 and 4000 B.C. In these woodlands a society emerged based on game, fish, and plants. The Ojibwa became food-gatherers who had a sophisticated relationship with vegetable food sup-plies—ranging from wild rice and berries to maple syrup—that supple-mented their basic diet of meat and fish. The higher standard of living made possible by extensive use of vegetation enabled the Ojibwa to multiply rapidly in pre-contact times, and to spread fairly widely geographically. Although their hunting territories may have been fairly plainly delineated, a certain sense of commonality was provided by a kinship system of family relationships. The basic organizational unit among the Ojibwa was the hunting band. The midwestern woodlands they inhabited, covering the Shield before it swings north to the Arctic Circle, were obviously more receptive to human habitation than the territory of their eastern equivalents. Nevertheless this environment had not encouraged the development of agriculture. It was still inhabited by a semi-nomadic hunting people who left, and returned to, the same areas again and again.

The Horticulturalists

The beginnings of agriculture totally changed the society of some of the woodlands Indians, particularly the Iroquoian people of southern Ontario. Although no Canadian natives developed the sort of urban culture based on corn production that characterized the Mississippi Valley, the Iroquoians did plant corn, beginning around A.D. 500. Cultivated plants came into the region either via the modern-day Windsor corridor, or through the Niagara peninsula. Domesticated plants provided a more stable food supply than hunting, and permitted a relatively large population to utilize a small area. The Iroquois—a linguistic family that included the Huron and several other peoples of the area—developed a horticulture that had started to proliferate in the centuries immediately before the European intrusion. These corn-farmers continued to hunt and fish, but lived in relatively permanent villages containing elaborate communal houses. Ceramic pots had begun to appear in southern Ontario and Quebec after 1000 B.C., and there is much evidence of the development of complex trading patterns among the early woodland people.[8]

In what is now central Canada, the only peoples who were supported by agriculture were the Iroquoian-speaking tribes: the Hurons who lived south of Georgian Bay, the Tobacco Nation or Petuns to the west, and the Attiwan-daronk or Neutrals along the north shore of Lake Erie. The famous Five Nations Confederacy of the Iroquois (the Mohawks, Oneidas, Onondagas, Cayugas, and Senecas) lived in present-day New York State. All these people were horticulturalists, relying on the cultivation of maize or corn, while the

Petuns also grew tobacco plants, whence came their appellation. Beans, squash, and sunflowers were also cultivated. This economy permitted the luxury of semi-permanent villages, located on well-drained sandy loam that was easiest to work with a type of slash-and-burn agriculture, planting a burned-over mass of land, which eventually exhausted the soil and required moving to another similar site every eight to twelve years. Large longhouses made of logs were constructed from the adjacent secondary forest. Inhabited by perhaps five families each, these houses were up to 25 feet wide and 100 feet long. A large village might contain upwards of 100 longhouses (and 3,000 people). Smaller villages were more common, however, and some settlements consisted of several contiguous, but agriculturally self-contained, units.[9]

The seasonal cycle in an agricultural economy was somewhat different than in a hunting one, although the men continued to hunt and fish throughout the year, while the women and children dealt with most of the planting, tending, and harvesting. Trees were cut and burned, if possible—the only part of the farming operation conducted by the males—and seeds were planted in holes made with a digging stick. Earth was hoed up around the plants into mounds, up to 2,500 per acre in fields as much as sixty acres in area. The process was not dissimilar to that practised by pioneer European settlers throughout eastern Canada when forested land was being opened to settlement. This was one technique the first Europeans did learn from the Indians, though in the course of time its origins were forgotten.

While unused land was held in common, families possessed their own farm plots—as much as they could reasonably cultivate. Land was a unit of production; it did not confer wealth and status, as it did in Europe. But the horticulturalists were able to accumulate goods, particularly food supplies for the winter, and produce did represent a form of wealth. Hoarding, however, was discouraged, and goods were shared through ceremonies and games of chance. Barter was conducted with neighbouring Indians. Shells and chert (a crystalline quartz) were the prized items of trade, much of which was mainly conducted with the Algonquin groups living to the north of the horticultural region. While these farming peoples often fought with one another in blood feuds and ritual warfare, before the arrival of the Europeans and the introduction of the fur trade, wars were not carried on for territorial purposes. With the coming of the Europeans, in the seventeenth and early eighteenth centuries, conflict between the well-armed and well-organized Iroquois peoples of upstate New York and their Canadian neighbours would assume alarming proportions.

✦ Western Peoples

In the huge hinterland of the western interior, between the Great Lakes and the Rockies—particularly on the Plains—hunting was the primary means of

An Assiniboine family and their lodge near Red River in the winter of 1848. A pen-and-ink drawing by George Finlay, an ensign with the 65th Regiment of Foot, who had been posted to Fort Garry in 1846 and while there made many sketches. Glenbow Foundation.

Paul Kane, *Assiniboine Hunting Buffalo*. Oil on canvas. In June 1845, Kane (1810-71) left Toronto for a three-year journey, which took him as far west as Fort Vancouver, to sketch the western Indians. The result of this trip was 100 canvases painted later from his sketches, and his classic *Wanderings of an Artist Among the Indians of North America* (1859), in which he described the subjects of this painting, whom he saw near Fort Edmonton: 'One day, whilst wandering some distance to the south of the fort, I saw two Assiniboine Indians hunting buffaloes. One was armed with a spear, formed of an ashpole about ten feet long, ornamented with tufts of hair, and having an iron head, which is procured from the trading posts; the other with a bow formed of ash, with the sinews of a buffalo gummed to the back of it. These they use with great dexterity and force; I have known an instance of the arrows passing through the body of the animal, and sticking in the ground at the opposite side.' National Gallery of Canada, 6920.

obtaining food. The mammoth, the earliest prey, disappeared into extinction, but it was replaced by mammals more familiar to our own time, including the Plains buffalo. Hunters were smoking and drying meat by 3000 B.C., and the gradual but severe shifts in climate forced them to look elsewhere than the Plains for meat during the protracted warm and dry millenia before that period. Much hunting was done by driving animals into gullies and over cliffs; gradually the hunters learned to contrive ways of trapping large beasts. Early hunters travelled on foot, but it was necessary to keep moving to follow the foraging instincts of the game, and semi-permanent habitations did not develop. Stone projectile points (or arrowheads), virtually the only evidence surviving of the presence of pre-European population, did change in style over time. The new styles spread geographically, indicating that cultures were not static and were influenced by developments in neighbouring regions to the south.[10] By A.D. 600 the points were being notched, and the use of ceramic pots spread from the south as far north as central Alberta in this later pre-contact period. On the western plains, burial practices were also influenced from the south, and the graves contained material, such as shells and copper, drawn from distant regions. Elaborate trade networks were obviously in existence. The horse was not introduced onto the Plains until the eighteenth century—well after the arrival of Europeans in the New World. Its impact on what is now the Prairie West of Canada is a classic illustration of the inherent capacity of the native population to adapt to new conditions. The horse ridden by an eighteenth-century Plains Indian was not native to North America but had been brought by the Spaniards to the southwest in the sixteenth century, and spread rapidly north in wild form. Before this time the animal did not exist anywhere in America; yet by the eighteenth century the Indians of the Plains had made it the centre of their society and culture. It is true that the horse was ideally suited to the nomadic lifestyle of a people whose major source of food came from hunting the buffalo; nevertheless, the speed with which the natives exploited its possibilities was impressive. The Plains Cree and Blackfoot had already adapted the dog as a beast of burden, and this doubtless simplified its replacement by the larger horse, although skills of horsemanship had to be developed. When Europeans finally penetrated the continent to the western prairies, they found a people whose relationship with the horse suggested a long development, rather than the relatively recent utilization of a windfall by-product of European intrusion.

Not all of Canada between the Great Lakes and the Rockies was prairie, and not all western Indians could base their economy on the buffalo. Between the Canadian Shield and the southern Plains was a heavily forested zone, separated from the prairie by hills, lakes, rivers, and marshy sloughs. This parkland, as it came to be called—alternating forest with open clearings covered with high grasses—extended west from the Red River to the north branch of the Saskatchewan, and ultimately into the Peace River country of modern British Columbia.

The western native peoples did not divide neatly into those who hunted the buffalo on the Plains and those whose food-gathering activities were more mixed and did not rely on the horse. The two largest groupings, the Assiniboine and the Cree, both had some bands in parkland and forest and some bands on the Plains, although the former were mainly based in the buffalo country and the latter in the woodlands. Horses were of little use in the boreal forest, or even in much of the parkland; only on the prairie did the horse, and horse culture, come into their own. The Cree spoke Algonquian languages, along with their western neighbours the Blackfoot, while the Gros Ventre and Sarcee—who, with the Blackfoot, inhabited what is now Alberta—were Athapaskan-speakers. The principal cultural distinction, however, was between those native inhabitants on the Plains—whose life was bound up with buffalo and horses—and those who lived in the parkland and woodland areas, whose lifestyles were closely akin to those of the woodland Indians of the East.

～～～ The Pacific Slope

John Webber, *The Inside of a House in Nootka Sound*. Webber accompanied Captain James Cook, as draftsman, on Cook's third voyage round the world in the *Resolution* and *Discovery*, in which they explored the northwest coast of North America, sailing as far north as Bering Strait. In March/April 1778 they anchored for nearly a month in Nootka Sound, on the west coast of Vancouver Island. This illustration was included in a portfolio of engravings of Webber's drawings, published in the 1780s. Metropolitan Toronto Reference Library.

The presence in the Far West of rivers and coastal waters teeming with fish and marine life (while relatively free of larger mammals) dictated a less-specialized process of food-gathering than was the case in regions with big-game animals that could be hunted. As the glaciers retreated, salmon began ascending the rivers to spawn, supplying a basic food source. This maritime environment was a relatively rich one, and the climate was the least harsh of any in the northern part of the continent. A large population, and increasingly complex social systems, therefore emerged over time. Specialized tools were developed and woodworking began to flourish, influenced by the diffusion of cultural traits from the south. Along the northern coast of what is now British Columbia the tradition of building wooden houses and cedar canoes, and of weaving baskets, was a very old one when the first white man arrived. In all areas of the Pacific Slope, where people did not need to follow a migratory food supply, villages appeared.

Recorded European contact along the Pacific Slope did not begin until very late in the eighteenth century, although Spaniards from the south and Russians from the north may well have visited there before the well-publicized arrival of Captain James Cook in 1778. What Cook found were semi-sedentary people who, despite the absence of agriculture, enjoyed a rich economic base centred on salmon and the cedar trees common to the region. He was greatly impressed by their trading sophistication, although others would be more fascinated by the furs they were offering for trade, particularly the pelts of the sea otter. The northern groups—the Tlingit, Haida, and Tsimshian—had more highly developed social organizations. The Kwakiutl, Bella Coola, and Nootka in the south were still cultures in the process of

Haida village on Skidegate Inlet, Queen Charlotte Islands, 1877, photographed by G.M. Dawson, a member of the Geological Survey of Canada, who made the first survey of northern British Columbia and the Yukon. British Columbia Archives and Records Service, HP33784.

developing. Nevertheless, all these coastal Indians had the most hierarchical society of any of Canada's native peoples, with divisions into nobles, commoners, and slaves. They also had extremely complex social systems based on kinship and centred on clans.

For all these Pacific Slope peoples, fish, sea mammals, and shellfish were available in relative abundance, and could be supplemented by berries and other natural vegetation. They had no need to farm. They lived in villages, in large houses built of cedar, and travelled the coastal waters in dugout canoes. Their prosperity introduced the concept of material wealth, and their houses and villages displayed evidence of a strong aesthetic sensibility, expressed in intricately carved house joists and in totem poles depicting ancestral symbols. Because of the lateness of contact with Europeans, and the speed with which the intruders moved to exploit the sea otter, the Pacific peoples were rapidly inundated with European technology and values. Adaptation to European values and customs, inevitably, was swift rather than gradual.

The peoples of the interior of what is now British Columbia were heavily influenced in their culture by the Pacific Slope peoples, but in their economy the Interior Salish, Kootenay, Chilcotin, and Okanagan groups, to name but a few, were rather more closely akin to the hunting and gathering peoples of eastern Canada. Most were Athapaskan-speakers. Despite social organization into clans, and even divisions into nobles, commoners, and slaves—probably taken from the coastal peoples—they were a semi-migratory folk dependent on hunting and fishing.

The Subarctic and the Arctic

In the basins of the Mackenzie and Yukon Rivers, north of the 56th parallel, lived other groups of woodland peoples—such as the Chipewyan, Dogrib, and Kutchin—whose lives were centred on the constant search for game animals: moose, caribou, bear, beaver, and smaller mammals. All were Athapaskan speakers and their historic thrust was southward, away from the Barrens—that vast barren area stretching from northern Manitoba to the shore of Coronation Gulf, an arm of the Arctic Ocean. In the west they had extended into the interior of British Columbia, but to the southeast they had found their way blocked by other groups. Some of these people fished as well as hunted, but their social organization was that of the hunting band and their lives were hard and insecure; their hunting territory could not sustain a high population density.

Finally, in the High Arctic and subarctic coasts of northern Canada resided the Inuit, a word that means 'people'. The earliest occupants of this region spread eastward from Alaska to northern Greenland, beginning about 2000 B.C. The expansion of these 'Palaeo-Eskimos'—the Pre-Dorset—coincided with a moderating climate and the eventual stabilization of the sea level that produced a regular food resource. The Arctic inhabitants began as land-hunters of caribou and muskoxen, but gradually shifted to marine resources as being more reliable. The Inuit's way of life was dependent on the sea mammals of the Arctic coast. In much of the Canadian Arctic prevailing movements of sea-ice produced scarcity of food supply, so that only a few localities where access was good were inhabited.

Because of their seemingly intractable environment, the Inuit (known to Europeans as 'Eskimos' or '*Esquimaux*', a derogatory word, acquired from the Indians, meaning 'eaters of raw fish') had been particularly ingenious in developing means for living in their ice-bound world. Their seal-hunting equipage was extremely complex. Their transportation systems employed at sea the speedy kayak and on land the dogsled. The Inuit used the dog as a beast of traction more than any other native people, except the Plains hunters before the arrival of the horse. They lived in the domed snow-hut—the

Snow Village of the Esquimaux, an engraving of a drawing by Captain G.F. Lyon, who accompanied Edward Parry's expedition in search of a Northwest Passage in 1821-3 and wrote a book about it, in which he described what he called 'snow-huts' or 'domes': 'The laying of the arch was performed in such a manner as would have satisfied the most regular artist, the key-piece on the top, being a large square slab. The blocks of snow used in the buildings were from four to six inches in thickness, and about a couple of feet in length, carefully pared with a large knife. . . . The raised places [inside] were used as beds, and covered in the first place with whalebone, sprigs of andromeda, and pieces of seal's skin, over these were spread deer pelts and deer skin clothes, which had a very warm appearance. . . . We soon learned that the building of a house was but the work of an hour or two, and that a couple of men, one to cut the slabs and the other to lay them, were labourers sufficient.' *Private Journal of Capt. G.F. Lyon of H.M.S.* Hecla *During the Recent Voyage of Discovery Under Captain Parry* (London, 1824). Metropolitan Toronto Reference Library.

igloo—in winter and in skin tents in the summer. Caribou hides served as the basic clothing material. The Inuit were also extremely skilful at tool-making, and their use of bone and ivory astounded Europeans. Their political and social organization was simple, as concepts of personal wealth had not entered their way of life.

Since the habitat of the Inuit was so obviously a difficult one, Europeans tended to be impressed by the ingenuity of their environmental adaptations. But the Inuit behaved no differently from any other native peoples in exploiting their surroundings. Native culture and society, native tools and clothing, even native religion, were all extremely sensible, sometimes ingenious, and always understandable responses to the world in which the original inhabitants of North America survived. The European newcomers would find, to their surprise, that much of what the native peoples had developed over centuries not only worked, but worked very well. For many years the intruders would benefit as much or more from taking over native ways as the natives would from the introduction of European technology. Europe brought firearms, but the Indians had the canoe. Europe had iron, but the Indians could cure scurvy.

The Europeans, of course, had difficulty in seeing cultural exchange in this light. At the same time, the native peoples lived in a symbiotic relationship with nature, and not much was required to upset the balance. What the Europeans brought with them was more than enough.

These watercolours by John White show three Baffin Island Inuit—a woman and her child and a man—whom Martin Frobisher took prisoner on his second expedition to the Arctic in 1577. All died a month or so after arriving in England. Copyright British Museum, 205220 and 234062.

✌ *The Problem of European Contact*

Although very isolated earlier contact with Europeans had occurred around A.D. 1000, when Viking adventurers, sailing out of Greenland and Iceland, recorded confrontations with people on the east coast of North America, regular European visitations to the northern shores of the continent began, off Newfoundland, only at the end of the fifteenth century, and accelerated greatly in the sixteenth. While the intrusion of Europeans greatly altered the dynamics of North American development, it also affected—in giving rise to misinterpretations—the subsequent understanding of the nature of the American population at the moment of Europe's appearance on the scene. Recorded history was after all monopolized by those who had written languages and could make records. In the centuries following European arrival, virtually everything written about the indigenous population of Canada was produced from the European perspective; and except in the oral traditions of the natives—only occasionally recorded at the time—no account of the reaction to the European exists. The oral tradition, however, could be surprisingly precise. Nineteenth-century investigators were able to determine the fate of a group of English sailors captured by natives almost three centuries after the event through oral reminiscence handed down from generation to generation.[11] But the spoken memories of native peoples could not compete with the spate of written observations by the newcomers. However well-intentioned, these records had many limitations, burdened as they were with colourful misconceptions and misinterpretations.

Any scholar would delight in being able to identify that important and definitive moment of first contact when a people was being observed totally uninfluenced and unaffected by a preceding European presence. But such a moment rarely, if ever, occurred. As European penetration of the continent continued over several centuries, there were innumerable episodes of 'first contact'. But in the relatively isolated and fragile ecosystems of North America, the European influence spread far in advance of the actual arrival of the first explorer—a point that the term 'first contact' tends to obscure. While Jacques Cartier may have been the first European to record the names of natives, he had also observed a number of fishing vessels in the Gulf of St Lawrence and found the people there eager to trade, probably because they had already traded with Basque fishermen. When British exploration had only just reached the Pacific Slope, Captain James Cook (1728–79) indulged himself in the thought that his party represented the first Europeans to visit the Nootka, although Spaniards had been travelling the West Coast for centuries. What Cook and other Europeans brought to North America was not the concept of trading, but European trade goods and a market for native goods such as furs. They also brought animals—and diseases.

However rapidly European artifacts and animals (such as the horse) may have spread ahead of the newcomers, what dispersed across the continent with even greater rapidity was disease. North America, in the seventeenth century, was a geographical isolate. A host of communicable diseases common to the 'known world' of international trade and commerce simply did not exist on the American continent, and its population had no immunity to them. Measles, smallpox, typhus, typhoid, and venereal disease—the last perhaps first contracted by Europeans in the Caribbean region—were as much European introductions as the gun and the horse. They spread rapidly among a population that lacked any natural protection. Trade and war, including the native custom of replenishing population losses by adopting captive women and children, spread disease far beyond points of actual European arrival. In fairness to the newcomers, they simply did not understand that their sexual promiscuity with native women, or their taking Indians back to Europe as prize specimens or native informants, were potentially devastating to the Indians. Europeans themselves had been forced to become callous about epidemic disease; it was part of life, and the concept of immunity was not understood. There was no reason to view the Indian propensity for dying 'in captivity' as something resulting from European intention or intervention.

The introduction of new disease renders all attempts to estimate the size of the indigenous population being 'contacted'—a dubious enterprise under the best of circumstances—totally useless. The indigenous pre-contact population of Canada was substantially larger than the sum total of the most generous estimates of all the first-contact observers. The east-coast population had been seriously reduced by epidemic during the sixteenth century, and demographic disaster preceded the Europeans right across the continent.

If the newcomers were ignorant of the effects of their entrance into North America, they were fully convinced that they were superior to the native inhabitants. Such a conviction was perhaps natural, although to a considerable extent unwarranted. The veneer of civilization covering the visitors was a thin one at best, and it often wore away quite quickly. While the master mariners and expedition leaders who have left most of the written observations during the first century of discovery were usually men of some cultural achievement—they could write, for example, which set them apart from their compatriots, and they were often well-connected at the royal courts—the sixteenth century was still a nasty, brutish, and violent age. Most Europeans, including the ordinary sailors on board the visiting ships, still ate with their fingers, bathed as seldom as possible, and enjoyed such amusements as bear-baiting, in which dogs were pitted against captive bears in fights to the finish. And the institutions of the ruling classes allowed heretics to be tortured in the name of Jesus Christ, witches to be burned at the stake, and the execution of thousands whose beliefs or backgrounds were different from those in charge of Church and State. Public executions were guaranteed crowd-pleasers, especially if the victim could be drawn-and-quartered before hanging and burning. In some parts of Europe a popular entertainment at fairs was watching blind men in pens attempt to beat each other to death with clubs.[12] Garbage and animal excrement were piled high in the streets of European cities, 'piss-pots' were emptied into the streets, and one of the major motivations behind European expansion was the search for new and more powerful spices to help disguise the stench of daily living by means of scents. The word '*sauvages*' (savages), which the European used to refer to the native peoples of North America, is to the modern mind not only brutal but ironic, and to natives of today insulting.

At the same time, Europe had achieved a different stage of development than the indigenous peoples of Canada. It had advanced to a new level of technology, based on the book and the wheel, although much of its technological glitter would prove relatively useless in the wilderness of the New World. Successful Europeans in Canada would for several centuries adopt Indian inventions in order to survive. Nevertheless, their technology helped to give them a sense of superiority, as did their emerging capitalistic economic order, their new political organization into nation-states, and especially their Christian system of values and beliefs. These pronounced differences between Europeans and indigenous Canadians prevented the visitors from comprehending the people they encountered, whose world views and successful ways of life they unconsciously, often quite subtly, judged by their own standards.

With the possible exception of the horticulturalists of south-central Canada, and the fisherfolk of the Pacific Slope, the economy of the native inhabitants was quite a simple one. It was organized around the food supply and offered semi-nomadic people little scope for the acquisition of material possessions that would only have to be abandoned at the next—and imminent—move. Nevertheless it *was* an economy, and those within it functioned according to its inner logic. Food was not cultivated, but pursued. The movement of game and fish had certain rhythms, but was at least potentially capricious. When food was available, the population was galvanized into action, gathering as much as possible and then consuming it in what seemed overindulgent orgies. When food ran out, energetic questing for new supplies did not necessarily begin immediately. The natives knew the general behaviour patterns of the wildlife they sought, and hurry often did little good: for example, it was useless to hunt for berries in February. In any event such an economy did not put a premium on the disciplined pursuit of goals, or on the deferral of expectations; nor did it encourage the sort of continual hard labour familiar to the European newcomers. Even after the Europeans had introduced new elements into the consumer patterns of the Indians—such as guns, alcohol, and tobacco—consumer demand tended to be (in the language of the modern economist) inelastic, or fixed. While furs and pelts were the currency with which such goods were purchased, the Indians would not pursue them unremittingly, since their wants remained simple.[13] Throughout much of Canada the Indian economy encouraged brief concen-

trated periods of activity, culminating in orgy, and much lying about. European observers, naturally, tended to interpret such behaviour as shiftless and
indolent rather than economically sensible.

Similarly, the nature of the Indian economy did not produce political
institutions on a European scale. Semi-sedentary people had no need for
political organizations larger than the band, which was itself based on the
coming together of a few family units. Larger organizations could not travel
together in the unremitting quest for food. Even where horticulture was
developed, with its resultant large semi-permanent villages, political structure was not complex by European standards, although some specialization of
function occurred. 'Chiefs' were not kings, although the visitors treated
them as such. They may not even have been 'head men' in any European
sense; such a concept was introduced and imposed on the indigenous population by the newcomers. As is now well known, the native notion of property,
especially land, was well beyond the comprehension of the Europeans. While
some Indian groups could conceive of territory as 'belonging' to them, this
was a concept of usage rather than ownership. Natives erroneously identified
as kings were quite happy to 'sell' to the European newcomers land that
neither they nor their people owned, as Europeans understood ownership.

Lacking much inclination to create expanding hierarchical political organizations, the Indians practised war according to different rules than those
employed in Europe, where institutions of Church and State inculcated
obedience to established authority. Indian wars were mainly raids by a few
warriors, conducted partly because success in battle was an important test of
Indian manhood. They were often used to take women and children captive
to replace those lost within the band. Individual prowess in battle was valued,
long-term military strategy and objectives were not. Indians had their own
military agendas, and were notoriously fickle allies from the European
perspective. Only the Iroquois—who, in the seventeenth century, may have
developed a militarily viable form of political organization that was partly
based on European models—were able to compete with the newcomers and
withstand their military power.[14]

The almost total absence of seeking complex long-term goals through
deferral of expectations was easily one of the most marked features of Indian
society from the European perspective. Given the way in which children
were raised among indigenous people in Canada, this absence was hardly
surprising. Europeans believed that goals had to be inculcated at an early age,
through a series of repressive tactics that included heavy reliance on corporal
punishment, though monastic orders were continually proving that results
could be achieved without the overt use of force. Children were put to work
at an early age. Native Canadians, on the other hand, treated their children
with affectionate indulgence, seldom inflicting reprimands and totally
eschewing corporal punishment. Despite such nurture, or perhaps because of
it, native children learned quickly and thoroughly from their elders what had

to be known. For young warriors the schooling became intensive and painful as it inculcated a stoic self-control and an ability to endure hardship and physical pain. This training had much in common with the self-discipline of the missionaries, and was one of the reasons the Iroquois admired the Jesuit martyrs while they were torturing them to death. But Indian self-control was more the ability to endure than the capacity to obey. Though circumscribed, controlled, and regulated by ritual, tradition, and custom (what we would call 'socialization'), most Indians nonetheless hated taking orders, particularly from Europeans.

While commenting on the freedom that children were allowed, European observers of every native group from coast to coast also wrote that women were badly exploited. European society at the time could scarcely be called liberal in its attitude to women, but what the newcomers saw as exploitation reflected an inability to comprehend the divisions of labour within the Indian economy and in a warrior society. Men hunted and fought, while women did everything else. Interestingly enough, when European women were captured by raiding parties and integrated into Indian life, many chose to remain with their captors instead of accepting repatriation back into colonial society.[15] What this says about the treatment of women by the respective races can only be surmised.

As for morality, particularly sexual, the Europeans and the natives seemed about equally matched. The generosity of the males of some tribes in permitting their women to bestow sexual favours on the newcomers speaks volumes about the male prerogative in native society. While some observers felt obliged to remark on Indian promiscuity, a few had the decency to recognize that Europeans were not blameless in this regard. In the saga of European intrusion around the world over the centuries, Europe sent only males, particularly as exploiters and traders in the pre-settlement period, and so native females were used for sexual purposes. The pattern in western Canada of European male coupling with Indian female produced a mixed-blood society that had its parallels in other parts of the world.

Nowhere was the gulf between natives and the European newcomers more apparent than in the spiritual realm. Indian religious beliefs were complex, and not readily apparent to the external observer. They were part of an intricate religio-magical world that the native peoples inhabited and shared with the flora and fauna. Given the hunting orientation of most tribes, it is not surprising that animals were endowed with spiritual significance. The very process of food consumption often acquired deep religious meaning, becoming a form of worship of the spirit world through everyday activity. Many tribes had legends about the origins of the world, and a few may have believed in a single Creator—though this is what missionaries wanted them to believe. The mixture of authentic Indian lore with European thought and missionary teaching that has coloured Indian legends and tales over the last 350 years has made it difficult—perhaps impossible—to separate one from the other. Formal religious ceremonies were not readily apparent to the eyes of the visitors, except for the activities of shamans, who claimed supernatural powers and engaged in several kinds of folk medicine, ranging from herbal treatment to exorcism. Shamans were no more priests than native leaders were kings, but Europeans tended to consider their activities to be at the centre of native religion. They found it impossible to grasp that for the native peoples objects in nature were alive, and had their own powers, and that rituals connected with the ordinary round of daily life had deep religious significance. That native religion had no buildings, no hierarchy, and no institutional presence helped further to disorient the European.

Tolerance for alternative spiritual values and belief systems was hardly one of Europe's strong suits in the Age of Discovery. The period of European arrival in North America coincided with the Protestant Reformation and the Catholic Counter-Reformation. Christianity was undergoing profound alteration, with traditional Catholicism being subject to reform from both within and without. Protestant and Catholic alike were quite capable of fierce persecution of any deviation from official belief and practice, and both could agree that what was being observed in Canada was pagan supernatural-ism that needed to be uprooted as quickly as possible and replaced with the 'true faith'. That Europeans could not themselves agree on the truth per-plexed some native peoples, such as the Iroquois, who were exposed to French, English, and Dutch missionaries, or in a later period the people of the Pacific Slope. But the European intruders could not possibly appreciate the extent to which indigenous religious beliefs and practices—so difficult to uncover, much less to understand and appreciate—served as the basis for native existence. Views of the world and one's place in it were as integral to existence for Indians as they were for Europeans, and the way in which the native peoples related spiritually to their environment was a critical part of their culture. Europe could not attempt to convert them to a well-developed European value system without undermining the very basis of their exis-tence. Naturally the Indians resisted.

Almost from the outset, European observers and newcomers to Canada had two contradictory responses to the peoples they were contacting and describing. On the one hand, much of what they saw of native life, particu-larly beyond merely superficial observation, struck them as admirable and gave rise to the idea of the 'noble savage': the Indians exhibited none of the worst features of European capitalistic society, such as covetousness and rapaciousness, and they revered freedom, while eschewing private property. On the other hand was the equally powerful image of the Indian as brutal savage and barbarian, particularly in the context of war. Even those who dealt lovingly with the natives frequently lapsed into such characterizations, as did Mère Marie de l'Incarnation, the head of the Ursuline school at Quebec, in 1668:

It is a very difficult thing, not to say impossible, to make the little Savages French or civilized. We have more experience of this than anyone else, and we have observed that of a hundred that have passed through our hands we have scarcely civilized one. We find docility and intelligence in these girls, but, when we are least expecting it, they clamber over our wall and go off to run with their kinsmen in the woods, finding more to please them there than in all the amenities of our French houses. . . . We have had. . . Hurons, Algonkins, and Iroquois; these last are the prettiest and the most docile of all. I do not know whether they will be more capable of being civilized than the others. . . . I do not expect it of them, for they are Savages and that is sufficient reason not to hope.[16]

Neither characterization produced a policy towards the Indians that did any credit to the newcomers, and perhaps none could be found.

For long after, and perhaps even before Jacques Cartier's identification of individual natives, Europeans blundered on in their attempts to come to terms with the indigenous population of North America. The natives would prove tenacious in maintaining their own identity and culture in the face of much effort to Europeanize them. But they lacked the physical power to prevent either constant encroachment on their territory, or the gradual undermining of the basic physical and spiritual ingredients of their way of life. The cultural contact between European and native Canadian was a true tragedy in the ultimate meaning of the term, for reconciliation of the two cultures was quite impossible, and the failure of reconciliation echoes still today.

chapter two

The Explorers of the Sixteenth

and Seventeenth Centuries

About the first of October 1578 a fleet returned to England from the land called '*Meta Incognita*' in the Arctic waters of North America. Its principal cargo consisted of 1,350 tons of rocks, collected with great effort and at considerable expense on Baffin Island. The expedition that had filled countless bags with these rocks was led by Martin Frobisher, an experienced English mariner, who on two earlier voyages to the region had brought back samples of rock that had been assayed as gold-bearing. Accounts of the return appeared in print before the experts had a chance to examine the cargo and everyone was demanding to be paid. The owner of one vessel wrote desperately to the government for money to pay his crew, noting, 'Chrystmas beynge so nere, every man cryeth out for money'![1] No money was forthcoming and for five years the sponsors of the expedition tried without success to find evidence of value in the cargo. The rock was nothing more than sandstone flecked with mica. The business degenerated into an unseemly exchange of recriminations and accusations among the investors, and the rock itself was eventually used in Elizabethan road construction.

Such an outcome was typical of most early European endeavours in North America—with enthusiasm, fuelled by greed, eventually turning into seeming failure. Europe's voyages of 'discovery' were a strange mélange of intrepid seamanship and astounding credulity, constantly increasing geographical knowledge of the New World without ever succeeding in achieving the aims of those who financed them: quick returns of great wealth to match the treasure taken by the Spaniards from the great Indian empires of Central and South America.

~~~~ The Viking Explorers

Although countless legends about American landfalls abound—originating with the ancients and their medieval successors—the first documented European visitations to North America were made by Norsemen. Contemporary evidence is to be found in the great Icelandic epic sagas, confirmed in our own time by archaeological excavations near L'Anse aux Meadows on the northern tip of Newfoundland. The two great sagas describing the Norse expeditions are the *Saga of Eric the Red* and the *Saga of the Greenlanders*, the latter probably written down from oral tradition before 1263.[2] In the tenth century Eric the Red left Norway for Iceland, already well colonized by the Norse, and from 982 to 985 explored Greenland, which he colonized over the next two or three decades with his second son Leif Eriksson. About the year 1000 Leif, pursuing stories about land to the west of Greenland, set sail in a Norse *knarr* (a broad-beamed open boat with one square sail and auxiliary oars) into the western unknown. He landed on Baffin Island (Leif called it Helluland, 'rocky land') and on the southern coast of Labrador (Markland, or 'wooded land'), and then headed south to another region he called Vinland, after the wild grapes and vines he found, and wintered there. Its location has given rise to much speculation, but as the site near L'Anse aux Meadows, which dates from about the year 1000, is the only confirmed Norse settlement in North America, it is the prime candidate for Leif's Vinland. Further expeditions were undertaken about 1003-4 by Leif's brother Thorvald (he was killed there) and between 1003 and 1015 by Thorfinn Karlsefni, who led some 160 colonists. Although the Icelanders found the climate of Vinland more hospitable than that of Iceland, they were intimidated by hostile natives ('Skraelings') and left after about a year. Vinland then virtually disappeared from the record.

Later Greenlanders may have timbered on Baffin Island—such ventures are referred to in the annals of Iceland. They may also have intermarried with the Inuit; attempts have been made to attribute the Thule culture of the Inuit to such racial mixings.[3] But Greenland itself gradually lost contact with Europe, and the Icelanders' settlements there died away in the fifteenth century. For all intents and purposes the Norse discoveries were a dead end. In our own time the uncovering of a world map executed in the mid-fifteenth century, showing a realistic Greenland and westward islands, with inscriptions referring to Vinland, created much speculation about Europe's geographical knowledge before Columbus. But this 'Vinland Map' has never been completely authenticated, and many experts have come to regard it with considerable suspicion.[4] Such evidence of pre-Columbian knowledge of the New World, even if genuine, merely becomes part of the murky geography of the late Middle Ages.

None of the various attempts to argue for North American landfalls before Columbus—except for the Vikings in Newfoundland—can be indisputably documented. Prince Madoc of Wales, for example, is credited with a Welsh colony in Florida in the twelfth century, a legend associated with repeated later accounts of contact with Welsh-speaking Indians in the interior of North America. Various tablets with runic inscriptions on them have been 'uncovered' in regions settled by Scandinavians in the nineteenth century—

like the Kensington Rune Stone, discovered in Minnesota in 1898. Pre-Columbian landfalls have become a minor industry for writers with vivid imaginations. In the fifteenth century the Portuguese did locate the Azores Islands, almost halfway between Portugal and Newfoundland, and made many attempts without success to find other islands further west. The prevailing winds from the Azores, however, did not favour serendipitous landfalls on the American continent. Nevertheless, European world maps of the fifteenth century were full of still mythical islands waiting to be properly discovered. The Portuguese—along with their commercial allies, the English—would undoubtedly have made a landfall eventually if Christopher Columbus had not beat them to it.

The Background to the European Discovery of America

The 'discovery' of the Americas at the close of the fifteenth century was a collaborative effort of mariners and scholars of many nations. The very notion of the need to 'discover' lands already inhabited by millions of people was, of course, profoundly Eurocentric, explained by the surge of intellectual confidence and the explosion of knowledge associated with the Renaissance. By the last quarter of the fifteenth century, geographers—led by an Italian cosmographer in Portuguese service, Paolo dal Pozzo Toscanelli—were arguing that Europe and Asia were closer than the ancients had imagined. The schemes of Columbus were influenced both by Toscanelli and by Portuguese notions of oceanic islands. Not merely geographical speculation, but ship design and navigational aids, pointed towards transatlantic voyages. The Germans contributed the development of the *cog*, a single-masted ship, decked over and fitted with rudder and tiller, sometime in the twelfth century; in the early fifteenth century the cog's hull was lengthened and the vessel was given two additional masts, becoming the carvel (or caravel or *nef*). Explorers found smaller ships more manoeuverable than larger ones, and came to prefer them on their voyages. Rigging also improved, particularly with the addition of the square sail to the earlier lateen (triangular) variety.

The art of navigation showed parallel development to ship design, a gradual result of trial and error by countless mariners. The greatest advance was in written sailing directions based on the taking of latitudes in relation to Polaris and the sun; longitudes were still based largely on guesswork, mainly on a mariner's estimates of the speed of his vessel. In addition to the compass, seamen used quadrants and astrolabes to determine latitude, and were familiar with the need to transfer their data on latitude and longitude onto charts ruled for these variables. *Routiers*—coastal pilot charts of European waters—were readily available. But none of the early explorers who reached North America had the faintest idea of the hazards of the coasts he was visiting. The most remarkable feature of the first known voyages was the infrequency with which mariners ran into serious problems with rocks, shoals, and tides. Master mariners had a 'feel' for the sea; they were able to read and deduce much from its colour and surface patterns with considerable accuracy.

Though the early explorers inevitably had blind spots, they were without exception skilled sailors, suitably cautious in uncharted waters—which may explain many glaring failures to uncover rivers and bays that are obvious on any modern map. Once ashore, however, the first Europeans to reach North America threw caution to the winds, particularly in collecting rumours of rich mineral deposits, or routes to Asia. Neither they nor their sponsors were at all interested in the scientific accumulation of knowledge. What they sought was wealth, equivalent to the riches the Spaniards were taking out of their territories to the south. While other motives—such as national advantage and missionary fervour, directed at native inhabitants—also entered the picture, and the desire to become rich and famous certainly inspired men, like Christopher Columbus, who led the early voyages of discovery, the easy and rapid exploitation of the resources of the New World long remained dominant. Although the rich fishing grounds reported in the 1490s by John Cabot off Newfoundland were quickly exploited, commodities such as fish and furs, valuable though they were, were less compellingly attractive throughout the sixteenth century than mineral wealth. Well over a century passed before European ambition focused on settling the newly discovered territory.

The great voyages of discovery—largely completed by the end of the sixteenth century, even though much of the North American continent remained to be mapped and charted—occurred against a complex European background of dynastic manoeuvering, the rise of the modern nation-state, the religious disputes of the Protestant Reformation and the Catholic Counter-Reformation, and the growth of capitalistic enterprise fuelled by the infusion of new wealth in the form of gold and silver bullion from the Indies. In the sixteenth century Henry VII and Elizabeth I of England, and Francis I of France, were important patrons of master mariners who set sail for the West, hoping to obtain national advantage from the voyages they sponsored. The dissolution of an earlier alliance between Spain and England in the wake of the latter nation's becoming Protestant, and the complex relationships between the ruling houses of the two countries, encouraged Elizabeth to turn her 'sea dogs' loose on the Spanish Empire. English exploration was inextricably bound up with 'singeing the Spanish beard', and with political hostility to Spain heightened by religious sentiments, English adventurers often combined the activities of explorer, pirate, and even colonizer. France—after Cartier's pioneering voyages of 1534, 1535-6, and 1541-2—became more involved in its internal dynastic struggles than in overseas adventuring and did not show much state interest in North America until the end of the century. In both France and England, however, overseas investment by an emerging mercantile class took over from the earlier thrusts of discovery by intrepid mariners backed by the Crown. Cartier's third voyage marked for France the transition from public to private enterprise, and the 1576 voyage of Martin Frobisher in search of a Northwest Passage to the East demonstrated the new importance to the English of mercantile investment.

John Cabot and the Portuguese Mariners

As with most of the early master mariners who sailed to North America, the early years of John Cabot's life are shrouded in mystery. He was probably an Italian, perhaps even a Genoese like Columbus himself, although he became a citizen of Venice in 1476. Giovanni Caboto (1449/50-1498/9) was a merchant employed in the Mediterranean trade, and like many another fifteenth-century Italian merchant sailor, he was prepared to go wherever employment beckoned. In the 1490s, known as Juan Caboto Montecalunya, he was in Spain, involved in plans for the building of a new harbour at Valencia. The success of Columbus meant that Caboto would have little chance in Spain of pursuing his own plans to sail west to Asia. He would need other patrons, perhaps from more northerly nations. He and his family were attracted to Bristol—an English port long associated with Atlantic seafaring. Bristol traded more dutiable goods than any other provincial port in the kingdom, and its merchants were aggressive, always seeking new trade.

In 1497 an anglicized John Cabot obtained the support of Henry VII for a voyage to uncover a short route to Asia, in one small ship of fifty tons with a crew of eighteen. Bristol had long been involved in the Icelandic trade, and its seamen were familiar with the prevailing winds, which blew easterly in the spring. Cabot, therefore, left Bristol in mid-May, and on 24 June 1497— as a later chronicle put it—'was newfoundland fowend by Bristol men in a ship called the *Mathew*'. Except for the date, and the time (supplied by Cabot's son Sebastian half a century later), no details survive for the 1497 landfall in Newfoundland. Cabot apparently went ashore briefly, declared possession for England, and then sailed along the coast, observing the land and the great schools of fish from the deck of his tiny vessel. As soon as he returned to Bristol in early August 1497, he hastened to London to inform the king of his discovery.

Cabot had little enough to display to Henry VII, having made only a brief landfall and lacking any kidnapped natives to verify his story. His belief that he had landed in Asia, however, was perhaps given plausibility by the fact that he saw none of the local inhabitants. He emphasized that he had found an island, although he had not coasted completely around it. So Henry's reward of ten pounds 'to hym that founde the new Isle' was not only reasonable, but generous. Cabot subsequently got an annual pension of twenty pounds, which came from the Bristol customs receipts. He also received royal support for a follow-up voyage, the king and various London merchants fitting out one ship and Bristol merchants adding four more carrying 'course cloth,

Caps, Laces, points and other trifles' to trade with the 'Asian' inhabitants that Cabot had not yet seen. The little fleet left Bristol in May 1498. One ship put into Ireland in distress and subsequently returned home. The remaining four, along with John Cabot, were lost at sea. Much subsequent confusion over the facts of the Cabot ventures was caused by the boastings of Sebastian Cabot (*fl. c.*1484-1557), a likeable fellow who traded on his father's name but had little regard for truth.[5] In the long run, John Cabot's discovery would prove of enormous significance to England. But it could hardly compete with the news of the conquest of Mexico in 1519 by Cortés, and of Peru in 1532 by Pizarro. Codfish were simply not as compelling or commercially exciting as silver and gold, or pearls.

From the standpoint of northern Europe, the main objective to be pursued was not the island Cabot had found, but what theoretically lay beyond it. Cathay was the goal and, with a few exceptions, those who followed Cabot for most of the succeeding century sought a passage through North America to the fabled riches of the East. In the immediate wake of Cabot's disappearance, much of the activity came from Portugal, or more precisely from Portugal's outlying islands in the Azores. João Fernandes, a *lavrador* or small landholder of the Azores, sailed with Portuguese royal approval in search of new islands in 1500, finding only Greenland, which he named *Tierra del Lavrador*. The name would later be applied to the mainland area of eastern Canada. Fernandes was followed by Gaspar and Miguel Corte-Real, both of whom were raised in the Azores. To Gaspar, who landed at *Tierra Verde* (Newfoundland) in 1500, goes the dubious honour of kidnapping the first native inhabitants of North America in order to display them in Europe. He captured 57 Beothuk on his 1501 voyage, and they ended up at the Portuguese court. This large number of captives suggests that Corte-Real had some other plans for them besides using them as evidence of his landfall— they were probably intended as slave labour. But, like most other North American natives, they did not flourish in captivity. As for the Corte-Real brothers, they never returned from *Tierra Verde*.[6]

João Fernandes abandoned Portugal in the face of the competition from the Corte-Real brothers, moving to Bristol, where he joined with other Azoreans and English merchants in 1501 in petitioning Henry VII for support in new American voyages. Henry's grant allowed the petitioners to take possession for England of any place unknown to 'all Christians', and insisted that they take action against any 'who shall rape and violate against their will or otherwise any women of the islands or countries aforesaid'— one of the few instances of concern shown for the native peoples among early voyages of exploration. The resulting expeditions accomplished little, although in 1502 three Indians were brought back from the 'Newe Found Ileland'. Initially 'clothid in beastys skinnys' and behaving like 'bruyt bestis', according to one observer, they settled in rather comfortably at the royal court in fancy courtier's dress, enjoying their life as living exhibits of the wonders of America.[7] In 1521 Sebastian Cabot attempted to organize an expedition to Newfoundland, but two London guilds advised Henry VIII against the project, on the grounds that Sebastian had never been there himself, and 'He sayls not surely that sayls by an other manny's compas'. The maps of the first quarter of the sixteenth century began to show a more clearly defined Newfoundland, but most of the place-names were Portuguese rather than English.

Portugal actually attempted to settle a colony on the Newfoundland coast under the leadership of Juan Fagundes, who had earlier sailed as far as the Gulf of St Lawrence. Fagundes ended up on Cape Breton Island, where his little settlement was destroyed by natives who 'killed all those who came there'. Nevertheless, by 1536 Newfoundland was sufficiently familiar, if exotic, to Europeans that a tourist voyage to the island was organized. London merchant Richard Hore (*fl.*1507-40) signed up 120 passengers, 'whereof thirty were gentlemen'. When provisions ran short on the Newfoundland coast, some participants allegedly resorted to eating their compatriots. Those surviving were understandably pleased to get back to England.[8]

Jacques Cartier

At approximately this point the French entered the picture. Although France—since it contained a large agricultural hinterland and was not dependent to the same extent on overseas trade—was not a maritime nation in the same sense that England and Portugal were, the northern and western provinces of Normandy, Brittany, Saintonge, and Guyenne (or Guienne) had a long seafaring tradition. Normandy contained the seaports of Dieppe, Rouen (situated on the Seine, near its mouth on the English Channel), and Le Havre, which by the sixteenth century had many mercantile families and a considerable international reputation for shipbuilding and commerce. Brittany was the home of small fishermen and coastal traders, famed for its pilots and sailing skills. To the south of Brittany, on France's exposed Atlantic coast, was the great trading port of La Rochelle, whose mariners engaged in the fishery and the wine trade, and whose inhabitants turned to a Calvinist Protestantism that would eventually involve the city in bitter religious wars with the French Crown.

France first became involved in North America through the activities of an Italian master mariner, Giovanni da Verrazano (*c.*1485-*c.*1528). Unlike most of his fellow mariners, Verrazano was well born and a gentleman, perfectly at ease in the French court. But like Columbus and Cabot, he was also an experienced and a highly skilled seaman. In 1523 he persuaded Francis I to sponsor a voyage of exploration to North America, getting one ship on loan from the French navy and another from private backers in Lyons and Rouen. He eventually left France in *La Dauphine* in early January 1524, making his first landfall around Cape Fear in North Carolina and coasting north to avoid running into the Spaniards, who claimed a monopoly of the New World. At one point a young sailor, who was cast ashore and was unable to swim back to the ship, was found by Indians, who dried him out in front of a fire (he was convinced they were preparing to cook him) and assisted him to return to his comrades. Such accounts of native friendliness were far more common in the early days of discovery than tales of hostile inhabitants. Verrazano wrote that his intention 'was to reach Cathay and the extreme eastern coast of Asia, but I did not expect to find such an obstacle of new land as I have found; and if for some reason I did expect to find it, I estimated there would be some strait to get through to the Eastern Ocean.'[9] In coasting from North Carolina to Newfoundland, however, he succeeded in missing every important opportunity to penetrate into the interior of the continent. Nevertheless, Verrazano was convinced by the end of his voyage that what he had visited was not part of Asia, but a totally new continent. He made two more voyages, searching for a passage to Asia and for some natural resource that would bring a return to his investors. On the third voyage in 1528 he was reportedly killed by natives in Florida or the West Indies. His last two voyages succeeded in opening a French trade with Brazil, chiefly in 'logwood', used in Europe for dyeing cloth, and his North American ventures prepared the way for Jacques Cartier.

Cartier (1491-1557) was born in Saint-Malo, a small seaport on the northern Brittany coast. He went to sea as a young man, and his supporters claimed he had been to Brazil and Newfoundland. Suggested to Francis I in 1532 as a suitable leader of an expedition to North America, he was ordered by his monarch in 1534 to uncover new lands 'where it is said that a great quantity of gold, and other precious things, are to be found'.[10] While a passage to Cathay may have been part of the assignment, there is no evidence of any French concern to Christianize the Indians, and precious little to suggest that France had any intention to claim any new-found territories for the Crown by right of discovery. Cartier would make three voyages: one to make a new discovery, a second to locate some mineral resource there that would attract investors and the royal court, and a final large-scale effort that failed to satisfy the greedy.

The account of his first voyage of 1534 made clear that Cartier was thoroughly familiar with Newfoundland waters. He was able to draw a map of the Gulf of St Lawrence, fully aware that there was much to see inland from it. Bringing back the two sons of Donnacona was his principal evidence of success, but the two men would also serve as interpreters for another summer's effort. Cartier had found enough in the Gulf to stir the imagination of the king, who provided 3,000 *livres* for a follow-up voyage the next year. Cartier departed from Saint-Malo with three ships on 19 May 1535, and on 15 August entered the St Lawrence River, guided by Domagaya and Taignoagny, who said that here was 'the beginning of the Saguenay and of

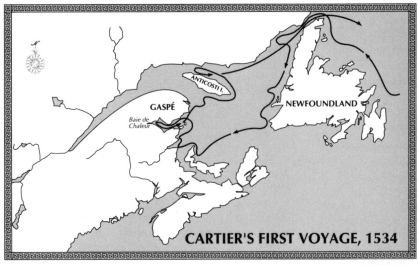

CARTIER'S FIRST VOYAGE, 1534

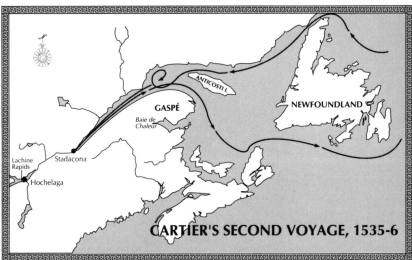

CARTIER'S SECOND VOYAGE, 1535-6

the inhabited region'. They spoke about copper, adding that up the river was 'the route towards Canada, and that the river grew narrower as one approached Canada; and also that farther up, the water became fresh, and that one could make one's way so far up the river that they had never heard of anyone reaching the head of it. Furthermore that one could only proceed along it in small boats.'[11] In early September they anchored off the Île d'Orléans and landed on the north shore of the river. They were met by Iroquois, living nearby in a small fortified village called Stadacona, who welcomed Taignoagny and Domagaya with dancing and ceremonies. The next day the visitors were greeted by many Indians, including Donnacona, who approached the ships in twelve canoes. Cartier found a place to lay up his two largest ships for the winter and in the *Émirillon* sailed upriver to find the village he had heard of called Hochelaga. He reached it on 2 October, met by 'great numbers' of friendly Indians who conducted Cartier and his party to the square in the centre of the village. There they were invited to sit down, on a mat the women provided, to receive the chief, called Agona, who was carried in seated in a deerskin: though only some fifty years old, he was paralysed. He, and many other sick people who came forward, hoped to be cured by the visitor. 'Seeing the suffering of these people and their faith, the Captain read aloud the Gospel of St John, namely "In the beginning, etc.", making the sign of the Cross. . . .' Hochelaga was a circular palisaded village and behind it was a high hill, which Cartier climbed and named Mont Royal. From there he viewed 'the most violent rapid it is possible to see, which we were unable to pass.' After mentioning another large river that came from the north (the Ottawa), the Indians 'seized the chain of the Captain's whistle, which was made of silver, and a dagger-handle of yellow copper-gilt like gold, that hung at the side of one of the sailors, and gave us to understand that these came from up that river.'[12]

The winter at Stadacona was difficult and longer than the one Europeans knew—from November to April. The river froze. Twenty-five men died and most of the others took sick from scurvy. The cure, provided by Domagaya, was perhaps the first gift from Canadian Indians to the white man: a drink made from the juice (filled with vitamin C) from the leaves of the white cedar. During the long nights of that Canadian winter the French heard much more about the Saguenay, mainly from Chief Donnacona. The inhabitants were white men, fabulously wealthy in gold, silver, and rubies. A neighbouring region was the home of people who, 'possessing no anus, never eat nor digest, but simply make water through the penis'. Old Donnacona probably enjoyed himself enormously acting out this description. Cartier determined to sail for France as soon as possible in the spring, taking Donnacona, his two sons, and other Indians back with him as witnesses to the possibilities. He also had some pieces of 'gold'.

Cartier had more to report from this second voyage than from his initial one. He had found an inland water route that took him far into the interior of the continent, had familiarized himself with its inhabitants, and had apparently penetrated to the margins of some sort of fabulously wealthy civilization. Whether the reports of the Saguenay in fact reflected native stories about affairs in Peru and Mexico has never been determined. Certainly the French court listened attentively, and believed, even when Donnacona elaborated still further on the great kingdom of Saguenay. There were gold and silver mines, as well as rich spice crops and some inhabitants who flew like bats, although only from one tree to another. Francis I was convinced. The Indians had never been caught in error, and besides, every-

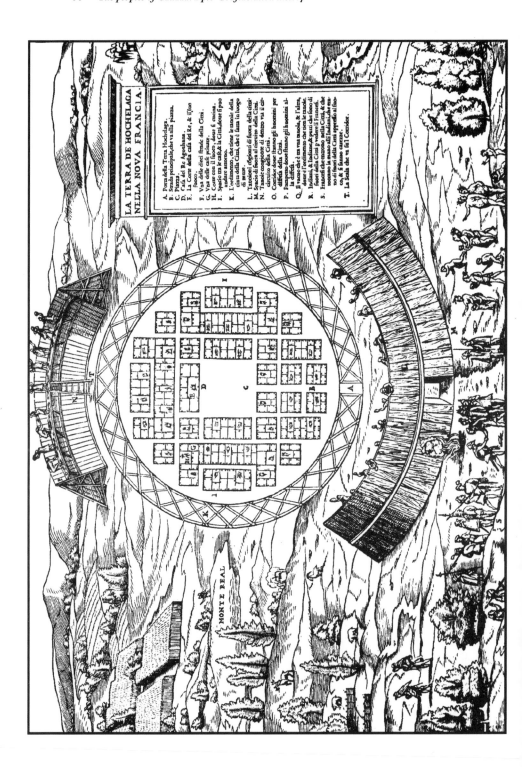

thing had been sworn before a notary. Belief was made easier by the knowledge that the Spaniards had indeed found Indian cities in Mexico and Peru—where gold was prized booty—and the French doubtless stimulated Donnacona's imagination with authentic Spanish information.[13]

The inevitable third, and substantial, colonizing expedition followed in 1541, led by a great nobleman, the Sieur de Roberval (c.1500-60), who had been appointed Viceroy of Saguenay. It was a disaster. Francis did not make the mistake of Ferdinand and Isabella of Spain, who permitted Columbus, a mere sailor, to have a monopoly over his discoveries. Cartier was initially put in charge, but then in 1541 was made pilot and no more. Roberval's commission included an explicit command not only to colonize the region but to Christianize the native inhabitants (Roberval, interestingly, was a Protestant); a necessary gesture, since the French were defying an earlier Papal bull that had divided the New World between Spain and Portugal. The rumours of Saguenay's riches were if anything exceeded by the talk of the enormous scope of the impending French expedition. Francis informed one Spanish complainant who opposed the venture 'that the sun shone for him as for others, and he would like very much to see Adam's will to learn how he divided up the world'![14]

Cartier sailed from Saint-Malo, with five ships, in late May 1541, leaving Roberval behind to find more money to support his expedition. Cartier brought with him none of the natives he had taken to France in 1536, for they had all died. He built two forts, upriver from Stadacona, called Charlesbourg-Royal, and made his way as far as Hochelaga and the Lachine Rapids, but soon turned back. The winter at Charlesbourg-Royal was fraught with scurvy, which was overcome, and hostile Indians. In June 1542 Cartier peremptorily broke camp and sailed for France, meeting Roberval's three

◀ **This diagrammatic rendering of Hochelaga—one of the best-known images associated with the discovery of Canada—was drawn from the description of Hochelaga in the account of Cartier's second voyage, and appeared in Giambattista Ramusio's Italian translation published in Venice in 1556, the year before Ramusio died. It is an interpretation of the following: 'And in the middle of these fields [of corn] is situated and stands the city of Hochelaga, near and adjacent to the mountain, the slopes of which are fertile and are cultivated, and from the top of which one can see for a long distance. . . . The village is circular and is completely enclosed by a wooden palisade in three tiers like a pyramid. . . . There is only one gate to this village. . . . Over this and in many places about the enclosure are species of galleries with ladders for mounting to them, which galleries are provided with rocks and stones for the defence and protection of the place.' The key refers to such things as: 'A. Gate to city of Hochelaga.' 'D. House of King Agouhana.' 'E. Courtyard of said royal house, and his fire [the fire is clearly in the house, not the courtyard].' R at the bottom refers to the meeting of Indians and Frenchmen—Cartier and Agona are shown shaking hands, as though at some grand reception in Europe. (Agona's paralysed state is ignored.) National Library of Canada, Rare Book Collection, C-68757.**

ships anchored in the harbour of St John's, Newfoundland. He told Roberval that he had with him 'certaine Diamonts, and a quantitie of Golde ore, which was found in the Countrye', and said that his small company could not withstand the Indians, who 'went about dayly to annoy him', which was why he had left. He 'commended the Countrey to bee very rich and fruitful', but refused to return. According to the account in Richard Hakluyt's *Voyages and Discoveries* (1600): '...hee and his company, mooved as it seemeth with ambition, because they would have all the glory of the discoverie of those partes themselves, stoll privily away the next night from us, and without taking their leaves, departed home for Bretaigne [Brittany].'[15]

Roberval carried on, establishing himself on the site of Cartier's Charlesbourg-Royal, renamed 'France-Roy'. He was not a proven leader or colonizer; harshness and cruelty seemed his principal attributes. In fairness, most of his 200 colonists had come from French gaols, and so it was hardly surprising that he was very cruel in dealing with his men, forcing them to work; otherwise they were deprived of food and drink. If anyone failed in his duty, Roberval had him punished. One day he had six of them hanged and some he ordered to be banished to an island, in leg-irons, because they had been caught in petty thefts involving not more than five *sous*. Others, both men and women, were flogged for the same offence.[16]

But he had acted with equal harshness against his kinswoman Marguerite de La Roque, who accompanied him on the voyage and fell in love with a young man on the ship. Roberval dumped the girl on a remote island (Île des Démons in the Strait of Belle Isle) with a maidservant; they were joined by the young man. Marguerite bore a child, who died. Only she had survived two-and-a-half years later, when she was discovered by fishermen and taken back to France, where she told her extraordinary story to the historian André Thevet:

> It was from her own lips that I learned this pitiful tale of her punishment. . . .She also told me that when she boarded the Breton fishing boat to return to France, she was overcome with a desire to go no farther, to stay and die on that lonely island as her lover had done, and her baby and servant. Overcome as she was with sadness when she talked to me, she still felt that way, she said.[17]

Roberval's severity with his colonists was sharpened by his failure to find anything to exploit. In June 1543 he did some exploring, going up the St Lawrence towards Hochelaga in search of the Kingdom of Saguenay. But this venture led to nothing, and his ships left in July and were back in France in September 1543. The aftermath of this expedition was predictable, with the usual recriminations and royal commission to examine the accounts. Roberval was financially ruined, and was eventually assassinated leaving a Calvinist meeting in Paris.

As for Cartier, the 'gold and diamonds' he had gathered turned out to be iron pyrites and quartz. 'False as Canadian diamonds' become a common expression of the time. Cartier clearly benefited from Francis I's decision not to put him in charge, which meant that he did not become chief scapegoat. He was never given another major command, however, and retired as a *noble homme* to his estate at Limoëlou, near Saint-Malo, always willing to talk about his adventures with those who sought him out. The disastrous third voyage put the French off further overseas ventures until early in the next century, although the internal political problems that arose after the death of Francis I in 1547 also played their part in delaying further colonizing ventures. Nevertheless Cartier had established a French claim to the St Lawrence region, and the French would ultimately return there.

Later English Activities

With the French effectively neutralized for half a century, the spotlight was turned on the English, who were enjoying one of those periodic flowerings of achievement and releases of energy that come to nations. English activity in Newfoundland, inaugurated by Cabot, continued without publicity while Cartier was investigating the St Lawrence. But English adventurism in the second half of the sixteenth century was spearheaded by a confluence of efforts to expand legitimate markets for trade, with highly successful raiding forays against the overseas trade of others, particularly the Spanish. The combination of the quest for markets and booty produced Martin Frobisher (1539?-94), and his search for a Northwest Passage in the Canadian Arctic.

Frobisher (or Furbusher, as his name was often spelled in contemporary records) came from the English gentry, as did other English adventurers of the period like Drake, Raleigh, Gilbert, Hawkins, and Grenville. Frobisher's 'great spirit and bould courage, and naturall hardnes of body' led him onto the high seas.[18] In the early 1550s he participated in two English trading ventures to the Guinea coast of Africa, and was held as a hostage by the natives for some months before being released. By 1564 he was one of England's leading 'sea dogs', a master mariner whose activities encompassing both legitimate trade and questionable privateering made his name, according to English Admiralty Court records, 'as well known to Philip of Spain and as well hated as that of Hawkins himself'. He was at least three times charged with piracy, although never brought to trial, and English merchants trading with France complained of his depredations against their vessels, commenting that 'no six of their ships were fit to cope with Frobisher'. Like others of his generation, Frobisher had long been fascinated by the possibility of a short route to Cathay through North America. The potential for profit from such a route would dwarf even the rich returns from slaving or privateering, and Frobisher spent many years attempting to interest investors in an expedition to find one. The English monopoly on such ventures was held by merchants trading to Russia as the Muscovy Company. It sent several parties to seek a Northeast Passage in the 1550s, and eventually Frobisher succeeded in persuading it to license an expedition. With the assistance of Michael Lok, the Company's director, he raised funds for three small vessels.

Dr John Dee—that curious figure of Elizabethan science who combined skills as a mathematician and hydrographer with an interest in astrology and the occult—instructed the Frobisher party in the latest navigational aids. Although the little fleet lost one vessel near Greenland, while another turned back from fear of the ice, the *Gabriell*, with Frobisher aboard, carried on westward, 'knowing that the Sea at length must needes have an endyng, and that some lande should have a beginning that way'. On 28 July 1576 he sighted land, to the north of which was a 'great gutte, bay or passage', into which the ship sailed.[19] Nearly a month later Frobisher climbed a hill on the coast of of the narrow 'strait' he was sailing. Looking west he 'saw far the two head lands at the furthest end of the straiets, and no likelyhood of land to the northwards of them and the great open betwene them which by reason of the great tydes of flood which they found comming owt of the same, land for many other reasons they judged to be the West Sea, whereby to pass to Cathay and to the East India.'[20]

Unfortunately Frobisher took his sighting not from the outer coast of Asia but from Baffin Island, and the 'strait' he was navigating (which would be named for him) was actually a deep bay. Equally unfortunately, Frobisher ran into trouble with the local Inuit, losing five of his crew to the natives and

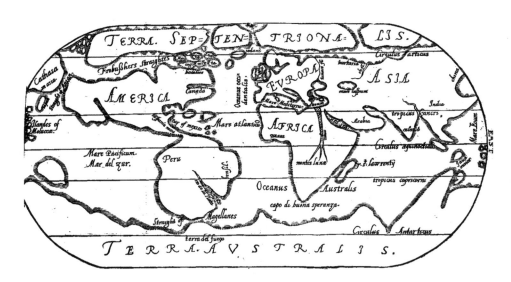

This map appeared in *A True Discourse of the Late Voyages of Discoverie, for the Finding of a Passage to Cathaya, by the Northeast, under the Conduct of Martin Frobisher. . .*(London, 1578) by George Best, Frobisher's lieutenant on the second voyage. Rare Books and Manuscripts Division, The New York Public Library: Astor, Lenox and Tilden Foundations.

capturing one Inuit (and his kayak). As he had hoped, his return to London with this 'strange man and his bote' created 'such a wonder onto the whole city and to the rest of the realm that heard of yt as seemed never to have happened the like great matter to any man's knowledge.'[21] The captive soon died, however, having caught a cold at sea. Such treatment of the Inuit was typical of English visitations to the Arctic that followed, and contributed to an ongoing hostility between natives and the visitors.

Perhaps most unfortunately of all, Frobisher's backers, led by Michael Lok,

This watercolour-and-ink drawing by John White shows Inuit attacking the Englishmen with bows and arrows and being fired on by muskets—a conflict that was described in accounts of Frobisher's second expedition. Copyright British Museum, 202756.

chose to publicize a promising rock brought back from Baffin Island. Although three experts were unimpressed, a fourth—who by his own account knew 'how to flatter nature'— pronounced it gold-bearing.[22] Why Lok knowingly permitted this dubious assessment to encourage eager investment in a follow-up voyage is not clear. A willingness to use gold as a lure for financing an expedition that would end up in Cathay was understandable, but Frobisher was instructed to concentrate on 'the Gold Ore, and to deferre the further discoverie of the passage until another tyme'. Perhaps Lok became trapped by his own deceptions. In any event, Frobisher set out on a second voyage in May 1577, with three ships and 120 men. To his credit, he spent much of the time in the summer of that year searching for his lost sailors. On this voyage he was accompanied by artist John White (born *c.* 1540-50), who produced the first pictorial representations of native North Americans in their home environment, including a sketch of an armed confrontation between the English and Inuit at Frobisher Bay. Frobisher returned with 200 tons of ore and three more Inuit (who died within a month of arriving in England). On his third and final voyage of 1578 he brought home quantities of ore that eventually led everyone to admit failure. Despite the controversy around this venture, Frobisher returned to an active and successful career as a buccaneer, serving as Drake's second-in-command in a 1585 privateering expedition against Spain and as a principal commander in the English defence against the Spanish Armada in 1588. He died in 1594 from a wound incurred in besieging a Spanish-held fortress in France.

Fascination with the possibility of a Northwest Passage continued to lure mariners for centuries into the icy Arctic waters, and over the next fifty years a series of explorers—mainly Englishmen, backed by English capital— greatly expanded Europe's knowledge of these northern regions. In three voyages (1585-7) John Davis (1550?-1605) entered and named Davis Strait (1585), the first link in the Passage, and crossed Hudson Strait (1587) without entering it. His log books were shown to Henry Hudson (d. 1611), who used them for his last voyage of 1610 under Dutch auspices. Hudson sailed into the Strait, entering Hudson Bay, and navigated its eastern coastal waters southward into James Bay—named by Thomas James (1593?-1635?), who visited it twenty years later—where he wintered. In the spring of 1611 Hudson's crew, experiencing the usual scurvy and rebelliousness of sailors too long at sea, cast their captain adrift in a small boat, along with his son and six others. His ship *Discovery* was sailed back to England by Robert Bylot who, with eight other crewmen, was tried for the murder of Hudson and pardoned. In 1615 and 1616 Bylot commanded two voyages on the *Discovery* with William Baffin (1584?-1622) as his pilot. They sailed in 1616 through Davis Strait, discovered Baffin Bay and Lancaster Sound to the north of it, without realizing that this was the entrance to the Northwest Passage for which so many had searched.[23] It would not be discovered for another two centuries.

Apart from expanded geographical information, the only result of these daring feats of seamanship was to anticipate an English claim of discovery to Hudson Bay and James Bay. This would prove useful when Frenchmen, particularly Pierre Radisson and Médard Chouart Des Groseilliers, had identified the potential value of the region for fur-trading.

The Overland Explorers

Although the High Arctic remained a focus for intrepid explorers until well into the twentieth century, by the end of the sixteenth century the opportunity for Europeans to make major new findings on the eastern coast of North America had come to an end. For the moment Europe had established that no wealthy native civilizations existed to be conquered on the eastern coast, and that no readily apparent sources of rich mineral wealth could be exploited. But when it was realized that the continent possessed fish and furs, a more complex pattern of exploitation was developed that required the year-round presence of settlers. Both France and England shifted their energies from maritime thrusts to colonization. The existence of a settled European population desperately seeking commodities to market in the Old World would lead to another century of exploration—this time overland, into the vast interior of the continent.

The geographical shakedown of European colonization activity in the late sixteenth and early seventeenth centuries determined that it would be the French who would take the lead in overland exploration, and that their activities would extend far beyond the boundaries of what is now Canada. While the English, Scots, Dutch, and Swedes established settlements along the eastern seaboard, the French—prudently, if belatedly, acting on Cartier's discoveries—founded their settlements on the St Lawrence River. Providing access to the Great Lakes and to most of the major river systems of the continent, this river would confer enormous power and influence for over a century on the nation that controlled it. It pre-eminently focused the French need for new sources of furs to supply the major export commodity of New France, and the ability of young Frenchmen to adapt themselves to the ways of the native inhabitants. It therefore ensured that most of the great feats of overland discovery would be executed by the French.

For many years French overland explorers have figured prominently in the primary-school curriculums in Canadian history and geography, and have acquired an unfortunate reputation that says more about the way the material has been taught than about its intrinsic interest. Many Canadians in primary school have had to 'research' the career of one or more of these explorers, using encyclopedias and standard reference works—an exercise that taught them precious little about historical research and even less about these men, who are commonly shorn of their humanity and individuality.

The first major French overland explorer was Étienne Brûlé (*c.*1592-1633), who lived with the Hurons near Georgian Bay, Lake Huron, in 1612, and may have been the first European to sight Lake Superior and Lake Erie. A rather elusive figure, Brûlé, like many early explorers, left no written accounts of his life or adventures. It is likely that he had volunteered in 1610 to live with the Indians and to learn their language, and he was probably the young man to whom Champlain referred in 1611 as accompanying an Indian party to meet with the French:

> I also saw my French boy who came dressed like an Indian. He was well pleased with the treatment received from the Indians, according to the customs of the country, and explained to me all that he had seen during the winter, and what he had learned from the Indians. . . . [He] had learned their language very well.[24]

In 1615 Brûlé accompanied a party of Huron braves into the territory of the Susquehannah to the south of the Iroquois, in what is now southwestern New York State. He took advantage of the opportunity to investigate the neighbouring regions, perhaps reaching Chesapeake Bay, and certainly tramping around modern Pennsylvania.

Brûlé subsequently journeyed to the north shore of Georgian Bay, and then in the early 1620s along the St Marys River to Lake Superior. Like many Europeans who 'went native', Brûlé was respected as an interpreter by his compatriots, even though they were intensely suspicious of his new persona. In Brûlé's case, his moral character and behaviour were criticized by Champlain even before his final 'treachery' of 1629, when he entered the employment of the Scottish Kirke brothers who had successfully captured the French colony. He had thus established a familiar pattern for those early Europeans who had come to terms with North America—such as the La Tour family in Acadia, and Pierre Radisson—by pursuing his own agenda rather than observing the abstract national loyalties dear to European hearts and values. By 1633 Brûlé was dead, reportedly killed and eaten by Hurons.

Over the course of the seventeenth century the interpreter, as represented by Brûlé, was transformed into the *coureur de bois*—the 'runner of the woods', or 'bushloper', as the English often called him. These men were responsible for most of the constantly broadening geographical knowledge of the North American continent. Their desire, however, was less to improve cartography than to exploit new sources of wealth, particularly furs, and above all to enjoy a free and adventurous life in the woods. Whether or not these wilderness braves became completely assimilated into Indian society and culture—some did—they all learned skills from the native peoples that made them crucial figures in the economy of New France. Sighting latitude or reading the surface of the water were joined by the ability to live off the land, to paddle a canoe for long distances with few breaks, to hunt animals for food, and of course to communicate successfully with a local Indian population—not merely at the level of language but at one of genuine empathy.

These inland explorers travelled in exposed small parties and had no defensive structure such as a ship to protect them from attack. They lived by their wits and had to be constantly adaptable. They made splendid guerilla warriors, as the English discovered to their dismay in the subsequent wars for control of the continent.

Few *coureurs de bois* had the time or the inclination to keep detailed records of their adventures or even of their personal lives. But one of the greatest, Pierre-Esprit Radisson, has left accounts of his six 'voyages' into the interior in the form of a series of autobiographical narratives, the first four of which he dictated in his imperfect but vivid English.[25] They constitute some of the most fascinating documents of the early period of European settlement and expansion across the continent, a window onto another world where the rules of life were quite different from those of 'civilization'.

Radisson (c.1640-1710), who was born in France, was living in Trois-Rivières as an eleven-year-old in 1651 when he was captured by a Mohawk raiding party and was adopted into a prominent family, rapidly acquiring the Indian ways. Meeting another Frenchman in similar circumstances on a hunting trip, the two young men murdered their Indian companions and escaped, but were soon recaptured. Radisson was tortured—in ways meticulously described in his account—but was saved by his adoptive parents. Later, as a member of a raiding party into the country of the Dutch, he initially rejected an offer of repatriation from a Dutch trader, but changed his mind when he returned to his village. He determined to escape while he was still trusted. As he put it in his account:

> I repented of a good occasion I let slip, finding myself in the place with offers of many to assist me, but he that is of a good resolution must be of strong hopes of what he undertakes, and if the dangers were considered which may be found in things of importance, you ingenious men would become cooks.[26]

Radisson had no intention of becoming a cook. He escaped and in 1654 was back in Trois-Rivières, where he found that his widowed half-sister had married Médard Chouart Des Groseilliers (c.1618-96?), who would become his associate in a series of wilderness expeditions and adventures.

In 1657 Radisson accompanied some Jesuit missionaries to the Iroquois village at Onondaga in present-day New York State. Relations between the visitors and the Iroquois were tense over the ensuing winter, so Radisson employed his knowledge of Indian psychology to plan an escape. In the spring the Indians were invited to a great feast given by the French, who provided large quantities of food, drink, and entertainment, insisting their guests could not sleep until everything had been consumed. Eventually, according to Radisson, the Indians could

> hold out no longer; they must sleep. They cry out, 'Skenon'!—enough. 'We can bear no more'. ('Let them cry skenon. We Will cry hunnay!—we are agoing,' says we.) They are told that the French are weary and will sleep awhile.

They say, 'Be it so.' We come away. All is quiet. Nobody makes a noise after such a hurly-burly. The fort is shut up as if we had been in it. We leave a hog at the door for sentry, with a rope tied to his foot. He wanted no meat for the time.[27]

The Jesuits prevented their secular companions from slaughtering the sated and perhaps drugged natives and their families, a possible strategy Radisson considered without qualms, writing simply: 'It was no great matter to deal with five or six hundred women and maybe a thousand children.' Instead, the party stole silently away.

In 1659 Radisson began his partnership with Groseilliers, his brother-in-law, on a journey to Lake Superior that excited their interest in exploiting the fur-bearing region that they knew extended as far north as Hudson Bay. The pair returned to Montreal in August 1660 with a vast haul of beaver skins that was seen as the colonys's salvation. The two fur-traders were not well received, however; their furs were confiscated and both men were prosecuted for trading without official permission. Groseilliers made a voyage to France to protest, but without much success. Not surprisingly, Radisson and Groseilliers wound up in 1664 in Boston, where the English were far more supportive and enthusiastic than the French about their interest in Hudson Bay. Taken to London, the two Frenchmen succeeded in convincing English merchants in 1668 to send two ships to Hudson Bay, discovered earlier by Henry Hudson but offering no economic incentive for further exploitation until the fur-trading potential was clearly understood. Radisson's ship turned

Pierre-Esprit Radisson, a line drawing copied from an old Paris print. National Archives of Canada, B-70.

back, but his brother-in-law carried on, returning in October 1669 with a superb cargo of furs. On 2 May 1670 the merchants founded by royal charter a formal trading company, 'The Governor and Company of Adventurers of England Trading into Hudson Bay', usually called the Hudson's Bay Company, which received title to the entire drainage basin of Hudson Bay—about forty per cent of modern Canada. Later that month Radisson and Groseilliers again went to the Bay, Radisson to the mouth of the Nelson River where Charles Bayly (c.1630-80), the overseas Governor of the new company, took possession of the land. In order to take up his new posting, Bayly had been released by the king, Charles II, from the Tower of London, where he had been imprisoned for seditious practices associated with his espousal of Quaker doctrine.[28]

French concern for this English competition in the fur trade, which had established a direct route to the fur-bearing regions of the Bay that bypassed the interior channels into the continent controlled by New France, resulted in 1675 in overtures to Radisson and Groseilliers to return to French employ. Radisson complied, but he found himself treated with much suspicion, particularly because he had married an Englishwoman, a daughter of Sir John Kirke (a major Hudson's Bay Company investor and one of the Kirke brothers who had captured Quebec in 1629), and was unable to convince his wife to defect with him. He was allowed to join a French freebooting expedition to Africa, barely escaping with his life, but gaining neither riches nor position. For the next ten years Radisson and Groseilliers attempted to play English against French to their own advantage, but they were very small fish in the complex imperial intrigues of the day. In the wilderness Radisson was master. Indeed, one of his exultant phrases about his adventures in the interior—'We were Caesars, there being none to contradict us'—captures perfectly the best spirit of the seventeenth-century inland explorer. But he was out of his depth in international intrigue.

Although the French did succeed in employing Radisson for a time in the early 1680s, by 1684 he had returned to the English, who immediately sent him back to the Bay. There he persuaded his nephew—Groseilliers's son, in charge of a French post on the Nelson River—to defect to the English, and leave with Radisson and a great cargo of furs only one step ahead of a French relief expedition. Radisson spent the years 1685 to 1687 in Hudson Bay, retiring thereafter to a London suburb and living off stock dividends and an annuity from the Hudson's Bay Company until his death in 1710. Beginning his career as a simple *coureur de bois*, with unusual powers of endurance and a pragmatic adaptability—which, among other things, allowed him to change his allegiance, with little compunction, more than once—Radisson was unusual among his fellow bushlopers in becoming involved in international events that visibly altered the history of the wilderness he helped open up. And the record of his adventures in his own words has added to his singularity and fame.

As most Canadian schoolchildren are all too painfully aware, there were a good many overland explorers in the seventeenth century, some of whom even had automobiles named after them. One of Radisson's major competitors for French support was René-Robert Cavelier de La Salle (1643–87), whose background was quite different from that of the typical bushloper, but who shared the energy, independence, and flexibility of character that exemplified the successful adventurer in North America. Born in Rouen of a wealthy family, and educated by the Jesuits—who labelled him *Inquietus* while he was in minor orders—he received release from his vows on grounds of 'moral frailties', drifting in 1667 to Montreal, where he was given a seigneury. After a brief attempt at agriculture, he sold his property, except for his horse, and organized a western expedition 'in order not to leave to another the honour of finding the way to the Southern Sea, and thereby the route to China', thus giving rise to the mocking name for his seigneury of 'Lachine'.[29] La Salle was totally unequipped for such a venture, one clerical companion observing:

> M. de la Salle, who said that he understood the Iroquois perfectly, and had learned all these things from them as a result of the perfect knowledge he had of their language, did not know it at all, and was undertaking this voyage almost blindly, without knowing where he was going.[30]

La Salle left Montreal in July 1669, with nine canoes, and spent two years wandering in the western Indian territory, undoubtedly learning much about the native people and their ways, although probably not making any of the major discoveries later claimed by him and attributed to him.

In any event, supported by Governor Frontenac and the Jesuits, in 1675 La Salle obtained a letter of nobility for himself in France, and in 1677 was authorized by Louis XIV to explore the vast interior of the continent. On an expedition begun in 1679 and broken by several returns to Montreal, he managed to reach the Mississippi River early in 1682, taking possession of the Mississippi Delta country (to be called Louisiana after the king—who else?) in a splendid ceremony on 9 April of that year. According to one chronicler, 'The whole party, under arms, chanted the *Te Deum,* the *Exaudiat,* the *Domine salvum fac Regem*; and then, after a salute of firearms and cries of *Vive le Roi,* the column was erected by M. de la Salle, who, standing near it . . . with a loud voice, in French', made his proclamation, 'to which the whole assembly responded with shouts of *Vive le Roi* and salutes of firearms.'[31] The differences between this impressive possession ceremony and that of Charles

◀ **Perhaps the most beautiful map of the cartographer Jean-Baptiste-Louis Franquelin, who worked at Quebec from 1671 to 1692 as both 'king's geographer' and 'king's hydrographer'. Elaborately decorated and delicately coloured, it shows the known territory of New France in 1688, with the bonus of a portrait of Quebec. National Archives of Canada, Cartographical and Architectural Archives Division, PH/1000/1688.**

Bayly at Port Nelson are striking. Bayly went ashore, and in the presence of a few witnesses, including Pierre Radisson, silently nailed His Majesty's arms 'in Brasse' on a tree as a sign of possession.

La Salle sought to establish a French colony in Louisiana; but whatever his merits as an explorer, he was a terrible organizer and leader. He was eventually murdered in 1687 on the banks of the Trinity River by a colleague who held a personal grudge against him. Although his contemporaries saw him as a man who mixed 'great defects and great virtues',[32] nineteenth-century historians in both Canada and the United States, led by Francis Parkman of Boston, turned him into the quintessential western explorer.[33] La Salle's background and pretensions worked to his advantage for the nineteenth century, while Radisson, whose career was far more typical of the inland adventurers, was much too earthy and human to serve as a hero for the Victorians. And yet today Radisson is much better known than La Salle—with a TV series based on his career, and a hotel chain named after him. Such is the changing taste in heroes.

While exploration of the western and northern parts of North America would continue well into the nineteenth century—and of the Arctic into the twentieth—by 1700 the cartography of the eastern half of the continent had been largely completed, and the claims of the competing European powers were well established, if not entirely settled. The English had eliminated competition from the Dutch and the Swedes along the eastern seaboard, and controlled the coastal regions from present-day Maine to South Carolina—as well as Newfoundland. The Spanish held Florida. The French dominated Acadia (including the three Maritime Provinces of Canada), and above all the St Lawrence Valley and its river connections down to Louisiana. The interior country, between the Mississippi and the Appalachian mountains, was still in dispute, as was the Atlantic region and the Hudson Bay country.

Two patterns of European discovery, however, had been established. One (the English) emphasized a maritime approach, focusing on the skills of the master mariner and resulting in a direct transatlantic contact between Europe and America. The other (the French) moved overland, acquiring familiarity with the skills of the native inhabitants, frequently by prolonged residence with them. Both groups of explorers contained a remarkable breed of men: attracted by adventure and risk, they were driven by the desire for wealth, for fame—or simply to celebrate the glory of God. But they were seldom fitted for the less exciting, and far more mundane, work of transplanting Europeans to the New World. After all they were not cooks, but rather Caesars.

chapter three

Colonizers and Settlers

in the Early Seventeenth Century

Sitting at his desk in his mansion-house built of stone at 'Avalon', his plantation on the southeast coast of Newfoundland, George Calvert (c.1580-1632) dipped his quill to write a letter to his sovereign. He took great care with his penmanship, for the king, Charles I, had years before commented that despite the neat look of his handwriting, 'when any man came neare it they were not able to read a word.' Born in Yorkshire, Calvert had attended Oxford University and then advanced rapidly in the seventeenth-century equivalent of the civil service. He had begun in 1606 as private secretary to Sir Robert Cecil, the king's chief minister, and in 1619 became a secretary of state and key member of the Privy Council. An active leader of King James's party against Parliament, Calvert had resigned abruptly in 1625, the year the king died, because of his conversion to Roman Catholicism, and retired to Ireland as Baron Baltimore of County Longford. Before leaving office Calvert became involved in Newfoundland settlement, first obtaining land in 1621 from Sir William Vaughan (who in 1617 had begun a colony he called Cambriol) and in 1623 receiving a royal charter for his plantation of Avalon.[1]

Unlike most of the men and women in England and France who projected and financed North American settlement in the sixteenth and seventeenth centuries, Lord Baltimore actually crossed the Atlantic in 1628 and resided for a year and a half in his colony at Ferryland, some 50 miles south of St John's, supervising it personally after experiencing considerable difficulty with absentee direction and local agents. He brought with him a young wife and nearly a dozen children by a previous marriage. Baltimore's Newfoundland experience was in some respects hardly typical of that of an ordinary settler, for he was well supplied with food, drink, and servants, and had no need to work long hours at manual labour to survive. Nevertheless, Newfoundland was a considerable shock to him, as he explained to his sovereign on 19 August 1629:

I [have] met with greater difficultyes and emcumbrances here which in this place are no longer to be resisted, but enforce me presently to quitt my residence, and to shift to some other warmer climate of this new worlde, where the wynters be shorter and less rigourous. For here, your Majesty may please to understand, that I have found by too dear bought experience, which other men for their private interests always concealed from me that from the middest of October, to the middest of May there is a sadd face of wynter upon all this land, both sea and land so frozen for the greatest part of the tyme that they are not penetrable, no plant or vegetable thing appearing out of the earth untill it be about the beginning of May nor fish in the sea besides the ayre so intolerable cold, as it is hardly to be endured.[2]

Calvert thereupon left Newfoundland for Virginia. He would ultimately receive a royal grant for territory north of the Potomac River called Maryland.

Lord Baltimore's complaints suggest some of the conceptual difficulties Europeans had with North America as a region for colonization. For a people accustomed to great dynastic struggles over land—which was related to political, social, and economic power, as well as to a constant demand by the ever-increasing population of common folk for access to enough ground on which they could eke out a living—the vast expanses of North America claimed only by native peoples seemed highly attractive. At a time when relatively few Europeans had attempted to live permanently year-round on the 'new' continent, little thought was given to the possibility that one might 'possess' thousands of acres of this wilderness and still not have enough food to make a decent meal. Ignorance bred optimism, not least among those who had no intention of serving as the guinea pigs.

The Motives for Colonization

The enthusiastic early promoters of North American settlement were largely absentee colonizers. Their motives for pursuing their grand projects were both varied and complicated, both laudable and despicable. National advantage, religion, humanitarianism, greed, and ambition jostled one another in the rhetoric of early colonization. Richard Whitbourne's *Discourse and Discovery of New-Found-Land*, which was recommended in 1620 for publication by the English Privy Council 'to bee distributed to the severall parishes of the Kingdom for the Incoridgment of such as shalbee willinge to assist that Plantation ether in there persons or other wise', expressed the official view of colonization well:

The Seas are so rich, as they are able to advance a great Trade of Fishing; which, with Gods blessing will become very serviceable to the Navie; and the increase of fishing there, cannot despaire of finding ports enow to vent the commoditie at profitable rates. Now if you would understand what motives wee have at home with us to carry us thither; doe but look upon the populousness of our

Countrey, to what a surfet of multitude it is subject; consider how charitable for those that goe, and how much ease it will be for those that stay, to put forth some of our numbers, to such an imployment of living. . . .There is another motive also, which amongst our Ancestors was wont to find good respect, namely the honour of the action, by the enlarging of Dominions; and that which will crowne the worke, will be the advancement of the honour of God, in bringing poore Infidels (the Natives of that Countrey) to his Worship, and their own salvation.[3]

The Crown—be it English, French, or Scottish—was the source of the charters and grants upon which early settlement was based. European sovereigns invested virtually nothing in the first colonies established in North America under their auspices. The documents of territorial title and trade monopoly given by monarchs to their subjects contained performance clauses that were seldom met, providing a justification for revocation when another promoter appeared. Moreover, given the vagueness of the promotions, which lacked serious planning, and the huge uncharted territories involved, it is not surprising that monarchs were unconcerned about duplication, particularly in the earliest period. The Marquis de La Roche de Mesgouez (1540-1606), for example, on 12 January 1598 was granted by Henri IV of France title to the territories of Canada, Newfoundland, Labrador, and Norumbega (the Penobscot region of Maine), as well as a monopoly of the fur trade in these regions. The French king, only a year later, made an almost identical grant to Pierre de Chauvin de Tonnetuit (d. 1603). Such instances of competing claims, even within the purview of a single European nation, were common. When the claims involved promoters from different countries, they were often settled by force.

If European monarchs and their advisers were happy to leave the establishment of a national presence in North America to the shock troops of private enterprise, they equally were flattered to think that they were encouraging God's work. Much of the earliest talk of missionary activities to the native inhabitants was pure rhetoric. Richard Whitbourne wrote about converting natives, but John Mason, in his *A Brief Discourse of the New-Found-Land* (1620), argued that one of Newfoundland's advantages was the 'securitie from foraine and domesticke enemies, there being but few Savages in the north, and none in the south parts of the Countrie.'[4] Certainly few of the early English ventures to Newfoundland included a clergyman, and most of the first French expeditions—including Champlain's to the St Lawrence River in 1608—did not carry any priests with them.

Although religious motivations to save the souls of native peoples were not very important to most early colonial promoters, religion did play its part in some of the early ventures. The initial English attempt at settlement in what is now Canada—the ill-fated and little-remembered colony of 'Ramea' in the Îles de la Madeleine, in the Gulf of St Lawrence, begun in 1597—was organized by religious dissenters who wanted to go 'to a foreign and far country which lieth to the west from hence in the Province of Canada' in order 'to worship God as we are in conscience persuaded by his Word.'[5] The English Crown authorized a group of 'artificers and other persons that are noted to be sectaries...to plant themselves in an Island called Ramea or thereabouts' as an alternative to conforming in religion at home. The vanguard of this project were four English dissenters who had separated from the Church of England, led by the Johnson brothers—Francis (1562-1618) and George (1564-1605).[6] The party were driven off the islands by Basque and Breton fishermen, assisted by Micmac allies. After returning to London, they led their awaiting compatriots to Amsterdam, some of them returning to America in 1620 on board the *Mayflower*. Lord Baltimore's conversion to Roman Catholicism and his ambition to turn Avalon into a religious refuge were well known at both the English court and the Vatican in the 1620s.[7] The French Crown was far more circumspect about its support for dissenters as potential colonizers and colonists, since Henri IV was a recent convert from Protestantism to Catholicism in order to consolidate his position on the throne. But several of the early recipients of royal support for North American ventures were prominent French Calvinists, such as Chauvin de Tonnetuit and Pierre Du Gua de Monts, although there is little evidence that they were attempting to do anything more than take advantage of their support for Henri IV in the French religious wars.

The possibility of employing North American settlements as an outlet for unwanted population at home influenced many colonial promoters. The Marquis de La Roche de Mesgouez, who established the first French colony in what is now Canada on Île de Sable (Sable Island, off the Nova Scotia coast), had attempted to recruit hardened criminals by offering those of 'considerable means' their freedom in return for payment of a substantial sum of money. The French courts eventually refused to turn prisoners over to him under such conditions.[8] He then selected his settlers in 1598 from among 250 'vagabonds and beggars' handed over to him by the Parlement of Rouen. On the whole, however, it was the English who seemed more alert to the prospect of transplanting unwanted population to North America, doubtless because England and Wales appeared, during the period of early colonization, to be overpopulated.

Agricultural transformations had displaced many from the land and turned them into a transient body of 'sturdy vagabonds'—or worse. In 1596 in England, for example, a Somerset Justice of the Peace complained that, despite the execution of forty felons in his county, many more had escaped, adding:

> And these that thus escape ynfect great numbers, ymboldenynge them by ther escapes. And they will change both name and habytt and commonly go ynto other sheeres [shires] so as no man shall know them....I do not see how yt ys possible for the poore cuntrymean to beare the burthens dewly layde upon hym and the rapynes of the Infynyt numbers of the wicked wandrynge Idell people of the land.[9]

The Welshman Sir William Vaughan in *The Golden Fleece* (1626) saw in Newfoundland— 'neer unto Great Britane, the next *Land* beyond *Ireland*, in a temperate Aire'—an opportunity for those driven from their farms and for younger sons lacking any inheritance. His colony of Cambriol, first projected in 1616, was to be a new Wales founded in North America, 'where the *Golden Fleece* flourisheth on the backes of *Neptunes sheepe*, continually to be shorn. This is *Great Britaines Indies*, never to be exhausted dry.'[10] If indeed peasants were those he recruited in the hope of turning shepherds into fishermen, his 'welch fools'—as one contemporary referred to them—did not prosper.[11]

More than one promoter of colonization appreciated the possibility of upward mobility for those who got in at the beginning. None pressed this matter further than the Scottish colonizer Sir William Alexander, Earl of Stirling (c.1577-1640). His reputation as a poet and scholar brought him to the notice of the court, and in 1624 King James instructed the Privy Council of Scotland to offer a barony and the title of Baronet of Nova Scotia to any Scot who would undertake to finance six settlers for two years in Alexander's 'New Scotland'. When no takers came forward under this scheme, the Crown offered to grant a barony to anyone paying 3,000 marks (a mark was worth thirteen and one-third pence in English money) directly to Alexander, who would bring out the settlers himself. Even after Charles I made it possible for canny Scots to take up baronies three miles by six miles in extent without travelling to America—by incorporating Nova Scotia into the Scottish Kingdom and instituting a ceremony at Edinburgh Castle—an insufficient number of buyers came forward to finance the settlement. New Scotland was turned over to the French in 1631, with only 85 baronies sold; nevertheless, an additional 25 titles were conveyed between 1633 and 1637 when the scheme was little more than a way of raising spending money for a beleaguered monarch unwilling to summon his Parliament. Although the American titles were regarded with suspicion, they remained part of the inheritance of those who had invested in them.[12]

Behind all the early colonization schemes, including those that were mixed with religious and humanitarian motives, was the expectation that great profits were to be made in North America. In the sixteenth century, fishermen from many nations sailed annually for the Grand Banks off Newfoundland, and some made their way into the Gulf of St Lawrence. In 1591 an English privateer captured a French-Basque vessel, the *Catherine de St Vincent*, returning from northern Atlantic waters with a cargo of oil, salmon, fish, and 'a great store of rich furs, as beaver, martenes, otters and many other sorts.'[13] Many of the early French 'colonizers' were merchants who had been active in the region as fishermen and traders. La Roche, for example, had been involved in exploiting '*Terres-Neuves*' since 1577, when the French monarchy granted him a commission to take over any territories 'of which he could make himself master', and a year later appointed him viceroy of New France with political powers.[14] A few years later, in 1583, Étienne

Fisherman and trapper, two archetypal figures of northern North America in the mid-seventeenth century—one of 100 engravings in *Orbis Habitabilis Oppida et Vestitus* (The Towns and Costumes of the Inhabited World), commissioned by Carel Allard, who published this collection of topographical and costume plates in Amsterdam around 1695. This illustration, which purports to be located in Davis Strait, is described in the Old-Dutch caption as showing cold-weather working clothes in an 'unliveable country'. Rare Books and Manuscripts Division, The New York Public Library: Astor, Lenox and Tilden Foundations.

Bellenger, a Rouen merchant, undertook a voyage to Cape Breton in association with the Archbishop of Rouen and the Duc de Joyeuse, intending to plant a small trading post to serve as the nucleus of a colony. He acquired so many furs after his arrival, however, that he abandoned his plans and returned instead to France with his cargo.[15] Chauvin de Tonnetuit, the founder of Tadoussac, by 1596 owned four vessels operating profitably in the North Atlantic fur trade and fishery.

The Colonization of Newfoundland

While the French dominated the trading activity on the northern mainland coasts of North America in the late sixteenth century, and obviously had much familiarity with them, the English were most knowledgeable about Newfoundland and turned their efforts in that direction. In 1578 Sir Humphrey Gilbert (c.1539-83) had executed a plan for laying claim to Newfoundland, appreciating that any exercise of sovereignty had to be based on some sort of land settlement that could enforce the licensing of fishermen. Sailing on the *Squirrel*, with four other vessels, he landed in 1583 at present-day St John's and took possession of the island in the name of Queen Elizabeth. On the return voyage his vessel was 'devoured and swallowed up by the Sea'. Gilbert was last seen with a book in his hand—perhaps Sir Thomas More's *Utopia*—calling, 'We are as near to Heaven by sea as by land.' Sir Humphrey was brilliant but unstable (it was said that his violent temper could be soothed only by providing him with a young boy to satisfy him sexually).[16] The serious colonization of Newfoundland was to be in the hands of far more prosaic men, mainly London merchants anxious to diversify their commercial interests.

Of all the early colonization ventures in what would become Canada, the one set under way by the London and Bristol Company for the Colonization of Newfoundland (founded in 1610) was the best conceived and financed, and economically sound in its conception. Newfoundland clearly had a marketable commodity to exploit in codfish, caught on the Grand Banks and dried by English fishermen on shore, along the coastline of the Avalon peninsula. Europe was desperately short of a protein food within the financial reach of the poor, and dried cod found a ready market in Catholic countries. The forty-eight subscribers of £25 each who organized the Newfoundland Company hoped that permanent settlers would have some advantage in the fishery over the English West Countrymen who came out to the fishery every spring and returned home every autumn. The first settlement of the Company was established on a strict business-like basis by John Guy (d. 1629), who led forty colonists from Bristol to Cupid's Cove on Conception Bay in July 1610, only months after the Company was granted the whole island, and the venture was funded by sale of stock. Benefiting from experience acquired in earlier colonization further south, particularly that of the Virginia Company, this Newfoundland settlement was well provisioned and led by a shrewd merchant who understood the need to diversify the contents of the cargoes returning to England. Fish, of course, would have an assured market.

Despite much advance planning, the Newfoundland Company was soon faced with the realities of planting a European settlement in a total wilderness. The expectation that the colonists would rapidly achieve self-sufficiency was not met. The soil was neither fertile nor extensive, the climate was unsuited to European seed, and it was difficult to keep settlers as landless employees labouring under difficult conditions solely for the profit of their masters. Continual injections of new manpower and provisions would be required: the Newfoundland Company, like most commercial operations in North America, expected fairly rapid returns on investment rather than constant capital outlays. The venture quickly turned into a series of mutual recriminations between those on the spot and those at home, the former demanding more financial assistance and the latter insisting on profits. The settlers constantly feared armed attack from 'pirates'— often summering

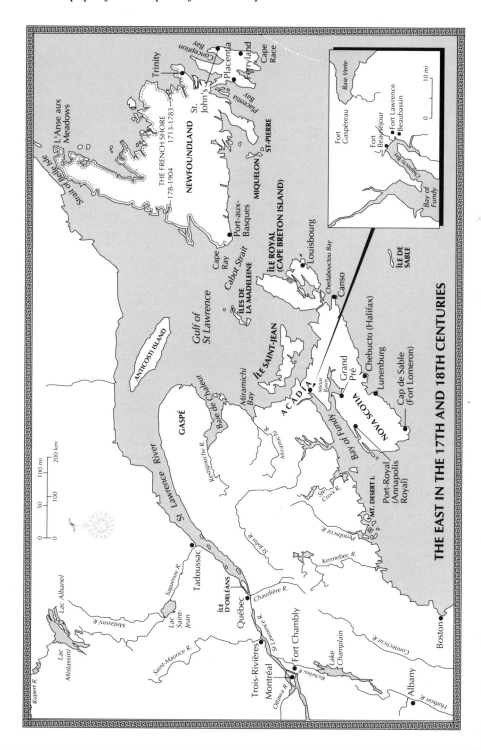

THE EAST IN THE 17TH AND 18TH CENTURIES

fishermen who were becoming increasingly concerned about competition. The truth was that the Newfoundland fishery did not require permanent settlement. Colonization might produce some marginal advantages, but the cost of establishment was higher than investors were willing to pay.

Neither John Guy's settlement nor a series of successors sponsored by both the Newfoundland Company and private promoters flourished. By the 1640s a handful of more or less permanent settlers survived on a year-round basis along the rocky coast. But throughout most of the seventeenth century no communities worthy of description developed. Although Newfoundland had been one of the earliest sites in North America for English colonization, the focus had quickly shifted south, where the English by 1650 had developed a number of successful colonies with a population in excess of 100,000. The 'new-found' island continued to provide enormous wealth to the British Empire in the form of fish, but as an area of settlement it had become extremely marginal.

Acadia

For the French, producing anything other than trading factories in the northerly Atlantic region of the New World was hardly any easier than for the English. French efforts focused first on the exposed Atlantic seaboard, then moved to the Bay of Fundy, and finally migrated to the St Lawrence. But the idea of a permanent St Lawrence settlement did not become pre-eminent in French thinking until well into the seventeenth century. For most of the period before the 1650s the Maritime region the French called 'Acadia'— vaguely bounded by the St Lawrence to the north, the Atlantic Ocean to the east and south, and the St Croix River to the west—was as important to French colonization and colonizers as 'Canada' in the St Lawrence Valley and its hinterland.

Few settlements had as violent an internal history as that of La Roche on Sable Island. Though the colonists there had been drawn from the mendicant classes, they flourished initially on local fish and game, as well as on 'french gardens', while they traded for furs on the mainland. In 1602, however, La Roche failed to send the annual shipment of supplies, and over the winter of 1602-3 the settlers murdered several of their own numbers and their leaders. When relief arrived in 1603, only eleven colonists remained. Brought back to France with their furs, they were rewarded by the king. La Roche could only sputter that 'instead of their being hanged for their misdeeds, they have been given money, although they have themselves admitted to the murders'.[17] Winter had also wreaked havoc on Chauvin de Tonnetuit's settlement at Tadoussac, at the mouth of the Saguenay River. The sixteen men left there in 1600-1 soon found 'what difference there was between France & Tadoussac', and having quickly run out of food, took to quarrelling with one another.[18] Reduced to dire straits by lethargy and sickness, they took refuge with the Indians. Five of them managed to survive.

In 1603 Pierre Du Gua de Monts (1558?-1628), a Calvinist supporter of Henri IV who had been at Tadoussac in 1600, was granted a trading monopoly 'of the coasts, lands and confines of Acadia, Canada, and other places in New France.' In return he was obliged to settle sixty colonists there each year and to establish missions among the native peoples. De Monts organized a trading company in the French coastal cities, and among the settlers he first recruited was a young draftsman, Samuel de Champlain (c.1570-1635), who had been to Tadoussac in 1603 and would serve as geographer and cartographer for de Monts's expedition. Arriving on the Nova Scotia coast in May 1604, de Monts and Champlain searched the shore of the Bay of Fundy for a suitable site. They were much impressed with the Annapolis Basin, but their initial settlement was placed at Île Saint-Croix (Dochet Island, Maine), in the mouth of the Saint-Croix River. The colonists constructed buildings (of French lumber), and planted gardens and

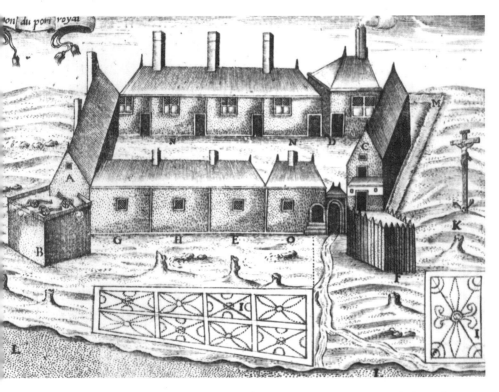

Champlain's rendition of the *Habitation* at Port-Royal, built in 1605 on the north shore of the Annapolis Basin. The parts of the closed quadrilateral complex are identified in his *Voyages* in an accompanying key. For example, 'A. Artisans' quarters'; 'B. Platform for cannon'; 'C. The storehouse'. At the top (north) were the dwellings of de Monts and (on the right) Gravé Du Pont and Champlain. National Archives of Canada.

wheat. But the crops were damaged in the severe winter of 1604-5. Over the winter de Monts lost 35 of his 80 colonists on this island colony, mainly to scurvy. In 1605 he moved his settlement to Port-Royal in the Annapolis Basin and built an *habitation* there, while continuing to search the eastern seaboard for a location that offered a milder climate, fertile soil, exploitable mineral wealth, and co-operative natives. Such a combination was hard to find. Champlain sailed along the New England coast as far as Cape Cod with Micmac guides, but his report was distinctively unenthusiastic.

De Monts, to protect his interests in France, left Port-Royal in September 1605. His deputy, François Gravé Du Pont (*c.* 1554-d. after 1629) — well experienced with the New World — administered the settlement in his absence, with Champlain merely an observer. Having received more backing, de Monts returned at the end of July 1606 with a young nobleman, Jean de Biencourt de Poutrincourt (1557-1615), Poutrincourt's young son Charles de Biencourt (1591?-1624?), and Marc Lescarbot (c.1570-1642), a Paris lawyer who wanted to sample life in the New World and acted as a sort of resident historian and poet. Lescarbot wrote shortly after their arrival, 'All this month [August] we made merry. Monsieur de Poutrincourt did set up and opened a hogshead of wine, one of them that was given for his own drinking, giving leave to all comers to drink as long as it should hold, so that some of them drunk until their caps turned round.' The merriment continued into the next year, particularly when Champlain founded *L'Ordre de Bon Temps* (the Order of Good Cheer) — a kind of dining club with extemporaneous entertainment — as a morale booster. Lescarbot also tells of the masque he wrote (the first play composed and performed in North America) to celebrate Poutrincourt's return to Port-Royal after an extended trip of exploration:

> After many perils. . .Monsieur de Poutrincourt arrived in Port Royal the 14th day of November, where we received him joyfully, and with a solemnity altogether new in that part. For about the time that we expected his return (with great desire, and that so much more that, if any harm had happened him, we had been in danger to have confusion among ourselves) I advised myself to show some jollity going to meet him, as we did. And forasmuch as it was in French verses made in haste, I have placed them with the *Muses of New France* by the title of *Neptune's Theatre*, whereunto I refer the reader. Moreover, to give great honour to the return and to our action, we did place over the gate of our fort the arms of France, environed with laurel crowns (whereof there is great store along the woods' sides). . . .[19]

At the end of July 1607 the colonists were obliged to leave because de Monts, unable to prevent illicit trade in furs by Basques, was forced by his backers to relinquish his monopoly. Lescarbot's interesting and lucid narrative, *Histoire de la Nouvelle France* (1609; revised 1611-12, 1617-18), contains a sympathetic and informative account of de Monts's ill-starred venture in Acadia.

De Monts's failure did not end the matter. In 1610 Poutrincourt and his son Biencourt re-established a post and settlement at Port-Royal. They were accompanied by Claude de Saint-Étienne de La Tour (c.1570-after 1636), his son Charles (1593-1666), and this time by the Jesuit priest Jessé Fléché (d. 1611?), the result of successful pressure by Poutrincourt on the papacy. Because Father Fléché did not understand the native languages, he did not make much headway in his mission to the local Indians. In 1611 Antoinette de Pons, Marquise de Guercheville, raised money in France for missionary work in Acadia, intending that profits from the fur trade would be used partly to support the Jesuits' efforts with the native inhabitants. Instead, the missionaries Guercheville sponsored, Fathers Pierre Biard (c.1567-1622) and Énemond Massé (1575-1646), found themselves opposed by Biencourt and engaged in unseemly disputes with him. In May 1613 the Jesuit fathers joined a small colonizing expedition, ordered by Madame de Guercheville, that settled at Saint-Sauveur opposite Mount Desert Island (now in Maine). In July it was attacked by Captain Samuel Argall, admiral of Virginia, who acted under instructions from the Virginia authorities to expel the French from all territory claimed by England.

Argall (c.1572-c.1626) was a typical seventeenth-century thug who openly employed intimidation and violence in an environment in which power belonged to the stronger. Before this attack on Saint-Sauveur he had journeyed up the Potomac and abducted Pocahontas, the daughter of the Indian chief Powhaten, to exchange her for English prisoners taken by her father. The tiny French establishment at Saint-Sauveur was easily surprised and overcome, but not without a brief battle in which several Frenchmen were killed. On a second expedition, Argall totally destroyed Saint-Sauveur and then looted Port-Royal, devastating the crops and burning most of the buildings to the ground. Biencourt nonetheless rebuilt and continued to operate Port-Royal as a fur-trading headquarters. His close friend and lieutenant Charles de Saint-Étienne de La Tour, who inherited Biencourt's claim as governor when Biencourt died in 1624, wanted to establish a trading post at Cap de Sable, on the southeastern tip of present-day Nova Scotia, and built Fort Lomeron there. According to his own testimony, La Tour trained and led a group of armed Frenchmen and Indians to enforce French fishing and trading rights against English encroachments, thus responding in kind to bullying tactics like those of Argall.

The confusing history of Acadia after 1624 is inextricably bound up with the exploits of the La Tour family. In 1629, when Quebec was captured by the English, Charles de La Tour's tiny trading post would be all that was left of a French presence in North America. In 1621 James VI of Scotland (James I of England) granted Nova Scotia to Sir William Alexander. In 1626 Claude de La Tour, who had remained in Acadia, returned to France to make claims for supplies on behalf of his son Charles. On his return voyage his vessel was captured by a squadron led by Sir David Kirke (c.1597-1654) and he was taken to England, where he quickly made himself at home. The senior La

Tour was accepted at court and married one of Queen Henrietta Maria's ladies-in-waiting! Impressing Sir William Alexander with his knowledge of Acadia, he accepted Nova Scotia baronetcies for himself and his son, and accompanied Alexander's son William to Acadia. They stayed for some seven months in 1629, building Charles Fort near the remains of the habitation at Port-Royal.

Returning with his bride to Acadia in May 1630 as part of a Scots-English expedition, Claude stopped at Cap de Sable to persuade his son to join him. Charles replied that 'he would rather have died than consent to such baseness as to betray his King.' Declaring his son an enemy, Claude led an attack on the fort at Cap de Sable. 'The ensuing battle between father and son', one historian has written, 'lasted two days and a night and has no parallel in the history of the New World.'[20] Charles put up a successful resistance and his father retreated to Port-Royal, only to discover that the English planned to abandon it. Seeing his prospects in 'Nova Scotia' disappear, the elder La Tour

> ...did not dare to return to England for fear lest he should be made to suffer. His wife was also a great embarrassment to him; to her he did not dare confess, though in the end he was obliged to do so, telling her that he could find nothing better, nor any other course to take, than to remain with his son, for there was no more safety for him in France than in England after the attempt he had hazarded.[21]

Madame de La Tour not only forgave her husband, but promised not to abandon him. Claude also came to terms with his son, who by now had received a formal governor's commission from the French Crown. The elder La Tour was permitted to live at Cap de Sable in a house outside the fort. Re-establishing his position with the French, he remained there with his English wife until his death around 1636. Nicolas Denys (1598-1688), a fisherman-trader and author, who visited Claude in 1635 and is the source for most of the above account, found the La Tours very hospitable and 'very amply provided'.

Although patricidal conflict had ended, Charles de La Tour continued to lead an embattled life. The chief bone of contention was not settlement but trade, for Charles never displayed any real interest in transplanting colonists into the territories he claimed. In 1631 he built Fort La Tour (also known as Fort Saint-Marie, at the mouth of the Saint John River), but after Acadia and Canada were returned to France by the Treaty of Saint-Germain-en-Laye in 1632, Isaac de Razilly (1587-1635) was appointed the new governor instead of La Tour. Charles, who got on with Razilly, returned to France and managed to get their respective spheres of authority regularized by the Company of One Hundred Associates (Compagnie des Cent-Associés, also known as the Compagnie de la Nouvelle France), which controlled French North America at the time. But Razilly died in 1635, and his interests passed to his cousin and lieutenant Charles de Menou d'Aulnay (*c*.1604-50), who almost immediately came into conflict with La Tour. The situation was exacerbated in 1638, when an attempt by the French Crown to divide Acadian territory between the two men put the central base of each on the other's land. There ensued one of several intricate La Tour episodes, in which d'Aulnay, resenting a visit Charles made in 1640 to check the furs at Port-Royal (the profits from which, it had been understood, he shared with Razilly), looked upon this appearance as an act of aggression, convinced the king of Charles' unfaithfulness, and took command of Fort Lomeron at Cap de Sable. When Charles tried to respond by sending an emissary to Boston to negotiate rights to trade and to recruit mercenaries, d'Aulnay rushed to France to add to his complaints about Charles and in August 1642 returned to Acadia with the official order that La Tour appear before the king to answer charges of treason.

La Tour decided to send his wife, Françoise-Marie, to represent him at the royal court. A member of the lesser French nobility, Françoise-Marie Jacquelin (1602-45) had been wooed by La Tour *in absentia*, and came out to marry him in 1640.[22] She successfully argued her husband's case in 1642, then returned in a French warship, carrying supplies for La Tour. In 1644 she again went to France, but this time was unable to protect her husband's interests. Escaping to England with borrowed money, Françoise chartered an English ship to carry her and supplies back to her husband. Off Cap de Sable the ship was detained and searched by d'Aulnay, but Madame de La Tour hid in the hold. In Boston she successfully sued the ship's captain for unwarranted delay, and used the money to hire ships to reinforce La Tour at Fort La Tour. Early in 1645, with her husband again off in Boston seeking assistance, Madame de La Tour commanded the defence of Fort La Tour against an attack by d'Aulnay. Her forty-five defenders held out for four days against an invading force of 200, but she eventually surrendered on the understanding that d'Aulnay 'would give quarter to all'. The victor, however, went back on his word. All the captives were hanged. Madame de La Tour, who was forced to witness the executions with a rope around her own neck, died scant weeks later. After his wife's death, Charles de La Tour retreated to Quebec, where he was warmly welcomed. He remained there until 1650.

With La Tour out of the picture, d'Aulnay took over Fort La Tour, trading 3,000 moose skins there in one year. He also assumed La Tour's connections with New England, signing a peace treaty and eventually receiving symbolic reparation—in the form of a sedan-chair captured by a pirate in Mexico—for the Yankee assistance to his rival, while remaining well connected at the French court. D'Aulnay was made governor of all Acadia in 1647, and given a monopoly of the fur trade—a privilege he was already forcibly asserting against the protests of the rival Company of One Hundred Associates. Upon d'Aulnay's death in 1650 at Port-Royal, his wife Jeanne Motin (c.1615-c.1666) resided there and assumed her late-husband's empire, as well as his enormous debt of more than 300,000 *livres* and guardianship of their eight children.[23]

As for Charles de La Tour, he returned to France to demand an enquiry into his case. With the support of the Company of One Hundred Associates, he was completely vindicated and was received again into royal favour. Returning to Port-Royal with a few new colonists in 1653, he successfully courted d'Aulnay's widow, ending their rivalry by merging their interests (and their debts); the couple had five children over the ensuing years. But La Tour's troubles were hardly over. Pursued by his debtors, he was forced in 1654 to surrender his garrison of seventy at Fort La Tour to an invading English expedition of 500 men. La Tour was taken to England, where Oliver Cromwell refused to restore his property in Acadia but did agree to recognize the long-dormant baronetcy of Nova Scotia—earlier negotiated by Claude—if Charles would accept English allegiance and pay his English debts. Twenty-five years after denying his father and asserting his loyalty to the French Crown, Charles de La Tour felt compelled to accept Cromwell's terms. He eventually sold out his rights in Acadia to English partners, and retired to Cap de Sable with his wife and family. The French Crown belatedly (in 1700) recognized the Acadian rights of La Tour's children, suggesting some sympathy with his tribulations.

For more than forty years La Tour and his family had kept French interests alive in Acadia. But he was a trader, not a colonizer. The few settlers he brought to the New World were only incidental to his economic and military activities. Unlike Champlain in Canada, La Tour had no particular vision of a settled agricultural presence in Acadia, and after his surrender to the English in 1654 the scattered Acadian settlers were very much on their own, until formal French occupation was restored in 1667. While the period of English control from 1654 to 1667 left little internal impress on the region, it did isolate Acadia from official French rethinking of its American empire in the early 1660s. Thus Acadia was not initially part of the decision of the Crown in 1663 to take a more active interest in its American colonies. As a result, its subsequent status was never properly clarified, leading to an administrative weakness that encouraged an autonomous outlook on the part of its population.

Canada

In 1607 Pierre de Monts received a one-year extension of his fur-trading monopoly on the condition that he found a post on the St Lawrence River. Champlain had already explored the river in 1603, up as far as the Lachine Rapids, and de Monts sent him there in 1608 to carry out this new initiative. After leaving the Île d'Orléans at the beginning of July, Champlain tells us in his *Voyages* that

> I searched for a place suitable for our settlement, but I could find none more convenient or better situated than the point of Quebec...which was covered with nut-trees. I at once employed a portion of our workmen in cutting them down that we might construct our habitation there: one I set to sawing boards,

another to making a cellar and digging ditches, another I sent to Tadoussac with the barque to get supplies. The first thing we made was the storehouse for keeping under cover our supplies, which was promptly accomplished through the zeal of all, and my attention to the work.[24]

The men toiled into the fall, erecting below a high cliff three buildings of two storeys—connected by a gallery around the outside, 'which proved very convenient'—surrounded by a moat and palisades.

Soon after their arrival at Quebec a conspiracy was uncovered, led by the locksmith Jean Duval. The plan was to murder Champlain and deliver the establishment at Quebec to the Spaniards. Duval was tried, convicted, and then 'strangled and hanged at Quebec, and his head was put on the end of a pike, to be set up in the most conspicuous place on our fort.'[25] His co-conspirators were sent back to France. In February scurvy broke out. When spring arrived, only nine of twenty-five had survived the first winter. It had not been a good year.

For a century the native nations who lived north and south of the St Lawrence were part of a trading network that exchanged furs, with fisher-men and traders, for European objects. They fought to gain control of this trade, for which the St Lawrence was the crucial channel. The Iroquois Confederacy of five nations—Mohawks, Oneidas, Senecas, Onondagas, and Cayugas, all living in present-day upstate New York—were in conflict with the natives who lived north of the St Lawrence. They included the Iroquoian-speaking Hurons, living in settled agricultural communities east of Georgian Bay off Lake Huron, as well as the wandering hunting tribes of Algonquins and Montagnais who ranged as far northeast as the Gulf of St Lawrence. These peoples were the allies Champlain sought to cultivate in order to ensure the success of his fur-trading establishment. In the spring of 1609 he wanted to explore 'the country of the Iroquois', but the Montagnais wanted to make war on them. He co-operated, accompanying them up the Rivière des Iroquois (the Richelieu River) to the lake that he named after himself. At Ticonderoga (Crown Point, NY) a miniature battle took place. 'When I saw them [the Iroquois] making a move to fire [arrows] at us, I rested my musket against my cheek and aimed directly at one of the three chiefs. With the same shot two fell to the ground; and one of their men was so wounded that he died some time after.' The Iroquois fled into the woods, 'whither I pursued them, killing still more of them.'[26] Thus ended the first armed conflict with natives in New France.

In May 1610 Champlain took part in another contest between his Indian allies and the Iroquois at the mouth of the Richelieu River, at a place where the Iroquois had built a circular barricade to catch the Algonquins on their way to Quebec with furs. There was an assault, an arrow piercing Cham-plain's neck, and the Iroquois fled. Champlain's final confrontation with the Iroquois took place in October 1615. The previous July, for 'the strong love which I have always cherished for the exploration of New France', he had

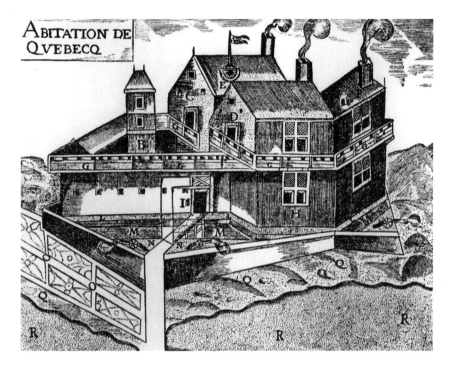

Champlain's drawing of the *Habitation* at Quebec. The accompanying key in his *Voyages* identifies, among other things, his garden (O) in the lower left—above the R for the St Lawrence River; a dovecote (B); sun-dial (E); and gallery (G), 'made all round our buildings, on the outside, at the second story'. National Archives of Canada, C-90711.

Champlain's drawing of the first armed conflict between Europeans and natives of North America, in which Champlain led a party of Algonquins, Hurons, and Montagnais, on 31 July 1609, against 'nearly two hundred' Iroquois—a battle that was very much desired by Champlain's Indian allies. In the early morning hours 'they dispatched two canoes by themselves to the enemy to inquire if they wished to fight, to which the latter replied that they wanted nothing else.' National Archives of Canada.

made his way to Huronia, just east of Georgian Bay, and in the fall he accompanied a party of Hurons to the southeast, travelling by way of Lake Couchiching, Lake Simcoe, the Trent River, across Lake Ontario, into the heart of the Iroquois country. On the east side of Lake Onondaga they found an Iroquois fort protected by four stockades. The disorderly Hurons attacked it without success. When Champlain was wounded in the leg they retreated, and Champlain, carried part-way, returned to Huronia, where he spent the winter.

There were about 50 Frenchmen on the St Lawrence in 1615. Among the early settlers, only Louis Hébert (1595?-1627), who came to Quebec in 1617 after lengthy service at Port-Royal as a surgeon, showed any interest in cultivating the land, using hand tools for farming until he died. But Hébert was most useful for his medical and apothecary skills; the trading company actually attempted to discourage him from agriculture.[27] Not until 1618— when in reports to the king and the French Chamber of Commerce, Champlain outlined a grand scheme for the colonization of New France—did anything approaching the plans of the Newfoundland company enter the French vision. Earlier French activities, including those of Champlain himself, had been under-financed by a succession of individual entrepreneurs and small syndicates. Trading posts, rather than settlement colonies, were the goal.

Until 1618 Champlain had served as an agent for others rather than as a colonial promoter in his own right. In that year he combined arguments for major investors with a scheme designed to appeal to the imperial pretensions of the Crown. New France and the St Lawrence not only constituted the possibility of a short route to Asia, but could produce 'a great and permanent trade' in such items as fish, timber, whale oil, and furs. The annual income was projected at 5,400,000 *livres*, virtually none of it coming from agriculture and less than ten per cent coming from furs. Champlain requested that priests, 300 families of four persons each, and 300 soldiers be sent to his base on the St Lawrence. French response was enthusiastic, and Louis XIII instructed the syndicate employing Champlain to expedite his plans. The partners and Champlain, however, were unable to agree upon terms, or make any progress in establishing the colony. Not until 1627, when Cardinal Richelieu assumed supervision of New France and established the Company of One Hundred Associates, did Champlain's grandiose schemes receive substantial backing.

Richelieu's company—unlike the Newfoundland Company—was organized from the top of the government rather than from grass-roots interest in the profits of colonization. It was to be capitalized at 300,000 *livres*, each participant contributing 3,000, and profits were not to be initially distributed. Of the 107 members listed in May 1629, only 26 were merchants and businessmen, mainly from Paris. The remainder were courtiers and state officials. The Company's initial venture—at a cost of 164,270 *livres*—was to send off to Quebec in 1628 four ships containing 400 people and carrying 'all necessary commodities & quantities of workmen & families coming to inhabit & clear the land and to build & prepare the necessary lodging.'[28] Unfortunately England and France went to war in 1627, and in July 1628 the Company's ships were captured off Gaspé by an Anglo-Scottish armed expedition led by the brothers Kirke. A year later, in July 1629, Lewis and Thomas Kirke forced Champlain's starving outpost to surrender. The Kirkes' occupation of the St Lawrence was extremely profitable: they left not only with Champlain and most of the settlers but with much booty and nineteen fishing boats.

Champlain was exiled from New France for the next four years. An effort by the Hundred Associates in 1629 to reoccupy Quebec was totally destroyed by shipwrecks and armed depredation, at a cost of 103,796 *livres*. The French company had spent virtually the entire original capital without planting a single colonist—the only profits from the venture had been made by the Kirke brothers. For the next 33 years colonization was subcontracted out to undercapitalized private companies, none of which were able to mount a scheme so ambitious as that of the Company of One Hundred Associates in the late 1620s.

The colony was restored to France in 1632, under the treaty of Saint-

This map of New France by Champlain appeared in the last volume of his *Voyages*, published in 1632, three years before his death. It includes the territories he explored, which are rendered with considerable accuracy—he was an excellent geographer—along with inevitably inaccurate renderings of regions he had only heard about. Archives National (Quebec), N-973-70.

Germain-en-Laye, and in July Father Paul Le Jeune (1591-1664), who had recently been appointed superior-general of the Jesuit missions in Canada, was one of the first arrivals at Quebec. In that year he began the first of the annual reports, the famous *Jesuit Relations*, that were sent until 1791 to the Provincial Father of the Society of Jesus in Paris to explain and promote the missionaries' efforts in the mother country. They combine a wealth of detail about life in New France, the native peoples, Iroquois warfare, the Huron missions, exploration and travel, as well as accounts of what were seen by the priests to be miraculous conversions in the native settlements they visited. Le Jeune described his arrival at Quebec:

> The English, who came to this country to plunder and not to build up, not only burned a greater part of the detached buildings which Father Charles Lallemant had erected, but also all of that poor settlement of which nothing is now to be seen but the ruins of its stone walls. We celebrated the holy Mass in the oldest house in the country, the home of madame Hébert, who had settled near the fort during the lifetime of her husband. She has a fine family, and her daughter is married here to an honest Frenchman. God is blessing them every day; he has given them very beautiful children, their cattle are in fine condition, and their land produces good grain. This is the only French family settled in Canada. They were seeking some way of returning to France; but having learned that the French were coming back to Quebec, they began to regain courage. When they saw our ships coming in with the white flags upon the masts, they knew not how to express their joy. But when they saw us in their home, to celebrate the holy Mass, which they had not heard for three years, good God, what joy![29]

Champlain returned to Quebec in May 1633. The palisade of Fort St Louis, which he built on the cliff in 1620, was still standing, but the *Habitation*, which he had rebuilt in 1624, had been destroyed.

In a letter to Cardinal Richelieu of 18 August 1634, Champlain described his reconstruction of the colony, beginning with

> ...the sorry state in which I found these places after their total devastation by the English. This will assure you, my Lord, that I have rebuilt the ruins, enlarged the fortifications, increased the number of buildings, erected two new habitations, one of which is 15 leagues above Quebec and commands the entire river so that it is not possible for a ship to sail up or down it without being stopped by the fortress I have built on an islet that duty obliged me to name for you, and henceforth it will be called Richelieu Island by everyone here, as a lasting reminder that these lands will be settled and the people converted to our holy faith. The other [Trois-Rivières] is placed in one of the best parts of the country, 15 leagues above Richelieu Island, where the climate is more moderate, the land more fertile, the fishing and hunting more abundant than at Quebec. Such has been the work of the last year, in which I have been much encouraged by the care and vigilance of Monsieur de Lauzon [one of the Hundred Associates], who lost no time in seeing to it that the project was carried out in accordance with your intentions. Also, the confidence that I have

observed among all the associates has guided me greatly, and it gives me fresh courage to see the many craftsmen and families they have sent out this year and intend to send later for the aforementioned habitations, with plentiful supplies of munitions and food. . . .[30]

The Company of One Hundred Associates was unable to maintain its trading monopoly, and despite its titular ownership of the territory of New France it lacked capital and energy to take an active part in development. It did, however, grant to Robert Giffard de Moncel (1587-1668) one of the first seigneuries in New France, 'a league of ground to be taken up along the shore of the St Lawrence River for a depth of a league and a half inland, at a place where the River called Notre Dame de Beauport flows into the said St Lawrence River, the first-mentioned river being included within the area.'[31] Giffard, his wife and two children, with over thirty other colonists all from the Perche region of France, arrived in 1634. Two families of Juchereaus arrived at the same time, with relatives and friends, and were joined by others. Giffard too brought other settlers later. In 1653 his seigneury of Beauport was expanded to a depth of four leagues.

While settlement was painfully slow, the fur trade prospered. In 1634 Champlain sent Jean Nicollet (c.1598-1642) on a peace mission to the western Indians, necessitating a long voyage of exploration, which was to include looking into the possibility of reaching the China Sea. Nicollet reached Lake Michigan, the first European to see it. Indicative of his expectations was 'a great robe of Chinese damask, with flowers over all & birds of various colours', which he carried in case he should reach Cathay. Though the robe was never returned to the Chinese, it did lead the Winnebagoes of Green Bay to believe the explorer a god and to agree to smoke the pipes of peace with him. Nicollet returned to Quebec in the autumn of 1635. But Champlain, who had suffered a paralytic stroke shortly before the young explorer's arrival, never heard of Nicollet's exploration.

Champlain died on Christmas Day 1635. Unlike his English contemporaries William Bradford at Plymouth Plantation or John Winthrop at Boston, he had not been permitted to employ his energies and abilities in leading a prospering colony through the problems of internal growth and establishing colonial institutions. Instead, much of his career was spent dealing with the preliminaries of settlement, in the interests of which he sailed nine times to France to further his plans for colonization, or to resist attempts to oppose them. A tireless fighter for his vision, he had the misfortune not to see it fulfilled. Although he had spent half his life in the commercial phase of colonization, in 1635 there were but 150 settlers on the St Lawrence. Nonetheless, Champlain had fostered the foundation on which Canada was built. A successful geographer and intrepid explorer who was equal to the most arduous demands of wilderness life, capable in complex dealings with the native peoples, and a respected leader of men, he also left a literary legacy. The three volumes of his *Voyages*—published in Paris

in 1613, 1619, and 1632—provide much of what we know about New
France in his period.

If both the emerging French state and private enterprise were failing in the
effort to expand settlement, there remained Catholic evangelical initiative to
help to fill the void. A missionary effort by the Société Notre Dame de
Montréal was organized in 1639. Led by Paul de Chomedy de Maisonneuve
(c.1612-76), a small group of settlers in two ships left La Rochelle on 9 May
1641. Jeanne Mance (1606-73), later the founder of the Hôtel-Dieu at
Montreal, was in one ship, which reached Quebec on 8 August. Maisonneuve's ship did not arrive at Tadoussac until 20 September, and he and his
companions were forced to winter at Sillery, near Quebec. The party arrived
at Ville-Marie (Montreal) on 17 May 1642, and the next day, Sunday, the first
mass was celebrated. The seventeenth-century historian of Montreal, the
Sulpician priest François Dollier de Casson (1636-1701), recorded the event.
A small group—including Maisonneuve; the nurse Jeanne Mance; Madame
de La Peltrie (1603-71), who had arrived at Quebec in 1639 and founded the
Ursuline Convent there; and the governor of New France, Charles Huault de
Montmagny (c.1583-1653)—heard Father Barthélemy Vimont (1594-
1667) deliver a sermon in which he told his audience:

> . . .what you see is but a grain of mustard seed, but it is sown by hands so pious
> and so moved by the spirit of faith and piety that Heaven must doubtless have
> vast designs since it uses such workmen, and I have no doubt that this seed will
> grow into a great tree, one day to achieve wonders, to be multiplied and to
> spread to all parts.[32]

A second contingent of settlers arrived by ship in August, and the feast of the
Assumption was celebrated with the thunder of cannon. Later in 1642 the
island of Montreal was nearly inundated by flood waters from the St
Lawrence; but flooding was far less a menace than the Iroquois, who made
their first raid on the settlement in June 1643.

For the next two decades the long rivalry between the Iroquois and the
Indian trading allies of the French created much fear and havoc, with
disastrous consequences for the Hurons. The compact area where they
lived—east of Georgian Bay and north of Lake Simcoe—was crucial to the
fur trade in the first half of the seventeenth century. The Hurons had access to
a seemingly inexhaustible supply of furs from the northwest, and the French
were determined to keep the supply flowing to Montreal and Quebec. The
Hurons had once greatly outnumbered the Iroquois—30,000 as against
15,000 of the latter—but in the 1630s their numbers were reduced to 12,000
by diseases contracted from the French who lived among them. In 1634, the
year the Jesuits set up permanent missions in Huronia, the natives suffered an
epidemic of measles. In 1639 the Jesuits oversaw the building of an elaborate
fortified headquarters, Sainte-Marie-aux-Hurons, on the Wye River. It
eventually comprised twenty buildings, including a residence for priests, a

An aerial view of the modern reconstruction of Sainte-Marie-aux-Hurons near Midland, Ontario — begun in 1964 after excavations that started in 1941 — showing the European compound (top); the work area (middle); and the Indian compound, with the Church of St Joseph, a longhouse, the hospital, a longhouse frame, and a bastion. Sainte-Marie-Among-the-Hurons, Huronia Historical Park; photograph by Michael Odesse.

church, a hospital, outbuildings for farming, residences for lay workers and Indian converts, as well as a canal with three locks. The first substantial religious settlement north of Mexico, in 1649 it housed 18 priests, 4 lay brothers, 29 workers and servants (*donnés*), 11 domestics, 4 boys, and 6 soldiers.

The Iroquois—supplied by the Dutch with firearms, which the French were reluctant to give to their Indian allies—were equally determined to control the flow of furs. They ambushed the Huron fur-fleets on the Ottawa River and between 1640 and 1645 they blockaded the river, while also attacking the settlements on the St Lawrence. 'In former years', wrote Father Vimont in 1643,

> the Iroquois came in rather large bands at certain times in the Summer, and afterwards left the River free; but this present year, they have changed their plan, and have separated themselves into small bands of twenty, thirty, fifty, or a hundred at the most, along all the passages and places of the River, and when one band goes away, another succeeds it. They are merely small troops well armed, which set out incessantly, one after the other, from the country of the Iroquois, in order to occupy the whole great River, and to lay ambushes along it everywhere; from these they issue unexpectedly, and fall indifferently upon the Montagnais, Algonquins, Hurons, and French.[33]

Ville-Marie would become one of the key trading sites for the continental interior, but it was initially dedicated to missionary efforts. Its centre-piece was the Hôtel-Dieu, the hospital founded by Jeanne Mance in the autumn of 1642, though the hospital building was not constructed until 1645. In the autumn of 1651 the Iroquois, according to Dollier de Casson,

> ...with no more cruelties to carry on above us, since there were no more Hurons left to destroy...turned their faces towards the Island of Montreal, which they looked on as the first object of attack in descending the river. Therefore, when the winter was over, they began to attack us in good earnest, and with such obstinacy that they scarce left us a day without an alarm. We had them on our hands incessantly, not a month of this summer passed without our roll of slain being marked in red at the hands of the Iroquois.[34]

The hospital was temporarily closed and Jeanne Mance retired to the fort. She gave money to Maisonneuve to recruit help in France, in the form of soldiers and workmen, but they did not arrive until two years later.

The Company of One Hundred Associates virtually withdrew from New France in 1645, when it gave its fur-trading monopoly to the Communauté des Habitants, an organization of Canadian merchants, which agreed to continue to pay for the administration of the colony. While the local devolution of the fur trade was a positive move for the colony, the new company soon felt the effects of Iroquois hostility, which hampered the fur trade for an entire decade. The Iroquois soon turned their full attention to Huronia. In July 1648 Senecas destroyed the mission of Saint-Joseph and killed 700

Hurons. In March 1649 a party of 1,200 Iroquois destroyed Saint-Louis and Saint-Ignace, where Fathers Jean de Brébeuf (1593-1649) and Gabriel Lalemant (1610-49) were tortured to death. The weakened Hurons were killed, surrendered, or fled. Before the Iroquois could reach Saint-Marie, the Jesuits there 'applied the torch to the work of our own hands' and fled with some 300 families to Christian Island in Georgian Bay. Most died of starvation or malnutrition. The next year the missionaries returned to Quebec with a few hundred Hurons—the pathetic remnant of a once-powerful nation.

The Hurons were early victims of European colonization and missionary endeavours. As for the missionaries themselves, only the Jesuits' profound faith and misguided intentions to educate the native inhabitants in French ways and induct them into a completely alien form of religion kept them on their indomitable rounds of travel and living in extremely harsh and tense conditions. Many of the natives turned against the missionaries—blaming their problems with disease, and with the Iroquois, on the Christian interlopers. Indeed, by exposing the natives to disease and weakening their culture by introducing other religious beliefs into it, the missionaries may have inadvertently contributed to the destruction of Huronia.[35] From the Jesuit perspective, conditions had become almost intolerable even before the final Iroquois assault. In 1636 Father Paul LeJeune wrote:

> . . . our lives depend upon a single thread; and if, wherever we are in the world, we are to expect death every hour, and to be prepared for it, this is particularly the case here. For not to mention that your Cabin is only, as it were, chaff, and that it might be burned at any moment, despite all your care to prevent accidents, the malice of the Savages gives especial cause for almost perpetual fear; a malcontent may burn you down or cleave your head open in some lonely spot. And then you are responsible for the sterility or fecundity of the earth, under penalty of your life; you are the cause of droughts; if you cannot make rain, they speak of nothing less than making away with you.[36]

While Jesuit missionaries were leaving Quebec to visit the native peoples, Marie Guyart—better known as Mère Marie de l'Incarnation—founded an Ursuline school there, intended to educate both Europeans and '*sauvagesses*'. A towering figure of the generation that succeeded Champlain in New France (and venerated since her death), Mère Marie has been prevented only by her gender and spiritual vocation from receiving more attention from secular Canadian historians.

Born in Tours, the daughter of a master baker, Marie Guyart (1599-1672) was a devout child who married at the age of seventeen. Her husband died two years later, leaving her with a son. Soon afterwards she had a mystical experience of conversion. Having taken vows of chastity, poverty, and obedience, she lived for some years with her sister and brother-in-law and worked with them in their carrier business. But at twenty-seven she had another experience of the 'inner paradise' and joined the Ursuline Order of nuns. Her son was left with her sister, though the separation was painful. After taking her vows in 1633, Marie had a dream in which God told her to go to Canada. She sailed there in 1639, founding her school and spending the remainder of her life running it successfully. Mère Marie had an extraordinary ability to combine her fervent spiritual life and the care of souls with her skills as a competent administrator and as a perceptive observer of the secular

Marie de l'Incarnation, 1672. This oil portrait has been attributed to Abbé Hugues Pommier (1637-86). Archives des Ursulines de Québec, Quebec.

life around her. As well as educating young girls, providing food for hungry natives and catechizing them, studying native languages, preparing dictionaries in French-Algonquin and French-Iroquois and an Iroquois catechism, she wrote extensively. Her works included spiritual autobiographies, lectures on faith, notes on prayer—and over 13,000 letters, most of them to her son, of which relatively few survive.

Prominent in Mère Marie's letters was a mystical inspiration. On one occasion she was asked to explain a line in the Song of Solomon (1:2): 'Let him kiss me with the kisses of his mouth':

> Without further ado I began with these words: *Let him kiss me with the kisses of his mouth*: this led me to an address, so that, starting from this quotation, no longer being in control of myself, I spoke for a very long time, under the influence of the love which possessed me. Finally I lost my voice, as if the Spirit of my Jesus had wanted the rest for Himself. I could not restrain myself on this occasion, which subsequently caused me much confusion, something which has since happened to me unexpectedly on other occasions.[37]

Fortunately for modern historians, Mère Marie's correspondence dealt not only with spiritual matters but with the entire life of the colony. After the arrival in 1659 of François de Laval as vicar-general of the Pope in New France, Mère Marie eventually came into conflict with him over rules for the Ursulines. Laval (1623-1708) was appointed bishop in 1674, after a lengthy struggle within the Church in France over the autonomy of the Jesuit Order in Canada—he became the candidate of both the Crown and the Jesuits. But he spent the rest of his active life in Canada until his retirement in 1688, attempting unsuccessfully to free the colony's church from the influence of the state and to exert episcopal control over all religious organizations within it. Mère Marie held fast against his interventions in the Ursuline Convent, while recognizing that 'we are dealing with a Prelate who, being of a very exalted piety, will never give up if once he is persuaded that God's glory is in question....'[38] Perspicacity and ardent devotion intermingle throughout Mère Marie's letters—which are one of the two best sources, along with the *Jesuit Relations*, for the history of New France in the mid-seventeenth century.

By the early 1660s the tensions experienced by the colony were appearing in strange forms. In 1661 New France was afflicted by an incident of alleged witchcraft, when a recently arrived Protestant miller allegedly used his 'diabolic art' to cast a spell over a young girl whose parents refused to allow him to marry her. The incident produced a general state of panic. Mère Marie was prepared to associate the work of the 'sorcerers' with the appearance of an epidemic of whooping cough, which 'was so universal that there is a strong foundation for the belief that those wretches had poisoned the air.'[39] In the midst of carnival season in February 1663 the colony was struck by an earthquake. Mère Marie described it vividly:

Thick dust flew from all sides. Doors opened of themselves. Others, which were open, closed. The bells of all our churches and the chimes of our clocks pealed quite alone, and steeples and houses shook like trees in the wind—all this in a horrible confusion of overturning furniture, falling stones, parting floors, and splitting walls. Amidst all this the domestic animals were heard howling. Some ran out of their houses; others ran in. In a word, we were all so frightened we believed it was the eve of Judgement, since all the portents were to be seen.[40]

The tremors continued for many months.

About this time the French Crown withdrew trading privileges and land ownership from the Company of One Hundred Associates and made New France a Crown colony. Since 1647 Canada had been governed by a central Council, and elected representatives of the districts of Quebec, Trois-Rivières, and Montreal for consultative purposes. Such a government was both responsive to the wishes of the inhabitants and autonomous of the mother country, but the arrangement was more a result of emergency conditions than a positive reform. Most of the colony was happy to trade autonomy for French financial and military assistance. Mère Marie refused to become too encouraged by the royal takeover, commenting '. . .all this has an impressive sound and is beginning well, but only God sees what will be the issues, experience having shown us that the outcome is often very different from the ideas conceived.'[41] The immediate results of this change were indeed satisfactory, though Mère Marie was quite right to be skeptical about the eventual outcome. In any case there landed in June 1665 four companies of the Carignan-Salières regiment to quell the Iroquois. In September of that year an Intendant, or chief civil administrative officer, Jean Talon (1626-94), arrived to transform the colony. One of his first aims was to increase the population, and the *filles du roi*—orphan girls who had been raised at the king's expense—were sent over to bring this about. 'The hundred girls that the King sent this year', wrote Mère Marie to her son in October 1665,

> have just arrived and already almost all of them are married. He will send two hundred more next year and still others in proportion in the years to come. He is also sending men to supply the needs of the marriages, and this year full five hundred have come, not to speak of the men that make up the army. In consequence it is an astonishing thing to see how the country becomes peopled and multiplies. It is said that His Majesty intends to spare nothing. . . .[42]

How long the French Crown would continue its unstinting support was still uncertain, but it had certainly rejuvenated the colony.

An assessment of the early colonization efforts in northern North America produces contradictory results, depending on which year in the 1660s is employed for the task. For example, in 1661, before the royal takeover of New France, the estimate of population would not be very impressive: while the English colonies to the south contained more than 100,000 inhabitants, there were fewer than a thousand year-round settlers in Newfoundland, no more than 500 settlers and fishermen in Acadia, and just over 3,000 people in Canada, nearly two-thirds of them in the Quebec area. Neither France nor England appeared to have any real interest in their northern Atlantic colonies. The English held Acadia, but were really concerned about their empire to the south, on the coastal mainland of North America, and especially in the West Indies. The possession of Acadia was a legacy of the Puritan Commonwealth in England, which had just collapsed and been replaced by a restored Stuart monarch. As for the French, they had expended much in the Thirty Years' War and had experienced considerable internal dissent, with the nobility rising in unsuccessful revolt against the Crown. Neither European power seemed really in control in North America. Indeed, in Canada it could be argued that Europe was slowly losing a war of attrition to the Iroquois, who boasted that the French 'were not able to goe over a door to pisse' in safety.[43] Overall, a contemporary observer might legitimately have predicted that the English would inherit the continent by default, through the sheer weight of numbers.

Only five years later, however, the situation had changed quite dramatically. The English Crown had clearly decided to give up Acadia, although it would not be restored to the French diplomatically until the Treaty of Breda in 1667, and it displayed no serious ambitions towards turning Newfoundland into a settlement colony. Not only had England, to all intents and purposes, withdrawn from the northernmost parts of North America, but the French had infused a new energy into their possessions there, particularly in Canada. Between 1663, when a census showed 3,035 inhabitants, and 1666, the population of Canada had nearly doubled to 5,870, mainly through injections of immigrants and soldiers sponsored by the Crown. Moreover, the government had begun making a concerted effort to deal with the Iroquois menace and to reform both the administrative and economic structure of New France. It would shortly attempt to establish a foothold in Newfoundland and regain control over Acadia. Although success would hold within it the seeds of destruction, the French in 1666 were on the eve of almost a century of expansion and dominance in North America.

New France: War, Trade, and Adaptation

When the Swedish Academy of Sciences decided to send a representative to North America to find new plants hardy enough to survive in Sweden's northern climate, Carl Linné (better known to us as the famous botanist Linnaeus) recommended his student and friend Peter Kalm (1716-79) for the mission. Kalm arrived in Philadelphia in September 1748 and spent two years and a half travelling in Pennsylvania, New York, New Jersey, and from July to October 1749 in southern Canada. A journal of his peregrinations was published in Sweden in 1753, and in English translation in London in 1770.[1] Unlike most contemporary observers of the French regime in Canada, who were either Frenchmen or Englishmen with a military interest in the country, Kalm was an outsider with a commitment to neither of the great antagonists in North America. His concerns, moreover, were essentially botanical rather than political, although he invariably found himself commenting on the society and culture of the colonies he was visiting. The dual perspectives of his European point of view and his broad experience in the English and French colonies produced an unusually objective appreciation of the places he visited.

What most struck Kalm about Canada was its civility and prosperity, both at the level of the colony's élite leadership, and particularly among its ordinary inhabitants. In diary entries not published in his lifetime, he observed:

> The common man in Canada is more civilized and clever than in any other place of the world that I have visited. On entering one of the peasant's houses, no matter where, and on beginning to talk with the men or women, one is quite amazed at the good breeding and courteous answers which are received, no matter what the question is. One can scarcely find in a city in other parts, people

who treat one with such politeness both in word and deed as is true everywhere in the homes of the peasants of Canada.[2]

It is interesting that this assessment came from a man who had already spent some time in Benjamin Franklin's Philadelphia.

Kalm was also impressed, however, at the extent of mutual cultural influence between the French inhabitants and the native peoples:

> Though many nations imitate the French customs, I observed, on the contrary, that the French in Canada in many respects follow the customs of the Indians, with whom they have constant relations. They use the tobacco pipes, shoes, garters, and girdles of the Indians. They follow the Indian way of waging war exactly; they mix the same things with tobacco; they make use of the Indian bark boats and row them in the Indian way; they wrap a square piece of cloth round their feet, instead of stockings, and have adopted many other Indian fashions.[3]

Many of Peter Kalm's comments suggest that New France—particularly that part along the St Lawrence known as 'Canada'—was very difficult to appraise fairly. This was partly because of the continual tension that existed between its European background and its North American environment. Its French origins provided institutions, a terminology in which to express them, and a set of assumptions about how society ought to be ordered and ought to operate: those of an ordered and hierarchical society in which the several social orders stayed in their place and subordinated themselves to the good of the whole, as defined by the Crown. To some extent these principles were successfully implemented, particularly when the colony was compared with British North America. 'The difference between the manners and customs of the French in Montreal and Canada', Kalm wrote, 'and those of the English in the American colonies, is as great as that between the manners of those two nations in Europe.'[4] However, the environment provided a set of daily realities that worked against European institutions and assumptions, modifying and altering—while never totally negating—efforts to imitate the mother country. As a further complication, the French Crown did not simply attempt to replicate the familiar institutions of the Old World in North America, but to reform them, particularly by eliminating centuries of European tradition that decentralized power and limited royal authority.

The result was a society that refracted the metropolis in France through the dual prisms of deliberate royal reform and North American reality. The external observer was often struck at first glance by the presence of familiar European institutions and terminology, while beneath the surface different patterns of operations and relationships had evolved. New France was modified by the cumulative effect of new pressures. Over the centuries, commentators like Peter Kalm have responded in various ways to the contradictions.

The Royal Takeover and the New Political System

This portrait of Jean Talon is a nineteenth-century copy attributed to Théophile Hamel (1817-70) of a seventeenth-century painting by Frère Luc (Claude François, 1614-85). National Archives of Canada.

The royal takeover of 1663 put French administrative policy for the colonies and its execution in the hands of two men, Jean-Baptiste Colbert and Jean Talon. Colbert was Louis XIV's chief bureaucrat, a highly experienced civil servant, whose major tasks both at home and abroad were to strengthen centralized royal government and to expand the French economy. As minister of marine, he served as the seventeenth-century equivalent of colonial secretary, amidst a myriad of other responsibilities. To implement policy in the colony, Colbert decided not to focus on the Governor, but instead to establish the position of Intendant, a royal official who in France had been appointed to cut through the accretion of centuries of devolution of royal power and to act on behalf of the state. Beginning with Talon's first appointment as Intendant in 1665, the colony's administration was greatly reorganized and centralized. The Governor, although still the titular head, was responsible for military affairs, external matters, and the colony's relations with the Church (which included education); over the years he would invariably be a member of the French nobility and an experienced military man. But routine administration was in the hands of the Intendant, a career civil servant. There would be some classic confrontations between intendants and governors, particularly during the regime of Louis Buade de Frontenac (1620-98; governor 1672-82 and 1689-98). But the royal regime always backed the former.

Colbert and Talon not only managed to put the colony on its feet, but established its administrative and institutional outline for the entire century of French royal control of New France. Their task was no easy one. Political institutions had to be established that would be simultaneously responsive to the royal will and satisfactory to the inhabitants; external threats had to be confronted; population growth had to be encouraged through both immigration and natural increase; and some kind of economic viability had to be created that would not threaten the mother country. Out of all these factors would emerge a society and culture of enormous tenacity, possessing many resources for regeneration and change.

The Political System

The political system that developed in seventeenth-century Canada, while centralized and autocratic, was not totally insulated from the popular will. The old governor's council was reorganized by Colbert as the Sovereign Council, with membership made up of the Governor, the Bishop, the Intendant, several legal officials, and five councillors (later raised to twelve). After 1675 the councillors served at the king's pleasure, and the Intendant (rather than the Governor) presided at meetings. The Council had both legislative and judicial responsibilities, but over time it concentrated most heavily on the judicial side. Most of the councillors appointed over the years were seigneurs and merchants, members of the colony's élite. Such a Council, both in function and membership, was typical of every colonial government in America; but in Canada the control of the Council by the Intendant (rather than the Governor) was unusual.

Canada did not have a regularly elected political body representing the inhabitants. The absence of such an institution, however, did not mean that those who governed New France did so in defiance of public opinion in some profoundly and unusually anti-democratic manner. Assemblies in the English colonies—made up of men quite similar in status to those on the Sovereign Council, but elected by adult male property-owners—were themselves not very 'democratic'. Indeed, the very absence of a truly 'representative' body forced the government of Canada to develop alternative ways of testing public opinion. Public gatherings were summoned on a number of critical occasions to comment on current affairs. The merchants of Quebec and Montreal had institutionalized access to the government through *chambres de commerce*, and the *habitants* were encouraged to meet frequently on local matters, often under the leadership of the *capitaine de milice*, who was employed by the Intendant as his community deputy.

Such devices did not necessarily come to terms with the grievances of the common people, but there was an outlet for popular discontent in the form of the public protest (or 'riot') that at the time was a typical feature of life in both Europe and America. Most of the riots in early French Canada followed the common patterns of the age, being touched off less by deep-rooted political critiques than by immediate problems. Oppressive taxes, the most frequent reason for European protest, were not an issue in Canada, since such levies were never collected. Unpopular *corvées* and food shortages did produce an effort to '*representer la misère*', as one observer put it. Complaints in the wake of bad harvests, often by women, were the most common form of collective protest in Canada. In December 1757, for example, attempts by the colonial authorities to eliminate the distribution of bread in Montreal and to sell half the price-regulated meat supply in the form of horse-meat, produced a demonstration of women at the door of the Governor's residence. Governor Vaudreuil (1698-1778) attempted to reason with the protestors, but in the end sent them away with the threat of gaol and hanging if they rioted again. Women mobilized against a reduction in the bread allowance in Quebec in April 1758, and 400 women demonstrated outside the Intendant's palace the following winter, forcing that official to promise an increased supply of bread and wheat. The government had the power to meet such actions with force, and even to punish the ringleaders, but it generally chose to be lenient unless violence or property damage ensued. That French Canada, under the *ancien régime*, did not have more such protests—only about a dozen serious ones were recorded in 100 years, mainly in the last years of French control—demonstrates the extent to which the government was responsive to public opinion, and to the needs of the population as a whole.[5]

The Church

Government did not simply mean secular rule. One of the institutions comprising the government of Canada was the Church. As in France, the Roman Catholic Church in Canada had both an indirect political and a direct spiritual role in society. Politically, the Church had a number of tasks. One was to help establish, within the ranks of the populace, due subordination to spiritual and secular authority, a job that was frequently beyond its capabilities. Most of the recorded injunctions of the Church in Canada against public misbehaviour and immorality suggest *post facto* impotence. Thus, when Bishop Jean St Vallier (1653-1727) thundered in 1719 about 'the Bad Habit you had acquired against all Well-being of appearing in underwear without bottoms during the summer to avoid the Great Heat', threatening 'the damnation of a large number of heads of families as well as of children, if you do not have regard for our remonstrance and paternal Exhortations', the impression he left was that instant obedience could not be assumed.[6] There were similar injunctions against immodest dress among young women, and against the racing of horses outside the churches during mass. Nor was the

Church able to prevent the use of liquor in the fur trade, despite its assertions of the grave evils of the traffic, particularly its harmful effects on the Indians. The Crown found the continued use of alcohol essential to trade, and so it remained.

The Church had other functions beyond its moral one. It was responsible for education and health care in the colony. Hospitals were run by the Church and were staffed mainly with nuns. Priests living with the Indians often acted for the Governor as agents, and some were sent to the English colonies for diplomatic negotiations and may even have acted as spies. New France, however, was certainly not priest-ridden. Although there were many women in religious orders in Canada, ordained priests were usually in short supply. In 1759 fewer than 200 clergymen served a population of between 75,000 and 80,000: such a small number could scarcely have much contact with, or authority over, the people. Only seventy-three of these 200 clergymen were actually parish priests, most of them Canadian-born—hardly a sufficient number to provide religious services for everyone in the colony, especially outside the towns. The average *habitant* simply did not have regular access to the sacraments, such as mass and confession.

In the symbiotic relationship between Church and State that characterized Canada after 1663, the state was clearly the dominant partner. It appointed bishops, granted seigneuries, and provided much of the revenue (up to forty per cent) of the Church. At the same time the subordinate role of the Church did not mean that Canada was irreligious or that Catholicism did not permeate deeply the lives of most of its inhabitants. Unlike France, Canada never experienced heresy, at least among its European population. There were no unorthodox beliefs to extirpate, for none were ever introduced. Canada had been born in deep Catholic piety, and Catholic orthodoxy remained the norm.[7]

The Role of the Military

Almost from its inception New France existed in a state of siege. The immediate defence problem in 1663 was with the Iroquois. Protecting Canada from them could be achieved only with a show of force, provided by the initial assignment of troops, backed by 1,100 veteran soldiers of the Carignan-Salières regiment. The regulars discovered that the Indians were not easy to defeat; but in 1666, without managing to engage a single native in battle, the soldiers razed four Mohawk villages to the ground. Conscious of the presence of a new French military resolution and under pressure from Algonquian nations to the west, the Iroquois agreed to peace in 1667. But they were never entirely removed as a threat, particularly given the continuation of warfare between England and France on an intermittent basis throughout the colonial period. The English could always count on Iroquois allies. After 1667 the French kept up a military posture less because of the natives than because of the English, whose notorious inability to work together was all that saved New France on more than one occasion. In the mid–1660s a colony with a population of little more than 3,000 was support-ing 1,300 regular soldiers required for its defence. Although this ratio diminished, the military presence in New France was always an important and influential factor in the colony's development.

As has so often been the case in the history of nations, France was prepared to accept expenditures on the military that it would not have countenanced for civilian matters. Colbert had set the civil budget of New France at 36,000 *livres*, for example, but was willing to allocate another 150,000 *livres* merely to feed and support the regular troops. The army always received the lion's share of financial support from the mother country, but without this infusion of funds the colony would have been less well off economically. The soldiers' pay was an important source of money for the Canadian economy, and the army was the best local customer for Canadian merchants. Mère Marie de l'Incarnation noted, as early as 1665, that 'money, which was rare in this country is now very common, these gentlemen having brought a great deal with them. They pay for everything they buy with money, both their food and their other necessities, which suits our *habitants* very well.'[8] Colonel Louis-Antoine Bougainville (1729-1822), towards the end of the French period, echoed these comments when he remarked pithily, '*La guerre enrichit le Canada.*'

Regular soldiers not only provided defence for the colony and necessitated constant injections of money to pay and supply them, but they also served as a source of labour and as potential additions to the population. Except at border fortifications and during times of national emergency, the troops were billeted with the *habitant* population from October to May, and 'the *habitant* who provides only the tools to his soldier employs him ordinarily for felling trees, uprooting stumps, clearing land, or wheat-threshing in the barn during that period, at a salary of ten *sols* daily plus food.'[9] Whenever funds to support the troops were temporarily exhausted, as they often were owing to the primitive complexity of contemporary accounting and budgeting practices, the soldiers were again sent off for billeting. An ordinance of 1685, wrote one officer, gave

> the soldiers. . .the freedom to work and to live with the said habitants to earn thus their board and lodging, whilst waiting that His Majesty send us the werewithals to pay their salary as usual. This obliges us to inform all the habitants of this Colony that they may hire such soldiers as they wish to work with them according to what they consider reasonable, prohibiting them to pay each of the soldiers more than 10 or 12 *livres* per month.[10]

The soldiers not only mixed freely with the civilian population, but were from their first arrival encouraged to join it upon expiration of their enlist-ments. In some cases it was possible to get out of military service to become a colonist. In 1698, for example, the King through his Intendant ordered that those who find it possible to establish themselves through marriage to women or widows born or settled in the said colony be discharged from the said companies at their first request, and that they keep the clothing which they have without the officers using any pretext to withhold it. And in order to give them the means to settle and to survive while awaiting that the lands they will be given be cleared and produce wheat and the other necessities for their subsistence, His Majesty has granted them one year's salary.[11]

Many inhabitants, particularly among the religious orders, complained of the licentiousness of the troops, but few suggested that they be recalled.

In the years after 1663, French North America found itself regularly at war with the English, and their native allies the Iroquois. Between the royal takeover and the English conquest, there were but forty years of peace. Only between the Treaty of Utrecht (1713) and the opening of a new round of warfare in the 1740s did the French colonies experience a protracted period free from threats of foreign invasion—and even then the Iroquois were a constant danger. War and its tensions were by far a more familiar condition to the population than peace. Regular troops were not regarded as a sufficient military force, and from 1669 the entire adult male population of the colony, between the ages of 16 and 60, was required to serve in the militia, locally commanded by *capitaines de milice* chosen from the ranks of the inhabitants. Not until 1684 was the militia actually called into action, but from then until 1760 it was used regularly. Virtually every able-bodied Canadian male served in at least one campaign.

And campaigns were never hard to find, against both the Indians and the English, for which there were never enough professional soldiers. Moreover, throughout the seventeenth century the troops sent to Canada were poor specimens, suitable mainly for garrison work. The Canadian militiamen did the bulk of the fighting and suffered the heaviest casualties. The large number of independent widows in Canada reflected the heavy mortality suffered by their men in war. Nor was active fighting the only danger. In the first conflict involving the militia on a large scale, Governor Le Febvre de La Barre (1622-88) in 1684 mustered nearly 800 men at Montreal, and led them against the Iroquois cantons in New York. The troops were laid low by a virulent influenza epidemic rather than by battle, and the governor negotiated a humiliating peace treaty with the enemy. His successor, the Marquis de Denonville (1637-1710), gathered an even larger force in 1687, including 930 Canadian militiamen, and marched them overland into the country of the Seneca. After a brief skirmish the Senecas fled into the woods and Dennonville's Indian allies refused to go after them. The Seneca villages and food supplies were thereupon destroyed. Two years later the unsuspecting village of Lachine was devastated by 1,500 Iroquois, who disappeared when a relief expedition approached the area.

But expeditions against the Indians—or even against the English—were not the only occasions for summoning the militia. Guerilla raids involving

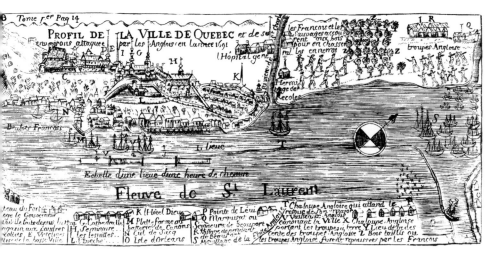

This crude but delightfully clear map depicting Phips's attack on Quebec in October 1690 appeared in Baron Lahontan's *Nouveaux Voyages* (1703). Metropolitan Toronto Refrence Library.

joint parties of *Canadiens* and Indians were a feature of every Anglo-French war, intended chiefly to keep the English colonies off balance and prevent them from using their superior numbers to invade the St Lawrence, as Sir William Phips had done in 1690 with thirty-four sailing vessels from Boston and a large army. Only a week before the English arrived at Quebec, the town was defended by little more than 150 men. But the militia swarmed to Quebec from Montreal and from their farms. Governor Frontenac succeeded in persuading the invaders that the French were prepared to fight, with his well-known rejoinder to an English officer demanding his surrender: 'I have no reply to make to your general other than from the mouths of my cannon and muskets.' Because of the lateness of the season, the invading fleet withdrew ahead of freeze-up. An even larger expedition, led in 1711 by Sir Hovenden Walker, was equally unsuccessful. In both instances virtually the entire able-bodied male population of the colony had been fully mobilized.

Foreign observers were always impressed with the martial spirit of the Canadians. One British officer in the mid-eighteenth century complained: 'Our men are nothing but a set of farmers and planters, used only to the axe and hoe. Theirs are not only well trained and disciplined, but they are used to arms from their infancy among the Indians; and are reckoned equal, if not superior in that part of the world to veteran troops.'[12] As is often the case, this reputation persisted long beyond the point where it was deserved. While the militia had been a powerful military aid to the French authorities in the earlier period, especially in guerilla warfare, by the middle of the eighteenth century and the introduction of tactical warfare, it was being regarded by French officers as a liability rather than an asset. The aide-de-camp to

Montcalm, Colonel Bougainville, writing in late 1758, reported that the militiamen 'become disgusted; they wish to return home, to sow and to harvest; soon they declare themselves sick. Either they must be sent home or they become deserters.' Moreover, he maintained, 'there is among the militia men no order and no submission' to their officers.[13]

New France—whose chief industries were war and military preparedness, which overshadowed agriculture or even the fur trade in terms of economic importance—possessed more than a bit of the appearance of an armed camp. One of the most important effects of this situation was on the career paths of able and ambitious young members of the Canadian élite. For many families, military service in an officer class was preferable to entrance into commerce and industry, just as in France itself. Unlike the English colonies, which had less of a military tradition and did not encourage a class of professional soldiers, Canada lionized its native officers. Young men began their training early in life, and there were constant pressures to reduce the age of entrance into the military: after 1729 it was set at age 15. For several decades in the eighteenth century there existed an *expectative* listing behind every rank from cadet to lieutenant, which enabled the young sons of leading families to fill the first vacancies. By the eighteenth century the *Canadien* élite provided most of the officers of the *Troupes de la Marine*, and even expected commissions to be reserved for the sons of serving officers.

Probably the most renowned Canadian military family was the Le Moyne clan, whose most distinguished member was Pierre Le Moyne d'Iberville (1661-1706), 'the first truly Canadian hero'.[14] Iberville was hardly a typical Canadian soldier, even of the officer class, but his career was a legend, beginning in his own time. He has remained fascinating ever since—no native Canadian from the French period has been the subject of more biographical study[15]—and has come to symbolize the spirit of martial heroism so characteristic of his time and place.

Pierre Le Moyne d'Iberville was a younger son of Charles Le Moyne de Longueuil et de Châteauguay and Catherine Thierry. His father was the son of a Dieppe innkeeper who spent his early years in Canada in the Huron country and settled at Ville-Marie. Renowned as an Indian fighter, Charles Le Moyne led the settlers in several campaigns against the Iroquois, and in later years often served as an interpreter and negotiator with the Five Nations. He was rewarded with several major land grants, and in 1668 was elevated to the nobility. On his death in 1685 Charles not only held many thousands of acres of land, but left a personal fortune valued at 125,000 *livres*—much of it apparently made in the fur trade. He was one of the shareholders in the Compagnie du Nord, formed in 1682 to exploit the rich fur-lands of Hudson Bay. Charles's success was a perfect illustration of how immigration to North America could permit extraordinary upward mobility. He and his wife had fourteen children. Most of his twelve sons emulated their father in both military activity and heroism. Pierre was usually accompanied by one or more of his brothers in most of his military endeavours.

Born in Montreal, Pierre Le Moyne d'Iberville began his career in his father's service. Somewhere in early life he acquired experience as a seaman. On the eve of his first campaign after his father's death, he was found guilty by the Sovereign Council of seducing a young woman and fathering an illegitimate child (he was made responsible for this child until she was 15). Such charges of philandering would continue to plague him throughout his life, although they could be seen as merely the obverse side of his public career. Iberville flourished at the margins of Europe's American empires in an age when governments did not make tidy distinctions between public and private sectors, thus encouraging military adventurism by entrepreneurs if it could be viewed within a larger imperial context. He was, in short, a buccaneer or *filibustier*, rather than a professional soldier in the conventional sense of the term—closer in spirit to the Kirke brothers or Captain Kidd than to the Marquis de Montcalm.

In Iberville's first campaign he led a party of Canadian *voyageurs* to James Bay as part of a French expedition under the command of Pierre de Troyes. The expedition—set under way in 1686 while England and France were attempting to resolve their American differences—utilized the Ottawa River and connected waterways to travel to the Bay, a perilous journey that lasted 85 days. At Moose Fort (Moose Factory), Iberville singlehandedly gained entrance to the fort, but once he was inside the palisade the seventeen Englishmen there closed the gate; while his companions forced it open again, Iberville distracted the Englishmen with his bravado until his men entered and the fort surrendered. His reputation for intrepid heroism was born, and he was put in command of this and two other James Bay posts captured by the French, Rupert and Albany (renamed Saint-Jacques and Sainte-Anne). In 1687-8 he was in France, returning to James Bay in command of a French vessel. On the Albany River in 1688 he added to his reputation for bravery one of total ruthlessness towards the enemy. When two armed English ships blockaded his own fur-laden vessel in the river in September, and all three ships became immobilized in the ice for the winter, Iberville's arbitrary conduct led to the deaths of many of the Englishmen, mostly from scurvy. Arriving back in Quebec in late October 1689 with booty and furs, Iberville was almost immediately made second-in-command of a French campaign to raid the English settlements in New York. Pouncing on the unguarded village of Corlaer (now Schenectady) in February 1690, the French killed 60 inhabitants in their beds and took many prisoners and much booty. This sort of guerilla warfare, consciously emulating the tactics of the Indians, made the French much feared in the English colonies, and was the secret of most French military successes in North America.

Iberville sailed with three vessels to Hudson Bay in July 1690, but was driven off York Fort in late August; and in 1692 his naval squadron, complete with French frigates—unable to sail to the Bay before winter ice—was ordered to harass the English coastal colonies. He returned to the Bay in

1694, this time under a buccaneering agreement with the French Crown, and captured York Fort (renamed Fort Bourbon), again with charges of ruthlessness in violating the terms of surrender. Returning to France as a hero, he was ordered to take his squadron to the Atlantic coast and Newfoundland, where, in the winter of 1696-7, he led his *Canadiens* to the destruction of thirty-six English settlements, with the usual heavy loss of life and the taking of prisoners and booty. Leaving Newfoundland for Hudson Bay ahead of the arrival of English reinforcements, his ship *Pélican* became separated from its companions. Iberville was forced to fight a naval battle with three English warships at the mouth of the Hayes River, sinking one and capturing another, while a third fled the scene. This triumph over the European nation that now regarded itself as master of the sea was the crowning glory of Iberville's career.

He was next sent by the French ministry—on two voyages in 1699 and 1701—to fortify and defend the mouth of the Mississippi River. Iberville proved less successful as a colonizer than as a *filibustier*, though he argued at length for French expansion in Louisiana. In 1706 he was placed in command of a squadron of twelve vessels ordered to the British West Indies. He led a force of several thousand regulars, Canadian *voyageurs*, and buccaneers in a successful conquest of the Island of Nevis, again conducted with much ruthlessness and looting. This expedition had begun under a cloud of accusations of improper outfitting and preparations for illicit trade. But Iberville, whose health had been bad for years, died shortly after the Nevis capture, and a posthumous royal commission dealt harshly with him. It found him guilty of many improper acts, particularly of embezzlement of supplies for the West Indies expedition. Other accusations of financial malfeasance would also surface, and his widow spent much of his fortune attempting to avoid orders for financial restitution.

In many respects Iberville's exploits were a dead end, for they achieved virtually nothing of lasting significance. The English recovered from his victorious depredations in Hudson Bay, Newfoundland, continental North America, and the West Indies. Others would succeed in colonizing Louisiana where he had failed. But this record, in a sense, could hardly have been otherwise. Iberville's intrepid buccaneering was made possible only by imperial conflict. While he demonstrated the extent to which Canadians could succeed in such enterprises, as well as their adaptability and bravery, the Atlantic world was changing. Later success would come to others less daring.

The Demographic Problem

The size of its population was the pre-eminent factor that underlay the defensive posture New France found itself in throughout a century of confrontation with the British colonies to the south. An anonymous French writer wrote in 1706:

> If anyone gives considered attention to the progress the English have made in the case of their New England colonies, he will have good reason to tremble for our colony in Canada. There is no single year but sees more children born in New England than there are men in the whole of Canada. In a few years we shall be facing a redoubtable people, one to be feared. As for Canada, her people will not number many more than they do today. Whether we must seek the reason in that mildness of climate which is so favourable to agriculture, stock-raising and all-the-year round navigation, or whether we must seek it in the demesne of specialized industry, this is certain: on those shores the colonies of England have become as solidly established as England herself.[16]

The problem had its roots in the first half of the seventeenth century, when France had failed to provide a population base for its continental American colonies in any way approximating that of the English. Only five per cent of the French immigrants arrived without public subsidy, while at least half of British colonists financed their own immigration. The New England colonies were established without a penny of public funding.[17] While the French were counting 3,215 in Canada, the English could have enumerated several hundred thousand people in their colonies, many of them black slaves. Given these comparative numerical bases—and the twin facts that between 1608 and 1760 the total immigration to New France did not exceed 10,000, while immigration to British North America during the same period came close to one million—high birth rates could not compensate.

After 1660 French Canada matched the British colonies by doubling its population every twenty-five years, but it could never keep pace numerically. By 1715 the population of New France was 20,000, and that of the English colonies 434,000. In 1754 the gap had grown still wider, with 70,000 in New France and 1,485,000 in the American colonies.[18] Between 1663 and 1672 the French Crown did send annually to Canada up to 500 men and 150 girls—the so-called *filles du roi,* who were intended to correct the severe shortage of women in the colony, under government subsidies. But after 1672—apart from a few artisans, merchants, and some soldiers—few French immigrants arrived, either publicly sponsored or privately motivated. Attempts to assimilate the native peoples in order to increase the population base did not prove successful.

While our anonymous Frenchman of 1706 offered observations explaining the superior attraction of the British colonies for newcomers—the so-called 'pull factors' of immigration—he failed to address the other key part of the equation, the 'push factors'. From the sixteenth century onward, the British Isles experienced continual dislocation of population, both urban and rural, as it shifted gradually but inexorably into a new capitalist economic phase of individual initiative and entrepreneurialism in which older paternalistic relationships were broken down. In France the relative absence of such a transformation on a universal scale, combined with the insatiable demands of the French military for cannon fodder, prevented the development there of a discontented and displaced population that was available for colonial migration on a massive scale. British immigration was not typically state-supported. Potential British settlers crossed the Atlantic on their own initiative or with the assistance of private enterprise, often contracting their labour to pay for their passage. For the French, deliberate government policy and action were required to make settlers available for the colonies, and France usually had other priorities.

Moreover, the ethos of individual enterprise transferred by the British to America made their colonies seem more attractive to immigrants outside the British Isles, and the needs of agriculture in most of Britain's American colonies encouraged the importation not only of large numbers of people under long-term labour contracts but also of many who were in permanent bondage. The French had no built-in opposition to slavery, and indeed sent large numbers of Africans to the West Indies. But only a handful of blacks— slave or free—ever resided in New France, while the British colonies had nearly half a million within their bounds by the time of the Conquest. In short, the entire economic and institutional structures of Britain and her American colonies encouraged massive immigration, while the immigration efforts of the French were relatively paltry.

In many ways, however, the traditional juxtaposition of the French and British colonial experiences is unfair and misleading. In relation to the colonies of most European nations in America—Spain, Portugal, the Netherlands, Sweden, Scotland—New France was a successful and not atypical settlement colony. It was the British colonies that were distinctive and different in their numbers, size, and dynamism. Unfortunately for the French, the British had not two or three colonies in America but at least thirteen, which were both economically vibrant and located on the exposed flanks of New France and Louisiana. In the inevitable imperial rivalries that ensued, the French were at a considerable disadvantage.

Economic Development

After the royal takeover of New France in 1663, the importance of economic diversification was emphasized. The colony's heavy dependence on the fur trade worried many. Colbert and Talon did not wish to end the trade; but they hoped to encourage an agricultural surplus and the exploitation of timber resources that would permit the colony to supply the French West Indies with goods currently being obtained from the English. Indeed, from Colbert's perspective the fur trade was a potential menace. 'It is to be feared', he wrote, 'that by means of this trade, the *habitants* will remain idle a good part of the year, whereas if they were not allowed to engage in it they would be obliged to apply themselves to cultivating their land.'[19] But in fact the colony's economy was slow to diversify. Royal success in penetrating the interior, in establishing good relations with the Indians there, and in setting fixed prices for fur encouraged the expansion of the trade. Colbert recognized the danger of embracing 'too vast an area whereby one would perhaps one day be obliged to abandon a part with some reduction of the prestige of His Majesty and of the State.'[20] But the constant westward press of the *coureurs de bois* continued unabated, contributing to a circular effect, in which the successful French quest for furs brought the colony into conflict with the English to the south; and the ensuing struggle made it virtually impossible to limit the fur-traders, since they were the ideal shock troops for dealing with the enemy. Furthermore, investment in the trade by royal officials, including Governor Frontenac, contributed to its relative immunity from serious restraint.

The Seigneurial System

Agriculture in New France functioned around the French seigneurial system, first introduced in Acadia and extended to the St Lawrence Valley in 1627. Seigneurial institutions after 1663 were governed by the *Coutume de Paris*. In Europe the seigneurial system ordered the social hierarchy, while also providing an economic arrangement between landlord and tenant. But in North America it operated predominantly as a means of granting land and ordering settlement, and here it was not very effective. As was often the case in the European colonies of North America—English as well as French—the state made its property concessions to landlords, who were supposed to find settlers to serve as tenants. In Canada, seventy seigneuries were granted to 1663; over 150 more were allocated before 1740. The most successful seigneuries were those along the banks of the rivers, particularly the St Lawrence. Roughly one-quarter of the seigneurial land was in the hands of the Church, which was more assiduous in its management than individual owners.

Although the *censitaire*, or tenant, owed various rents and feudal dues to his seigneur, these amounted to very little, except on the best land in the most prosperous years. Mutual obligations regarding community services, such as ovens and mills, worked for the most part to the advantage of the tenant, for he was able to insist that the seigneur provide these capital-intensive fixtures whether or not they would be immediately profitable. After 1711, with the Edict of Marly, seigneurs could no longer withhold land from settlement legally (in anticipation of rises in prices) if there were *censitaires* who demanded it. This royal attempt to prevent land speculation and encourage orderly settlement was not unusual in North America. In principle, however, it interfered with the autonomous power of the seigneur, who actually had very little independent authority over his *censitaires*, as the Intendant often interfered to settle disputes.

Not until the very end of the French period, when the population had grown to over 70,000, was there sufficient pressure on the land to benefit the seigneur substantially.[21] His position would become far stronger under the

British than under the French royal regime. What the seigneur possessed during the French period was status, for he was regarded as a member of the colonial upper class. Whether one became a member of the élite because of being a seigneur, or whether one became a seigneur as a member of the élite is not entirely clear, although the latter seems more common. The seigneurial system did have social and economic implications, however. Not only did seigneurs acquire a special social status by virtue of their landholding, but *censitaires* were hardly encouraged to treat agriculture as a business enterprise, since they did not own the means of production. They were still peasants, not American petty capitalists like New England or Virginia farmers. Their obvious European-ness was what led Peter Kalm to prefer them to the bumptious Americans.

The seigneurial system may not have been very onerous for the tenant or

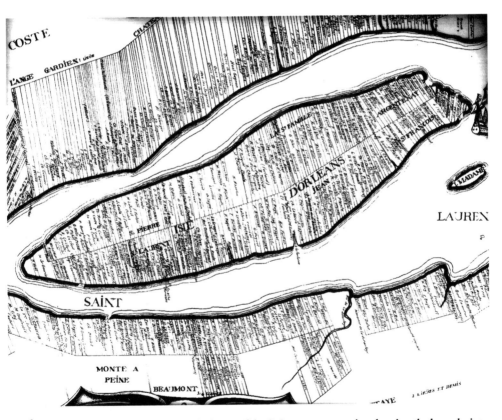

The Île d'Orléans and the north and south shores of the St Lawrence opposite, showing the boundaries of the land grants with names of the seigneurial families in 1709, mapped by Gédéon Catalogne (1662-1729) and drawn by Jean-Baptiste de Couagne—a detail of a larger map of the Quebec region. Archives nationales du Québec, neg. no. 111274-34.

financially rewarding to the landlord, but it was also not completely feudal, since military obligation in the colony was not tied to land tenure.[22] What its effects were on agricultural production is less certain, but plainly it neither tied people to the soil—large numbers of young men went off into the fur trade—nor encouraged the large-scale staple-crop farming that was practised in many English colonies to the south. In the short run, the system produced family farms on small holdings. Slash-and-burn agriculture was common, and given land abundance and labour shortages, farming practices tended to be extensive rather than intensive. Wheat was the preferred crop, although other grains and legumes were also grown, and every farmer kept livestock; the *habitants* lavished much attention on their horses. Markets for this produce (especially outside the colony) were limited, partly by transportation costs and partly by the constant disruption through war of overseas trade. While the *habitant* has often been criticized for his low yields and his generally slovenly agricultural practices—he often did not manure his fields, and they were planted annually without resting or rotation—these were characteristic of the age and were perhaps encouraged by the availability of land and the lack of ownership. Not until the 1720s was there enough land in cultivation to produce a dependable surplus, and bad harvests were always a threat.

The system did not produce the small agrarian capitalist who pressed for maximum production and speculated eagerly in land. On the other hand, the seigneurs sought to speculate, and did so increasingly in the eighteenth century. Few seigneurs lived on their land, for the seigneurial system under the French did not produce enough revenue to permit the emergence of a landed aristocracy. By the eighteenth century the typical seigneur was an absentee landlord who lived in one of the towns and was involved in a variety of economic and political activities.[23] A seigneury was part of a diversified portfolio of investment for an élite in whose ranks little specialization of function had yet occurred.

One typical seigneurial type was represented by Nicolas–Gaspard Boucault (c.1689-1755), who was royal attorney, merchant, and seigneur rolled into one. Boucault arrived in Quebec in 1719 and rose rapidly in the colony's legal service, collecting a number of remunerative offices along the way to appointment as lieutenant of the provost court and lieutenant-general of the admiralty court. He was equally active in commercial matters, helping to sponsor seal-hunting expeditions and becoming a major figure in the Louisbourg trade. His seigneury, on the Chambly River, was obtained in 1723 from Charles Le Moyne. He also owned a large stone house in Quebec, which he built on rue Saint-Paul in 1733. Boucault obviously saw his landholding as part of a total investment strategy, although he does not appear to have made money from his seigneury. He retired to France in 1754. Another familiar seigneurial type was represented by Louis Charly Saint-Ange (1703-67), one of the heirs to a Canadian fur-trading business. Charly invested heavily in an unsuccessful western copper-mining enterprise and continued to be active in the western fur trade. The owner of a house in Montreal, he acquired the small seigneury of Îles Bourdon in 1751. In 1764 he sold his Canadian estate to an incoming Englishman and retired to France.[24] Not all seigneurs were either as diversified or as mobile as Boucault and Charly, who represent the royal/official and merchant type of seigneur respectively, but most engaged in a variety of business and administrative activities. Such complex economic strategies occurred in most colonial situations, and would characterize the élite of Canada/British North America—whether French or English—until well into the nineteenth century.

Commerce and Industry

While most Canadians were farmers, and agriculture was the dominant form of economic activity in the colony, there was a complex commercial and small-scale industrial (mainly artisanal) life in New France as well. Commercial activity was not very specialized, and it required an enormous amount of continuous effort, but few members of the colony's élite failed to engage in it. There was a small merchant class in Canada, particularly at the transatlantic level. As the principal industry of royal New France, for much of its existence, was war, troops had to be supplied. In both war and peace, imports far exceeded exports, so that the overseas trade of the colony, within the French mercantile system, regularly showed an unfavourable balance of payments. Nevertheless, there was a substantial and constantly increasing volume of transatlantic shipping, and considerable traffic between Canada, Louisbourg, and the French West Indies. Overseas trade was complex and dangerous, the more so because the merchant never had up-to-date information about markets and prices. He compensated by diversifying cargoes and enterprises as much as possible, and attempted to deal with the problems of distance by operating as much as possible through family and clan connections. Marriage alliances established new branches of family firms in distant ports, and after the deaths of their husbands, women took over local enterprises. But in imperial terms the Canadian merchants were small fry, without much capital or status. They were petty entrepreneurs rather than major capitalists, linked to merchant families in France, both Catholic and Protestant.[25]

The economy over which the merchants presided was a relatively fragile one, although it steadily expanded throughout the French regime. Unlike the vibrant economy of the British colonies to the south, however, that of New France required peace and stability to perform best. Although transatlantic trade grew, by the early 1740s only a dozen ships per year were sailing from France to Canada. Smaller vessels plied the St Lawrence, and the Atlantic from Louisbourg to the West Indies, and this relatively local trade was both more difficult to measure and of greater consequence than that with Europe. 'Coasting' in small vessels, picking up cargoes wherever they could be found and depositing them wherever they could be sold, was a North American way of economic life. The trade deficit with the mother country was endemic, although it did decrease substantially in the latter years of the peace between 1713 and the 1740s. In wartime, when government expenditure increased enormously, the deficit skyrocketed.

Like most other colonial economies, that of New France suffered not only from chronic international deficits in the balance-of-payments equation, but also from a stripping-off of all available hard money (i.e., gold and silver) to service the deficit. The result was another chronic shortage: of a circulating medium of exchange. The colony's efforts to deal with this problem are the stuff of legend. It was typical of colonial monetary policy that European coinage was greatly overvalued in an attempt to hang onto it. But beginning in 1685 the colony, in effect, printed its own currency supply by using decks of playing cards inscribed in various denominations as paper money and signed by the Intendant. Officially the cards initially represented public promissory notes, to be redeemed when the mother country eventually sent the cash. But by the eighteenth century the supply of card money greatly exceeded any possibility of swift redemption, and the playing cards were joined after 1735 by military *ordonnances* (orders) that circulated as legal tender.[26] Both cards and orders were inflationary, and their issuance, especially of the latter in the final war with the British, merged into the so-called

In the late seventeenth century, when Quebec lacked currency, playing cards, marked with amounts, were turned into money — refundable when funds arrived from France. These copies were painted in watercolour and ink by Henri Beau (1863-1949). National Archives of Canada, Picture Division, C-17059.

'corruption' of the administration of the Intendant François Bigot (1703-78, Intendant 1748-59), which was long held to be partly responsible for the ultimate fall of New France.

Bigot was the grandson of an important and wealthy citizen of Bordeaux; his father was a lawyer and court clerk, a member of the French *noblesse de robe* (a 'law lord'). François was educated as a lawyer, and after several minor posts set sail for Louisbourg in 1739 as its financial commissary. Achieving considerable success in the newly built Atlantic port, he was transferred to Quebec in 1748 and promoted to Intendant. His career there demonstrated an insatiable appetite for personal gain, but his eventual downfall needs to be placed in perspective and tells us much about the latter years of the Old Regime. Bigot operated mainly in wartime, when the opportunities for corruption, but also the problems of financial administration, were most severe. He got things done, managing to supply the troops and the civil population throughout most of the years of war. While his financial policies were both venal and inflationary, they were also creative and necessary, given the failure of the government at home to provide adequately for the colony. Bigot's venality must also be balanced against an appreciation of the inability of eighteenth-century accounting practices to distinguish adequately between the personal and public transactions of an official like Bigot.[27] In the end, he was made the scapegoat for the loss of Canada, although others, including the Marquis de Montcalm, had a much more direct role in the débâcle. The government in France naturally connected Bigot's corruption with an inflationary spiral that was quite independent of his operations, and then added charges (for defeat) that really ought to have been levied against the military. Found guilty as charged, Bigot spent his last years in Switzerland, in disgrace. His corruption was substantial, but so were his administrative achievements. He was blamed for far too much.

Although both government and private entrepreneurs occasionally attempted to create large-scale industrial operations, they seldom succeeded. Nevertheless there was a constant demand for the local production of skilled artisans, and they flourished. At the apex of the artisan pyramid were those master craftsmen whose work, mainly for the Church, reached consciously for high aesthetic standards. Such a man was the master woodcarver François-Noël Levasseur (1703-94), who, beginning in 1740, turned out religious furniture and sculpture from his shop in Quebec. To furniture of simple design he and his brother, Jean-Baptiste-Antoine, added classical decorations and motifs. Their shop produced, in substantial numbers, crosses, statues, reliquaries, communion tables, and pews, and its production did not end with the defeat of the French, but carried on until 1782—one of the many continuities between the *ancien régime* and its successor.

Two major attempts to industrialize New France were encouraged in the 1730s by the Intendant Gilles Hocquart (1694-1783), one an ironworks near Trois-Rivières (Les Forges du Saint-Maurice), the other a shipyard at

Quebec. The former was a private enterprise, the latter was state-supported. Both 'succeeded' in the sense that they produced iron and ships respectively, but they required large amounts of state subsidy to continue. The royal shipyard, indeed, may have smothered private shipbuilding in the colony. Both enterprises demonstrated that Canadian workmen could be mobilized for industrial activity and could manufacture serviceable goods on a large scale. The main trouble with the ships was the use of green or badly selected wood, a common defect of Canadian shipbuilding throughout the colonial period. The number of specialized occupations and individuals employed in these industries expanded greatly in the eighteenth century. The iron works and shipyard employed several hundred men each, a substantial portion of the labour force in a colony of little more than 50,000 people. The ironworkers of Saint Maurice resided in their own separate community, a primitive 'company town', and the shipyard employees worked within locked fences governed by a time-clock. But while both ventures succeeded, neither was profitable.[28]

Men engaged in the fur trade (the *voyageurs* and *engagés*) also grew substantially in number, from 200 at the end of the seventeenth century to nearly 1,000 in the 1740s and 1750s. The work was both physically and emotionally demanding. Perhaps as many as 20 to 25 per cent of able-bodied Canadian males were involved in the western trade at some point in their lives, usually in their younger years before they settled down with a wife and family in sedentary occupations along the St Lawrence. A few rose to be specialists in the trade, some remaining in the West throughout their lives, and about twenty becoming *marchands équipeurs* (or outfitters), who organized the parties and provided the credit. Unlike the transatlantic merchants, the fur-trade merchants were almost exclusively Canadian-born. Considering the limited access to credit and the number of years required to realize returns from a western 'outfit', substantial markups on trade goods could not alter two realities: partnerships were necessary, and profit margins were small.[29]

∿∿∿ *Society*

In the mid-eighteenth century Peter Kalm was able to describe the heartland of French Canada along the St Lawrence as 'a village beginning at Montreal and ending at Quebec, which is a distance of more than one hundred and eight miles, for the farmhouses are never above five *arpents* [293 metres] and sometimes but three apart, a few places excepted.'[30] Each farmhouse, usually of three or four rooms built of stone and timber, stood alone. Tiny villages occasionally, but uncommonly, gathered around the churches. Three towns punctuated this continuous village: Quebec towards the eastern end, Trois-Rivières in the middle, and Montreal towards the west. Quebec and Montreal especially contained impressive and concentrated public and private buildings; but by our standards, both towns were quite small in population

The village of Château-Richer, on the north shore of the St Lawrence north-east of Quebec, about 1785 — a watercolour by Thomas Davies (*c*.1737-1812), the most gifted of all early topographical painters in Canada. This view shows part of the Côte de Beaupré, with white-washed stone farmhouses, wooden barns, and eel traps in the river. National Gallery of Canada, 6275.

and area. On their peripheries the dominant landscape pattern of the separate but contiguous farmstead was quickly resumed. Thus French Canada replicated neither the European medieval village, whence many of its rural settlers had come, nor the English colonial tendency towards isolated farmsteads separated by considerable distances. The typical Canadian holding was long and narrow, fronting on the St Lawrence or another river, and population was slow to move into the *rangs* (ranges) behind those along the waterfront.

Though not large, Quebec and Montreal were the centres of government, of the direction of economic activity, and of the Church and its social services, such as health care and education. They inevitably contained a heavy concentration of the upper classes of French Canada: royal officials, clergy and nuns, military officers, merchants, and seigneurs. The polite society that was concentrated in Montreal and Quebec favourably impressed visitors like Peter Kalm. But these towns, which had grown rapidly in the seventeenth century, were not so dynamic in the eighteenth; their growth-rates remained well behind that of the colony as a whole. Public buildings, like churches and

QUEBEC

A . Le Fort
B . les Recollets
C . La plate forme
D . Les Jesuittes
E . La Cathedralle
F . Le Seminaire
G . l'Hostel Dieu
H . L'éveché
I . La Redoute
K . Le magasin apoudre

This view of Quebec in the early 1700s was included in La Pothérie's *Histoire de l'Amérique Septentrionale* (1722). In all such early depictions of the town, the height of the spires was greatly exaggerated. National Archives of Canada.

hospitals, were important sources of employment. The construction trades employed the largest number of workers and were the largest single element of the local economy—as would be the case in Canadian towns until well into the nineteenth century. Large numbers of domestic servants were also employed by those who could afford them.[31]

While there were undoubted gradations of wealth and status, New France was fundamentally divided into two orders: those with, and without, access to government largesse and patronage. But the law was available to all, and in a society without trained lawyers, it was administered with a fair degree of equity. At the same time, only *some* Canadians could expect public appointments (particularly in the military), government contracts, and seigneurial status. On the other hand there was a certain degree of social mobility: an individual of humble origin could advance up the social ladder much more easily than in France itself, thanks to the availability of land and economic opportunity. Such had been the case for Iberville's father. Upward mobility, however, required an economic singlemindedness that was not typical of the *habitants*. Most observers agreed that the average *Canadien* worked no harder than necessary, spending a disproportionate amount of time pursuing his own pleasures and interests. Both the aristocratic presumptions of the upper orders, and the non-acquisitive behaviour of the lower, suggest that the values of the mother country had not been entirely transformed in the New World.

As for the roles and status of women, they received no remarkable transformation in the fresh air of the New World. The organization of Canadian society continued to be fundamentally patriarchal, with farms and businesses passed on from fathers to sons. The traditional European role of woman as helpmate and child-bearer, however, was moderated by several factors. One was the shortage of marriageable women throughout most of the French regime. Another was the absence of men on the frontier and in the military. The legal code of the colony, the *Coutume de Paris*, provided some limited protection for the property rights of married women, particularly by denying to the husband the sole right to dispose of the family estate. And the autonomous rights of widows were well protected by law and custom: many widows ran successful businesses or farming operations after the deaths of their husbands. In theory, women ought to have been at least slightly better off in New France than in the mother country, not only because there were proportionately fewer of them, but also because the unspecialized nature of the colonial economy prevented them from being shunted to one side and exploited. In truth, however, historians do not have very much detailed knowledge about women in New France, chiefly because of the limitations of the documents, which are more concerned with masculine than feminine activities.[32]

While early Canada always had a substantial number of women in holy orders, most women in the colony did marry (at the average age of 22)—earlier than in France itself. Early marriage was primarily encouraged by economic and social factors, particularly the absence of a recognized role for single women outside the Church. If marriage and remarriage rates were high, so too were birth rates and the number of children. Throughout the eighteenth century, raw birth rates ran over 50 per 1000 inhabitants, and women on average bore 7 children. Couples had 5.65 surviving children, while in France they averaged 4.5. But these demographic characteristics were typical of colonial societies, and were not distinctive to French Canada. Winter and spring were the peak periods of conception. Childbirth was difficult and dangerous. While Canada's men were constantly exposed to the dangers of warfare, their wives faced equal or greater danger and pain every time they gave birth.[33]

Observers agreed that the typical Canadian was more prosperous, and enjoyed considerably more personal liberty, than his European counterpart. As one royal official wrote towards the close of the French regime:

> The ordinary *habitant* would be scandalized were he called a peasant. In fact, they are of a better cloth, have more spirit and more education than those in France. The reason for this is that they pay no taxes, have the right to hunt and fish, and that they live a sort of independence. . . . The *Canadien* is haughty, self-seeking, mendacious, obliging, affable, honest, untiring for the hunt, trips and voyages that they make to the upper country, [and] lazy in agriculture.[34]

According to another commentator, the higher standard of living and independence of behaviour of *Canadiens* were the result of 'the fact that they were born in a country with a good climate, fed on good and abundant food and that they have the liberty, from childhood, to exercise in fishing, in hunting and in canoe trips.'[35] Against all the typically North American characteristics that coloured the *Canadien's* way of life must be set one fundamental fact: he lacked the brutal economic acquisitiveness that dominated in the English colonies to the south.

Culture

Perhaps the single most difficult feature to comprehend in early French Canada has been its culture. The most striking cultural characteristic of French Canada has always been its language. In New France, language came to be the French of the Paris region, spoken extremely well. 'All are of the opinion', wrote Peter Kalm, 'that in Canada the ordinary man speaks a purer French than in any province in France, yes, that in this respect it can vie with Paris itself.'[36] That Parisian French would dominate on the banks of the St Lawrence had by no means been assured from the beginning of settlement. In seventeenth-century France a variety of regional dialects, and even some distinctive tongues (like Breton), were spoken; the supremacy of Parisian French as the national language did not occur until well into the eighteenth century, guaranteed by reforms of the revolutionary and Napoleonic eras. Given the origins of most of the early French-speaking immigrants to Canada from rural districts of the north and west of France, where regional dialects were strongest, the early speech of the colony must have been quite mixed.[37] Here the *filles du roi* exerted their influence. Almost without exception, they came from Paris; and as the mothers of a generation of French Canadians they raised their children to speak—quite literally—the mother tongue.[38]

If French Canada was unmistakeably Parisian in language—although with modified accent and a wonderful new vocabulary, taken over from the Indians, chiefly the Algonquians—it did not approximate Paris in any of its other cultural attainments. Nor ought this reality to occasion either any surprise or sense of inferiority. Generations of Anglo-Canadians have been taught that French Canada was culturally backward, with a key piece of supportive evidence being the absence anywhere in the colony of a printing press—that emblem of 'progress'. Such a focus on indigenous literary culture is unfair in several respects, as well as anachronistic. New France was numerically a small colony, closely linked to the mother country. Its need for books and printed matter could easily be met by France itself, and the colony was no more a cultural backwater than some of those western French provinces from which its original settlers had come. True, it did not have a newspaper, as did all the English colonies to the south by the time of the Conquest; but most of those newspapers had only recently emerged as part of a communications revolution within the British Empire.[39] Perhaps even more to the point, the concentration on the written word ignores the locus of the artistic and aesthetic life of New France as it was associated with the ritualistic requirements of the Church. It also ignores the fact that early Canada did have a literary culture in its folk-tales and songs—but it was oral, part of a folk tradition rather than high culture.

Because of the religious impulse behind much of the early settlement of Canada, and the substantial numbers of priests and nuns who represented the learned element of the population, the Church inevitably supplied much impetus for artistic life in the colony, as well as serving as chief patron for creative artists. An emphasis on music, for example, was both practical and aesthetic. The Indians were extremely receptive to music, and it became a central feature of missionary activity. Thus Father Jean Enjalran reported from the Huron seminary at Sillery in 1676: 'One is charmed to hear the various choirs, which the men and women form in order to sing during mass and at vespers. The nuns of France do not sing more agreeably than some savage women here; and as a class, all the savages have much aptitude and inclination for singing the hymns of the church, which have been rendered into their language.'[40] The racism of this passage should not obscure its point that much music was performed in the Church. The first organ appeared in the colony by 1660, and music at the mass was not confined to the Indian missions. As early as 1664, Bishop Laval reported:

> There is here a cathedral [Notre-Dame-de-la-Paix] made of stone; it is large and splendid. The divine service is celebrated in it according to the ceremony of bishops; our priests, our seminarists, as well as ten or twelve choir boys, are regularly present there. On the more important festivals, the mass, the vespers, and the eventide Salve are sung with instrumental accompaniment in counterpoint with viols, and each are arranged according to its own style; blending sweetly with the singers' voices, the organ wondrously embellishes this harmony of musical sound.[41]

In other areas of culture, the most vibrant activity occurred among the common people, who brought with them to the New World a rich heritage of song, dance, and music for dance. Indeed, most of the Québécois folk-songs collected in recent years have their origins in the period before 1673. They have been revised and constantly adapted as part of an ongoing oral tradition, some having upwards of one hundred different local variants.

While most literary and artistic activity was served from the mother country, the culture of ordinary *Canadiens* was an ongoing and dynamic expression of the rituals of daily life, and of experience in *habitant* households in rural parishes. One of its manifestations was in vernacular domestic architecture, which had evolved its own style in rural Canada by the end of the seventeenth century. An observer described it in the middle of the eighteenth century:

> The greater part of the houses in the country are built of wood, and sometimes plastered over on the outside. The chinks in the walls are filled with clay instead of moss. The houses are seldom above one story high. The windows are always set in the inner part of the wall, never in the outer, unless double windows are used. The panes are set with putty and not lead. In the city glass is used for the windows for the most part, but further inland they use paper. . . . In every room is either a chimney or a stove, or both. . . . The smoke from the stoves is conveyed up the chimney by an iron pipe in which there are no dampers, so that a good deal of their heat is lost. In summer the stoves are removed. The roofs are always very steep, either of the Italian type or with gables. They are made of long boards, laid horizontally, the upper overlapping the lower. Wooden shingles are not used since they are too liable to catch fire, for which reason they are forbidden in Quebec. Barns have thatched roofs, very high and steep. The dwelling houses generally have three rooms. The baking oven is built separately outside the house, either of brick or stone, and covered with clay. Brick ovens, however, are rare.[42]

Furnishings were simple and made of wood; those few examples that have survived are much admired today for their elegant, functional lines.[43] By the mid-eighteenth century iron stoves came into common use, beginning the characteristic Canadian practice of overheating houses during the winter months.

At least one aspect of *habitant* life remained firmly rooted in the culture of the mother country: the use of epithets and pejorative slang, as revealed in contemporary court records. Here the patterns of spoken abuse corresponded closely to those of France itself, and there is little evidence of a particular North American influence, apart from a tendency towards functional simplification.[44]

The centre of New France, on the St Lawrence River, had considerable vitality, and left to its own devices could have led the colony in one of several new directions. But New France itself was eventually overwhelmed by the exigencies of imperial rivalry—to find herself no longer an integral part of France overseas, but rather an alien component of a vastly expanded British Empire in North America.

chapter five

The Atlantic Region:

The Cockpit of Empire, 1670–1758

In early July 1755 the Executive Council of the British province of Nova Scotia met in the residence of Governor Sir Peregrine Hopson (d. 1759), one of the few public buildings in the town of Halifax, which had been founded six years earlier. The governor himself had left Nova Scotia in 1753 because of serious eye problems, and the meeting was called to order by the lieutenant-governor, Colonel Charles Lawrence (1709-60), a successful career officer who had spent some years after the return of the Louisbourg fortress to the French in 1748 readying the defences of the Bay of Fundy region for the day when war would again break out. By the time of this meeting it was clear that the temporary peace between Britain and France cobbled out at Aix-la-Chapelle in 1748 was rapidly breaking down around the world, and that the two European antagonists—and their empires—would soon again be openly fighting, as they had been sporadically for centuries.[1]

Despite the importance of the meeting, only four members of the Council were in attendance that day, all royal officials resident in Halifax. Benjamin Green (1713-72), a New Englander born in Salem Village (where the Salem witchcraft affair had occurred in the 1690s), was the provincial treasurer and naval officer of Halifax. John Collier (d. 1769), an Englishman, was a retired army captain and judge of the Halifax Court of Vice-Admiralty. William Cotterell was provincial secretary, and Jonathan Belcher (1710-76), son of a former governor of Massachusetts, was chief justice of the province's Supreme Court. This distinguished gathering was, to a man, fully persuaded of the potential threats to the province posed by the French, both those outside its bounds and those commonly called 'Acadians' who resided within them.

The meeting had been summoned as part of the process, already in motion, of dealing with the 'Acadian menace'. The lieutenant-governor placed before the Council two memorials signed by the deputies and inhabitants of several Acadian communities in the Minas Basin. The signers declared that they had remained faithful to the British despite the efforts of 'another power' unnamed, and insisted that they would remain loyal providing they were able to continue to enjoy the same 'liberties' previously allowed them. The petition did not elaborate on the earlier liberties, but they included a full acceptance of their rights under the Treaty of Utrecht of 1713, *de facto* recognition of their property rights, and exemption from the burden of bearing arms. Such an arrangement, they could have argued, had been worked out in the late 1720s when the Acadian people had taken an oath of allegiance on those terms. One of the petitions went on to demand the return of arms seized in the spring of 1755, insisting: 'It is not the Gun the Inhabitant possesses, which will lead him to Revolt, nor the depriving him of that Gun that will make him more faithfull, but his Conscience alone ought to engage him to maintain his Oath.' This eloquent appeal to the right of conscience raised the ire of the Council, and the Acadian deputies were called into the meeting room and 'severely reprimanded for their Audacity in Subscribing and Presenting so impertinent a Paper.'[2]

According to the Council minutes, '. . . in Compassion to their Weakness and Ignorance of the Nature of our Constitution, especially in Matters of Government', as well as because of the Acadians' past submissiveness, the government was still prepared to treat them with leniency. 'In order to shew them the falsity as well as Impudence of the Contents of their Memorial', that document was read to them paragraph by paragraph, and 'the Truth of the several Allegations minutely discussed.' The Acadian deputies were in no position to debate on equal terms with the Council, and what followed was more of a harangue than a dialogue—an exchange of the sort familiar to errant children.

The Acadians were asked to produce an example of hardships imposed upon them by government, and then to advance a single instance of service to that government. To both questions there was no reply. They were then informed that conditional fealty was impossible: 'All His Majesty's Subjects are protected in the Enjoyment of every Liberty, while they continue Loyal and faithfull to the Crown, and when they become false and disloyal they forfeit that Protection.' As for the guns, by the laws of England, Roman Catholics were forbidden to bear arms. What right had they to expound to the government on the 'nature of Fidelity, and to prescribe what would be the Security proper to be relied on by the Government for their Sincerity'?

The Council then told the Acadian deputies that they must immediately take the oath of allegiance in its common form. The deputies replied that they were not ready, and must return to consult the body of people on the question, for 'they could not do otherwise than the Generality of the Inhabitants should determine.' The Council quickly rejected this 'extraordinary' reply, sending the deputies away for an hour to consult among themselves. They returned to answer that they were prepared to take the oath they had always taken. This reply was deemed unacceptable, and the Acadians were sent away until ten o'clock the following morning.

The next day the Council informed the deputies that new representatives of the French inhabitants would be summoned, given one more chance to take the unconditional oath, and if they refused to do so, 'effectual Measures ought to be taken to remove all such Recusants out of the Province.' At this point the Acadians from Minas offered to take the oath required. The Council refused to administer it, saying 'that as there was no reason to hope their proposed Compliance proceeded from an honest Mind, and could be esteemed only the Effect of Compulsion and Force', they 'could not now be indulged with such Permission.' The die was now cast, and Lieutenant-Governor Lawrence set in motion the proceedings by which thousands of Acadians would be summarily deported from the province. A classic illustration of one of the most common confrontations of Canadian history, between the singlemindedness of the state and a collective minority requiring/demanding special treatment, was in the closing stages of resolution.

Acadia and Île-Royale, 1670-1748

The Acadian population residing in Nova Scotia in 1755 was a legacy of earlier machinations by imperial authorities. As we have already seen, Acadia—that ill-defined geographical region that included more than peninsular Nova Scotia—had been contested ground between the British and the French since the first days of European settlement. Returned to France in 1670, Acadia, and especially the village of Port-Royal, were commonly regarded in New England as 'a Nest of Privateers & a Dunkirk to New England'. Port-Royal had been captured in 1690 by an expedition of seven vessels and a 'foot regiment' of 450 New Englanders, but was returned to France by the Treaty of Ryswick in 1697. A subsequent New England force of 1,000 militia in 23 transports had failed to take Port-Royal in 1707, returning to Boston to the jeers of their neighbours. According to Governor John Winthrop of Connecticut:

> They landed at Scarlett's wharfe, where they were met by severall women, who saluted them after this manner: 'Welcome, souldiers'? and presented them with a great wooden sword, and said wthall 'Fie, for Shame. pull off those iron spitts wch hang by yor sides, for wooden ones is all the fashion now'. At wch one of the officers said, 'Peace, sille woman, etc.' which irritated the female tribe so much the more, that they cal'd out to one another as they past along the streets, 'is yor piss-pot charg'd, neighbor? Is yor piss-pot charg'd neighbor? So-ho, souse the cowards. Salute Port Royal'.[3]

Although the Yankees successfully captured Port-Royal in 1710, the earlier humiliations remained long in the collective memory of New England.

Acadian Society

Port-Royal was the frequent target of New England raiding parties in the years before its ultimate capture, but it was hardly all of Acadia; and indeed before 1700 it was not even regarded as its official capital. The period between 1670 and 1713 saw considerable Acadian expansion, both in terms of numbers and in territory cultivated. A census in 1671 counted 400 heads in the colony, mainly in the Port-Royal area of the Annapolis Basin, where there were 67 families (65 men, 67 wives or widows, 125 sons, and 91 daughters) cultivating 400 *arpents* and holding 650 cattle and 430 sheep. Perhaps another 100 souls were scattered thinly in the remainder of the Nova Scotia peninsula, mainly along the southwestern coast. By 1710 there were between 1,500 and 2,000 Acadians in the colony, with new concentrations along the Minas Basin, Cobequid, and Chignecto Bay. Although some immigration, in the form of soldiers and artisans, had occurred since 1670, the bulk of the population increase was natural. At least two-thirds of the Acadian population of the mid-eighteenth century were descended from those in the colony before 1670.

As would be typical of agricultural expansion in Canada until the twentieth century, most of the settlers moving to new land in the seventeenth century had been members of a younger generation pressing on the limits of existing resources in older communities. Formally there were seigneurs and seigneurial grants made by the French Crown, but in Acadia the seigneurial system meant less than in Canada, and the *censitaires* operated as if they held their land in freehold. The 'meadowland cultivation' pattern of the early Acadians was greatly assisted by the construction of dykes that controlled the inundation of the lowlands by the high tides of the Bay of Fundy, draining marsh to allow it to be used for farming.

As the Sieur de Dièreville explained in 1708:

> . . .five or six rows of large logs are driven whole into the ground at the points where the tide enters the Marsh, & between each row, other logs are laid, one on top of the other, & all the spaces between them are so carefully filled with well-pounded clay, that the water can no longer get through. In the centre of this construction, a Sluice is contrived in such a manner that the water on the Marshes flows out of its own accord, while that of the Sea is prevented from coming in. An undertaking of this nature, which can only be carried on at certain Seasons when the Tides do not rise so high, costs a great deal, & takes many days, but the abundant crop that is harvested in the second year, after the soil has been washed by Rain water compensates, for all the expense.[4]

As this description suggests, Acadian farmers went to considerable effort when returns on labour investment were considered high. Farms were relatively small in size, averaging twenty *arpents* each. Wheat and pease were the main crops, along with vegetables and fruit. In Port-Royal in 1698, the census noted 1,766 fruit trees on 54 of the 73 farms in the community. It was, claimed one visitor, 'as well planted with Apple trees as they would have been in Normandy'.[5] Even without dyking, tidal marshland provided large quantities of hay and grazing for livestock, the mainstay of the Acadian economy. Throughout the early period observers frequently commented on the failure to improve the forested 'uplands' away from the coast. Most blamed the lack of effort in the uplands on the indolence of the population, although inferior soils and the ready availability of marshland were doubtless more critical factors than laziness.

Livestock, especially cattle, provided the chief commodity traded by the Acadians. A trade with Canada in salted beef was legal; but much of Acadia's meat production was clandestinely supplied to the New Englanders, from whom the Acadians obtained most of their imported goods, especially tools and hardware: the censuses list a number of artisans in the major communities. Acadian farms were hardly self-sufficient. A good deal of specialized agricultural activity went on, and there was a lively commerce in grain and livestock with New England fishermen and coastal traders. Indeed, much Acadian produce ultimately found its way through Yankee hands to the French Antilles. Most of this illegal trade with New England was conducted on a barter basis, for currency was endemically in short supply in North America. Royal officials were convinced that the Acadians hoarded any gold and silver they obtained, one official writing in 1710: 'Therefore, as you inform me that there is plenty of money in Acadia, but that the inhabitants do not put it in circulation, it is your business to discover the means of getting it into circulation.'[6]

On the outskirts of the tidal settlements, and especially in the Cap de Sable district and on the southwest coast of Nova Scotia, were a number of precariously located fishing communities. (Little fishing was done by the French on the northeast coast in the Canso district.) These outports engaged not only in fishing, but also in hunting, fur-trading, and occasionally timbering—as well as privateering. Minimal effort was made to settle on Cape Breton Island (Île-Royale) or on the north shore of the Bay of Fundy before 1710. As would be the case in the Atlantic region until well into the nineteenth century, there were few roads and virtually no overland transportation links between settlements. Canoes and small boats (shallops) provided the basic means of movement in early Acadia.

Government sat fairly lightly upon this population. Between 1670 and 1710 at least eight authorized royal governors and administrators attempted intermittently to control Acadia, producing a continual flow of census data (which, although never complete, indicates that the inhabitants recognized some authority when it was exercised). The seat of government was often at Port-Royal, but even here nobody was in resident authority for long, particularly during the last ten years of the seventeenth century. Before 1710 there were between forty and fifty priests and missionaries in service at various times; parish priests worked at Port-Royal after 1676 and at Grand

Pré and Beaubassin from the mid-1680s. The priests served as informal agents of royal authority, providing some contact with Canada. Almost all the military activity carried on from the region, chiefly border raids against New England, was directed from Canada, often through missionaries to the native peoples in the region, who brought orders to their flocks from Quebec.

The bulk of Acadia's inhabitants came from a relatively small area of southwestern France, including the provinces of Vienne, Poitus, Aunis, and Saintonge, and spoke a southwestern dialect of French. The Acadians never did adopt the official parlance of the Paris region, unlike their compatriots along the St Lawrence. As this point indicates, they developed culturally as well as politically in isolation from French Canada; their ties to the outside world were preserved more through their priests than through their government. The family (*le clan*) and the local community were the important units. A closely knit peasant society, intensely conservative in most respects, Acadia had developed an inherent sense of autonomy from external forces that would serve it well in the first decades of British rule, when—in the vast chess game that imperial warfare represented in the eighteenth century—France found itself obliged to surrender territory in North America with the Treaty of Utrecht (1713).

The British and the Acadian Problem, 1713-45

Acadia was one of the pawns given to the British in 1713. The '*anciennes limites*' of Acadia mentioned in the treaty were not defined, and the French came to insist that the 'Acadia' surrendered did not include what is now New Brunswick and northern Maine; they formally retained the two islands of Île-Royale (Cape Breton) and Île-Saint-Jean (Prince Edward Island). On the former the French proceeded to construct a major fortified seaport at Louisbourg. As for the French-speaking inhabitants of the territory ceded to the British and called Nova Scotia, to indicate Britain's historic claims there, the treaty specified that the French inhabitants had one year to remove to French territory or to remain as subjects of their new masters. But the year expired with little change. Neither the Acadians nor the British Board of Trade (fearing a massive exodus would only strengthen the French at Île-Royale) really wanted removal. As a result, the Acadians were tacitly allowed to remain in Nova Scotia on sufferance. Questions such as their land, language, and religious rights—as well as their political and military obligations to their new rulers—went essentially unresolved. The government of Nova Scotia was permitted to deal with the Acadians on an *ad hoc* basis, accepting their insistence on being treated as political neutrals and failing to exercise much authority within the Acadian community. The deputies of the local populations with whom the British dealt were informally chosen by the Acadians themselves.

Lacking direction from London or the manpower to exert military pressure on the Acadian population, the Nova Scotia government permitted the situation to drift and the Acadians to translate unofficial tolerance, born of irresolution, into enshrined 'rights'. The most extreme illustration of the problems created by irresolution came in regard to Article XIV of the Treaty of Utrecht, which allowed to former French subjects in the ceded territory 'the exercise of the Catholic and Roman religion, conformably to the laws of Great Britain.' British laws proscribed Roman Catholics, but the French insisted that this clause gave the Bishop of Quebec the right to appoint priests to serve both the Acadians and the Catholic Indians of Nova Scotia—despite complaints from the British that the missionaries were mixing in politics, particularly in the disputed lands west and north of the Bay of Fundy.

The free pursuit of their religion and the question of political loyalty were the key issues over which the Acadians and their British masters conflicted. In the mid-1720s, Lieutenant-Governor Major Lawrence Armstrong (d. 1739) provoked a confrontation with the priests when he demanded that the French inhabitants take an oath of allegiance of his own composition. The oath enjoined the Acadians 'with all submission and obedience to behave our-selves as Subjects of so good and great a King and Crown of Great Britain Which we swear ever to be faithfull to.' At Annapolis in 1726, Armstrong attempted to administer this oath, which the Acadians insisted be read to them in French. They then demanded 'that a Clause whereby they might not be Obliged to carry Arms might be Incerted', and despite protests, Armstrong, on the advice of his council, 'Granted the same to be written upon ye Margent [margin] of the french translations in order to gett them over by Degrees.'[7] This concession, however, was not communicated to the British authorities in London. Subsequent efforts to administer an oath of allegiance to Acadian communities, including one at Annapolis early in 1730, met with similar responses from the population.

In 1730 Armstrong's successor, Colonel Richard Phillips (1661-1730), successfully secured from 194 inhabitants over the age of 16 what he announced to Britain as an unconditional oath of his own devising. A Welshman, Phillips undoubtedly thought he understood about appeasing minorities. The oath read: 'I promise and swear sincerely in the faith of a Christian that I will be entirely faithful and will truly obey His Majesty George the Second, whom I recognise as the sovereign lord of Nova Scotia and of Acadie. So help me God.'[8] On this occasion, as on subsequent ones, Phillips orally reassured the inhabitants not only that they would be undisturbed in their religion and their property if they took this oath, but that they would never be called upon to perform military service. The first two promises were authorized by London—although the exact wording of the oath was not—but the last was completely unofficial. Nevertheless, the Acadians after 1730 had good reason for believing that both the religious and the loyalty questions had been resolved to their satisfaction.

Louisbourg, 1713-1748

Unfortunately for the French population in Nova Scotia, their ancient loyalties were being constantly tested by France, which had turned its attention after 1713 to Île-Royale, and particularly to building a fortress at Louisbourg on the southeastern coast. In 1716 Louisbourg contained about 600 people, mainly fishermen brought there from abandoned Placentia on Newfoundland. After 1720 it grew rapidly as the French government fortified the town, garrisoned it, and employed it as the military and economic nerve-centre of the Atlantic region. By 1734 the townsite — four east-west streets on about 100 acres — was surrounded by walls on three sides, with impressive gates. The fortifications — poorly located and poorly built — were never completed. Inside the walls were the huge and stately King's Bastion and barracks (the largest building in New France), and numerous stone dwellings and other structures.

In the 1740s the Louisbourg population was made up of 600 soldiers (increased to 3,500 in the 1750s) and some 2,000 administrators, clerks, innkeepers, artisans, fishermen, and families. Its complex urban society, heavily subsidized by the Crown, included a wide variety of tradesmen and a substantial servant-keeping class, headed by twenty '*marchands*'. Always a major fishing port, serving as the centre of the French fishery after the surrender of Placentia in 1713, Louisbourg in its prime was also an important naval station harbouring French warships as well as fishing vessels. Since its hinterland was completely undeveloped, supplies had to be imported from afar: from Canada, France, Acadia, and New England. The Yankees even

◀ This commemorative medallion — on which is inscribed (in translation) 'LOUISBOURG FOUNDED AND FORTIFIED 1720' — was buried in that year at Louisbourg and recovered by archaelogists in the 1960s. Fortress Louisbourg.

The Porte Dauphine, ▶ the entrance to the reconstructed Louisbourg, with the clock-tower of the King's Bastion and barracks in the distance. Parks Canada photo, D-11-1.

supplied much of the building material for the fortifications. By the time open warfare was resumed between Great Britain and France on 27 April 1744, Louisbourg had become a major military and commercial entrepôt in northern North America, one on which the New England colonies to the south cast fearful and covetous eyes.

Proposals for a military expedition against Louisbourg had been made by a number of New Englanders and Nova Scotians before King George's War (the North American version of the War of the Austrian Succession) had officially begun in May 1744, when French troops from Louisbourg attacked Canso and in August (with the help of their Indian allies) Annapolis Royal, formerly Port-Royal. The Massachusetts assembly took swift action early in 1745. One of the principal arguments for a reduction of Louisbourg, which seemed so threatening, was the parlous state of the garrison. In the words of contemporary historian Thomas Hutchinson it 'was disaffected, provisions were scant, the works mouldering and decayed, the governor an old man unskilled in the art of war.'[9] This information, reported to New England by Yankee sailors captured by French privateers over the summer of 1744, proved more accurate than the Americans themselves could appreciate. In December 1744, for example, Swiss mercenaries stationed at Louisbourg had instigated a mutiny, ostensibly over inadequate food, clothing, and firewood. Joined by the French *troupes de la marine*, the revolt forced the authorities to capitulate to their demands, underlying which was a long history of exploitation, by officers and the town's civil government, of those sent to this isolated and unpopular posting.[10]

Massachusetts hastily raised over 3,000 troops, joined by recruits from Connecticut and Rhode Island, under the command of William Pepperrell (1691-1759), and the expedition was fortunate enough to have the full assistance of a substantial naval squadron commanded by Admiral Peter Warren (d. 1752). Assistance was not necessarily co-operation. 'So striking was the mutual independence of the land army and fleet', wrote one inhabitant of the fortress, 'that they were always represented to us as of different nations.'[11] As, in a sense, they were.

The motivations of those responsible for organizing the Louisbourg expedition of 1745 are readily understandable. They included personal career advancement and military glory, against a backdrop of larger economic and strategic advantages. Less clear is why thousands of young New Englanders volunteered for service in the operation, although it is a truism that the young have no sense of their own mortality. One youthful volunteer explained in his journal:

> The News of our Government's Raising an army (Together with the Help of the other Neighboring Governments) in Order to the Reduction of Cape Breton (Viz Louisbourg, which was Like to prove Detremental if not Destroying to our Country so affected the minds of many (together with the Expectation of Seeing Great things, etc.) As to Incline many, yea very Many to Venture themselves and Enlist into the Service. Among whom, I was one, which was the 14th of March 1745.[12]

Part of the 'etc.' was, of course, plunder; and 'our Government' and 'our Country' plainly did not refer to Great Britain.

Unlike most Anglo-American expeditions against the French in North America, this attack on Louisbourg succeeded beyond the wildest expectations of its proponents. One Bostonian commented of this 'wild goose chase' that it was justified only because 'we got the goose'.[13] Casualties were light— only 53 French and 101 American troops were killed, most of the latter from the inexperienced use of captured cannons—and, after a two-month seige, the fortress surrendered on 28 June 1745. One observer wrote, in some exasperation:

> Those who were on the spot, have frequently in my hearing, laughed at the recital of their own irregularities, and expressed their admiration when they reflected on the almost miraculous preservation of the army from destruction. They indeed presented a formidable front to the enemy, but the rear was a scene of confusion and frolic. While some were on duty...others were racing, wrestling, pitching quoits, firing at marks or at birds, or running after shot from the enemy's guns, for which they received a bounty.[14]

Admiral Warren's naval commanders, and the officers of the American militia, were allowed the luxury of squabbling over the responsibility for a victory, for a change, rather than the more customary débâcle. For their part the French were able to find the perfect scapegoats in the leaders of the 1744 mutiny: after the fall of the fortress, many soldiers were court-martialled.

This successful attack on Louisbourg had substantial implications for all the players in the longstanding imperial struggle in the Atlantic region. The Acadians in Nova Scotia were heavily criticized for their lack of support for the British; and the triumphant Americans in the expedition were confronted with territory that was clearly ripe for settlement and economic exploitation. The French, however, were not yet prepared to abandon the region, and in 1746 sent a major naval armada to America that was ravaged at sea. The British saw the capture of Louisbourg as an embarrassment, since it would prevent the French from sitting down to discuss peace until they had something to exchange for it. A proposed British invasion of Canada in 1746 was rejected as being too provocative, although its supporters began talking openly of the need to secure the American colonies through 'the entire expulsion of the French out of the Northern continent of America.'[15]

In the end, Louisbourg was exchanged for Madras (India) in the Treaty of Aix-la-Chapelle of 1748, a peace arrangement that left North American issues unsettled. New England was outraged. One Boston newspaper editorially thundered: 'Who can tell what will be the consequence of this Peace in times to come? Perhaps this goodly land itself—Even this beloved country, may share the same fate with this its conquest—may be the purchase of a future peace.'[16] Nevertheless, after the peace a key faction in the British government pressed for a new commitment to North America. The Duke of Bedford, for example, recommended that disbanded British troops be encouraged to enlist and settle in Nova Scotia,

> ...after having served in a military capacity for some limited time in that province, for the entire reduction of the inhabitants of it to his Majesty's obedience. There seems to be no method so likely to succeed toward effecting this necessary work as the settling in that country [of] a sufficient number of British subjects, to be intermixed with the French inhabitants, who are inured to the use of arms, and able to endure the northern climate.[17]

In December 1748 the Board of Trade and Plantations drew up a plan for the settlement of 'Chebucto', to be raised in defiance of Louisbourg. Supplied with settlers the next year, it was called Halifax after the president of the Board, the Earl of Halifax, who oversaw the settlement from England. With the founding of Halifax, the process of redistributing power in Nova Scotia would be completed.

A long series of continual warnings to the British authorities from many quarters that the French population in Nova Scotia should be either secured to British allegiance or removed—as well as that the province required both a substantial military force and larger numbers of British settlers—was finally heeded after 1748. As early as 1720 one British officer in Nova Scotia had pointed out that 'the great expence the Government has been at already on account of this country, and the little benefit that has accrued from it owing for the most part, to its being peopled with Inhabitants that have been always enemies to the English Government, for its evidence from what has been said of the temper of the Inhabitants, and the underhand dealings of the Government of Cape Breton, that what orders are or may be given out by the Governor of this Province, without they are backed by a sufficient force, will always be slighted and rendered of non effect.'[18] Governments have always had difficulty appreciating that minorities may have their own agendas. In 1745 the Nova Scotia Council had joined the invading Americans in criticizing the Acadians, arguing:

> ...if they are not absolutely to be regarded as utter Enemies to His Majesty's Government they cannot be accounted less than unprofitable Inhabitants for their conditional Oath of Allegiance will not entitle them to the Confidence and Privileges of Natural British Subjects nor can it even be expected in several generations especially whilst they have French priests among them.[19]

Beginning in 1745, therefore, British settlement and Acadian removal were commonly coupled in the minds of British governments on both sides of the Atlantic, and with the founding of Halifax an almost inexorable sequence of events, culminating in '*le grand dérangement*', was set in motion.

Newfoundland, 1670–1760

From the British perspective, the decision to spend large sums of public money on peopling Nova Scotia marked a new departure in policy, both towards the French and towards the Atlantic region. Nova Scotia and Newfoundland had previously been treated with considerable indifference by Britain, especially as settlement colonies. After 1749 the 7,000 permanent residents of Newfoundland, who had settled in that place without the approval or assistance of the British government, would be substantially augmented by additional British colonists.

Newfoundland had been one of the earliest centres of English colonization activity, but the settlements had failed and attention had shifted further south. Many of the sites of the early ventures, however, continued to be visited by summering fishermen sailing from England each year, and the French continued to be active in the southern coastal region, particularly at Placentia. In 1687 Placentia contained 256 of the 640 inhabitants of Newfoundland, including a small garrison. Although at the time of the Treaty of Utrecht (1713), the French had nearly as many permanent (or wintering) residents as the British in Newfoundland, and despite some notably successful French naval activity around the island in the 1690s (led by d'Iberville), the overall French position internationally, at the time of peace negotiations, forced them to surrender any sovereign rights they claimed to the island. In return for permanent fishing rights, the French agreed to evacuate their inhabitants and to maintain neither permanent residences nor fortifications. The French fishermen were removed to Île-Royale, chiefly to Louisbourg, and the British were left in unchallenged territorial control of Newfoundland.

Obtaining exclusive sovereignty over Newfoundland did not imply that Britain had decided to treat the island as a colony or to encourage settlement there. The debate between English West Country interests, which sent fishing expeditions to Newfoundland each summer, and the advocates of full-scale colonization that would compete with the summer visitors, continued throughout most of the eighteenth century. The British authorities allowed settlement to occur, but deferred to the West Country by refusing to establish a year-round government. As a result, the substantial growth of permanent population on the island developed independently of any govern-ment policy or supervision. It was the product of the decisions of countless fishermen (and a few women and children) to remain behind rather than to return home with their vessels. Population grew, to 3,500 by 1730 and to 7,300 by the 1750s. The percentage of permanent residents in the total summering population increased as well, from 15 per cent in the 1670s to 30 per cent in the 1730s to at least 50 per cent by 1753. The cultural background of the residents and the conduct of the fishery changed as well over these years.[20]

In the seventeenth century almost all residents were of English origin, chiefly from the West Country counties of Cornwall, Devon, and Dorset. As late as 1732, 90 per cent of the permanent population remained English; but

A painting — possibly by Michael Corne, who visited North America in 1799 — of Benjamin Lester's fishing establishment at Trinity. Between Lester's arrival in Newfoundland from England, in 1737, and his departure in 1776, he built up a large fishery centred at Trinity, with a fleet of 12 ships in the 1770s and 30 in 1793, many of them built in Trinity. Dorset County Museum, Dorchester, England; 1974.8.2.

most of the eighteenth-century additions came from southern Ireland, through the increasing connection between Newfoundland and the Irish ports of Waterford and Cork. One census of wintering inhabitants in 1753 showed 2,668 Irish and 1,916 English. The Irish were being pushed out of Ireland by famine and unemployment, and were attracted to Newfoundland by cheap (and available) transportation and work prospects.[21] By 1750 Newfoundland had become a conduit by which Irish Catholics could make their way to North America, and it remained so until 1815, though not all who jumped ship remained permanently on the island.

With the increase in population, Newfoundland began to develop a deep schism in its population that was simultaneously ethnic, religious, and economic. The chief economic division was between those who owned boats and those who laboured on the boats of others. Not all Protestant West Countrymen were boat-owners, but few of the Catholic Irish were.

A development parallel to the increase in permanent population was a shift in fishing practice. Throughout the seventeenth century the quest for codfish, the mainstay of the Newfoundland fishery, was conducted entirely from shore, whether by year-round residents or by summering fishermen. Fishing vessels from England would arrive in a harbour and send out their fishermen in small boats called shallops, manned by crews of three to five and venturing no further than 'a Cannon shott' from shore. By 1714 the English ships had abandoned this inshore fishery and turned instead to fishing directly from the offshore banks. The 'bankers' salted far more heavily than fishermen who practised the traditional inshore process of drying fish on wooden platforms called flakes; and although the quality was lower, so too were the expenses. The expense of one banker with ten hands (plus staff on shore) was calculated to be £70 per season, while a lesser quantity of fish caught inshore would require seven shallops employing thirty-five hands and costing £400. Until 1750 fish stocks inshore held up fairly well, but after that year diminishing catches further encouraged labour-saving offshore techniques. Inshore fishermen were forced to expand onto the north of the island, and to diversify into salmon, furs, and especially seals. The seal fishery was carried out in December, using nets. After the fixing of the nets, wrote one witness,

> ...the people carefully watch the appearance & motions of the seal shoals as they approach the Pass, either in coming up or in going down the River, and so soon as the bulk of the Seals have got over the outmost or end nets, all hands are set to heave these nets to the surface of the water, by which means the Seals are enclosed, and entangle themselves in the nets till they are caught.[22]

The seal oil resulting from these dangerous efforts was highly prized. Diversification, however, seldom extended beyond maritime resources, and was hard to achieve. Newfoundland's economy remained totally dependent upon the sea.

✎✎ *The Founding of Halifax, 1749-1755*

In 1749 Newfoundland had a British population but lacked a proper colonial government. Nova Scotia, on the other hand, had a government—though it lacked a representative assembly—but few British settlers. The British ministry's decision in 1748 to settle Nova Scotia at public expense was a turning point in North American history. It marked the first time, in Britain's involvement in America, that the public purse, rather than private capital, would be employed to people a British colony. Between 1749 and 1764 over £600,000 were invested in establishing a non-French population in Nova Scotia. The settlement of Halifax in 1749 marked a new British interest— perhaps not yet a firm policy—in the northern part of the continent, and certainly Britain's first show of interest in the Atlantic region since the previous century. In providing a preferred population to contend with the Acadians for control of land and resources, and bringing a military force that could be swung into action to do something about the French 'neutrals', it also stiffened backbones within the Nova Scotia government of governor and council.

For Halifax, Britain—making promises of land and support—hastily recruited settlers among soldiers and sailors recently disbanded from the nation's military services, and also among London's artisans. Over 2,500 people left England with the first fleet of 1749—many of them from Ireland, providing an Irish tinge to the Halifax population that was subsequently enhanced by arrivals from Newfoundland, and by other Irish immigrants. A number of New England merchants, many already active in the Louisbourg trade, also arrived in Halifax, helping to establish the town as a northern subsidiary of Yankee commercial patterns. The New Englanders were not universally admired by the British newcomers to the province, one observing, '...of all the people upon earth I never heard any bear so bad a character for Cheating designing people & all under the Cloack of religion.'[23]

Each transport that left England in May 1749 had its own Mess List of settlers aboard, totalling 1,174 heads of families, only 509 of whom were accompanied by their spouses. There were 414 children under the age of 16, and 420 servants, mainly males. Of the total heads of families, 654 were soldiers and sailors. The largest single civilian occupation given was farmer (161 names), with 107 in the building trades, and a vast assortment of other occupations.[24] The town of Halifax they arrived at—which had been laid out by surveyors—was very far from meeting the description in a contemporary English magazine of a 'city...of 2,000 houses, disposed into fifty streets of different magnitudes', in its centre 'a spacious square with an equestrian statue of His Majesty.' The immediate reality meant huts, tents, and primitive conditions. The new governor, Lord Edward Cornwallis (1713-76), wrote home that 'amongst these [settlers] the number of industrious active men proper to undertake and carry on a new settlement is very small—of soldiers

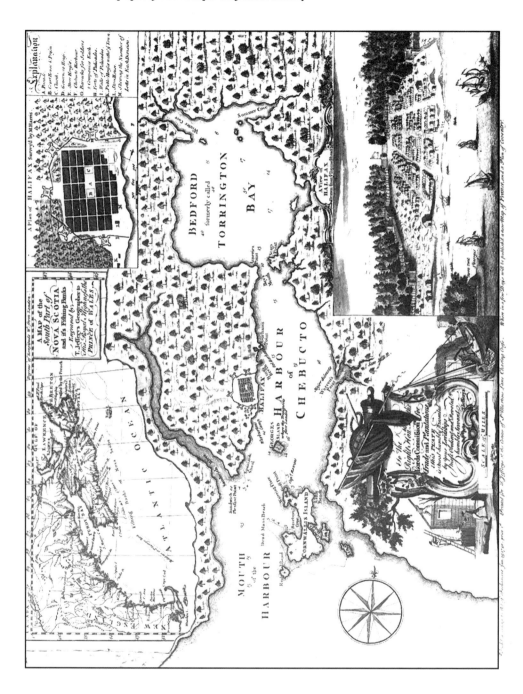

there are only 100, of tradesmen, Sailors and others able and willing to work, not above 200.' The remainder, he claimed, 'were poor idle worthless vagabonds that embraced the opportunity to get provisions for one year without labour, or sailors that only wanted a passage to New England. Many have come as into a hospital to be cured, some of Venereal Disorders, some even Incurables.'[25] The arrival of the garrison from Louisbourg, which had been returned to the French the year before, further complicated matters by bringing a swarm of camp-followers who were mainly devoted to supplying the thirst and physical desires of the troops. Many settlers died over the first winter, and hundreds left for New England. Persons objecting to assisting in burying corpses in St Paul's Cemetery were ordered struck off the ration list. Disbanded soldiers here, as elsewhere, proved unsatisfactory settlers. While Charles Lawrence doubtless exaggerated, he had a point when he asserted in 1760 that 'every soldier that has come into the Province, since the establishment of Halifax, has either quitted it or become a dramseller [seller of spirits].'[26]

The British government soon sought a new source of settlers, turning to projects, long mooted, of settling Nova Scotia with 'Foreign Protestants' — chiefly Swiss, French Huguenots, and Germans. It employed as recruiting agent the young Scotsman John Dick (d. 1804), who would subsequently assume, unjustifiably, a dormant knight-baronetcy of Nova Scotia and spend many years as British consul at the free port of Leghorn, Italy. Knighted in the order of St Alexander Nevsky in 1770 by Catherine the Great of Russia for some unspecified service to the Russian fleet, he also became involved in a scheme by which a purported illegitimate daughter of the Empress Elizabeth of Russia was carried off in a pretended marriage by a Russian adventurer. Over the winter of 1749/50 John Dick, at this time a merchant in Rotterdam, was empowered by the Board of Trade to recruit up to 1,500 'Foreign Protestants', who would receive land, a year's subsistence, arms and tools, but not free transportation. Dick protested that free passage was the main inducement, but in 1750 he managed to dispatch to Halifax one ship with 322 passengers, permitting the emigrants to finance their passage by contracting their labour to the government.[27]

One of the first in a long line of recruiting agents whose work would provide settlers for Canada, Dick was severely criticized for collecting 'in general old miserable wretches', misleading them about conditions in the New World, exploiting their labour, and overcrowding his vessels. Such problems would become a familiar part of immigration, and were especially common when the agents had no stake in the settlement itself. In 1751 Dick dispatched four vessels with 1,000 passengers and sent another 1,135 in 1752, while other agents dispatched additional immigrants recruited among young men in Switzerland. The total came to over 2,700 'Germans and Swiss', many of the latter actually French Huguenots from Lorraine.

These immigrants were composed of 40 per cent adult men, 25 per cent adult women, and 35 per cent children; most of the adults were under the age of 40. As was typical of European immigrants to Canada throughout its history, those in family groups settled more easily than single individuals, especially males. The largest single occupational component—well over 60 per cent—described themselves as farmers; but there were over fifty other trades and professions represented, including carpenters, surgeons, watch-makers, schoolmasters, and clergymen. Few unskilled labourers appeared on the passenger rolls. The government intended to settle these newcomers in agricultural communities, chiefly on the Bay of Fundy. But most remained in Halifax because of the uncertainty over Acadian land titles. They did not like that shanty town. One memorial of 1752 complained of an inability to obtain land and building materials, and of high rents and exorbitant prices. Assistance with victualling, sought by the newcomers, was reluctantly granted by the Nova Scotia (and British) authorities. Because of the many problems caused by these 'Foreign Protestants', the British ceased active recruitment of them in 1752, and never resumed it for any other North American colony. A good idea was seen to have gone awry, although the Board of Trade never did appreciate that much of the problem in Nova Scotia began with an absence of cleared land that these emigrants had been prom-ised. This difficulty was better understood by the Nova Scotia government, which tended to focus its attention on those Acadians who continued to inhabit that land—despite their refusal to commit themselves fully to British allegiance.

Desperate for some solution to the 'foreigner' problem, Governor Hopson and his council, in the spring of 1753, determined to remove the Protestants to Merliguish (or Merligash)—about fifty miles west of Halifax, and renamed Lunenburg—where there were ostensibly several hundred acres of cleared land and decent soil. The first contingent of settlers left Halifax in a flotilla of tiny vessels, under the direction of Charles Lawrence. On 19 June 1753 they were given town lots and two months later Lawrence reported: 'Most of them are well under cover. All of them have gardens and many of them good Framed Houses.'[28] But the people were 'inconceivably turbulent, I might have said mutinous,' Lawrence added—as could have been expected, given the treatment they had received. In mid-December of that first year, the settlers rose in armed rebellion. The incident was apparently touched off by rumours of a letter from London, concealed by one resident, that the people were not receiving all the support authorized by the British Parlia-ment. The Nova Scotia government moved quickly to quell the uprising, but it never could deal with its underlying causes. The Lunenburg rebellion became yet another mark against the Acadians, who continued to farm the lands intended for the newcomers, while seeking political neutrality.

Acadia and the Expulsions

The British settlement policy for Nova Scotia was only one in a series of new pressures brought upon that province's Acadian population. The French government had begun to reinforce Louisbourg, the fortifications of which had not been totally destroyed. It also constructed new forts (Fort Beauséjour and Fort Gaspéreau) on the disputed Chignecto peninsula. The French also started encouraging those Acadians in Nova Scotia to remove to French territory, particularly the previously neglected Île-Saint-Jean. Despite its obvious agricultural potential, the isolation of that island prevented its settlement until after 1719, when the French government attempted to people it through private proprietors. One of these entrepreneurs, Jean-Pierre Roma (fl. 1715-57), actually took up residence on the island and supervised the clearing of land for a substantial community on its eastern tip. A man with 'so much causticity' in his character (wrote one contemporary) 'that it is to be feared he could not reconcile himself to anyone', Roma fought successfully against isolation and natural calamity, but saw his settlement fall in June 1745 to imperial policy in the form of Yankee raiders from Louisbourg. After the return of Louisbourg to France in 1748, the population of Île-Saint-Jean grew rapidly, from less than 800 to over 2,000 residents by 1752. Most of the new arrivals were Acadians—previously living in the borderlands of Nova Scotia—who were caught between British and French demands for their loyalty and sought to escape conflict. (The French authorities, for example, after 1748 had forced Acadians near Fort Beauséjour to bear arms under threat of deportation.[29]) The refugees then replicated their 'meadowland cultivation' on the marshlands along the island's coastal rivers, and began to prosper.

After 1748 the bulk of Nova Scotia's Acadian population hung tough— though some migrated, and others succumbed to French blandishments. In 1749 they forced Governor Cornwallis to back down from an attempt to administer an unconditional oath. But it was by now plain that the French 'neutrals' could not be turned into model British subjects, and it was equally apparent that new settlers could not (and would not) take up lands in areas of Acadian concentration while the question of titles remained unclarified. In 1754 the renewal of undeclared war in North America, between France and Britain, helped solidify the thinking of the Nova Scotia authorities. The British campaign against Fort Beauséjour in 1755 completed the process, especially when 300 armed Acadians were found inside the French lines when that fortress was captured in June of that year. Lieutenant-Governor Lawrence promptly decided to resolve the Acadian question, forcing the confrontation on 3 July between the Council and the Acadian deputies discussed at the beginning of this chapter.

As so often happens when men finally resolve in their own minds a dilemma that has persisted for some time—in this case for over forty years—the confrontation with the Acadian deputies in 1755 produced swift and ruthless action, allowing no time for reconsideration. Charles Lawrence did not bother to consult the British government on the question of the Acadian removal. Although the Board of Trade had often mentioned the possibility, it had never actually recommended it. Nor did Lawrence inform the Acadians of the result of their failure to take the unconditional oath at their meeting on 3 July. When news of the defeat, on the Monongahela River in western Pennsylvania, of General Edward Braddock arrived after the July confrontation, Lawrence only stiffened his position. On 25 July a group of newly selected Acadian deputies were told by the Council that 'they must now resolve either to take the Oath without any Reserve or else quit their lands, for that Affairs were now at such a Crisis in America that no delay could be admitted.'[30] The deputies replied that they would rather quit their lands than take a new oath. In turn the Council warned them of the dire consequences ('if they once refused the Oath, they would never after be permitted to take it, but would infallibly loose their Possessions') and gave them three days to reconsider. While the inner workings of the minds of the Acadians cannot be probed, a sense of *déja vu* can fairly be assumed. The British had pressed before without effect, and the Acadians had resisted before with success. On 28 July the deputies refused to take the oath. They were summarily imprisoned, and the Council agreed unanimously that 'it would be most proper to send them [the Acadians] to be distributed amongst the several Colonies on the Continent, and that a sufficient number of Vessels should be hired with all possible Expedition for that purpose.'[31] The distribution of Acadians among other English colonies served to answer the British desire not to add strength to the French settlements, and seemed the obvious strategy to adopt.

The formal plan prepared for the Acadian evacuation spoke not only of attempting to persuade the Acadians that they were to be removed to French territory (any ruse was acceptable to prevent resistance), but also of destroying the Acadian settlements in Nova Scotia. The details of the actual process of removal are scanty, but the diary of Lieutenant-Colonel John Winslow (1703-74), who supervised the removal at Grand Pré, indicates that it was carried out with firmness and met little resistance. On 5 September 1755 Winslow summoned the Acadian men to the parish church, and from a table in its centre (surrounded by armed officers) informed them of their fate. While implementing instructions to keep families together in the same vessel, and declaring 'lands and tenements, cattle of all kinds and live stock of all sorts' forfeited to the Crown, Winslow allowed the Acadians to take their money and household goods, guaranteeing them security of their personal property. On 10 September he placed another 230 Acadians aboard five transports, although embarkation did not occur until a month later. By 3 November he had sent off 1,510 people, and followed subsequently with another 600.[32] Another 1,100 Acadians were removed from Piziquid, 1,664 from Annapolis Royal, and 1,100 from Fort Cumberland. The only serious resistance came at Chepody, where 300 Acadians and Indian allies success-fully drove the British forces back to their ship. More frequently, the Acadians abandoned their lands and houses, escaping to the woods to make their way to French territory—as far away as Louisiana—or to uninhabited districts of the province, mainly in what is now New Brunswick.

Over 6,000 Acadians were transported to southern British colonies, from Massachusetts to South Carolina, that were never advised of their imminent arrival. The first contingent reached Boston harbour in early November 1755. Massachusetts authorities discovered that six vessels, loaded with 1,077 Acadians bound for points south, had put in for repairs. The transports were 'too much crowded' and provisions were insufficient. Some Acadians were removed to reduce the congestion and placed in the care of towns in the colony, which were informed by newspaper advertisement that more were to come. One of the leading political figures in the province, Thomas Hutchin-son (a historian, and later a prominent Loyalist), not only temporarily shel-tered one family headed by an ailing widow, but kept her children under his care after she died. Moreover, he angrily organized a petition that the exiles be returned to their homes or be compensated for their losses, suggesting that the petition be placed in the hands of 'a proper person in England to solicit their cause.' The leaders of the Acadians rejected Hutchinson's legal efforts because they were afraid petition to the British Crown might damage their standing in France.[33]

On the whole the people of Massachusetts met the exiles with fairness and humanity, locating them in small groups throughout the province and pro-viding them with food, shelter, medical care, clothing, and employment. The Massachusetts government complained constantly of the cost, and of the failure of Nova Scotia to warn of the exiles' arrival. Further south, from New York to South Carolina, many vessels met an even less enthusiastic welcome, and were forced to return to Nova Scotia because the British colonies would not grant asylum to their passengers. These returning Acadians joined those who had escaped deportation in 1755 in their search for new homes in France and the various French colonies of North America.

Those Acadians who made their way to Île-Royale and Île-Saint-Jean would discover that they had only postponed their wanderings. The popula-tion of Île-Saint-Jean grew rapidly in the wake of the Nova Scotia actions, with more than 2,000 refugees from the mainland arriving on the island over the winter of 1755/6, and more than 1,400 of these folk remaining, depen-dent on the French king's bounty. On 26 July 1758, however, another British expedition against Louisbourg forced its surrender, and another expulsion began, this one virtually ignored and forgotten in Canadian history, although 6,000 Acadians were forcibly removed from their homes, over 3,500 of them from Île-Saint-Jean. Some parishes on the island escaped removal to begin the present Acadian population there, and the Îles de la Madeleine received other refugees—but most of the deportees were sent directly back to France, where they received little sympathy. The Acadian Expulsion of 1758 has created few legends. Unlike the earlier Acadians expelled from Nova Scotia, the 1758 exiles from Île-Royale and Île-Saint-Jean were merely the pawns of imperial warfare, dealt with according to the conventions of the day.

The British government was not pleased with Nova Scotia for its actions in 1755, but the Board of Trade did not remove or even chastise Charles Lawrence. Instead, on 25 March 1756, it wrote him, acknowledging his report on the removal of the Acadians, and adding, '. . .as you represent it to have been indispensably necessary for the Security and Protection of the Province in the present critical situation of our affairs, we doubt not but your Conduct herein will meet with His Majesty's Approbation.'[34] Approbation never came, but neither did any other comment.

Despite two rounds of forcible removals, the British never quite succeeded in eliminating the French population from the Atlantic region. Many had escaped their potential captors by heading into the bush, and others returned from the destinations to which they had been sent. What the expulsions did accomplish was the permanent elimination of the Acadians as an impediment to the settlement of a new population on their traditional lands.

❧❧❧ *The Fate of the Indian Population*

The founding of Halifax—with its clear implication that Nova Scotia was to become an important British settlement colony—had a substantial effect on the native population, particularly the Micmacs. That impact was sealed by the defeat of the French in 1758. In Nova Scotia, as elsewhere, the Indians wanted to maintain their traditional lives and lands, while having access to European trade goods. They had discovered in the seventeenth century that the strategic ambitions of one European power could be played off against another. Before 1749, and especially in the period 1713-49, they were able to take considerable advantage of the ongoing imperial rivalry, despite their relatively small numbers; by 1750, probably no more than 1,000 Micmacs lived in peninsular Nova Scotia and 2,000 natives remained in the entire Atlantic region, exclusive of Labrador.

That the Micmacs attempted to pursue their own policies is demonstrated by their refusal to be removed from the territory when it was transferred to the British in 1713. They were not impressed by French blandishments to persuade them to migrate, however much they were influenced by the missionaries who had long toiled among them. To move was to sacrifice the land. Ironically, during the period of eighteenth-century rivalry Catholicism gained in importance among the Micmacs, chiefly because the French put increased effort into missionary work and the British resolutely refused to court the natives with either missionaries or extensive gift-giving. The British attitude in Nova Scotia anticipated later insistence in other regions that sovereignty took precedence over native land claims, and that occasional formal treaties of friendship and submission could serve in place of the constant cultivation of native goodwill. Treaty negotiations turned on oaths of allegiance and native acceptance of European settlement, not on promises to maintain Indian autonomy.

Insensitive British treatment further assisted the French and hardened native resistance—even into open conflict. The years between 1715 and 1725 saw a series of violent incidents in Nova Scotia that eventually merged into a larger Indian war with New England from 1722 to 1725. Micmacs, Malecites, and Abenakis fought together to stem British incursions into their territories. The natives were never totally defeated, but they made a peace in Boston late in 1725 that was ratified in Nova Scotia a few months later. The British promised not to interfere in Indian territory, and the natives in turn acknowledged King George as 'the rightful Possessor of the province', to whom they submitted. Whether either party understood the other's interpretation of these commitments is doubtful. Certainly after the founding of Halifax the possibility that Indian lands would remain free from extensive British settlement became increasingly unlikely.

By 1749 the Indians were convinced that British concepts of land ownership and settlement were disastrous to their interests. A Micmac declaration of war against the British in 1749 was studiously ignored in Halifax, the Council declaring that the Indians could not be allowed to become 'a free & independent People', but had to be 'treated as so many Banditti Ruffians or Rebels to His Majesty's Government.' The British, led by Lord Cornwallis, responded instead with a policy of extermination, with orders proclaimed 'to Annoy, distress, take or destroy the Savages commonly called Mic-Macks, wherever they are found.'[35] Bounties for Indian scalps were added inducements, and the Micmacs were hounded into French territory. At least one band agreed to peace in the early 1750s, and was allowed to settle at Shubenacadie with promises of non-interference. The remaining Micmacs, deprived of French support and arms by the surrender of Louisbourg in 1758, were forced to submit to British power.

The final Nova Scotia peace treaty with the Micmacs was concluded in 1761, but it was in effect only a renewal of that of 1726 by a 'merciful Conqueror'. The agreement did not really deal with land rights. Although in 1762 the Nova Scotia government proclaimed that it would maintain rights to Micmac land 'reserved or claimed' by the Indians, such claims were not clearly agreed upon by both parties at the time and would not be accepted by incoming settlers. The Nova Scotia authorities would remain aware of the

Micmacs for the next few years because of fears that they would respond with violence to settlement on their land. They didn't. But after 1761 the Indians were not an important military threat, and in time they would cease to be regarded as a factor of any importance whatsoever in the affairs of the province or region.

Nova Scotia in 1758

In 1758 Britain took Louisbourg once and for all. An expedition under Major-General Jeffery Amherst, one of whose three brigade commanders was James Wolfe, was made up of a force of 15,000 soldiers and more than 150 ships, and the siege lasted from the landing on 8 June to the surrender on 26 July. Wolfe remarked: 'If it had been attacked by anybody but the English, it would have fallen long ago.'

In October, with Louisbourg finally in British hands, the government of Nova Scotia again turned to settlement. Unhappy both with the Halifax experiment and with the Foreign Protestants, the authorities looked to New England, that other obvious source of settlers, with its surplus population and close ties to Nova Scotia. The governor's advertisements in October 1758 of Nova Scotia's new availability for settlement found a ready audience, especially in eastern Connecticut, southern Rhode Island, and southeastern Massachusetts, where available land was in short supply and a younger generation was eager to move. Transportation to new homes would be by water rather than over land, the land was already cleared and improved (so the Nova Scotia government claimed), and transportation costs and initial support in the new settlements would be met out of the public purse.

Only a few days before the advertisements were published, a legislative assembly—the first widely elected governing body in what is now Canada—met in Halifax. It had long been insisted upon by the British authorities, who had noted in instructions to Governor Richard Phillips as early as 1719 the need for 'such reasonable laws and statutes as hereafter shall be made and assented to by you with the advice and Consent of our Council and Assembly of the said Province hereafter to be appointed.'[36] The creation of an assembly had been long delayed by the continual turmoil in the province. Particularly critical had been the presence of a French-speaking Roman Catholic population that was either ineligible for participation, given British law, or required precedent-setting exemptions. (A similar foot-dragging would be seen in Quebec after 1763.) But following the influx of settlers in 1749 and the removal of the Acadians, there was little excuse for not summoning an assembly. By 1757 denunciations of the Nova Scotia government were reaching London, one claiming that 'We are, the Shamefull and Contemptible By-Word of America; The Slaves of Nova Scotia; The Creatures of Military Gov'rs; Whose Will, is our Law, & whose Person, is our God.'[37] In early 1758 the Board of Trade virtually ordered Governor

Lawrence to establish an assembly, writing: 'We think it of indispensable necessity that it should be immediately carried into execution.' When it was established in October, the twenty legislators who met—almost to a man New Englanders resident in Halifax—voted to serve without remuneration and quickly settled down to the passage of legislation. One of the assembly's first acts was to establish a court of divorce for the province, with far more liberal rules than existed in the mother country.[38]

Nova Scotia was now a full-fledged British colony. This point had not been reached without considerable brutality. The *grand dérangement* would resurface in the nineteenth century as a major blot on the copybook of Governor Charles Lawrence and his associates, even though it evoked little official reaction at the time. But if the Expulsion has become part of Canadian mythology, the government's 1750 policy of Indian extermination remains known only to a handful of scholars.

By 1758 the British were clearly in the ascendant in North America. On 12 January 1759 James Wolfe, fresh from his success at Louisbourg, was appointed major-general and commander-in-chief of the land forces in the expedition against Quebec. A concerted military campaign to defeat the French in North America and drive them out of the continent forever was already formulated. The British, no longer treating the northern part of the continent as an afterthought, were well on their way to converting all of it into an integral part of their burgeoning North American Empire.

chapter six

The Expansion and Contraction of Britain's

North American Empire, 1759-1781

Around dawn on 13 September 1759 a Canadian militia man rushed to the outskirts of the French defences north of Quebec and the Plains of Abraham to report that the enemy had reached the heights. Because of the difficulties of a serious assault at that place, reported one French witness, 'people did not believe a word of this man's story, thinking that fear had turned his head.'[1] But the intensified sound of guns and the rapid movement of French troops towards the heights soon made his account more credible. The French commander-in-chief, the Marquis de Montcalm (1712-59), rode out just after seven a.m. to survey the situation, silent and preoccupied. He said nothing as he looked over the field of scarlet uniforms still forming on the plains: nearly 4,500 British regulars, mainly crack regiments of Highland Scots, Britain's best soldiers. Montcalm returned to his headquarters to organize his response, and about 9:30 a.m. he commented to one of his officers: 'We cannot avoid action; the enemy is entrenching, he already has two pieces of cannon. If we give him time to establish himself, we shall never be able to attack him with the sort of troops we have.' Soon after, the officer to whom Montcalm had spoken saw the French forces begin moving, 'M. de Montcalm at its head and on horseback.'[2] The military showdown that had been building for nearly a century, between the French and the British for the control of North America, was about to begin.

The series of abortive and aborted British attempts to seize Quebec, the administrative capital of New France—in 1690, 1711, and 1746—had not prevented another major expedition under General James Wolfe (1727-59) from trying again. The largest and best-equipped military force that North America had ever known, it assembled at Louisbourg over the winter of 1758-9, while the frozen ice of the St Lawrence isolated the French. It consisted of 8,600 troops, most of them regulars, and 13,500 sailors on board 119 vessels, including twenty-two ships of the line and five frigates. This great armada required six days simply to clear Louisbourg harbour in early

June 1759. On 27 June, Wolfe landed his army on the Île d'Orléans without serious French opposition. A flotilla of French fire-ships, which cost Louis XV a million *livres*, was sent downriver a day later to wreak havoc among the British transports, but they were fired prematurely and caused little damage. There followed over two months of skirmishing, as Wolfe attempted to find a place to land his army closer to the French forces and Montcalm sought to prevent such a move. Meanwhile, Wolfe and the British admiral Sir Charles Saunders (1713?-75) were at constant loggerheads, and Montcalm saw considerable evidence that his forces, mainly French-Canadian militiamen, would not stand up to offensive action. The British navy kept up a continual bombardment of the fortified town, in which 'above 180 houses had been burnt to the ground which was more than one half of the town, in the best quarter of it, and the finest Houses in Quebec.'[3]

Wolfe tried a number of plans, all without success. He was becoming desperate. As the end of summer approached, the length of time the massive British fleet could remain in the St Lawrence was quickly lessening and its commanders were pressing for a final confrontation. In August, Wolfe began deliberately destroying the French villages along the south shore of the St Lawrence from Kamouraska to Pointe-Lévis, and by mid-month the sky was continually full of smoke from burning houses. One of his subordinates complained, 'I never served so disagreeable a Campaign as this. Our unequal Force has reduced our Operations to a Scene of Skirmishing Cruelty &

◄ James Wolfe, aged 32. This is said to be a copy of a sketch by John Montresor, a British engineer, drawn from life at the Montmorency camp on 1 September 1759 — two weeks before Wolfe died. National Archives of Canada.

Louis-Joseph, Marquis de Montcalm. National ▶ Archives of Canada, C-14342.

Devastation. It is War of the worst Shape.'[4] This critic thought Wolfe's leadership little better than the general's health, which was very bad. Never blessed with a strong constitution, Wolfe for years had had a strong premonition of an early death. Shortly before taking to his bed in Quebec with a fever, he commented: 'I would cheerfully sacrifice a leg or an arm to be in possession of Quebec.' If Wolfe thought he was dying, but wanted to depart this world a hero, his opposite number Montcalm had spent several years struggling with bouts of depression over the 'miserable dissensions' and lack of preparedness of the colony he was defending. 'I should like as well as anybody to be Marshal of France,' he wrote to a friend after his victory at Ticonderoga in 1758, 'but to buy the honor with the life I am leading here would be too much.' He despaired of returning home: 'When shall I see my château of Candiac, my plantations, my chestnut grove, my old mill, my mulberry trees?'[5] Only a few days before the final showdown against Wolfe and the British, Montcalm complained to an aide: 'My health is going to pieces.'[6]

Not until Wolfe's partial recovery from his fever—the doctors had bled him profusely and fed him opiates, the standard treatment of the time—did the British commander galvanize himself into action for a final effort before the inevitable freeze-up of the St Lawrence. His brigadiers recommended cutting off supply lines 50 miles above the town, at Batisian, placing the British army 'betwixt' Montcalm 'and his provisions'—thus forcing a confrontation in which 'Quebec and probably all Canada will be ours.'[7] Wolfe accepted their recommendations, writing to his mother:

> The enemy puts nothing at risk, & I cant in conscience put the whole army to risk. My antagonist has wisely shut himself up in inaccessible entrenchments, so that I cant get at him without spilling a torrent of blood, and that perhaps to little purpose. The Marquiss de Montcalm is at the head of a great number of bad soldiers, And I am at the head of a small number of good ones, that wish for nothing so much as to fight him.[8]

The British found a path up the cliffs to the plain above at the Anse au Foulon, and managed to pass the French sentries unmolested. According to George Townshend's account, when 'the french Centries on ye bank's challeng'd our boats, Captn Frazer who had been in ye Dutch Service & spoke french—answered—la france & vive le Roy, on which the French Centinels ran along the Shore in ye dark crying laisser les passer ils sont nos Gens avec les provisions.'[9] The French had not prearranged a password. Beginning the climb at 4 a.m., Wolfe's army reached the top of the cliffs by 8 a.m.—though not without opposition from a French detachment, which was made to disperse. The British battle lines were drawn, only two deep instead of the normal three, covering the plain.

Montcalm ranged his forces for battle, a militia unit within each regular battalion, and gave the order around 10 a.m. for the three columns to advance at a run. He himself was in the lead. Not until the French were at close range

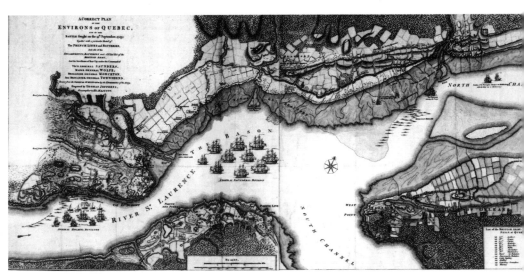

This 1760 map by Thomas Jefferys, who was then geographer to George III, illustrates the Quebec campaign in 1759. Wolfe set up camp on the Île d'Orléans (lower right); failed in July in his attempt to land at Montmorency on the north shore (above the North Channel); moved his fleet upriver past Quebec in September; and landed at l'Anse au Foulon (extreme left) to wage the brief battle on the Plains of Abraham (above). National Archives of Canada, 128079.

Richard Short, *A View of the Bishop's House, with the Ruins as they appear going up the Hill from the Lower to the Upper Town, 1759.* Short accompanied Wolfe's forces to North America and served at the siege of Quebec. He made twelve sketches of the town, showing the results of the devastating bombardment, that were later engraved. National Archives of Canada, C-352.

(different accounts say 40 and 60 yards) did the British fire—not quite as one man, although they did achieve a reasonable degree of co-ordination. The French broke ranks and, retreating back towards the city, were pursued by what was obviously a victorious British army. Wolfe, who had recklessly exposed himself in the midst of his troops, was hit several times by musket balls; one in the chest was almost immediately fatal. His last words—after some hasty orders—were 'Now, God be praised, I will die in peace.' Soon after, Montcalm was himself mortally wounded, dying the next day. The initial British volley and French reaction were not the end of the fighting, which went on fiercely for some time, with considerable loss of life. Nor was it the end of the war, for the bulk of the French army escaped and would fight valiantly on for nearly another year. But the British possessed the fortress of Quebec and would never relinquish it.

The Battle of the Plains of Abraham is one of history's most famous battles and much has been written about it. Many tantalizing questions can never be completely answered. Why did Montcalm attack without waiting for reinforcements, which were on their way? Why did he attack at all? Unopposed, the British would have run out of food very quickly, while being subjected to sniping shots from by the French. Did Wolfe deliberately expose himself to a hero's death? But in the end the battle came out much as could have been predicted. It was probably the first engagement in North America that was fought almost totally in European, rather than American, terms, and when a fully professional army, well disciplined and on the day well led, defeated a partly untrained one. Fully backed by a government at home with regular troops and naval support, the British finally breached the defensive position that the French had enjoyed for nearly a century.

ᴗᴗᴗ From the Plains of Abraham to the Proclamation of 1763

Both Britain and her American colonies responded to the news of Wolfe's victory with enthusiasm. In London, printers were setting in type a dispatch of Wolfe dated 2 September that spoke of stalemate, when word of triumph, reaching Portsmouth by fast frigate in only four weeks, arrived in William Pitt's hands on the evening of 16 October. 'All was rapture and riot; all was triumph and exaltation,' commented novelist Tobias Smollett. But celebration was a bit premature, particularly given the common assumption that the British had won not only the battle, but the war. The French continued to fight valiantly on many fronts, and would be joined by the Spanish, who would lose heavily in the Caribbean. Even in Canada, where Brigadier-General James Murray (1721-94) was installed as military governor of Quebec, the French were not yet beaten. Montcalm's successor, the Duc de Lévis (1719-87), rallied the French forces, marshalling an army of 7,000 men, half of them regulars, the remainder composed of militia and Indians. He led them from Montreal to Quebec, hoping to retake the town before

Murray could receive reinforcements after the spring breakup of the St Lawrence.

On 28 April 1760 Murray was forced to return his troops to the Plains of Abraham, where—in the Battle of Ste Foy—he proceeded to repeat Montcalm's mistakes, attacking the enemy and seeing his men retreat in disarray. But there was no repetition for the French of the previous year's British victory, and both sides waited to see which would first receive reinforcement. In the meantime Lévis began to bombard the devastated town yet again, and Murray answered with superior fire-power. In London news of the disaster came as a bit of a shock. 'America was like a book one has read and done with,' noted diarist Horace Walpole, 'but here we are on a sudden, reading our book backwards.' On 9 May a vessel was sighted rounding the final point in the river before Quebec. At first the French were hopeful, but she flew the British flag. The frigate *Lowestoft* was soon followed by other warships, and it really was over for the French. A traditional three-point attack on Montreal—anchored by a large army led by General Jeffery Amherst (1717-97) from New York—forced the surrender of that town, the final French stronghold, in early September. The fifty-five articles of capitulation would govern the British occupation of Canada until the governments

Thomas Patten, *An East View of Montreal in Canada*, 1760. Patten was a British officer who accompanied General Amherst's expedition for the capture of Montreal in 1760. His watercolour of the walled city was engraved and published by Thomas Jefferys in 1762. National Archives of Canada.

in Europe settled matters by the Treaty of Paris in 1763. But in the autumn of 1760, no one knew how long it would be before a final peace could be made.

Until Europe made a final determination on the future of Canada, Britain would have to deal with the colony with a fairly light hand. In the capitulations, General Amherst had readily granted freedom of worship, security of property, and the people's right to remain in their own homes (an important consideration in view of the recent events in Nova Scotia). His response to requests for neutrality and the continuation of customary law was: 'They become Subjects of the King.' But in the short term, such concessions were generally observed by the three military administrators of the colony, all of whom continued to accept French as the 'language of the country', especially in the military courts, which administered civil justice under local precedents; and the military garrisons proved quite generous to the conquered in terms of informal assistance. The capitulation immediately forced French royal officials to abandon the country—some of them, like François Bigot, returning to France to face disgrace, for they would be made the scapegoats for the débâcle of 1759-60. Many of the colony's landed and commercial élite also left, after it became clear that France would not retain Canada, and the Jesuits had been expelled by General Murray in 1759. But for some of the French-Canadian élite, especially the merchants, a decision to depart was difficult, and adaptation to the new order seemed possible. However, the victorious armies brought in their wake—ominously—a new group of suppliers, mainly American colonials tied to British and American trading patterns. These connections were far more substantial than those of the *Canadiens* with their familiar French firms, which had become restricted, if not made impossible. And in the closing years of the war their fortunes would be affected by the collapse of not only the Canadian but the French economy.

Before 1761, uncertainties about the final outcome of the war persisted, and the possibility that Canada would be restored to France remained alive. That option was seemingly fuelled by a great discussion in the British press over the value of Canada, particularly in comparison with West Indian sugar islands. This 'Canada versus Guadaloupe' debate, as it has been called, had little impact, however, on the British government in its peace negotiations. This was particularly so after the coalition ministry—headed by William Pitt and the Duke of Newcastle—which had successfully fought the war, was replaced by one dominated by the Scotsman Lord Bute, the former tutor of the new British king, who took the throne in 1760. George III (1738-1820) wanted peace, and it was Bute's task not only to provide it, but more importantly to sell it to a British public that was greedy for new territorial acquisitions as the symbols of victory over the enemy. Peace negotiations in 1761 had proved abortive, not because the French had balked at sacrificing North American territory, but because William Pitt wanted much more. When the French West Indies fell totally and the British began an assault on Spanish Havana, the French and Spanish had their backs to the wall. The

French offered to sacrifice more continental American territory. Louisiana east of the Mississippi was surrendered for Martinique and Guadaloupe. The French were granted fishing rights in Newfoundland and the islands of St Pierre and Miquelon in exchange for the surrender of all claims to territory in the northern part of the American continent. The Spanish proved no problem after the conquest of Havana. In a complicated arrangement, Britain returned Havana and Puerto Rico and kept Florida, while France compensated Spain for its losses by ceding it the western half of Louisiana and the port of New Orleans.

The final arrangement was sold by the Bute ministry to the British public by emphasizing the great gains made in North America, while ignoring the absence of other territorial acquisitions that might legitimately have been demanded, given the international British victories. Having stressed the North American theatre, and the security that had been won for the American colonies as a result of the Seven Years' War—at tremendous expense to the British people in manpower and money—the government needed an American policy. The addition to the British Empire of a sizeable number of French-speaking Roman Catholics in Canada, as well as the acquisition of complete responsibility for the Indians of the North American interior, meant that regular troops would have to be stationed in America, and Indian affairs properly regulated. The Americans would have to provide at least a token revenue to support the military. Over the winter of 1762-3 the government debated an American tax to support the army, but paused to seek more information before proceeding.

George Grenville succeeded Lord Bute as prime minister in 1763. Proposals for an American policy came to him from all directions, many advocating an integrated approach that combined solutions to all the outstanding imperial problems: administering the new territories, the Indians, the military, a colonial revenue, and administrative reform of the North American colonies. One adviser argued:

> It might also be necessary to fix upon some Line for a Western Boundary to our ancient provinces, beyond which our People should not at present be permitted to settle, hence as their Numbers increased, they would emigrate to Nova Scotia, or to the provinces on the Southern Frontier, where they would be useful to their Mother Country, instead of planting themselves in the Heart of America, out of the reach of Government, and where, from the great Difficulty procuring European Commodities they would be compelled to commence Manufactures to the infinite Prejudice of Britain.[10]

Commitments to the Indians seemed to coalesce with Britain's other interests regarding both its old and its recently acquired colonies. Indian policy and general policy—as John Pownall, secretary of the Board of Trade, observed—'do, in the present object, by a happy coincidence of circumstances, meet the same point, and form an exact union of system.'[11] The government put aside the far-reaching proposals for reorganization, probably because it could not rouse itself to such an effort, and the immediate result of all the advice and deliberations was the notorious Proclamation of 1763, the first attempt by the British to produce a policy for its new territories and responsibilities.

The Atlantic Region, 1763–1775

Richard Short, *Part of the Town & Harbour of Halifax in Nova Scotia, looking down Prince Street to the Opposite Shore. . .*, one of six prints of drawings of Halifax made by Short in 1759. National Archives of Canada, C-4294.

Like most British policy for what is now Canada produced over the next few years, the Proclamation of 1763 was not directly intended to effect fundamental alterations for Britain's older seaboard colonies. (The notorious Stamp Act of 1765 — requiring a tax stamp for publications and legal documents — was simply cosmetic tinkering.) For the moment, four new governments were created out of the American acquisitions, including Quebec, which was limited to the St Lawrence settlements. This truncated province was to be governed by British law and, as soon as possible, an elected assembly. The Island of St John and Cape Breton were attached to Nova Scotia. Land grants to retired officers and disbanded servicemen were to be made readily available. In the west, beyond the river systems of the Atlantic coast, no land grants were to be made. This territory was to be reserved for the Indians, and any traders in it were to be regulated by the imperial government. The Proclamation had ramifications beyond the territory ceded by the French, however. It was preceded by a major Indian uprising in the interior, known as 'Pontiac's Rebellion'. And both the declaration of limits to American western settlement and the need to finance Britain's new military responsibilities would enrage the American colonials, who soon began a series of provocative responses to Britain that, within a dozen years, would escalate into an organized colonial rebellion or 'revolution'. It soon became apparent that policy for Britain's northernmost colonies could not be effected by Great Britain in isolation.

Although neither the Proclamation of 1763 nor any other British document ever elaborated a fully articulated settlement policy for what is now Canada, the outlines of that policy were perfectly clear. The British did not wish to populate their northernmost colonies with emigrants from the mother country itself. Great Britain was at the beginning of a major economic shift, usually called the Industrial Revolution, and it wanted to retain its own people, both as a labour force and for military purposes. The British, however, were prepared to make land grants to disbanded servicemen; professional soldiers were not regarded as economically very useful at home. They were also willing to accept 'foreign Protestants' as settlers, although they hoped that colonial Americans, already acclimated to the New World, would become the principal newcomers. As a result of their experience in Nova Scotia, the British had learned two lessons: first, the best way to deal with a population alien in language, religion, and customs was by outnumbering it; second, the state could not afford to subsidize a large movement of people to a new colony.

The treatment meted out to the Acadians remained to haunt the British for many years. Forcible removal of an alien population was not a humane policy. As for publicly subsidized settlement, to the first Halifax settlers and the 'foreign Protestants' Nova Scotia had added a third contingent of newcomers in the person of New England 'Planters' who were brought to the province between 1759 and 1762. Governor Lawrence took advantage of a substantial annual parliamentary grant for Nova Scotia to recruit over 8,000 Yankees, providing them with land, transportation, and subsidies until 1762, when the financial tap was turned off. The New Englanders came mainly from land-hungry areas of Rhode Island, Connecticut, and southeastern Massachusetts. They saw migration to Nova Scotia—an alternative to movement to northern areas of New England—as particularly attractive because it was being financed by the government instead of out of their own pockets. The migrants tended to move in kinship groups, and often as entire communities. Most were farmers anxious for more or better land, although others were fishermen looking for improved access to superior fishing grounds in Nova Scotia. The farmers settled on Acadian land in the Minas Basin, while the fishermen moved to south-shore outports they named Yarmouth and Barrington after their New England counterparts.

The Planters had been promised not only cheap land but liberty of conscience and a government 'like those of neighbouring colonies'—a guarantee they took to mean that they could replicate their New England practices of allocating land to the community's 'proprietors' and developing a strong local democracy around township government. They managed to distribute land according to their traditional concepts of freehold tenure, but soon found that the government of Nova Scotia did not intend to permit strong local government. Political disillusionment was added to disappointment over the quality of the new land, and perhaps half the new arrivals were gone within a few years of the termination of subsidies. The newly founded townships were not very prosperous initially, particularly after the bottom dropped out of the postwar economy. In their religious life the settlers often found themselves unable to afford a paid ministry, to which they were accustomed, and in many communities there was a vacuum into which lay-preachers—and eventually a form of religious revival—moved.

Population turnover in newly settled Planter districts was heavy, as was speculation in land—which was endemic in Nova Scotia, from the top to the bottom of society. Among the ordinary folk, within the recently established communities, Yankee proprietors wheeled and dealed in small parcels. For the élite office-holding classes (both inside and outside the colony), large parcels of wilderness land were acquired—three million acres in the last few days before the Stamp Act became effective in 1765. Only a handful of these large-scale speculators became active in either settlement ventures or commercial development, and those who did were a rather heterogeneous group of Britons and Americans.

After 1763, the active British contingent among those who acquired land grants in North America tended to be interested in settlement rather than commerce, reflecting the dominance of landowners in British society, and the need for some men within the ranks of the landholding class to establish themselves anew. They were committed to replicating a European pattern of landholding, with aristocratic landlords and peasant tenants—a pattern that competed with freehold everywhere in the newly acquired territory. Before the eventual arrival of the Loyalists, there was no reason to assume that freehold would triumph.

Captain William Owen (1737-78)—a younger son of a family of Welsh country gentry who had gone into the naval service of the East India Company and had lost an arm at the battle of Pondicherry—found himself at loose ends after 1763. He came to Nova Scotia in 1766 as the private secretary and naval aide of Lord William Campbell (c.1730-78), with whom he had served in India, who had been appointed the colony's governor. The next year Campbell granted Owen an island—which he named Campobello Island—at the entrance to Passamaquoddy Bay, near the border of what would become Maine and New Brunswick. Returning to Britain, Owen enlisted the backing of Liverpool merchants and began a settlement on

Campobello in 1770 with people recruited in western England and adjacent Wales. Similarly John MacDonald (1742-1810) of Glenaladale, a senior tacksman of a prominent Highland clan, found himself being squeezed out of his traditional middleman role between his chief and the tenantry. As a Roman Catholic, he was also under pressure from his Church to help tenants who were being pressured to convert to Protestantism by finding them a refuge from persecution. MacDonald managed to obtain through purchase one of the lots on the Island of St John distributed by lottery in 1767, and with his brother Donald began organizing an immigration of Highland Catholics to the Island in 1771. The result was a major settlement of Catholic Highlanders in the Tracadie area of what would be named in 1799 Prince Edward Island.

Neither Owen nor MacDonald had any intention of selling land to the people they recruited. Instead, both sought to establish new landed estates in America where they could be landlords over a subordinate tenant population. Such designs went against the grain of American experience, and both men would ultimately fail in their efforts. Owen did not remain on Campobello for more than a few months, and the tiny settlement was on the verge of collapse when the American rebellion began. Captain Owen returned to active duty, and was killed at sea in 1778. MacDonald's settlement at Tracadie would not survive the war, at least not in the form envisaged by its founder. Most of the colonists in both settlements moved on elsewhere to acquire their own land. MacDonald tended to blame the failure of these ventures to recreate European society in America on the difficulty of obtaining proper managers. Landed proprietors in America, he insisted, had to be in continual residence, for 'When one succeeds to or Acquires an Estate, he takes up a trade—the trade of a Land Lord, or manager, of that Estate, which if he does not attend to regularly will be sure to fail; for it is a very minute trade requiring intimate Acquaintance with the Subject, renewed occasionally as former Circumstances alter or new ones occur.'[12] Such an analysis was too simplistic, but not entirely inaccurate.

Unlike the British Owen and MacDonald, American speculators who moved into the northern colonies after 1763 tended to concentrate on commercial activity. The post-1763 careers of the Hazen brothers illustrate the difference. Born in Newburyport, Massachusetts, into a mercantile family, William (1738-1814) and Moses Hazen (1733-1803) both served as volunteers in the British army during the Seven Years' War, and recognized the possibilities of the northern provinces in the course of their campaigning. Following the war, William set up in Newburyport as a merchant with two cousins—James (1735-1830) and Richard Simonds (d. 1765)—all of whom had visions of opening up the trade of the St John River Valley. The mercantile firm organized in 1764 established its trading outpost at Portland Point on the site of modern Saint John, New Brunswick, although William remained in Massachusetts. The operation gathered fish, fur, and feathers in the Bay of Fundy region in exchange for manufactured goods, selling the fish in the Caribbean. It began quarrying limestone, supplying scattered British military outposts, and moved into timbering, sawmills, and shipbuilding. William had intended to move to Portland Point in 1771, although he did not actually do so until the very eve of the American rebellion, and then chiefly to protect his investment. Nevertheless he would remain loyal to Britain throughout the war. Brother Moses, who had served in Quebec during the war against the French, was attracted to the upper Richelieu River Valley, where he and other British officers bought lands from the French seigneurs of the district.

Quebec, 1763-1775

The influx to Quebec of men like Moses Hazen was too substantial to be totally ignored by the British authorities. Moses Hazen assumed some role as landholder, on his property and that of others he managed, becoming a justice of the peace in 1765. But an appointment as assistant surveyor of the King's forests that same year helped lead him into timbering on a grand scale. Cutting was usually done on someone else's land, and like his brother, Moses was soon running a sawmill and proposing to build ships on Lake Champlain. But he did not prosper, and spent increasing amounts of energy in acquiring land all across the northern frontier, from what would become New Brunswick to the future Vermont. In the end, large debts forced him back to his own seigneury and its manor at Bleury-Sud, where he nevertheless built a sawmill, forge, and ashery for the manufacture of potash. Many of Hazen's fellow Americans in Quebec, however, moved into the fur trade.

At the same time, anglophone newcomers to Quebec were too limited in numbers to resolve the many outstanding problems facing British administration in the province. The overall design of the Proclamation of 1763 had been to remodel Canada as a British province. But until a large number of British or Anglo-American settlers arrived in Quebec, the colony's population consisted of French Canadians, accustomed to the practices of the Old Regime, who could not be expected to respond favourably to a grand reconstruction of their laws and religion. The colonial authorities in Quebec understandably temporized, introducing some British elements into the system while confirming many French ones. Thus, while a British-style judicial system was promulgated in 1764, applying to the province the laws of England and the principles of English justice (including the jury system), an inferior court of common pleas was permitted to apply French law in cases involving Canadian-born residents. Initially this court was to apply French law only in cases originating before 1 October 1764, but the continuation of the principle was implicit in the new regulations.

That the vast majority of 'His Majesty's subjects' were Roman Catholic French Canadians both limited change and forced concessions when application of British rules worked hardship on the so-called 'New Subjects'. (In a curious reversal of terminology, the newly arrived British were the 'Old Subjects'.) Governor James Murray, who continued after the end of the military occupation as first civil head of Quebec, refused to summon an elected assembly—that essential symbol of British government in the colonies. Since the Catholic *Canadiens* would be ineligible either to vote for or sit in such an institution, its presence would enable the legislation of the colony to be dominated by a small number of anglophones who chafed at the tolerance being shown to the French. Murray and his council, mainly men sympathetic to the *Canadiens* who would become known as the 'French party', waived the religious disqualification of Catholics from serving on juries, since it would have meant that a few Protestants would be 'perpetual judges of lives and property' for the impotent majority. The British authorities in London sympathized with the problems, and official legal opinions were offered in the mid-1760s that British laws against Catholics did not extend to Quebec and that respect for property rights implied the confirmation of French law on such matters. Finally, there was the problem of the Church in Quebec, which had been drifting since the death of its last bishop in 1760. In the end, Grand Vicar Jean-Olivier Briand (1715-94) was chosen by his Canadian colleagues for 'presentation' at Rome, and with both Murray's support and the tacit acceptance of the British government, he was consecrated bishop near Paris on 16 March 1766. Officially Briand would be only 'superintendant' of the Quebec Church, but in practice he was accepted as its bishop, and the collection of tithes was officially supported.

James Murray had moved somewhat cautiously in the direction of concessions to French Canadians and restructuring the Old Regime. But an increasingly loud chorus of objections from the British inhabitants of the colony to his policies, particularly his *Canadien* sympathies, led to his recall in 1766. (As long as governors had real power and discretion in British North America, opposition to their policies would ultimately unite in criticism and hostility, and the British government would respond by finding a replacement.) Murray's successor, Guy Carleton (1724-1808), had fewer compunctions. Like Murray, Carleton was a professional soldier who had served under Wolfe. An Anglo-Irishman, he was also a member of the British gentry, a firm believer in a landed aristocracy, the subordination of a tenant class, and the close connection between Church and State. Carleton might have turned against the *Canadiens* and the Old Regime, but instead he came to see that, with slight adjustments to circumstance, his overall vision for society was quite compatible with the active continuation and even the extension of Murray's policies. Moreover, Carleton was led to see the *Canadiens* as ideal subjects when contrasted with the emergence of the 'mobocracy' that was behind the turmoil in the American colonies. Finally, Carleton's task was of course to keep his province quiet and loyal in the face of the great movement of rebellion and potential separatism in the Thirteen Colonies. To achieve these goals he would inevitably turn to the handiest instruments at his disposal, the Catholic Church and the traditional seigneurs. Alienating the natural leaders of the *Canadiens* in Quebec was hardly in his best interests.

There were no policy documents or academic literature on how to rule alien populations in an imperial context in the eighteenth century. But Carleton, building on the actions of his predecessor, instinctively grasped a strategy that would be common within the British Empire long afterwards. Essentially the ruler's task was to find and co-opt local collaborators from the 'alien population' into the governing process. In Quebec such a strategy involved extending support for the remaining natural leaders among the *Canadiens*, chiefly the seigneurs and the clergy of the Roman Catholic Church, and protecting as many of the rights and privileges of the French inhabitants as was consistent with the new situation of the colony. It also involved undoing some of the economic damage to the economy resulting from the geographical dismemberment of Quebec in the Proclamation of 1763. Hence the Quebec Act of 1774. Most of the ancient boundaries of Quebec, both to the west and east (including those given to Newfoundland in 1763), were restored to the colony. His Majesty's subjects in Quebec, 'professing the Religion of the Church of *Rome*', were granted free exercise of their religion, exempted from the traditional oaths of supremacy with a new one supplied, while the Catholic clergy were allowed 'their accustomed Dues and Rights, with respect to such Persons only as shall profess the said Religion.' Provision was also made for the support of a Protestant clergy. All matters relating to property and civil rights were to be decided by the traditional laws of Canada. This clause, in effect, preserved the seigneurial system intact. English criminal law was continued, and the province was to be governed by a legislative council; there was no provision for an elected assembly.

Not surprisingly, debate in Parliament concentrated on the civil law and the absence of an assembly, although the issue of boundary provisions and the privileges extended to the Catholic Church were also raised. Lord North, the prime minister, argued for the Act:

> The bulk of the inhabitants are Roman Catholics, and to subject them to an assembly composed of a few British subjects would be a great hardship. Being, therefore, under the necessity of not appointing an assembly, this is the only legislation you can give the Canadians, and it is the one under which they live at present. . . .It has been thought better calculated to secure the happiness of Canadians, and more beneficial for all who live in the country, that they should have the civil law of Canada, and not that of England. . . .It has been the opinion of very many able lawyers, that the best way to establish the happiness of the inhabitants is to give them their own laws, as far as relates to their own possessions.[13]

Critics of the administration—mainly 'friends of the American colonies'—complained that the Act 'carries in its breast something that squints and looks dangerous to the inhabitants of our other colonies in that country.' Its most famous critic, the parliamentarian Edmund Burke, added:

> I, for one, will never give my vote for establishing the French law in that country. I should be sorry to see his Majesty a despotic governor. And am I sure that this despotism is not meant to lead to universal despotism?. . .When we are sowing the seeds of despotism in Canada, let us bear in mind, that it is a growth which may afterwards extend to other countries. By being made perpetual, it is evident that this constitution is meant to be both an instrument of tyranny in the Canadians, and an example to others of what they have to expect.[14]

Most of the attacks on the legislation assumed some connection between it and the American turmoil to the south, and while Burke was incorrect in his assertions that Britain intended to extend its 'despotism', he and others were quite accurate in understanding that French Canada was not being governed in an absolute vacuum.

Sixty-five years later, Lord Durham (1792-1840) would encapsulate the typical explanation of British policy towards French Canada when he wrote:

> . . .the conquest of Canada was almost immediately followed by the commencement of those discontents which ended in the independence of the United Provinces. From that period, the colonial policy of this country appears to have undergone a total change. To prevent the further dismemberment of the Empire became the primary object with our statesmen; and an especial anxiety was exhibited to adopt every expedient which appeared calculated to prevent the remaining North American Colonies from following the example of successful revolt.

Such an analysis was quite sensible. Unfortunately, Durham (and others) went further, insisting that 'the nationality of the French Canadians was therefore cultivated, as a means of perpetual and entire separation from their neighbours.'[15] This argument assumed far more deliberate policy than any British government of the eighteenth century was capable of achieving. In any event, if the British government intended by the Quebec Act to secure the loyalty of the *Canadiens*, the strategy was not entirely successful.

ᔑᔑᔑ *The First American Civil War*

In early April 1775 British troops, attempting to raid clandestine colonial arms depots in Massachusetts, were fired upon by the Americans, and a long-festering imperial political crisis turned into a shooting war. From the vantage point of the leadership of the Americans, they were involved in a 'revolution' to secure their rights against the arbitrary authority of the British Crown. From that of the British government the Americans were engaged in a 'rebellion' against duly constituted authority. But many of the inhabitants of British North America, including those in the northernmost colonies, were forced into involvement in a great 'Civil War' in which brother fought brother, friend opposed friend, and many were eventually pushed into exile. Indeed, the proportion of exiles from the new United States exceeded that from France after 1789, from Russia after 1917, and from Cuba after 1955.

One of the great problems for Canadian historians is to comprehend the realities of public opinion, particularly on the part of those members of the population who were not among the articulate élites. Even in our own time, assessing public sentiment is scarcely a science; but before opinion polls and regular elections, this objective was a virtual impossibility. What the average French-Canadian *habitant* was thinking on the eve of the Anglo-American War remains as much a mystery as what the English-speaking population of the northern provinces, especially in the Atlantic region, felt about the events swirling around them. Only an occasional glimpse of opinion can be obtained—sometimes from the written record, more frequently from patterns of behaviour. Clearly few of the inhabitants of Britain's American empire north of the Thirteen Colonies had much information about, or experience with, the issues that led the southern colonies inexorably towards rebellion and civil war.

The Invasion of Canada

The American colonists had been gradually escalating their conflict with the mother country, and turned from political protest and scattered acts of violence to armed rebellion in April 1775. They were already organizing an alternative government through their Continental Congress when Massachusetts militiamen clashed at Lexington with British regulars attempting to seize an illegal stockpile of arms at the neighbouring town of Concord. Two Connecticut hotheads, Ethan Allen (1737-89) and Benedict Arnold (1741-1801), both had the idea of attacking Fort Ticonderoga (NY) and raised small forces of their own—Allen from among his Green Mountain Boys, while Arnold formed a company of local militia. The rivals joined forces and led some hundred men to the fort on the morning of 10 May 1775, when the garrison was still asleep, and took it without firing a shot. The second Continental Congress hastily began organizing an army, under the command of George Washington of Virginia, and while that force was still in embryo, authorized an invasion of Quebec as a move to bestow 'the *coup de grâce* to the hellish junto' governing Great Britain.[16] Washington was somewhat more enthusiastic about this plan than he was about subsequent proposals to invade Nova Scotia. On 27 June Major-General Philip Schuyler, commander of the troops in upper New York, was ordered to proceed to Quebec by way of Lake Champlain and the Richelieu River. Later in the summer Arnold received orders from General Washington to lead another army, going by way of the Kennebec and Dead Rivers in Maine and along the Chaudière to the St Lawrence. With over a thousand men, Arnold began his disastrous march to Quebec on 19 September.

The sudden turn of events put the government of Quebec in a state of shock and confusion. Governor Carleton, only recently returned from London the previous September, with the Quebec Act in his dispatch case, transferred his troops from Quebec to Montreal and set up headquarters there. He surveyed his colony along the St Lawrence and informed Britain that he had 'not six hundred Rank and File fit for Duty upon the whole Extent of this great River, not an armed Vessel, no Place of Strength; the ancient Provincial Force enervated and broke to Pieces; all Subordination overset, and the Minds of the People poisoned by the same Hypocrisy and Lies practised with so much Success in the other Provinces.'[17] A public *mandement* from Bishop Briand, ordering the population to ignore American propaganda under threat of denial of the sacraments, had little effect, and the seigneurs appointed to raise a militia found it difficult to do so. Carleton's alliance with Quebec's traditional leaders proved useless, largely because he misunderstood their position under the Old Regime. He described the *habitants* as 'wretched People...blind to Honor, Duty & their own Interest.'[18] The Church had seldom had much influence on *habitant* behaviour, and the seigneurs had never had much to do with the militia. The British merchants, who had never been cultivated by Carleton, proved singularly unco-operative. Not even the Indians leapt into action on Britain's behalf. Virtually the only positive military response the British received was when a Scottish-Canadian army officer, Colonel Allan Maclean (1725-84), was given permission to raise two battalions of disbanded Highlanders, the Royal Highland Emigrants. The first—which took part in the defence of Canada that was soon to follow—was recruited in Canada and New York; the second in Nova Scotia and the Island of St John (later Prince Edward Island), where Maclean had a land grant but never lived.

Fortunately for the British, the Americans were neither as well organized nor as lucky as Wolfe's expedition had been in 1758-9, and the Québécois were not as enthusiastic about liberation as the invaders had hoped. In September 1775 an unauthorized attack on Montreal, led by Ethan Allen, failed miserably, and Allen was sent back to Britain in chains, along with several of the town's American supporters. But after the British surrendered Fort St Jean, on the Richelieu River, to the invading Americans on 2 November, Carleton abandoned Montreal and left for Quebec. Meanwhile, General Richard Montgomery (1736-75) was struggling to bring an invading army up the Lake Champlain route, writing that 'the privates are all generals', and of his 'unstable authority over the troops of different colonies.'[19] He was concerned that the Canadians had not turned out in larger numbers to support their liberation. And Benedict Arnold was bringing his army across what is now the state of Maine under horrendous late-autumn conditions, losing nearly half his troops in the process; he did not cross the St Lawrence until the night of 13 November. On 11 November, Montgomery and his troops arrived near Montreal—which was pretty neutral, almost equally divided between pro- and anti-Americans—and two weeks later pressed on to Quebec, though Montgomery's soldiers were constantly deserting him to return home. In Quebec, Colonel Maclean had stiffened resistance by convincing the inhabitants that the Americans were 'the worst of Banditti', eager to loot and pillage; and Carleton, on his return, purged the city of 'useless, disloyal, and treacherous persons.' Montgomery joined Arnold at Pointe-aux-Trembles on 3 December and quickly determined that he lacked the force and supplies to lay siege to Quebec. Instead, he decided to storm the town. The assault on 31 December was a desperate move by the Americans, who were suffering from smallpox as well as problems of logistics and morale.

The garrison held, and the result, wrote one British officer, was 'A glorious day for us, as compleat a little victory as ever was gained.'[20] General Montgomery's frozen body was found not far from the barricade against which he had led the charge, General Arnold took a ball through the left leg at the first battery, and over three hundred Americans were taken prisoner. The American forces, now under Arnold's command, remained in military occupation of more than fifty parishes over the winter of 1775-6. By spring one American officer reported: 'The peasantry in general have been ill-used. . . . It is true, they have been promised payment, from time to time; yet they look upon such promises as vague, their labour and property lost, and the Congress and the United Colonies as bankrupts.'[21] The use of paper currency, argued one American, cost the occupying army 'the affections of the people in general.' A commission from the Continental Congress, headed by Benjamin Franklin, wrote from Montreal: 'Till the arrival of money, it seems improper to propose the Federal union of this Province with the others.'[22] At Saint-Pierre-de-Montmagny, the early spring found rival military parties of Canadians skirmishing with one another. But in May British reinforcements arrived at Quebec, and by mid-June 1776 the Americans had completely retreated, never to return.

Warfare in the Atlantic Region

The Americans had desperately wanted Quebec. George Washington wrote to Benedict Arnold early in 1776: 'To whomsoever it belongs, in their favour, probably will the balance turn. If it is ours, success, I think, will most certainly crown our virtuous struggles; if it is theirs, the contest, at least, will be doubtful, hazardous and bloody.'[23] The rebel leaders did not feel the same way about Nova Scotia: partly because of its protection by the British navy; partly because there was less visible evidence of enthusiastic residents ready to support an invading army. Some of the Yankee settlements on the Bay of Fundy had long chafed under Halifax's refusal to allow them their traditional New England forms of local government, and several American agitators attempted to channel this discontent in more visible and specific directions. Legislation calling up militia and imposing a tax for its support produced a petition of objection signed by 250 inhabitants of the Chignecto area, protesting against having to march 'into different parts in arms against their friends and relations.' Despite the suspension of the laws by the governor, discontent continued to simmer, local leaders complaining that some residents had 'a chaise and six horses, postillion and a flag of liberty, and drove about the isthmus, proclaiming the news and blessings of liberty.'[24]

For active American sympathizers like Jonathan Eddy (1726/7-1804) and John Allan (1747-1805), the introduction of rebel troops would soon settle the question, and the two attempted unsuccessfully to lobby with the American authorities for a general invasion. Instead, they had to settle for a private freebooting army recruited chiefly from Machias (now in Maine) and Maugerville (now in New Brunswick) and consisting of some 80 men, who marched overland from the St John River towards the British outpost at Fort Cumberland in late October and early November 1776. This 'invasion' was joined by a few Chignecto residents, but was quickly suppressed by British reinforcements, leaving those Nova Scotians who had supported the Americans either abjectly explaining away their actions or quickly departing for American lines, leaving behind their wives and families to be sworn at and 'often kicked when met in the street'.[25] Not until 1779 were these refugee families exchanged for Loyalist prisoners. Rebel farms were seized in lawsuits for damages, and anonymous letters were written to legal officers threatening violence if more writs were executed. Civil wars were truly nasty ones.

The Fort Cumberland business was more typical of this war than was the American invasion of Canada. Away from the armies, the opposing parties, rebel and loyalist, fought vicious little battles with one another for control of the 'neutral' population, often paying back old personal injuries along the way. On the high seas, legalized pirates called 'privateers' captured unarmed ships and attacked undefended settlements along the coasts. Between 1775 and 1781 the privateers literally brought commerce to a halt in the Atlantic region for most of the period, causing a number of food shortages, particularly in Newfoundland and the Island of St John. Both these colonies went for long periods without the arrival of a single vessel from overseas. On the borders between loyal and rebel territory, guerilla raiders (often including native allies) struck farms and villages. Since most of the population of the northernmost provinces of British North America lived on the coast or near a border with the United States, everyone lived in constant fear of attack.

The need to make decisions about loyalties was largely confined to the earlier years of the rebellion and to those areas under military threat from the Americans, real or potential. The vast majority of those residents of the northern provinces who preferred the American side to that of the British Crown left for the south in the first months after Lexington. Among those who remained, some found that their commitment to their place of residence was tested. Such was certainly the situation for the fishing communities of Newfoundland, where American vessels that had supplied most of the island's foodstuffs before the rebellion had disappeared by 1776, and where

British recruiters were extremely active on behalf of both army and navy. Between the press gang and the privateer, the offshore fishery—particularly the bankers—was virtually wiped out for the duration. As late as 1781 a British official reported 'an amazing number of privateers when I arrived off the coast,' and indeed in that year sixteen privateering vessels were captured in Newfoundland waters.[26]

The offshore fishery was also the migratory fishery, and one of the major results of the American Revolution was to guarantee that the dominant population in the fishery would be the resident one. The year-round residents of Newfoundland who survived the war had their loyalty to the island severely tested because it was so difficult to bring in sufficient supplies of foodstuffs from outside. Local land improvement and agriculture was encouraged, but could not in the short term fill the need. Prices of food skyrocketed, and one observer reported that Newfoundlanders were actually eating their own fish. In Conception Bay, over the winter of 1779/80, there was 'a raging Famine, Nakedness & Sickness.' The local missionary wrote: 'None can express the heart felt woe of Women & Children mourning for want of Food.'[27] Many of the inhabitants of the outports removed to St John's, where they hoped to find work and food. The population of the town grew considerably during the war, many finding support by enlisting in the Newfoundland Volunteers, a militia group organized partly to provide government assistance for the unemployed and impoverished. Whatever the attitude of the population in a region in 1775, by 1781 those sympathetic to the American cause had left, converted to loyalism, or learned to keep very quiet about their allegiances.

The Ranges of Response

For most people in British North America, survival was probably the foremost priority, even before war actually began. When pressed to choose sides by the logic of events, survival no doubt continued to be uppermost in most minds. How one sought to survive, of course, depended largely on circumstances. The responses of six inhabitants of the northern colonies—John and Helen MacDonald of Tracadie, Island of St John; Simeon Perkins of Liverpool, Nova Scotia; Henry Alline of Falmouth, Nova Scotia; Moses Hazen of St Jean, Quebec; and Joseph Brant of Canajoharie, New York—indicate the range of possible reactions to the complexities of the period.

The Loyal Soldier

One of those who responded to the emergency by supporting the British was John MacDonald of the Island of St John. MacDonald, it will be recalled, had organized a large contingent of Catholic Highland Scots who immigrated to the island in 1772, partly on behalf of the Scottish Catholic Church and partly on his own account. Like most Highland Catholics, he had quickly adjusted to British supremacy after the abortive 1745 rebellion in Scotland, and by the time of the American rebellion had come to view the British Crown as the best protection for both his landholding pretensions and his religious persuasion. Constantly short of money to develop his estate, Tracadie, MacDonald saw service as a British officer as a way of improving his financial situation and ultimately providing a pension. He sought and received approval from the leaders of the Scottish Church to take whatever oaths were necessary to become an officer. Moreover, the American colonists, he was fully convinced, were a pack of Protestant sectaries desirous of extending their domination into the realm of politics.

Thus in 1775 John MacDonald of Tracadie responded with alacrity to the opportunity to serve his king against the American rebels, taking a number of his 'tenants' with him to Halifax to join the second battalion of the Royal Highland Emigrants. Given the rank of captain, MacDonald served in the Halifax garrison throughout the war while his sisters attempted to maintain the family property. Late in 1777 he wrote a lengthy position paper for the British minister in charge of the war, which argued the value of Highland Catholic settlements such as his own for ensuring the loyalty of America should the rebels be successfully defeated on the battlefield. While he was away on military service, MacDonald very nearly lost his property to the machinations of the local government on the Island and spent the years after demobilization fighting to secure its restoration. Although somewhat unusual among inhabitants of the northern provinces in his officer rank, John MacDonald was only one of many from the region who served the Crown in a military capacity, neglecting his own land in the process. According to the operational definitions of the time, he was not a 'Loyalist'. But he was certainly a loyalist.

The Loyal Woman

Helen (Nelly) MacDonald (c.1750-1803), John MacDonald's sister, was one of countless women everywhere in North America who were required to manage family affairs when the males went off to war. She had come to the Island of St John with her brother Donald, and three years later when her brothers were commissioned in the Royal Highland Emigrants, she was left to supervise the Highland settlement at Tracadie and the complex MacDonald business interests. Her brother John—who did not return until 1792—was not simply a farmer but a self-conscious Highland laird who was responsible for a number of dependent tenants. Nelly's responsibilities were many during a stewardship that eventually lasted for seventeen years. There was the family farm with its 90 head of cattle. There was the estate, with its rents to be collected—often in kind, which had then to be marketed. (Nelly stored money from the rents in a strong-box in her cellar.) She saw to the construction of a house for Captain John, according to his specifications. There was also the need for gathering local political intelligence for her brother, since the Island's officials had long cast covetous glances at the MacDonald property.

A constant flow of advice, orders, and remittances went from Halifax to Tracadie. 'You & the People should have dances & Merriment Among Yourselves,' wrote John MacDonald in 1780, for 'it is very reasonable that You Should be innocently Merry, & make the Time pass Smoothly.' When Nelly met a young loyalist officer at a dance and contemplated marriage, however, her brother became very agitated. The young man had no capital but his commission, and no family background. 'You had better not throw yourself away' and 'make yourself & me look silly in the Eyes of world,' he warned. Nelly's mother subsequently assured her in a letter that 'One comfort I have marrage is not nesesary to salvation—so my Dear Nelly you may...be happie els wher if not in marrage here.' She eventually married in 1792. As well as advice and orders, Captain John sent 'care packages', which on one occasion included eight pairs of shoes and two pairs of galoshes. Although she had hoped to find a more congenial place to spend the years of the war, Nelly MacDonald never left the Island and suffered for years from its many privations.[28]

The Rebel Soldier

Moses Hazen took a different course of action from Captain John Mac-Donald, partly because his loyalties were more confused than MacDonald's, partly because as a resident of Quebec his situation was different. Recommended early in 1775 for a commission by Guy Carleton, Hazen initially acted on behalf of the British. He was responsible for informing Carleton of the impending American invasion, and subsequently met with the American general Philip Schuyler to discourage the American advance. Attempting to play both sides without an open commitment, Hazen was on succeeding days arrested by the Americans and then the British, ending up spending 54 days in a Montreal gaol refusing British offers for his loyalty. He was ultimately freed by the advancing American army that unsuccessfully attempted to beseige Quebec in late December 1775. Sent as a messenger to the American Congress with the news of the failure of the attack and the death of General Richard Montgomery, Hazen was appointed by the Congress to command a regiment to be raised in Canada; he was promised indemnification for any loss of British pension he would sustain by entering American service.

Returning to Canada, Hazen was initially successful in recruiting *habitants* for his regiment, stopping at 250 men only because he ran out of money. The offer was for forty *livres* in bonus plus a monthly stipend, recruits to find their own clothing and equipment. But Hazen soon discovered the limitations to *Canadien* enthusiasm. By April 1776 he was complaining that the *habitants* were only 'waiting an opportunity to join our enemies', since they were upset by the looting and seizure of property by an American army living off the land and paying only in worthless paper currency. In June 1776 Hazen retreated from Canada with the American forces, spending several years attempting to clear his name from charges of irregularities raised against him by Benedict Arnold and others. His regiment, in which French Canadians were augmented by later American recruits, fought at the Battle of Brandywine, losing four officers and 73 men in what became an American rout. Hazen was forced to fight hard to keep his regiment from being disbanded, his strongest argument being that his Canadians were men 'without Friend, without Acquaintance, without Money; drove from their native Country by the Active Part they have took, in Consequence of an Invitation by Congress and a Promise of Support.' The Canadian volunteers, he insisted, 'have no Parent State to reward their meritorious Services, or provide Bread and Shelter for them.'[29] Hazen's regiment never fought in a major engagement after October 1777, but served in a variety of non-combative capacities until it was disbanded at White Plains, NY, in November 1783.

Hazen spent the years after the war in ill health and in constant financial difficulties. He lost his Canadian lands—not to confiscation for political decisions, but to satisfy his creditors—and they were resettled, ironically enough, by incoming American Loyalists. As for the *Canadiens* who had enlisted and served in his regiment, they and their families ended the war stateless and as the wards of the American Congress, which asked the State of New York to accept most of them as citizens. When the state legislature in 1784 passed a law providing land bounties for its citizens who had served in the war, the Canadian refugees were specifically included. One of the Marquis de Lafayette's last actions before returning to France in 1784 was to urge an inquiry for Canadian families displaced by the war, and the American Congress in 1785 set aside three townships bordering Lake Erie for refugees, while another tract was established on the western shore of Lake Champlain just south of the border. Not until well into the nineteenth century were the claims of Canadian and Nova Scotian refugees in the United States finally settled. Their experiences during and after the Revolution are a useful reminder that, in civil war, loyalties become greatly confused. Not all the refugees from the American Revolution were United Empire Loyalists settling in British North America. The Loyalists had their counterparts in the United States.

The Loyal Civilian

Like Moses Hazen, Simeon Perkins (1734/5-1812) of Liverpool was a native of New England, born in Norwich, Connecticut, to a prominent local family. Perkins joined the pre-revolutionary Yankee migration to Nova Scotia, arriving in Liverpool on the southwestern coast of the province in May 1762 as one of 142 proprietors. Liverpool—where Perkins built a house in 1766-7 (extended in 1781) that has been preserved—was one of the fishing and lumbering communities of the colony, and he actively engaged in both trades as a merchant. He also acquired positions of political importance that included acting on the township committee in 1770 and being commissioned as lieutenant-colonel of the militia in 1772. As a merchant engaged in trade with New England and the mother country, Perkins was more conscious of the developing conflict between his homeland and Britain than most Nova Scotians. His comment on the repressive measures adopted by Parliament in 1774 in response to the Boston Tea Party was to fear the 'disagreeable consequences', and he was in New England in 1775 at the time of the affair at Lexington that provoked open rebellion.

Despite his awareness of the implications, Perkins returned to Liverpool on 28 May 1775, and carried on with both his own business affairs and the local administrative duties ordered from Halifax. His emotional confusion over loyalties is revealed in entries in his diaries, such as one in 1776 about American privateering depredations on his vessels, commenting: 'This is the fourth loss I have met with by my countrymen.'[30] Perkins mobilized the local militia, attended meetings of the Nova Scotia Assembly at Halifax to defend his community from charges of disloyal behaviour, and carried on with his affairs. His position was perhaps best revealed in a diary entry early in 1777, when he wrote: 'I should be happy to be in a private station in these times of difficulty, but as I had been a Magistrate many years in times of tranquillity, it might be out of character to resign in times of difficulty.'[31] Despite obvious conflicts of allegiance, Simeon Perkins remained consistently loyal to his community, his colony, and his monarch. As the war continued, his position and that of his community became considerably less complicated, for when American privateers raided both Liverpool itself and its vessels at sea, the United States was forcibly established as 'the enemy'. The Nova Scotia government was slow to provide Liverpool with adequate protection, and the town was forced to defend itself. Later in the war Liverpool even mounted its own privateers, in some of whose enterprises Simeon Perkins had invested. By 1780 he was appointed a local marshal of the provincial court of admiralty, authorized to auction vessels and cargoes captured at sea by British privateers: overcoming any personal feelings about his native land, Simeon Perkins found his duty and his self-interest eventually coinciding. The epitaph on his gravestone quite properly describes him as 'LOYAL to his KING', adding, almost parenthetically, 'and A SINCERE CHRISTIAN.'

The Radical Drop-out

If Simeon Perkins placed political loyalty ahead of his genuine religious commitment, Henry Alline (1748-84) of Falmouth reacted to the confusions of the revolutionary period almost entirely in spiritual terms, although such a response made an implicit political statement of its own. Born in Newport, Rhode Island, Alline had come to the Minas Basin area of the Annapolis Valley in 1760 with his parents, who received 500 acres for themselves and their seven children. Falmouth was located in some of the richest agricultural land in the Atlantic region, and it was a farming community. As his parents aged, young Henry took over supervision of the family enterprises, including a farm and perhaps a small-scale tanning operation. Unlike Simeon Perkins, Alline was not politically active, although he served one term as a local constable. Instead, he spent his free time in youthful activities and in study of the Bible and the few religious writings available to him in a remote farming village.

While political turmoil swirled around him, Henry Alline's conflict was internal, concerned with the state of his soul. Although he continued to be 'chief contriver and ringleader of the frolicks' of his contemporaries, he was actually uneasy and 'would act the hypocrite and feign a merry heart.' By the time of escalation of the American revolutionary conflict he was still unmarried, though in his mid-20s, and his chief concern was with 'carnal passion'. He had a series of visions, including one he described in great detail in his posthumously published autobiography:

> . . .there was represented to my view a beautiful woman (one whom I had seen before, but had no great acquaintance with) and the happiness that I thought I might enjoy with her stole away my affections from thinking much of God or my state. The devil told me that I need not commit any sin for to enjoy her; that I might marry her, which was lawful: yea, I so acquiesced in the temptation, that my affections were after her, and she appeared the most beautiful object that ever I beheld. My passions were so inflamed with the prospect, that I thought I would not omit the first opportunity to go see her and propose marriage to her. I thought I would be the happiest man on earth, if I might but have her for a companion for life.[32]

Alline was able to overcome this conflict, which for him demonstrated 'the subtilty of that grand adversary, who might by this temptation have proved my eternal ruin, if God had not interposed.' Nevertheless, he walked around for several years 'groaning under a load of guilt and darkness, praying and crying continually for mercy.' He found release through a religious experience on 26 March 1775, writing that suddenly 'redeeming love broke into my soul with repeated scriptures with such power, that my whole soul seemed to be melted down with love.' Such a conclusive experience hardly resolved Alline's problems, however, for he had become extremely suspicious of the traditional teachings of the New England Puritanism in which he had been raised, particularly the picture of a vengeful rather than a loving God, and the insistence on the preordained election of the saints. Moreover, while Alline's experiences called for him to go forth to preach the gospel to others, his upbringing told him that only those with formal educational credentials were allowed to become ministers.

Alline's wrestling for a year with the inconsistencies between his own thinking and traditional New England doctrine paralleled the confusion in Nova Scotia resulting from the outbreak of armed rebellion in New England.

He noted about the call to preach, soon after his conversion in March 1775, that 'the prejudices of education and the strong ties of tradition so chained me down, that I could not think myself qualified for it, without having a good deal of human learning.'[33] He tried unsuccessfully to find passage for Boston, and rejected the offer of a commission in the Nova Scotia militia, deciding that his only commission should be one 'from heaven to go forth, and enlist my fellow-mortals to fight under the banners of Jesus Christ.' On 18 April 1776, a day set aside by the Nova Scotia government for 'fasting and prayer'—coincidentally the first anniversary of the Lexington battle—Henry Alline decided upon a public preaching career. He had successfully rejected both New England and Nova Scotia in favour of offering to others what he himself had found: a spiritual assurance that rejected and transcended the tribulations of the secular world. In the struggle for loyalty, many routes were possible.

For the first three years of his brief career as an 'Itinerant Preacher' Alline focused his efforts on the region around the Bay of Minas, including the Chignecto area, although he made occasional and sometimes controversial forays to the south-coast fishing communities. Alline's principal opponent and critic was Jonathan Scott (1744-1819), the pastor of the Puritan Church at Jebogue (Yarmouth), who saw in Alline's anti-Calvinist doctrine and emphasis on free will a dangerous alternative to New England theology.

Apart from Scott and some local supporters and opponents in the communities Alline visited, no one in official Nova Scotia appears to have paid much attention to him or to the movement of Christian pietism and rejuvenation he began. Not until well after his death in 1784, on a preaching tour to New England, did the authorities in church and state begin to recognize the dangers of the levelling egalitarianism espoused by Alline, which rejected secular affairs in favour of the self-government of the godly. Alline deliberately denied that 'earthly dignity, the esteem of man or a conspicuous station in the world' made a man of God, insisted that political leaders would have no special privileges on the day of judgement, and emphasized that Christ commanded his followers 'to salute no man by the way.' For those who shared his vision and spiritual experience, Alline insisted on withdrawal from 'this ensnaring world' on the grounds that 'you have no continuing city here.' In his own way Henry Alline was a radical leveller, not without populist overtones. He travelled the countryside composing and singing hymns, regarding music as a way to attract and hold an audience, as well as a useful vehicle on the road to salvation. To the Atlantic region he left a legacy of evangelism and revivalism—his followers were called 'New Lights'—although his theological concepts had their major appeal among the Free Will Baptists of the United States. In a period of confusion in Nova Scotia, however, when it was being subjected to fallout from the American Revolution, Alline—whose own life was a form of rebellion against society—offered an alternative path to public declarations of political allegiance.

The Native Loyalist

Joseph Brant (Thayendanegea, 1742-1807) was born in what is now Ohio, son of a prominent Mohawk warrior. He was marked out as a bright young man by New York Indian Superintendant Sir William Johnson (1715-1774) and in 1761 was sent to an Indian Charity School in Connecticut, where he was described as 'of a Sprightly Genius, a manly and genteel Deportment, and of a Modest and benevolent Temper.' He rejoined his people in 1763, and participated with other Iroquois allies in several British campaigns against recalcitrant natives before marrying and settling down on a farm in Cana-joharie, New York. Brant helped missionary John Stuart translate the Gospel of St Mark and a catechism into the Mohawk language, and was renowned as an interpreter and translator. When American hostilities broke out, he remained loyal to the King and in 1775-6 was part of a native delegation to London (where he was painted by George Romney and interviewed by James Boswell), which was told that grievances could be redressed only after the rebellion had been settled.

Brant became persuaded that only continued active alliance with the British could protect Indian interests, and he preached this doctrine among the Iroquois in the summer of 1776 against the prevailing policy of neutrality. He recruited a force of about 300 Indian warriors and 100 loyalist settlers, which was active in scouting and raiding operations, and in 1778 collaborated with Butler's Rangers in guerilla raids in the Mohawk Valley of New York.* On one occasion, at Cherry Valley, Brant tried desperately to prevent Butler's Senecas from killing non-combatants. The Americans responded to such activity in 1779 with a major expedition into the land of the Iroquois, led by General John Sullivan, who was ordered by George Washington to lay waste the countryside. The Indians, including Brant, were forced to retreat to Fort Niagara, where they became supplicants for British assistance. Brant continued to fight as a successful Indian war chief—latterly as an officially commissioned captain of the Northern Confederate Indians—until the end of hostilities.

Joseph Brant's support of the British had been predicated on his understanding that only Great Britain could preserve Indian lands from the encroachment of European settlement. He was shocked to learn that the peace treaty between Britain and the United States had not only ignored the natives but had ruthlessly transferred to the Americans much land claimed by Britain and inhabited solely by natives. He worked desperately to organize an alliance between the Six Nations and the western tribes, but was never entirely accepted as a leader by all parties. Recognized as a warrior chief, he was not a sachem and derived much of his authority among his own people

---

*John Butler, the deputy superintendent of the Six Nations, was ordered to collect a force and he did, from among the Indians, mostly Senecas—they were called Butler's Rangers.

William Berczy, *Joseph Brant*, *c*.1807. This full-length oil was painted — perhaps as a tribute — after Brant died on 24 November 1807. Berczy painted him at least once from life, however, when they met at Newark in 1794. The Mohawk chief has his arm outstretched in a gesture of imperial authority and is majestic in a bright red blanket. Berczy wrote of Brant in 1799: '. . . he is near 6 feet high in stance, of a stout and durable texture able to undergo all the inconvenience of the hardships connected with the difficulties to carry on war through immense woods and wildernesses — His intellectual qualities compared with the phisical construction of his bodily frame — He professes in an eminent degree a sound and profound judgement. He hears patiently and with great attention before he replies and answers in general in a precise and laconic stile. But as soon as it is the question of some topic of great moment, especially relative to the interest of his nation he speaks with a peculiar dignity — his speech is exalted energy and endowed with all the charms of complete Retorick.' National Gallery of Canada, 5777.

from the positions of his sisters and his wives. The British authorities in Quebec, however, realized that the displaced Iroquois (as much Loyalists as anyone else) would have to be given new lands, and Brant led his Mohawks to the Grand River in Ontario in 1784.

The above sketches only suggest the very wide range of responses in this first American civil war. The position of neutrality, which was almost impossible, seemed to require the sort of extreme non-political reorientation in which Henry Alline engaged. For most people, black or white choices were required, and had to be made.

Opening Up the West

The fur trade of the northern peripheries, from Labrador to Hudson Bay, was virtually immune from the direct influence of war. The Proclamation of 1763 should have had a considerable impact on the fur trade in the traditional 'up-country' region of the St Lawrence watershed, by setting off that territory as an Indian reserve and requiring licences to trade. Theoretically the licences were open to English and French alike, but Anglo-Americans who had come to Quebec with the army had better connections with the English market, and soon came to dominate the trade. Controlling the traders became increasingly difficult for the British government, since it required the co-operation of all the colonies—which was difficult to achieve even in better times. Gradually Quebec's control of the trade was increased, until the western Indian territory was returned to it administratively by the Quebec Act. But the typical fur trader had never been a man who took very seriously the rules of the civilized world, and colonial Americans like Peter Pond (1740-1807?) seemed relatively unaffected by the American Revolution, continuing to ship their furs through Montreal regardless of the political changes that had occurred. What did matter was that the western movement of the Montreal-based fur traders had built up momentum. By the time of Lexington and Concord, they were pressing up the Saskatchewan River into the basin of the Churchill, and in 1778 Peter Pond made the breakthrough into the richest fur-trade country of North America: the Athabasca region. The competition of the 'Pedlars from Quebec', as one Hudson's Bay Company man contemptuously referred to them, galvanized the English company into more aggressive action, and it moved inland from its posts on the Bay to ones up the Saskatchewan.

Competition was always a mixed blessing to the Indians, the primary labour force in the fur trade. On the one hand, rivalries among fur traders gave them a choice; and as modern consumer organizations always insist, choice offers control. On the other hand Indian consumer demand for trade goods was relatively inelastic, limited by their needs and by their itinerant way of life, which made many possessions an encumbrance. Guns and ammunition, knives, cooking pots, and blankets were the sorts of material goods desired by the Indians, and there were clear saturation points. Competition meant higher prices and constant bidding for favour on the part of the fur traders. The result of such rivalry was always to increase the amount of non-material consumer goods—particularly tobacco and alcohol—introduced into the trading system. The increased incidence of such deleterious and addictive commodities in the trading system was a far from positive result of competition.

The military conflict of the American revolutionary period had one curious spinoff in Hudson Bay. A great French fleet had been beaten off Jamaica by the British in 1781, and three of the dispersed French ships from that engagement were ordered to the Bay, where they appeared in high summer of 1782, easily capturing Churchill Factory and razing York Factory. But this French visit was brief: the fleet soon retreated, its commander hopeful that sufficient damage had been done to force the Hudson's Bay Company into bankruptcy. The Company was disrupted, but neither its inland goods nor its furs were damaged, since both had already been shipped. Far more serious than the French depredations was a development of the same period that had nothing to do with the American troubles. A major smallpox epidemic hit the Indians of the Hudson Bay drainage basin, rapidly spreading during 1781 and 1782. Few of the European traders were affected, having obviously built up some immunities to the dread disease. But the Indians died in large numbers, and dealing with the sick was almost more than the Company could manage.

Equally remote from the events of the Hudson Bay region were those on the Pacific coast. The British Admiralty's decision in 1776 to send Captain James Cook (1728-79) on another quest for the Northwest Passage, while partly motivated by an increased European activity in the Pacific region, was based more particularly on new information that had led Parliament in 1775 to offer a £20,000 reward for discovery of the fabled waterway. Samuel Hearne (1745-92) of the Hudson's Bay Company had published in 1771 an account of his overland trek to the mouth of the Coppermine River, where he saw the Arctic sea; and while Hearne had crossed no obvious passage, there might be one to the north. This possibility was enhanced by the appearance of a Russian map, ostensibly based on first-hand information from Russian fur traders, that showed Alaska to be an island separated from the mainland by a wide strait that might run into the Arctic.

James Cook had spent his early years as a hydrographer, surveying the coast of Newfoundland, and he had already made two important voyages to the South Pacific that had completely changed European perceptions of the region without the loss of a single man to scurvy. Cook sailed again in July 1776 (at the same time that the Americans were signing their Declaration of Independence), rounding the Cape of Good Hope, and crossing the Pacific Ocean to the northwest coast of America. He arrived off the Oregon coast in

March 1778, and anchored later that month in Resolution Cove, Nootka Sound, off the western coast of Vancouver Island. Here he and his crews observed the Nootka Indians who inhabited the shores of the cove, being much impressed with their trading acumen and especially their principal trading commodity, the sleek, thick fur pelt of the sea otter. Cook left Nootka Sound on 26 April and on his continued voyage north found no passage. On his return to England via the Pacific, he was mysteriously murdered by usually peaceful natives in the Sandwich Islands (now Hawaii). But his men continued on, and an impressive account of the voyage was published in England in 1784. Cook had worked out the outline of the northwest coast of North America with some accuracy, and his officers provided much detail about the region's Indians, including some wonderful first-hand drawings by the artists attached to the expedition. What most struck many readers of the official account, however, were the sea-otter pelts, and there was soon a rush to cash in on their obvious value, particularly in the difficult Chinese market.

M.B. Messer, *Capt. Cook's Ships Moored in Resolution Cove, Nootka Sound, Vancouver Island, March 1778*, a watercolour after a drawing by John Webber. National Archives of Canada.

‿⌒⌐ The End of the War

While James Cook's crews were still on the high seas returning to England, the British lost the war of the American Revolution. Whether they could ever have won it is an open question, but certainly few contemporaries were as realistic as Captain John MacDonald, who wrote in 1777 that even if the British achieved a complete military victory, it was almost impossible to conceive of a post-war policy that would return the Americans to their earlier loyalty.[34] MacDonald had the advantage of starting from the assumption that, whatever the reasons, the American thrust for independence was a broad-based popular one. Most British statesmen, and most American loyalists, always held that a few hotheaded agitators had stirred up and misled the common people, whose deep-seated allegiance to the Crown would reassert itself as soon as the scheming politicians were removed. Throughout the war the British chased the chimera of the silent majority, forgetting that advancing eighteenth-century armies not only liberated the populace from its misguided leaders but also ran roughshod over them, making as many enemies as friends in the process. Military solutions to movements of national liberation worked no better in the eighteenth than in the twentieth century. Moreover, once the Americans had hung on long enough against typical military stupidity and inefficiency, they found allies in Europe, particularly among the French, who signed a treaty with the United States in the wake of the abortive invasion from Canada led in 1778 by 'Gentleman Johnny' Burgoyne (1722-92), which resulted in the surrender of an entire British army at Saratoga. The American victory at Saratoga helped bring the French into the war. Fortunately for the British in Quebec, the Americans were suspicious of the intentions of their new allies, and various proposals to mount a joint expedition to invade Quebec came to nothing.

Unable to beat the Americans with regular troops, the British increasingly came to rely on provincial loyalist units to do the fighting, thus increasing the sense of civil war that was implicit from the outset. On the New York and Carolina frontiers, Loyalists and Rebels fought fierce battles in which no quarter was asked, or given, and in which the ostensible reasons for fighting were submerged in a host of other issues. With the assistance of the French navy, the American army finally succeeded in 1781 in trapping another British army under Lord Cornwallis in Virginia. Cornwallis's surrender, suitably accompanied by a regimental band playing a popular tune of the day entitled 'The World Turned Upside Down', was really the end of the line for the British government. Under heavy criticism for years—less on the principle of fighting the Americans than because of the heavy expenses and taxes the war necessitated—the ministry could no longer pretend that ultimate victory was right around the corner. The British government fell, and its critics took office to negotiate the peace.

The process of making peace with the Americans took a long time, from mid-1781 to 30 November 1782, when provisional articles of peace with finally signed. British recognition of the independence of the United States was among the least of the issues to be negotiated. There were questions of boundaries, of fishing rights, of Indian rights and territory, of the blacks; and, of course, the thorny problem of the Loyalists. While the emissaries from the two sides met, rumours about the terms of the ultimate arrangement ran rampant across North America. British authorities in America were forced to deal with many matters in advance of the final peace terms; but until those terms were formally accepted and announced, it was impossible to adopt an overall policy for what remained of Britain's American empire. That policy would have to take the Loyalists into account.

chapter seven

The New Immigrants:

Peopling British North America, 1783-1845

On 6 May 1783 General George Washington, commander-in-chief of the American army, met at Orangetown, New Jersey, with Sir Guy Carleton, British commander at New York, to discuss one of the articles of the preliminary peace treaty signed between His Majesty's Government and the United States late in 1782. The meeting was at Washington's instigation, and the article discussed was not the provision (or rather lack of one) for the Loyalists, but Number VII, which called for the liberation of all prisoners and the speedy withdrawal of the British 'Armies, Garrisons, and Fleets, from the said united states'. The clause specified that the British should not carry 'away any Negroes or other Property of the American Inhabitants', which Washington insisted meant that any slaves who had at one time been the property of Americans should be abandoned by the British. Carleton, in his turn, maintained that he would evacuate any slave claiming protection under the various proclamations issued by His Majesty regarding slaves. But, he assured Washington, he had kept a record of blacks being removed, and was willing to allow American representation on a board, to meet regularly in New York, that would examine the standing of every departing slave.

Thus every Wednesday between 30 May and 7 August 1783—from 10 a.m. to 2 p.m.—blacks who already held certificates as refugees were liable to be challenged at board meetings at New York City's Fraunces Tavern. Their name, age, description, story of escape, military record, and other personal details were entered in a 'Book of Negroes'. In the end only fourteen cases were disputed; most were decided in favour of former masters, who were permitted to resume their proprietary interest. Those blacks who had not been summoned before the board understandably felt they had passed a final test and were now entitled to regard themselves as full Loyalists. Over 3,000 blacks were included in the 'Book of Negroes', and probably more removed to Nova Scotia on the Loyalist ships. They represented over ten per cent of the total number of Loyalists who made their way to that province.[1]

✐✐✐✐ *The Loyalists*

The Loyalists have a place in the first story of Canada learned by every school child. While the Loyalist migration has always been the subject of considerable controversy and mythologizing, several points stand out fairly clearly. The first—as the 'Book of Negroes' suggests—is that there was no such thing as the 'typical' Loyalist. Perhaps 40,000 people received land grants and assistance under the British Loyalist assistance program, with about 30,000 settling in Nova Scotia (part of which would become the province of New Brunswick in 1784), 750 on the Island of St John, 1,000 on Cape Breton, and the remainder in 'Quebec'— mainly in what would become Upper Canada. Of this total of 40,000, well over 3,000 were black, and almost 2,000 were Indians who were ultimately settled in Upper Canada. Something over half the 40,000 were civilian refugees; the remainder were officers and men, either from former Loyalist regiments or from British regiments disbanded in America. A large proportion were neither American nor English in origin. Quite apart from the blacks and the Indians, a disproportionate number of new settlers, especially those in the military, came from Scotland, Ireland, or various German principalities. Anglican clergyman Jacob Bailey (1731-1808) characterized his new neighbours in the Annapolis Valley as 'a collection of all nations, kindreds, complexions and tongues assembled from every quarter of the globe and till lately equally strangers to me and each other.'[2]

And, surprisingly, most newcomers did not expect to benefit from the policy of His Majesty's Government, announced in 1783, to compensate Loyalists for property in the United States that had been lost to the rebels. Less than ten per cent of New Brunswick Loyalists, for example, submitted a claim to the Loyalist Claims Commission; almost none of the immigrants to the Island of St John bothered to claim at all; and the other colonies had relatively few claimants—in spite of the fact that, as the lieutenant-governor of Quebec put it in 1786: 'The Loyalists in the Province, with a few exceptions do not consist of Persons of great Property or consequence. . . . A small compensation for their Losses would restore to the greater part of them all the Comforts and Conveniences they have lost.'[3] The same might have been said for most Loyalists in most parts of British North America.

Many Loyalists were not well-to-do, but had nonetheless experienced many trials and tribulations because of their allegiance. The American Revolution was one of the bloodiest civil wars ever fought, and dissenters were handled roughly. In the early days of the war the typical treatment of Loyalists in the rebellious colonies often involved mob persecution and vigilante justice. In August 1775, for example, soldiers from the southern colonies, on their way to Boston, met a man in New Milford, Connecticut, who called them 'd—d rebels'. According to his later account,

> They. . .made him walk before them to Litchfield, which is twenty miles, and carry one of his own geese all the way in his hand. When they arrived there,

they tarred him, and made him pluck his goose, and then bestowed the feathers on him, drummed him out of the company, and obliged him to kneel down and thank them for their lenity.[4]

George Washington refused to discourage such proceedings, on the grounds that they were in the interests of liberty, and that only an enemy to his country would oppose them.

Later in the war, the fighting between Loyalist and Rebel in New York and the Carolinas was extremely bitter. Guerilla leader Sir John Johnson (1742-1830, son of Sir William) reported in 1780:

> We burned several houses on our return to Johnstown, where we arrived about one o'clock the same day. After providing Provisions, &c., we marched back by the same route we came to the Scotch Settlement. The Number of houses, Barns, Mills, &c., Burnt amount to about one Hunded and Twenty. The Indians contrary to my Expectation Killed only eleven men.[5]

Shortly thereafter, at the battle of King's Mountain in the Carolinas, a unit of Loyalists attempting to surrender heard the answer: 'Tarleton's quarter!'—a reference to Sir Banastre Tarleton's earlier massacre of patriots at Waxhaws, North Carolina—and many of them were promptly dispatched. The Loyalist casualty list was a long one that day. In Westchester County, New York, the Loyalist forces were known as 'cowboys' and 'cattle rustlers', while their patriot counterparts were called 'skinners' because of their tendency to skin victims of all possessions. Small wonder the officers of the provincial Loyalist regiments insisted on their units' being included in any Loyalist removal to the northernmost colonies: 'The personal animosities that arose from civil dissension have been so heightened by the Blood that has been shed in the Contest, that the Parties can never be reconciled.'[6] Such a view was certainly valid in early 1783—but in this context, memories were short.

Like the policies that created many of the Loyalist contingents, those that resettled them were for the most part *ad hoc* responses to immediate circumstances, rather than part of any carefully conceived long-term strategy. The first Loyalist settlements in Quebec began before the war had even ended, in the Niagara district. By the time of the Battle of Yorktown in 1781, a number of Butler's Rangers were already preparing ground there for spring planting. News of the impending peace treaty in 1782 galvanized the Loyalists into action—particularly in New York, which was occupied by the British and would serve as the springboard for most Loyalists heading northwards. Initially, arrangements for resettlement were made by private organizations of Loyalists (such as the Westchester Refugees, the Port Roseway Associates, and the Bay of Fundy Adventurers) with the British authorities in New York and Nova Scotia. These associations elected boards of agents, who formally requested assistance in the form of food and tools from Sir Guy Carleton, who granted it as far as supplies permitted.

The first contingent of Loyalists left New York for Annapolis Royal, Nova

Scotia, in late 1782. They were joined in 1783 by six fleets of transports carrying more exiles—the 'Spring Fleet' of fifty sail, which left New York in May with eighteen transports intended for Port Roseway in Nova Scotia (subsequently called Shelburne) and eleven carrying passengers to the Bay of Fundy. A second fleet left a few weeks later, and a third followed in July. Two additional fleets departed New York in August, and another in October. All passengers—including both civilian 'refugees' and soldiers from Loyalist units—were 'victualled' by the New York authorities before embarkation. In no case were those departing given land in advance. The process of land-granting in Nova Scotia (and Quebec) would be a slow one, causing much 'Discontent and uneasiness' among those who felt they had been unceremoniously dumped and abandoned in a total wilderness.[7]

The Loyalist migration was very much one of both visible and invisible minorities. Among the invisible were women, who represented a substantial proportion of the newcomers but left very little evidence to mark their presence. Perhaps none among the Loyalists had more difficulty in becoming resettled, however, than the more visible black and native Loyalists—chiefly because the British had even less policy for them than for the other exiles.

The Women Loyalists

Many of the records in which the names of Loyalists appeared omitted women, almost by definition. Land grants were made to adult male applicants, military records listed the names of males, and Loyalist muster-rolls almost invariably gave only the names of males. One place where women's names could be found was among the Loyalist claimants to the British government for compensation. Claimants were not necessarily typical of all Loyalists, and not all of them had settled in British North America. But 468 of the 3,225 people who presented claims were women, and their evidence suggests much about the place of women in the Loyalist migration. They, of course, submitted claims only because there was no male to do so for them. Although they often had considerable knowledge about property, particularly in the context of the home, most women claimants had difficulty in supplying detailed financial information about their family's total losses—with the result that they tended to receive less than males. Nearly ten per cent of the female claimants had worked outside the home, but most of their activities revolved around their immediate households. The loss of them, and of their familiar and cherished contents, was probably more traumatic for Loyalist women than were property losses for men—and for women the gradual re-creation of stability was much more difficult.

During the American Revolution women alone, without male protection, experienced many difficulties; both Loyalist women in patriot areas and rebel women in Loyalist ones (such as the women in the Fort Cumberland region after 1776) complained frequently of abuse and threats. Exile provided a different kind of nightmare, and many claimants observed that, as they left their homes, their 'severest trials were just begun.' While male Loyalists typically described themselves as 'unhappy' or 'distressed', female claimants labelled themselves as 'helpless'. The difference in terminology was important. Men did not perceive themselves as dependents, or alone, or as being in a situation that was beyond their power to correct. But women, understandably, did. Men could re-establish relationships in meeting places outside the home, but women usually could not. Women—usually without having been consulted about the decision to emigrate—had sacrificed for a principle. They had every right to be bitter about their fate.[8]

Black Loyalists

In the first days of the war against the Americans, the British authorities on the scene attempted to enlist some of the half-million slaves to fight against their masters, although the British government was not entirely enthusiastic. In November 1775 Virginia governor Lord Dunmore declared free 'all indented servants, negroes, or others...that are able and willing to bear arms, they joining his Majesty's troops.'[9] Within a week, Dunmore had more

Caroline Bucknall
Estcourt, *The Good 'Woman
of Colour' of Lundy's Lane,
Upper Canada*, 1839.
Watercolour. The artist's
husband, James Bucknall
Estcourt, was a
lieutenant-colonel in the
43rd Foot posted to
Lundy's Lane, near
Niagara Falls, for a few
months in 1839. National
Archives of Canada.

than 300 blacks in his 'Ethiopian Regiment'. The slogan carried on the front of their uniforms, 'LIBERTY TO SLAVES', thus became a British policy— though this declaration was not predicated on abolitionism but on military necessity. After 1779, when the British again returned to the American South as a theatre of war, they encouraged all blacks to their side, and not only those capable of active military service. Sir Henry Clinton, British commander-in-chief, issued his famous Philipsburg Proclamation, promising 'to every NEGRO who shall desert the Rebel Standard, full security to follow within these Lines, any Occupation which he shall think proper.'[10] The intention was to open schisms in the southern slave economy.

Thousands of blacks found their way to British lines by whatever means possible, drawn by promises of freedom that only the British could possibly honour. About one-third of those recorded by the British in 1783 at Fraunces Tavern had experienced military service. Given the reasons for British policy, it was hardly surprising that they did not always treat the blacks well. Many slaves seized as confiscated property from the Americans were resold into slavery, mainly in the West Indies, although 43 were brought to Montreal in 1783 to be sold for an average price of £33.15 each. Nevertheless, loyalist blacks were usually evacuated when the British withdrew from an American district, because—as one British officer argued— 'however policy may interfere in favour of the Masters, an attention to Justice, and good faith, must plead strongly in behalf of the Negroes, many of whom have

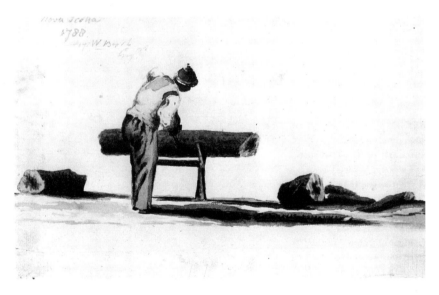

William Booth, *A Black Woodcutter at Shelburne, Nova Scotia, 1788.* **Watercolour. National Archives of Canada, C-40162.**

certificates of services performed.'[11] On such grounds were the black Loyalists enumerated and removed to Nova Scotia.

What all Loyalists wanted and needed in British America was land, and the blacks were perhaps even more desperate than the remainder of the Loyalist population. Unfortunately, despite the presence of more than 26 million acres of wasteland in Nova Scotia, making it available for settlement was no easy matter. In September 1782, from his command post in New York, Sir Guy Carleton had sketched out a Loyalist land policy, insisting that grants were to be 'considered as well founded Claims of Justice rather than of mere Favor', and were to be made without quitrents or fees. Because so much of Nova Scotia's best land had been given away in the 1760s, it had to be returned to the Crown by the legal process of escheat, which was done expeditiously but was still time-consuming. Procedures for administering grants were cumbersome, there were scarcely enough qualified surveyors to prepare them, and priority was given to those who had lost the most property in the United States. Attempting to save money in the welter of 'accumulating expenses' of resettlement, the authorities in London reduced the number of deputy-surveyors who actually laid out the grants. The blacks were at the bottom of everybody's list of priorities; even British officials themselves admitted that they 'laboured under some disagreeable Circumstances with respect to their Lands.'[12]

At Port Roseway, where confusion over land reigned supreme for several years, the blacks had been given their own community of Birchtown to the northwest of the main settlement. A special board dealt with applications for land, and completed its assignment in late 1786, 'except for those for the Negroes at Birch Town'. While white settlers waited several years for their land, fully two-thirds of the blacks of Birchtown never received any at all, and the grants given to a fortunate few were much smaller than those promised by Carleton. At Digby, blacks were not located on land until June 1785, and were then removed because the land had been reserved for a church glebe and a school. In the end, except for one-acre town lots granted to blacks in the early days of settlement, they never received any farm land in the area. Blacks had similar experiences elsewhere in the colony. Most ended up either without land or with inadequate portions. Of the more than 3,000 black Loyalists transported to Nova Scotia, only 1,155 actually received land grants for a total acreage of 12,015 ½ acres, or less than eleven acres per grant. Blacks became part of the mobile population of the region, many of them moving into the Guysborough district of the Halifax area, where they took up whatever employment was available.

As well as failing to obtain enough land to become independent farmers, black Loyalists suffered other disabilities. Although many paid taxes, they were not entitled to trial by jury. In what became New Brunswick they were not allowed to vote in elections for representation to the general assembly. In Shelburne, Nova Scotia, the magistrates forbad 'Negro Dances, and Negro

Frolicks in this Town'. Blacks brought to British North America as slaves by Loyalist masters continued in their status until the start of the nineteenth century, when local courts ruled slavery out of existence in the colonies by extending English laws. Freed blacks, however, were treated more harshly by the courts than whites convicted of the same or similar crimes. They responded to these limitations, in the short run, by turning to religion. The 'new light' of Henry Alline was especially appealing, and so was the preaching of the black Baptist David George (d. 1810), whose message of equality before God was a powerful one for black congregations. Along with their own schools, their chapels were institutions of some importance to an alienated segment of the population. In 1791 nearly half the Nova Scotia black Loyalists would accept with alacrity a chance to immigrate to the African colony of Sierra Leone.

Native Loyalists

In its own way the native experience paralleled that of the blacks. For Canada the most important native Loyalists were those from the Iroquois Confederacy, who ultimately settled in what would become southern Ontario. Despite some individual British supporters among the Mohawks—especially members of the Brant family who had intermarried with the Johnson family of upstate New York, which had long dominated British superintendency of the Iroquois people—the bulk of the Six Nations had attempted to remain neutral. The British put far greater pressure on the Iroquois to break their neutrality than did the Americans, arguing that the 'covenant chain' had long ago united the two peoples in perpetual alliance. Not all natives were persuaded, and their families were often as divided as European ones. But those natives who did join the British were soon enmeshed in the brutal warfare of the New York frontier, and acquired reputations for 'barbarous butchery'. An American expedition in the late summer of 1779 laid waste the native villages as far as the Genesee River, thus destroying the heart of their prosperity. Hundreds of native refugees were driven to Fort Niagara, becoming dependents of the British in the process. Throughout the war the British were able to play on natives' fear of American retaliation, and on their fear that the Americans intended to settle in large numbers on native lands that the new United States had never recognized as belonging to the First Nations.

Like the Loyalists themselves, who got nothing more out of the peace negotiations than a promise by the American negotiators that they would take Loyalist claims to the several states for consideration, the First Nations were virtually abandoned by their British allies in the rush for extrication from an unpopular and expensive war. Britain transferred to the Americans sovereignty over land south of the Great Lakes and as far west as the Mississippi River, totally ignoring the fact that most of that land was claimed by Indians who could reasonably argue that they had never given it up to the

Europeans. Even that loyal friend of the British, Joseph Brant, was bitter about the treaty, insisting that the British 'sold the Indians to Congress'. Part of the problem was that land ownership and sovereignty were not identical, and Europeans and natives had quite different interpretations of these matters. The general British attitude was well demonstrated by the efforts of colonial officials to accommodate Indian refugees in what would become Upper Canada. Governor Frederick Haldimand (1718-91) found available land by a series of hastily concluded treaties with the Mississauga, and the bulk of the native exiles were given a grant of land along the Grand River. Here a 1785 census showed 1,843 native residents, including more than 400 Mohawks. The grant never actually matched the land available, since the government had mistakenly failed to purchase much of it from the Mississauga. Moreover, the British government of Upper Canada insisted that the land was earmarked solely for Indians and could not be sold to European settlers, while Joseph Brant maintained that if Indians were truly sovereign, they could do what they liked with the land. The issue was never, from the Indian standpoint, satisfactorily resolved, either for this territory or for other territories set aside for the First Nations by the British.

James Peachey, *Encampment of the Loyalists at Johnston, a New Settlement on the banks of the St Lawrence River, June 6, 1784.* This watercolour was painted when Peachey was deputy surveyor-general, surveying and laying out lots for disbanded troops and Loyalists in the future Upper Canada. National Archives of Canada.

❧ The Loyalist Impact

The three largest contingents of Loyalist exiles from New York settled in three 'instant towns' in Nova Scotia and Quebec: Port Roseway (or Shelburne) on the southwest coast of the Nova Scotia peninsula; Saint John at the mouth of the Saint John River in what would soon become the Province of New Brunswick; and Cataraqui (later Kingston) on Lake Ontario. The two Nova Scotia communities contained large numbers of artisans and shop-keepers, and there was a rapid replication of the relative urbanity of New York itself. Especially in Saint John, there was also an emergence of a serious political struggle between those Loyalists who sought to import aristocratic values based on landholding, and those from the artisan/shopkeeping ranks who were far more committed to Americanized democratic values; this urban class had been one of the most active and radical in the turmoil leading up to the American Revolution, although not all sought ultimately to break with the British Crown. Gradually the proto-aristocrats would move upriver and find their centre in the new provincial capital at Fredericton. While initially all these new communities experienced boom-time conditions based on the availability (and future promise) of British largesse, their long-term success depended on becoming the centres of some kind of economic activity in their regions. Located in some of the poorest agricultural land in Nova Scotia and lacking any exploitable resource except fish—which hardly required or generated much economic sophistication—Shelburne quickly declined as a major community, its failure assisted by the many problems of land-granting in the area. Saint John would find some economic viability through the rich agricultural hinterland of the Saint John River Valley and through the seemingly inexhaustible timber resources of the province. Kingston would struggle on as an administrative centre, but with little economic vitality until well into the nineteenth century.

Few of the newcomers stayed where they first settled. The tendency of some Loyalists to leave the towns they initially attempted to create—the constant movement of individual Loyalists looking for a better situation—was one of the most characteristic features of the Loyalist migration. Their mobility was encouraged by the administrative failure of the governments welcoming them to provide them with land grants, much less acceptable land. In most cases this was caused by lack of organization and administrative bungling, although in some instances, as on the Island of St John, govern-ment officials attempted to use the settlement of Loyalists to enhance their own nefarious land dealings. In any case, the 1780s saw continual Loyalist relocation, sometimes within the colony of original settlement, sometimes to another colony of greater promise, and often eventually back to the United States after subsidies ran out and the initial hostility to the Loyalists had died down.

Shelburne, a town of over 10,000 people at its height in the mid-1780s, was little more than an oversized village ten years later. In Adolphustown, in upcountry Quebec (later Upper Canada), a quarter of the households turned over every two years. On the Island of St John fewer than 25 per cent of Loyalist land grantees were still on the Island for the first nominal census of

1978. In Wallace, Nova Scotia, on the south shore of Northumberland Strait, 40 per cent of grantees never actually took up their lands, and another 36 per cent were gone within two years. In the Maritime region, disbanded soldiers (who for the most part did not have families) were more likely than refugee settlers to move off their land grants. In Quebec, where a larger proportion of soldiers brought their families, chiefly from New York, the most transient were the American-born Loyalists, as opposed to those who were relatively recent arrivals in the New World. The recent immigrants were for the most part tired of moving and eager to settle down, while the American-born, with less experience of being uprooted, became more quickly dissatisfied with their situations. The most stable newcomers were members of the office-holding élite, who tended to cluster in the provincial capitals.

One important consequence of Loyalist settlement was the renewed emphasis on freehold tenure everywhere in what remained of British North America. Freehold had not been an important aspect of British policy under the Proclamation of 1763. Most of the land grants of the post-1763 period had been made to large proprietors who were expected to settle tenant farmers. The proprietorial system instituted on the Island of St John was typical of British policy during these years. In Quebec, the seigneurial system had been retained and even strengthened. The policy of giving the Loyalists small freehold land grants marked a shift in British policy, and there were enough such grants in most colonies to establish the practice.

If the Loyalists were by and large a restless population in a geographical sense, they were also a discontented and highly vocal one in political terms. While only a fraction of the new arrivals would be formally compensated by the British government for lost property in the United States, all felt that they had suffered for their allegiance to the Crown and were highly deserving of both land and government assistance. Moreover, since most of the Loyalists were former American colonials, they were accustomed to certain levels of political participation and shared many political values with their former neighbours. It must be remembered that most ordinary Americans had supported colonial criticisms of British policy up to the point of the open break with the mother country. They did not like oligarchic government and expected to be allowed full participation in the political process. They also detested any landholding principles except freehold tenure. Loyalist political activity thus occurred at several levels simultaneously.

At one level there were demands to be allowed to share in government. Quebec Loyalists complained bitterly about the absence of a representative assembly in the province, and Nova Scotia Loyalists about the domination of the government by the older inhabitants. Criticisms of the government of Nova Scotia were spearheaded by the Loyalist élite, who fulminated at its incompetence and distinguished between old and new inhabitants. As Edward Winslow (1746-1815) put the case in 1784:

A large proportion of the old inhabitants of this country are natives of New England or descendants from New England-ers. They from their situation never experienced any of the inconveniences which resulted from the violence of political animosity. They remained in quiet during all persecutions in the other provinces. They retained a natural perhaps laudable affection for their country. The rebel part were more industrious in propagating their opinion and their doctrine. . . . From the nature of their government & a conviction of the policy of being quiet they did not meddle in the controversy but they were evidently hearty well wishers to the Cause. Of this complexion are the public officers (generally). On our side the principal people are men who have served in a military line—irritable from a series of mortifications—scarcely cooled from the ardor of resentment—jealous to an extreme—perhaps illiberally so.[13]

From Winslow's perspective, the 'old inhabitants' had not suffered sufficiently. Thus the leading Loyalists of Nova Scotia pressed for their own province, which they could dominate and in which their values would prevail. They would soon be given New Brunswick.

On another level Loyalists were often divided among themselves politically, with the chief divisions existing between the old élite, who sought to re-establish themselves as the natural leaders of society, and the more articulate among the rank-and-file, who sought a more democratic and open future. The most public example of this conflict occurred in the town of Saint John. In the summer of 1783 fifty-five leading Loyalists—men of 'the most respectable Characters' by their own assertion, and including a number of the principal Loyalist agents of the private associations—petitioned Sir Guy Carleton for large 5,000-acre grants in Nova Scotia in order to regain their old standing. Such grants, the petitioners added, would be 'highly Advantageous (to the colony) in diffusing and supporting a Spirit of Attachment to the British Constitution.' A counter-petition, organized among several hundred Loyalists at Roubelet's Tavern in Saint John, argued that acceptance of such requests would produce nearly 'a total exclusion of themselves and Familys, who if they became Settlers must either content themselves with barren or remote lands. Or submit to be Tenants to those, most of whom they consider their superiors in nothing but deeper Art and keener Policy.'[14] Public discontent with the agents continued in Saint John, and in early 1784 an anonymous author printed a poem, publicly circulated in the town, that openly attacked the agents:

> The main design that they're upon,
>> To keep us easy at St. John,
> Till we have eat our bread and pork,
>> And then the D—l goes to work.
> To them we'll go instead to Pharrow,
>> But we shall soon behold a Nero,

To them we'll make our cries and moan,
　　Instead of bread they'll give us stone.
Except you'll give them all your living,
　　And every thing that's worth a giving.
Like slaves you cannot then resist,
　　Your lands likewise, except the Priests.[15]

A combination of British policy and the ultimate scattering of ordinary Loyalists would limit the success of the critics of the ruling élite. But from time to time such sentiments would reappear in post-revolutionary politics.

After the Treaty of Paris of 1783 pressure from the Loyalist leadership would contribute to an eventual political reorganization of British North America. The first stage came in 1784, when a governor-generalship was established to administer Britain's remaining North American colonies. Sir Guy Carleton, now Lord Dorchester, was the first appointee to this position in 1786. Britain also created two new provinces. New Brunswick was hived off from Nova Scotia in 1784 and given a set of political officials chosen from the 'needy' Loyalist élite, with the capital laid out at Fredericton in 1785, the year the first governor, Thomas Carleton (brother of Sir Guy), arrived. Cape Breton was ruled by a lieutenant-governor and council without an assembly, but in 1820 the island was reunited with Nova Scotia. In the initial reorganization of the Island of St John the governor was demoted to lieutenant-governor and his administration was placed under the jurisdiction of Nova Scotia. No changes were made in the government of Newfoundland, which was still being administered by officials who were resident in St John's only during the summer months and which functioned without an assembly. Nor were alterations made immediately in Quebec, although Dorchester arrived in 1786 with a new chief justice in the person of Loyalist William Smith (1728-93) of New York. Smith's political views were distinctly Anglo-American, and he was known to have little sympathy for the Old Regime.

In 1787 a former Loyalist polemicist, the Reverend Charles Inglis (1734-1816), arrived in Halifax as the first North American bishop of the Church of England. Although most Loyalists were not Anglicans, the British government did wish to continue a close connection between church and state, and Inglis worked uphill for years to bring Anglicanism to a level worthy of state support. The Loyalists also pressed for institutions of higher learning in the colonies. William Smith of Quebec advocated a secular university for his province, Inglis helped establish King's College in Windsor, and Benedict Arnold (who lived in Saint John as an unpopular Loyalist refugee from 1786 to 1791) spearheaded a movement for a university in New Brunswick, which did not take root at that time.

In the western part of Quebec, demands from the up-country districts for British institutions, particularly an assembly, eventually produced the second stage of reorganization: the Constitutional Act of 1791. This parliamentary legislation split Quebec into Upper and Lower Canada, giving the former a lieutenant-governor (John Graves Simcoe), both an executive and a legislative council, and an assembly. In theory, Upper Canada's lieutenant-governor would be responsible to the governor of Quebec. But Britain's efforts in this period to create an administrative hierarchy of colonies were not very effective. Each colony of British North America continued to turn directly to the British government as the source of real authority. An earlier act for Quebec that gave the colony revenue from commercial activity, prior to the establishment of an assembly, was not repealed, and so Lower Canada collected duties from Upper Canada.

Despite self-denying legislation by Parliament in 1777 that no direct taxes would be collected in British North America without the consent of the governed in a legislative assembly—a belated attempt to deal with the American cry for 'No Taxation Without Representation'—and however much eighteenth-century British statesmen were committed to the principle of colonial assemblies, Great Britain was still not prepared to universalize their institution. French Canadians got an assembly in 1791 less because they were entitled to one than because the Loyalist settlers of the up-country insisted on having one, and the need for symmetry between the two provinces was strongly voiced in Quebec. Cape Breton, because of its small size and remote location, would have to grow into an assembly. From the British perspective, assemblies implied that colonies had come to full maturity, having a revenue to control. As for Newfoundland, Britain still hesitated to grant it full colonial status partly because it had a large population of Roman Catholics. The Loyalist period, however, saw the achievement of full political privileges for Roman Catholics in most of British North America, partly through local legislative initiative but also by parliamentary fiat (for Quebec). Only on the Island of St John—which in 1786 passed laws permitting Catholics to own land but refused to allow them to vote—and in New Brunswick until 1810 were they still disenfranchised politically.

The Loyalist migration was over by 1786, when compensatory land grants and provisioning ceased virtually everywhere in British North America. But in one decade the loyal provinces of British North America—to their great benefit, and through no action of their own—had received a substantial contingent of American settlers, well subsidized by the British government, that they had not been able to attract before the American troubles. So-called 'Late Loyalists' would continue to be attracted to Upper and Lower Canada by offers of land, but the Maritime region would never again experience a substantial American influx. For all colonies of British North America immigration and settlement would long have crucial importance, but the post-Loyalist wave would have to be managed under quite different circumstances.

∿✄ Post-Loyalist Immigration

Early statistical data for Canada—for population as well as for other variables—is notoriously unreliable, even when figures are available. Censuses were taken irregularly, at different times in different colonies, and were both extremely incomplete and limited in the kinds of information collected. Nevertheless the available data indicate that the population, of European origin, of British North America grew from over 250,000 in 1791 to over 1,600,000 in 1845, as illustrated by the following:

c. 1791		*c. 1845*	
Newfoundland	15,000	Newfoundland	96,000 (1845)
New Brunswick	20,000	New Brunswick	155,000 (1840)
Nova Scotia	40,000	Nova Scotia	202,000 (1838)
PEI	6,000	PEI	47,000 (1841)
Cape Breton	2,000	Upper Can.	432,000 (1840)
Quebec	171,000	Lower Can.	697,000 (1844)
		The West	10,000

Source: *Census of Canada, 1870-71* (Ottawa, 1876), Volume IV, *passim.*

In addition, there were perhaps 50,000 Indians in the settled parts of British North America in 1790, and in 1845 approximately 150,000 in the outlying British territory. Of the population of European origin in 1791, 140,000 were of French and the remaining 110,000 chiefly of British origin. By 1845 the French population was around 600,000 and the British close to one million. In 1790 half the population of British origin had come by way of the thirteen American colonies, while in 1845 those of American origin were less than ten per cent of the 'British' total, with extensive concentrations only in Upper Canada, where only 32,000 in the 1842 census were listed as having been born in the United States. For the French population (both *Canadiens* and *Acadians*), the growth between 1790 and 1845 was the result almost exclusively of natural increase, while for the British natural increase had been less important than a massive immigration from the British Isles, particularly after 1815.

Immigration figures are even less reliable than population data. Records were not systematically kept for what is now Canada until well after Confederation, though after 1815 the British began keeping approximate track of their emigrants. Since many from the British Isles sailed to British North America, but had the United States as their ultimate destination, the British count is singularly undependable as a measure of the number of actual new arrivals who stayed in British America. Nevertheless, between 1790 and

1845 probably over 750,000 Britons settled in Britain's American colonies, close to half of them from Ireland. Of the remainder, English and Welsh outnumbered Scots, but given the relatively small population of Scotland, the Scots represented the British population that was statistically most likely to emigrate in this period. The fact that the newcomers came overwhelmingly from the British Isles did not imply that they were in any way a homogeneous population. Britain was really a collection of quite distinctive countries, and the bulk of the new arrivals came from the least-integrated parts of the nation, particularly in a cultural sense. Some spoke languages other than English, and even those who spoke English usually did so with distinctive accents and vocabularies; most were not adherents of the Church of England. Once in British North America, Scots and Irish especially retained a clear sense of a distinctive identity, which they have never entirely lost.

This first massive wave of immigration to what would be Canada— beginning in the post-Loyalist period and almost entirely British in origin— really took off after 1815, when the Napoleonic Wars ended and the British government shifted from a policy of hostility to colonial emigration to one of enthusiastic support. Emigration quickly gained momentum, increasing in magnitude after 1830. According to British sources, 70,000 left Britain for British North America between 1815 and 1820, 139,000 between 1821 and 1830, and 522,000 between 1831 and 1845. After 1840 the Irish famine fuelled an even greater increase up to 1855. From 1790 to 1815 most immigrants to British North America were small property holders with enough capital to self-finance passage to the New World. After 1815 the number of immigrants without capital continually increased, as the cost of passage declined considerably and various British schemes for subsidization of emigration came into effect. Earlier immigrants could expect to become landowners and farmers, while many later ones had to begin life as labourers in resource industries and on the increasing number of public-works projects that began in British North America in the 1830s.[16] In neither period was much attention paid to the prior claims to land of the First Nations, regarded as nomads who had never properly utilized the territory in which they resided.

1790-1815 and the Selkirk Settlements

Before 1815 there was considerable pressure from inhabitants of the Scottish Highlands and Ulster to depart for America, but the British authorities viewed the departure of emigrants with an attitude ranging from lack of enthusiasm to positive alarm, depending chiefly on the immediate military situation. Both the Highlands and Ireland were major recruiting grounds for the British army, and mercantilist views still prevailed in most British circles. Population was needed at home and ought not to be encouraged to leave. A groundswell of concern over the loss of tenants from the landlords of the

Scottish Western Highlands and Islands resulted in 1803 in the passage of the first British legislation regulating the transport of emigrants across the Atlantic. Officially intended to improve conditions on the emigrant vessels, the law of 1803 was really designed to raise the price of passage beyond the reach of those seeking to leave.[17]

The British authorities not only refused to support emigration at home, but failed to press the several colonial administrations to make land available for—or in other ways to welcome and assist—the new arrivals. More than one colonial governor wrote home complaining about immigrants, who put pressures on provincial budgets. Some colonies, particularly Upper Canada, did at least make land available, but many allowed existing land arrangements to govern the situation. Thus in Prince Edward Island (the Island of St John was renamed in 1799), land could be obtained only from the proprietors, who wanted tenants and were not eager to sell land to prospective purchasers. As a result of British policy—or, more frequently, the absence of positive policy—and of the almost continual warfare during this period, immigration to British North America before 1815 was spotty, occurring from the British Isles only during the brief periods of peace, particularly from 1801 to 1803. In these years American immigration was more important than it would subsequently become, and an absence of direction permitted Acadians to re-establish themselves in large portions of New Brunswick, as well as in Nova Scotia and Prince Edward Island. By 1803 a religious census showed nearly 4,000 Acadians in Nova Scotia, nearly 700 in Prince Edward Island, and nearly 4,000 in New Brunswick. Left virtually to fend for themselves, the Acadians developed both their own culture and the institutions to support it before the authorities were fully conscious of what was happening.

Before 1815 immigration from the British Isles came chiefly from the Scottish Highlands and from Ireland. Most of the Scots were drawn to the Maritime provinces, where they had already established beachheads of settlement, but some went to eastern Upper Canada to join Scottish communities there. The major movement that occurred in the years 1801 to 1803 was chiefly to the northeast shore of Nova Scotia, to Cape Breton, and to Prince Edward Island. Prosperity in Newfoundland and New Brunswick during the period 1812-15 drew many Irish to those colonies. More Protestant than Catholic, most came from northern Ireland. Unlike the American experience with the Irish later in the century, British North America drew heavily from the Protestant districts.

In this early period (as later) previous settlement and kinship ties were important factors in decisions to migrate and in choice of destination. The Scots immigrants particularly travelled in extended family groups: successful immigration and settlement begat more immigration from the same districts. After 1806, when the closure of the Baltic timber region to Britain encouraged the development of the timber industry in British North America, the availability of ships sailing westward across the Atlantic to pick up timber suddenly increased substantially. For most shipowners, sailing with passengers was preferable to sailing in ballast, and costs of passage decreased considerably. They would not increase until changing British trade policies in the 1840s ended the favouritism shown North American timber in the British market.

Before 1815 few immigrants were attracted to Lower Canada, both because of the presence of a dominant French culture and because the continued strength of the seigneurial system made it difficult for newcomers to gain access to freehold property, except in the isolated Eastern Townships. In Upper Canada the major stream of new arrivals in the period was American in origin—partly Late Loyalists, but mainly Americans moving westward who were attracted by a generous land policy. As tensions between Britain and the United States grew after 1807, British authorities in both London and the colony began to be worried by the predominance of Americans. The onset of the War of 1812-14, of course, forced those Upper Canadians who were not of Loyalist origin to choose sides. Those who remained in the colony during the conflict had made a commitment, but in the post-war period continuing hostility to Americans would make it difficult for them to gain full citizenship.

In the period before 1815 the key transitional figure was undoubtedly Thomas Douglas, Fifth Earl of Selkirk (1771-1820), who sponsored three settlements in British North America: in Prince Edward Island and Upper Canada, and on the Red River. The youngest son of a Scottish peer who came unexpectedly to the title because of the early deaths of four elder brothers, Lord Selkirk was educated at the University of Edinburgh, and spent considerable time in Paris during the French Revolution. Because of one notoriously radical brother (Lord Daer, who was responsible for bringing Thomas Paine to England in 1792), and a brother-in-law (Sir James Hall) who was a leading scientist, Selkirk was on familiar terms with many of the leading *philosophes* of the revolutionary period. He always regarded himself as a 'political economist' who sought to harmonize the obvious need for social reform of his time with both personal self-interest and imperial utility. His was an almost solitary voice in Britain in support of immigration to the British colonies. Between 1796 and 1801, when he experienced at first hand the results of uprooting people in the Highland clearances, leaving them helpless, as well as the aftermath of a rebellion in Ireland in 1798 that had been brought on by starvation, Selkirk became convinced that colonizing North American lands with oppressed and disadvantaged Britons was the ideal way of touching all bases. The colonies would benefit, the colonial promoter would benefit (either with public approbation or personal profit), and Britain would rid itself of unwanted people who very likely would eventually turn to crime or otherwise cause trouble.

Selkirk's best-known book, *Observations on the Present State of the Highlands of Scotland, with a View of the Causes and Probable Consequences of Emigration*

Thomas Douglas, Earl of Selkirk. This portrait is based on a painting by the distinguished Scottish artist Sir Henry Raeburn. National Archives of Canada, C-1346.

(1805), made a persuasive case for the advantages of emigration to both colonies and mother country, at the same time as it criticized the Highland landlords for their lack of adequate calculation of their own best interests. Selkirk insisted that it was quite senseless to prevent people who would soon become useless at home from departing for a new opportunity abroad. As one newly appointed Commissioner and Emigration Agent of the British government would report in 1815: 'His book was received at the time with some prejudice & excited considerable opposition. But it has been found that it contains much truth.'[18]

Selkirk became interested in North American colonization at the beginning of the century, proposing at first to lead a party of Irish rebels to Louisiana. When the British government rejected this plan, he turned to Prince Edward Island, buying land from proprietors and recruiting more than 800 Highlanders. Selkirk hoped to use Prince Edward Island to prove the efficacy of his theories on emigration: Highlanders could be transported to North America and successfully transplanted in agrarian circumstances. In July 1803 Selkirk set sail with his Highland emigrants for Prince Edward Island and arrived in August. Leaving them in September, he travelled from Halifax to Boston; to York, Upper Canada; and then to Montreal, where he learned much about the fur trade from fellow Scots. While he was in

Upper Canada he was granted 1200 acres plus land for Highland settlers in an area, chosen by him, on Lake St Clair that he called Baldoon; he visited and made plans for the site in June 1804 and settlers followed. On his way home in July he visited his Prince Edward Island settlers and found them well established. But early the next year he learned that Baldoon had proved an expensive failure, chiefly because its manager had no intention of supervising it personally, and could never find reliable agents to run it for him. Selkirk came to regard the unscrupulous behaviour of agents as the 'American disease', and never did find a solution for the problem.

Both the Prince Edward Island and Upper Canadian schemes were dwarfed by the sheer audacity of Selkirk's last and largest promotion: the establishment of a colony at the forks of the Red and Assiniboine Rivers, roughly on the site of the present city of Winnipeg. To facilitate this venture, Selkirk and his family gained a substantial interest in the Hudson's Bay Company, which at the time was at a serious disadvantage in its rivalry with the Montreal-based North West Company. From the HBC, Selkirk in 1811 received a grant of 116,000 square miles covering parts of present-day Manitoba, North Dakota, and Minnesota. Miles Macdonell (*c.*1767-1828) was named the first governor of Assiniboia, as the territory was called, in June 1811. On 26 July he and the first colonists left for Hudson Bay, arriving two months later at York Factory. After wintering on the Nelson River until the break-up of ice towards the end of June, they did not arrive at the junction of the Red and Assiniboine Rivers until 30 August, founding Fort Douglas. The colony quickly ran afoul of the North West Company, which employed the Red River region as the source of pemmican for the provisioning of its traders on the vast inland canoe routes. In 1813 Selkirk came very close to persuading the British government to finance the recruiting, equipping, and transporting to the Red River of a Highland Regiment to be commanded by himself. The scheme had won ministerial approval, but at the last minute was vetoed by the Commander-in-Chief, the Duke of York. Selkirk was reduced to sending to the Red River Settlement, at his own expense, people for the regiment recruited from the estates of the Duke of Sutherland.

When the Selkirk settlers were forced to rely on buffalo meat and pemmican for food—and, in January 1814, when Macdonell proclaimed that pemmican could not be exported from the region without his permission— the North West Company's men, whose supply of pemmican to the north-western Athabasca country was thus endangered, resorted to aggressive opposition. They encouraged the local Métis community, under Cuthbert Grant (*c.*1793-1854), to destroy the colony and very nearly succeeded in 1815, when Governor Macdonell was forced to surrender to them and was taken to Montreal under arrest. In November 1815, Robert Semple (1766-1816) arrived as governor-in-chief of the HBC territories. The next May, Grant set out with a force of 60 Métis horsemen to interfere with HBC activities, ambushing its pemmican boats on the Qu'Appelle River, capturing the HBC's Brandon House, and heading for Fort Douglas. On 19 June 1816, at Seven Oaks, Semple went out to meet them with a small force. A shot was fired, a small but bloody battle ensued, and in a quarter of an hour Semple and 20 of his men were killed.

Selkirk learned of this disaster—on 25 July at Sault Ste Marie—while on his way to Fort William with a small flotilla of soldiers and boatloads of supplies and arms for Red River. He arrived at Fort William, the headquarters of the North West Company, seized it, made some arrests, and occupied it for the winter. On 1 May he left for Red River, where he stayed until August, when he left for Upper Canada, arriving at York on 10 January 1818. The charges against him, the legal proceedings that followed, and ill health led to Selkirk's departure from Canada later in the year.

Despite the North West Company's hostility, and the British belief that the conflict between Selkirk's colony and the North West Company was a trading rivalry being conducted outside the jurisdiction of the government (which held Selkirk himself principally to blame for the crisis), Assiniboia survived, with French Canadians arriving in 1818 to found St Boniface, across the river from Fort Douglas. After the union of the North West Company with the Hudson's Bay Company in 1821, Fort Garry (built in 1817-18) superseded Fort Douglas as the headquarters of the Settlement.

Selkirk's *A Sketch of the British Fur Trade in North America, with Observations Relative to the North-West Company of Montreal* (1815) was perceptive and accurate in its demolition of the claims and pretensions of the North West Company. Its comments and evidence have been neglected chiefly because Selkirk was a notorious rival and enemy of that company. Although both his *Observations* and *British Fur Trade* were polemics, they were exceedingly well documented and well argued.

Selkirk died in France in 1820 virtually bankrupt and unvindicated— though he had succeeded in placing before the British public a powerful set of arguments about emigration and colonization that gained much acceptance in the years after 1815. He had insisted that the usual policy of government—'to take no charge whatever of emigrants, even of those who embark for our own colonies, but to leave to every one to provide for himself as he best can'—was a mistake. He further maintained: 'There are still in Canada millions of acres of fertile land in the disposal of Government; there is a great surplus of population at home, who might be employed to cultivate those lands; and there is also a great deal of unemployed capital in the hands of individuals, who, upon equitable arrangements, would find it for their interest to employ their capital in the cultivation of these waste lands, and in colonizing them with the surplus of our own population.'[19] Selkirk was thus a proponent both of government involvement in emigration and settlement as an imperial matter, and of the development of colonial land by large land-holders as an investment. In both respects he anticipated the future.

The Post-1815 Period

The War of 1812-14 divided the two periods of immigration mainly because the threat of privateering on the high seas reduced ocean traffic. After 1815 circumstances combined to alter completely the resistant attitude to emigration of both the British government and the British ruling classes (the common folk of Britain had always been enthusiastic about starting afresh in the New World, given half a chance). Immediately after the Napoleonic Wars, the shift from an overheated wartime economy to a peacetime one produced considerable unemployment; and even after the post-war depression had ended, a new round of industrialization and agricultural rationalization left many without work in their traditional occupations and places of residence. For large numbers of villagers and small farmers migration was inevitable—either within the British Isles to other forms of employment or to North America, where there was a chance of continuing their agricultural pursuits. The growth of the factory system threw many artisans with traditional skills out of work, and the new industrialists did not employ workers when they did not have orders to fill. Pressures on Britain's long-standing arrangements for relief of the poor increased, and among those who ran both local governments and the nation it became commonly accepted that Britain was once again overpopulated. As the influential *Edinburgh Review* argued in 1826: 'What is wanted is, the adoption of a system that will effectually relieve the immediate pressure of pauperism, without throwing it upon Great Britain and which will, at the same time, enable such further measures to be adopted as will ensure the future and lasting prosperity of the country.' Increasingly, emigration was seen as the answer. But whether this relocation of population should be officially sponsored and funded by the British government was another matter. The burgeoning of the North American timber trade provided the shipping capacity for the transatlantic movement of immigrants at relatively low cost, and many private entrepreneurs were brought into the picture in several capacities.

In British America the relationship between immigration and land policy—particularly the ways in which 'waste' or wilderness land was transferred from the Crown into the hands of individuals—was always a close one. The traditional British pattern was to devolve the cost of immigration onto the private sector. Before 1775 the government had reserved large grants of land for prospective sponsors of immigration; after 1783 land was typically made available to anyone applying for it at the cost of the expenses of transferring it. Occasionally, as in Nova Scotia or with the Loyalists, the British government sponsored settlement schemes. Characteristically, before 1830 the advocates of 'assisted' emigration combined actual settlement on the land with the process of relocation, and there were a number of underlying assumptions: that the people so aided would need to be supported until their land was improved; that the newcomer would ultimately farm his own land; and that he somehow had to be made to pay back the funds invested in this expensive process. Relatively few emigrants benefited from assisted emigration, either public or private, and most of the cost of the overall process of transplantation—in terms of both money and, especially, suffering—was borne by the emigrants/settlers themselves.

The immigrants came for a variety of complicated reasons, although the principal one was to gain access to land, something that was becoming increasingly difficult to obtain in the British Isles. Such access meant different things for different groups of settlers. For some, it meant 'independence'. As one former Glasgow weaver put it in 1821, in Scotland

> I had to labour sixteen or eighteen hours-a-day, and could earn about six or seven shillings-a-week—here, I can, by labouring about half that time, earn more than I need: there, I was confined to a damp shop,—but here, I enjoy fresh air: there, after I had toiled until I could toil no more, I would have the mortification of being a burden,—but here, two or three years' labour will give me more than will keep me in sickness, as well as in health: there, it is all dependence,—here, it is a fair prospect of independence.[20]

Not all new arrivals hoped to become full-time farmers. Many sought to return to a half-remembered past when artisans had enough land to supplement their wages with subsistence agriculture. Combining farming with some other occupation was quite common in British North America.

The British often had an extremely idealized picture of the wilderness. For example, Thomas Carlyle (1795-1881) offered in *Chartism* (1839) a typically romantic vision of North America, which he described as

> a world where Canadian Forests stand unfelled, boundless Plains and Prairies unbroken with the plough; on the west and on the east green desert spaces never yet made white with corn; and to the overcrowded little western nook of Europe, our Terrestrial Planet, nine-tenths of it yet vacant or tenanted by nomads, is still crying, Come and till me, come and reap me![21]

Carlyle's view was distinguished for both its romantic images of the wilderness and its vague, dismissive reference to the native inhabitants, who were obviously not taking full advantage of their birthright. Such a perception of the First Nations fit perfectly with the policies advocated for them in the settled and settling regions. Natives, according to colonial governments, should either settle down on small holdings and become farmers alongside the new immigrants, or alternatively hang on to their old ways on reserves located out of the way of onrushing settlement. In the summer of 1836, Sir Francis Bond Head—lieutenant-governor of Upper Canada—met with assembled Ottawas and Ojibwas of his province to sign a treaty that surrendered Manitoulin Island to the Crown. As Head explained to his audience, '. . .an unavoidable increase of white population as well as the progress of cultivation have had the natural effect of impoverishing your hunting grounds', making it necessary 'that new arrangements should be entered into for the purpose of protecting you from the encroachments of the whites.' The problem was that 'In all parts of the world farmers seek for uncultivated land as eagerly as you my red children, hunt in your forest for game.' He concluded: 'If you would cultivate your land, it would then be considered your own property,...but uncultivated land is like wild animals, and your Great Father who has hitherto protected you, has now great difficulty in securing it for you from the whites who are hunting to cultivate.'[22] For those few white men, chiefly colonial officials and missionaries in the settled colonies, who gave any serious thought at all to the people of the First Nations, turning them into small farmers seemed a reasonable solution to the conflicting needs for land of both native peoples and new immigrants.

The Patterns of Post-1815 Immigration

Basically, four patterns of emigration and settlement developed after 1815. One involved government assistance, which was often a combination of official British recruitment of emigrants and settlement, with public aid, on land made available by the several colonial governments. Such schemes, frequently either involving soldiers disbanded after the War of 1812-14 or excess Irish population, continued sporadically until 1830. A second pattern involved private landholders, or more often well-capitalized land companies, who occasionally arranged a package of transatlantic passage and land for settlers, but more commonly sold land locally to emigrants recruited by other means. Occasionally the land companies worked with private landholders in Britain, especially Scotland, who were willing to pay the passage of their 'excess' tenantry in order to clear them off the estates. Often the land was sold on credit, but this process was intended to appeal to emigrants with at least some capital, rather than to the impoverished. A third pattern involved the recruitment and transportation of emigrants by private entrepreneurs, usually shipowners, with little thought or commitment given to the disposition of the passengers when they arrived in British North America. In some cases passage money was paid by local authorities or landlords, although most emigrants dealing with private recruiters found enough money to pay their own passage. Finally, many emigrants arranged their own passage and frequently they came to British North America with no fixed plans or destination. Sometimes they intended to join relatives or friends who already had taken the step. If they had capital, they found land. It was generally estimated that at least £100 was required to make a farm from wilderness land, and even more was needed to purchase one already improved. Those who could not afford this expense joined the ranks of the labouring class in their new land. A more detailed look at examples of each of these patterns will illustrate the complexities of the process.

Assisted Immigration

Despite its unwillingness to resettle Highlanders to serve as a military force in the West at Lord Selkirk's Red River Settlement, the British government as early as 1813 began making plans for demobilizing soldiers on lands in its American colonies. The first formal scheme was undertaken early in 1815, when the government advertised in Scotland, offering passage to Upper Canada, land grants of 100 acres to each head of family, agricultural implements at cost, and a publicly supported minister and schoolteacher. Prospective emigrants had to provide a substantial deposit refundable in Canada two years after actual settlement—the scheme was obviously not intended for the very poor. More than 700 passengers on four government vessels were sent to Quebec, and housed over the winter of 1815-16 at government expense in Cornwall, eventually making their way to lands recently purchased from the Indians in Lanark County. The newcomers, however, had lost a year's planting time. The government had to continue with assistance to prevent them from being lured off to the United States, but this proved so expensive that the ministry abandoned the scheme, awaiting 'a Season of less financial Difficulty'. Subsequent ventures, including one involving unemployed weavers in 1819-20, required the co-operation of government and private emigration societies. In the case of the weavers, who also settled in Lanark County at New Lanark, the government advanced over £22,000 to them and in 1836 was eventually forced to cancel the debts.

In spite of the reluctance of the British authorities to invest large sums of money in settlement or resettlement schemes, the problems of Ireland and its dispossessed tenant farmers seemed too pressing to be ignored—at least in the mid-1820s. In 1823 the ministry of Lord Liverpool proposed public sponsorship of Irish emigration and settlement to the provinces of Canada, offering to 500 acceptable applicants from the rebellious south of Ireland inducements of free passage, land, and free conveyance to it. Irish landlords initially opposed the plan, on the grounds that 'the most industrious and best disposed' would take advantage of the scheme. They recommended that those selected for emigration be 'only those, who, if not actually connected with the disturbances' came from districts likely to erupt in violence. Peter Robinson (1785-1838)—a prominent resident of York and brother of the Attorney-General of Upper Canada—was placed in charge of recruitment, which focused on County Cork, where the Insurrection Act was in force.

After initial resistance from the Irish, Robinson found 'a perfect mania for going to Canada'. A party of 568 left Ireland in July 1823, arriving finally on their lands in the Bathurst area in October, too late to plant and nearly too late to house themselves. Local residents had to be employed to assist the newcomers in preparing for winter. Within two years, a third of these 182 families had departed; the average expense of settling one person had been more than £26. A subsequent scheme of 1825, again led by Robinson, involved 2,024 Irish from 'the most disturbed part' of that troubled country, who were transported to what became Peterborough. In this case, a third of the adult emigrants were dead within three years, and there was much local violence between the Roman Catholic newcomers and the Protestant Irish already in the district. Costs again were high, publicity about the venture negative, and the governor of Lower Canada spoke for many when he described the whole enterprise as having 'no other end than relieving the South of Ireland of a burden which [was] thrown upon the industrious classes of this young country.'[23]

The various government experiments with assisted emigration simply demonstrated that the cost of establishing British emigrants in British North America was high. Even those who argued that costs could be reduced estimated £60 for a family of five. Some members of the British government—particularly the parliamentary undersecretary at the Colonial Office, Robert John Wilmot-Horton—insisted that such government sponsorship was essential, notably to rid the country of unwanted paupers. Wilmot-Horton brought his own emigration plan before parliamentary committees several times and in 1828 before Parliament itself. It called for the expenses of transatlantic resettlement to be met by local authorities that were encumbered by the poor, the money raised by an annuity debited to the rates. Three factors worked against Wilmot-Horton's scheme: first, the ratepayers were not enthusiastic about footing the bill at the local level; second, many complained that populating British North America would only speed the congress of those colonies with the United States; finally, an attractive alternative to Wilmot-Horton's ideas emerged in the late 1820s. Its chief advocate was Edward Gibbon Wakefield, who focused less on emigration than on the disposal of colonial land. Unlike Wilmot-Horton's plans, which were attacked as nothing more than the 'shovelling out of paupers', Wakefield's scheme concentrated on land policy, abandoning the idea of giving land away in favour of charging a 'sufficient price' that would ensure a revenue for colonial improvements, as well as guaranteeing that those acquiring land had some capital.

Private Landholders and Land Companies

Wakefield's ideas were never fully implemented in British North America, although they lurked behind the commentary on land policy in Lord Durham's famous *Report* of 1839 that was drafted by Wakefield himself, who was one of Durham's aides. But the notion of selling Crown lands to provide a colonial revenue was always an attractive one, gaining more support after the parliamentary failure of Wilmot-Horton's emigration proposals. Before the 1820s most schemes for the sale of land involved free grants to proprietors, who would develop the land and sponsor emigrants to settle on it. Over the years this process underlay many of the large grants to proprietors made by several colonies, such as the Island of St John.

The best-known private proprietor in British North America—apart from Lord Selkirk—was Colonel Thomas Talbot (1771-1853), an Anglo-Irishman who attempted to replicate his family's aristocratic heritage, centred on Malahide Castle, in British North America. He was introduced to Upper Canada in 1792 as a military officer who was appointed private secretary to John Graves Simcoe, the first lieutenant-governor. This position lasted until 1794, when he was promoted to major, recalled to England, and spent the next six years in European service, selling his commission at the end of 1800, when he returned to Upper Canada. In May 1803—promising to settle Britons rather than Americans, thus checking the 'growing tendency to insubordination and revolt'—Talbot obtained 5,000 acres in Dunwich and Aldborough townships and settled at the mouth of Talbot Creek in Dunwich. This was the site of Port Talbot, where he lived until near the end of his life. Taking advantage of the Upper Canadian policy of rewarding with additional land grants those who brought settlers, and of his friendship with Lieutenant Governor Francis Gore (1769-1852), Talbot by 1821 had acquired ownership or control of hundreds of thousands of acres of land in the two townships, including a 'palatinate' of 65,000 acres. His settlement practices were informal, amounting to little more than the pencilling in of the name of a new settler on a large-scale township plan. A provincial report in 1836 indicated that he also held, quite apart from the 'palatinate', more than 500,000 acres on 3,008 lots in 28 townships of southwestern Upper Canada. From this land he drew considerably more status than revenue. Unlike Lord Selkirk, however, Talbot did not often assist emigrants with their passage, but rather made land available to them after they had arrived on initially inexpensive terms. Even so, the cost of development, particularly of the best-developed road network in the province, was considerable. The 'Talbot Roads' linked Port Talbot with the Niagara District, the Upper Thames Valley, and Amherstburg.

As Selkirk and Talbot discovered, a private landlord's costs in developing land were heavy. In the 1820s privately funded land companies—which could raise larger amounts of capital than a single proprietor—partially replaced the earlier individual entrepreneur. Of the three largest companies—the Canada Company, the British American Land Company, and the New Brunswick and Nova Scotia Land Company—the earliest and most energetic was the Canada Company, in which Scottish novelist John Galt (1779-1839) played a leading role. This Company, which in 1826 initially purchased most of the Crown reserves and half of the clergy reserves of Upper Canada, subsequently also bought a large block of unsurveyed land on the shore of Lake Huron (the Huron Tract). Its payment for these lands—to be spread over sixteen years—provided an annual revenue to Upper Canada. Although the Canada Company nearly went bankrupt on several occasions, and despite criticisms that its payments to the colony for land were not commensurate with the concessions made to it, the Company did settle large numbers of people on its lands. The towns of Guelph, Galt, and Goderich were founded, and by 1840 there were nearly 6,000 settlers, 23,000 acres under cultivation, and numbers of gristmills, sawmills, tanneries, and distilleries.

The British American Land Company was incorporated in 1834 to develop and settle nearly 600,000 acres of Crown land in the Eastern Townships of Quebec. In 1837 Colonel Duncan McDougall advocated the establishment of 5,000 Scots Highland families on 150,000 acres of Company land, at a cost to the British taxpayer of £227,500, arguing that the removal of protective duties on alkali had destroyed the Highland kelp industry, much as the abolition of slavery had destroyed the sugar planters. This scheme did not win favour, but the Company did begin co-operating with Scottish landlords, like Lord Seaforth, in making land available for emigrants whose passage was paid by their former lairds. The Company's success was limited by the availability of competing government grants, and it moved gradually into more diversified investments.

Of the three major companies, only the New Brunswick and Nova Scotia Land Company—formed in 1831 to settle several large tracts in New Brunswick—actually advanced money to emigrants, mainly Scots from the Isle of Skye. The financial affairs of the New Brunswick Company, however, are shrouded (like those of its sister companies) in a mystery that combines chicanery with bad management. It was quite impossible for any of these ventures to know whether or not substantial profits from land improvement and settlement occurred. A modern assessment of their economic viability and financial operations is equally impossible.

The Transatlantic Transportation Contractors

From the beginning of the nineteenth century, much of the traffic in transatlantic migration was carried to North America in sailing vessels built for carrying freight (especially timber) that were temporarily converted to accommodation for passengers. Owners of such vessels would charter them to others who collected the passengers, or often would fill their own ships through advertisements or in distressed areas through door-to-door visitations. The brig *Albion* was built for a Welsh merchant family named Davies, residing in Cardigan and trading out of Liverpool. Registered in March 1815, just at the end of the Napoleonic Wars, she had one deck, two masts, and was 72 feet long by just over 22 feet wide. Her height at its maximum was about 13½ feet, and her burden was reckoned officially at 166 tons. Launched at the start of a lengthy economic crisis, the *Albion*, and other vessels like it, had to turn far afield for cargoes, such as British North American timber. The problem with the timber trade was that it was not easy to find an outgoing cargo, since timber was much bulkier than the finished goods exported to British North America. Not surprisingly, Thomas Davies turned to the distressed farmers of Cardiganshire, who had overused their land during the wartime demand and now found it suffering from soil exhaustion. Conditions worsened after the war, when the bottom dropped out of the grain market, and not even the introduction of the Corn Laws (which protected the market but raised the cost of grain for consumers) could help very much. According to observers in Cardiganshire: '...the poor are attempting to prolong life by swallowing barley-meal and water—boiling nettles, etc.', while the landed proprietors sent 'their Bailliffs with Distress warrants to Distrain upon their poor tenants', secure in the knowledge that a rapidly increasing population would provide new tenants prepared to pay more than their predecessors for the privilege of working the land.[24]

The surplus population of Wales would eventually be put to good use in the coal mines and factories of the Industrial Revolution, but in 1819 the prospect of starting again in America was an attractive one. Displaced or unhappy tenant farmers could be described as 'poor', but they were not paupers, for they possessed farm equipment and livestock that could be sold to provide passage money. Thomas Davies found 180 people—in response to his printed broadsides in English and Welsh—willing to take passage to New Brunwick. The voyages to America of the *Albion* were different from countless others of the period only in the fact that the participants wrote and published works about them. Someone, for example, wrote—in Welsh—a lengthy narrative about an 1818 passage to New Jersey entitled 'Hanes Mordaith y Brig Albion o Aberteifi'. The work hardly lionized the emigrants; instead, in the language of Welsh Protestant sectarianism, it worried about whether those departing were doing the right thing by abandoning their religion and their native land. It concluded:

And if you want to come after us, I want you to sit down and think. Leaving one's country and friends is no small thing. You have heard accounts of our leaving the land of our birth to go to the land of our death—a great change— but the greatest change is yet to come: the transition from the land of our death to the living eternity.... Let us therefore number the ones who wait, and search for the One who is coming.[25]

The 1819 voyage of the *Albion* produced a poem, 'Cân Sef Hanes y Brig Albion', that was far more positive:

I can tell you about New Brunswick,
Which is so full of trees, right across it;
I don't think there is anywhere in the whole world
A better place to be found. . . .
There are no rents or taxes here,
Everyone owns his own property.
O that the poor people of Wales
Could be here, all of them.[25]

The eventual reality, not described by the poet, was considerably different. Disembarking in Saint John, the *Albion* passengers had little money and no means of obtaining land. Most headed up the Saint John River for Fredericton, where they petitioned the government for land and became the objects of local charity, a society having been formed in 1820 'for the purpose of assisting the Welch families' by raising money through subscriptions and donations. A somewhat exotic group, these Welsh immigrants did receive assistance, and ultimately had to deal only with the trauma of adjusting to, and clearing, a total wilderness. Many other passengers deposited at seaports in British North America faced a far more uncertain future, and often far more public hostility. At the same time, the poverty and lack of direction of the self-propelled immigrant ought not to be overemphasized. Many new arrivals came with considerable capital—or at least access to it—and the funds they imported were a constant injection into the colonial economy, becoming as important as any other single economic factor in the period.

The Unassisted Immigrant

At least the passengers on board the *Albion* had the company and support of one another (this was probably critical, given their cultural background, which set them apart from the English-speaking society of New Brunswick), as well as public and private assistance in settlement. For new arrivals in British North America who sailed at their own expense and arrived alone— or at best, in isolated family units—adjustment was even more difficult. Probably most immigrants came to North America by themselves, paying their own costs out of often modest savings.

In 1876 a tiny volume was printed, by Messrs Hunter, Rose & Co. of Toronto, entitled *Life and Adventures of Wilson Benson. Written by Himself.* Born in Belfast in 1821, Benson and his young wife departed for Quebec in early 1841, making their way to Brockville by barge and deciding to settle there. The Bensons began with two sovereigns of ready money and a chest from which most of their personal possessions had been stolen on the way to Brockville. According to Benson:

> My wife hired out to do general house work. However times were so bad I could not find a stroke of work to do, neither in the town nor the country round about. My money was exhausted, and the first night in Brockville I took lodging in a tolerably respectable looking tavern; but after getting to bed, the fleas and bed-bugs appeared to be at war which of them should take possession of me. This was my first experience of bedbugs.[26]

As his account suggests, the Bensons had been forced to separate in order to find any employment. Benson moved quickly through a variety of jobs, none of any lasting duration. He tried storekeeping in Kingston, worked as porter on a river steamer, and finally opened a small store in Toronto and began a trade in vegetables and fruit with Kingston, while still working on inland vessels. Not until 1851 did he and his wife finally raise enough money to undertake to settle on some waste land—but it was probably the death of his father in Ulster that provided the necessary cash. Ultimately successful,

Wilson Benson was able to reflect in 1876 that 'it is a source of extreme gratification to me, as it no doubt will be to all the pioneers of my early days, that their sacrifice of worldly comforts and exposure to toil and suffering have so largely contributed to the development of our country and the welfare of succeeding generations.' Others who experienced Benson's peripatetic quest for employment and land with less success doubtless had a different view of the process. We hear mainly about those who eventually achieved their ambitions, not those who failed dismally along the way.

We also hear about the male, not the female, immigrant. While the preponderance of new arrivals was male, females came to British North America as wives, as children in family parties, and as single unattached newcomers. Wives and children played an important role in assisting their families, particularly in developing wilderness farms. From the outset of pioneering, the family farm was both the typical and the preferred unit of both settlement and production. While men's labour was required to do much of the heavy work of clearing the land, women and children did much of the planting, weeding, and caring for livestock. Women, of course, also bore and raised the children that were so essential as an unpaid labour force. An unattached woman arriving in British North America could look for

Philip James Bainbrigge, *Bush Farm Near Chatham*, *c*.1838. Watercolour. A 2nd Lieutenant in the Royal Engineers, Bainbrigge was posted to Canada in 1836 and remained for six years. He painted many watercolour views of Upper and Lower Canada and the Maritimes. National Archives of Canada, C-1181.

a husband in a gender-skewed environment, or obtain work among the servant class prevalent in every colony. Female servants were in great demand everywhere, particularly in the homes of the wealthier inhabitants of the larger urban centres. By the early nineteenth century, one in every five urban households in British North America employed at least one servant, and in Montreal and Quebec servants (two-thirds of them women) made up as much as eight per cent of the total population.

The difficulty of the transatlantic passage remained unchanged from 1790 to 1845. Even those few who could afford cabin accommodation faced voyages of six to ten weeks, cooped up in small quarters and living on bad rations; for the more typical poor emigrant in steerage, the discomfort and health dangers were greatly increased. As conditions worsened in Britain, especially in Ireland, more emigrants took passage whose long-term malnutrition made them particularly susceptible to contagious disease on overcrowded vessels. Moreover, after 1825 the British government abandoned efforts to regulate the passage in any serious manner. Given the fact that most new arrivals heading inland in British North America landed at Quebec, it was not surprising that there was a series of epidemics there in the 1830s, or that some of the population of the city became convinced that the British government was deliberately dumping its unwanted population on their doorstep. Conspiracy or not, mortality and suffering ran fairly high among the immigrants.

Since public policy was never mobilized to settle British North America, that process was achieved by the successes and failures of those who tried their luck. Most were not paupers, although many arrived without enough money to take up land, at least immediately. Out of their trials and tribulations, however, these immigrants from the British Isles, as part of the largest mass movement of population in human history, did succeed in transforming the colonies of British North America in the first half of the nineteenth century. Apart from their physical presence and the pressures they provided for the settlement process, the immigrants were also a great source of wealth for the colonies they settled in. If every immigrant brought on average only £10, between 1815 and 1845 that amount would total £10 million injected into the colonial economies. Catering to new settlers, mainly immigrants, accounted for one of the most vibrant sectors of the colonial economy.

chapter eight

The Resource Economy and Its Society, 1783-1840

Late in 1839 Sir George Arthur (1784-1854), lieutenant-governor of Upper Canada, asked his executive councillors for written recommendations on how land policy and immigration could best be reconciled. The result was a number of reports submitted in June 1840, including two diametrically opposed ones by Robert Baldwin Sullivan (1802-53) and William Allan (c.1770-1853). Sullivan, the son of an Irish merchant and a nephew of William Warren Baldwin, was one of the province's most distinguished lawyers; a member of both the Executive and Legislative Councils, he was once described as being 'liberally conservative'.[1] Scots-born William Allan, one of the province's leading businessmen, was the first president of the Bank of Upper Canada, heading that institution from 1821 to 1835, and first president of the Toronto Board of Trade on its founding in 1834; he too was a member of both councils. An ultra-Tory, he 'hazarded little in doubtful enterprises and had no fondness for speculation.'[2] The two men differed markedly over how best to develop their province economically, as well as over their vision of the ideal Upper Canadian society—two matters that in the minds of both Allan and Sullivan were closely linked. They offered two sharply contrasting models for economic and social development.

Sullivan suggested in his report that an agrarian society of independent yeoman farmers was the best way to achieve both stability and prosperity. He said that 'the only necessary inequality of condition is, between the small and the great, the poor and the wealthy land owner.' For him, any limitations on land granting 'to produce a greater inequality, founded upon reasoning applicable to other Countries appears in theory, as it has been found in practice, chimerical.' Moreover, he insisted that attempts to create a European-type society of 'master and servant, of Capitalist and hired labourer' would fail in a country where land was readily available, only retarding its progress by overpopulating it.[3]

William Allan, on the other hand, maintained:

The greatest drawback to the employment of Capital in this Country at present consists in the *high price of wages,* and the *extreme difficulty of procuring the labour* requisite for its profitable employment in *any* pursuit; and more especially in *agricultural* ones. Everything, therefore, that tends to lessen the *quantity of labor in the Market,* will also tend to *exclude capital from it.* But the main cause of the scarcity of hired labor in a new Country is the *Cheapness of Land,* and it seems to follow, as an irresistible conclusion, that the *Free gift of Lands,* must increase that scarcity an hundredfold.[4]

The British North America of 1840, from which these two different views were drawn, had developed over the previous fifty years along the lines of both simultaneously. Contrary to much opinion at the time and since, they were not necessarily contradictory. What is perhaps most notable about this confrontation of alternate visions was that both protagonists recognized a direct relationship between economic and social development.

British North America ended the wartime period of the American rebellion with an extremely limited economy and was in considerable disrepair. By the 1840s it could boast a very active, even vibrant, commercial economy based on its rich inheritance of natural resources and a growing transatlantic carrying trade. Without substantial economic growth, Britain's American provinces could never have attracted—and retained—the major additions of new immigrants who flocked into its seaports and filtered onto its waste lands. Economic development was always complex, never straightforward, and in most regions of European resettlement it was anchored from the outset by natural resources. Fish, furs, timber, and grain were particularly critical. These commodities did not constitute all economic activity in British North America in this period, but taken together with their ancillary industries, they represented well over ninety per cent of it. Natural resources, of course, require a market, and before the 1840s Britain's colonies found their market chiefly in the United Kingdom and within the British Empire, where trade policies tended to remain mercantilistic and favourable to colonial raw materials. In the 1840s, when Britain shifted to a policy of international free trade, British North America had to make significant adjustments to its economic and commercial patterns. But for infant colonies rapidly expanding in population, British preferential treatment for colonial raw materials constituted a major boost, and was at least as important an aspect of colonial growth as immigration policy.

The mother country provided not only the market but also much of the capital with which British North Americans developed their resource base. To some extent Britain's investment restricted her colonies to certain acceptable channels, perhaps ultimately constricting diversified economic development. But for a people desperately short of capital, early British investment was a boon to which there was little alternative. The American economy had not yet sufficiently matured to provide venture capital for foreign investment; the Americans used what capital they generated chiefly to develop their own internal market, which rapidly expanded into one of the world's most integrated ones. Subsequent American investment strategy in British North America/Canada suggests that had the Americans shown an earlier interest in their northern neighbours, it would have been in extending their own economy rather than simply in gaining returns on investment, which was the immediate goal of at least some British investors.

A colonial economy based on natural resources was inevitably one that ultimately depended on transatlantic and even international trade, but it also had substantial implications for society and its structure. The extraction and production of the raw materials of trade was a seasonal business, with the rhythms depending on the commodities being produced. Fish and grain required summer activity, while timbering flourished in the winter; the fur trade was sufficiently isolated as to have its own year-round cycle. Initial production was usually in the hands of small-scale commodity producers (such as farmers and boat-owners), who exploited casual labourers and were in turn exploited by the merchants who dealt with the commercial system of marketing. Most primary-resource producers had little connection with their international market and no control over the prices they received for their products, which tended to lead them to attempt to maximize production regardless of economic conditions.

As a small capitalist, however, the typical primary producer—whether boat-owner, farmer, or lumberer—identified himself with the commercial system rather than with his labour force, thus impeding the development of any working-class consciousness or the formation of an articulated class structure. Merchants had to be successfully entrepreneurial in order to survive, but tended to find it difficult to move beyond their immediate commercial horizons into wider industrial activity. Recognizing the value of processing raw materials, merchants were prepared to invest in such processing within their own sphere of influence, but not outside it, and the limited availability of capital further restricted their enterprise. The result was a highly exploitative and essentially conservative economy, with a fluid and somewhat fuzzy social structure. It was an economy that could celebrate the values of an independent yeomanry at the same time that it relied on a labour force that was itself dependent on the producers and merchants.

✌ Fish

The fishery was the oldest and most continually rewarding aspect of British North America's resource commodities, having been successfully exploited since the early years of the sixteenth century. Traditionally associated with Newfoundland, it continued to dominate that colony's economic picture throughout the nineteenth century, although in the period 1790-1840 fishing also became important for Nova Scotia and in the Gulf of St Lawrence, especially in the Gaspé region of Quebec. While in these years

Newfoundland cod continued to find its major market in southern Europe, Nova Scotia sent much of its fishing production to the West Indies, where Britain was able to exclude the Americans much of the time and give British North America some competitive advantage. Britain had also assisted her colonial fishery to a limited extent in the peace negotiations with the Americans, allowing the Yankees to fish on the Grand Banks and in the Gulf of St Lawrence, but restricting their right to dry fish on unsettled British shoreline, excluding Newfoundland. John Reeves, the island's first chief justice and first historian, commented in 1793 that the American Revolution

> has made an alteration in the value and importance of Newfoundland, which seems to me never to have been sufficiently considered. . . .It has become a sort of cul de sac; what does not stay there must come to Great Britain and Ireland; there is no longer the competition and interloping trade of the New Englanders so much complained of heretofore by the merchants.[5]

Great Britain would subsequently insist that the War of 1812 had negated the rights given the Americans in 1783, further increasing Newfoundland production: the fishery remained a bone of Anglo-American contention for many years.

The exclusion of the Americans was not the only change in the Newfoundland fishery that occurred in these years. By 1815 the dangers of warfare finished the migratory fishery of England's West Country, and the actual production of fish was almost totally in the hands of Newfoundland's residents, who grew rapidly in number in response to the situation. West Country merchants moved into St John's, which became the commercial entrepôt of both the fishery and the island, gradually eliminating both English and Jersey Islands interests. After 1815 the Newfoundland fishery stagnated for many years, forcing Newfoundlanders to diversify their methods and catches. Caught in the economic squeeze were outport entrepreneurs, who were replaced after 1830 by individual fishermen dealing directly with the larger merchants of Water Street in St John's. The Newfoundland fishery expanded into Labrador, combining fishing with sealing. Indeed sealing, which before 1815 had never represented more than ten per cent of the value of the cod fishery, increased rapidly in importance. In 1818, 165,622 seals were taken, and over 601,000 by 1831—when the value of dried cod and seal-oil exports were £360,000 and £197,000 respectively. Sealing employed 290 ships and 5,418 men in 1827. The markets for Newfoundland fish changed as well, with those in southern Europe declining in volume after 1815, those in the British West Indies holding steady, and those in British America and Brazil increasing substantially. Newfoundland's relatively unchanged production of dried cod was related less to declines in world demand than to increased competition, particularly from countries like Spain and Portugal that had formerly been major customers.[6]

While the rise of the Nova Scotia fishery did not directly compete with that of Newfoundland for world markets, it did prevent Newfoundland from gaining ground in the British West Indies trade, partly because Nova Scotia merchants were able to carry more diversified cargoes to the Caribbean. Nova Scotia had gained its West Indian advantage during the breakdown of Anglo-American relations that culminated in the War of 1812, and managed to insist that Britain restrict trade with the Caribbean islands after the war. In an attempt to expand its fisheries, Nova Scotia experimented with bounties and worked hard at building up a carrying-trade to the West Indies in goods from both the United States and Canada. A fishery that in 1790 had been mainly for local consumption employed 10,000 men by 1830, and was in volume about one-fifth of the Newfoundland totals.

The Gaspé fishery suffered from several disadvantages in this period, and probably never did recover the importance it had enjoyed under the French regime. As Americans were not excluded from dry-fishing on unsettled coastlines, such as on the Magdalen Islands, they were attracted to the Gulf of St Lawrence. In 1822, one of the major fishing merchants of Quebec complained:

> It is beyond any manner of doubt ascertained that many hundred American craft (chiefly schooners) catch their load of fish in the Gulf of St Lawrence and chiefly on the Orphan Bank, and many close to the islands of Miscou and Shippigan; as soon as the Gulf is free of ice, the American craft take their station so that before the 30th May there are generally several hundred on the Orphan Bank only and its vicinity.[7]

Moreover, in the assembly of Lower Canada attempts to support and protect the fishery ran up against opposition from the *Canadien* agricultural interests that were dominant in that body. According to Louis-Joseph Papineau, support for the Gaspé fishery 'was encouraging a species of industry the least proper for this country; for every fisherman they created they withdrew a cultivator from the soil, a pursuit that is infinitely more fit for Canada than any fishery.'[8] Despite this lack of enthusiasm, several large firms of merchants flourished in the Gaspé fishery, notably Charles Robin and Company at Paspébiac, which employed over 350 men between May and August and supported over 800 families in the district.

Between 1790 and 1815 the fisheries of British North America grew substantially, particularly in the early years of the nineteenth century when American competition was virtually eliminated. But after 1815 appreciable expansion did not occur. Nonetheless, the industry employed a considerable work force. It produced a significant export trade, and of course required a large number of sailing vessels, both large and small, which contributed both to the shipbuilding industry and to the carrying-trade capacity of British North America.

❧❧❧❧ Fur

That other traditional Canadian resource industry, the fur trade, was after 1790 a very minor one in economic terms; the total value of its export was only a small percentage of that of the Newfoundland fishery. Nevertheless, in a non-economic sense the fur trade was of enormous importance to British North America, since it provided the means by which Great Britain retained a claim to sovereignty over much of the northern part of the continent, especially in the vast districts west of the Great Lakes, extending across the Prairies to the Pacific Slope. The years between 1790 and 1840 were absolutely critical to the trade, for it then expanded geographically both northward and westward. Moreover, a bitter rivalry between the Montreal-based fur traders who gradually formed the North West Company, and the English-based Hudson's Bay Company, came to a head, the battlefields being Lord Selkirk's colony at Red River and the rich fur-trading territory of the Athabasca River system in what is now northern Alberta.

The North West Company

The Montreal-based fur trade—managed from the 1790s chiefly by the North West Company—had always been inherently expansionistic, utilizing its well-developed abilities to traverse inland waterways by canoe and portage to open constantly new territory offering higher-quality furs. After the American rebellion, the direction of the Montreal trade was largely in the hands of Highland Scots, while the labour force consisted almost exclusively of Canadian *voyageurs* and Indian trappers. The Montrealers constructed an elaborate, if flexible, corporate organization to run the trade, separating the market function from the trading one, and allowing successful traders who operated in the interior to rise rapidly to profit-sharing partnerships. Unlike other resource industries in British North America, that of the fur trade always tended towards monopoly, and the North West Company itself represented the end product of several decades of amalgamation of smaller trading concerns, with cut-throat competition and violence intimidating those who refused to co-operate. The Company always encouraged individual enterprise, and under its auspices there occurred a number of feats of overland exploration, including the journey of Alexander Mackenzie (1767-1830) to the Pacific in 1793, and in 1808 the descent to tidewater by Simon Fraser (1776-1862) of the river that bears his name. By 1812 the Company had successfully expanded to the Pacific Coast in the wake of the journey of David Thompson (1770-1857) down the Columbia in 1811. And after 1814 it largely controlled the Pacific fur trade, which to that point had been mainly conducted by American traders arriving by ship.

Despite its geographical expansion in the early years of the nineteenth century, the North West Company had serious problems, a product of over-expansion. These included a substantial increase in transportation costs and the lengthy time-lag between sending out traders with goods (the so-called 'outfits') and the bringing of the furs to market in Europe. The Company had no control over the depression in fur prices that resulted from Napoleon's closure of the Baltic in 1807, nor was it able to eliminate completely competition from the Hudson's Bay Company by reaching some agreement on the sharing of territory. Publicly the Nor'westers insisted that the chartered monopoly of the Hudson's Bay Company was irrelevant; but they knew full well that they were interlopers, and that if the English company ever gained the full backing of the British government in asserting its charter rights, the Montreal trade was in serious trouble.

The Hudson's Bay Company

For nearly 150 years the Hudson's Bay Company had paid very good dividends to its stockholders. Run from London by a board of directors who had never seen its fur-trading territories, the HBC was conservatively managed. Montreal-based competition from the North West Company had forced the HBC to move inland from its posts on the Bay, but it had not yet expanded into the rich territory of the Athabasca, and its total share of the trade was relatively small. In 1809 Lord Selkirk, and his family by marriage, succeeded in becoming important stockholders in the HBC, and attempted to reinvigorate the company and diversify its trading activities. After 1811, when Selkirk received a large grant of 116,000 square miles of western territory from the HBC, and began to organize his settlement at Red River—the very district where the Nor'westers provisioned their canoe crews before continuing their lengthy journeys from the St Lawrence to the fur-trading regions farther west—the Nor'westers regarded the colony as an open declaration of war by the Hudson's Bay Company. They, Selkirk, and the HBC were soon engaged in a desperate struggle for control of the West that lasted from 1815 to 1820. The British government refused to intervene in the dispute. In the end, with all parties physically and financially exhausted, the Nor'westers merged with their rivals in 1821, with the blessings of the British Colonial Office. The newly structured Hudson's Bay Company enjoyed the benefits of the HBC charter, access to capital and corporate management, combined with most of the personnel of its more energetic rival. Under the immediate supervision of George Simpson (c.1787-1860)—who was made governor of the Company's territories in 1821—the new HBC quickly became a force to reckon with in the fur trade, successfully freezing out occasional American and Canadian competition.

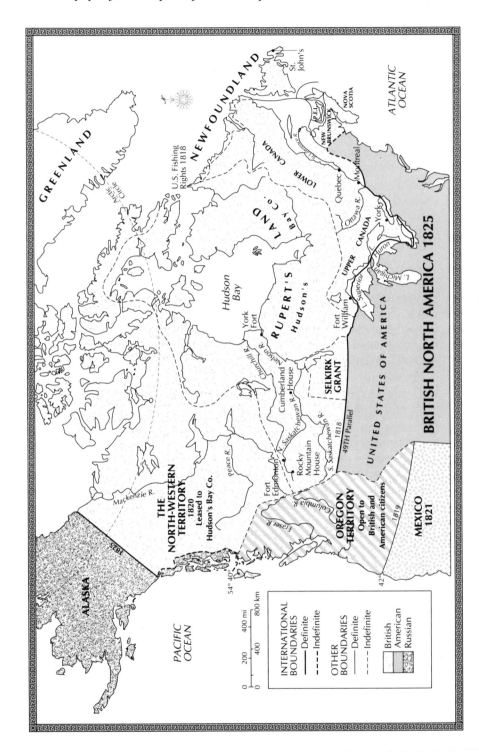

BRITISH NORTH AMERICA 1825

From 1821 to 1840 the Hudson's Bay Company attempted to maintain a monopoly position, not only in the territory of its 1670 charter, but as far east as Labrador, as far west as the Willamette Valley in what would become Oregon, and as far north as Alaska and the Arctic. It was not successful on all fronts, but it did succeed in controlling, both economically and otherwise, most of the territory that would become Canada's western and northern inheritance. Increasingly after 1821, the Hudson's Bay Company was employed by the British government as an informal instrument of imperial policy. Unfortunately the Company's settlement efforts, particularly west of the Rockies, proved less successful than its fur-trading activities.

One of the consequences of the disappearance of the North West Company was that Lower Canada, especially the ports of Montreal and Quebec, was forced to shift out of an industry that it had dominated but that had little economic future. Instead, timber and wheat became the wave of the future in eastern Canada, although the fur trade continued to be profitable for several generations, mainly providing British investors with a steady income. George Simpson quickly rationalized the personnel of the new company, retiring a number of men, some of whom settled in the tiny colony of Red River. Over-extended transportation routes continued to be a problem, but most of the traffic now went through Hudson Bay, or around the Horn, rather than through Montreal. The Pacific Slope became more important to the Company after 1821, as the Columbia River basin was deliberately overtrapped. Fort Langley was established on the Lower Fraser River as a major Pacific entrepôt in 1827, and in 1836 the first steam vessel arrived at Fort Vancouver—at the confluence of the Columbia and Willamette Rivers in what is now the state of Washington. Simpson pressed hard to produce self-sufficiency in foodstuffs at all posts, and by the 1830s the Pacific posts had joined Red River as sources of farm products.

By 1832 Fort Vancouver had over 400 cattle, and was producing 3,500 bushels of wheat, 3,000 of barley, 3,000 of pease, 15,000 of potatoes, and 2,000 of oats. New lines of trade, including the packing of salmon, were developed. The obvious agricultural attractions of the Far West, especially the Willamette Valley, led to the beginning of American settlement in the late 1820s. Pioneers trekked overland from the mid-continent in covered wagons across the fabled 'Oregon Trail'. The Company was able to hold its own against fur-trade competitors, but not against the constant stream of American settlers, and those in the Willamette Valley soon began organizing to demand territorial status and annexation to the United States. Given the relatively small value of fur production throughout the entire period, and the absolute decline that set in after 1840, the fur trade had a remarkable influence in the West, chiefly because furs were the only commodity that could be exported profitably; the entire region was organized politically and economically around the fur trade. In the organized provinces of British North America, however, the fur trade had little importance after 1821.

~~~~ Timber

Philip James Bainbrigge, *A Bush Road, Upper Canada*, 1842. Watercolour. National Archives of Canada, C-11818.

After 1790 fish and furs, the old staples of the northern colonies, were rapidly joined, and were exceeded in economic importance by, timber and grain. Both commodities benefited, particularly in the early years of production, from imperial preference, which gave them considerable advantage within the Empire, especially in the large and lucrative British market. Britain began colonial preference with a new Corn Law in 1791, and allowed colonial competitive advantage to grow, even with the famous Corn Law of 1815, which partially cushioned British North America from the general prohibition on the British import of wheat and wheat flour until prices became extremely high. In another Corn Act of 1828, the mother country allowed advantages outside Europe to all British colonies. By the 1840s Britain began talking about reducing the differential duty scales on wheat; in 1846 she ended, for all intents and purposes, preferential treatment for colonial grain.[9] A similar pattern prevailed for the timber trade, where differential duties were 'the sleeping partners of the Corn Laws'. The process of giving duty advantage to colonial timber began in earnest with Napoleon's closure of the Baltic in 1807, reaching its maximum effect in the period 1813-19. Extremely high duties on non-colonial timber were reduced in the early 1820s; but a distinct advantage to British North America was preserved until 1842, when the Peel ministry began to move towards free trade. A massive reduction in colonial preferences was introduced into Parliament in 1846, and thereafter the colonies' timber, like their grain, was forced to compete without much advantage in the British market.

Merchants in British North America lobbied constantly in Britain in favour of continued (or even enhanced) imperial preferences for their major resource exports. (It is worth remembering that while colonials may have been chained to the mother country economically, they revelled in the chains.) Every hint of change in imperial regulations brought a chorus of fears of economic disaster from the colonial mercantile community. The *Quebec Gazette* summarized several generations of argument in 1842 when it wrote: 'Our great ground of complaint is that British Acts of Parliament created the trade, caused capital to be invested in the trade, trusting to these acts, which by the uncertain character they now assume may ruin thousands. We never asked for protection; it was given on grounds of national policy.'[10] Not everyone in the colonies shared the mercantile concern, however— particularly for the timber trade, which was generally regarded as preventing young men from settling down to agriculture and encouraging dissolute living in the isolated timber shanties of the forests. But the fact remained that Britain did provide these industries with advantages in the start-up phase; her movement towards free trade came at a point when they had served—or at least ought to have served—their economic purpose.

While every province of British North America, except Newfoundland, became actively involved in the timber trade, cutting down primary-growth forests as quickly as possible with no thought for either conservation or reforestation, it was most important in New Brunswick, where the timber business permeated and dominated every aspect of life. Starting at an extremely low level, the colony's export of squared timber increased forty times within twenty years, to 400,000 tons by 1821, and its dependence on timber became almost total; in 1827, for example, over two-thirds of the value of exports from Saint John was in wood products. Expansion of settlement was closely connected to the opening of new timber territory, and jobs in the forests were available to incoming immigrants who had few other credentials but their willingness to work.

Although almost anyone could become a timberer, the industry quickly became dominated by those local merchant entrepreneurs with access to markets and to expensive licences to cut on Crown land. Licences required not only capital but political connections at Fredericton; and, not surprisingly, the timber princes became the leading politicians of the province. By 1836/7 twelve men held nearly half the province's licences. Below the large merchants, who were based in the port cities, was a variety of local entrepreneurs—storekeepers, brokers, sawmill operators—who organized hundreds of small parties that wintered in the woods, cutting trees and transporting them by river to the ports. It was in the best interests of the industry to do as much processing of the timber on the spot as possible, but the production of sawn planks (or 'deals') in place of squared timber developed only slowly. The British preferred squared timber, and little capital was required to cut it; it was more difficult to float and manage deals. Nevertheless, the shift to fully processed lumber was inexorable, and only enhanced the position of those with capital at the apex of the timbering pyramid in the province. By 1837 the sawmills of Samuel Cunard, on the Miramichi River in northeastern New Brunswick, were capable of cutting 42,471 feet of boards per day, 'the produce of 320 logs and 50 workmen.'[11] In that province, as in other prime timber territories such as the Ottawa River Valley, the production of timber was very much an industry.

Grain

All North American farmers needed a marketable crop or crops, but given the primitive state of transportation and the limited availability of markets, finding a profitable one was not easy. The growing demand abroad for wheat seemed to offer the ideal solution to the farmers' needs, and in the extensive agricultural lands of the St Lawrence Valley and Upper Canada, wheat quickly became the dominant crop. Indeed, many Canadian farmers of the first half of the nineteenth century were at least as specialized in wheat production as their later Prairie counterparts, exporting a substantial proportion of their crops into the international market. The marketing of wheat was much like that of fish and timber, in that the producers had little connection with the ultimate sale and distribution of their crops and were almost totally dependent on the commercial activities of the merchant exporters. Upper and Lower Canada had quite different experiences with wheat in terms of economic growth. The former re-invested the profits from great surpluses to produce further economic growth in non-agricultural sectors, while the latter not only became quite uncompetitive but was often even unable to produce enough wheat for home consumption. In this period wheat had strong internal and external markets, and it was virtually the only crop that could be transported for long distances and exported successfully. In 1840—admittedly a very good year—the St Lawrence mercantile system exported, mainly to the United Kingdom, over 1,700,000 bushels of wheat and flour.

Upper Canadian farmers quickly found that wheat was relatively well suited to their soil, although they also grew it in places where the soil was far less suitable because of its cash potential. Wheat prices depended on international and imperial variables, and Upper Canadian farmers quickly became accustomed to calculating their farming strategies in terms of the price of wheat. Relatively high yields were possible, particularly on virgin land, and farmers practised an exploitative style of agriculture that was not very much different from the way timberers attacked the forests. Instead of rotating crops, they exhausted the soil and then moved on, eventually to the Canadian West. By 1840, with the output of Upper Canadian farmers reaching new heights, the handwriting was already on the wall for the province's wheat economy. Within ten years the best soil everywhere in the bread-basket regions would be exhausted, and average wheat yields were already under twenty bushels per acre. Nevertheless, while the wheat boom lasted it provided for both commercial development and capital accumulation in the province. Most larger urban centres and major towns, such as Brantford and London, particularly in the more prosperous districts west of Belleville, served as export ports or terminals while supplying the surrounding wheat-growing region. As much of the western crop was shipped to overseas markets through Montreal via the St Lawrence, Upper Canadian wheat enabled Montreal to remain a major entrepôt, despite the uneven record of its Lower Canadian hinterland.

While Upper Canadian agriculture flourished, though lacking in sound agricultural practices, Lower Canadian farming passed through a series of crises in the first half of the nineteenth century. Until the first years of the nineteenth century *Canadien* agriculture was on a fairly small and diversified scale, producing for a limited local market, with wheat as the major crop. At the end of the eighteenth century a substantial overseas market opened up for Canadian wheat (which Upper Canada was not yet capable of exploiting), and Lower Canada was the first province to attempt to supply the increased international demand, although both the soil and climate further west were better suited to the crop. The older cultivated lands, often cropped for generations with bad agricultural techniques, quickly became exhausted when required to produce for this market; and the new lands were never very promising. As in Upper Canada, the pressures of a single cash crop operated against the less-extensive and exhaustive farming practices, and by the 1830s (if not before) the rapidly increasing population of Lower Canada consumed wheat more rapidly than it could be grown. The result was a permanent wheat shortage. Eventually this situation would produce a movement out of wheat by *Canadien* farmers, but in the short run the failure of wheat as a staple crop kept Lower Canada from using it as a basis for urban and economic development, as Upper Canada did. The wheat crisis was one of the reasons that agrarian discontent developed in Lower Canada, reaching its peak in the mid-1830s and fuelling the troubles of 1837-8.[12]

Despite the obvious importance of grain to many farmers, their dependence upon it should not be exaggerated. Farmers everywhere in British North America also produced much for their own consumption—cows, chickens, pigs, and the produce of kitchen gardens—that could be tended by the women and children of the household. The vagaries of the international market became a serious problem mainly if the farmer over-specialized, giving up self-sufficiency, or if he was in deep debt that had to be repaid. In such cases a prolonged fall in the price of wheat, such as occurred in the mid-1830s, could cause considerable stress and agrarian discontent. Some well-located farmers were able to supply meat and produce to adjacent urban markets, or to send crops like potatoes to places such as Newfoundland that were chronically short of food. In the Maritime provinces particularly, where farms had begun before the wheat boom and where neither land nor climate was well suited to that crop, mixed farming was far more common. Nevertheless, Maritime farmers devoted far more land to wheat and grain than was advisable.

The Mercantile System

The Merchant

Producing resource commodities internally anywhere in British North America would have been only a futile exercise without the capacity to sell them on the international market. Here the merchant capitalist was critical, for through him the production of the colonies flowed out and finished goods flowed in. The merchant had to deal with the transportation of goods in both directions, either employing the shipping of others or organizing his own. He needed reliable agents abroad, and had to deal with the vagaries of an unsophisticated international credit system that essentially relied on his own ability to turn goods around in an environment where it often took years to realize a return on previous investment. Merchants operated at a number of levels of volume and capital investment. Some—like Simeon Perkins in Liverpool, Nova Scotia, who continued to trade until his death in 1813—were small fry, protecting themselves against maritime disaster by operating and placing goods in several vessels and investing small amounts in a few more. The small merchant continued to find a place throughout the period, but increasingly the extent of the resource trade demanded larger entrepreneurs—such as Samuel Cunard in Halifax or the Buchanan brothers in Upper Canada. Large or small, mercantile entrepreneurship was both rewarding and financially dangerous. The ways in which failure could occur were many, ranging from disasters at sea, to miscalculations of the market, to inability to collect from creditors. The larger entrepreneurs were at greater risk than the smaller ones, and few merchant princes in the colonies survived to leave fortunes to their heirs. Because of the difficulties of finding trustworthy partners and agents, the extensive family network was still the international basis of much mercantile activity.

One of the few merchants who managed to leave a fortune to his heirs was Samuel Cunard (1787-1865), whose property at his death in 1862 was said to be variously £350,000 and £600,000. Cunard got his start in A. Cunard and Son, the Halifax firm of his father, founded in 1812, which was active in the timber and West Indian trade. He engaged in a variety of enterprises in British North America, diversifying and protecting himself relatively well. But even he experienced at least one financial crisis when the steamship company he had created in 1839 (the forerunner of the Cunard Line) with a number of Glasgow partners failed to make anticipated profits because of a British recession. He found himself overextended and in 1841 began borrowing money by mortgaging his property; a year later he furtively left Halifax aboard one of his own steamships to avoid a writ of attachment for £2,000. The Cunard family scrambled desperately to find enough cash—£4,000 was all that was required—to keep Samuel from being pushed by one creditor into involuntary bankruptcy. For many years Cunard's creditors hampered his free movement and prevented him from controlling his own enterprises; he liberated himself from them only in the 1850s.

The case of the Buchanan brothers is equally instructive and illuminating about the vagaries of merchant activity in this period. They were from a successful family of Glasgow merchants and industrialists. Younger son Isaac (1810-83) began in the Caribbean trade, but moved to Montreal with a partner to open a store in 1830. Quickly convinced of the possibilities in Upper Canada, Isaac opened a branch in York (Toronto) in 1832, and attempted to convince his elder brother Peter (1805-60), still running the family's affairs in Glasgow, to concentrate on Upper Canada. The two brothers opened a new partnership in 1834, based in Toronto and Glasgow, and liquidated other investments to provide an initial capitalization of

£12,000. They got credit from their family funds, a major merchant firm in Liverpool, and from banks in Glasgow and Upper Canada. The new venture—called Buchanan, Harris and Company—relied on Canadian wholesaling of imported dry goods and groceries (opening another branch in Hamilton in 1840) and was regarded as one of the largest mercantile firms in the province. From the outset the success of the business depended on Upper Canada's grain trade, although the Buchanans were initially not directly active in it. Concerned about government policy, Isaac ran successfully for the assembly in Toronto in 1840 as a representative of the business community. In the 1840s the firm expanded into the iron trade and grain exporting, and by the mid-1840s was one of Hamilton's largest enterprises, respected particularly for its close links to Great Britain. Although the Buchanans had negotiated successfully through the mine-fields of the international mercantile system in the 1840s, their prosperity was closely connected with the wheat economy of the province, and the company eventually went bankrupt in the 1850s.[13]

While the Buchanans began their Canadian operations on the importing side, other merchants joined Samuel Cunard in emphasizing the carrying-trade aspect, although seldom in steamships. James Peake (d. 1860) of Charlottetown emigrated from Plymouth to Prince Edward Island in 1823, and quickly became a major shipowner and shipbroker, selling Island-built vessels in the British market. Peake concentrated on smaller vessels, mainly schooners, for resale, keeping brigs for his own employment, chiefly in two trades: the timber trade between PEI/New Brunswick and England, and a general coastal trade, often between Nova Scotia and Newfoundland. Peake took advantage of 'fleeting opportunities'—as in 1845, when he bought potatoes from PEI for a New England market where crops had failed. But the basis of his success was diversification—into stores that sold goods he imported, into marine insurance, into ship chandlery and outfitting, which grew out of both his retailing and shipbrokerage operations, and into land speculation. Peake himself regarded his task as one 'to set an example and to encourage others to plan and build for the future in this place.' He added: 'Tho' others will no doubt have more capacity, still I feel it is my place, if I may say it, to be an engine, yet moderate.'[14]

Colonial Manufacturing

Merchants like James Peake were fully aware of their importance in the economic life of their regions, and in the period 1790-1840 commercial activity was the 'engine' of British North America's economic system, filling the Atlantic Ocean with sailing vessels with outgoing cargoes of resource commodities and incoming ones of manufactured goods. Some manufacturing activity did exist within the British colonies, however, involving relatively small establishments that engaged in two kinds of production. The first was by artisans producing goods and services that either could not be imported profitably or could not be imported at all: every town had its saddler, every village its blacksmith. Wheelwright Benjamin Chappell (1740/1-1825) produced over 700 spinning-wheels by hand for the Prince Edward Island market in the early years of the nineteenth century. But as well as the production of specialized goods for a local market, there was some processing of resource commodities. Grain was distilled into whisky, brewed into beer, and milled into flour. Wood from wasteland being cleared by farmers was burnt into potash, and timber was cut at sawmills into deals. But among many specialized manufacturing enterprises—both relatively small and ubiquitous—shipyards, which translated timber into sailing vessels, were the most extensive.

While shipyards were to be found everywhere in British North America where timber and open water combined—the commerce of the Great Lakes and the transatlantic traffic both required a good many sailing vessels—no place depended more on shipbuilding than Saint John, New Brunswick. 'Whatever Saint John is,' commented one of its newspapers in 1848, 'it must be admitted that shipbuilding and the timber trade have made it.'[15] Although Saint John was distinguished in the Maritime region for the large size of the vessels it produced, the shipbuilding industry there was craft-oriented rather than merchant-controlled. This characteristic was common everywhere in British North America. Merchants ordered ships, and sometimes—as did James Peake on Prince Edward Island—supplied material and capital advances. But they did not own the shipyards, which were controlled by master shipbuilders of limited resources. Before 1830 vessels built in British North America had a somewhat unsavoury reputation for bad workmanship and green wood, but after that year there was considerable demand at home and abroad for local production. The marine craftsmen who built the vessels became extremely skilful, and entered the élite among the artisans in Saint John and other places. By 1840 the Saint John merchant fleet was the largest of any port in British North America, and it was mostly home-produced. But since shipbuilding was done outdoors, it was as seasonal as the resource economy itself.

Shipbuilding was in many respects an ideal processing industry. It relied primarily on the rich timber resources that British North America had in abundance. It did not require excessive capital outlay for physical plant or materials, and its products could either be sold abroad or employed at home; the 'carrying-trade' was a major contributor to any mercantile economy. But during its heyday it was not an industry with either a future or a capacity to generate industrial spin-off. As early as 1840, with the construction of wooden ships poised on the verge of its golden age, technological developments of steam and iron had already begun to foreshadow the decline of wood. Moreover, some shipbuilders were content to import the finished goods employed in construction, such as iron fittings and sailcloth, and

Courtney Bay near East Saint John, NB, showing several types of ships under construction, *c*.1860.
Public Archives of New Brunswick.

Henry Francis Ainslie, *Entrance to the Rideau Canal at Bytown, Upper Canada*, 1839. Watercolour. An officer
in the 83rd Regiment of Foot, Ainslie served in both Upper and Lower Canada from 1838 to 1843.
National Archives of Canada.

secondary spin-off seldom occurred. Through the 1840s the industry was simply a monument to the mercantile resource economy that had so dominated British North America in the period from 1790 to 1840.

Internal Improvements

Trade and commerce required financial infrastructures, as well as what the Americans of this period were fond of calling 'internal improvements'. Banks could provide a common medium of exchange, but several attempts to establish them in British North America before 1817 ran into much political opposition from those who still remembered earlier French and Yankee uses of paper money. Finally the Bank of Montreal was founded in 1817, and was followed by the Bank of Upper Canada (chartered in April 1821, opened in July 1822) in York. Soon there were banks scattered across all the provinces, although they did not co-operate. The currency they issued was usually denominated in dollars, although most businesses kept their books in pounds, shillings, and pence. Banks also came to supply credit, first to merchants, then on behalf of governments, often for public enterprises or development.

Early commerce in British North America was limited by access to ocean and by navigable waterways with ocean outlets. An expanding internal economic system demanded roads, bridges, and canals to connect the bulk of the population with their markets and sources of supply. Most British North Americans wanted such facilities, but (as we shall see in the next chapter) they did not want to pay for them out of taxes. Canals were the great craze after the American success with the Erie Canal, which connected the Hudson River with Lake Erie and was opened in stages between 1820 and 1825. The Lachine Canal, begun in 1821 and finished in 1825, partially bypassed the rapids of the St Lawrence above Montreal. The Welland Canal, connecting Lake Erie and Lake Ontario, was opened in 1829. The Rideau Canal— linking the Ottawa River at Ottawa with Lake Ontario at Kingston—was a great military boondoggle, paid for by the British government, that was built with little regard to expense between 1826 and 1832; and the Chambly Canal, begun in 1833, bypassed rapids on the Richelieu River. The early canals either opened water access into Lake Ontario or improved the St Lawrence River system, and their whole thrust was to enable the economy to shift from a transatlantic focus to internal development—a process that would really take hold with the introduction of the railroad in the 1850s.

Early Cities and Towns

Trade and commerce, both internal and international, were the basis of urban growth in British North America in these years. Even a city such as Saint John, with a strong industrial component, founded its industry on the back of its trade. For the most part, the major cities of the British colonies in America were also the centres of political activity and influence as well as of its commerce, although it was easier to flourish without a government presence (Montreal, for example, or one of the growing cities of Upper Canada like Hamilton) than without trade (as Fredericton, the political but not the commercial capital of New Brunswick, well demonstrated). Despite its picturesque location and local political importance, Charlottetown in 1801 contained only about 45 families, including those of the officers of government and the garrison. No city dominated more than its immediate region and none was very large. Montreal's population of 40,000 in 1840 was at the top of the urban table. Nevertheless from the 1790s to 1840 most urban

Elizabeth Frances Hale, *Part of York the Capital of Upper Canada on the Bay of Toronto in Lake Ontario*, 1804. This watercolour shows Palace (now Front) Street, with Cooper's Tavern (facing what is now Jarvis Street), and the houses of Duncan Cameron, a merchant, William Warren Baldwin, and William Allen. In the distance can be seen the two government buildings and the town blockhouse, with flag. Elizabeth Hale, who lived in Quebec, was married to John Hale, then deputy paymaster to the British troops in the Canadas. Her painting of York—which circulated widely as a print—is somewhat similar to a painting by Edward Walsh, made the year before, and may be a copy. National Archives of Canada, C-34334.

centres in British North America grew rapidly. For example, York in 1795—two years after it had been founded—contained 12 cottages. Immigration halted during the War of 1812-14 and the population remained fairly static at between six and seven hundred; the town was occupied twice by the Americans in 1813 (the parliament buildings were burned), but it enjoyed an economic boom and some merchants became rich. By the time it was incorporated and renamed Toronto in 1834 it had over 1,000 houses, 100 shops, and its population was 9,252.[16] In 1837 Anna Jameson (1794-1860) wrote of Toronto: 'Two years ago we bought our books at the same shop where we bought our shoes, our spades, our sugar, and salt pork! Now we have two good booksellers' shops, and at one of these a circulating library of two or three hundred volumes of common novels.'[17]

All British North American towns and cities were still quite small in area as well as in population, many of them being collections of tightly packed buildings huddled around, and extending out from, port facilities. In 1834 Toronto was a rectangle bounded by Parliament Street on the east, Bathurst on the west, the lakefront on the south, and extending 100 metres north of Queen Street. In 1836 Anna Jameson described it as 'most strangely mean and melancholy. A little ill-built town [with] some government offices, built of staring red brick, in the most tasteless, vulgar style imaginable; three feet of snow all around; and the gray, sullen, wintry lake, and the dark gloom of the pine forest bounding the prospect.'[18] Montreal was not much better. One visitor in 1820 commented, 'The whole city appears one vast prison,'[19] and another added in 1833, 'the houses are all made of grey stone so that the long narrow streets look very dark.'[20] Americans were more impressed by Montreal than European observers, probably because so few cities on the continent had been built of stone.

Though urban conditions were everywhere still fairly primitive in the 1830s, they were improving. Saint John, for example, began constructing a wooden sewer system; but before 1840 few householders hooked up to it, partly because of the entry fee. The same decade saw in that town the development of a piped water supply, which in turn made possible improvements in fire-fighting capacity. Toronto was fairly typical for 1830 in lacking sidewalks, drains, sewers, water supply, and street lighting—which were all improvements of the late 1830s and the 1840s. Montreal got its drinking water from a series of aqueducts, first introduced in 1801 and converted to cast-iron in 1819; and Saint-Paul Street was lit with oil lamps from 1815 and with gas light after 1830.[21] Policing before 1840 remained largely undeveloped, consisting of a few ward constables and a night watch. Montreal got its first 24 'night watchmen' in 1818. For most urban centres in British North America, 1840 marked the break between remaining a town in the eighteenth-century sense, and becoming a city in the nineteenth-century one.

Thomas Young, *View in King Street [Toronto], Looking East*, 1835. The buildings on the left (north) are the jail, the court house, and St James' Church at Church Street (the steeple had not been built at this time). This drawing by Thomas Young (*c.*1805-1860), a Toronto architect, was included in his *Four Views of the City of Toronto*, a series of lithographs issued in 1836 by the newly founded firm of Nathaniel Currier in New York. National Archives of Canada, C-1669.

James Gray and Joshua Gleadah, *View of Montreal from St Helen's Island*, 1828. The Church of Notre-Dame, which had just been completed, can be seen on the left. Its two towers were not added until 1843. Drawn by Gray, the scene was aquatinted by Gleadah, along with the other views, and the set was published in London. National Archives of Canada.

❧ The Resource Society

The resource society of the time was dominated by two élites, having to do with government (including military officers) and commerce. It is not difficult to distinguish them, or to understand the bases of their power, although in most colonies their identity sometimes became confused when they battled politically, employing rhetoric that suggested deeper chasms than actually existed. By far the majority of the population belonged to the non-élite: small shopkeepers, artisans, minor civil servants; owners of small industries such as gristmills, tanneries, soap factories, and breweries; and resource workers and farmers. In the British context of making distinctions between those who held land and those who did not, few 'landholders' in British North American possessed anything but farms in the process of becoming, and most were forced to hold other employments, often working side by side with the landless. Women in this society acquired the status of their husbands, but those without spouses were severely limited in any upward mobility. Finally, native peoples lived outside the social structure, although missionaries kept trying to bring them into it.

The Governing Élite

At the top of the élite ranks of British North American society were two groups: the major appointed colonial officials of government, military officers, and the merchants, who usually lived in the capital cities close to the officials. Within the ranks of the officials, the governor or lieutenant-governor was at the top—by virtue of his position, the size of his salary, and his station in Britain. The first lieutenant-governor of Upper Canada was John Graves Simcoe (1752-1806), who founded York in 1793. Though he left Canada only three years later, he had hoped to establish an aristocratic society there. In fact his assistant Peter Russell (1733-1808)—who came to York as receiver-general of Upper Canada in 1793, was appointed to both the Executive and Legislative Councils, and from 1796 to 1799 was administrator of the province—perhaps unintentionally had a good deal to do with creating an élite in the town, where at first connections, but then mainly ability, mattered. Russell himself laid out the plans for York. In the process he acquired a large property stretching north from Queen and Peter Streets to Eglinton Avenue (including the present-day Russell Hill Road). To farm part of it he brought from England John Denison (1755-1824), who founded a leading Toronto family. He also brought his cousin John Wilcocks, the Mayor of Cork, to York. Wilcocks, who became prominent as a merchant and the first postmaster, induced another Irish family to emigrate in 1798: Robert Baldwin Sr and his son William Warren Baldwin (1775-1844). William Warren—a doctor, lawyer, and architect who married Phoebe Wilcocks, the inheritor of the Russell property—became very influential in Upper Canadian politics, as did his son Robert. The growth of an élite was

John Strachan about 1827, when he was forty-nine. This small oil by an unknown artist is owned by Trinity College (which Strachan founded), University of Toronto. Metropolitan Toronto Reference Library.

John Beverley Robinson, 1856, a sketch for an oil painting by James Richmond. Metropolitan Toronto Reference Library.

William Warren Baldwin. A lithograph, made after Baldwin's death, of a portrait by Théophile Hamel (1817-70), printed in the 1830s and now hanging in Osgoode Hall. Metropolitan Toronto Reference Library.

Robert Baldwin, 1846. This portrait was both painted and engraved by Hoppner Mayer, who dedicated it to 'the Reformers of Canada'. Metropolitan Toronto Reference Library.

also sustained by the native-born. John Beverley Robinson (1791-1863), the brilliant son of a Virginia loyalist whose father died when he was seven, was educated first in Kingston in a school run by John Strachan (1778-1867), an ambitious man who later became an Anglican priest and a powerful figure in his own right. Robinson became solicitor-general in 1815, attorney-general in 1818, and chief justice in 1829, an office he held until 1862.

The income, the access to credit and the style of living it brought, all encouraged colonial officials to emulate British values, particularly those of the landed gentry. They were anglophiles to a man. (The locally born Nova Scotia Supreme Court Justice, Thomas Chandler Haliburton, actually managed to retire to the mother country, though he had to write a number of best-selling novels in order to do so.) Their houses—typically designed in late-Georgian symmetry, with a columned front portico and extensive grounds—reflected their aspirations. Peter Russell's frame house, built for him in 1797 by William Berczy on Front Street West, was imposing enough to be given the name 'Russell Abbey'. John Strachan's magnificent house, also on Front Street, west of York, was popularly known as 'The Palace' even before Strachan became Bishop of Toronto in 1839. In 1819, the year after it was built, his brother visiting from Scotland is alleged to have commented: 'I hope it's a' come by honestly, John.'[22] These two dwellings disappeared long ago, but the degree of architectural distinction attained in the 'gentlemen's houses' of other members of the colonial élite of Toronto can today be seen in 'The Grange' (1817-18), owned by D'Arcy Boulton Jr, the son of a judge, and in 'Campbell House' (1822), owned by Judge William Campbell.

Not surprisingly, colonial officials believed in the balance of interests, and above all in order. John Beverley Robinson argued in 1830 that order

> . . .lies at the foundation of good government in the social state. . .by all who are concerned in making or administering the laws for this rapidly increasing country, it should be felt that we, in this generation, are laying the foundations of a social system which is to extend its advantages or entail the consequences of its imperfections upon millions who will soon succeed.[23]

Such men were well educated and usually very able. But they governed British North America with an extremely narrow and limited vision, though usually without soiling themselves in graft and corruption.

The most successful merchants—such as William Allan and Joseph Cawthra (1759-1842) in York—and a few professionals shared the lifestyle of the major colonial officeholders, but without their status. In part, British ambivalence about 'trade' carried over to British North America; but what really limited the social positions of the merchants was the impermanence of their incomes, which could be greatly affected by conditions in the market. The British system associated status with land because an income from landed estates was rightly regarded as far more permanent and inheritable than income from commerce or industry. British North America was never able to replicate the British landed aristocracy; the colonial official was one equivalent, but his income was only for life. Offices were occasionally passed on from father to son, but only by dint of special pleading and not through inheritance. In theory, the seigneur of Lower Canada ought to have been viewed as a landed aristocrat, but the typical seigneur was a good deal like the typical Scottish country laird described by Sir Walter Scott in his novels—too poor to try to cut a figure in the town and reduced to a seedy rural gentility. The Lower Canadian agrarian crisis had done considerable damage at the top of the seigneurial system as well as at the bottom.

Another problem with land was its sheer availability; an Upper Canadian back-country farm consisted of a larger acreage than many an English landed estate. Most land was held for speculation rather than status, although because of the tendency to emulate British values it remained important. Dr William Warren Baldwin in 1815 built a house on an estate three miles west of York that extended north from present-day Queen Street to Eglinton Avenue. He described it a year later as follows:

> I have a very commodious house in the Country—I have called the place Spadina, the Indian word for Hill—or Mont—the house consists of two large Parlours Hall & stair case on the first floor—four bed rooms and a small library on the 2d. floor—and three Excellent bed rooms in attic storey or garret— with several closets on every storey—a Kitchen, dairy, root-cellar, wine cellar & man's bed room under ground—I have cut an avenue through the woods all the way so that we can see the vessels passing up and down the bay—the house is completely finished with stable &c and a tolerable good garden.[24]

The sense both of satisfaction and of British gentry values is palpable in such a description.

Lacking a permanent upper class based on land, British North America instead began developing a social structure based on wealth and conspicuous consumption, which might be temporary but was certainly visible. Not all social standing was based on money, of course. British North America had more regard for education, professional training, and the life of the mind than did Britain, and the concentrations of professional men—doctors, lawyers, clergymen, educators—in the larger towns and cities were admitted to the ranks of élite society, although usually in an inferior position to that of the elected and appointed officials and the leading merchants.

The Regional Élites

While colonial officials and most of the merchants lived in the political capitals that were also the great commercial centres of British North America—York, Montreal, Halifax, St John's—a sprinkling of others in the hinterlands also assumed the functions of leadership. Every province had its retired half-pay officers attempting to carve landed estates out of the wilderness, and Lower Canada had its seigneurs. Every province also had its local merchants and professional men, as well as a few prominent farmers who had exhibited particular acumen or abilities, often in the context of a church organization. Thus Elihu Woodworth (1771-1853), who was deacon of the Grand Pré Presbyterian Church in Wolfville, Nova Scotia, was a farmer and cordwainer (shoemaker) with a sense of his own worth obviously shared by his fellows. Early in 1835, for example, he entered in his diary:

> Attended the Temperance Society in the evening. Was warmly solicited to join the Society—but I observed to them that the general disposition of mankind was to ascend in office rather than descend and as I had been President of a Temperance Society upwards of 20 years it would be rather degrading to become a private in my old age....Mr. A. DeWolf said if I would allow my name to be put on the temperance records I then would be appointed President.[25]

Somewhat different pecking orders prevailed in small villages than in the political capitals.

These regional élites were the men who were elected to the provincial houses of assembly, where they came to contend with the governing élites for political control of the colony. They were also the men who served as local justices-of-the-peace (or magistrates), and they tended to be militia officers as well. Sometimes such honours came as a consequence of local success, but in most instances appointments as magistrates or militia officers, made in the political capitals by members of the governing élite on principles never entirely clear, preceded other accomplishments. In most provinces these were alternative routes to regional prominence, which was recognized by election to the assembly and by appointment to permanent local civil office. Before 1840 most members of the regional élites would have described themselves as farmers, although they usually engaged in a variety of occupations, hoping through diversification to succeed and survive. Perhaps the most striking feature of most British North Americans was their lack of occupational specialization. Over the course of a lifetime most colonials would hold many different jobs, both in succession and simultaneously.[26]

The Non-élite

Sorting out the élite is considerably less complicated than coming to terms with the remainder of society in British North America. Theoretically, in a frontier society with so much wilderness or wasteland available at relatively low cost, the bulk of its population ought to have been yeoman farmers, or at least individuals on their way to becoming such. A number of factors prevented this ideal from being realized. One was the fact that in many places freehold land was simply not available. Such was the case in Newfoundland, on Prince Edward Island, and in large parts of Lower Canada still under the seigneurial system. A second factor was that unimproved freehold land, while often cheap enough to obtain, cost a great deal in labour and cash to develop. The less cash one had, the longer the process took. Farms could be carved out of primary-growth forest at the rate of only a few acres a year, at best, and in the 1830s the typical farm in British North America did not grow a substantial surplus for the market but was still struggling at the subsistence level, while its family of owners continued desperately to clear enough additional land to produce a marketable surplus. Further complicating the situation, fishing and timbering provided an alternative to farming for employment in the resource economy. Non-agricultural employment had several results. It could exploit a landless worker and prevent him from ever earning enough to gain land. While providing the small landholder with the cash income he had not yet obtained from his farm, it could also slow down his clearance of the land that would enable him to become a market farmer himself. Market farming, of course, brought its own set of problems, connected with external prices and demand, however much the farmer with large marketable surpluses was usually the envy of his peers.

The Poor

At the bottom of colonial society were the poor, who fell into three categories: permanent, immigrant, and casual; and into two major groups: those who had relations or friends to look after them in their distress, and those who did not, so that they had to fall back on public sympathy. While British North America was in some senses a 'land of opportunity' and a 'good poor man's country', it was absolutely essential to be healthy, or to have kinfolk prepared to assume responsibility for one's welfare. Those who through disability, incompetence, or misfortune (such as young orphans) could not look after themselves and had no one to do it for them, became the objects of charity or lived in squalor, like the child Maria Louisa Beleau, who died in Quebec in the winter of 1816/17, according to one witness, in a hovel

> NOT FIT FOR A STABLE. It is open in many parts of the roof, and on all sides. There is no other floor than the bare earth. It is a mere wooden shell; it has no window, nor any chimney. In the middle is a shallow hole made in the earth, in which there are marks of a fire having been made; and the smoke escaped through the open parts of the roof and sides.[27]

A second category of poor were recent immigrants who arrived without capital resources, and settled into the ranks of the impoverished in whatever port they disembarked. Unable to obtain enough money to move on, these newcomers (often Irish, who were less likely to meet sympathetic locals than English, Welsh, or Scots) merged into the third category, the casually employed. Because of the seasonal nature of most Canadian employment, however, the winter saw the body of unemployed greatly augmented by skilled artisans temporarily out of work; in some places, by resident fishermen unable to work for seven months of the year; and, increasingly in western Canada, by Indian bands that camped outside fur-trading posts in the coldest months and expected to be looked after by the traders inside.

Winter was always the most likely time to be seasonally unemployed—though timbering crews were active in the woods, snow, ice, and cold weather slowed down most economic activity—and also the worst time to be poor. Food costs increased; wood, no longer obtainable close to settled areas, became the largest single expense of the urban poor, who could not afford to obtain it in large quantities. Rural farmers managed to keep warm, though they could be just as short of food as the urban poor. Malnutrition and inadequate clothing, combined with under-heated housing, provided a ready-made recipe for the spread of illness and contagious disease in the winter. The poor were 'relieved' partly out of charitable instincts, but largely to prevent their turning 'by despair to commit depredations', or by infecting the entire community with contagious disease.[28] The preferred relief was some sort of make-work employment, combined with charitable dispensations.

Contemporary society in British North America tended to identify poverty as an urban problem, because in towns it was both more visible and easier to conceptualize. How could a family that was able to grow its own food and cut its own wood possibly be poor? In Lower Canada, however, decades of misuse of the soil on many seigneuries had produced serious problems, and combinations of crop failures, bad prices, overpopulation, and unremitting exaction of seigneurial rents did render many *habitant* families more or less permanently impoverished by the 1830s. The principal causes of poverty in this period—unemployment and soil exhaustion—remained untouched by a society that saw the poor in moral rather than economic terms.

Occupational Pluralities

Between the poor and the prosperous independent farmer at the top of the non-élite ladder were numerous occupational and social groups that defy rational ordering by any scheme but the most rigid and unrevealing of Marxist categories. A detailed examination of a few—such as the Newfoundland fishing-boat owner—suggests some of the difficulties. A property owner and an employer, the boat-owner was probably landless except for a small house-lot for which he held no deed. Moreover, he was typically in debt to the merchant who bought his fish and supplied him with essentials for both the fishing season and the winter. Encouraged to contract a debt, the fisherman soon found himself in 'slavish servitude'. This 'truck system' operated virtually everywhere in the fishery until well into the twentieth century.

In the timber districts and the fur trade as well, the truck system was not uncommon. But even if decent wages were paid and carried home by the individual worker, home was frequently a semi-developed farm on marginal land, or an improved farm of insufficient acreage to support a large or extended family. Huge portions of territory—such as in most of New

Brunswick, much of Prince Edward Island, and the Ottawa Valley in the Canadas—were dominated by neither agriculture nor timbering, but by a combination of the two. In these agro-forestry districts, timber-workers in the summer off-season did not join the ranks of the urban unemployed, but maintained subsistence farms, where they attempted to grow enough food to feed themselves and their families. Such farms did not have to face the market, for their cash income came from outside employment.

A similar situation prevailed in French-Canadian parishes that supplied large numbers of *voyageurs* for the fur-trade. In 1814 a British traveller wrote of the parish of Sorel in the Lower Richelieu Valley:

> The country people in the vicinity are mostly employed as voyageurs in the North-west fur-trade, and the cultivation of their farms is left to their wives and children. When they return home, they seldom bring more than enough to support them during the winter. The soil is thus neglected, and the town is badly supplied with provisions.[29]

Such an observation partly missed the point. Sorel's agriculture was characterized less by neglect than by the subdivision of extensive landholdings, a product of a rapid population growth after 1790. Neighbouring parishes producing for the market exported population, while Sorel's fur-trade income permitted its inhabitants to survive on holdings that were not really viable farms. Large areas of Nova Scotia, New Brunswick, Lower Canada, and Upper Canada (especially east of Kingston) consisted of uneconomic farms that were kept operating on a subsistence level by women and children—whose labour went unpaid and unrewarded, except when children were ultimately given parts of the family property to begin their own adult lives.

Even in districts of exceptionally fertile soil with access to markets, new farms being carved out of wasteland produced few surpluses or prosperous farmers. As Catharine Parr Traill noted in 1838, writing of Upper Canada:

> Even a labouring man, though he have land of his own, is often, I may say generally, obliged to *hire out* to work for the first year or two, to earn sufficient for the maintenance of his family; and even so many of them suffer much privation before they reap their reward.[30]

Traill discovered, to her surprise, that few farms in the making were capable of feeding a family, much less earning any return: she was advised to be patient and cheerful in the meantime.

As with the élites, houses illustrated the situation graphically. Settlers hoped to progress from log shanty to log house to permanent dwelling built of stone or brick. Most had seldom reached the final stage in the period of the resource economy. In 1831 Upper Canada had 36,000 dwellings, of which 75 per cent were made of logs and less than 1,000 were built of brick and stone. Most houses were small, with dimensions varying from 300 to 600 square feet. Size was a factor of cost. When Lord Selkirk, at the beginning of the nineteenth century, solicited carpenters' estimates for building a house—'30 by 40—2 Stories (20 Feet sidewall) cellar and garret'—the quotations he received ranged from £920 to £1065. A typical substantial 'dwelling house', thirty feet by twenty, might have an adjacent kitchen, often added onto the back of the structure. Length of settlement was the principal factor in the choice of construction techniques, although few Americans lived in hewn-log houses, and English newcomers were on the whole able to construct more substantial dwellings than their Irish or Scottish counterparts, reflecting the larger amounts of capital they brought with them. In 1841, more Irish lived in shanties, suggesting both their poverty and the lateness of their arrival as immigrants.[31]

An Ontario Farm with Partial Improvements, an illustration in *The British Farmer's and Farm Labourer's Guide to Ontario*. . .(1880), issued by authority of the Government of Ontario. National Archives of Canada, C-44625.

The Disadvantaged

Women in Colonial Society

Catharine Parr Traill also discovered that men found it easier to be in good spirits about the future than women. She reported that both

> are discontented and unhappy. Few enter with their whole heart into a settler's life. They miss the little domestic comforts they had been used to enjoy; they regret the friends and relations they left in the old country; and they cannot endure the loneliness of the backwoods.[32]

But women had more to be discontented about than loneliness. They seldom shared legally in any of the fruits of their hard labour; they were subject to control of their persons by their husbands; and they were expected to produce many children in an age when maternal mortality rates ran very high. Most women preferred marriage to the alternatives, despite the risks. In this period women married at age twenty-two on average, and thereafter gave birth to many children—more than seven for French Canada, on average, and more than six elsewhere.

At the same time, for an increasing number of women in relatively prosperous circumstances there was the beginning of a 'domesticization' of the household, where the home became the central social unit for cultural transmission and the pursuit of happiness; work-life became something quite separate. While males went away to work, women remained home, running the household and supervising family members—performing, often simultaneously, the roles of wife, child-bearer, mother, and household manager. The nineteenth-century tradition of placing women on a pedestal, particularly as keepers of culture and as civilizing influences, made them the focus of superhuman expectations, and many women became silent martyrs. It is not surprising that they were religious, and the dominant force behind much of the charitable and missionary outreach of churches.

As an institution, marriage hardly united equals. At least among the articulate middle and upper classes, the permanent and calculating aspects of marriage—property, status, children—were increasingly joined by elements of romance and intimacy. But despite the emphasis on mutual affection in marriage, men still thought that submissiveness and obedience were important qualities in a beloved bride. One prospective groom in 1829 wrote to his mother of his expectation that his new wife would not only 'unite affection & prudence in her conduct as respects myself' but 'that she will be an excellent & dutiful daughter-in-law.' Another male, contemplating marriage in 1832, hoped to find in his wife 'a true friend, a rational companion, and a useful assistant.'[33] For the most part women appeared to have accepted their role, although not always comfortably. Marriage, wrote one prospective bride to her sister in 1830, 'costs me something even in prospect to give up my independence, my power of motion, my hermitage, my philosophizing life, my general utility & alas some of my more particular associations.' But, she continued, 'I am more and more contented to make these sacrifices,' adding her feeling 'that it is perhaps the work assigned me by providence to promote his more important interests whilst I am at the same time convinced that I should in return incur no hindrance but receive assistance & encouragement on my own onward progress towards the great goal.'[34] The rationalization in these words is obvious.

Native Peoples

Between 1790 and 1840, in the settled regions of British North America, the native peoples were seen as being brought from beyond 'the pale'—but then they were systematically marginalized. Nova Scotia's superintendent of Indian Affairs, George Monk, well explained the process in 1794, when he petitioned the government on behalf of the Micmacs. In earlier days there had been room for all, wrote Monk, and the Micmacs had merely to learn to live in peace with the whites. By the century's end, however, settlement had eliminated hunting grounds and there was no place for the natives to go. They now had to be treated as objects of 'general relief'—at least until the authorities could 'rehabilitate the rising Generation to labour in some of the various works of farming till they know how to earn a livelihood for themselves.'[35] Thereafter, the Micmacs would never be at the centre of government or public concern. They were given handouts of provisions and land in the form of unsurveyed local reserves, on which land-hungry settlers would squat at will. In 1841 an aged Micmac chief, Peminuit Paul (1755-1843), wrote directly to the young Queen Victoria for assistance:

> I cannot cross the great Lake to talk to you for my Canoe is too small, and I am old and weak. I cannot look upon you for my eyes do not see so far. You cannot hear my voice across the Great Waters. I therefore send this Wampum and Paper talk to tell the Queen I am in trouble. My people are in trouble. . . .No Hunting Grounds—no Beaver—no Otter. . .poor for ever. . . .All these Woods once ours. Our Fathers possessed them all. . . .White Man has taken all that was ours. . . .Let us not perish.[36]

Within five days of its receipt at the Colonial Office, a dispatch requesting more information was on its way to the lieutenant-governor of Nova Scotia. But further information was not immediately available, and by the time it was collected British ardour had cooled.

Similar appeals might have been sent from native leaders in all the settled provinces, although in Upper and Lower Canada in 1840 it was still possible for native peoples to retreat constantly northward, beyond encroaching settlement. But in Newfoundland, retreat had not prevented extinction. When Shawnadithit (c.1801-29), the last Beothuk, died in Newfoundland, her remains were not fully interred: local surgeon William Carson (1770-1843) presented her skull and scalp to the Royal College of Physicians in London, presumably for research purposes.

Those native peoples who managed to remain 'beyond the pale' continued to have some independence and autonomy, although the reverberations of extensive settlement could be felt at long distances from the actual European presence. On the Prairies, the Cree and Assiniboine suffered extensively from a smallpox epidemic in 1838, while on the Pacific Slope the Haida began fabricating 'curiosities'—particularly wood carvings and cedar canoes—for sale. In the settled colonies, as well as in British Columbia, native artwork and crafts were becoming a major source of revenue.

Mobility

If the presence of large numbers of semi-proletariat, unclassifiable women and native peoples muddied the clarity of British North American society in the resource period, so too did the constant mobility of the population of the colonies. Some of this occurred in the form of outmigration from overpopulated districts, especially in Quebec, but much is extremely difficult to explain. For whatever reasons, the people of British North America were constantly on the move, seldom remaining in one location for very long. The constant turnover of population in almost any area had a profound effect on those who did not move, because the persisters were much more likely to be successful, both economically and socially. Perhaps they stayed because they were already on the road to success. But it is equally possible that those who could not bring themselves to be patient and cheerful, as Mrs Traill's informant had advised, contributed by their own movements to the success of those who stayed put. The notion is at least intriguing.

The overall impression one receives of the British North American colonies between 1790 and 1840—both from the reports of first-hand observers and from the detailed reconstructions of later historians—is of a great state of fluidity, of constant flux. Little was secure, and virtually nothing was permanent. French Canadians still remembered the Conquest, while most English-speaking settlers were either first- or second-generation immigrants. Fortunes could be made rapidly, and lost virtually overnight. Sickness and physical injury lurked everywhere. Given the vagaries and volatilities of life, it is scarcely surprising—as we shall see in the next chapter—that British North Americans took their religion and their politics very seriously, incorporating them inextricably into the culture of the time. Also unsurprisingly—as the contrasting reports of William Allan and Robert Baldwin Sullivan in 1840 suggest—politics continually reflected society and its economic verities.

chapter nine

Politics and Culture, 1783-1840

On 1 January 1835 Joseph Howe's *Novascotian* printed a letter signed 'The People', charging that the magistracy of Halifax had 'by one stratagem or other, taken from the pockets of the people, in over exactions, fines, etc. etc., a sum that would exceed in the gross amount of 30,000 pounds.' Those criticized requested that the governor prosecute whoever was responsible for the charges. Howe refused to divulge the name of his author, and the attorney-general of Nova Scotia began to proceed against him for criminal libel. Consultations with several lawyers produced little comfort for Howe, for as he himself later wrote, they told him: '*No*, there was no doubt that the letter was a libel; that I must make my peace, or submit to fine and imprisonment.' In 1835, as this incident suggests, truth was not a defence against libel charges at common law, and any criticism that belittled public officials or disturbed public order was criminally libellous.

Joseph Howe (1804-73) was the son of a Halifax Loyalist printer, largely educated by his father and through his own efforts, who had entered the family firm in 1818 and begun publishing a newspaper in 1828 at the age of twenty-four. Like most early newspapers in British North America, Howe's *Novascotian* was from its inception well integrated into the political culture of the day. The paper carried some international news, mainly clipped from newspapers brought to Halifax by merchant shippers, and reported on local politics in an official tone. It also pressed for local economic development, carried much mercantile advertising, and occasionally its editor allowed himself to publish a bit of poetry or a literary essay, often his own. Gradually Howe became more daring in his attacks on local and provincial politics, although always from the position that reform was needed to bring the institutions of government up to British models. When, in January 1835, lawyers told him his case was hopeless, Howe spent a week reading in the law. He may have acquainted himself with earlier British and American cases on liberty of the press, some of which were seminal. In any event he discovered that he did have a defence—of sorts. As he wrote to his wife, if he 'had the nerve and power to put the whole case before a Jury, as it rested in [his] own mind, and they were fair and rational men, they must acquit.'[1]

When the court met, Howe quickly admitted all the facts of publication, called no witnesses, and went straight to the jury. As a prominent layman, he had to be given a certain leeway by the court, and he employed it mercilessly to argue his case. For over six hours he spoke, at several points reducing jurors to tears. (People had longer attention spans in those days.) As a legal defence the case he presented was irrelevant, for as the attorney-general remarked when court reconvened the following morning, Howe had 'stated a great variety of things which could not be evidence, which are mere hearsay, and which the court would not have permitted counsel to use.' The verdict would hinge on the chief justice's charge to the jury, and that worthy—who had been one of those included in the blanket accusations of Howe in his lengthy speech—refused to exercise his power. He merely told the jury:

> In my opinion, the paper charged is a libel, and your duty is, to state by your verdict that it is libellous. You are not bound by my opinion. . . . If you think that this is not a libel, as a consequence, you must think that it bears no reflections injurious to the complaining parties. If this is your opinion say so; I leave the case in your hands.[2]

Within ten minutes the jury had acquitted Howe, and all Halifax celebrated, as if freedom of the press had been established in Nova Scotia and everywhere else. But it had not. Only in 1843 did the British Parliament pass legislation permitting truth of the libel as a defence, and even after that date newspaper editors in British North America were subject to many constraints on their freedom to say what they chose about public officials. The *Novascotian* case is important, for it reminds us about the limits of action within the pre-modern political culture of British North America in the first third of the nineteenth century.

ᴄᴧᴧᴧᴧᴄᴧ *Politics*

In pre-modern societies, government and politics were themselves the highest expression of the culture of those who engaged in them on something resembling a full-time basis. Such was certainly the case for the élite groups actively involved in politics in British North America between the arrival of the Loyalists and the beginning of the collapse of the oligarchies that had dominated the governments of the period. A full-time political appointment—with salary, pension, and the chance to be succeeded by sons or kin—was the ultimate ambition of most men engaged in politics in these years. Gaining access to such a world was no easy matter, and given the ways in which the colonial political system conspired against either reform or change, it was not surprising that some critics ended up trying to bring the system down through open rebellion. The principal political institutions in the colonies were the governor, his council or councils, and the assembly, with the Colonial Office an important element.

One of the obvious characteristics of colonial government was that ultimate authority rested in the mother country, which itself was controlled in this period by the British landed aristocracy, with a bias towards order and tranquillity wherever possible. The British government held an ultimate veto on every piece of colonial legislation (the 'royal disallowance'); made most major political appointments in the colonies (including governors and councillors) and paid them through the civil list; and influenced colonial affairs in a variety of formal and informal ways, including the parliamentary legislation that made colonial preference possible. When the British organized a Colonial Office in the first decades of the nineteenth century, a colonial secretary sat in most British cabinets, and supervised a small bureaucracy of civil servants who maintained the files of Empire.* What the British government desired above all else from its colonies was that they operate without causing crises small or great—certainly without introducing issues from afar into the British political situation. Armed rebellions were taken seriously enough, although what British politicians wanted when they responded to such troubles was resolution as quickly and expeditiously as possible.

Given modern practices, and the oligarchical nature of British government at the time, one might expect the British government and the Colonial Office to be susceptible to the lobbying of pressure groups with colonial interests, including the colonial assemblies. Such lobbying occurred, but was not particularly effective. British civil servants concerned with colonial affairs were not very numerous or powerful. The British system's real imperviousness to outside pressure was due to the fact that most demands for serious constitutional change originated with colonial (rather than British) elements—perceived to be either mercantile or populist in nature—with the result that the natural landholding bias of the parliamentary system came into play. Colonial lobbies, such as the landed proprietors of Prince Edward Island, were victorious less because they influenced the Colonial Office than because those who supervised colonies had a deep-seated commitment to land and to the preservation of private property. The decisions of the Colonial Office were more likely to coincide with the interests of some colonial lobbies than to be influenced by them.

Certainly the predilections of the British government were well illustrated by both the choice of colonial governors and the inevitable decision to replace them. Invariably Britons, colonial governors came to the attention of

---

*The originals of those files, collected in large ledger volumes, are still to be found in the Public Record Office in London, where they may be consulted by researchers.

those who appointed them through a variety of routes—often the patronage of major British politicians, but occasionally through their own efforts. For example, Sir Francis Bond Head (1793-1875, lieutenant-governor of Upper Canada, 1836-8) called attention to himself by writing a book about his exploits in the Argentinian pampas, and Sir John Harvey (1778-1852, lieutenant-governor of Prince Edward Island, 1836-7, and of other colonies afterwards) by doing well in a minor administrative appointment in Ireland. Most appointees to colonial governorships in British North America had some sort of military experience. All, however, found their situation inherently impossible. Colonial governors were expected simultaneously to be the local representative of the British Crown (i.e., head of state) and the local head of government, the equivalent of a first minister heading his executive. Inevitably the governor would find himself torn between British orders and local demands. Whichever side he chose produced conflict, and since the prevention of conflict was one of his principal duties, its emergence eventually produced his recall. Governors had a chance of success in this system only by dominating both houses of their legislature, but they seldom had sufficient patronage to accomplish this degree of control.

Governors worked most closely with the networks of colonial officials and merchants who made up their councils. In some colonies, such as Upper and Lower Canada, a distinction was maintained between executive and legislative functions by having two councils, but in most provinces one council served both purposes. The councils, centres of the élite political establishments of the colonies, were more or less self-perpetuating oligarchies that were described in terms of derision by their critics: the 'Family Compact' in Upper Canada, the '*Château Clique*' in Lower Canada, the 'System' in Nova Scotia and New Brunswick, and the 'Cabal' in Prince Edward Island. These groups were never as closely related or as tightly organized as their opponents seemed to think, but with the governor they did run the administrative affairs of their colony and also served in the upper house of the legislature. In the first third of the nineteenth century the councils increasingly opposed any attempts on the part of the popularly elected assemblies to wrest control of provincial affairs from their hands—sometimes by co-opting assembly leaders into their own ranks as one way to avoid confrontation. The various oligarchies tended to be composed of men of Tory stripe, who often referred to the levelling 'republicanism' of the American or French Revolutions with a combination of fear and disdain. Only in Lower Canada and Newfoundland was the oligarchy composed of a different ethnic group than its critics. In Lower Canada the critics were largely French Canadian, in Newfoundland frequently Irish.

The British had extended to their colonies the conventional constitutional wisdom of the time: the theory of mixed or balanced government, in which—in a single legislature—the governor represented the monarchical element, the councils the aristocratic, and the elected assemblies the demo cratic. All three branches were to act in concert in any legislative endeavours, thus preventing one from becoming dominant. In practice the veto given to each element quickly frustrated the assemblies, which sought unsuccessfully to obtain the right to initiate taxation and oversee financial expenditures. The British themselves did not understand clearly how their government had altered since 1688, with a monarch gradually slipping into a more ceremonial role and a ministry headed by a first minister owing its continuation to support in Parliament, especially in the House of Commons. British North America continued to be governed by the conventions of the late seventeenth and eighteenth centuries, which allowed the 'court' interests of governor and council far more power than the 'country' interests of the popularly elected branch of the legislature. No provision was made—and none was really comprehended—for co-operation between the colonial executive and the assembly. Lord Durham was quite accurate when he observed in 1839 that 'the natural state of government in all these Colonies is that of collision between the executive and the representative body.'

In most colonies of British North America the obstacle to the cozy working of élite politics was the popularly elected assembly. Newfoundland was not granted an assembly until 1832, although once it obtained representative government it quickly joined the others in the pattern. But we must not confuse popular election with democracy in the modern sense of the term. While the political franchise was relatively broad in most colonies, extending to most adult male property owners (perhaps eighty to ninety per cent of all adult males), only members of the local élites normally ran for election to the assembly, since only they could afford the time and money necessary to serve constituents in the often-distant political capital. Assemblymen were not paid and in most colonies not even reimbursed for their travel and living expenses. Most voters were prepared to accept this arrangement, and a 'politics of deference', in which it was tacitly agreed that only those near the top of the social pyramid were suited for political service, applied in most provinces.

Election proceedings of the time were quite different from today, particularly in the blatant purchase of votes. Despite the theoretically broad franchise, only a relative handful of men ever voted in any assembly election. This was chiefly because polling was centralized at the chief market town, balloting was open to public scrutiny rather than conducted in secret, and voting was frequently manipulated by election officials (usually sheriffs) in favour of one candidate. Voters were bought with liquor and stayed bought, since they voted publicly. Protests about electoral abuses were common, both in Lower Canada and elsewhere. As one *Canadien* candidate complained, following the Quebec City elections of June 1792 (which he lost by 26 votes): '62 Voters more on the spot presented themselves in my favor and formally protested even in the building where the election was held, from which they were chased by some gentlemen who demolished it by force, but they continued their protest and finished it in the neighbourhood.'[3]

The War of 1812-14

This war did much to cement the dominant position of the oligarchies in central Canada, where most of its battles were fought on land and lake. The Americans declared war on Britain on 18 June 1812 partly in response to Britain's searching American ships on the high seas during the Napoleonic blockade, and removing British subjects aboard them and impressing them into her navy; partly because the Yankees coveted Canada, which they once again invaded in 1812 and 1813. A succession of invading armies were thrust back through the major entry points: the Detroit/Windsor corridor, the Niagara peninsula, and Lake Champlain. In the process York (Toronto) was burnt, Washington was sacked in retaliation, and Fort Michilimackinac (on western Lake Huron) was taken and held by Canadian *voyageurs.* The British, however, were unable to win control of the lakes in 1814, and both sides agreed to a stalemated peace: the Treaty of Ghent was signed on 24 December 1814. By a diplomatic convention in 1818 the two sides would agree to declare the lakes an unarmed zone and the 49th parallel to be the Anglo-American border from the Lake of the Woods to the Rock Mountains. During the fighting the oligarchies in Canada—especially in Upper Canada—were able to appropriate the notion of their monopoly on Loyalism against a popular opposition led by Americans, and after the war to perpetuate the belief that they, as colonial soldiers and sailors, and not the Indians or the British regulars, had won it virtually single-handed.

Political Conflict: Early Opposition

While serious political conflict between the assemblies and the provincial oligarchies that governed in British North America was almost inevitable, given the constitutional arrangements, it was much slower to develop than in the thirteen American colonies half a century earlier. No tradition of constitutional political opposition had yet developed in British North America, and the British experience was in most respects not particularly useful in this regard. The aspirations of the assemblies in all colonies were associated by the oligarchy with the worst aspects of levelling republicanism, using two revolutions as evidence. Criticism of government was immediately rejected and critics were silenced by any means necessary, including violence. In most cases, however, removal from appointed office seems to have been sufficient.

In all the colonies of British North America with assemblies, early political opposition to the government interest was sporadic, and for the most part conducted from within the ranks of the élite according to fairly clearly defined rules of the game. It was acceptable to criticize one's opponents within the confines of the House of Assembly, not so acceptable to publish such criticisms in a newspaper, and it was totally unacceptable to organize to replace the people in power. Only occasionally did an opposition leader turn to the general electorate for support, but never with a concerted campaign over time. The absence of persistence can be partly explained by the swiftness with which critics who became too vociferous were suppressed or co-opted by the local government in power, partly by the difficulty in keeping together loose coalitions of legislative opponents without any consistent political program—except dislike of the ruling oligarchy, from which most of them were obviously excluded.

Most of the early efforts at opposition to the local governments emanating out of the assemblies were led by outspoken political gadflies who received precious little support from their fellow assemblymen: James Glenie in New Brunswick, William Cottnam Tonge in Nova Scotia, Robert Thorpe in Upper Canada, and William Carson in Newfoundland. The last three were all dismissed for their political agitation, complaining bitterly about such treatment. That all had held major offices—and thought they could use them as a platform for their criticism of government—says much about the political culture of the day.

Tonge (1764-1832) was a native Nova Scotian, a distinguished representative of the regional élite of the province based in Hants County. At the turn of the century he elevated his personal dislike for Lieutenant-Governor Sir John Wentworth (1737-1820) into a broader constitutional struggle over financial control of the provincial revenue and expenditures. In 1806 Tonge was rejected by his fellow assemblymen for his narrow obstructionism and was then unceremoniously dismissed by Wentworth from his major office as the colony's naval officer. Tonge used every resource at his command—including public meetings of supporters, petitions, and string-pulling among the highest authorities in Britain—to bring about his reinstatement, but to no avail. He fared better, however, under Wentworth's successor, Sir George Prevost (1767-1816), who arrived in Halifax in April 1808 and by December had appointed Tonge to office in the West Indies, where he died.

The Irish-born William Carson (1770-1843) wrote in 1812 and 1813 several pamphlets of political protest in Newfoundland, complaining about the arbitrary behaviour of officials and calling for the introduction of civil government. Governor John Thomas Duckworth (1747/8-1817) dismissed Carson from his position as surgeon to the Loyal Volunteers of St John's, an action that Carson was totally unable to comprehend.

Robert Thorpe (1764-1836), another Anglo-Irishman, was appointed in 1801 Chief Justice of Prince Edward Island, where he was not only critical of the colony, which he hated, but quarrelsome. Appointed a judge of the Court of King's Bench in Upper Canada in 1805, he quickly found sympathetic companions in a few Anglo-Irish critics of a government that he took it upon himself to disparage from the bench. Nominated to the assembly in 1807, he campaigned on the slogan 'The King, the People, the Law,

Thorpe, and the Constitution' and was elected. But his time there was brief, once he tried to form an opposition party. Thorpe's overall conduct was considered scandalous by Lieutenant-Governor Gore (1769-1852) and the executive council. Finally permission was received to suspend him from office. (He went on to more agitation in Sierra Leone.) Self-important and high-handed though he was, and lacking any sense of practical politics, Thorpe was nevertheless intelligent, and propounded some sound ideas: for example, the vesting of executive authority in a cabinet responsible to the local legislature, and the amalgamation of Prince Edward Island, Cape Breton, and Newfoundland into one colony.[4]

A decade later, government leaders in Upper Canada felt the sting of another gadfly. Robert Gourlay (1778-1863) was a self-admitted agrarian radical—he had studied agriculture after receiving his M.A. in Scotland and wrote an official report on the conditions of farm labourers in two English shires. He arrived in 1817 in Upper Canada, where his wife had inherited land. Land questions were a sensitive issue, causing much discontent. Crown reserves made huge areas useless; immigration from the United States had slowed down because of a decision to deny land grants to Americans; and militiamen in the War of 1812-14, who had been promised land, had received none. Deciding to become a land agent, and applying for a land grant, Gourlay prepared a list of 31 questions for resident landowners (drawn from Sir John Sinclair's *Statistical Account of Scotland*). He was allowed to publish them in the *Upper Canada Gazette*, appended to an address in which he contrasted the possibilities of Upper Canada with its actual state. In a second address, in February 1818, he was more strident, encouraging American immigration, thus challenging a government policy, and accusing the colonial government of 'paltry patronage and ruinous favouritism'. When he was refused a land grant (because he did not intend to settle in Upper Canada) his rage knew no bounds. His writings in the *Niagara Spectator*—against 'the vile, loathsome and lazy vermin of Little York', with special words of invective for Archdeacon Strachan—reached a provocative climax in April 1818 when he wrote: 'It is not the men, it is the system which blasts every hope of good and till the system is overturned, it is vain to expect anything of value from change of representatives or governors.'

For a while Gourlay attracted many supporters, whom he charged to organize township meetings; he was twice arrested for criminal libel and acquitted. He was finally stopped by a clause in the Alien Act of 1804 that allowed the banishment of anyone who disturbed the tranquillity of the province. Gourlay—who by this time had lost most of his allies and was subject to periods of mental disorder—refused to leave the province and was jailed for eight months. He finally departed in August 1819. He lived out his long life, besieged by mental problems, in Scotland, England, and the US—returning to Canada for two years, 1856-8, when he unsuccessfully ran for office. He died in Scotland. His legacy to the province was two-fold: his

Robert Gourlay in his late
seventies. Metropolitan Toronto
Reference Library.

Statistical Account of Upper Canada. . .(2 vols, London, 1822), the result of the
questionnaire, which contains a rich fund of information, drawing attention
particularly to the large areas of unused land; and, for later reformers, his role
as a martyr created by a ruthless oligarchy.[5]

The political experience of James Glenie (1750-1817) in New Brunswick
was as symptomatic as Gourlay's of the period before 1820. The province had
a built-in conflict between Saint John and Fredericton: the former the home
of vociferously democratic Loyalists; and the latter—established in large part
to insulate the government from such notions—gaining support from the
intending aristocrats who resided in and around the capital. Glenie was a
Scots-born former military officer (in the engineers) who had trouble with
the concept of blind obedience to orders on several occasions before his
ultimate settlement in Sunbury County in 1788. Glenie wanted to pursue an
aggressive trade in ships' masts, but soon ran afoul of Lieutenant-Governor
Thomas Carleton (1735-1817) and the loyalist élite of Fredericton. He
turned to fighting the government from the assembly—of which he was a
member from 1789 to 1803—proposing the appointment of new councillors
with 'European Gentlemen very well qualified who will not be Tools like
those recommended.' By 1795 he had shifted to public campaigning in order
to carry the differences between the assembly's program and the administration's behaviour 'into every County and to every Man's door as much as
possible'. The conflicting political issues—extremely difficult to identify—
were chiefly connected with objections to the oligarchical way the government operated.

Glenie was able to point to constant vetoes of assembly legislation by the legislative council, and to the need to control wasteful spending by an internal clique. He agreed that 'our Legislature consists of three distinct Branches, like that of Great Britain', but insisted that the model did not apply in British North America, 'where two Branches of the Legislature are in a great measure thrown into one scale.' After some years of leading the assembly to a deadlock with the government, Glenie was unable to sustain the opposition and was nearly defeated in an 1802 election (with 101 votes against 87 for his opponent); the next year he disappeared from politics, and he returned to England in 1805. The opposition Glenie put together was basically a collection of all those opposed to Thomas Carleton's loyalist New Brunswick. He therefore counted among his supporters—briefly—religious dissenters, merchants, pre-Loyalists, Saint John and coastal area people, and Loyalists out of power. But rhetoric could not hold such a coalition together in the absence of major issues or in the quest for the spoils of office.[6]

Only in Prince Edward Island and Lower Canada did something approximating political parties form before the War of 1812. From the very founding of the colony on the small island in the Gulf of St Lawrence, there had been bitter political infighting, and a brief attempt in the 1780s at an assembly-centred opposition to the corrupt government of Walter Patterson (1735-98). While there were plenty of potential public issues on the Island, the one that struck the most responsive chord with the ordinary inhabitant was escheat, a legal process by which the Crown recovered earlier land grants made to the proprietors. Other issues finally provoked a political organization, called the Loyal Electors, which established itself in 1809 within a society of 7,000 inhabitants, fewer than 300 eligible voters, and perhaps fifty members of the élite—officeholders, professional men, merchants, and large landholders in residence. The Loyal Electors proposed to consider 'proper legislative measures, to bring about the introduction of upright, independent men and persons of unimpeachable character in the House of Assembly' (the similarity to James Glenie's earlier call in New Brunswick is striking), and the reformers quickly came into conflict with the Island's administration—although not with its octogenarian lieutenant-governor, J.F.W. DesBarres (1721-1824), who supported the Electors.

On 18 October 1811 the province's attorney-general sent DesBarres a legal opinion on the constitutionality of the society of Loyal Electors. It was, he insisted, a 'self created permanent political Body organized after the manner of Corporations and associated for the purpose of controlling the Representatives of the People in the House of Assembly, as well as the appointment of Public Officers.' Claiming that the society's purpose was to 'obtain possession of the whole power of Government', he considered its views and principles not to be 'consistent with the Genius and Spirit of our Constitution.' As a result, the British government was easily persuaded that the Loyal Electors were a 'Confederacy of a very dangerous description', and the society was quickly suppressed.[7] That any organization should be officially crushed for attempting to behave like a political party speaks for itself.

Lower Canada was the most likely place for distinct political organizations to form, because race and language differences in themselves created both sharp divisions and informal political bonds quite different from the usual links based on opposition between 'ins' and 'outs', or political 'hinterland' and 'centre'. Political divisions developed quickly when the anglophone merchants who had dominated the first assembly elected after the Constitutional Act of 1791 found themselves outnumbered by an active group of French-Canadian political leaders, mainly from the ranks of the liberal professions in both city and countryside. After 1800 the *Canadiens* became increasingly vocal in the assembly, and a *Parti Canadien* was soon opposing the alliance of officials and merchants that came to be known as the *Château Clique*. Each group had its own newspaper, and the *Quebec Mercury* and *Le Canadien* thundered at one another across a growing gulf. A new land tax to build a prison in 1805 served as a focus for criticism of government, and Governor Sir James Craig (1748-1812) attempted to suppress *Le Canadien*, which from 1808 to 1810 was feeling its way towards an ideology of opposition. However, the newspaper's editorial position, mainly articulated by its fiery editor Pierre-Stanislas Bédard (1762-1829), supported in these early years concepts of British liberty and British institutions, including the balance of powers.

For Bédard, writing in 1809, the British constitution represented 'perhaps the only one under which the interests and rights of the various classes composing society are so carefully arranged, so wisely set off against one another and linked to one another as a whole, that they illuminate and sustain one another through the very conflict which results from the simultaneous exercise of the powers that are entrusted to [these classes].' He argued, however, that the way in which power was being administered in his province was wrong, for it did not reflect the balance of interests. He also recognized that maladministration jeopardized the position of the governor in the balanced constitution, for 'it lays the king's representative open to the danger of losing the people's confidence through his ministers' errors.' But unlike his compatriots in other colonies, who did not face a racial split, Bédard also recognized that 'a governor cannot have the English party, the party of the government, on his side without adopting all its ideas, prejudices, and plans against the Canadians.' Bédard's successor as leader of the *Canadien* party—Louis-Joseph Papineau after 1815—built more on his racial analysis than on his constitutional theory: and when Bédard retired in 1819, he insisted that 'Mr Papineau and Mr Viger [another spokesman for the *Canadiens*] are no real friends of mine.'[8]

◞◟◞◟◞◟ *Political Conflict After 1820*

Upper Canada

As a result of the election of 1824, the assembly of Upper Canada had a majority of members critical of the executive—for the first time in its history. They included Peter Perry (1793-1850), a public-spirited land-owner; Dr John Rolph (1793-1870), an English-born lawyer and doctor; and Marshall Spring Bidwell (1799-1872), an American-born lawyer, son of Barnabas Bidwell (1763-1833), who had sat briefly in the assembly in 1821. In the election of 1828 these critics, now known as reformers, increased their majority with the addition of (among others) the American-born business-man Jesse Ketchum (1782-1867) and Dr William Warren Baldwin—who was very much a member of the élite in the sense of being wealthy, educated, and a considerable landowner, but who was also a dedicated reformer, highly critical of the 'arbitrary, oppressive, and high-handed conduct of the Colonial Executive'.[9] These men were moderate reformers, most of them profession-als who could debate with the Tories more or less as equals and mix with them socially. This was not true of another new member, a self-styled independent, the Scots-born William Lyon Mackenzie (1795-1861), whose increasingly radical voice had been heard in his newspaper the *Colonial Advocate* for four years, and who had campaigned for this election by distributing a pamphlet entitled 'The Legislative Black List of Upper Canada:

William Lyon Mackenzie, an oil portrait painted in 1834, after he became mayor of Toronto. Mackenzie House, Toronto.

or Official Corruption and Hypocrisy Unmasked', in which he rated members of the assembly according to the way they had voted in past sessions. Over the next nine years Mackenzie became more and more of a disruptive influence on the work of the other reformers, most of whom gradually distanced themselves from him.

When Sir Peregrine Maitland (1774-1854) give up the office of lieutenant-governor of Upper Canada in November 1828, he may have taken pride in the fact that during his tenure the population had increased greatly; progress had been made in creating new townships and building roads, schools, mills, and canals; and a provincial bank had been established. On the other hand, more and more people had grievances, and these had caught the attention of the British House of Commons, which appointed a commission of inquiry. Its *Report*, which preceded Maitland's departure by a few weeks, accepted many of the reformers' criticisms of his administration.

Among their grievances was the Naturalization (or Alien) Bill, passed in 1826, which refused British citizenship and its privileges to Americans who had not lived in the province for seven years, declared allegiance to the King, and renounced allegiance to the United States. Many long-established Upper Canadians—the Bidwells, for example—could therefore be considered aliens, although some of them sat in the assembly. They, and Mackenzie's *Colonial Advocate*, attacked the bill and a petition was taken to England. The next year the colonial secretary, Lord Goderich, disallowed it, making it possible for the Canadian legislature to pass a law automatically conferring citizenship on settlers who had come into the province before 1820, and requiring a seven-year waiting period only for those who had arrived after that year.

There were other grievances, such as the clergy reserves, provided for in the Constitutional Act of 1791, which set aside one-seventh of the public lands of Upper Canada 'for the Support and Maintenance of a Protestant Clergy' (interpreted as the Church of England). The reserved land created large tracts that few people wanted to rent, because land was so easily purchased; moreover, this unused land separated settlers from each other, created drainage problems, and made difficult the building and maintenance of roads. Though the reserves were virtually non-productive of income, the Presbyterians objected to them as a matter of principle, and because the potential of their more than two million acres was very great. (The House of Commons committee denied the exclusive claims of the Church of England to the clergy reserves; they were secularized in 1854.) There was also the fact that the judiciary was not independent of the Crown, with the chief justice sitting on the executive council and other judges on the legislative council, of which the chief justice was speaker. (The committee ruled that judges, except for the chief justice, should not be on either council.) Yet another grievance was that control of most of the revenues raised in the province belonged to the executive: the committee recommended that public revenue be placed under public control. Of all the grievances, the paramount one was perhaps the stranglehold of the governing élite, the so-called Family Compact, with its fear of the 'unbridled democratic will' of the assembly and its rejection of anyone who criticized the government in any way.[10]

COLONIAL ADVOCATE.
Thursday, Nov. 22. 1832.

HUZZA FOR MACKENZIE!!!

To the Poll! To the Poll!!
Gentlemen—*We expect to see you next Monday at the Election! Herein fail not!! Huzza for the County of York!!! Wake up! and awaken your sleepy neighbours!! Your rights are invaded!!! To the Poll!! To the Poll!!!*

In the election of 1830 the reformers were greatly reduced in number, but their morale was sustained by the election in Britain of a Whig government in 1831, and by the introduction of the Reform Bill, its defeat followed by its victory in 1832—the year Mackenzie visited London, where he met the leading radicals and presented his grievances to Lord Goderich. Mackenzie's spirits, and his hatred of government, had risen to new heights when he published in the *Colonial Advocate* (1 December 1831) a piece that contained the statement:

> Our representative body has degenerated into a sycophantic office for registering the decrees of as mean and mercenary an executive as was ever given as a punishment for the sins of any part of North America in the nineteenth century.[11]

This comment was considered libellous and Mackenzie was expelled, to be triumphantly re-elected a few weeks later by the York County farmers and tradesmen who were his followers, and who presented him with a medal 'as a token of their approbation of his political career'. He was almost immediately expelled again, and re-elected—a pattern that was repeated several times more. Of his expulsions, Peter Perry was reported to have said publicly: 'No two persons disapproved more at times of Mr Mackenzie's occasional violence than Mr Bidwell and himself, but they both supported him on principle, seeing that the people had been insulted in his person.'[12]

But in March 1834 Mackenzie became the first mayor of Toronto, and in October he was returned to the assembly, which once again had a majority of reformers, who were now seen to be made up of both moderates and radicals. When the two groups united in passing various reformist bills that came to nothing once they reached the legislative council, Mackenzie then began to think in terms of pressuring the government from outside the assembly. In the meantime, he persuaded that body to set up a Committee on Grievances, with him as chairman, allowing him to summon a parade of government officials and other citizens (from February to April 1835) to answer his pointed questions. The 500-page *Seventh Report from the Select Committee of the House of Assembly of Upper Canada on Grievances* was jumbled, often inaccurate, and filled with impractical schemes, but it was nevertheless a highly detailed and revealing account of the condition of Upper Canada. Two thousand copies were printed, and it found its way to the new colonial secretary, Lord Glenelg. Receiving it as the voice of the assembly—Glenelg did not know that it was only reluctantly endorsed by that body, or that some moderate reformers, including Peter Perry, voted against it because of its inaccuracies and virulent exaggerations and indictments—he recalled Sir John Colborne (1778-1863), who had succeeded Maitland as lieutenant-governor.

The Radical Reformers

The new generation of political critics that emerged in British North America between 1820 and 1840 were both more stubborn and more willing than their predecessors to invoke popular support on behalf of their attacks on the prevailing oligarchies. Three reformers stand out in this period besides Mackenzie of Upper Canada: Louis-Joseph Papineau (1786-1871) of Lower Canada, Joseph Howe of Nova Scotia, and William Cooper (1786-1867) of Prince Edward Island. Only Howe would actually survive the political turmoil he created to run a colony. Mackenzie and Papineau would spend years in exile after abortive rebellions they had sponsored out of frustration at being unable to change the constitutional system. Cooper eventually drifted off to California, his political movement finished with little to show for it. None of these men actually overturned the political system of the élites, but they made some inroads against it—anticipating in a variety of ways a gradual democratization of politics in British North America.

All four reformers were radical-sounding in their rhetoric, with Papineau—seigneur of Montebello on the Ottawa River, a lawyer and member of the assembly since 1809 and three times its Speaker—the most socially conservative, and William Cooper the most profoundly democratic. These men all believed in the importance of Cooper's ideal of the 'independent cultivator of the soil', displaying profound hostility to commerce, the merchant classes, and expensive economic development by the public sector. Equality of conditions was what mattered. Both Papineau and Mackenzie turned to the American ideas of Jacksonian democracy in the 1830s when

Louis-Joseph Papineau.
National Archives of Canada,
C-5435.

they found themselves unable either to persuade the British government of the inadequacy of existing constitutional arrangements, or to alter the system by political activity. As Papineau explained, the aristocratic nature of the political constitution went against the democratic nature of the social constitution in the Canadas, 'where every one is born, lives and dies a democrat; because every one is an owner; because every one has a small piece of property. . . .'[13]

In Prince Edward Island, where not everyone was an owner, William Cooper led a political party devoted to escheat, a process by which the large landholders would be stripped of their holdings and the land redistributed to those who actually tilled the soil. Once his party was triumphant in the assembly in 1838, Cooper himself became an official delegate to the British government to put the case for the tenants before the ministry. He crossed the Atlantic in a timber vessel in steerage to save money, and when the British authorities refused to consult with him, he was helpless. He returned to the Island and could do nothing but encourage his party to legislation, petitions, and memorials—all of which were rendered useless by the refusal of the legislative council and the lieutenant-governor to endorse them.

What all these reformers shared was a desire to overturn the 'corrupt' oligarchies that ran their respective provinces, replacing them with administrations that were 'responsible to the province'* as represented in the House of Assembly. They could also agree, as a result of their agrarian and anti-mercantile assumptions, that public 'improvements' paid for out of the public purse or sponsored by the government—such as canals and banks—were not only imposed on their provinces by the oligarchies, but represented an unnecessary financial burden on the taxpayer, since they were in effect 'class legislation'. As Mackenzie argued, the 'true source of a country's wealth' was 'labour usefully and prudently applied'. This assertion led to the rhetorical query:

> In what way are the services of a Bank, like the Bank of Upper Canada, the Kingston Bank, or any other institution issuing promises to pay gold and silver on demand in almost unlimited quantity, required to produce the wealth and prosperity I have shewn to be the result of labour and industry usefully applied?

His answer, of course, was simple: 'In no way whatever.'[14] For Papineau in Lower Canada, an active economic state was being dominated not only by the mercantile class, but by a *British* mercantile class, which promoted capitalism in all ways.

In December 1834, when Papineau told the electors of Montreal West to withdraw their money from banks, he declared:

> They will call that destroying trade, whereas in reality it will merely be escaping from enemy hands to fall into friendly ones. Producers will continue their habits of work and economy, the only important sources of a country's wealth. Whether there are banks or not, there will not be one acre more farmed, or one acre less. From the moment that there is a surplus of exchangeable produce, the European capitalists, in view of the profit they would derive from it, will have bought it up.[15]

It is in this context—the struggle between commercial capitalism and agrarianism—that we must understand both the Tory commitment to public involvement in economic activity and the reform opposition. These reformers were in no way precursors of socialism, for they had no conception that public economic development could be executed on behalf of the people, any more than they had a general conception of any positive role for the state in ensuring the social well-being of its citizenry. These men were instead nineteenth-century liberals who sought to reduce the influence of government on the lives of the population, as well as the temptation to insist on special privileges. As Mackenzie wrote in a broadside entitled *Independence* in late November 1837: 'We contend, that in all laws made, or to be made,

---

*This phrase, of September 1830, is Mackenzie's. But the idea of responsible government was first articulated, in letters of 1828 to colonial authorities, by William Warren Baldwin, influenced by his son Robert—under whose ministry in the Province of Canada (shared by Louis-H. La Fontaine) it came into effect in 1848.

every person shall be bound alike—neither should any tenure, estate, charter, degree, birth or place, confer any exemption from the ordinary course of legal proceedings and responsibilities whereunto others are subjected.'[16]

Political Violence and Rebellion

Political violence was hardly something invented in 1837—it was common throughout this era. Though sometimes spontaneous, it was often carefully calculated for partisan purposes. The age was itself a violent one, with tensions always exacerbated by ethnic and religious divisions carried over from the Old Country, fuelled by liquor, and often harnessed by the élite for its own purposes. Occasionally members of the élite themselves engaged in mob activity, although almost always disguised. Thus a 'mob' of fifteen young Tories, dressed as Indians, smashed William Lyon Mackenzie's printing press in 1826, partly as retaliation for his scurrilous attacks on leading members of the Family Compact. At one 1832 poll on Prince Edward Island voters began to be noisy in mid-afternoon and threatened to pull down the hustings. They were quieted by threats, 'except when the Returning Officer was administering the Oath, which generally excited a noise.' Finally, about 7 p.m.,

> while the Returning Officer was speaking to an Elector as to his qualification, the Hustings were pulled down—the Deputy Sheriff and the Candidates thrown to the ground—and the Boards of which the Hustings were made, and the barrels which supported them, were thrown into the air—a barrel in falling struck the Returning Officer on the shoulder.[17]

Although polling was again resumed, the onlookers began to throw sticks and stones at both doors of the barn in which the voting was taking place, eventually forcing the returning officer to close the poll without proclaiming candidate William Cooper (who spent the time of the riot hiding in the barn) duly elected. A year later in Farmersville, Upper Canada, a political meeting was interrupted by a gang of Orangemen wielding a 'number of Shillalahs', in the course of which 'a number of persons received contusions and the Chairman was severely cut on the head.'[18]

Most large-scale violence erupted in conjunction with nominating meetings and electoral polling. It was common in districts where ethnic or denominational groups conflicted, and was particularly intense where ethnic lines overlapped with denominational ones, producing what contemporaries usually referred to as 'sectarian' controversy. Before 1840 sectarian conflict was kept to a minimum by the tendency for cohesive ethnic and confessional groups to settle together in nodes of population separated from their neighbours by large extents of waste land. This sort of settlement pattern meant that the conflicting groups came together only on a few occasions, notably election day. But in places like Newfoundland—where Protestant and Catholic, English and Irish, boat-owner and non-owner, tory and liberal, all contended together—electoral violence was part of a way of life.

The Rebellions of 1837

The mob was the political expression of the ordinary inhabitant, who was not usually at the centre of political events in this period. Nevertheless, the dominant cultural expression in the British colonies between 1790 and 1840 was in politics, where the élite culture suffered a crisis in the late 1830s that would not so much transform it as liberalize it. This change was brought about in Upper and Lower Canada by rebellions, which were a conflict between élite leadership and vernacular opposition. These uprisings can be viewed in a variety of ways: as political events, as cultural manifestations, as illustrations of subterranean pressures resulting from agrarian discontent; or, in Lower Canada, as an expression of English-French animosity. They were a combination of all these things. Had the rebellions not been so quickly suppressed, similar uprisings might well have broken out in the eastern provinces, particularly in Prince Edward Island, where agrarian and political discontents were also strong.

The Rebellions of 1837 challenged the stable political culture of the élites in the Canadas. The ostensible leaders, William Lyon Mackenzie and Louis-Joseph Papineau, became completely frustrated in their attempts to wrest control of the government from the hands of the powerful cliques of Toronto and Quebec and put it into the hands of the popularly elected assemblies. The so-called 'popular parties' in the assemblies of the Canadas (or elsewhere) were in large part dominated by regional élites, discussed in the previous chapter, representing more the grass-roots countryside than the traditional power structure. They were prepared to come to terms with a more pluralistic political culture than was contemplated by the oligarchies. In this sense the rebellions marked the first of a series of movements in Canadian history to decentralize government and political power.

If home rule was one ambition of the reformers, the accommodation of partisan rivalries that extended beyond the ranks and ken of the governing élite was another. When Upper Canada's new lieutenant-governor, Sir Francis Bond Head, arrived in January 1836, he began promisingly by attempting conciliation and reform, as he had been instructed to do: fashioning a more representative executive council based upon 'principles of Justice and impartiality, independent of party'—by which he meant including some reformers. Dr William Warren Baldwin was not interested, since in his view responsible government—which he had been advocating, along with his son Robert, since 1828—was the only means of reform. In a letter to his son, he described telling the lieutenant-governor that

> ...as the Government of England has, so must every free Government and especially these Provinces, have two parties: a governing party and a party in

check; it was no matter what the parties were called, whig or tory, parties will be, and must be,. . .therefore it became important [for the executive] to have the concurrence of the Assembly.[19]

Three moderate reformers — Robert Baldwin (1804-58), Dr Rolph, and the receiver-general, John Henry Dunn (1792-1854) — finally accepted Head's invitation to join the executive council, along with three Tory members. They were sworn in on 20 February, but three weeks later they had all resigned. Baldwin had objected to Head's saying that as lieutenant-governor he would simply *consult* his council, that the responsibility for government was his alone. The council thereupon presented a brief to Head, arguing that responsible government (making the executive responsible to the assembly) was consistent with the constitution. Head disagreed. As a result all six councillors resigned (the three Tories less forthrightly than the reformers). This event greatly disturbed the assembly, and all reformers throughout the province, inflaming anti-government sentiments.

The assembly was also infuriated by the discovery that Sir John Colborne, before he was recalled from Upper Canada, had established 44 rectories for Anglican clergymen, encompassing some twenty-one thousand acres. A select committee, headed by Peter Perry, was set up to investigate and report on the resignations. It criticized the lieutenant-governor harshly, calling him a liar and a tyrant who conducted 'our affairs' according to his own 'arbitrary and vindictive' will. The assembly then voted to stop the supply of money for the day-to-day expenses of government. Head responded angrily, reviewing and justifying his policies and denouncing the assembly's insulting demand for an explanation of what he called the 'firing' of his executive council as well as its decision to stop supply, which he said was a direct attack on the monarchy. He dissolved the assembly a month later and in the ensuing election, a bitter one, he actually campaigned against the reformers, most of whom — including Mackenzie, Perry, and the Speaker, Marshall Spring Bidwell — were swept out of office. In 1837, therefore, Baldwin and many of his fellow moderates were effectively removed from politics, unable to put curbs on hotheads like Mackenzie.

The political situation was even more serious in Lower Canada, where the *Parti Canadien* and its successor, the *Parti Patriot,* had more consistently dominated the lower house than had the reformers in Upper Canada and the party conflict had long since taken on racial overtones. The *Parti Canadien* was also dominated by members of the regional élites, chiefly French-Canadian professionals with neither the hope nor the ambition to be co-opted into the ranks of the *Château Clique* — such as Denis-Benjamin Viger (1774-1861), a Montreal lawyer (related to Papineau) and member of the assembly, who financed *La Minerve*, a newspaper that published nothing to discourage the accelerating rebellious activities. When they spoke of autonomy for their province and the right to rule themselves, their intentions differed from those of reformers in Upper Canada. What was needed, argued Papineau in December 1834, was 'a local, responsible, and national government for each part of the Empire, as regards settlement of its local interests, with supervisory authority held by the imperial government, to decide on peace and war and commercial relations with foreign countries; that is what Ireland and British America ask for.'[20] The reference to Ireland, rather than Upper Canada, was crucial.* In February 1834, Ninety-two Resolutions, prepared by Papineau and three others, were adopted by the assembly of Lower Canada and submitted to London. They catalogued grievances and requests, among them control of revenue by the legislature, responsibility of the executive to the electorate, and the election of legislative councillors. The British government's reply of 2 March 1837, in the form of Ten Resolutions of Parliament, was in effect a rejection of Papineau's demands: among other things, it allowed the governor to take funds from the provincial treasury that the assembly refused to vote. This response energized the radicals into activities that led to rebellion before the end of the year. A year earlier in Upper Canada—when the assembly had a letter from Papineau read to them by the Speaker attacking British governing authorities—Mackenzie agreed with his fellow radicals in Lower Canada that action must be taken against British authority.

Beyond their political and constitutional significance, the rebellions were also manifestations of popular, especially agrarian, discontent. The mid-1830s saw the collapse of the international wheat market, which put pressures on Upper Canadian farmers and additional pressures on Lower Canadian farmers, whose wheat economy was in crisis even before this latest bust. Rural districts had been restive for several years in both provinces, and some protest meetings held in early 1837 were attended by armed farmers. An attempted rural uprising near Brantford, Upper Canada, led by Dr Charles Duncombe (1792-1867) dispersed on 13 December when he heard of the defeat of Mackenzie's motley group on 8 December at Montgomery's Tavern north of Toronto. Both Mackenzie and Papineau persistently denied that they had carefully planned insurrections, though they wished to take credit for providing the initiative as leaders. This led Dr Wolfred Nelson (1791-1863), a supporter of Papineau's, to comment:

> You have to fight liars, whether with their own weapons or with trickery. Frankness is a fine thing among honest men and in private life; in public, it leaves us too exposed. I am annoyed by Mr Papineau's and Mackenzie's admission that we had decided to rebel. That is to justify our opponents and to deprive us of any right to complain that we were attacked.[21]

---

*What Lower Canada's political leaders wanted in the 1830s was little different from what they demanded in the 1980s: an autonomous place in the weakest possible federation.

THE

HISTORY

OF THE

BATTLE OF TORONTO,

WITH ILLUSTRATIONS AND NOTES, CRITICAL & EXPLANATORY, EX-
HIBITING THE ONLY TRUE ACCOUNT OF WHAT TOOK PLACE AT
THE MEMORABLE SIEGE OF TORONTO.

POWELL SHOOTING ANDERSON.

MR. ANDERSON WAS A CAPTAIN IN THE PATRIOT
ARMY AT THE TIME HE WAS MURDERED.

ROCHESTER:

PRINTED AND SOLD AT NO. 7, FRONT STREET.

1839.

Certainly the rural districts in Lower Canada provided their own rationale and impetus for rising in arms against the government. What appears clear is that when both Mackenzie and Papineau escalated legal agitation in 1837, most reformers could support them. But when agitation turned to insurrection, many moderate members of the élite leadership of the reformers fell away, to be replaced by armed farmers.

Unfortunately for the rebels in both the Canadas, their self-declared leaders had a fairly narrow agenda of political change, rather than a broad-ranging concept of social and economic reconstruction. The uprisings were led by men who sought little more than to replace the existing élites with themselves. Neither Papineau nor Mackenzie had any notion of how, practically, to turn a spontaneous uprising into an organized rebellion. Both became caught up in their own hysteria, panicked, and fled to leave others to face the music. In Lower Canada the *Patriotes* were prepared to see their cause as being in the best interests of the French-Canadian 'nation'; but the leaders of the rebellion in 1837, and again in 1838, were not really revolutionaries, prepared to suffer and die for their cause. On 16 November 1837 warrants were prepared for the arrest of the *Patriote* leaders, and Viger, in his own home, warned Papineau of this. Much later, the deposition of a servant in the Viger household, Angélique Labadie, stated:

> I also heard M. Papineau say that he would never be satisfied until he was president in this country, and that he would be soon, and that if the government seized the country from him he would snatch it back. M. Viger then told M. Papineau that he should keep calm and wait for freeze-up and then he would just have to whistle and all the *habitants* and thousands of Americans would espouse their cause and they would soon be masters of this country.[22]

Soon after, Papineau rushed across the border dressed as a woman.

The rebels in Upper Canada were little braver. Mackenzie fled at the first sign of trouble, clad in his great-coat to ward off the bullets; and Charles Duncombe, telling his followers that only leaders would be prosecuted, demonstrated his leadership by galloping off to Michigan when armed supporters of government marched into the region.

The leaders were incorrect in thinking that only they were in danger.

◀ **After Mackenzie fled Upper Canada he wrote his own account of the rebellion. First published in a newspaper in Watertown, NY, it was published as a booklet in Toronto in 1838 under the title *Mackenzie's Own Narrative of the Late Rebellion*. It reappeared the next year in Rochester with the title and cover reproduced here. The woodcut illustration (bearing no resemblance to the actual incident) represents what happened when Alderman John Powell, on a reconnoitring mission from Toronto up Yonge Street, on 3 December 1837, was met by Mackenzie, captured, and taken to Montgomery's Tavern by two men, one of them Anthony Anderson, a leading rebel. As they approached the tavern, Powell drew a pistol and shot and killed Anderson. (Far from being punished, Powell became mayor of Toronto and held this office for three years.) Metropolitan Toronto Reference Library.**

Though there were no real 'battles' in either province in 1837 *or* 1838, many rebels died in the course of the skirmishes. The government moved quickly to suppress dissent, behaving far more categorically in Lower than in Upper Canada. To sort things out, in December 1837 the British prime minister, Lord Melbourne, appointed Lord Durham (1792-1840) governor-in-chief of British North America. But Durham's residence in Canada lasted only three months. One of his major problems in Lower Canada had to do with dealing with captured rebels: he resigned over the British government's refusal to authorize his transportation of eight prisoners to Bermuda as an alternative to executing them at home.

The Lower Canadian Rebellion of 1838

The rebellions of 1837 were relatively easily suppressed by the authorities, using mainly volunteer forces. One response of the British government to the crisis was to increase the number of regular soldiers stationed in British North America, ostensibly because of the threat of invasion by Americans in league with exiled rebel leaders. Reinforcements did not arrive in time to prevent a second uprising in Lower Canada in November 1838, led by Wolfred Nelson, who crossed the border from the United States with a few supporters in hopes of finding an army. He met up with several thousand badly armed *Patriotes* at Napierville, and this force was quickly routed by a much larger one led by Sir John Colborne, who was now commander of the British forces in the Canadas (soon to become Durham's successor as governor). The government army did a good deal of burning, particularly in the county of Laprairie, which the *Montreal Herald* said 'presented the frightful spectacle of a vast expanse of livid flames, and it is reported that not a single rebel house has been left standing.' Colborne was awarded the nickname of 'Old Firebrand' for this effort.

As in the earlier rebellion, the government allowed the leaders to escape, going instead after the rank-and-file rebels.* Such a strategy reflected the governing élite's sense that there had been a conjunction of popular discontent with the constitutional wrangling. This time 753 men were captured and 108 brought quickly to court martial, resulting in 99 death-sentences. In the end, twelve were executed and fifty-eight were banished to Australia. But

◀ Katherine Jane Ellice, *The Rebels at Beauharnois, Lower Canada* , 1838. The family of Katherine Balfour's husband, Edward Ellice, owned the Beauharnois seigneury, and in 1838, when he was appointed secretary to Lord Durham, she accompanied him to Lower Canada. In early November the house was seized by 'picturesque ruffians' and Katherine was briefly kept under house arrest. While gazing at her captors out the window, she painted them. National Archives of Canada.

---

*Both Papineau and Mackenzie were eventually allowed to return to Canada, and they were elected to the Canadian legislature in 1848 and 1851 respectively. But events had passed them by, and their colleagues paid them little attention.

even this government response (for its time, relatively mild) was typical of both British North America and its successor, the Dominion of Canada: for many decades there was a tendency to react to violent expressions of discontent with disproportionate brutality.

Lord Durham and His Report

Yet another typical response to the insurrections—this time by the British government to the earlier manifestations—had been to dispatch a fact-finding commission, headed by Lord Durham, who was given extraordinary powers to settle down the colonies and to bring about necessary reform. Though he did not remain long in Canada, his famous *Report on the Affairs in British North America*, filed in January 1839, was a thorough and eloquent examination of the problems of the Canadas. The solution he saw was responsible government, having been persuaded by Robert and William Warren Baldwin, on a visit to Upper Canada, of its necessity. Otherwise, Durham did not propose any major alterations to the élite political culture that existed everywhere in British North America, much less to the social and economic systems that lay behind it. But he did propose the legislative union of the two Canadas, being more impressed by the racial conflicts in North America than by other causes of discontent. As he wrote:

> I expected to find a contest between a government and a people: I found two nations warring in the bosom of a single state: I found a struggle, not of principles, but of races; and I perceived that it would be idle to attempt any amelioration of laws or institutions, until we could first succeed in terminating the deadly animosity that now separates the inhabitants of Lower Canada into the hostile divisions of French and English.[23]

Once the two colonies were unified, the next step would be the assimilation of the French Canadians into Anglo culture.

In recommending that the internal government of the colonies be placed 'in the hands of the colonists themselves', Lord Durham dealt more with the relationship of colonies to the mother country than with the details of local constitutional arrangements. His assessment did not comprehend the importance of political parties, or of political pluralism, in either Upper or Lower Canada. Durham harboured the mistaken belief that governors could maintain considerable power so long as they altered the make-up of their councils to reflect the shifting situation in the House of Assembly. Though he basically felt that the situation of the Canadas could be dealt with by constitutional reform, Durham also considered questions of land policy, recommending an end to the proprietorial system in Prince Edward Island and strongly supporting a general system of land reform involving the sale of Crown lands at sufficient price.

While the rebellions did little more than focus the attention of Britain on the need for change, Durham's recommendations for the union of the Canadas and for responsible government were eventually heeded—though it would be left to other forces to remake British North America. Free trade, railroads, and industrialization, in the end, were just as powerful engines of change as either political uprisings or constitutional reform.

✎ *Religion*

Next to politics between 1790 and 1840, religion was the most familiar form of cultural expression in the colonies of British North America. Humankind has long held a deep need for explanatory constructs that give order and meaning to life. For British North Americans in the early nineteenth century these were to be found chiefly in Christianity of various denominations. The francophone population was almost exclusively Catholic, while the English-speakers were both Protestant and Catholic. In many ways a more useful division than Protestant/Catholic was between those denominations that supported the establishment and those that did not.

The Established Churches

The élite culture of privilege was supported not only by the constitutional arrangements of the provinces of British North America, but also by the clergy of the established churches. Such support was, of course, one of the reasons the British government felt so strongly about the need for establishment in the American colonies. Indeed, an established churchman was almost by definition a conservative Tory, a supporter of the status quo. For many years it was tacitly agreed that the established church in Upper Canada—entitled to receive the financial support of the state—was the Church of England, and this understanding was of course devoutly upheld by Archdeacon John Strachan of York, who in 1824 solemnly expressed his belief to Maitland, the lieutenant-governor, that the form of worship and the doctrine of their Church 'was the most pure form of Christianity existing in the world, certainly the most compatible with our form of government.'[24] Significantly, not only the Church of England, but Presbyterians and Roman Catholics were also inherently conservative in their views. Like Strachan, Bishop Alexander Macdonell (1762-1840), his Roman Catholic colleague on the legislative council from 1831 to 1840, also believed in a social hierarchy.

For these conservatives,

> To meditate the establishment of equality..., that splendid delusion of the present age, the vision of the weak, and the pretext of the wicked, is in fact to meditate war against God, and the primary laws of creation....In society inequality is just as natural as in the forest, but productive of much more salutary effects. Without inequality what would become of the necessary distinctions of parent and child, master and scholar, the employer and the employed![25]

While Strachan and Macdonell would certainly have agreed with such sentiments, they were actually proclaimed in Halifax by a Presbyterian minister, Andrew Brown (1763-1834), in 1794. Strachan's version of this belief was only slightly different:

> Subordination in the Moral World is manifest and this appearance of nature indicates the intention of its Author. The beauty and advantages of this arrangement are obvious and universally acknowledged. . . .The various relations of individuals and Societies require a mutual exchange of good offices. . . . Hence it would appear that they who labour in the inferior departments of life are not on that account the slaves of their superiors. The Magistrate requires the aid of his people—the Master of his Servant. They are all dependent upon one another, as they subsist by an exchange of good offices. . .The lowest order enjoys its peculiar comforts and privileges, and contributes equally with the highest to the support and dignity of Society.[26]

Established church leaders—like Strachan, Bishop Jacob Mountain (1749-1825) in Lower Canada, and Charles (1734-1816) and John (1777-1850) Inglis in Nova Scotia—all understood that they needed to develop their churches at the local level in order to justify the public favour they were able to gain from the political élite of which they were a part. All succeeded to a considerable extent, although a vigorous local presence did not necessarily translate into popular acceptance for the Church of England.

For those British North Americans who were not associated with established churches—the majority in most provinces, although in Lower Canada, Catholics were obviously overwhelmingly dominant—the pretensions of the ecclesiastical establishment, particularly in maintaining such traditional monopolies as marriage rites and education, were constant irritants that were frequently blamed on the oligarchic constitutional system. Dissenters chafed under arrangements that granted 'liberty of conscience' to all Christians, but denied to them full powers to act in such matters as the solemnization of marriage. The Church of England fought a rearguard action unsuccessfully, ultimately losing any pretense to monopoly in the 1820s and 1830s but clearly demonstrating, in the process, its privileged position.

The years before 1840 saw a number of developments within the Catholic Church. In Lower Canada, the Church further solidified its position within the political structure, especially under Bishop Joseph-Octave Plessis (1763-1825, bishop and archbishop 1806-25), who was appointed to the legislative council of the province in 1817. Plessis continued to have trouble with shortages of priests even after the earlier arrival of a number of French priests exiled by the French Revolution, and with lay opposition to Church administration. He also presided over the devolution of the Church in British North America, as Rome in 1819 elevated him to an archbishopric at the same time that it created new dioceses in Upper Canada and Prince Edward Island, both headed by Highland Scots. Plessis was not himself an ultramontane—he was not one of those who believed that the Church, as the guardian of moral law, must be heeded in all matters relating to politics. But he did attempt, with some success, to strengthen the structure of his Church by educating more clergy, by obtaining government recognition of its legal position (especially in Lower Canada), and by reforming its far-flung governance.

The Dissenters

For the most part, dissenters in every colony not only chafed at the conservative social vision of the established churches and their support of hierarchy and privilege, but also objected to the view of God they promulgated. The most numerous dissenters were Methodists and their itinerant ministers, who were constantly on the move, covering as large a circuit as possible. In the eyes of John Strachan, another objection to Methodists was that many were Americans and possibly republicans, and he accused their ministers of 'preaching the Gospel from idleness or a zeal without knowledge. They are induced without any preparation to teach what they do not know, and which, from their pride, they disdain to learn.'[27] Strachan was scornful of the fact that there were no educational requirements for entering the Methodist ministry (a candidate only had to satisfy a Conference committee that he had absorbed a set list of books). Other dissenters included Baptists, some schismatic Presbyterians, and a handful of other groups, such as the Society of Friends (Quakers) and the Mennonites (who kept to themselves and did not enter any debates, political or religious).

E.S. Shrapnel, *Camp Meeting Scene,* an illustration in *Upper Canada Sketches (1898)* by Thomas Conant. Ontario Archives, S13885.

For most of the dissenting Protestants, the fundamental disagreements with the established churches were epistemological, centring on how one came to know God: many were evangelicals who believed that God had to be felt emotionally rather than comprehended rationally. These feelings were 'awakened' in revivals and in the 'camp meetings' of the Methodists that were so common in Upper Canada. Such occasions were characterized by mass participation, and concentration on ultimate salvation, in a highly charged and emotional atmosphere. The preachers emphasized 'Christ crucified' and strove for a crisis conversion experience that was often quite intense and expressed in noise and movement. Many preached (as one witness put it) as if battling a swarm of bees. Naturally those who preferred their religion well-ordered and sedate found themselves dismayed and appalled by extravagances that need not—indeed often could not—be explained in rational terms, making the convert into what John Strachan once described as 'the slave of unruly passions and appetites'. The evangelicals were not only irrational and passionate, but inherently populist in their attitude. For many in the establishment, violent passion and populism went hand in hand with revolution.

Education

Another area of conflict between the privileges of the establishment and the needs of an expanding population appeared over education. In every colony Crown lands had been set aside for the support of 'a Protestant clergy' and of education, and both their disposition and the use of the resultant revenue became bones of contention. In Upper Canada, John Strachan fought on behalf of the Church of England's exclusive use of the revenue from the clergy reserves, both against the pretensions of other 'established' churches, such as the Church of Scotland and the Roman Catholic Church, and against efforts to use the funds for secular purposes.

As for the structure of education itself, it was naturally divided between institutions designed to educate the few and those intended to deal with the many. Over the former—universities, colleges, academies—the established churches insisted on maintaining a close control, on the grounds that higher education involved more than merely technical knowledge. (This pattern was broken in Nova Scotia, however, where the University of King's College was founded at Windsor by the Church of England in 1789, and in 1818 Lord Dalhousie founded Dalhousie College in Halifax as a non-denominational alternative.) Over the latter—common and elementary schools—the relationship with the established churches, particularly the Church of England, was rather more complex and tenuous.

At the start of this period the Church of England saw the establishment of an elementary school system as the responsibility of a state church. Thus the views of Bishop Jacob Mountain in Lower Canada were reflected in the founding in 1801 of the Royal Institution for the Advancement of Learning, intended to supervise schools within the province that were under Anglican auspices. Catholics, for their part, established private schools. A bequest of land and £10,000 from the Montreal merchant James McGill (1744–1813) to the Royal Institution to begin a university led to a charter's being granted in 1821 to McGill College, which opened in 1829.* John Strachan had his own ambition for a university in Upper Canada, which was to be mainly a 'Missionary College' for the training of clergymen. In 1826, authorized by the provincial government, he went to England to obtain a university charter, and the next year a royal charter was announced for the University of King's College, which was to be firmly under the control of the Church of England, with the lieutenant-governor as chancellor and the Archdeacon of York as president. (Mackenzie's angry response appeared in the *Colonial Advocate* on 11 October 1827.) But Sir John Colborne, who arrived as lieutenant-governor in 1828, thought a university was premature, and opted instead for a preparatory grammar school, participating in the founding of Upper Canada College in 1829. The plan for King's College lay dormant until after the Rebellion.** Strachan had earlier taken the lead in encouraging the legislature to appropriate money for the support of common schools, and he was president of the General Board of Education established in the colony in 1823 to supervise public education.

Both the élite and ordinary people could agree on the desirability of education, although for somewhat different reasons. As one Quebec citizens' petition of 1787 complained, government after the Conquest did not continue to emphasize

> the education of youth, from whom heretofore civil officers, good militia officers, commercial persons, navigators, and intelligent tradesmen were formed. All, for want of a public education, remained in ignorance of the laws divine and human, of reading, writing, and even of the English language. . . .[28]

While many farmers may have seen little advantage in sending their children to school, others recognized that education was inseparable from upward mobility. For William Lyon Mackenzie—whose *Catechism of Education* was published in 1830—'Intelligence is power' and the aim of education was to produce happiness. On the subject of free schools, he argued:

---

*McGill was the brother-in-law of John Strachan's wife by her first marriage. Strachan had advised McGill to leave this bequest, was a trustee of his will, and was on the board of the planned university, of which he had hoped to become principal.

**In April 1842, on the grounds of the present Ontario Parliament Buildings, the cornerstone was laid for King's College, and the next year it opened. Strachan resigned as president in 1848. In 1849 the College was secularized and brought under government control, and the University of Toronto came into being on 1 January 1850. The King's College building was demolished in 1886.

The beneficial effects attending such a system are incalculable. Additional stability would be given to free institutions, the sum of public and private happiness would be greatly increased; the power of the people extended; crime diminished; an inviolable respect for the laws maintained; and a constitutional vigilance more increasingly exercised, against all encroachments upon national or individual rights.[29]

Mackenzie also maintained that entrusting schooling to the government meant that the youth 'are trained generally to habits of servility and toleration of arbitrary power, in as far as precept and example can influence their minds.' But fortunately the young obtained 'those keys of useful knowledge, the faculties of reading and writing, by means of which, "the liberty of the press," and the intelligence of the age, they are prevented from becoming instruments of evil. . . .'[30]

If for common folk and their liberal spokesmen, education represented the means of mobility and liberation, for the authorities education was necessary for social order. There was considerable overlap between the two ambitions, for even Mackenzie saw the reduction of crime and a respect for law— 'additional stability', he called it—as resulting from education. For those members of the élite concerned about social order, the need was even more pressing. Two systems of education were thus brought to the colonies from Britain after 1815, both of which offered the merit of teaching large numbers of students at relatively low cost, and both based on teaching the older children, who in turn passed their lessons by rote to the younger.

One scheme, the Bell system of National Schools (also called the 'Madras' system, since it was first employed in India), was fostered in Britain by the National Society for Promoting the Education of the Poor in the Principles of the Established Church, and was promulgated in British North America by the Anglican Society for Promoting Christian Knowledge (SPCK). The other was the 'Monitorial' system promoted by Joseph Lancaster (1778-1838), a London educator who came to Lower Canada in 1829 and whose educational experiments in the province were supported by men as diverse as Papineau, Mackenzie, and Lord Aylmer (1775-1850, governor of Lower Canada, 1831-5). Unlike the Bell System, the Lancastrian one had the merit of being unassociated with any denomination. Neither system ever won sufficient favour to shape directly an educational structure, although parts of both were incorporated into common school arrangements in various colonies. Only in the 1830s, however, did demands for broadly based public education—such as those led by the Methodist minister and educational administrator Egerton Ryerson (1803-82) in Upper Canada—become prominent anywhere in British North America, and the great landmark School Acts belong to the post-1840 period.[31]

Before 1840 the curricula of schools in British North America were extremely eclectic, reflecting the nature of the colonies both in terms of absence of central direction and pluralistic cultural influences. Immigrants brought with them their educational experiences in England, Ireland, Scotland, or America, and those experiences were often coloured by a substantial class bias as well as ethnic and denominational ones. Lower Canada had its own system, based on the *collège classique*, which trained young men for the priesthood and the professions, especially the law. Philippe-Joseph Aubert de Gaspé (1786-1871) wrote with considerable affection and respect in his memoirs about the Séminaire de Québec, where he was educated at the end of the eighteenth century.[32]

Textbooks imported from both Britain and the United States—and in Lower Canada from France—shared many common assumptions about virtue and morals, but differed in such basic matters as spelling and currencies employed in arithmetic problems. As they increasingly reflected a conscious attempt to inculcate values of nationalism and patriotism for their targeted population, they became even more undesirable for use in British North America. Not until the 1840s did the British colonies begin to produce their own schoolbooks, and in them religion tended to dominate at every opportunity. Thus *An English Spelling Book with Reading Lessons,* published in Saint John in 1841, began its first lesson:

> All sin. I sin. You sin. Sin is bad. Do not sin at all. Sin is not hid. God can see it.
> Go not in the way of sin. The way of sin is a bad way.[33]

The relationship of such readings to religious catechism was transparent.

Culture

The cultural activities of British North America—beyond the predominant political culture of every colony—were as diverse, eclectic, and pluralistic as its educational patterns. While a common stereotype identifies this period as one of extremely limited and primitive cultural and artistic production—in no way to be compared with the flowerings of literature, art, and music in Europe and the British Isles, or even in the United States—such an interpretation reflects a particular set of assumptions about culture. Indigenous high culture was understandably rare—foreign models were usually employed. There was, however, a substantial folk culture, which included a well-established oral tradition, in the form of tales and songs, handed down from generation to generation, from group to group, as well as in the work of craftsmen. As an example of the devolution of people's appreciation of this culture, the simple pine furniture of clean, uncluttered, functional lines produced by hundreds of anonymous craftsmen during the colonial period found little favour in succeeding generations that regarded heavy ornamentation and the use of highly polished wood veneers as exemplary. But today we recognize that the aesthetic values of those anonymous furniture-makers were on a level with their high craftsmanship.

For the most part, the élite culture of British North America is not very compelling in today's eyes, in either its originality or its dynamism. Nor could it be otherwise. European models were imitated because it was virtually impossible to conceive of any others. Indeed, most of the producers of élite culture were trained and educated abroad, as were most of the élite in this period. Of the 538 people given entries in Volume VII of the *Dictionary of Canadian Biography*, covering those who died between 1835 and 1850—and including the leaders of British North America in the second quarter of the nineteenth century—fewer than 200 were born in the colonies, and most of these were born in Lower Canada. The remainder came mostly from the British Isles and the United States (although some were born as far away as India and Senegal). Even young people educated in British North America were usually trained by seniors who were educated abroad, usually with emphasis on slavish replication of both form and content. Outside the circles of the élite in the larger cities, there was a very small appreciation of artistic, literary, theatrical, or intellectual expertise. What the public wanted in painting, theatre, and books was work that mirrored contemporary European taste, and a few people made a decent living in the larger cities catering to the gentry and the leading merchants. But there was no substantial market for works of art or refinement.

Most high culture was produced by people who made their living in some other way, and who often regarded their artistic activity as diversion or byproduct rather than as either conscious art or professional activity. The relative absence of institutions of higher learning in the eighteenth century—those few that existed were more like secondary schools, employing small staffs—meant that they could not provide employment for artists and intellectuals. In 1787, David Owen (1754-1828), senior wrangler at Cambridge University and tutor to William Pitt the Younger, was attracted to New Brunswick by the prospect of a university appointment. But when the university failed to materialize, he retreated to family property on Campobello Island, and spent the remaining forty-three years of his life as an eccentric hermit and semi-feudal landlord, publishing occasionally in the newspapers of Saint John.

Literature

Some of the best-known writers of the colonial period were women from the gentry class who managed to find the time to continue their literary endeavours amidst the turmoil of pioneer life, while their husbands were engaged in 'men's work'. The first novel by a native British North American—*St. Ursula's Convent; or, The Nun of Canada*, published in Kingston in 1824—was written by Julia Catherine Hart (1796-1867)—née Julia Beckwith of Fredericton, NB. Nearly 150 subscribers paid 9s. 4d. for copies of the two-volume work. Hart tapped a rich vein of Protestant suspicions of what Catholics 'got up to' in convents, although her tale was more melodramatic than immoral and today has only historical significance.

The Strickland sisters—Catharine Parr Traill (1802-99) and Susanna

Moodie (1803-85)—were more polished, and each sister wrote a classic work. Traill's *The Backwoods of Canada* (London, 1836) is made up of eighteen letters home to family and friends in Suffolk. It is a sensitive early account of the pioneer experience: never complaining, she left readers with the overall impression of a cheerful adaptation to the rigours of life in a previously unsettled area of Upper Canada, where she willingly made do with whatever was at hand. Upper Canada, however, is portrayed as a land 'with no historical associations, no legendary tales of those that came before', and the impenetrable forest all around her is 'desolate', 'interminable', 'a maze'. It simultaneously isolates and liberates her.*

If the forest took on forbidding characteristics in Traill's deliberately factual account, both it and its inhabitants assumed an almost grotesque presence in John Richardson's novel *Wacousta; or, The Prophecy*, which was first published anonymously in London and Edinburgh in 1832. Born in Queenston, Upper Canada, Richardson (1796-1852) served as a gentleman volunteer in the British army in Upper Canada. Captured by the Americans in 1813, he spent the following years in England—between demobilization (in 1815) and his return to Canada in 1838—using occasional military activity and a pension to supplement an unsuccessful attempt to become established as a writer. Like many another exiled artist, he found British North America wanting on his return, even more than Britain, as a supporter of his literary pretensions. After many disappointments—described in his autobiography, *Eight Years in Canada* (1847)—he travelled on to New York, where he died in 1852 of erysipelas induced by undernourishment.

Most of Richardson's large body of writing—seven novels and two long poems, in addition to memoirs and journals—was in some way autobiographical; or, to put it differently, his experiences in the War of 1812, which were both formative and adventurous, were frequently employed in fictional ways. He was captured at Moraviantown in October 1813, after the defeat and death of the great Indian warrior Tecumseh (1768-1813), and he had obviously heard accounts of the Indian warfare on the western frontier from kinfolk and military colleagues. Richardson's *Wacousta* combines a sentimentalism that was common in eighteenth-century English fiction with an element of the unreal/fantastic clashing with the real—a literary equivalent of the 'picturesque' that has come to be called the 'grotesque'. To the extent that *Wacousta* juxtaposes the ordinary and the deformed, producing a sense of terror, the grotesque becomes the Gothic.

For today's reader, what Richardson chose to see as the fantastic elements in the story are of great interest. The Canadian setting and its native

---

*Susanna Moodie's *Roughing It in the Bush: or, Forest Life in Canada*—which is notable both for its more trenchant (and discouraging) descriptions of the pioneering experience and for its memorable sketches of people and events—was published after this period, in 1852.

inhabitants, who surround a little enclave of Europeans at Fort Detroit, are emphasized. Wacousta himself—a confidant of Pontiac—is 'this formidable mysterious enemy' who 'might have been likened to the spirit of darkness presiding over his terrible legions.' Nature in *Wacousta* is a presence, both frightening and full of energy, though it is never described in detail. But the overriding impression of the novel is the sense that the Canadian environment—both man and nature—had eventually overwhelmed the tiny outpost of Europeans at Fort Detroit. Richardson suggests that having to come to terms with Canada was both frightening and isolating. Wacousta, the dreaded native leader, is finally confronted with his past. He is identified as an English officer, Sir Reginald Morton, who had become maddened by an injustice inflicted on him twenty years before by his friend Charles de Haldimar, now the commander at Detroit. Consumed by hatred and vengeance, he is at last murdered by his adopted people in full sight of the garrison.

Richardson stood virtually alone in Upper Canada. The real intellectual and literary centre of British North America in this period was Nova Scotia, the home of Joseph Howe, Thomas Haliburton, and Thomas McCulloch. By the 1830s the province also was the location of three colleges and several important academies. It contained a number of subscription libraries established in the 1820s, and literary and scientific societies organized in the 1830s. It supported numerous newspapers and, between 1826 and 1833, two literary magazines, the *Acadian* and the *Halifax Monthly*. The cement that held much of the literary community together was provided by Joseph Howe, himself a poet and essayist as well as a newspaper publisher and printer. In 1829 Howe published *An Historical and Statistical Account of Nova Scotia* by Haliburton, most of whose Sam Slick sketches would appear in instalments in Howe's weekly *Novascotian* before Howe published them in book form. Howe was a leading member of 'The Club', a group of writers in Halifax who often contributed to his newspaper. The common topic for Nova Scotia's best writing was the development of the province itself, and the common approach was to make fun of Nova Scotians for their follies and foibles—gently in Howe's 'Rambles', which ran serially in his newspaper between 1828 and 1831, but satirically in the writings of McCulloch and Haliburton.

Born in Scotland, Thomas McCulloch (1776-1843) was a Presbyterian minister who came to Pictou, Nova Scotia, in 1803, accepted a call there, and led the Presbyterians in their fight to establish an interdenominational institution of higher learning at Pictou: McCulloch was the first principal of Pictou Academy, founded in 1809. He was continually embroiled in public controversy over religious and educational matters, usually in opposition to the Halifax establishment and supportive of ordered reform. Despite his public involvements (an extremely influential educator, he was, among other things, the first president of Dalhousie College in 1838 after the Academy folded), McCulloch wrote on educational and religious subjects as well as some fiction. His major literary success was in the form of short sketches, *The Letters of Mephibosheth Stepsure*, originally printed in the pages of the *Acadian Recorder* in 1821, 1822, and 1823. (They were not published in book form until 1960, as *The Stepsure Letters*.) McCulloch created a fictional observer, the decidedly self-righteous and distinctly Scots Presbyterian Stepsure, to comment on the affairs of 'our town', and the resulting satire was double-edged, in that the reader learned of the foibles of both the community and the narrator, as well as pawky (a Scotticism meaning shrewdly and dryly humorous).

The subtle humour, which depends on a thorough understanding of the pretensions of the time, is difficult for modern readers to appreciate, even though McCulloch made a social and didactic point in mocking the materialism, upward mobility, and immorality (especially alcoholism) of Nova Scotians who forsook agrarian values—usually without much success—in their search for the presumed greater wealth of commercial enterprise. Northrop Frye has written that 'McCulloch is the founder of genuine Canadian humour: that is, of the humour which is based on a vision of society and is not merely a series of wisecracks on a single theme.'[34] His *Stepsure* influenced Thomas Haliburton's Sam Slick sketches, which were

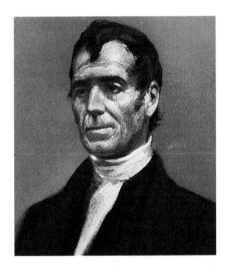 

Thomas McCulloch. A pastel portrait made in 1845, two years after McCulloch died, by Sir Daniel Macnee. (This is presumably a copy of another portrait.) Atlantic School of Theology, Halifax; photo courtesy the Nova Scotia Museum.

Thomas Chandler Haliburton. Lithograph by E.V. Eddie. National Archives of Canada, C-6087.

first published some fifteen years later and continued a tradition of Canadian humour that had its culmination in the writings of Stephen Leacock.

Thomas Chandler Haliburton (1796-1865)—born in Windsor, Nova Scotia—was a Tory in the eighteenth-century tradition of the squirarchy. After an early career as a lawyer and politician, he succeeded his father on the bench as a judge in the Inferior Court of Common Pleas in 1829, and in 1841 was appointed to the Supreme Court of Nova Scotia, where he served until his retirement to England in 1856. Haliburton nevertheless made time for writing, and his output was prodigious, beginning with *A General Description of Nova Scotia* (1823), which was enlarged into *An Historical and Statistical Account of Nova Scotia*. Haliburton's romantic account of the expulsion of the Acadians inspired Longfellow to write *Evangeline: A Tale of Acadia* (1847). In 1835-6 Haliburton wrote 21 sketches about Sam Slick—a literary character that would rival those of Dickens. When they first appeared in Joseph Howe's *Novascotian*, they became so popular that Haliburton enlarged them into *The Clockmaker; or The Sayings and Doings of Samuel Slick, of Slickville* (Halifax, 1836). Slick is a wise-cracking Yankee clockmaker from Connecticut who tours Nova Scotia gulling the gullible and commenting on Nova Scotia society, employing 'soft-sawder' and an understanding of 'human natur' in his dual role as con-man/commentator. He achieved international popularity when *The Clockmaker* was published by Joseph Bentley in London.

Possessed of a far more ribald and anecdotal sense of humour than McCulloch—the reader can sense the tavern as the place where these sketches had their origin—Haliburton can still be read with enjoyment today, particularly by those who know a little about the society he was satirizing. He created Sam Slick for a purpose, which was as double-edged as McCulloch's. Sam embodied the worst features of Americans (their loud braggery, their opportunism), but his criticisms of Nova Scotians grew out of his admiration of the best American traits (their energy and entrepreneurial adaptability). Haliburton agreed with McCulloch that Nova Scotia was living beyond its means, exhausting itself in useless squabblings. Through Sam Slick he offered the Tory alternatives of collective adjustment to changing conditions and the development of existing resources. While he did not succeed in reforming his province, he created a memorable stage Yankee, possessing a colourful dialect and an unlimited fund of aphorisms and epigrams, who became one of the most popular comic literary characters of the nineteenth century.

Ironically, both McCulloch and Haliburton produced their major work for a local audience without giving much thought to the larger world. When their local successes gave them confidence and they wrote self-consciously for markets in Edinburgh (McCulloch) and London (Haliburton), they were less imaginative and inventive. The fault was not entirely theirs, for to the outside world, writers like McCulloch and Haliburton were colonials, with all that appellation implied. McCulloch, for example, followed up the success of

Stepsure at home with two novellas published in Scotland under the title *Colonial Gleanings:William and Melville* in 1826. With these works he moved in the direction of Scottish writing of the day, dominated by Sir Walter Scott and John Galt and anchored by a historical realism that resurrected the Scottish past and its people. McCulloch's next work was more ambitious: a three-volume novel entitled 'Auld Eppie's Tales'. It was rejected by a Scottish publisher, as was a revised version of *Stepsure*, the latter because of the coarseness of the humour, which had 'the pungency and originality of Swift' but was felt to be unacceptable to an audience that had become accustomed to Scott. The publisher did suggest that McCulloch rewrite *Stepsure* for Scottish publication, omitting all references not only to breaking wind but to previous publication in 'any of the Canadian papers'.

As for Haliburton, after the first series of Sam Slick sketches, his use of the character changed and the fields for his satire expanded. The result was popular success but not much critical acclaim, at that time or since. A work without Slick, *The Letter-Bag of the Great Western; or Life in a Steamer*, which Haliburton published in 1840, was heavily condemned because of its coarseness and descent into popular humour, including the dialect of the uneducated and frequent use of the pun (although these were features of the Slick books as well). Its real problem was that, without Slick, Haliburton's reactionary Toryism was all too apparent. Haliburton would produce one more masterpiece, *The Old Judge; or, Life in a Colony* (1849), which the subtitle accurately describes: it is a nostalgic, rather romantic, but very graphic portrait of colonial society in the form of sketches and stories that reveal the narrative skills of Haliburton at their best.

Painting

In the non-literary arts even more than in literature, the official culture of British North America was derivative and unadventurous. Painters inevitably emphasized European styles and techniques, sometimes acquired from working with established masters, and the market had little interest in anything else. But within this tradition a few fine painters emerged, some of whose works form the historical roots of Canadian painting.

William Berczy (1744-1813) was born in Germany, trained in Austria, worked in Florence, and claimed that he had spent some time in a Turkish harem before 1790, when he arrived in England, where he exhibited work in the Royal Academy of Arts. As the bit about the harem suggests, his career was more than a little chequered—something he had in common with many other talented newcomers to British North America in the nineteenth century. In 1791 he became a recruiter of emigrants from northern Germany for a British group attempting to develop land in upstate New York, and chose to join his settlers in the New World. In 1794, representing another land company, he came to Upper Canada with his German settlers and accepted a commission from Governor Simcoe to finish building Yonge

William Berczy, *The Woolsey Family*, 1809. Oil on canvas. The curiously detached appearance of each member of the family group is explained by the fact that Berczy first drew each figure separately in pencil, then traced it onto the canvas. Once they were all painted, the background—the mirror, the window opening onto the St Lawrence beyond, the classical mantel, and the painted canvas floor-covering—was filled in around them. National Gallery of Canada, 5875.

Street from York north to Lake Simcoe. Berczy's settlement scheme failed and he was left badly in debt. A polymath, Berczy spent some years in Montreal attempting to pay off his creditors with whatever he could sell. In 1803 he won an architectural competition for Christ Church, Montreal, and he painted a number of very fine miniatures and portraits, including a famous one of Joseph Brant (page 160). In 1809 Berczy was invited by a Quebec merchant, John William Woolsey, to paint his family. The artist produced a formal grouping, in the then-fashionable neo-classical style, of Woolsey, his mother, his wife, his brother-in-law, his four children, and a dog (Berczy was paid £10 per figure; the dog was free)—with, behind them, a high window open to a view of the St Lawrence. The work is a masterpiece of early Canadian painting.

Berczy's landlord in Montreal was Louis Dulongpré (1759-1843), who apparently came to America as a musician with the French army that supported the Americans during their war for independence. After the war he settled in Montreal, where he taught music and dancing and in 1789 helped to found the Théâtre de Société in Montreal, which quickly ran into opposition from the Church. Unable to earn a living teaching the arts, Dulongpré went to the United States to learn how to paint from what he later described as 'the best Academicians'. Over the years, working in both Montreal and Quebec, he produced more than 3,000 portraits—over ten a month—and much decoration for Roman Catholic churches. He eventually retired to the parish of Saint-Hyacinthe.

Robert Field (1769-1819), born in England, was a well-trained artist who was initially lured to the United States after independence. He spent fourteen years painting miniatures in the eastern states, apparently disliked by American competitors. When he removed to Halifax in 1808, he certainly faced few rivals, advertising his plan to 'exercise his profession, as portrait painter, in oil and watercolours, and in miniature.' There was no shortage of commissions, and over the next few years he painted more than 50 oil portraits of the Nova Scotia élite, all of which were professionally competent if not inspired. Field wandered off in 1816 to the West Indies, and, succumbing to yellow fever, was buried three years later in an unmarked grave in Kingston, Jamaica.

Newcomers like Berczy, Dulongpré, and Field exposed local artists who had not trained abroad to new standards and techniques, and perhaps through example or advice even encouraged some to undertake foreign study. At least two native-born painters working in Lower Canada studied in Europe: François Baillairgé (1759-1830) and Antoine Sébastien Plamondon (1804-95). Even after working in Paris during the American Revolution, Baillairgé was conscious of his limitations, advertising in the *Quebec Gazette* in 1785 for 'amateurs and experts in the art of painting' to examine his work, adding, 'Being deprived in this country of the lessons needed to guide me in this art, I hope that the criticism and advice of experts will lead me to the perfection to which I aspire.' He never achieved personal satisfaction or public success as a painter, however, and eventually found his métier as an architect and woodcarver. Plamondon had studied in Paris with a teacher trained by the great David, and became the most celebrated and sought-after artist in Lower Canada, with studios in both Montreal and Quebec. Plamondon's portraits—including those of Cyprien Tanguay, Louis-Joseph Papineau, and Julie Papineau and her daughter—are austere, beautifully modelled works in the classical style. His masterpieces, *Soeur Saint-Alphonse* (1841) and *La Chasse aux Tourtes* (1853), were painted after this period.

British officer-artists and other visitors produced most of the landscape paintings of the period because, for native artists, there was little money to be made from non-portraits. Most surviving landscape work from these years was really done by skilled amateurs—some ability and training in sketching and watercolour were almost essential for the well-equipped traveller in the years before the camera; even Lord Selkirk could produce a competent sketch. Joseph Bouchette (1774-1841), a survey engineer (he studied with

Baillairgé in 1796), who succeeded his uncle as surveyor-general in 1817, painted some fine, sweeping views of the Quebec countryside and its villages. But the most exciting painter of scenes was Joseph Légaré (1795-1855), with whom Plamondon studied for six years. Secure financially because of astute real estate speculation—most artists, like most British North Americans, invested in undeveloped land and property whenever possible—he acquired a collection of European paintings and spent much time restoring, cleaning, and eventually copying them. He achieved some later repute for depictions of Canadian historical events, painted in the dark European style of the time, for copying portraits (of Lord Elgin, George IV, Queen Victoria), as well as for religious pictures. But we remember him today for some eerie paintings that were inspired by threatening events, such as the cholera plague of the 1830s—which produced a brooding study of the Market Place in Quebec by moonlight, with dead bodies being loaded into carts and the population obviously agitated—and fires that swept the Quebec City suburbs of Saint-Roche and Saint-Jean. Légaré was virtually forgotten or ignored until the 1970s.

Architecture

The architectural style that pervaded the settled parts of Canada from the late eighteenth century well into the nineteenth—for government buildings, the homes of the élite, and simpler houses and shops—was Late Georgian. The grand Late Georgian buildings were essentially brick (sometimes frame or stone) boxes that were lent dignity and even nobility by such external features as pediment, door-case, and portico, handled in such a way that kept symmetry and proportion in dynamic balance. In official buildings Late Georgian bespoke permanence, tradition, social and political power; in the mansions, which were usually two storeys high and five bays wide, it conveyed the standing and pride of the owner; in its more modest expression in streetscapes of houses built to the same two- or three-storey height up against the front of the lot—with little distinction between houses, shops, and other commercial buildings—it bespoke regularity and order. For the craftsmen who built them it was part of their basic knowledge, the only way of building. The streets of Montreal, Quebec City, York, Kingston and the cities of the Maritimes were all gradually built up with simple Georgian houses, most of which have vanished. (Rue Notre-Dame in Montreal, however, and rue Saint-Louis, among many other streets in Quebec City, retain their Late Georgian appearance.)

Many—perhaps most—builders got their ideas from English and American pattern books, which circulated widely in North America. The most widely used pattern book was James Gibbs's *A Book of Architecture* (1728), which was the source for at least two early churches, the Anglican Church of St Paul (1750) in Halifax, and Holy Trinity Cathedral (1800-4) in Quebec City; the former was modelled on St Peter's, Vere Street, in Marylebone,

James Patterson Cockburn, *St. Louis Street, Quebec*, 1830. Watercolour. The mixed use of the street is evident. Abraham Roberts' grocery store is on the left. Next to it is a small log house where Richard Montgomery's body was prepared for burial after his unsuccessful attack on Quebec on 31 December 1775; it bears the sign of innkeeper William Dobbins. The two large three-storey Georgian houses were built from 1814 to 1816, when the novelist Phillipe Aubert de Gaspé lived in one of them. The large house on the right was once owned by Mme Péan, the mistress of François Bigot; it served as officers' quarters in Cockburn's time. Cockburn, perhaps the most prolific of the talented English officer/artists, served six years as commanding officer of the Royal Artillery in Canada from 1826 to 1832. His *Quebec and Its Environs; Being a Picturesque Guide to the Stranger* (1831) was illustrated with his own views. Royal Ontario Museum, 942.48.82.

London, and the latter is an elegant simplification of St Martin-in-the-Fields in Trafalgar Square. Both London churches were designed by Gibbs. Their Canadian imitations, by very reason of their sources, were seen as unmistakable symbols of British authority.

The Late Georgian style—which, by way of military and other craftsmen, came to the Maritimes from England, to Newfoundland from Ireland, and to Upper Canada from the US—conveyed this message even more forcefully in

Province House, Halifax, in the 1860s — the oldest seat of government in Canada. John Merrick prepared the plan and elevation, and the architect/builder Richard Scott supervised construction, which took eight years, from 1811 to 1819. National Archives of Canada, 8555.

the new government buildings of the period: for example, in the imposing Government House (1800-5) in Halifax, raised to be visible from the harbour. This was the work of the master builder Isaac Hildrith (1741-1807), an Englishman who had moved to Virginia and had come to Nova Scotia as a Loyalist. He probably interpreted details from pattern books in constructing the building. Also in that seaport city, Province House (1811-19), Canada's oldest seat of government, is a superb example of Palladian-Georgian architecture, perhaps built to designs procured in England.

Other kinds of public buildings displayed a more domestic use of Georgian. The first Bank of Montreal (1818-19), on Montreal's rue Saint-Jacques, had the appearance of a classically inspired Georgian house, three storeys high and six bays wide, with a low Doric portico standing in front of two central doors. (It was demolished in 1870 and the much more impressive second bank, which still stands, was built next door in 1846-8.) The Bank of Upper Canada in York, on Duke Street (now Adelaide Street East) at George Street, was designed—by Dr William Warren Baldwin—as a gentlemen's townhouse in Regency London, with stone steps leading up to a porch and a double-door entrance with a fanlight above.* Osgoode Hall (1831-2), the home of the new Law Society of Upper Canada in York, was designed by John Ewart (1788-1856) and built on a large garden site purchased from John Beverley Robinson on Lot Street (Queen Street West), on the east side looking south down York Street facing the harbour. Its design also reflected that of a London mansion. An extension to the northwest, containing a three-storey wing for offices and student rooms, was designed by Dr Baldwin and built in 1833. (Additions in the 1850s and in 1888-90 completed the building we know today.)

Georgian dwellings of the more elaborate type can still be found, not only in larger cities but sprinkled throughout the provinces. On Brunswick Street in Fredericton, the house of Jonathan Odell (1737-1818)—Church of England clergyman, writer, Loyalist, one of the founders of Fredericton, and secretary of the province—was built between 1785 and 1795 and was perhaps the first house in New Brunswick to reflect the importance of its owner. Many owners of elaborate houses were merchants with political connections. In Saint John the Loyalist House (1817), at Union and German Streets, was built by Daniel David Merritt. Acacia Grove (1811-17) in Nova Scotia's Annapolis Valley was the earliest Georgian country house in that province, built for the Honourable Charles Ramage Prescott, a retired merchant who later served in government. The Black-Binney House (c. 1815-19) in Halifax was built—on Hollis Street, next to Government House—for John Black, another merchant and member of the legislative council. In York the castle-like Holland House (1831) was a suburban villa on a large property on the south side of Wellington at Bay, facing the harbour, the home of Henry John Boulton (1790-1870), who was appointed attorney-general in 1829 and was elected to the assembly the next year.** Holland House established the importance of its owner not by a classical portico—as in The Grange, the home of Henry John Boulton's elder brother—but by means of a three-storey curved tower with a Gothic arched loggia.

The taste for a more up-to-date version of Georgian architecture was satisfied by the arrival in British North America of a number of English

---

*The Bank of Upper Canada, which was chartered in 1821, had close links with the élite of York. William Allan was its first president, D'Arcy Boulton Jr, and his brother Henry John, were directors, along with Dr William Warren Baldwin. Two years after Baldwin died, in 1846, John Howard completed work on the Doric portico, with a wrought-iron railing above the cornice, that can be seen today.

**Boulton was dismissed as attorney-general in 1833 for his part in the repeated expulsions from the assembly of William Lyon Mackenzie—after Mackenzie had been to London and reached the ear of the colonial secretary, Lord Goderich, with his grievances.

architects who established careers there. John Howard (1803-90)—architect, surveyor, and artist—was responsible for designing, in and near York, many Regency villas, a variant of Late Georgian that was adapted to a country setting. His own Colborne Lodge (1836-40) is a superb example of the style, with its verandas and French doors opening out onto his estate, which he called High Park.*

Perth, on the Rideau Canal, retains prime examples of Late Georgian town building. It had the advantage of being able to employ Scottish stonemasons, one of whom presumably built a Georgian-related house-type, the Ontario Cottage, called Inge-Va ('Come here' in Tamil). This stone house, 1½ storeys high, with principal gables on the sides, a secondary gable (added later)—over a doorway having both a fanlight and sidelights—and a broad veranda, was built in 1824 for the Anglican rector, the Reverend Michael Harris. The Summit (1823) was built of brick in the newly laid-out town for James Boulton (the seventh child of D'Arcy Boulton Sr), who became a lawyer and moved to Perth in 1822, buying the choicest property in town to build a house that he modelled on The Grange, the home of his elder brother in York. (Implicated in the last fatal duel fought in Canada—because he had not prevented it—Boulton had to leave Perth for Niagara in 1833.) A block away is the much grander red-brick house (c. 1830-2) of the second lawyer in Perth, Daniel McMartin, in which three bays of the five-bay façade are contained within an elegant engaged arcade. White marble was used for quoins as a belt course between the two storeys, and for the window heads, and three wooden cupolas originally crowned the truncated hipped roof—combining late-eighteenth-century British classicism with the American Federal style. One explanation for this elaborate treatment may have to do with the rivalry that existed between McMartin and James Boulton, who had both attended Strachan's Grammar School in Cornwall and were at loggerheads until Boulton left Perth.

Late Georgian, though predominant in this period, was accompanied by other fashionable styles, among which Gothic Revival began to be used for churches. Perhaps the greatest monument of the period was the Church of Notre-Dame de Montréal (1823-9), on Place d'Armes. Designed by James O'Donnell (1774-1830), an Irish architect imported from New York, it is the earliest surviving example of a Canadian church designed in the Gothic Revival style. With its twin-towered façade and monumental entrance, it was for some time the largest church in North America. Its towers were completed in 1843, after O'Donnell's death. The interior was renovated in 1872-80 in a colourful High Victorian style.

Popular Culture

Other currents were stirring in British North America besides élitist imita-

---

*Howard gave High Park to the city in return for an annual salary until his death.

tion. Most of them had some connection with the vernacular culture of the common people, which tended to be oral rather than written, traditional rather than mimetic, and often connected either with artisan conventions or religious energy of the evangelical variety.

For all inhabitants of British North America, singing—both religious hymns and secular songs—was an important part of their culture. Most of what was sung was inherited from Europe, both music and lyrics, although the latter were frequently altered by time and to suit new circumstances. People sang as they worked in the fields, the *voyageurs* sang as they paddled their canoes, fishermen as they pulled up their nets. From the time of Henry Alline onward, hymn singing was central to any revival meeting in British North America, and at least in the period before 1840 hymns and hymn tunes were remembered rather than sung from books. Whenever people got together around a campfire or a stove in the evening of a Canadian winter, songs were sung, poems were recited, and stories told. Many of the pioneers sprang from ethnic backgrounds in which the bard—often a combination of poet and songster—represented an important folk memory.

Among no people were the bards more important than for the Gaelic-speaking Highland Scots, and there was perhaps no more important poetic voice in British North America in the period 1790-1840 than that of John MacLean (Iain MacGhilleathain, 1787-1848). MacLean's inherited task, like that of most bards, was to record the life of his chief and family, although in the disintegration of the clans at the beginning of the nineteenth century he found it necessary to move in other directions. In 1818 he published in Edinburgh a collection of poems by himself and other bards, and soon after immigrated to Pictou, Nova Scotia, moving thence to Merigomish, and eventually to Antigonish County. MacLean wrote extensively in the genre of the spiritual song, but in Nova Scotia he produced much 'village verse', based on local events and especially on the complaints of his people at their tribulations in the New World and their yearnings for their native land. A typical poem was 'The Deception' ('Am Mealladh'), which begins:

> On a sunny, mild, pleasant day,
> I went for a walk
> to take a look at the place,
> this land of tall trees and valleys.
> Alas, I was deceived;
> it is unfortunate that I left my beloved kin.
> Alas, I was deceived.

It concludes:

> In my heart I said sorrowfully:
> a pity I left the land of happiness
>
> to come west to dwell here
> even though I had wanted property.

In my folly I had thought
when I left with the Colonel,
that I would be going about with spur and boot,
gathering gold from every treetop.

I soon discovered that far-away fields
are not so green as reported.
Imagine what a trying experience it is
to lose one's ears in the cold spring.[35]

Vernacular culture expressed itself not merely in spiritual song and secular poem but in various other forms as well. One of the most tangible was a rich heritage of crafting in wood, the material that was so readily available everywhere in British North America. We have recently become more aware of this heritage, as examples of wooden sculptures—including the figure-heads of the great sailing ships of the time, carved by anonymous craftsmen—have become available in many Canadian museums. The sailing vessel itself was a monument to the skills of carpenters and builders, and while there was not much room for originality, British North America began producing vessels distinguished for their speed and for a great deal of regional variation. Even more ubiquitous than the ship was the house, the sum total of the assimilation of existing canons of style and taste combined with the possibil-ity of local or even individual variation. One of the most common places for distinctiveness was in the roof dormer, such as the 'Lunenburg bump' commonly found on the south shore of Nova Scotia southwest of Halifax. Another was in the back hallway leading to the kitchen, the preferred entrance way to most houses everywhere in the colonies and rendered in a host of styles and fashions. Housing tells us much about the ethnic traditions of any region, as well as about its prosperity. Acadian houses from this period are externally very similar to those of the British, for example, but their interiors are quite different.

Although élite culture in this period was imitative, popular culture sug-gested the rich possibilities for creative adaptation of the inherited past to the North American present. By 1840, for example, Scottish settlers familiar with the sport of curling had not only imported the game into a climate ideally suited for it, but had made great strides forward in its popularization. The first organized curling club in British North America was founded in Montreal in 1807, and by 1840, when the first Canadian book on curling was published, most urban centres had a club. So successful was the game in British North America that sometime around 1840 the world's first indoor curling facilities were constructed, probably in Montreal.

One of the predecessors of ice hockey—'bandy', 'shinty', or 'hurley'—was known to have been played in Dartmouth, Nova Scotia, in the 1830s by members of the garrison, who had learned it from the natives, as well as on the frozen harbour of Kingston. And a public ice-hockey game ('the ice-hurtling game') was described in the *Montreal Gazette* in February 1837.

Nor were all the games being developed and refined in British North America direct imports from Europe. The *Montreal Gazette* of 1 August 1833 reported an all-Indian lacrosse game between the Iroquois of Caughnawaga and the Mohawk of St Regis; this sport would soon be taken up by non-natives. Baseball was first played in Canada in a recognizably modern form in Beachville, Upper Canada, on 4 June 1838 as part of Militia Muster Day—a year earlier than Abner Doubleday's famous game in Cooperstown, New York.[36]

Given the vastness of the country, its division into a number of different colonies with varying ethnic backgrounds, and the large number of recent immigrants in various stages of assimilation—as well as the presence of marginalized groups and a very high residential and occupational turnover—it was hardly surprising that feelings of nationalism to rival those in the United States were fairly slow to develop. For most British North Americans in 1840, a sense of place did not extend very far beyond their immediate surroundings. The highest expression of love of country was for one's own province, reflected in the motto of Sir Walter Scott—'This is my own my native land'—which Thomas Haliburton attached to his history of Nova Scotia in 1829. No British North American was more ardently patriotic than Haliburton's publisher Joseph Howe. One of Howe's first editorials after he began publishing a newspaper in 1827 was entitled 'My Country', and in 1834 he lectured an audience at the Halifax Mechanics' Institute on the subject 'Love of Country a Stimulus to Enterprise'. In this address Howe argued that it was an 'unerring law of nature' that the colonial-born would transfer their allegiance and sense of attachment to their native land. And when Howe returned from a visit to England in 1838, he reminded his readers that however 'fascinated' he was 'by the splendours and novelties of an old nation', what he really loved was that 'small countrie that we wot of, far over the billow...that small spot of earth, between Cape Sable and Cape North'.[37] Such ardent local patriotism—but little more—could be found everywhere in British North America by 1840.

chapter ten

Developing the Economy, 1840–1865

On 3 July 1863 a prospectus for a reorganized Hudson's Bay Company was issued to the public in London, with capital fixed at two million pounds. The principal attraction of the stock was an opportunity to construct a transcontinental telegraph line across Hudson's Bay Company territory, arrangements having been made 'through Her Majesty's Government (subject to the final sanction of the Colonies) based on a 5 per cent. guarantee from the Governments of Canada, British Columbia and Vancouver Island.'[1] Shortly thereafter the government of Canada refused to have anything to do with the telegraph scheme, and the venture—which had been promoted by English businessman Edward Watkin (1819-1901)—for the moment came to nothing, beyond the acquisition of the assets of the Hudson's Bay Company by a new set of British businessmen. At the time of this promotion of stock shares, Watkin was president of the Canadian Grand Trunk, having begun in 1861 a salvage attempt for this financially troubled railway on behalf of its principal English creditors, the Baring brothers. The 1863 scheme was part of his effort.

The Grand Trunk Railway—initially intended to run between Montreal and Toronto—had been first projected in 1852 with great enthusiasm and hoopla. Ultimately it was intended to connect the eastern provinces of British North America with Canada by rail, but the British government refused to guarantee loans, and the Canadian government, under Premier Francis Hincks (1807-85), borrowed capital in British money markets against its own guarantees for a line from Montreal to the western end of Lake Ontario. Shareholders were promised a substantial annual dividend of 11.5 per cent, and the initial offering was oversubscribed. But like many such schemes, the Grand Trunk soon got out of hand, adding more track and borrowing more money. The contractors cut corners, and traffic never measured up to the expectations (some said, claims) of the promoters. The Canadian government demanded and got its own gauge, to prevent its stock from running on American lines. However, it forgot that the reverse also held: American stock could not run on its track. By 1857 the government of Canada was in debt for the Grand Trunk to the tune of $25,000,000, and four years later the road survived only with public assistance, while the investors more than grumbled.

Edward Watkin—who had been involved with railroads in Britain since 1845—had acted successfully on behalf of British investors when the Erie Railway in the United States was bankrupted, and his appointment in 1861 as president of the Grand Trunk was a natural one. Even before his arrival in Canada that same year, he had been attracted by arguments that 'nothing would serve the Grand Trunk Company so much as the opening of the western prairies.'[2] Watkin soon became involved in negotiations for an eastern railway extension called the Intercolonial Railway, not built until later, which was intended to increase intercolonial railroad traffic. He was also cognizant of the ambitions of the Canadian government to open telegraph and postal routes to British Columbia, as part of its plan to make the West available for settlement. In 1862 Watkin had sounded out the Hudson's Bay Company about purchasing it, and he pressed ahead on behalf of a syndicate in organizing the matter. All these schemes were part of the overall need, perceived necessary by Watkin and other businessmen of the time, to make over-capitalized central-Canadian railroads profitable by increasing their business and by tying them into larger transportation and communication systems. As Watkin put it, 'some effort *westward*' was required, for 'Intercolonial is. . .absolutely essential to Grand Trunk: and Intercolonial is, under present circs [circumstances] in Canada, dependent upon this other movement.'[3] Prospective investors in speculative ventures reacted well to impressive-sounding schemes, and British investors were easily persuaded to support Watkin's operations.

High finance, huge public debts, railroad construction, and westward expansion—all were characteristic of the new economic order in British North America after 1840, and they were all inextricably connected. The financial troubles of one railway, in eastern British North America, thus led in the first instance to the apparently disconnected purchase by British financial interests of the great fur-trade company that controlled western British North America, and would eventually lead in 1869 to the purchase by Canada of the Hudson's Bay Company's vast territory. Along the way, the Grand Trunk's debt-load would contribute to the unification of British North America.

The Demise of Mercantilism

By 1840 the mercantile economy of British North America—based on an unremitting exploitation of colonial raw resources for the international market, particularly Britain—had reached its apex, and was about to undergo considerable change. That alteration would be based on a number of factors, of which the most important were clearly the demolition by the British government of the imperial trading system that had prevailed since the seventeenth century, a shift into seeking advantage in the burgeoning American market, and the rise of new technologies that began to resolve the long-standing transportation problems of internal development. Instead of mercantilism, Britain moved to free trade, and in the process wiped out the protectionist advantages for her colonies. As a result, in place of a transatlantic economy based on the sailing ship, much of British North America was forced to think in terms of a continental economy. Fortunately the railroad came along at exactly this time, providing visions of both internal development and internal markets. And also fortunately, long-standing differences with the Americans were resolved, making possible the negotiation of a trade treaty that provided some access for British North America into the lucrative American market. Inherent in the reorganization of the commercial economy was the rise of industrialization. Internal markets within the continent required not raw materials but finished goods, and colonial businessmen sought to oblige.

The Rise of Free Trade in Great Britain

The old mercantile system of Britain, which had essentially been in place since the first round of colonial expansion at the start of the seventeenth century, had been under attack since the period of the American Revolution by a number of political and economic thinkers. The rebellion of the colonists merely substantiated the critics' basic arguments: mercantilism was, in Josiah Tucker's words, 'THE GREATEST INFATUATION'. According to Tucker, arguing in 1776 against those who bemoaned American separatism, England would be better off purchasing raw materials at the best possible prices instead of paying bounties to encourage inferior colonial production. Tucker further insisted that 'When all Parties shall be left at full Liberty to do as they please, our *North-American* Trade will rather be increased than diminished, because it is Freedom, and not Confinement, or Monopoly, which increases Trade.'[4] Adam Smith's *Wealth of Nations* (1776) provided a thoroughly reasoned theoretical framework for free trade, and offered a vision of international expansion based upon it. In the years following Smith, a number of classical political economists in Britain—Malthus, Chambers, Ricardo, Mill—expanded on earlier critiques of mercantilism, always insisting that freedom worked best, even in the market-place.

Despite the intellectual demolition of mercantilism in the first quarter of the nineteenth century, British governments found protectionism difficult to give up for political reasons, since it artificially supported influential sectors of the economy. Eventually, however, the free-traders won out, largely because of Britain's industrial successes after 1815. With the most dynamic industrial economy in the world by the 1840s, the British could no longer afford the luxury of protectionism, which limited their access to foreign raw materials; they could no longer maintain that they required its converse, guaranteed colonial markets. By 1841 only twenty-two per cent of the British labour force was employed in agriculture, forestry, or fishing, as opposed to thirty-five per cent in 1801; and forty per cent were employed in mining and manufacturing, up from thirty per cent in 1801. Cotton textiles accounted for about half of all British exports, and Britain had become 'the Workshop of the World'.

The overall strategy for the British economy had not changed since the seventeenth century; it still emphasized importing cheap raw materials and exporting finished goods to overseas markets, 'vast territories in North and South America, in the plains of Buenos Ayres, in the hills and dales of Australia and New Zealand'.[5] One of the leading free-traders, John MacGregor (1797-1857), originally from PEI, emphasized in a study entitled *British America* (1832) that Britain's American colonies, especially the lands west of the Great Lakes, could support an enormous population and control 'the umpirage of the Western World'. What turned Britain to free trade in the 1840s was a realization that it would work to British advantage. The ministry led by Sir Robert Peel therefore gritted its teeth and systematically removed protection for corn and other raw materials (including timber), justifying the repeal of the Corn Laws in terms of the famines of the 1840s. 'I am fairly convinced', Peel wrote in 1846, 'that the permanent adjustment of the Corn Laws has rescued the country and the whole frame of society from the hazard of very serious convulsion.'[6] While British free-trade policies made possible a new wave of British overseas expansion—wedded to economies rather than territories—they also had a tremendous impact, perhaps more psychological than actual, on colonial merchants and their political allies, especially in the rich heartland of British North America. Britain's industrial needs also contributed to the need for international peace and bilateral understandings.

Anglo-American Entente

British policy since the War of 1812 had been to seek *entente* with the Americans, a process that gained impetus in the period of free-trade innovation of the 1840s, and by 1846 most of the outstanding boundary questions between the two nations were resolved. In 1842 the Webster-Ashburton Treaty had sorted out the complex eastern boundary issues along the Maine-New Brunswick border. This dispute had simmered since the 1783 Treaty of Paris, which had confused matters by drawing a line that did not match the geographical realities of the region. By the 1830s there was much tension in the disputed territory, and the desire of both parties to resolve matters was demonstrated by the fact that each side suppressed its official maps (which showed the area in question to belong to the other party) to avoid public outcry over a compromise decision.

The boundary problem was even more intense west of the Rocky Mountains, where the two nations had agreed in 1818 to share occupation until there was need for a formal decision. Many Americans had already settled in the Oregon territory south of the Columbia River, and presidential candidate James Polk had in 1844 rattled American sabres with his campaign slogan of '54°40' [the southernmost Russian boundary on the Pacific slope] or Fight'. American administrations of the 1840s were quite aggressive over continental expansion—the Polk government would go to war with Mexico in 1846 in the aftermath of the 1845 annexation of Texas—and the British were prepared to come to terms. Again a 'compromise' was reached, this time one less even-handed than in the East. Under the Oregon Boundary Treaty of 1846 the border across the Rockies to the Pacific was continued from the Great Lakes at the 49th parallel to the Pacific (excluding Vancouver Island), thus allowing the Americans to possess what would become the State of Washington, in which they had virtually none of their nationals, and which had been partially occupied by the Hudson's Bay Company. The forty-ninth parallel artificially bisected the Pacific territory, where mountain ranges and river valleys ran north and south rather than east and west. But apart from a few protests from the Hudson's Bay Company, British North Americans were not concerned with the Oregon Treaty, except insofar as it pacified the Americans.

The Reaction to Free Trade in British North America

The Early Response

Most merchants appreciated the nature of the revolution that had been going on in Britain since 1842, and those in Canada especially waited apprehensively for news about the future of the Corn Laws in 1846. 'We do not believe', observed one colonial newspaper, 'that since Canada became a Province of the British Empire the arrival of any vessel from Europe was ever looked for with half the anxiety as that of the *Hibernia*'—the vessel that would report that Peel had been returned to office. The situation seemed particularly difficult, since the Americans had been engaged in their own commercial revisions, in 1845 and 1846, passing legislation remitting duties on goods imported into the United States from foreign countries and re-exported to Canada. Everyone rushed to export wheat and timber under the old system and, predictably, oversupply and the uncertainty resulting from the repeal of the Corn Laws and the Timber Duties, both in 1846, resulted in a collapse of prices in 1847 that was to last for the remainder of the decade. Wheat exports fell from 628,000 bushels in 1847 to 238,000 bushels by 1848, and flour exports dropped from 651,000 to 383,000 barrels. Further complicating matters for colonial governments was the arrival of thousands of impoverished Irish immigrants, refugees from the Great Famine of the

1840s, bringing death and expense to the colonies along with their anguish. The result of all these blows was a conviction that the old Empire had collapsed, indeed had been subverted by the mother country. Canadians themselves helped complete the demolition of the old mercantilism when they argued for the repeal of the British Navigation Acts, which regulated shipping, in favour of opening the St Lawrence to the Americans. Those shipping laws were abandoned by Britain in 1849.

Because of the reliance on wheat exports of the Province of Canada, Canada East and Canada West (Lower and Upper Canada having been reunited by the Act of Union of 1840), the crisis seemed much more serious there than elsewhere in British North America, although all colonies turned instinctively from the mother country to that other obvious trading partner, the United States. The Americans had been engaged for decades in their own economic development, and by the 1840s had applied Manifest Destiny to expand their geographical empire to include much of the North American continent, from coast to coast. They had taken what they wanted of the southwest from Mexico in the Mexican-American War of 1846, and what they needed of the northwest from Britain that same year, utilizing American pioneers settling beyond existing territorial limits as the foot-soldiers of their expansion. The Americans had a vision of an integrated continental economy, and their energy was consumed more in internal development than in the search for overseas markets; after 1846 they seemed reasonably satisfied with their territorial situation.

Canadian policy in the 1840s, in the wake of British free trade, was to attempt to come to terms with the Americans. Indeed, in 1848 the Montreal Board of Trade insisted that Canadian-American interests 'under the changed policy of the Imperial Government are germane to each other, and under that system must sooner or later be politically interwoven.'[7] The Canadians pressed on with the improvement of their internal transportation system, largely through expensive canal construction that increased the Canadian debt considerably, and argued for reciprocal free trade between British North America and the United States in the natural products of each.

The Annexation Movement

In 1849, in a fit of desperation, four of the leading English-language newspapers of Montreal, speaking for the mercantile community of Canada East, editorially supported annexation to the United States. The demand for annexation followed an extremely intense political debate over compensation for Lower Canadians who had not rebelled but had lost property in 1837. The anglophone press viewed the Rebellion Losses Bill of 1849 with contempt, regarding it as 'the famous outrage, the damning insult to the loyal people of Canada, the Bill by which traitors, rebels, and murderers, are to be indemnified for supposed losses incurred by them in consequence of their crimes.'[8] Mass meetings in Montreal to protest the passage of the legislation

Burning of the Houses of Assembly, at Montreal. The burning of the parliament buildings, and the riot by a Tory and Orange mob, followed the passage of the Rebellion Losses Bill on 25 April 1849. This engraving (and the caption) appeared in the *London Illustrated News*, 19 May 1849, which editorialized: 'The Ultra-Tory, and formerly ultra-loyal party in Canada, have proceeded at last from rebellious speeches to rebellious acts. They have grossly insulted and assaulted the Queen's representative, they have burned down the Houses of Parliament. . . and committed a series of acts which would have disgraced the most ignorant mob of the most lawless city in Europe.' Metropolitan Toronto Reference Library.

led to a mob attack on the Parliament Buildings, in the course of which they were set on fire and burned to the ground. Supporting annexation was another way of protesting against the current state of affairs, and while it may have seemed ironic that those who had so often proclaimed their loyalty to the Empire were now suggesting another strategy, there was a certain consistency in the position. As one manifesto of the annexationists explained:

> The truth is, that between the abandonment by England of her former system of protection to Colonial produce, and the refusal of the United States to trade with us on a footing of reciprocity, Canada, to use the old proverb, is between the devil and the deep sea, and we must own—it may be perhaps from our terrible blindness—that we can see no way to get out of the scrape, but by going to prosperity, since prosperity will not come to us.[9]

The arguments are familiar to any Canadian. 'What matter is it', asked one newspaper, 'whether you number yourself among the millions of Anglo-Saxons that obey our gentle Queen Victoria, or among those other millions who have delegated the supreme administration of their affairs for four years to plain old [US President] Zachary Taylor?'[10] The cause was occasionally taken up outside Montreal. The Toronto *Examiner*, for example, was prepared to allow that 'However strongly many may cleave to British Connexion as a matter of choice, all agree that the great interests of the country must be sustained even at the sacrifice of such a connexion.'[11] The wide circulation of such opinions in the mother country merely confirmed the views of those opposed to a political empire that ungrateful colonials would always leave the mother country at the first hint of denial of their demands.

～✦～ Reciprocity

Annexationism, however, was a far less widespread movement than that of reciprocity, which flourished in the economic and commercial uncertainties of the late 1840s, seeming to become less popular as the depression that had accompanied the British free-trade actions ended in 1851. Many British North Americans saw annexation as the inevitable result of the failure to achieve reciprocity, rather than as a desirable end in itself. Canadians, especially those dependent on the wheat economy, viewed internal markets— which they initially considered to be in the United States—as the only alternative to markets in Britain that had been lost with the repeal of the Corn Laws. The leading Canadian spokesman for reciprocity, William Hamilton Merritt (1793-1862) of St Catharines, argued the case in the Canadian parliament in 1846:

> Were our products admitted into their markets. . .the Canadian farmer would at all times be placed on an equal footing, in all respects with the western farmer. . .he would realize the advantages he possessed and resist any political change.[12]

In New Brunswick, where the timbering industry was reeling from the ending of imperial preference in 1846, reciprocity would allow colonial shipbuilders access to the American market and provide an outlet for the province's timber. Both Nova Scotia and Prince Edward Island were also enthusiastic, demanding that they be 'included in any measure of reciprocity that may be obtained for Canada.'[13] Only Newfoundland initially remained aloof, on the grounds that 'no advantage, to be derived from a reciprocal free trade with the United States of America, would compensate for the concession to the citizens of that Republic of a participation in the Fisheries of this Colony.'[14] But Newfoundland would ultimately become enthusiastic.

In the United States, Israel D. Andrews published in 1851 the first of several reports favouring reciprocal free trade in natural products between the United States and Canada, stating that 'this measure recommends itself strongly to American interests and magnanimity'. Andrews saw the two countries as economically complementary, and maintained that a product that had a large surplus to be controlled by the international market could not be protected by domestic duties. Thus Canadian wheat was no threat to American prices. Andrews was very bullish about the prospects of British North America as a market for American finished goods.[15]

Economic prosperity returned to British North America in the 1850s—when reciprocity, like annexationism, lost much of its support. But there were some who kept the scheme alive, and the various colonial governments, especially the Province of Canada, began looking for ways of pressuring the Americans. Newfoundland's assembly, in 1852, suddenly awoke to the possibility of being left out of a treaty and kept insisting on being included at the same time that other provinces were having second thoughts, mainly over fisheries concessions that the Americans had made clear were an essential part of any trade negotiation. Although the British government generally supported reciprocal arrangements between British North America and the United States—partly on grounds that any freeing of trade was a good thing, partly as an ingredient in Anglo-American *entente*, but mainly to gratify very unruly colonials—the American government showed almost no interest in the matter until 1852, when the British government decided to toughen its fisheries policy. What little American political opinion there was about reciprocity was supportive, although for contradictory reasons. In the northern states reciprocity was seen as the first step towards annexation of the British colonies. Horace Greeley's New York *Tribune* declared editorially: 'Expansion in the direction of the north star—expansion for the purpose of union with more than two millions of liberty-loving slavery-hating people. . .is not a prospect to cry out against at the present moment.'[16] On the other hand, the southern states saw reciprocity as the only way to prevent annexation, which would greatly upset the delicate political balance between North and South in the United States.

The Reciprocity Treaty, as it was ultimately negotiated in 1854, was hardly a very broad-ranging free-trade agreement. It removed tariff and other barriers on a variety of enumerated goods, mainly raw materials common to both countries, such as grain, meat, flour, livestock, coal, fish, and fish-oil. These had previously been the principal items of export to the United States as well as the principal items of import from the Americans. The treaty did not remove barriers on finished goods ('dutiable items', as they were called), although the Americans hoped the increased prosperity of British North America under the treaty would lead to greater imports. Instead, the volume of trade in dutiable items did not increase, and several provinces of British North America (including Canada) increased duties, ostensibly for revenue purposes, during the life of the treaty. What the treaty did was open markets for raw materials in both directions, as well as make possible several re-export commodity trades abroad, such as the shipment of American wheat through Canadian ports. This result, of course, was much more beneficial to British North America than to the United States, which explains why the Americans were so anxious to abrogate the treaty at the expiration of its initial ten-year term. But it does not appear to have increased trade considerably in either direction. British North America did not aggressively market its raw materials and agricultural produce in the United States, even during the Civil War years when prices and demand were high. In particular, the so-called 'lower provinces' (the Atlantic provinces) failed to increase their exports to New England significantly.

British North America Under Reciprocity

Although the Reciprocity Treaty produced few important changes in the patterns of north-south trade, statistics are not the entire story. Psychologically the arrangement was far more critical for British North America than for the United States. It encouraged merchants, entrepreneurs, and politicians—especially in the Province of Canada—to continue the process of reconceptualizing their economic orientation: from an imperial context, in which the British market was critical, to a context in which continental markets were dominant. Once turned from the traditional transatlantic economy to a continental one, Canada began to emphasize industrialization and the need for its own internal markets. Indeed, one of the principal reasons why American trade in dutiable items did not expand during the ten years of the agreement was that the manufacturing capacity of British North America—again, particularly in the Province of Canada—grew substantially in this period. But this process of economic reorientation was not uniform in all of British North America. Canada and the Atlantic provinces moved in somewhat different directions. While the Canadians became immersed in internal development—even territorial expansion into the Prairie West— the Atlantic provinces continued to find the older transatlantic economy quite comfortable, basing their prosperity on a shipping industry oriented around the wooden sailing ship, which the region was successfully producing. The period from 1840 to the early 1870s was the 'Golden Age of Sail' in the Atlantic region.

Agriculture

While agriculture continued to serve as the basis for much of the economic vitality of British North America, particularly in central Canada, the period after 1850 saw several significant and related shifts in agricultural development. First, by 1850 Canada West had joined Canada East in reaching the limits of expansion of land that could profitably be brought under wheat cultivation. Second, the commercial reorientation from the international to the internal market, accompanied by great improvements in internal transportation through canals and railroads in the 1850s, permitted agriculture in Canada West to shift out of monocultivation of grain into mixed farming. The new produce of mixed farming, particularly in the dairy area (for example, butter and cheese), often found markets in Britain. In 1854 the seigneurial system in the St Lawrence Valley was brought to an end by legislative fiat, with traditional seigneurial obligations replaced by a quitrent, and tenants given the opportunity to purchase their lands. The gradual elimination of the seigneurial system provided further evidence that agriculture needed to be modernized, at the same time that commerce and industry were undergoing major changes. As agriculture was transformed, along with other economic activity, the percentage of the population of central Canada that depended on it decreased, from about two-thirds of the total population in 1850 to under sixty per cent by 1870.

Given the greatly expanding population of British North America throughout the mid-nineteenth century, combined with distinctly limited amounts of really productive agricultural land, the opportunities for farm ownership quickly became problematic throughout most parts of the provinces. One result was a substantial outmigration to the United States (discussed in detail in Chapter 13), beginning in Canada East in the 1840s and in the Atlantic region in the 1850s. It would eventually put substantial pressure on the economies of the several provinces to employ intending migrants so that they would stay at home. By 1860, when the pressure was most felt in Canada East, the nature of the problem had not yet hit the Atlantic region, which still thought of itself as dynamic and prosperous because of its international commercial success in shipbuilding.

The Golden Age of the Atlantic Provinces

Despite the development of new technologies, the wooden sailing vessel remained the dominant element in shipping until later in the nineteenth century. Atlantic Canada enjoyed not only the raw materials, but also the skilled expertise for building and sailing such vessels that enabled it to benefit from both the local and the international need for a carrying trade. The most important shipping advantage the region enjoyed, its access to cheap vessels, was enhanced even in the early days of competition with iron steamers. In the 1860s, for example, a large new sailing ship could be purchased in Atlantic Canada for between a quarter and half the price of an iron steamer built on the Clyde, and so long as the speed and efficiency of the latter was not double that of the former, sailing vessels remained profitable. For the Atlantic region, then, the key to expansion was not in the traditional export of resources, but in the opportunity to carry goods produced anywhere in the world. Atlantic shipping flourished during the early 1860s, when the United States was engaged in a bloody civil war and its merchant marine decreased substantially in size.

With hindsight, it is possible to recognize the inherent weaknesses in the Atlantic situation, even at the point of its greatest success and prosperity. The carrying-trade was an industry of high risks and fairly rapid capital depreciation; the life expectancy of a wooden sailing vessel was no more than fifteen years. Moreover, this trade was an international one, part of the transatlantic rather than the continental economy, and subject to international developments over which Nova Scotia and New Brunswick had no control. The most important elements in the carrying-trade, during its heyday, did not directly involve the economy of British North America at all, because it concentrated on traffic with the United States and markets in Britain and Europe, transporting bulk commodities such as wheat, cotton, and petroleum. The Atlantic shipping industry was plugged into an international economy, and its success or failure was totally dependent on such factors as bulk freight rates and technological innovation by competitors. Nonetheless, the carrying-trade was for some time a substantial and profitable economic enterprise in the Atlantic region. It provided employment for thousands, both in the shipyards and on board the sailing vessels. It also produced an outward-looking international orientation rather than one that focused on internal continental development: for Atlantic entrepreneurs, freight rates in Boston were more important than territorial expansion into the western hinterland. While the Atlantic provinces (not so much Newfoundland) were eager to expand transportation links with Canada, they thought first of the implications for the carrying-trade between Europe and America, not of supplying an internal market with their own production.

Canada and the Railway Mania of the 1850s

The Province of Canada, on the other hand, became fascinated by the internal market because transportation improvements were one key to internal development. Canals had proved a most unsatisfactory means to achieve the necessary integration, since they could be tied only to existing waterways. The new technology of the steam engine riding on rails, first developed in Britain in the 1820s and in the United States in the 1830s, was ideally suited to Canadian needs.

Canadian railroad expansion would not occur in earnest until after 1850, by which time the old imperial trade system had obviously been demolished. The thrust for internal improvement was influenced by imperial reorientation, so that what was actually attempted did not have to include overseas linkages. British North Americans had always recognized the potential advantages of railroads, but had managed to construct only several short lines in the early years of the railway era. The Champlain and St Lawrence Railroad Company opened a line around the Richelieu Rapids in 1836, employing an imported steam engine and wooden rails. A railway around Niagara Falls was built in 1839, but with grades too steep for primitive locomotives. Several lines in Nova Scotia operated to carry coal short distances. More ambitious projects were often discussed, one from Saint John to Quebec as early as 1827. In the 1830s territorial disputes prevented actual construction of a railroad from Saint Andrew's, New Brunswick, to Lower Canada, despite approval from the assemblies of both provinces and British financial support for a survey (the land surveyed went to Maine in 1842). A

The Bytown and Prescott Railroad, 1851. National Archives of Canada, C-28864.

The Great Western Railway Station in Toronto, facing southwest on Yonge Street at The Esplanade. Designed by William G. Storm in the Romanesque style, this wooden building was completed in March 1866. In 1882, when the Great Western amalgamated with the Grand Trunk Railway, the station became a depot for freight, then for wholesale produce; it was in use as recently as May 1952, when it was destroyed by fire. This engraving of a Notman and Fraser photograph appeared in the *Canadian Illustrated News* on 2 April 1870. Metropolitan Toronto Reference Library.

number of charters were granted in Upper Canada, but no construction was actually begun. By 1850, therefore, only 60 miles of track were in operation in Canada. The obstacles had not been technological, but financial and psychological. Railroads were expensive capital investments, few routes in British North America promised to be immediately profitable, and finding investors was not an easy business—at least until the railway boom of the 1850s.

The most advanced thinking on railroads in Canada was expressed in a pamphlet by the civil engineer Thomas Coltrin Keefer (1821-1915), appropriately titled *The Philosophy of Railroads* (1850). Keefer was a St Catharines boy, educated at Upper Canada College in Toronto. He apprenticed on the Erie Canal, worked on the Welland Canal, but was basically unemployed in 1849 when he wrote a prize-winning paper that was published as *The Canals of Canada* (1850). This visionary pamphlet not only saw the St Lawrence waterway as the best outlet for the western interior, but argued for free trade in agricultural products and a moderate tariff to encourage industrialization. His *Philosophy of Railroads*, written on behalf of the Montreal and Lachine Railroad, argued strenuously for the developmental advantages of rail, employing the vision of the born promoter. Keefer saw railroad stocks as ideal investments, arguing that 'if universal ruin be inevitable, *they* will be the last public works to succumb to the general prostration.'[17] He visualized railroads—these 'iron civilizers'—converting sleepy agricultural villages into manufacturing centres, and bringing their inhabitants into the modern world. With reference to the St Lawrence and Atlantic Railway, he emphasized its importance to Montreal, 'inasmuch as it will pass for upwards of 100 miles through an agricultural country naturally depending upon Montreal for its supplies', and added:

> As an outlet. . .for the agricultural productions of the districts through which it passes, and as a means of supplying the city with firewood, vegetables, fruits and articles which without a Railway would not reach the market, (*and as a means of promoting manufactures*) it will be successful beyond a doubt.[18]

Although much of his emphasis was on getting raw materials out of the interior, Keefer clearly recognized the railway's importance in supplying a market with manufactured goods.

In the 1850s a mania for internal development quickly captured the imaginations of Canadian politicians and investors, encouraged by promises of ultimate profits brought about by railroad construction. Keefer acknowledged that Canada was short on capital, but failed to add that railroads were extremely expensive to build, especially if the British practice of solid construction was observed—rather than the American one of building at cheap initial cost and upgrading only as traffic permitted. British North America opted for British practice, and the Great Western Railway, which opened in January 1854 between Niagara Falls-Hamilton-London-Windsor, cost

$66,000 per mile; the Grand Trunk Railway, incorporated in 1852 to build a railway from Toronto to Montreal (later extended), cost $63,800 per mile. By 1867 the total cost to Canada of 2,188.25 miles of track was $145,794,853, or roughly $66,000 per mile. In order to pay for construction, money had to be raised on the British exchanges, and governments had to both guarantee the loans and eventually contribute themselves. The Canadian government alone, by 1867, had incurred a provincial debt on railway construction of over $33,000,000, and its municipalities added considerably more.

Not only was construction expensive, but the sums of money involved in the manipulation of such high finance encouraged the worst in many businessmen and politicians (who were often the same people). This period has often been criticized for the lack of leadership—and the extent of venality—of its politicians. Allan MacNab (1798-1862), for example—who was seven times chairman of the Canadian assembly's railroad committee between 1848 and 1857 and served the province as co-premier in 1854-6—was at various times president of three railway companies, chairman of another, and director of two more. It was MacNab who coined the immortal phrase, 'All my politics are railroads.' He profiteered in stock shares in his own companies, sold land to them at inflated prices, organized construction companies to build his roads, accepted 'retirement gifts' to leave boards of directors, and while premier took cash payments from railway companies. Although 'conflict of interest' had not yet appeared as a political concept, MacNab's career made him, for one associate, 'an excrescence which cannot be got rid of.'[19]

Interlocking directorates of politicians and businessmen, engaged in the various aspects of railroad construction, were common. So too were bribes to assembly members. As Sir Edmund Hornby, who administered the Canadian business of the Grand Trunk, wrote of the political manoeuvering over one unnamed railroad bill in his *Autobiography* (1928):

> The Canadian Ministers were willing enough but weak—the majority a doubtful quantity, and although up to the last moment I felt there was a chance of getting the Bill through, I was always doubtful, since it was clear that some twenty-five members, contractors, etc., were simply waiting to be squared either by promise of contracts or money, and as I had no authority to bribe they simply abstained from voting and the Bill was thrown out. Twenty-five thousand pounds would have bought the lot, but I would rather somebody else had the job than myself. . . . As usual it was a Psalm-Singing Protestant Dissenter who, holding seven or eight votes in the palm of his hand, volunteered to do the greasing process for a consideration. Upon my word I do not think there was much to be said in favour of the Canadians over the Turks when contracts, places, free tickets on railways, or even cash was in question.[20]

Thomas Keefer himself later wrote in 1863 of the boom period of railroad construction: 'No machinery could be better devised for launching a doubtful project,. . .viewed as a commercial undertaking, than that possessed by the colossal railway contractors, the modern and unique results of the railway era.'[21] And, he added, 'During the Grand Trunk era of construction, from 1853 to 1859, the first Canadian age of iron, and of brass—the utmost activity was displayed in running into debt.'[22]

Construction over-runs were common, corruption rampant. But, Keefer emphasized, 'the great want of the Canadian railways is a paying traffic,' and he was highly critical of expensive construction well in advance of settlement, resulting in what he called 'colonization roads'. By 1863, looking back, Keefer would have preferred an alternative strategy of 'national' railways, such as the Intercolonial, to link the lower provinces with central and western Canada. Such a railroad would, he insisted, 'promote immigration, develop the resources, and provide for the defence of the country.' He recommended giving large endowments of land to companies willing to construct such roads, but admitted that without western immigrant travel, a Canadian road would have large numbers of cars travelling west as 'empties', the landlocked equivalent of sailing in ballast.

All railway promoters insisted that their lines would promote manufacturing by reducing transportation costs to a minimum. As Keefer earlier had rhapsodized:

> A town has been built and peopled by the operatives—land rises rapidly in value—the neglected swamp is cleared and the timber is converted into all sorts of wooden 'notions'—tons of vegetables, grains, or grasses, are grown where none grew before—the patient click of the loom, the rushing of the shuttle, the busy hum of the spindle, the thundering of the trip-hammer, and the roaring of steam, are mingled into one continuous sound of active industry.[23]

He might almost have been thinking of Collingwood (incorporated 1858), at the southern end of Georgian Bay, which was called by early settlers the 'impenetrable swamp'. It contained nothing but a tiny village until it became, in 1855, the northern terminus of the Ontario, Simcoe and Huron Railway. A similar success-story awaited Ingersoll, fifteen miles east of London, which prospered with cheese-making and agricultural-implement manufacturing after the arrival of the Great Western Railway in 1853.

Industrialization

The extent to which the railroads were themselves responsible for the increasing industrialization of British North America, particularly Montreal and Canada West, is a moot point, because railroads and industrialization emerged together in the 1850s. Railroads not only closed the distance between markets, they also served as a major market for industrial goods and were industrial manufacturers themselves. The Grand Trunk, for example, began by building its own cars, but by 1857 decided to produce its own rails, constructing an iron foundry and rolling mill in Hamilton. By the late 1850s

Steam-forging Hammer in the Great Western Railway Works, Hamilton, Ontario — an engraving that appeared in the *Canadian Illustrated News* on 14 February 1863. From the accompanying article on the workshops: '. . . one would scarcely suppose that those small scraps of iron scattered about, many of them weighing but a few ounces, were in process of becoming important parts of a locomotive engine, but so it is. The process is thus: the scraps are piled on boards two or three feet long. These are placed in the furnace. Soon the heat fuses the scraps into a lump, which is pulled out and placed under the hammer, which with a few vigorous thwacks kneeds them together as a baker would his dough. They are then beaten into layers of about an inch thickness, and the requisite number welded together to form a crank, axle, or the parts of a driving wheel, as the case may be. Our sketch of the hammer shows the forging of a large shaft for the stationary engine, fourteen feet long and weighing sixteen hundred-weight.' Courtesy Special Collections, Hamilton Public Library.

both the Grand Trunk and the Great Western were building their own locomotives in their own shops. Not only were railroads some of the largest manufacturers in Canada, but they were also involved in the heavy-industry sector of the economy. The Great Western's car factory at Hamilton was described as 'not only the largest workshop of the kind, but perhaps, the most extensive manufacturing establishment of any description in Western Canada.' A journalist marvelled in 1857, after a tour of the plant:

> The first room we entered seemed to be the general hospital, in which the sick giants were disposed in long rows and supported at a considerable height, on

wooden blocks and beams. Passing in we came to two rows of ponderous machines. There were drilling machines, boring holes of various sizes through any thickness of metal. There were planing machines which dealt with iron and brass as if they were soft wood, and rapidly reduced the blocks of metal to the necessary form—machines which cut iron as if it were paper, and punched holes through quarter inch plates as easily as you would punch a gun-wad from a piece of paste-board.[24]

The physical plant for this operation was huge; the carpentry shop was 165 feet long by 83 feet wide, and the body-building shop 300 feet by 50.

Before 1850 industrial enterprises in the Province of Canada had been small (most employed less than five people), scattered (nearly half of those working in them lived outside the major towns), and limited in variety (two-thirds of the industrial work force in 1851 were involved in textile manufacturing, blacksmithing, and the resource trades). The cities were still chiefly commercial centres, and manufacturing supplied mainly a local market. In 1850 shipbuilding was the only large-scale industry, with seven shipyards in Quebec City employing over 1,300 men.

The diverse business activities of John Molson (1787-1860) were characteristic of entrepreneurs in the transitional period from commerce to manufacturing. He was a member of the prominent Montreal business family founded by his father, John Molson Sr (1763-1836), which had interests that extended far beyond the Molson Brewery and were closely bound together in a series of unstable partnerships. Molson's engineering abilities were used in his father's shipping enterprise—John Molson Sr had launched the first steamship built in Lower Canada, the *Accommodation*, in 1809 and a few years later the *Swiftsure* (1812) and the *Malsham* (1814)—when the Molson family acquired majority control of the St Lawrence Steamboat Company, founded in 1822, which expanded to gain control of all shipping on the Ottawa River and the Rideau Canal. In 1826 Molson was elected to the board of directors of the Bank of Montreal; in 1836 he was appointed president of the Montreal Gas Light Company, which provided gas lamps for all the city's main streets the next year; and he moved into railroads ahead of most Canadians when he co-founded the Champlain and St Lawrence Railroad, of which he was named president in 1836, the year the railroad was inaugurated. Molson's interest in iron technology led him into iron-making, and in 1835 he began to manage the St Mary's Foundry, owned by his father, inheriting it when his father died the next year. (Though this foundry built heavy machinery, it had only seven employees.) Molson also owned a good deal of property in and around Montreal; his Montreal home was Belmont Hall, at the corner of Sherbrooke and Saint-Laurent. His career therefore embraced a great many of the activities that were bolstering the economy: brewing, steam navigation, iron-founding, railways, street-lighting, import-export, real estate, and banking.

After 1850—as manufacturers developed much larger plants, ceased supplying only local markets, and began producing for export, an enterprise that required substantial capital investments—the changes in Canada were both rapid and profound. In the Montreal region, which advanced most rapidly into industrialism after the 1850s, most of the large firms with large capital investments were relatively recent creations, initially involved in clothing production (especially boots and shoes) and agricultural processing. By the later 1850s Montreal had moved aggressively into large-scale heavy-metal production and fabrication, building on the earlier foundries like St Mary's and importing its iron ore and coal from the United States. By the mid-1860s the city had seven foundries and three rolling mills. Montreal industrialized rapidly for several reasons, but chiefly because of its labour supply and its access to capital. One promotional pamphlet of 1856 made the city's case well. It had a commercial base and access to water-power, wrote the authors, who continued:

> Another advantage Montreal possesses, is found in the density of the population of the surrounding districts. In many places the land has been subdivided until the holdings of each man are too small for profitable agriculture, and the people, deeply attached to the soil, are unwilling to leave the older settlements in the valleys of the St. Lawrence and Richelieu so long as they can obtain subsistence there....No where are there found people better adapted for factory hands, more intelligent, docile, and giving less trouble to their employers, than in Lower Canada.[25]

The expansion of population, and the subdivision of agricultural holdings—which had already begun in the 1830s and 1840s—produced an outflow of Lower Canadians into the factories of New England, and would also lead them into the factories of Montreal. To take advantage of this new labour force, Montreal entrepreneurs had little difficulty raising capital in what was the largest money-market in British North America.

Although the Molsons did move into banking in the 1850s, establishing the Molson Bank as a private bank in 1853 and restructuring it as a chartered bank in 1855, the great financier and industrialist of the post-1850 period was Hugh Allan (1810-1882), who was born in Scotland into a family with large shipping interests, operating vessels that sailed between Glasgow and the St Lawrence. Hugh came to Montreal in 1826, and in 1831 joined an importing firm with shipping interests. Four years later he became a partner and, with his father's assistance, expanded the firm's shipping operations until it had the largest shipping capacity of any Montreal-based firm, operating as part of the shipping interests of the Allan family. (In April 1863 it became H. and A. Allan—named for Hugh and his younger brother Andrew.) As president of the Montreal Board of Trade (1851-4), Hugh Allan pushed for a government-subsidized steamship line between Montreal and British ports that would provide mail service, transportation for immigrants, and shipment of imports and exports. Raising capital from a syndicate, Allan formed the Montreal Ocean Steamship Company, incorporated in 1854, and two years

***Immigrants Embarking at Liverpool for Quebec* on the Allan Line, an illustration in the**
***Canadian Illustrated News*, 4 April 1874. National Archives of Canada, C-61174.**

later, with the help of Conservative politicians, secured the contract (and the
£24,000 subsidy) to provide regular fortnightly service between Montreal
and Liverpool in the middle of the year and from Portland, Maine, and
Liverpool between November and May. By the 1870s the Montreal Ocean
Steamship Company, now known as the Allan Line, held contracts to carry
passengers into the interior, and Allan expanded into railway building.*

Allan also concentrated on financial institutions and manufacturing in the
1850s and early 1860s. He became particularly associated with the Bank of
Montreal, serving on its board of directors from 1847 to 1857, and later
established the Merchants' Bank of Canada (chartered 1861, opened 1864) as
a family enterprise: Allan ran the Merchants' Bank aggressively, and it paid
ten per cent returns on capital stock. He was also active in a number of
insurance companies, and had investments in many manufacturing concerns,
including the Cornwall Woollen Manufacturing Company, the Montreal

---

*Allan's connection with the Canadian Pacific Railway, and his involvement in the
notorious Pacific Scandal of 1873, are discussed on page 381.

Sept. — **FALL FAIR EDITION.** — **1883.**

THE MASSEY MANUFACTURING COMPANY

Build double the number of Reapers, Mowers, Binders and Horse
Rakes of any manufacturers in Canada.

10,300 MADE FOR 1883! - - - **11,500 to be Made for 1884!!**

The greatest number of Machines ever built by any one concern in the Dominion.

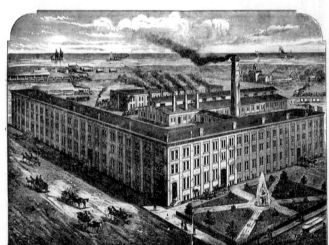

THE WORKS OF THE MASSEY MANUFACTURING COMPANY FOR 1883.

Now being greatly enlarged, 400 feet, 4 stories high, 50 feet wide,
being added to meet the demand of our celebrated machines
the coming season.

◆ ● ◆

☞ Read description of our Factories on Page 4, and visit them before leaving the City.

The expansion that took place when the Massey Manufacturing Company moved to
Toronto in 1879 is illustrated by the front cover of the company's promotional magazine,
which was distributed to dealers and employees. The building pictured still stands on
King Street West, Toronto. Courtesy Massey-Ferguson Archives, Ontario Agricultural
Museum Library/Archives.

Rolling Mills, and the Canada Paper Company. The secrets of his success were twofold. First, he was increasingly able to use his financial institutions to provide credit for his industrial ones. Second, he was perhaps the first Canadian entrepreneur to achieve both horizontal and vertical integration for his complex business empire: he was able both to diversify across enterprises and to control profitably most of the steps in the final production within any operation. That he spoke French fluently and had come to terms with the local French-Canadian élites was a distinct advantage.

In Canada West, industrial development was more dispersed geographically and less intensive in scale. No single entrepreneur was ever able to create quite so extensive an empire as Hugh Allan. Typical was the Massey family. Daniel Massey (1798-1856) began in a small way to manufacture labour-saving farm implements and eventually steam engines and other machinery in Newcastle, under the name Daniel Massey and Company. It became H.A. Massey and Company in 1856—the year he died, when his son Hart became sole proprietor—then the Newcastle Foundry and Machine Manufactory. The company expanded and flourished under the direction of Hart Massey (1823-96), who acquired production rights in the United States, between 1851 and 1861, for a mower, a reaper, a combined reaper and mower, and a self-raking reaper, which he not only manufactured but marketed successfully as a result of his early understanding of the need for effective advertising: the first well-illustrated Massey catalogue was issued in 1862. In 1870 the company was incorporated as the Massey Manufacturing Company, of which Hart was president and his son Charles vice-president and superintendent. The works were moved to Toronto in 1879.[26]

The world economic depression that contributed to the armed uprisings of 1837-8 lifted in 1841, and six years of prosperity and development followed (until another depression took hold in 1847 that lasted into the early 1850s). Prosperity was brought about, particularly in Toronto, not only by the stabilization of the political situation, but also by the opening up of grain, timber, and trapping resources, and of breweries and distilleries; by English investment, the development of banking and insurance systems, and immigration; and by the increase in import/export markets, provided by Toronto's free-trade access to international commerce via the St Lawrence, and by cross-lake shipping to New York by way of the Erie Canal and Hudson River. With the onset of the railway age, Toronto became the hub and commercial centre for the region.

While Toronto was the largest single industrial producer among western Canadian cities, it was never dominated by manufacturing as was Hamilton, which specialized in metal fabrication—particularly, although not exclusively, connected with the railways. Certainly Hamilton's earlier development as a wholesale supplier for the agricultural hinterland to the West, and its importance in the 1850s as a railway centre—when Hamilton merchants bought into the Great Western Railway and other lines—help explain how it initially got into metal fabrication. To some extent, the presence of a pool of skilled labour attracted other enterprises, and despite the importance of plants such as rolling mills, the manufacture of heavy consumer items, such as stoves and sewing machines, was the core of Hamilton's success.

Except in Hamilton, little specialization occurred anywhere within the industrial development of Canada West. Much of its industrial growth, particularly outside the larger cities, was determined by the agricultural sector. As one observer put it in the early 1870s,

> Agriculture in its several branches has been, and is now, the foundation on which rests the entire industrial fabric of Ontario. On its prosperity all classes depend—and with a good crop or a bad one, business operations, the abundance of money, and the social comforts of our whole people rise and fall, as do the waters of the sea with the flow and ebb of the tide.[27]

Nevertheless, increasing land shortages in Canada, combined with declining agricultural productivity, led to westward territorial expansion in the 1850s, as well as to industrial expansion because of the availability of cheap labour. Industrial expansion in turn produced pressures for a larger market. By the late 1850s many Canadian businessmen (and the politicians associated with them) saw the question of markets for industrial output as central to future policy. For example, the authors of *Montreal in 1856* argued, on behalf of Montreal manufacturers, that 'the sole difficulties with which they have to contend are a restricted market, and the competition of the larger, wealthier, and longer established factories in other countries.'[28] Thus agricultural overpopulation created (i) pressures for territorial expansion to provide new land for farmers, and (ii) urban workers who would become a proletariat.

❧❧❧ The Rise of Organized Labour

The growth of industrialization inevitably made labour relations an important issue in British North America. The resource economy, and particularly the construction of canals and railways, employed large numbers of men on a seasonal basis who had little opportunity to organize themselves. Their response to bad working conditions and employer exploitation was often either to move on, or to engage in general violence and rioting—directed not so much against the employer as against other targets. Before 1850, more than 200 labour riots occurred across the colonies, one-third of them involving the canals. In the same period only about fifty labour protests were sufficiently focused to be called strikes. Masons working on the Lachine Canal in 1823, for example, objected to working from 5 a.m. to 7 p.m. (They did not get the twelve-hour day they sought, but their wages were raised.) Several times in 1844 workers on the Lachine Canal marched in a body to Montreal to vote. In October of that year 400 marchers clashed with cavalry and 27 men were arrested.

Industrialization rationalized and stabilized the labour market. Manufacturing tended to be more continuous than seasonal, with much of it conducted indoors. Overhead costs encouraged employers to seek stabilization, and larger labour pools developed. Employers could afford higher annual wage bills than those in resource production, and their overheads simultaneously provided workers with leverage and themselves with a drive to minimize labour costs. The rise of a capitalistic labour market stabilized and settled the workers—but did little for their bargaining position. Those with highly developed skills were in the strongest position, so it is not surprising that labour organization first developed in British North America in industries employing such workers—printing, for one. The York Typographical Society was founded in 1832. It was initially supported by William Lyon Mackenzie, but by 1835 he changed his tune, writing: 'If all the journeymen were editors and each had a press of his own, a more resolute, determined, I had almost added *obstinate* body, would not be found on this continent.' His own workers had struck for higher wages, and Mackenzie railed against efforts 'to split up the community into so many selfish and mischievous monopolies.'[29]

While early trade unions emerged in certain skilled industries in various cities—for example, carpenters in Halifax in 1798, in Hamilton in 1832, in Montreal and Toronto in 1833, in Yarmouth in 1834—such unions almost never had any contact with one another, and could achieve only immediate and localized gains. Organization and communication were better in the Mechanics' Institutes, which had begun in British North America in 1828 and expanded greatly after 1840; but these were more fraternal self-improvement societies than militant unions. The core of a local Institute was its library, patronized by a mix of businessmen and artisans and frequently dominated by the former. In Saint John, for example, forty-two members of an élite Philosophical Society in 1838 joined 175 tradesmen in the birth of the local Mechanics' Institute, and by 1851 the organization had over 1,000 members. The 'mechanics' (mostly waged artisans) had to fight for years to gain control of the Saint John organization, which was able to mobilize tradesmen in non-union causes, such as temperance or Sunday Schools.

Throughout the 1840s and 1850s labour militancy was local, like the labour organizations themselves, and extremely limited. Most violence continued to occur among the unskilled navvies of the construction industry and the raftsmen of the timber industry, but it was seldom systematically organized. When it showed signs of being focused, the state quickly entered the picture. Despite business rhetoric about the free market in labour, few construction bosses objected to the use of informal spies to check on labour sentiment and of troops to enforce the peace. Navvies around the several canal projects of the 1840s were particularly restive, and a 'mounted police force' was created in 1845 to deal with labour violence on these quasi-public work projects. When the Great Western Railway began construction near Hamilton in 1851, that city raised a special police force to deal with labour troubles, and built a large barracks to accommodate a contingent of mounted police. When a company was prepared to pay for a police force, it usually got one. Though the navvies were frequently able to win extremely short-term goals with their strikes and walk-outs, they operated under distinct disadvantages when they attempted to behave in an organized fashion, not least because employers were willing to break strikes through the use of the civil power.

Despite the presence of workers' trade or craft organizations in the 1840s

Procession of Nine-Hour Movement Men — Hamilton steelworkers marching in support of a nine-hour day, along South James Street near the corner of King; *Canadian Illustrated News*, 8 June 1872. The short notice about this in the *Illustrated News* stated: 'In former issues we have fully discussed this important movement and endeavoured to prove conclusions which, while in themselves correct, were not adverse to the real interests of the workmen.' Metropolitan Toronto Reference Library.

and 1850s, there was a tendency for such unions to identify solely with the trade, rather than with fellow workers in other trades in other places. As one manifesto of the Toronto Typographical Society (TTS) stated in 1847: 'We are knit together by ties that should be considered as indissoluble, being in the words of our motto, "United to Support"—not combined to Injure.'[30] The development of industrial activity, and the rise of factories employing mechanization in the 1850s, brought considerable changes to the still incipient labour movement. A handful of international unions appeared that were occasionally British in origin (such as the Amalgamated Society of Engineers), though more frequently American (such as the International Molders Union). And unions with several local chapters—such as the Boot and Shoemakers Union and the Journeymen Cigarmakers Union—were organized. The TTS by 1865 was in contact with several British unions and a number of American counterparts, and a year later it affiliated with the American National Typographical Union. Mechanization was the principal issue behind labour organization, although the impersonality of the new factory system also created problems for labour, particularly when more and more juveniles and women were drawn into the labour market. In Montreal, for example, women and girls by 1871 constituted 34.5 per cent of the city's industrial workers: over 80 per cent of the work-force in the clothing industry, over 40 per cent in shoe-making, and over 60 per cent in tobacco processing. Girls especially were hard to organize because they typically worked only until they married, or engaged in piecework production at home rather than at the factory.

The West and Westward Expansion

Given the greatly expanding population of British North America in the mid-nineteenth century, and the limited amounts of really productive agricultural land, the opportunities for farm ownership quickly became problematic in most parts of the provinces. One result was a substantial outmigration to the United States, beginning in Canada East in the 1840s and in the Maritime region in the 1850s. Another was the emergence of a serious interest in the western territory controlled by the Hudson's Bay Company. As early as 1850, the Toronto *Globe* of George Brown (1818-80) was calling editorially for attention to the West. And on 10 December 1856 its subscribers were informed about 'the best method of taking possession of the vast and fertile territory which is our birthright, and which no power on earth can prevent us occupying.' The *Globe* went on to advocate the construction of an 'Atlantic and Pacific Railway, which has now become a necessity.' George Brown had obviously followed events in the West over the years with considerable interest.

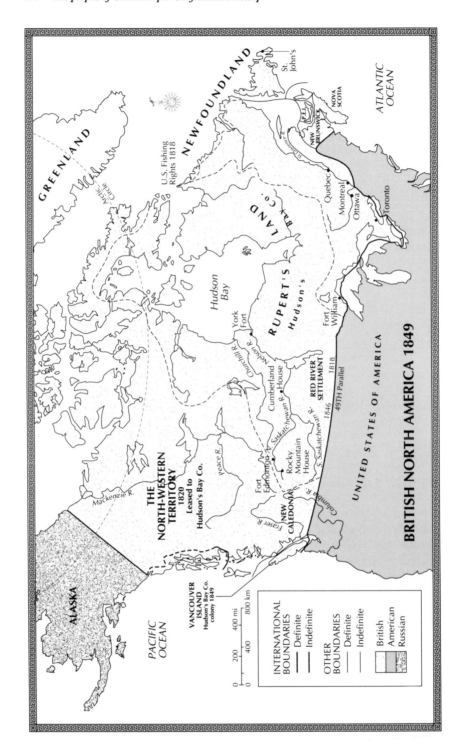

The Founding of Vancouver Island

One key development in the settlement of the West had been the establishment in 1848 of Vancouver Island as a British colony. Until then, Britain had been content to allow the Hudson's Bay Company to act as custodian of British interests in the West; but the Company had come under considerable attack, chiefly by James E. Fitzgerald, a clerk in the British Museum. Using knowledge he had acquired in the library stacks to call attention to himself as a colonial expert, he published a scathing attack on the Company in 1849, arguing that the country north of the 49th parallel, a 'frozen wilderness', had been exploited by the fur-traders for their own interests. He argued that the prairie district—'a broad belt stretching from Lake Superior, in a north-westerly direction to the Rocky Mountains'—was one region suitable for settlement, and that British Columbia and Vancouver Island were two others. He called for an expedition to survey the West, both for settlement and for transportation links, insisting that 'Canada would become the line of transit for emigrants, for all the commerce which colonies in the interior would necessarily create, instead of being, as she now is, planted against an impenetrable wall of desert, two thousand miles thick.'[31]

Fitzgerald was unsuccessful in his advocacy of a joint stock company to develop Vancouver Island, but his agitation did force the Colonial Office to permit the Hudson's Bay Company itself to organize a colony there: in January 1849 the Island was leased to the Company for an annual amount of seven shillings. In 1841, before the settlement of the western boundary, Governor George Simpson of the HBC had sent James Douglas (1803-77), who had been made chief factor the year before, from Fort Vancouver to establish a post on Vancouver Island as a fall-back position if the Oregon territory were lost. Douglas founded Fort Victoria in May 1843 as a fur-trading post, and returned to it in 1849 in his role as chief factor of the Company, becoming governor in 1851. The newcomers—so far mostly officers and clerks and their families—sought to reproduce British gentry conditions on the Pacific Slope. A few of them resented Douglas, who made some effort to deal responsibly—if not exactly generously—with the native peoples whom the British were displacing on Vancouver Island, and whose wife, the former Amelia Connolly, had Indian blood. One settler wrote home that Douglas 'has spent all his life among the North American Indians and has got one of them for a wife so can it be expected that he can know anything at all about Governing one of England's last Colonies in North America.'[32]

As so often happens in history, preordained developments intersected with immediate ones. In 1838 the British government had extended the Hudson's Bay Company's monopoly over the West for twenty-one years, and as a result a major parliamentary enquiry was held in 1857 on the affairs of the Company. The Report was not unsympathetic to the past performance of the Company, but recognized new circumstances, particularly 'the growing

Fort Victoria, 1854. Provincial Archives of British Columbia, 10608.

desire of our Canadian fellow-subjects that the means of extension and regular settlement should be afforded to them over a portion of this territory; the necessity of providing suitably for the administration of the affairs of Vancouver's Island, and the present condition of the settlement which has been formed on the Red River.'[33] It was recommended that the Company cease to have any connection with Vancouver Island, and also encouraged the annexation to Canada of the districts on the Red River and the Saskatchewan River. At the same time it maintained that for much of the West the continuation of the trading monopoly of the Company was desirable.

The Prairies

While the British Parliament was considering the future of the West, two scientific expeditions—one Canadian and one British—set out for the region to find out more about it. Captain John Palliser (1817-87), an Irish landlord who had spent a lifetime seeking excitement around the world, had travelled in the American West in 1847 and 1848, bringing home a menagerie of wild animals, including three buffaloes, an antelope, a bear, two Virginia deer, and a half-wolf Indian dog.* Such a 'splendid chap', in the Victorian context, could hardly be denied when he proposed to the Royal Geographical Society in 1856 to survey a large portion of North America.

---

*While in New Orleans, when a professional musician failed to appear, Palliser had sung both male parts in a charity performance of a Handel oratorio.

The Society got the Colonial Office to contribute £5,000 for an expedition, to pay for two scientific assistants and two royal engineers. The British understandably wanted to know more about their western possessions, particularly since Lorin Blodget, an American, had published data in 1856 suggesting that the Prairies were hardly as barren as most people had imagined. Eminent scientists were consulted, including Charles Darwin, and a team of experts recruited for the expedition, of which Palliser was naturally put in charge, formally receiving his commission during the parliamentary enquiry of 1857. They left England on 16 May on the Royal Mail Steamer *Arabia*, docking in New York and then heading west via American railroads and steamers. At Sault Ste Marie they picked up two canoes with their *voyageur* crews and made their way by steamer across Lake Superior, arriving at Isle Royale, Michigan, in mid-June 1857. A month later they had reached Lower Fort Garry on the Red River.

On 23 July of that same year the Canadian Exploring Expedition, under the titular command of retired chief trader of the HBC, George Gladman (1800-63), left Toronto for the West, accompanied by Simon James Dawson (1820-1902), an engineer, and Henry Youle Hind (1823-1908), an English-

Part of the Canadian Exploring Expedition at a camp on the Red River, 1 June 1858. This photograph was taken by Humphrey Lloyd Hime (1833-1903), a surveyor and photographer who accompanied the expedition. National Archives of Canada C-4572.

born and Cambridge-educated professor of chemistry and geology at Trinity College, Toronto, who acted as geologist and naturalist. Its sponsor was the Canadian government, eager to find out more about the Northwest, which many said should be annexed to Canadian territory.

The findings of these two expeditions, which were not published immediately, served their purpose in expanding geographical knowledge of the West and in helping to end the public perception of this vast region as unfit for human habitation. The final reports from Hind and Palliser, besides containing much scientific information, acknowledged the great potentiality of the West. Indeed, the aura of 'impartial science' that surrounded their large and stodgy documents gave their findings, in the eyes of enthusiasts for western expansion, greater cachet. Hind, for example, in his *Reports of Progress; Together with a Preliminary and General Report on the Assiniboine and Saskatchewan Exploring Expedition* (Toronto, 1859), waxed lyrical over the 'truly fertile valleys' of the West, calculating that between Red River and the south branch of the Saskatchewan there were over eleven million acres of fertile and arable land. Palliser's *Papers Relative to the Exploration. . .* were also published in 1859. And after three more explorations between 1858 and 1860, Her Majesty's Stationery Office published his *Journals, Detailed Reports, and Observations Relative to the Exploration* (1863) in an edition of less than 100 copies. Palliser made the same point as Hind, that millions of acres of the West were prime agricultural land, although he also identified what came to be known as 'Palliser's Triangle'—a drybelt area of the West that even today is the graveyard of farmers' hopes. Palliser also recognized how much easier it was to get into the British West via the United States, and he advocated a 'railway on the British side of the line to the northward and westward, through the southern portion of "the fertile belt" to the Rocky Mountains; at all events as soon as the country showed symptoms of becoming sufficiently populated to warrant such an effort.'[34]

Palliser and Hind accepted long-standing assumptions that the northern prairie was an extension of the Great American Desert; that parts of it were useful for settlement; and that a railroad was needed to open the region, particularly to connect Canada with the Pacific. Those in the Province of Canada who were interested in expansion found enough support in the work of these expeditions to document their case. Scientific exploration had now confirmed what continental expansionists had long known instinctively: the Northwest could not only be settled, but as the Canadian government claimed in 1864, it was 'capable of sustaining a vast population.'[35]

Mineral Exploitation

The British Columbia Gold Rush

While Victorian scientific explorers made great claims for the potential of the Prairies, sheer serendipity brought the Pacific Slope to the attention of the world. One of Vancouver Island's chief problems as a colony was the isolation of its resources. But in 1857 the discovery of gold in the mainland region, along the Thompson and Fraser Rivers, produced a sudden change. The California Gold Rush of 1848 was still fresh in everyone's mind, although when Governor Douglas exhibited a few grains of gold from the North Thompson at dinner in the Hudson's Bay Company mess-hall, only he seemed to appreciate its importance as an instrument of 'great change and busy time'.[36] The amount of gold easily available was quite small by California standards, and the ensuing rush was a pale imitation of the American one; nevertheless hundreds of men, mainly from California, made their way to the Fraser River in the interior of British Columbia in the spring of 1858 — altering forever perceptions of the western colony back east. Of the 450 men in the first rush inland, only 60 were British and under 100 were Americans (including 35 blacks); the remainder were an international mix of professional gold-seekers.

The quiet village of Victoria was almost instantly transformed, with over 200 buildings being thrown up virtually overnight. South of the 49th parallel, talk of American annexation spread rapidly. One American popular ditty was plain enough:

> Soon our banner will be streaming,
> Soon the eagle will be screaming,
> And the lion — see it cowers,
> Hurrah, boys, the river's ours.[37]

*View of Victoria, c.*1860, **a hand-coloured lithograph. National Archives of Canada, C-1893.**

Governor Douglas had already attempted to deal with such a threat late in 1857 by declaring that all gold mines in the interior were the property of the Crown and providing for a licensing fee. The British government was forced to rush through parliament legislation putting 'New Caledonia' under the direct jurisdiction of the Crown, and the mainland colony of British Columbia was formally embodied with royal assent on 2 August 1858. James Douglas was appointed governor of the new colony, which was initially kept administratively separate from Vancouver Island. Douglas had already taken the initiative to introduce British justice into a community of over 9,000 miners, and he would subsequently write to Sir George Simpson, with some satisfaction: 'Many changes have taken place in this Country since I had last [in 1841] the pleasure of travelling with you on the Coast, and works of a perfectly stupendous character have been executed.'[38]

The discovery of gold brought rapid, and unanticipated, changes to the Pacific coast. To the surprise of the local authorities, the miners, however rough in appearance, were not badly behaved. They were certainly a motley enough crew, described by one observer as '*Englishmen* (staunch Royalists), *Americans* (Republicans), Frenchmen, very numerous, Germans in abundance, Italians, several Hungarians, Poles, Danes, Swedes, Spaniards, Mexicans, & *Chinese*.'[39] The amount of gold obtainable with only hand tools and without capital investment was fairly small, and few became rich. Some settled down to work for mining companies with proper machinery, while others travelled across the new colony in search of fresh strikes. In any event, supplies had to be transported into the interior and the gold brought out, leading to the rapid construction of wagon roads from the Lower Fraser River, with the assistance of a contingent of Royal Engineers sent out from Britain. In 1860 the gold rush extended northeast into the foothills of the Cariboo Mountains, where a major strike was made at Keithley Creek. The next year Governor Douglas supervised plans for the construction of a long-distance wagon road, beginning at Fort Yale and passing through the Fraser Canyon to Lytton and going north from there.* But when Billy Barker made a spectacular discovery, in August 1862, on Williams Creek—near where the town of Barkerville developed—the plans were extended to take miners that far into the British Columbia interior.* A few other early arrivals did well, one team of prospectors earning $10,000 apiece for three months' labour. But again, most of the gold required expensive equipment to extract, and organized mining companies employing wage labour would take out far more gold than individual prospectors.

Many gold-seekers found employment and profits in other ways, because the developmental spin-off from the rush was substantial for awhile. James Thomson (1823-95), a Scottish-born baker who had immigrated to Canada

---

*This was the famous Cariboo Road, between Yale and Barkerville. An impressive construction supported by pilings or crib-work, or cut through rock, it was completed in 1865.

Frederick Dally, *The Aurora Gold Mine, Williams Creek, B.C., 15 August 1867.* Dally arrived in Victoria in 1862, and in 1866 became a photographer, documenting the native peoples and life in the goldfields. He left Victoria in 1870 and eventually returned to England. Metropolitan Toronto Reference Library, T 14321.

Main Street, Barkerville, before the fire of 16 September 1868. British Columbia Archives and Records Service, HP 10109.

in 1844 and travelled widely in search of his fortune, headed for California in 1850. While he did not get rich, he had made enough money from his efforts, mainly as a baker, to buy a farm in Edwardsburgh on the St Lawrence. He then made his way to the Cariboo in 1862, but he did not strike it rich in British Columbia either, reporting to his wife: 'We can make about six dollars a day each, but our provisions cost us about two dollars per day each.'[40] He spent most of his time sawing wood and shingles before leaving British Columbia in late November, arriving home before the end of the year.

The discovery of gold altered life irreversibly for the native peoples of the Pacific Slope, as serious mineral exploitation tended to do everywhere in British North America. Much of the remaining fur-trade territory—where the natives still maintained traditional ways of life, controlled their economic exchanges with Europeans, and most important of all, retained their lands— was not attractive for agricultural settlement. But remote and forbidding regions often contained great mineral wealth, and the land claims of native peoples were ignored in the rush to exploit the land itself. One British Columbia newspaper insisted that 'according to the strict rule of international law[,] territory occupied by a barbarous or wholly uncivilized people may be rightfully appropriated by a civilized or Christian nation.'[41] Few settlers disagreed with this proposition, or with the view that that the 'indolent, contented, savage, must give place to the busteling [*sic*] sons of civilization & Toil.'[42] The result of the ensuing displacement was for native peoples a serious cultural disruption, recovery from which would be extremely difficult.

The New Mineral Wealth

The Fraser River Gold Rush that began in 1858 in British Columbia— where the settlement of Granville (Vancouver) was founded and a capital was appointed on the site of New Westminster—presaged a new element in the resource economy of British North America: exploitation of the rich mineral wealth of the northern part of the continent. Iron ore had been mined in small quantities since colonial times, and rich coal deposits in Cape Breton and Vancouver Island had been tapped since the 1820s. New technologies provided a constantly expanding market for British North America's mineral wealth, as well as new means of extracting it from the ground. By the 1850s copper ore was being mined along Lake Superior, and petroleum was discovered in southwestern Ontario in 1855. (The chief problem facing producers—not resolved until later in the century—was the cost of transporting ore long distances for refining purposes.) There was an oil rush at Petrolia in 1862 after the discovery of a well that initially produced 3,000 barrels a day. By 1863 the production of crude oil in Canada ran to 100,000 barrels a year.

There were also small gold rushes in Nova Scotia in 1861 and in Canada along the Chaudière River in 1863. Unlike timbering, which mining gradually replaced as the principal economic activity and employer of labour in isolated districts, mineral production tended to be extremely capital-intensive, while requiring specialized scientific knowledge, particularly of geological formations and refining techniques. Until the twentieth century, when international demand made local refining and long-distance transportation expensive but profitable in Canada, production tended to be confined to a few minerals that were particularly well located for outward transportation in bulk. Thus Vancouver Island coal was shipped to California by the 1850s, and Nova Scotia coal to eastern American markets in the same period. But the burgeoning industrialization of the continent—which developed in British North America after 1850—demanded large quantities of mineral production, which in turn required access to raw materials. Here, as in so many other areas of production, the expansion of the railroad seemed critical to those who sought to develop the continent.

Exhaustion of eastern grain land, a shift from imperial to continental trade, the growth of industrialism, the expansion of railroad construction—all contributed, by the 1860s, to a new attitude on the part of many of the the political and economic leaders of British North America. Some form of political unification seemed to be required that would make possible both westward expansion and eastern integration. The probings of E.L. Watkin, in proposing an increased economic activity for central Canada by reaching out both eastward and westward, were symptomatic of the age. The economic climate was right for the creation of a national state out of the disparate colonies of British North America. And external and internal political pressures would help complete the process.

chapter eleven

Political Reform and Unification:

1840-1867

In 1859 George Brown, the editor of the Toronto *Globe* and the leading Reformer in Canada West, organized an Upper Canadian Reform Convention that would attempt to unify the various elements of the party—which ranged from radical Clear Grits to moderate Liberals—in an effort to prevent dissolution of the unsatisfactory union of the two Canadas. It began on 9 November in St Lawrence Hall, Toronto, and that evening a committee presented six resolutions, the fourth of which proposed federation: 'That in the opinion of this assembly the best practicable remedy for the evils now encountered in the government of Canada is to be found in the formation of two or more local governments to which shall be committed the control of all matters of a local or sectional character and a general government charged with such matters as are necessarily common to both sections of the province.'[1] The next evening George Brown gave a stirring address that was a historic and winning appeal for a federal union:

> I do hope there is not one Canadian in this assembly who does not look forward with high hopes to the day when these northern countries shall stand out among the nations of the world as one great confederation! What true Canadian can witness the tide of immigration now commencing to flow into the vast territories of the North West without longing to have a share in the first settlement of that great and fertile country, and making our own country the highway of traffic to the Pacific? But is it not true wisdom to commence the federated system with our own country, and leave it open to extension hereafter, if time and experience shall prove it to be desirable? And how can there be the slightest question, with one who longs for such nationality, between complete dissolution and the scheme of the committee? Is it not clear that the former would be a death blow to the hopes of the future union, while the latter may at some future day readily furnish the machinery of a great confederation?[2]

After Brown's triumph, the *Globe* promoted this idea all across Canada West. But the road to confederation was long, and it was not a smooth one.

❧ Reorienting Politics: The Achievement of Responsible Government

The British government gradually resolved the constitutional problems of the 1830s in British North America over the following decade. For the Canadas, the process had begun with the implementation of one of the main features of Lord Durham's *Report*, the unification of Upper and Lower Canada into one legislature by Act of Parliament in July 1840. Legislative union did not by itself satisfy Durham's other major recommendation, the right of the assembly to decide policy and its implementation through control of 'the persons by whom that policy was to be administered.' Neither Durham, nor anyone else in Britain, understood the importance of political parties in British North America, and their relationship to the operation of what came to be called 'responsible government'. This failure of understanding was compounded by Britain's aim to reconcile cabinet government with its desire to continue to guarantee British perceptions of fairness and impartiality for all colonials. The British thus temporized by giving colonial governors more political freedom of action than they had ever before enjoyed, actually encouraging them to serve as party brokers under the new arrangements. Governors of the Province of Canada—Canada East and Canada West— were allowed to construct ministries, although local conditions forced them to accept in broad outline the personnel endorsed by the assembly.

In 1842 the new governor, Sir Charles Bagot (1781-1843), appointed two Reformers from Canada West and Canada East, Robert Baldwin and Louis-H. La Fontaine (1807-64), both believers in responsible government, to form a ministry. He saw that it was necessary to admit French Canadians to the ministry in response to a political alliance between these two Reform leaders. Although Bagot retained the right to select, he stated that 'Whether the doctrine of responsible government is openly acknowledged or only tacitly acquiesced in, virtually it exists.' Bagot resigned in January 1843, owing to ill health, and died a few months later. His successor, however, was instructed not to concede responsible government.

Sir Charles Metcalfe (1785-1846) began his term as governor in a harmonious relationship with the Executive Council, supporting its decisions to make Montreal the capital of the Province of Canada and to grant a general amnesty for all offences during the rebellions, except murder. But gradually a gulf formed between the governor and his ministers over a series of issues and mutual resentments. On 24 November, after Metcalfe had made a Tory appointment, La Fontaine and Baldwin demanded that he not make another appointment without taking their advice—a principle that was considered by all the councillors as essential to responsible government, and by Metcalfe as a surrender of the Crown's prerogative. Two days later all the councillors but one resigned. Metcalfe carried on alone until August 1844, when he formed a mainly conservative Executive Council, headed by William Henry Draper (1801-77), the former attorney-general for Canada West, and Denis-

Benjamin Viger.* He then called a general election, which resulted in the ministry's being sustained by a small majority in November 1844: the government itself had now assumed the mantle of a party, composed of the remnants of the conservative anti-Reformers of the 1830s. The next election was called in July 1847, and in January 1848 the Reformers won a sweeping majority: the Conservative ministry resigned. The governor, Lord Elgin (1811-63)—who had arrived twelve months before with the instruction to concede responsible government—called upon La Fontaine and Baldwin, as leaders of Reform parties in their respective constituencies, to form a ministry, which was sworn in on 11 March 1848. In placing himself, as a representative of the Crown, above party politics and leaving government in the hands of leaders of an organized party, Lord Elgin inaugurated responsible government in the Province of Canada. In April 1849 he signed the Rebellion Losses Act, a bill—passed in both houses of the legislature—indemnifying those in Canada East who had suffered losses in the recent rebellions.**

The British authorities were prepared to accept the dominance of the assemblies in other colonies, but sought initially to prevent, then restrain, the development of a party system. Despite London's best efforts, however, political parties did coalesce in the 1840s, rather loosely, around traditional local questions and the local political dynamic. Reformers found different issues to emphasize from colony to colony, anti-Reformers responded in slightly different ways; but the effect was the emergence of two parties in each province differing in their support of local reform. By and large the anti-Reformers (or Conservatives) had more difficulty in accepting the need for organization and party discipline, but they achieved them.

In 1847, the year Lord Elgin arrived in the Province of Canada with a clear mandate to preside at the inception of responsible government, the governor of Nova Scotia, Sir John Harvey (1778-1852), was maintaining that the 'minor' colonies were

> scarcely fitted for the strict application to them of a System of Government which not only contemplates the materials for the machinery of *two or more distinct administrations,* but involves the still more startling proposition of the surrender of their offices by all the heads of the Civil Departments of the Government upon every Political change by which the possession of a Majority, however inconsiderable, in the representative Branch of the General Assembly is obtained by any party.[3]

---

*Viger had had an ambiguous relationship with the revolutionary movement in Lower Canada and was imprisoned from 4 November 1838, when Sir John Colborne proclaimed martial law, until 16 May 1840—though he was uncharged.

**The immediate consequence of his doing so was that he was stoned by Tory and Orange mobs of demonstrators, who proceeded to burn the parliament buildings in Montreal. The capital was thereupon moved to Toronto, which alternated with Quebec City.

Yet that surrender is exactly what he and other governors were forced to accept. In fact, Nova Scotia—where Joseph Howe had been agitating for responsible government as a Reformer since 1836—finally achieved it after the election of 5 August 1847, which focused on that single issue. The Reformers were victorious, and when a Reform administration took office in late January 1848, the province became the first colony to achieve responsible government. It was granted to the Province of Canada in March of that year, to Prince Edward Island in 1851, and to New Brunswick in 1854.

The situation in Newfoundland was complicated by a British attempt at alternative constitutional arrangements in the 1840s. In 1842 that colony was given a legislature composed partly of elected and partly of appointed members, thus amalgamating the old Executive Council and assembly into one body. The experiment, however, was popular neither in Newfoundland nor in the British Parliament and was never given a proper chance to work. In 1848 the older constitution was restored, and Newfoundlanders immediately began agitating for 'a form of Government based upon enlarged and fairly divided Representation—with a departmental Government and Executive Responsibility similar in character to that form lately yielded to...Nova Scotia.'[4] Newfoundland eventually achieved this aim in 1855, however reluctant the British were to grant such a principle.

The Growth of New Political and Constitutional Problems

Although in the short run the constitutional revisions of the 1840s seemed to work best in the Province of Canada—which, as the largest colony in British North America, was regarded as the bell-wether—over the long haul responsible government in British North America produced a series of seemingly intractable problems. The lower provinces, even including Newfoundland, were sufficiently homogeneous to be able to live with a two-party system, particularly since the composition of the parties was still fluid and constantly changing to suit existing conditions. But Canada was not so fortunate. The alliance in 1842 of Robert Baldwin and Louis-H. La Fontaine on a reform platform was in some respects illusory, for it quickly transpired that Canada East (the former Lower Canada) had slipped back into older voting patterns that were not very supportive of reform; in other words, the principle of governing by a coalition, coming from each of the two sections of the united province, was inherently unstable. By the mid-1840s French Canada had become enamoured of the principle of the 'double majority', in which the province would be governed by an assembly majority in each of its two main sections. Such an arrangement naturally appealed to French Canada's sense of nationality, but it also implied that political parties in each section would develop along parallel lines. So long as the principle issue

George Brown. National
Archives of Canada, C-6165

remained the achievement of self-government, reformers in the two sections could make common cause. But by 1850, when responsible government was fully operational, new factors would emerge to complicate the Canadian political system. Two were important.

One was the rise, at the end of the 1840s, of a new political movement in Canada West, a radical Reform group known as the 'Clear Grits', with whom the Grits or moderate Reformers eventually merged, led by George Brown (1818-80). Centred in the western districts, the 'Grits' were thorough-going Reformers who embodied the principles of Upper Canadian agrarianism. But in many ways they were also the heirs of William Lyon Mackenzie* rather than of the moderate Robert Baldwin: they were democrats, populists, geographical expansionists, opponents of close connections between church and state in a Protestant rather than a secularist sense. Furthermore—and ominously—they were hostile to French Canada in traditional Upper Canadian ways. In 1840, when the population of Canada East was greater, each section of the United Canadas was given forty seats; in

---

*Mackenzie was pardoned in the general amnesty of February 1849. While his brief visit to Toronto in March, to test the waters, provoked some violence, he returned with his family in May 1850 to stay, and became an ally of the Grit radicals. In the spring of 1851 he stood in a by-election to fill a vacant seat in Haldimand County, and won—over his opponent, George Brown.

1849 the liberal *Rouge* party unsuccessfully demanded 'representation by population'. But when the census of 1851 showed that the population of the western section was greater, 'rep by pop' became a platform of George Brown when he stood as an independent Reformer in the general election in the autumn of that year—and was elected. However, an arrangement that had initially benefited Canada West quickly came to disadvantage it, producing a deadlock that was not resolved until Confederation in 1867, because the Grits perceived that French Canada stood in the way of the successful adoption of their platform. As Lord Elgin, who was governor until 1854, quickly realized: 'If clear Gritism absorbs all the hues of Upper Canadian liberalism, the French, unless some interference from without checks the natural course of events, will fall off from them and form an alliance with the Upper Canadian Tories.'[5]

The growing pressures of the Grits contributed to, but did not by themselves produce, the second development of the 1850s. This was the gradual withdrawal of French Canada from political principles of radical reform and the development of exactly the result Lord Elgin had feared: an alliance between the Canadian legislative majority and the Upper Canadian opponents of the Grits. In the 1850s French Canada had its own agenda, centred on the continued development of nationalist pretensions and the preservation of French-Canadian culture and society. By this time the leaders of the Catholic Church had come to recognize the importance of nationalism, and the necessity of separating it from its earlier reformist connections. In this process of separating nationalism and reform, the Grits—unwittingly—were extremely useful. Grit attacks on religious establishment came from evangelical Protestant principles, and their great shibboleth was 'voluntaryism': the idea that church and state should be separated, and that there should be no civil interference in ecclesiastical matters. In the Upper Canadian context voluntaryism was directed against the pretensions of the Anglican Church to control higher education and to benefit from the clergy reserves. For example, in 1849 Robert Baldwin (a former student and parishioner of John Strachan's) secularized King's College, Toronto—the Anglican university that Strachan had founded: on 1 January 1850 it became the University of Toronto.

Confessional Controversies of the 1850s

But ultra-Protestantism had even more implications for the Catholic Church in Lower Canada. Voluntaryism was neither areligious nor amoral. Despite its rhetorical objections to church establishment, it merely sought to replace one religious arrangement with another that was far more openly Protestant—religious reformers were quite unable to appreciate the political importance of this fact. Secularism, in their hands, was hardly neutral. At the same time that the voluntaryists sought to free the state from 'religious privilege', they could contemplate with equanimity the passage of legislation controlling the availability of alcoholic beverages (reflecting their support of temperance) and restrictions on work and other activities during the Sabbath (which they held sacrosanct in ways not shared by the traditional national churches). While God might not be eligible to hold land and be exempted from taxation, He could be used to justify state intrusion in moral matters. Even secular schooling, by the 1850s, had a religious dimension that could divide Protestants and Catholics, evangelicals and ecclesiastical statists.

The rise of denominational divisions as a factor in politics was not confined to the Canadas, although the sectional situation—with Roman Catholicism firmly entrenched in Canada East, and evangelical Protestantism in Canada West—gave such matters a special edge in that province. To a considerable extent denominational politics reflected the increasing democratization of the political process, for as the involvement of voters increased, politicians turned to issues that appealed to their prejudices. The venue for the expression of such disagreement was usually provided by a growing concern in the legislatures over public education.

Educational conflicts could take bizarre turns, as events in Prince Edward Island, beginning in 1856, showed. In that province the issue revolved around Bible reading in the schools, a procedure that was pressed by the evangelical Protestants and opposed by the Roman Catholics of the Island, who had not adopted the practice of separate schooling: having integrated into the 'mixed schools' of the province, they actually favoured the continuation of 'godless', or non-sectarian, principles in them. The Bible question helped re-align Island politics as Catholics and Protestant Liberals allied against evangelical Protestants, backed by the old Tories. Many felt that the Tories, in other ways a declining force in politics, were pleased to fish in the troubled waters of confessionalism. In any event, the principal issue of the 1858 election was for many voters 'between Protestantism and Romanism'; and a year later a prominent local newspaper commented that 'the two parties into which the people of this Island now are, and for some time to come will continue to be divided—[are] a Protestant and a Catholic party.'[6]

In Newfoundland as well, the contending political parties wore denominational faces—the Liberals backed by the Roman Catholics and the Tories supported by the Protestants—although in that island province, as in the Canadas, there were close identifications between religion and ethnicity: in Newfoundland, Catholics were Irish and Protestants English in origin.

The Growing Canadian Crisis

In the Canadas, La Fontaine and Baldwin retired from public life in 1851, and a new Reform government was confirmed in the general election of December 1851 (in which George Brown was elected in the southwestern county of Kent), headed by Francis Hincks (1807-85) and Augustin-Norbert Morin (1803-65). The Canada West Conservatives were led by Sir Allan MacNab (1798-1862), but the parliamentary leader and the brains of the party was John A. Macdonald (1815–91), the Scots-born lawyer from Kingston who had been that city's MP since 1844. In June 1854, amid charges of corruption and extravagance, and procrastination over key issues, parliament was dissolved. In the ensuing election Hincks and Morin, while winning the largest number of seats, did not win a clear majority: their minority government was soon defeated and they resigned. A coalition government was then formed, headed by MacNab and Morin; Macdonald (who did the real work of forming the new government) became Attorney-General for Canada West. When MacNab was forced to resign in 1856, Macdonald's leadership of the Conservatives was openly acknowledged.

John A. Macdonald in 1856.
National Archives of Canada,
C-6512.

On the Reform (now called the Liberal) side, George Brown took an increasingly prominent role. When, in May 1855, a new bill for separate schools in Canada West was passed at Quebec, after many western members had left for home, the Grits of Upper Canada were furious. At this point Brown argued most strongly for representation by population, gaining supporters from both the Grit and Clear Grit factions, as well as from the more moderate Liberals. At a convention for unity in January 1857, Brown emerged clearly as the Liberal leader.

Nothing unusual was suggested by the denominational, or even by the racial and sectional, nature of the divisions that existed in the Canadas. What *was* unusual was the acceptance of the principle of the double majority, which required that legislation affecting either Canada East or Canada West alone could not be passed unless it received majority support from members having constituencies in the section in question—though it was unlikely that any ministry in either section could garner enough votes to make this work. Its acceptance was an open admission of the sectional nature of the Canadian union. Sir Edmund Head (1805-68), governor from 1854 to 1861, quite properly regarded 'this quasi-federal question, which I am bound to treat as theoretically absurd', as an unnecessary complication—although he admitted 'in practice it must be looked to.'[7] Given the weaknesses of the *Rouges* in Canada East and the western strength of the Grits, as well as the difficulty of bringing about co-operation between these two disparate political groups—and considering their differing prejudices—the room for political manoeuvring, in the short run, was considerably reduced. Canadian politics had devolved into ingenious compromising. In 1856 Macdonald, who had emerged as the supreme political operator, was able to forge a new coalition from among the moderate (some said pragmatic) Tories from Upper Canada whom he led, and the *Bleus* of French Canada, led in 1859 by George-Étienne Cartier (1814-73). But the fact remained that Canada West was far more divided politically than Canada East. Most Canadian political leaders could agree with Governor Head that the double majority was, as Macdonald put it in 1856, 'in the abstract indefensible'. It was also politically difficult if followed slavishly. For example, as a result of the December 1857 elections—when Macdonald won a personal triumph in Kingston though the Brown Liberals, including Brown himself, won a clear majority, while in Lower Canada the *Rouges* were defeated by Cartier's *Bleu* Conservatives—the Macdonald-Cartier ministry could continue in office. But the double majority would have required a coalition of Brown's Grits with Cartier's *Bleus*. It was not enough that sectional parties would have to govern in tandem; to make the system really work, the sectional parties with affinities for one another would have to be elected with majorities at the same time. Yet within the union the only alternative seemed to be 'rep by pop', which was hardly acceptable to French Canada at a time when the population of Canada West was greater than that of Canada East and growing more rapidly.

John A. Macdonald would later describe the double majority with some affection, using another aspect of it to illustrate the working of a federal principle in Canada. Defending in 1865 the Seventy-two Resolutions that were drafted at the Quebec Conference on confederation in October 1864 (the basis of the British North America Act of 1867), he argued:

> We, in Canada, already know something of the advantages and disadvantages of a Federal Union. Although we have nominally a Legislative Union in Canada—although we sit in one Parliament, supposed constitutionally to represent the people without regard to sections or localities, yet we know, as a matter of fact, that since the union in 1841, we have had a Federal Union; that in matters affecting Upper Canada solely, members from that section claimed and generally exercised the right of exclusive legislation, while members from Lower Canada legislated in matters affecting only their own section. We have had a Federal union in fact, though a Legislative Union in name.[8]

As early as 1856 talk began to emerge of another alternative to the double majority: a proper federal union, perhaps even one that extended beyond the Canadas. In August 1856, Brown's *Globe* stated that 'If Upper and Lower Canada cannot be made to agree, a federal union of all the provinces will probably be the result.' By 1863 the political implausibility of the double majority had been accepted by most of the leading politicians of Canada. Some other form of union seemed the only solution.

The Background to Union

While the political problems of the Canadas were the immediate prod for Canadian politicians to begin to explore the possibility of a larger union with the eastern provinces, beginning at the famous Charlottetown Conference of September 1864, such a solution was not drawn from the sky. The political unification of the provinces of British North America—possibly under some sort of federal arrangement paralleling the American one—had been frequently advocated since the days of the Loyalists. While most of the schemes suggested had been political abstractions by men with vision, proposals for union had occasionally arisen in the context of attempting to resolve political impasses brought about by contemporary events. Thus, when the mercantile leaders of Lower Canada had pressed in 1821 and 1822 for the political unification of the Canadas as a solution to the economic and constitutional problems resulting from the British legislation of 1791, creating two Canadas, Upper Canadian Tories responded with calls for a larger union. John Strachan, when he was the Anglican rector of York, had argued in 1824 that in a parliament of all British North America, 'the French would be only a component part and would merge without any sacrifice of national vanity or pride &c.', and John Beverley Robinson, the Attorney-General of Upper Canada, added:

> It is believed that to unite the British North American Provinces by giving them a common legislature and erecting them into a Kingdom, would be gratifying

all those colonies: that it would add to their security, confirm their attachment to the present government, and make wider the distinction between it and the republican institutions of their neighbours.[9]

Robinson's plan for the unification of British North America into one 'grand confederacy', submitted to the Colonial Office in 1823, was summarily rejected by the British as impractical. The Colonial Office's internal commentator added that such a proposal contained 'within itself the germ of separation'.[10] Nonetheless, the idea re-emerged in 1849, and was advocated by a convention of the British American League—a Loyalist organization opposed to increased ties to the United States—as an alternative to annexation. Robinson had seen his proposal for confederation as a prelude to absorption of the British provinces into the mother country, and even resurrected an old suggestion of the Loyalists that British Americans should be represented in Westminster. Most of the early schemes for unification did not give much consideration to the question of whether a union would result in an independent national state. Most were not very detailed and could be supported in the abstract without much commitment to change.

A New Canadian Nationality

By the 1850s, however, there was emerging—particularly in the Canadas—some sense of the existence of '*a true Canadian feeling*—a feeling of what might be termed *Canadian nationality*, in contradistinction to a feeling of mere colonial or annexation vassalage' (the Montreal *Pilot*, 6 April 1850). Sometimes the spirit was couched in terms of high-flown rhetoric, as in Alexander Morris's lecture *Nova Britannia* (1858), which called for a new national patriotism for British North America, 'this new Britannia, this rising power on the American Continent.' Often the idea was couched in terms of economic or cultural protectionism. Thus Thomas D'Arcy McGee (1825-68)—in his newspaper *New Era*, published in Montreal in 1857-8—called for a revision of the Reciprocity Treaty, which had been made with the United States in 1854, on cultural grounds. In literature, said McGee:

> The Americans have an advantage in this market. . . . The consequence is that Montreal and Toronto houses are mere agencies for New York publishers, having no literary wares to exchange with Harper, or Putnam, or the Sadliers, or Appleton. Economically, this is an evil; intellectually, it is treason to ourselves. If the design is to Massachusettsize the Canadian mind, this is the very way to effect that end: if, on the other hand, we desire to see a Canadian nationality freely developed, borrowing energy from the American, grace from the Frenchman, and power from the Briton, we cannot too soon begin to construct a Grand Trunk of thought, which will be as a backbone to the system we desire to inaugurate.[11]

McGee's *New Era*, though short-lived, was a major voice in the advocacy of both a union of the provinces of British North America ('The future political being of Canada is bound up most intimately with that of the maritime provinces,' McGee insisted in 1857) and Canadian independence from the mother country. Simultaneously he called for the 'speedy and secure establishment of the Canadian nationality.'

No more ardent Canadian nationalist could be found in the 1850s than McGee, a Catholic Irishman who immigrated to North America in 1842 as part of the growing flood of Irish driven out of their mother country by famine. He worked in the United States as a journalist on Irish newspapers until 1857, when he moved to Montreal. By this time he was persuaded that the United States did not enjoy a political system that tolerated and encouraged minority groups such as the Irish Catholics, and he saw a need for British North America to develop an alternative system. To a considerable extent McGee transferred Irish nationalist ideas to the Canadian scene. When he was elected to the Legislative Assembly in December 1857, representing the Irish and Catholic interests of Montreal, he issued his political manifesto:

> In entering into public life in this province, we do so with the strongest desire to preserve the individuality of the British North American colonies, until they ripen into a new Northern nationality. We shall judge of all proposed changes, not only by their own merits, but by their applicability to this end. Representation by population—the maintenance of the union of Upper and Lower Canada—a union under proper conditions with the Maritime Provinces and Bermuda—the annexation of Hudson Bay territory—the education, employment, and civil equality of all classes of people—in fact, every important topic that can arise ought to be viewed by the light, and decided by the requirements of Canadian Nationality.[12]

McGee's vision was clearly one of Canadian dominance in any new political arrangements, but his shopping-list suggests the direction of thinking that was emerging in Canada in the later 1850s. As a recent arrival, he could do little more in his platform than synthesize the commonly expressed ideas of others, for he lacked the experience to do otherwise. Many of these planks were built into the principles accepted at George Brown's Upper Canada Reform convention held in November 1859 in St Lawrence Hall, Toronto.

The Road to Confederation

The American Civil War

Neither the bind of the double majority nor the Irish-influenced vision of D'Arcy McGee was alone sufficient to impel British North Americans to national unification. Events in the United States in the early 1860s rapidly altered both the continental and the international balance of power. The Americans had been blundering for years towards the break-up of their federal union, and it fell apart with surprising suddenness in 1861, with the secession of the southern states into their own Confederacy and the beginning of the American Civil War. A large segment of public opinion in British North America supported the Confederacy for several reasons, despite the fact that it was built on principles of slavery, which most British North Americans found abhorrent. But while French Canada sympathized with the problems of a beleaguered minority, English Canada had a long-standing hostility to American republican democracy, exemplified by the Northern Union, believing that a divided United States might prove an easier neighbour with which to co-exist. As for Britain, she found economic and political reasons for a neutral policy, which to the Americans seemed to favour the Confederates—especially after the Americans seized Confederate diplomats off the British mailship SS *Trent* late in 1861. Public opinion in the northern states, whipped up by American newspapers, was extremely hostile to both Britain and her colonies, and Abraham Lincoln's government refused to back down and release the prisoners. The stage was set for an Anglo-American war that could alter the history of the continent.

Despite clear provocation, the British government refused to take advantage of the *Trent* affair. In the larger sense, such forbearance demonstrated a genuine desire for neutrality. But given the military situation, Britain could hardly leave her North American colonies unprotected. Two possible scenarios seemed likely. In the first, the Confederacy would succeed in maintaining its independence, and the Union government would seek to replace it by turning its frustrated military machine northward to British North America. Alternatively, the Union government would defeat the secessionists, and then use the enormous army obviously required to achieve victory to annex British North America, employing as a pretext any number of incidents in which Britain and her colonies had 'supported' the Confederacy, including the occasional raids on American territory by southerners based north of the border. From the British perspective, defending British North America was expensive and dangerous. Despite the dispatch of British troops to the colonies following the *Trent* affair, what the British really wanted was for the colonials to organize their own defences, and to become sufficiently strong militarily to discourage the Americans from adventurism in the north.

In 1864 the military situation in the United States turned more dangerous for British North America. The Union forces gained clear victories over the Confederacy, at the same time as the Canadians had become totally frustrated by their own political impasse. The year 1864 also represented the expiration of the ten-year agreement for reciprocity with the United States, and motions for abrogation in the American Congress only just failed of passage in December. Although the Americans were hostile to British North America because of its perceived support of the Confederacy, a more relevant factor was a growing protectionism, combined with a notion that the British colonies had benefited more from reciprocity. In any event, the American Senate voted for abrogation early in 1865. In several respects the efforts of the Canadians to create a larger union fitted very well with British desires for lessened colonial responsibilities and expense, so that the full weight of the still-considerable influence of the British colonial system was placed on the side of unification.

The Canadian Coalition of 1864

The events of the American war influenced not only British but Canadian thinking as well. The difficulty experienced by the Canadian government in military mobilization, caught as it was by the double majority, was one of the factors that led George Brown to propose a political coalition with his political enemies, based upon commitment to a British American federal union. The achievement of this 'Great Coalition'—a ministry formed by a union of the Conservatives under Macdonald and the *Bleus* of Canada East under Cartier, with the Grits led by Brown, announced in the Canadian Parliament on 22 June 1864—broke the political deadlock. The new government moved on a variety of fronts over the summer of 1864. Most important was the preparation of the outlines of a federal union to be presented to a conference of Maritime delegates meeting at Charlottetown in September, which was called to discuss Maritime union with the Canadas. The *Trent* affair had stimulated the interest of many in the completion of the Intercolonial Railway linking the Maritime provinces and Canada; but despite negotiations in 1862—among the Canadas, Nova Scotia, and New Brunswick—that agreed on a cost-sharing formula, the Canadians had dragged their feet. A Maritime union that would enable the lower provinces to deal on a stronger footing with the Canadians was debated in the legislatures of the three provinces and discussed desultorily in the newspapers— though some voices called for a larger union.

It is impossible to measure where the Maritimes actually stood on the question of union at the time of the Charlottetown Conference in 1864. What we do know is that there was a considerable amount of abstract support for some form of unification, tempered by two realities: a strong feeling that any Maritime participation in a larger union must not work to the disadvantage of either the provinces or the region; and an equally strong feeling that the Maritimes were not doing so badly within the existing imperial system. Most of the economic interests of the Maritime region were transatlantic rather than intercontinental, and part of the problem of a British North American union was to find a way to offer economic advantages to the Maritimes that replaced those offered by trade with the outside world encompassed by the British Empire. The Intercolonial Railway, of course, could fit into just such an argument, providing a means of bringing western products to the carrying-trade of the Maritimes, at the same time as it dangled the prospect of new markets for Maritime goods in the interior. Canadian historians have always tended to view the Maritime position as one of parochial defence of local interests, but such an interpretation really misses the point. The region was already part of a larger political and economic system, known as the British Empire, and had legitimate reasons for not wishing to surrender local autonomy without receiving clear advantages in return. Ironically, many Maritimers feared a union that perpetuated local interests. More than one newspaper joined the *Halifax Citizen* in expressing distrust of 'that combination of union and disunion—that expensive double machinery of government, that attempts to neutralize sectional feelings and interests through a general government while perpetuating those feelings by means of local legislatures.'[13]

Canadian historians have also generally deprecated Atlantic Canada's hostility to union as parochial, while refusing to treat the opponents of Confederation with much respect or attention. Before the *Dictionary of Canadian Biography*, few anti-Confederationists in the Maritimes made their way into standard Canadian reference works, and their opposition to Confederation

The Charlottetown Conference, September 1864. On the left, Charles Tupper is standing against the first pillar and D'Arcy McGee against the second, with George-Étienne Cartier in front of him; next to Cartier, seated, is John A. Macdonald. National Archives of Canada, C-733.

was ignored or downplayed. Though the anti-Confederationist case was subsequently disproved by history—at least through 1990—in its own day it was certainly not unreasonable to view the unification of British North America as an impracticable visionary scheme, proposed by politicians in the Province of Canada to meet its needs, that was really not in the best interests of other colonies. Little analysis has ever been made of the backgrounds of those politicians and businessmen who opposed Confederation—compared with those who supported it—but one trend is plain. Anti-Confederationists in most colonies were far more likely to be Liberals than Conservatives, supporters of grass-roots democracy rather than of economic development. To some extent they reflected the suspicions of their constituents.

Despite the general love-in at Charlottetown, where the Canadians presented their scheme for a federal union to what seemed to be general approbation, there were several problems inherent in the proposals. One was the fact that central to the Canadian initiative was the need to escape the political problems of a united Canada, preferably by allowing the French their own province, and then balancing that concession by adding more provinces to the new union. The aggressive French-speaking representatives from Canada East made such a structure almost inevitable, and the ingenuity of John A. Macdonald and others was taxed in explaining why this federal union would work when the American one had failed. In addition, in any federal union operating on the basis of parliamentary responsible government and 'rep by pop', those provinces with smaller populations were likely to be overwhelmed.

The question of Senate representation proved critical, particularly at the second conference—which Newfoundland joined—held at Quebec in October 1864 to work out the details agreed to in principle at Charlottetown. After Quebec, almost all of the objections to Confederation, expressed in any part of British North America, were not to the general idea of union, but to the specific terms worked out at that conference and the procedures used to implement them. Critics complained not about union itself, but about '*this union*', which reflected the dominance of Canadian needs and Canadian thinking, and rode roughshod over the legitimate ambitions of the smaller (also the lower) provinces to protect themselves from the Canadian juggernaut. When Macdonald moved at the Quebec Conference that the three sections of British North America—Canada West, Canada East, and the four Atlantic provinces—each have 24 members in the Senate, the immediate response from the East was to ask to have its representation raised to 32. Eventually the Quebec Conference returned to the Charlottetown arrangement of three sections, each with 24 members, offering Newfoundland an additional four. Prince Edward Island made a big issue—without any success—over getting one more member of the Commons (six instead of five) than its population allowed. A further debate came over the powers of the local legislatures. The majority case was stated by Charles Tupper (1821–1915) of Nova Scotia:

> Powers—undefined—must rest somewhere. Those who were at Charlotte-town will remember that it was fully specified there that all the powers not given to Local should be reserved to the Federal Government....It was a fundamental principle laid down by Canada and the basis of our deliberations.[14]

But a number of Atlantic delegates disagreed. And those from Prince Edward Island became upset when a provision for money to buy out its landed proprietors (apparently agreed to at Charlottetown) was omitted from the final agreement.

However ungenerous the Quebec Conference was to Prince Edward Island, no one could accuse the Canadians of stinting on expenses to woo the delegates. Both supporters and critics of Confederation could agree on the conviviality at Quebec, although they obviously took away different interpretations. 'Picture it ye enthusiasts!' wrote a Hamilton newspaper satirically. 'What a Canadian prospect and Arcadian delight...a national Paradise....Mr Brown loving Mr Galt, Mr Galt loving Mr Brown, and Mr Macdonald loving everybody continually. What could be more lovely?'[15] According to *Barney Rooney's Letters*—a major anti-union publication from Nova Scotia, written in 'Irish' dialect—the whole conference came to life only after the delegates returned to the St Louis Hotel 'after a hard day's conspirocy', agreeing over the punch bowl that 'the well understood wishes iv [*sic*] the people are so notoriously in favour iv this scheme that it would be a reckless and infamous policy to put them to the trouble of expressing themselves.'[16]

As Barney Rooney suggested, selling the Quebec scheme to the lower provinces would be no easy matter, particularly given the reluctance of any of Confederation's supporters to take the question to the public, in the form either of an election on the question or of a plebiscite. The public debate was not particularly well informed, and the preliminaries to Canadian Confederation produced no supporting gloss nearly equivalent to the *Federalist Papers* of 1787 by James Madison, Alexander Hamilton, and company, which could be read by subsequent generations of Canadians. Some debate occurred over the question of whether the proposed union was federal or legislative, but most discussants had little real grasp of federalism in particular, or of political theory in general. Although the delegates at Charlottetown and Quebec had generally accepted that the new union was centralist, it was discussed in Canada East in quite different terms. While Macdonald (and others) sought to reduce the powers of the provincial legislatures to 'municipal' proportions—something many in the Atlantic region did not like—in French Canada a different apprehension prevailed. For example: 'The power will be sovereign, no doubt,' wrote the *Courrier de St-Hyacinthe* in September 1864, 'but it will have power only over certain general questions clearly

defined by the constitution. This is the only plan of confederation which
Lower Canada can accept . . . . The two levels of government must both be
sovereign, each within its jurisdiction as clearly defined by the constitution.'[17]
The proponents of union in Canada East made quite clear that Confederation
meant giving French Canadians their own province. According to George
Cartier's *La Minerve,* 'as a distinct and separate nationality, we form a state
within the state. We enjoy the full exercise of our rights and the formal
recognition of our national independence.'[18] The general acceptance of this
argument meant that little French-Canadian opposition was to be found
when the union was debated in the Canadian legislature. The chief Lower
Canadian opponent and critic of the scheme was an anglophone Protestant
MLA from the Eastern Townships, Christopher Dunkin (1812-81).

The Debates Over Union

Given the general agreement of Confederation's proponents that provincial
acceptance of the new arrangement could be achieved by legislative fiat, the
debates over the union within each provincial assembly constituted the most
telling forum for opinion about the new scheme. What they demonstrated
most of all was the success of the proponents of union in capturing most of
the positive ground. Critics like Christopher Dunkin and A.-A. Dorion
(1818-91), leader of the *Rouges*, and also an MLA, could dissect the Quebec
proposals and reduce them to rubble—as Dunkin did in a series of two four-
hour speeches to the Canadian Parliament in 1865—but they had little that
was positive to suggest in their place. For Canada, the absence of alternatives
was in some ways more significant than in the Atlantic provinces. Those
colonies could stand pat, and Newfoundland—convinced it would be little
more than 'the contemptible fag-end of such a compact' with Canada, after
an election on the question in 1869—remained outside Confederation until
1949. Not even a substantial annual income in return for the colony's Crown
lands was a sufficiently persuasive argument. Sir Stephen Hill, governor of
Newfoundland, wrote the Colonial Office in November 1869:

> The mass of voters in the Colony as already stated by me in a former Despatch
> are an ignorant, lawless, prejudiced body. The majority of whom living as they
> do in the Outports in almost a primitive state of existence are unfit subjects for
> Educated and Intellectual man to attempt to reason with on the advantages of
> Confederation. I therefore consider that it was a fatal error to have submitted to
> such a population the decision of such an important question as the Union of
> this Country with Canada.[19]

In Prince Edward Island, the issue was simple. The Island's population was
small and likely to remain so. Given the principles of representation by
population built into the Quebec proposals, the Island would have no clout in
the federal legislature. Moreover, the local legislature would be reduced to

the importance of a town council, while the Island was not sufficiently compensated for 'the surrender of a separate Government, with the independent powers it now enjoys.' Prince Edward Island, like Newfoundland, recognized that Confederation was essential to Canadian interests rather more than to its own, and did not join.

The situation in New Brunswick and Nova Scotia was considerably more complex—and more volatile. In New Brunswick, as one Canadian reporter wrote in 1864, 'Party politics do not run high. There are no great questions dividing parties and the battles of Parliament are mainly of a personal nature, except when railway matters are introduced.' The Intercolonial Railway was an important matter in New Brunswick, however, for it symbolized a continental commercial connection. But such a connection cut both ways. One 1865 poster in an election fought over union put the question thus: 'Do you wish Canada Oats, Beef, Pork, Butter etc. to come into this country at one half the price you are now receiving? Do you wish the whole Revenue of this country to be handed over to...the dishonest Statesmen of Canada?'[20] And the route taken by the Intercolonial itself through New Brunswick was an important matter, for politicians recognized that those districts served by the railroad were more likely to prosper. The political leader of opposition to union, A. J. Smith (1822-83) of Dorchester, was not only critical of a scheme cooked up in the 'oily brains of Canadian politicians', but had an alternative in continued reciprocity with the Americans—providing the Yankees would play the game. In the election of 1865 Smith, and Confederation's opponents, blew the pro-Confederation government of Samuel Leonard Tilley (1818-96) away.

A non-partisan government whose only platform was opposition to union with Canada was not likely to do very much, or survive very long, and the Smith administration went back to the polls in April 1866. The campaign was conducted against the background of threatened invasions of British North America, particularly New Brunswick, by thousands of Irish nationalists (the Fenians), many of them veterans of the American Union army who had kept their arms when disbanded. If the Fenians had not existed, the pro-Confederation forces would have had to invent them. But there was just enough truth in the circulating rumours to fuel everyone's paranoia about American aggression and Irish volatility. Many in New Brunswick joined the Roman Catholic Bishop of Arichat (on Cape Breton), who wrote Charles Tupper on 12 April 1866: 'Altho' no admirer of Confederation on the basis of the Quebec Scheme, yet owing to the present great emergency and the necessities of the times, the union of the Colonies, upon a new basis, we receive with pleasure.'[21] The Smith government was defeated, and the new administration headed by Tilley moved an address favouring Confederation, not—it must be noted—the union of the Quebec Resolutions, but 'upon such terms as will secure the just rights and interests of New Brunswick, accompanied with provision for the immediate construction of the Intercolonial Railway.'

From this point opposition to union in New Brunswick melted away. Given its location, it is not surprising that New Brunswick had always been ambivalent about Confederation and a continental vision to replace the traditional imperial one. The Fenian threat provided an excuse for replacing the Smith government, which in office had exemplified no vision whatsoever.

The situation was different in Nova Scotia, both in terms of the intensity of opposition to union and in its longevity. Nova Scotia was the most populous and prosperous of all the Atlantic provinces, with its mixed economy spearheaded by a shipping industry that was still extraordinarily profitable. By the mid-1860s Nova Scotia owned one ton of ship for every one of its 350,000 inhabitants. With its sailing ships able to go everywhere in the world under the protection of the British Empire, Nova Scotia had little enthusiasm for continentalism. Surely, argued Joseph Howe, there was no need to replace London as Nova Scotia's capital. 'We need not seek for another in the backwoods of Canada, and may be pardoned if we prefer London under the dominion of John Bull to Ottawa under the dominion of Jack Frost.' The province's lieutenant-governor in the years following the Quebec Resolutions, Sir Richard MacDonnell (1814–81), offered a similar point, writing that the Great Coalition ministry in Canada 'seems not to have cared how

Joseph Howe in 1851, a copy of a portrait painted by T. Debaussy in that year. Public Archives of Nova Scotia.

Canadian—selfishly Canadian, they may have appeared to Bluenose who is very happy as he is.' The government headed by Charles Tupper in 1864 was unpopular, and embraced union as a policy that might keep it in office. But, as the Halifax *Herald* asked after the Quebec Conference: 'We have the trade of the world now open to us on nearly equal terms, and why should we allow Canada to hamper us?'[22] In Nova Scotia that question was not an easy one to answer. Nova Scotians opposed to unification initially attacked on two fronts: first, any union was ridiculous; and second, *this* union smacked too much of Canadian concerns, giving Upper Canada rep by pop, Lower Canada provincial autonomy, and the Maritimes nothing but trouble.

Before long the opposition had moved the discussion to economics and finance. As one Halifax newspaper soberly observed:

> The financial portion of the Confederation scheme is its most important feature. Since no real Union is in contemplation, but rather a careful bargain between Canada and the Lower Provinces—free trade and an Intercolonial line offered by the former, and a Union which will loose Canada's political deadlock by the latter—the fiscal portion of the agreement assumes a gigantic importance.[23]

Nova Scotians spent far more time on the details of finances than on the shape of the bargain, although after the entrance of the powerful voice of Joseph Howe in opposition, and the defeat of the pro-Confederation government of Tilley in New Brunswick, the Tupper government backed off early in 1865 from introducing motions on union with Canada.

A variety of circumstances put unification back into contention in Nova Scotia, chiefly British pressure and the Fenian threats. Even the opposition gave in a little. Anti-Confederationist William Annand (1808-87), a friend of Howe's, wrote to A.J. Smith in March 1866, observing that 'Like yourself, I desire no political Union with Canada, because I feel that the Maritime Provinces, in any scheme that may be matured, must be seriously injured by a connexion with a colony which must necessarily exercise a preponderating influence over all the others.' At the same time, added Annand, circumstances might force union, and if so, he wrote, 'let it be one that has some more redeeming features than the Quebec Scheme.'[24] Charles Tupper seized on the Fenian threat and opposition waffling, introducing a motion that ignored the Quebec Resolutions and called for 'a scheme of union' in which 'the rights and interests of Nova Scotia' would be ensured. It passed 31-19. Unlike the situation in New Brunswick, the opponents of Confederation in Nova Scotia did not at this point disappear. They went on to complain about the failure of the Tupper government to take Confederation to the voters, and eventually to elect full slates of candidates provincially and federally committed to taking Nova Scotia out of the union in which she had become involved.

Two related observations about Confederation in Nova Scotia and New Brunswick are perhaps worth making. One is that neither province had displayed any enthusiasm for the Quebec Resolutions, and the legislative actions supporting union had quite pointedly avoided any endorsement of them. The pro-Confederationists in these provinces found it politically expedient to talk about renegotiating terms, however, and were prepared to allow the Canadians to offer a slightly better financial deal without changing any of the basic fundamentals of Quebec that were found wanting in so many different quarters. Thus the second point: though Nova Scotia's and New Brunswick's legislatures accepted the principle of union with Canada—but not the union worked out at Quebec—what those two provinces got was the Quebec scheme with all its imperfections. Since all but the most ardent unionists in New Brunswick and Nova Scotia recognized that the Quebec proposals consigned their provinces to political impotence, it is hardly surprising that the region later complained when its voices in Ottawa were ignored.

Confederation Becomes a Reality

In November 1866 delegates from Canada, Nova Scotia, and New Brunswick—the three provinces committed to union—met in London to work out the final details, basically the Quebec Resolutions, with more money (and an Intercolonial Railway) for the Maritimes. The possibility that Prince Edward Island and Newfoundland might join later was left open. Everyone agreed the new country should be called by the name of its largest progenitor, thus openly announcing the importance of Canada in the united government and causing confusion ever afterwards for students of Canadian history. Under pressure from the Colonial Office, which in its turn was under pressure from the Americans, the delegates scrapped Macdonald's preferred terminology 'Kingdom of Canada' in favour of the less monarchical 'Dominion of Canada'. The resulting piece of legislation, the British North America Act, passed quickly through the British Parliament in 1867, the MPs barely looking up from the order paper as they voted. The Queen signed the bill into law on 29 March 1867; the date of proclamation was to be 1 July. Joseph Howe, who had been in London lobbying against the legislation, returned to Nova Scotia, writing:

> We must submit of course, because we cannot fight the British Government, but if the Queen's troops were to withdraw I would die upon the Frontier rather than submit to such an outrage. . . . Our first duty will be to punish the rascals here who have betrayed and sold us. If then convinced that the Canadians are disposed to act fairly, we may try the experiment.[25]

The governor-general, Lord Monck (1819-94), not surprisingly called upon John A. Macdonald, the man everyone associated with the union, to be the first prime minister. On the morning of the first of July—a day of celebration and military parades in all the four provinces—the new country was proclaimed in the recently completed Parliament Buildings in Ottawa, and Macdonald received a knighthood. Launching the new nation was not the same as ensuring its success, however.

Mid-Victorian Society

On 23 February 1883, a Queen's University medical student entered into her diary a litany of deepest despair:

> Every day things look blacker as regards a tithe of justice for us in the future, near or remote. We have given up all hope of making any high standing even if we were allowed wh. every day seems more doubtful. We will have the same papers, but if they will not class our marks with those of the boys the outside public will not understand & the boys will virtually hve gained their point. And then the humbugging we have rec[eived] as regards lectures & then injustice & calummy we have so wrongly suffered. None but Heaven knows or can know what we have suffered & do suffer daily...When we are fighting in a good fight & should have all support to aid us, to be turned on by all, with such mistaken zeal, with such injustice it is hard, so hard If I can only fight it out till I get home I'll be glad.[1]

Elizabeth Smith (1859-1949) was born into a prosperous farm family in southwestern Ontario. Like many ambitious young women of her generation, she became a teacher, attending the Model School of Hamilton Collegiate Institute between spells of teaching in Ontario's rural school system. By 1878 she had decided to become a doctor and was advised to attend medical school in the United States, since the Canadian system was so hostile to women. Instead she joined several other young women at Queen's Medical School in Kingston, which had reluctantly opened its doors to women—who were taught separately—in 1880. Financing her medical education with further teaching assignments, Elizabeth struggled uphill against male hostility, her despair culminating in the diary entry quoted above.

Elizabeth Smith would ultimately not graduate from Queen's, but from the newly established Toronto Woman's Medical College in 1884. She opened a general practice in Hamilton, then became a lecturer at the Kingston Women's Medical College, which had opened in 1883. Marriage to the pioneering scholar of economic history Adam Shortt (1859-1931) in 1886 produced three children, and she resigned in 1893 to concentrate on her family. She never resumed her formal medical career, achieving distinction instead through volunteer service in a variety of women's and social organizations. Her later history belongs in a subsequent chapter, but her early struggles to obtain a medical education well demonstrate the changes, opportunities, and limitations within Canadian society in the years immediately after Confederation. Elizabeth Smith's brief practice as a doctor, and her subsequent employment as a teacher of medicine, represented one of the major shifts in employment of women during the mid-nineteenth century: aspiring to be a medical doctor in 1840 would have been unthinkable. In this context Canadian society had advanced. Nonetheless, the obstacles Elizabeth Smith encountered were those of a society that was hardening its structure. New social rigidities, particularly affecting women, were all part of Victorian society, in Canada as elsewhere.

Between 1838 and 1885 British North America changed from a collection of loosely connected colonies in the northeastern sector of the continent, heavily dependent on the mother country both economically and politically, to a transcontinental nation with a rapidly diversifying internal economy anchored by substantial industrialization. The era witnessed some spectacular technological advances—particularly associated with the steam-engine on sea and land—that radically altered perceptions of distance in a vast domain separated from Europe by three thousand miles of ocean. The discovery of telegraphy, and the eventual laying of a transatlantic cable from Newfoundland in 1866, also affected the perception of distance. It was now possible to communicate within North America and to Europe almost instantly. Although the mid-nineteenth century was a period of ever-escalating technical developments—including the practical application of principles of telephony, electricity, sound recording, and even motion pictures—few of these 'inventions' had as yet risen above the experimental stage and most were seen, as were earlier technologies, mainly to have value for commerce and industry rather than for individual private users. The great age of the democratization and domesticization of technology was still in the future. The relationship between political unification and social change was a complicated one, but there were some common causes, particularly in the economic sphere. The transition to industrialism in the economic arena was matched in the social one.

Three major themes dominate the society of these years. First, there was an unmistakable sense of the constant geographical mobility or transiency of the population in every part of British North America, but mainly out of the older and more settled rural districts. Second, the class structure of society began to take shape and even solidify, with the chief changes being the emergence of a working class (or proletariat) associated with urbanization and industrialization, and the rapid professionalization of certain educated and skilled segments of what was developing into a middle class (or bour-geoisie). Along with the development of social classes went a concurrent hardening of certain caste lines, associated with class but not identical with it. Here women and certain racial minorities, chiefly native peoples and orien-tals, were the chief factors. Finally, this period saw the enormous expansion of private organizations—fraternal, humanitarian, religious, and even cultural.

One of the major ironies of historical scholarship, in Canada and elsewhere over the last twenty years, has been the way in which developments in social history that were intended to make the past more accessible and humanized have had exactly the reverse effect. Scholars have reacted against the tenden-cies of the old history to focus on traditional masculine pursuits—and the élites who dominated them—in favour of recovering more information about the lives of ordinary people, including various hitherto invisible groups. Much of the work of recovery has been quantitative and statistical, establishing trends among large numbers of anonymous individuals, or else has dealt with the daily lives of ordinary people—typically unexciting, and often oppressive. The products of the 'new social history' are not only substantively different from those of the 'old history', but often less interest-ing to read about for anyone but the committed. Establishing some sort of balance between the preference of many readers for the unrepresentative anecdote or example that is interesting simply because it is unusual and atypical, and the tendency of scholars to prefer more abstract generalizations, is obviously no easy matter.

Mobility

The years 1840 to 1880 saw a series of substantial movements of population, into the country from Europe, out of the country into the United States, and within the country into new rural districts, as well as into the industrializing cities. After 1870 the westward movement into the Prairie West began in earnest. Indeed, probably the single most important social factor in the era was the sheer extent of the movement of people, responding to a variety of forces both positive and negative. We tend to associate geographical mobility with our own society, forgetting that a pattern of movement—of people constantly searching for better conditions—existed in Canada 150 years ago and more.

Immigration and Internal Migration

Throughout the 1840s and 1850s British immigration to North America continued at high levels, fuelled especially by the potato famines in Ireland, which reached a peak in 1846. Much of the outflow of Catholic Irish from the south of Ireland made its way initially or eventually to the United States, mainly to the cities of the eastern seaboard, although some indeterminate percentage of immigrants settled in British North America, many of them on small farms located in the more marginal districts of the various provinces. Between 1840 and 1860 well over 600,000 British immigrants arrived in British North America, most of them seeking land on which to build a new life. Combined with the natural increases within the colonies, the arrival of this horde of new settlers put enormous pressure on available agricultural land, particularly land that was suitable for staple crop farming for the market. Second-generation farmers were forced to accept less-desirable land or move to the United States where a more rapid industrialization than existed in British North America had opened up new jobs. Thus, at the same time that thousands of land-hungry immigrants were moving in, thousands of disillusioned members of the younger generation within the colonies were moving out.

By the 1860s most immigrants were arriving in British North America on board steamships rather than sailing vessels, which cut the length of the transatlantic journey from weeks to days. The result—despite often horrendous steerage conditions for the poorer passengers—was less chance of illness and disease. Another 800,000 immigrants came in the years between 1867 and the mid-1880s, with a substantial increase in numbers after 1882. Most of these newcomers also originated in the British Isles. Many came in response to recruitment campaigns by the federal government, by provincial governments, and by private enterprise (especially western land and railway companies). After 1882 the immigrants would tend to bypass the Atlantic region and Quebec, heading for Ontario and the newly opening West.

French Canada   The first sign of serious outmigration came from the seigneurial districts of French Canada, the heartland of French-Canadian culture, language, and religion. There the agrarian crisis, combined with the failure of the rebellions of 1837/8—which had been partly caused by that crisis—forced many to leave their native province. Some of the migrants were political exiles, but most were young French Canadians, both male and female, pushed by the unavailability and unproductivity of land in the traditional seigneurial regions and pulled by the opening of textile mills in cities of New England like Manchester, New Hampshire, Lowell, Massachusetts, and Woonsocket, Rhode Island. Almost any opportunity was superior to a future on a farm of less than 100 acres, a limitation faced by the vast majority of inhabitants of the seigneuries. In the 1830s upwards of 40,000 of them left the province for the United States, and that figure jumped to 90,000 in the 1840s and 190,000 in the 1850s. This population loss was regarded as critical in French Canada, one cleric calling it 'the cemetery of the race', for it marked the disappearance of a population that would respond rapidly to American assimilationist pressures, and signalled an end to over two centuries of unremitting expansion of the French-Canadian people. Today the visitor to these New England towns and cities can still see standing—usually empty and forlorn—the extensive brick buildings that housed the nineteenth-century factories in which these French Canadians worked.

The movement to the United States was not the only migration out of the seigneurial districts. Thousands of French Canadians also moved into the Eastern Townships of Canada East, which were originally intended as English-speaking enclaves, while others continued to fill up unpopulated regions in the Laurentians and around Lac Saint-Jean. Colonization of these regions was promoted by both state and church as an alternative to migration to the United States.

Because most of the land in the Townships was held by speculators, much of the first French-Canadian settlement there was in the form of squatting. Once the Townships were opened by railroads in the 1850s, sawmills and textile mills rapidly grew up along the rivers of the region. In Sherbrooke the largest woollen factory in Canada—employing 500 workers—was opened in 1866, and French Canadians had the choice of being exploited south of the border or at home. The arrival of large numbers of French Canadians in the Townships helped drive many British settlers, often non-Anglophone Gaelic-speakers, further west. As early as 1871 the former had come to outnumber the latter rather substantially. In the upper St Francis district of the Eastern Townships, for example, the French-speaking population grew from 9.7 per cent of the district in 1844 to 64.1 per cent by 1871.[2]

As well as moving out of the country or into regions like the Eastern Townships, thousands of Quebeckers, mainly French Canadians, moved into the cities and expanding towns of the province. Overall the number of non-rural Québécois nearly doubled between 1851 and 1881—a period when the population of Montreal more than doubled, from 57,715 to 140,747, and the number of towns increased from fourteen to twenty-two, each of them growing steadily in population. Trois-Rivières, for example, nearly doubled in population (from 4,900 to 8,600), and by 1871 it had 124 manufacturing establishments employing just over a thousand workers. The most significant change occurred, of course, in Montreal, where thousands of rural French Canadians, the majority of them female, moved to the city in search of employment. Some found work as domestic servants, the numbers of which nearly doubled between 1844 and 1881; but most were employed in a few burgeoning industries, particularly clothing manufacture, textile production, and the making of tobacco products. The result was a significant gender imbalance within the city, making husbands hard to find. But since few rural French-Canadian males could aspire to a decent farm, the situation was probably no worse in the city than in the countryside, and perhaps a little better.

Canada West/Ontario   French Canada was hardly alone in the extent of its migratory patterns, although particularities varied from region to region. In Canada West/Ontario, for example, most of the movement into the United States was into the agricultural districts of the American Midwest, a migration that was to some extent arrested by the opening of Manitoba after 1870.

A key factor behind the constant mobility was the inherent instability of that much-admired institution the family farm, which has been always regarded as the basis of rural society. Its entire structure revolved around the perform-ance of most, if not all, of the work by family members. Large numbers of children were therefore desirable and by and large achieved. In Peel County, Ontario, between five and six children per family, of the total of eight to nine born, survived to maturity. In this simple demographic fact lay the success of the farmer who enjoyed such a family; but it also created pressures for the expansion of landholdings and led to the eventual removal of some of the younger generation. While maturing, children could be retained on the farm as a captive work force, but as they grew up they would stay only on the understanding that they would eventually inherit enough land to become independent farmers themselves. In this male-oriented society males nor-mally inherited productive farm land, and their expectations could be deferred for only so long. Hence the tendency in all rural societies in British North America/Canada to throw off a disproportionate number of females (usually between ages 15 and 21) into the cities and non-agricultural work. If the family enjoyed the advantages of a number of sons, it either had to provide landholdings for them or expect that they would join their sisters in departing.

In 1852, for example, farmer John Snell of Chinguascousy Township in Peel County was 41 years old, with eight children—four of them boys— under the age of fourteen. His farm of 100 acres had cost $1,300 to assemble, and he would add another 100 acres over the next few years at a cost of $60 per acre. Although the farm was economically viable for a growing family, it was not large enough to be subdividable for more than two of the sons, while the pressure on land in his district had raised the cost of assembling enough land for additional farms (at $60 per acre) to a prohibitive amount.[3] Thus, while agricultural districts everywhere produced large numbers of children, not all of them could expect to be accommodated on the family farm, however prosperous. At the same time, the need to accommodate children led farmers to accumulate land whenever possible. The average farm size in Peel County increased by 40 per cent from 1851 to 1861, while in that decade the number of males aged 15 to 30 increased even more rapidly.[4]

Not every agricultural district, or every family within it, followed a single pattern of development. Farms growing staple crops on extended and exten-sive acreages were less subdividable than more complex mixed farms, although even the latter had a minimum size for viability. And over time it was possible in Ontario, as it had always been in parts of French Canada and the Atlantic region, for families living on farms too small for an economic return to be supported through the outside employment of some members, often the family head or older children. But the pressure on some of the younger generation to depart was always strong, whether in search of a future or because of the lure of adventure and excitement. Those family farms that

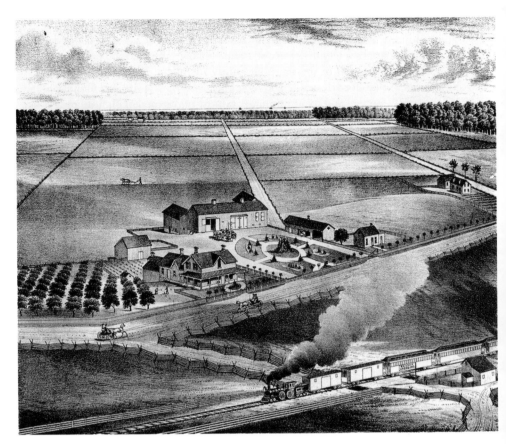

The residence, farm buildings, and farm of Hugh McQuoid in Durham Country, near the the Bay of Quinte on the north shore of Lake Ontario, 1878. The drawing appeared in one of 29 county atlases (on Northumberland and Durham), published in Ontario between 1875 and 1881, containing maps, biographies of residents and illustrations of their properties (for which they presumably paid), and offering a vivid, if idealized, glimpse of rural life at the time. The railway is the Great Western. Metropolitan Toronto Reference Library.

did not enjoy a large number of children put different pressures on young people, who were unable to leave and were expected to take over the farm and help support aging parents.

Under most circumstances women could not expect to inherit farms, even from deceased husbands; and, indeed, they usually could not share in the proceeds of sale. The right of the male head of a household to own, sell, and control the inheritance of land was accepted in law and practice everywhere in Canada, and few fathers chose to treat daughters equally with sons, however much they had contributed to the family's prosperity. Although

Elizabeth Smith's family established a famous preserve business (E.D. Smith Company) in the 1880s, she never received much benefit from the family farm or business in pursuing her career. Land went to the sons, and daughters could expect little more than a small cash bequest out of the liquid assets of the operation. Small wonder young women were even more likely than young men to leave rural communities. Land accumulation and its inheritance were key issues in rural society, and the dynamics of farming were an inherently destabilizing force in Canadian society for most of the population. Elder sons (and the women they married) could expect to become pillars of the community, local leaders in political, religious, and cultural terms, and could even become part of the rural élite in their community. But for most of the children of farmers, adulthood meant moving on, in search of new land on which to begin the cycle again, or of non-agrarian opportunities.

Some new land within Canada West/Ontario was available to the north, and settlement moved rapidly after mid-century up to Georgian Bay and into the Muskoka country, heedless of the prominent outcroppings of the Canadian Shield. The father of Stephen Leacock, for example, after unsuccessful attempts at farming in South Africa and Kansas, in 1876 settled his family near Orillia in the Lake Simcoe region. The construction of the CPR through north-central and northwestern Ontario in the 1870s encouraged the opening of this and neighbouring areas; but they were agriculturally marginal (because of both soil and climate), and though they were initially settled with great optimism, many farms were subsequently abandoned. Leacock's father abandoned his farm—though he left his wife and eleven children on it, to survive mainly through family remittances from England.

Those who sought to grow grain, the staple crop of southwestern Ontario, usually moved west instead of north, at first into adjacent states of the American Midwest, such as Michigan and Illinois, where immigration from Upper Canada began in earnest in the 1830s. One community near London, originally settled by Welsh immigrants in the 1820s, was by the 1850s exporting most of its younger generation into the American grainbelt. After the American Civil War a constant stream of Upper Canadians made their way beyond the midwestern states onto the American prairies, contributing to the rapid settlement of states such as Nebraska and the Dakotas—though some of these families, or their children, would eventually re-immigrate back into the Canadian Prairie West.

As was true everywhere in British North America/Canada during this transitional period, Ontario migration into the province's own cities and towns was substantial. Between 1850 and 1870 alone the number of towns in Ontario with populations between 1,000 and 5,000 people more than doubled, from 33 to 69. Toronto, the largest city, grew commensurately, from less than 40,000 in 1840 to over 86,000 in 1880. Of its population of 56,000 in 1870, just over half were native Canadians, most of them drawn from the surrounding countryside. Toronto had a gender skew in favour of females, although not as substantial a one as Montreal, to which women were drawn by domestic service and opportunities for employment in retail trade and manufacturing. By 1880 over 12,000 Torontonians were employed in 932 industrial establishments.

The Atlantic Region   The years before 1860 saw considerable internal expansion in the Atlantic region as settlers moved into less desirable and more remote parts, while others moved into the major urban centres. Population growth-rates continued extremely high, although they had ominously begun to decline for Nova Scotia as early as the 1850s. By the end of that decade very few of the older settled districts could support their natural increases in population, much less sustain incoming immigrants. In Newfoundland, for example, there was considerable movement out of the eastern districts into the largely unsettled western part of the island, and a vast increase in a seasonal migration into the Labrador fisheries; in some outports over two-thirds of the working males became seasonal workers in Labrador. Similar patterns persisted in the Maritime Provinces, as people in New Brunswick moved northwards and in Prince Edward Island westwards. Seasonal migration for timbering declined somewhat in intensity in these provinces as forests became depleted. Neither expansion onto new (and frequently marginal) land, nor seasonal migration, could in the end provide a livelihood for a growing population. As agriculture, fishing, and shipping reached the limits of their capacities to employ the young, many turned to migration—either out of the region, usually to the United States, or to urban centres—to find employment.

Although there were always British North Americans who slipped away across the border, the 1860s saw the exodus from the Atlantic region, especially the three Maritime Provinces, begin in earnest. Probably only the uncertainties of the American Civil War prevented it from taking off before 1865. While in the 1850s only a few districts were losing population, in the next decade over one-third of the counties in the Maritime Provinces experienced population losses, and that figure climbed to over half in the 1870s. The correlation between rural counties (with economies largely dependent on farming and fishing) and depopulation was very strong.

The lost population often moved in two stages: first, from the countryside to the nearest town or city; and second, out of the region entirely. While outmigration was a general phenomenon, Scots and Irish were over-represented in the exodus and Acadians under-represented. Most of those departing were young. One 1873 study of Nova Scotians going to the United States found over one-quarter under fifteen years of age, and less than fifteen per cent over forty. Significantly, considerably more than half (831 out of 1,524) were women, with the majority in the under-fifteen category. Most men leaving Nova Scotia were farmers and unskilled workers, although a minority came from artisan trades, which were declining in economic importance.

By 1880 just over 100,000 native Maritimers resided in the United States, chiefly in New England, and only 30,000 in the remainder of the Dominion. Boston was the chief American city that drew them.

The West   While the great increase in population west of Ontario would begin after 1885, substantial settlement began in the years after 1870. Between the 1871 and 1881 censuses, the number of people in Manitoba more than doubled from 25,228 (of whom over half were natives) to 62,620, and the population of British Columbia increased substantially as well. In both provinces native peoples rapidly ceased to be numerically dominant. In Manitoba, the bulk of the new settlers were Canadians, chiefly from Ontario and the Maritimes. In British Columbia, the post-1865 period saw the beginning of settlement in the interior of the mainland, with the Nicola and Okanagan Valleys experiencing the arrival of pioneers mainly from Britain. One young Irish immigrant wrote from Nicola Lake in 1868 that 'a young Englishman and I were the two first white men who came to this district,' adding, 'When we came here our nearest neighbour was from 40 to 50 miles from us. Since then quite a number of settlers have located in the valley. . . .'[5]

Transiency

Population movement in the mid-nineteenth century was not only the result of the futureless younger generations' response to lack of agrarian opportunity. Another whole dimension was provided by a large group of constant transients, shifting from one frontier area to another, or from rural, to urban, back to rural. By and large, those who remained permanently fixed in one place prospered and were reasonably successful. Those who moved continually tended to be the failures, or at least people whose constant movement prevented them from becoming permanently established and hence successful. In Hamilton, Ontario—an emerging city that has been as thoroughly studied for the mid-nineteenth century as any in North America—a remarkable correlation prevailed between transiency and poverty. Similar findings over a similar period occur for Peel County, Ontario, northwest of Toronto. In both rural Peel County and its market-town, Brampton, persistence of residence was the most important factor in economic success measured by wealth. In Peel County, as in Hamilton at mid-century, residential persistence also meant that one was likely to have been involved with the community virtually since the beginning of its prosperity. Not all founders stayed, but those who did tended to prosper.

Even before the shift to industrialization got into high gear, Victorian society was composed of two socio-economic groupings that transcended specific economic relationships between people and their work: the more successful persisters and the less successful transients. Thus, while much movement of population can be understood in terms of particular population displacements caused by overpopulation and underemployment, another whole category of transiency was a fairly perpetual movement of the less successful. Whether such people failed because they were continually 'in motion', or constantly moved in search of better opportunities they almost never found, is debatable. So too is the question of whether or not their failure was structural; that is to say, so deep-rooted as to be transmittable to their children.

Historians of Canada have not, until recent years, paid much attention to those people who were constantly on the move. It is axiomatic that their very movement prevented them from making much of a mark on the records of any particular community, and their general economic insignificance equally militates against their study, except in quantitative terms. The careers of few such people grace the pages of Canadian encyclopedias, or the *Dictionary of Canadian Biography*. But the occasional individual transient does emerge.

Wilson Benson, whose biography was mentioned earlier, was one such figure. Beginning in Ireland at age fifteen, Benson changed his district of residence eleven times (six in Ireland and Scotland between 1836 and 1838 and five in Canada West between 1838 and 1851) before finally settling on a farm in Grey County in 1851 at age thirty. He had changed occupations twenty-nine times and apprenticed to at least six different trades in the 1830s and early 1840s, eventually moving back and forth between storekeeping and cooking seasonally on a lake vessel in the later 1840s.[6] In his later years, on his farm, he also kept a store in the community.

James Thomson, whom we have also met earlier in the British Columbia Gold Rush, had a similar experience. Like Benson in at least several of his occupational reincarnations, Thomson was a baker. He emigrated from Aberdeenshire to Montreal in 1841, and from there to Edwardsburgh, Canada West, as a baker. In 1849 he headed west to Chicago, clerking for a timber merchant, and a year later crossed the continent to California, where he tried gold mining and ended up baking. Thompson returned to Edwardsburgh in the early 1850s and at the age of thirty-one married, intending to settle down permanently as a farmer. But he was on the gold-dust trail again in 1862, working at a variety of occupations in the Cariboo until he returned virtually penniless in 1863. By 1865 Thomson had a job as assistant bookkeeper in the Edwardsburgh Starch Company. This time he stayed put, eventually serving on the town council and ultimately as reeve of Edwardsburgh.

A third transient was Félix Albert (1843-1924), born in the old seigneury of L'Île Verte on the St Lawrence, northeast of Rivière-du-Loup. Félix's parents owned an 84-*arpent* farm, of which less than 16 *arpents* were under cultivation. The land could not support a large family, much less provide for their futures. In 1857 Félix joined his father and one brother in colonizing land in St Éloi, a newly established parish to the east. Through hard work the family survived and even prospered. Félix married and came into sole possession of the family farm. But bad harvests, caused by drought and frost, demoralized him, and in 1880 he went off to Maine to work for the winter.

The following year he and his family abandoned their land and headed for Lowell, Massachusetts. There his children found employment in the textile factories, and Félix worked at odd jobs, mainly involving woodcutting. Then he began building tenements and achieved some reputation as a businessman, until financial reverses drove him back to the land outside Lowell. In 1909 an illiterate Félix Albert dictated, and hawked on the streets of Lowell, his own autobiography.[7]

For Thomson, Benson, and Albert, residential and occupational persist-ence eventually brought a modicum of success. But in the process of achiev-ing this modest result, they had been constantly on the move. All had moved in and out of urban areas, and each eventually ended up on a farm, supple-menting a meagre agrarian income with other work. Wilson Benson, James Thomson, and Félix Albert are all participants in a number of trends of mobility in this period. They immigrate; they move to cities. Thomson moves to the United States (and back again) and then heads off into the Canadian West; Albert moves to Massachusetts. But while they are statisti-cally countable in several respects, what they most typically represent is the extent of transiency in Canadian society.

A Stratifying Social Structure

By contributing to economic inequality in this period, transiency had some impact on social structure. But it was industrialization, and a new sophistica-tion of commercial and business practices, that created a working-class. For all of Canada in this period, the exodus from older settled rural districts, with traditional agrarian and resource-oriented economies, into towns and cities within and without the region demonstrated the extent to which the older mercantile economy was unable to support the rate of population growth that was achieved by the combination of immigration and high rates of natural increase. Rural overpopulation produced migrants that would settle and attempt to tame undeveloped regions, as well as those who would provide a labour force for industrialization and an internally oriented com-mercialization. While the farming pioneers remained small-scale commodity producers indeterminately related to the solidifying class structure, the urbanized workforce swiftly turned into a landless working class. Over the middle decades of the nineteenth century the older social structure of élites and non-élites was swept away, to be replaced by one that was far more clearly stratified.

The Rise of the Rich Businessmen

As had always been the case, the potential for great gains and great losses was considerable among businessmen throughout the middle of the nineteenth century. Nevertheless, successful businessmen—including the ubiquitous bankers—were highly esteemed in this age of economic transformation,

achieving high status partly by self-ascription and partly by their acknowledged economic and political power. That power was evident in all political
arenas, but was uppermost at the municipal level, where businessmen formed
a mutually supportive élite that took the lead in all aspects of the life of the
city, including its development and its land market. In this period, most
business leaders were self-made men—not in the sense that they had risen
from rags to riches, but in the sense that they had achieved their position in
the community by their own efforts and without benefit of direct inheritance—though some merchant princes like Sir Hugh Allan of Montreal and
George Gooderham of Toronto represented a second generation. Scots were
over-represented in business ranks and Protestantism predominated.

While before the 1830s the wealthiest members of the élites tended to be
found within the ranks of the office-holders, after 1840 merchant princes
began to appear who were able to engage in considerable conspicuous
consumption, particularly in the larger cities of British North America/Can-
ada. In Montreal's 'Little Mountain' district (later known as 'Westmount'),
where the wealthier members of society had been building large houses since
the eighteenth century, by 1850 the older military/officeholding class had
begun being supplanted by merchants. One Regency brick house, built
around 1836 for a garrison officer, by 1852 was owned by T.C. Panton,

'Ravenscrag', *c.*1902, the conspicuous mansion of Sir Hugh Allan on Pine Avenue, overlooking
Montreal. From the tower Allan could view the ships of his own Allan Line. Notman Photographic
Archives, McCord Museum, 143/395/II.

grocer and wine merchant, who named it 'Braemar'. Other choice villas included 649 Côte St Antoine (built in 1869 for Richard Warminton, who sold plumbing equipment), and 'Riverview' (built in 1876 for William Simpson of the Bank of Commerce). Both these houses mixed classical and Gothic styles with unexpected embellishments in the Victorian fashion.[8] Two mansions on Dorchester Street were the Donald Smith house, built in the late-Victorian baronial style around 1880, and the house of Harrison Stephen, who made a fortune as an importer and retired at the age of forty-five; it was designed in the Florentine palazzo style and built around 1860. No house in Montreal, however, was more impressive than Hugh Allan's 'Ravenscrag', built in 1860-1 on the site of the old Simon McTavish house on the slope of the mountain, where it dominated the city. This mansion of over seventy rooms was designed in the 'Tuscan Villa' style; its separate classically designed coach house could stand beside other mansions of the time.[9]

Although not begun until 1889, the Romanesque Revival mansion of George Gooderham (1820-1905), at St George and Bloor Streets, was one of Toronto's comparable monuments to conspicuous wealth.* Gooderham succeeded his father as president of Gooderham and Worts distillery, and was also active in commercial and financial enterprises, including the Bank of Toronto, of which he became president in 1882. He was able to travel abroad for the winter—to Egypt, the Riviera, the United States—and was renowned as a yachtsman, owning at one time the champion sailboat *Canada*. Though possessing fortunes that were millions of dollars less than those of their richest American contemporaries, Toronto moguls like George Gooderham, Hart Massey, and Timothy Eaton—and Montreal's Sir Hugh Allan and Sir William Van Horne, who became president of the Canadian Pacific Railway and was knighted in 1894—adopted extravagant lifestyles that were in many respects comparable to those of their American counterparts.

The New Proletariat

As Canadian cities began the shift from commercial entrepôts to industrial centres, they already contained significant inequalities, particularly in terms of wealth and income. In Hamilton, for example, the most affluent ten per cent of the city held eighty-eight per cent of the propertied wealth, drew nearly half its income, and controlled about sixty per cent of the wealth within the city. On the other hand, the poorest forty per cent earned only one per cent of the city's total income and controlled about six per cent of its total wealth. Most of the poor in Hamilton were Irish and Catholic, doubtless recent arrivals to the province. Over half the adult males of

---

*All these houses have been demolished except Ravenscrag, which is now the Allan Memorial Institute of the Royal Victoria Hospital, and the Gooderham house in Toronto, which is now the York Club.

Hamilton did not own enough property to meet the property qualification for voting, and few of the poor ever enjoyed any political office. At the same time, rich and poor in Hamilton in the 1850s still lived in close proximity to one another; the flight of the wealthy from the urban core had not yet begun.

In any Canadian city, before industrialization, considerable social and economic diversity could exist within a relatively small circumference. In Toronto, just one block away from a street sporting 3 gentlemen, 3 merchants, a professor, a broker, a registrar, a civil engineer, an auctioneer, and a widow, was another street where there resided six labourers, 2 widows, a tailor, a shoemaker, a cooper, a moulder, an innkeeper, a clerk, and a carver.[10] Only as the cities developed an expanding middle class that could afford to move out of the urban centre, and a working class sufficiently propertyless to cram into the buildings evacuated by the middle class, would the industrialized city emerge—with its clear sectional divisions between rich and poor, and between one economic function and another. During industrialization, not only did residential housing begin to be differentiated on the basis of wealth, but economic functions began to separate as well, with commerce remaining 'downtown' in the older urban core, and industry moving to the outskirts of the city as it then existed, where land costs were lower.

In the pre-industrial city the role of women and children within the labour force was fairly limited. In Hamilton in 1851, 72 per cent of employed women were domestic servants, and another fourteen per cent were seamstresses and dressmakers. Hamilton had no particular economic use for young children, but its employment of youths reflected the fact that, outside the ranks of the very wealthy, there was no adolescence. Children matured into adulthood at the age of fourteen or fifteen, and at that age entered into the bottom ranks of menial employment. Industrialization—with its rational division of labour into a series of simple, repetitive tasks that supplemented the machines—could and did employ both women and children. In typecasting, for example, a machine produced the type at the rate of 200 characters per minute, but with small imperfections that human labour could eliminate. Young boys could remove the small 'jet' left on each type as its umbilical cord to the machine was severed, and young girls could rub the type on stone to smooth the surface. In Montreal, one-quarter of boys between 11 and 15, and ten per cent of girls, were part of the labour force in 1871. The use of children, from a factory-owner's perspective, was a way of getting work done for extremely low wages. From the perspective of the child's family, such work supplemented the family income and perhaps permitted the family unit to retain echoes of its pre-industrial togetherness. Many rural families, migrating to an industrial situation, insisted that employers take on the entire family, particularly in the textile trade. As one employer explained:

...a man will be working at the mill, and his daughter working there also, and he may have a small child, whom he desires to have there, for instance, in the spooling room. Often you don't want to take the child, but if you do not, he and his daughter will go out, and they will go to some mill where the whole three will be employed.[11]

While such family employment served some social functions, its main importance was to supplement incomes: '...many are necessitated to do so,' argued one charity worker, 'from the fact that their parents probably earn very little, not sufficient to keep a large family unless the little fellows are sent to work at tender years.'[12]

In the end, the major characteristic of families on the unskilled side of industrialization was their vulnerability to poverty. Employers paid low wages, and felt little compunction about laying off workers—particularly in Montreal, with the winter closure of the port to commerce. Work by the entire family was often required to make ends meet, and to some extent the rural French-Canadian family was the ideal instrument for the industrial economy. Not only was it accustomed to having all family members working, but it was also used to sharing housing with kinfolk. As one Montreal observer put it, '...under the present state of things, overcrowding is inevitable, and only the cheapest and most inferior class of rookeries can be paid for out of the current rate of wages.'[13] Montreal had an especially high percentage of families who shared dwelling space with others; but such crowding was typical of the tenements of the labouring poor, with 'two to three families, or sometimes two families using one stove between them, and if there are several families, each family will have one room for a sleeping room, and use the kitchen for a dining room—the kitchen and stove in common with others.'[14] The family economy of rural Canada, especially rural French Canada, was thus carried over into the industrializing city. Within such families, of course, formal education was extremely limited; learning on the job was all that most children could expect. Opportunities for mobility out of industrial poverty were also fairly limited, being achieved less because of education than of occupational serendipity.

Not all the working-class poor were employed in industry, of course. Opportunities for women especially were strong at the lower end of the labour force in 'domestic service', as well as in business and clerical occupations. The Victorian age saw remarkable economic changes, and not merely in the rise of industrialism. Commerce, particularly at the retail end, altered dramatically in this period, and the structure of business operations began to change as well. The reshaping was most observable in shopkeeping, particularly in the expanding cities. In 1840 retail establishments were relatively small, concentrating for the most part on supplying goods within a specialized range—such as dry goods, groceries, and drugs. Beginning around 1870, however, general merchandising spawned the department store, which offered a multitude of goods, segregated into appropriate departments, under one roof. The T. Eaton Company was founded in Toronto in 1869, and was soon joined by Simpsons, Ltd., founded in 1872. In the West, the Hudson's Bay Company moved into general retail merchandising in the early 1880s.

The department store was characterized not only by its expansion of categories of goods carried, but by two other features. One was the mail-order catalogue, which was first issued by Eaton's in a 32-page format in 1884 and was designed to send its supply of goods into rural communities; it depended on cheap and efficient delivery of mail by the Canadian Post Office, and was the first large-scale merchandising catalogue in North America.[15] The other feature of the department store was its increasing employment of women as shop clerks, at relatively low wages. As in most other areas where women found employment, the substantial wage differentiation between males and females encouraged the hiring of the latter. In a department store a large number of relatively inexperienced and poorly paid women could by supervised by a few men. Women could also handle the filling of mail orders.

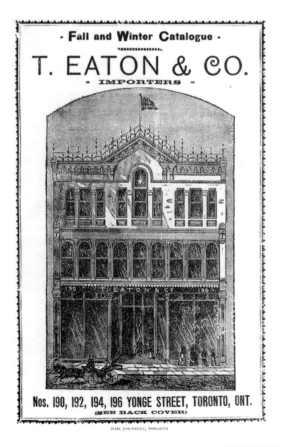

The front cover of the first Eaton catalogue, 1884 — published, the prefatory note says, 'owing to the immense increase in our Mail Order Department'. Its page size was small, 5 3/4″ x 8 1/2″, and it had no illustrations. Metropolitan Toronto Reference Library.

Similarly, new occupations for women, at the lower end of the clerical scale, were made possible by the expansion of the administration of business that accompanied sheer growth, aided by the application of new technologies. Gradually, as the structure of business became sophisticated, male clerks of the Bob Cratchit variety were replaced by women in the lower clerical ranks who were often typists. New technologies—like the typewriter, which was developed in the 1870s—would create occupational avenues for women in increasing numbers after 1885, although for most of the nineteenth century clerical jobs remained largely a male domain. What remained was the inequitable wage: women were paid between fifty and sixty per cent less than men for the rest of the century. The question of equal pay for equal work had not yet emerged, for the work was not equal. A number of factors contributed to inequality. One was the tendency of women to accept piece-work to be done in the home; or to prefer to work only until marriage, a factor that combined with the new compartmentalization of labour in interesting ways. Women could be kept at the bottom of any structure in the belief that they were not making a career, and hence did not require the same sort of training as male workers might demand. Obversely, the absence of training kept women at the bottom, and underpaid, not only for the work they did but because they were unable to advance.

The Middle Classes and the Rise of Professionalization

In between rich and poor, the middle class came to be increasingly composed of members of the educated professional occupations, although it also included urban property owners such as artisans and small merchants, substantial small-town merchants and small industrialists, and in the rural areas owners of larger farms and boats. The relative dependability of income for professionals tended to set them apart from other members of the middle class. Professionalization was the chief development within the middle classes in the Victorian era.

As elsewhere in the educated occupations, the trend was both to increase the number of qualified practitioners through formal education, and then to limit them to those with acceptable formal education who had met stringent licensing requirements, often set by the occupation itself. Nowhere was this process more advanced in this period than in the medical profession. Until the beginning of the nineteenth century, medicine was practised by men with suitable medical credentials and by a host of others, some of whom simply declared themselves doctors, and still others—such as midwives who handled most medical ministrations at childbirth—who simply functioned in a minor medical capacity. Canada had experienced a good deal of conflict over attempts at licensing doctors, partly because of differing educational systems in Canada East and Canada West, partly because of disagreements between doctors educated in Canada and those trained abroad.

An attempt in 1839 to create by legislative enactment a College of Physicians and Surgeons of Upper Canada was disallowed in 1840, although another attempt in 1847 to produce a similar institution in Canada East to examine and certify potential practitioners succeeded. Perhaps significantly, doctors were one of the first groups to organize nationally: the Canadian Medical Association was formed in the very year of Confederation. Ontario succeeded in establishing a certifying College in 1869, and was followed by other provinces in fairly short order. By 1885 only Prince Edward Island lacked such an institution. Most of the legislative licensing acts in the provinces automatically accepted as doctors those who were already practising, but imposed stringent requirements on new applicants. Lawyers engaged in a similar policy, and although the Law Society of Upper Canada (which came to regulate admission to the practice) was formed in 1797, most such provincial societies were created between 1846 and 1877. There were few formal law schools before the 1880s, and most lawyers were trained by a form of apprenticeship (articling) to practising lawyers and examined by the law societies under provincial statutes.

The rise of professionalism produced higher standards of practice—or at least guaranteed that practitioners had some appropriate training—but it also enabled the professions to control their numbers to some extent, and to create a public sense of professional status that justified incomes and raised esteem. By the 1880s doctors, lawyers, and educators had joined clergymen (who usually had lesser incomes) as the backbone of the Canadian middle class.

While Canadians often assume that most of their ancestors had live-in servants, only the rich or more affluent members of the professional middle class could afford to hire the labour of others and house them. In the 1871 census, only between ten and fifteen per cent of urban households contained live-in servants, and two out of three of these homes had only one servant. A very small percentage of households (less than five per cent) had four or more servants, even in large cities like Quebec or Halifax.

The Marginalized Invisibles

While the Canadian class structure was taking shape in the middle years of the nineteenth century, the era's treatment of women suggests the difficulty of adopting a simple class model for any complete analysis of Canadian society. Gender discrimination—which would today be labelled 'sexism'—was extremely powerful in Canadian society, and provided an additional variable that set women apart as a separate caste from the society as a whole. Racial discrimination—which today would be called 'racism'—also set certain elements of the population aside. In this period there were three such groups excluded from a full life in Canada: native peoples (both Indians and Métis); Chinese; and blacks (or Negroes, as they were then called).

Women

Women were regarded in Victorian Canada as equal to, but distinct from, men. They were not only the bearers but the nurturers of children, and their proper place was considered to be in the home as wife, helpmeet, and mother. 'Women's first and only place is in her home,' argued one magazine writer in 1874. 'She is destined by Providence to make her home. . .a cloister wherein one may seek calm and joyful repose from the busy heartless world. . . .The land she governs is a bright oasis in the desert of the world's selfishness.'[16] So far so good. But while it was true that most women sought marriage and children, not all of them were prepared to be content in the role of Victorian housewife, separated from the real world of 'manly' activity. Escaping, however, was not easy.

Woman's liberation from menial occupations came most readily in 'nurturing' or 'service' work that accorded with the overall perception of the 'woman's sphere'. And women had few rights in law. A wife could not expect automatically to inherit a deceased husband's property, even if that property were a farm into which she had put considerable labour over the years. In most provinces a husband could sue a wife for divorce on grounds of adultery, but a wife could sue a husband only if he were adulterous *and* had committed some other heinous offence. Wives were expected by courts to reform violent husbands rather than prosecute them, and could not expect single rights of guardianship over children unless they were unwed mothers. Nevertheless many women managed to take some action to escape the confinement of the domestic pedestal. As we shall see, many found an outlet through religion and the churches. Others acquired education—in many school systems more females stayed longer than males—and some enrolled in the growing number of woman's academies or in Normal Schools.

The most invisible women within the labour force were those working in domestic service, who were virtually ignored in records kept by most of their employers. On call fifteen to sixteen hours per day, most servants by the 1870s (over ninety per cent were women) worked in the kitchen. The typical domestic servant in the census of 1871 was female, lived in the house, was young (in her 20s), and single—and could both read and write. Wages were competitive with those of industry, given the fact that these women received room and board as well as five to six dollars a month in cash. But they had little time off and often felt isolated from their peers.[17]

The way in which women could take over an occupation—and the limitation that ensued—is perhaps best illustrated in the teaching profession between 1845 and 1875. The increased demand for teachers, brought about by the expansion of the common-school system towards universality in the middle years of the nineteenth century, was followed by the sophistication and streaming of the educational system, accomplished by dividing schools into grades. This practice permitted the first grades to be taught by less-experienced teachers whose need to establish discipline through technique and even physical presence was less than in ungraded schools. Once the schools were graded, the thrust of any educational authority for lower costs made the hiring of women at the elementary level a very attractive notion. Women worked for less, and the money saved could be employed to raise the salaries of male supervisors and upper-level teachers. Their employment at the lower grades could be viewed as part of the 'nurturing' process in which women excelled. This 'feminization' of teaching began in the urban schools, and only gradually worked its way out into the rural districts. Not until the 1870s did rural 'schoolmarms' assume the predominance we associate with the one-room school. But while women were actively recruited into the teaching ranks, it was clearly intended that they remain at the lower end in terms of both salary and responsibility.

A few women made their way to universities, often fighting to obtain a degree or professional training. In 1875 Grace Annie Lockhart (1855-1916) received the first bachelor's degree anywhere in the British Empire (from Mount Allison College); and as we have seen, Elizabeth Smith entered medical school at Queen's University a few years later. Smith was not the first woman doctor in Canada. That honour goes to Emily Howard Stowe (1831-1903), who, when she was refused admittance to Canadian medical schools, went off to the New York Medical College for Women and obtained a degree there in 1867. She set up practice in Toronto, but was initially refused certification by the College of Physicians and Surgeons of Ontario on the grounds that she had not attended classes at a provincial medical school, none of which would admit her. She was not properly accredited until 1880, and her refusal to take provincial examinations allowed another women, Jennie Trout, to become licensed before her. Her experiences led Stowe to organize Canada's earliest formal suffragist organization, the Toronto Women's Literary Club in 1876, and the Woman's Medical College in Toronto in 1883.

Blacks

The first major influx of black people, both slaves and freemen, came to Canada as part of the Loyalist migration to Nova Scotia. In the provinces of British North America slavery was gradually abolished by judicial decision, but the Nova Scotia black community, which experienced much economic and other discrimination during the post-Loyalist years, continued under many disadvantages throughout the nineteenth century, particularly when it was augmented by Jamaican Maroons (ex-slave rebels against white rule in that island) in 1796 and by 2,000 ex-American slaves after the War of 1812. Although legally equal, Nova Scotia blacks were taught in segregated schools and generally kept in a subordinate position. Another movement of blacks entered Upper Canada between 1812 and 1860 via the famous 'Underground Railway', which smuggled escaped slaves from the American South out of the reach of American courts. In these years perhaps as many as 30,000 ex-slaves made their way to Canada—facing, as in Nova Scotia, little legal but much actual discrimination. Many of these immigrants returned to the United States after the Emancipation Proclamation of 1863, but those who remained in southwestern Ontario were effectively segregated from the remainder of that province's society. A few fugitive slaves made their way to British Columbia in the 1850s, some settling on remote islands off the coast of Vancouver Island, such as Saltspring Island, and becoming assimilated.

The Chinese

The Chinese began arriving in British Columbia from California in the late 1850s as part of the colony's gold rush. China was opened to Europeans in the first half of the nineteenth century, and its enormous over-population encouraged the recruitment of contract labourers by visiting merchantmen, many of whom were Yankee. Some Chinese came voluntarily to British Columbia, while others were brought in to work in the mines and at other menial occupations. As early as 1860 the colonies of Vancouver Island and British Columbia contained as many as 7,000 Chinese, and that number was greatly augmented over the ensuing years, particularly between 1880 and 1884 when over 15,000 Chinese entered the province of British Columbia,

Chinese construction workers on the CPR in their camp at Kamloops, BC. National Archives of Canada, C-2880C.

almost half of them to work on the CPR. Overwhelming male, most came from rural districts of South China, were largely unskilled, and spoke little English. They were regarded as unassimilable, the importers of every social vice imaginable, and unfair competitors for employment.

While many of these Chinese immigrants were merely 'sojourners' who hoped to earn enough money to return home, the growing feeling against them produced legal discrimination that made it very difficult for those who wished to do so to assimilate into local society. The British Columbia legislature disenfranchised the Chinese in 1875 and in 1884 denied them the right to acquire Crown land. A Royal Commission in 1885 gave evidence of much hostility to the Chinese in British Columbia, with even those defending their presence doing so in uncomplimentary fashion. Sir Matthew Begbie (1819-94), British Columbia's chief justice, testified: 'I do not see how people would get on here at all without Chinamen. They do, and do well, what white women cannot do, and do what white men will not do.'[18] Huang Tsun Hsien, an acculturated Chinese who testified before the Royal Commission in 1885, made little impression when he argued:

> You must recollect that the Chinese immigrants coming to this country are denied all the rights and privileges extended to others in the way of citizenship; the laws compel them to remain aliens. I know a great many Chinese will be glad to remain here permanently with their families, if they are allowed to be naturalized and can enjoy privileges and rights.[19]

Although in the 1870s and 1880s the federal government disallowed several pieces of British Columbia legislation that further discriminated against the Chinese, it responded to obvious provincial pressure in 1885 by imposing a head-tax of $50 on nearly every Chinese person entering the country. The same law added a clause allowing only one immigrant from China for every fifty tons of vessel capacity and requiring a certificate of entry for each new arrival. The year 1885 marked a sad watershed for the Chinese in Canada, for at this time the federal government joined British Columbia in setting them apart as a separate caste.

Native Peoples

New policies for dealing with native peoples were adopted by the Colonial Office and the various provinces after the early 1840s. Sir Francis Bond Head tried ruthlessly to remove natives to reserves, but met with considerable opposition from religious organizations in both Britain and British North America, and Sir Charles Bagot was instructed to examine policy in 1842. The result was a reaffirmation of Crown responsibility for natives in Canada and a recognition of their 'rights of occupancy', combined with an effort to persuade them to become freehold farmers. Because of the difficulty of educating natives, most schools by the 1840s had become residential ones. The native educational system of Canada was given its elaboration and justification in 1847 by Egerton Ryerson, who emphasized the need for a 'plain English education adapted to the working farmer and mechanic'.

Although the Province of Canada recognized native rights, that fact did not necessarily lead to much protection. As mineral exploitation around Lake Superior increased in the 1840s, for example, natives complained about

The Manitoba Indian Treaty — Conference with the Chiefs. The cover illustration for the *Canadian Illustrated News* of 9 September 1871, marking the speeches that were delivered and the ceremony that took place before a large audience at Lower Fort Garry from 25 July to 3 August. The article inside, which had a very racist tone, stated that the Indians were satisfied with the Commissioner's offer, made on behalf of the Canadian government: 'Three dollars a year per head in perpetuity to every Indian, man, woman and child; a hundred and sixty acres of land to every family; and to every one of the reserves set apart for each tribe some ploughs and harrows, and a pair of oxen to enable the Indians to cultivate the soil.' National Archives of Canada, C-56472.

trespasses on their property, leading Lord Elgin to comment that all Indian claims should have been extinguished before mineral concessions were granted. As a result, in 1850 the government negotiated new treaties with natives in northern Ontario that extinguished claims over vast territories, well in advance of settlement, in return for substantial reserves. In 1850 also the Canadian parliament passed legislation that operationally defined who was and who was not an 'Indian' within the meaning of the acts involved. The process of legislating *for* natives rapidly escalated after 1850. In 1857 the legislature of Canada passed the 'Act for the Gradual Civilization of the Indian Tribes in the Canadas', which contained many provisions that ran against the wishes of the natives. Canadian policy not only became devoted to removing natives from the paths of settlement, but did so by coercion and compulsion if necessary.[20] Most of these policies—which defined Indians, made them citizens when properly educated, and provided for land grants— were inherited by the Dominion of Canada from the Province of Canada after 1867.

The announced basis of Dominion policy towards the natives was 'to lead the Indian people by degrees to mingle with the white race in the ordinary avocations of life.'[21] At the same time, the transfer of Rupert's Land to Canada and earlier experiences led the government of Canada to set up a massive round of new treaty negotiations with western natives. These treaties were partly intended to sort out the native problem in advance of settlement, but were also a response to demands from natives for some protection, both from encroaching farmers and from the demise of the vast buffalo herds that had once roamed the plains. The government of Alexander Mackenzie boasted in 1877 that the treaty arrangements had guaranteed that—in contrast to the experience in the United States—'no difficulty has arisen with the Canadian tribes living in the immediate vicinity of the scene of hostilities'* against settlers and the American army along the border.[22] The government agreed to make annual payments to the natives, thus assuming responsibility for their well-being, in return for extensive reserves out of the way of settlement. Often the natives were told that the lands they had bargained away would not be immediately needed. Neither side could envision the speed with which the West would be settled.

Some West Coast natives had hoped that union with Canada would bring a more enlightened policy to British Columbia, but they were doomed to disappointment. The very words of the clause (number 13) of the Terms of Union dealing with such matters spoke of the assumption by the Dominion of 'a policy as liberal as that hitherto pursued by the British Columbia Government.' At best the status quo was preserved. Natives were specifically excluded from voting by provincial legislation in 1872 and 1875, and the

---

*The year before, in June 1876, General Custer and a detachment of over 200 men were killed in a campagin against the Sioux on the Little Bighorn River in Montana.

province systematically opposed every federal effort to introduce more equitable administration, which could only reflect the limited advantages of central-Canadian thinking on the subject of natives. In 1874, 110 native leaders of the Lower Fraser Valley protested the arbitrary behaviour of the British Columbia government, but received no satisfaction. The provincial government in 1875 attempted to suppress the documentary record of its behaviour over the previous twenty-five years, and finally agreed in 1876 to come to terms with Ottawa. The result was an Indian policy that was still settler-dominated. The absolute numbers of natives in British Columbia—as well as their proportion within the total population—began declining in the 1880s, and sometime in that decade British Columbia became much like provinces further east in that settlers no longer were sufficiently concerned about natives to pay any attention to their complaints.[23]

After 1885 the First Nations had been effectively pushed out of the sight of settlement and 'pacified', from the Atlantic to the Pacific. For nearly a century few Canadians would take seriously the complaints and protests of this invisible component of their nation.

The Need to Belong

The Victorian age in Canada was characterized by an enormous expansion in the number of private associations devoted to non-occupational goals. The state did not weigh heavily on the lives of most Canadians by the end of this period, and political allegiances were not as important to the average person as family, religion, and fraternal organizations. Churches continued to be most important. In Canada East/Quebec, the Catholic Church was overwhelmingly dominant. In the Atlantic region, Protestants and Catholics were more equally divided. Only in Canada West/Ontario were Protestants in such a clear numerical ascendency and position of power that the regional culture assumed obvious Protestant dimensions, although Ontario culture— particularly as it expanded westward onto the Prairies—began in some circles to be confused with Canadian Culture. But by the 1880s few Canadians—whether urban or rural—failed to belong to a good number of societies beyond their church membership, and most could count their other memberships, if not their actual participation, in the dozens. In an earlier period—before the 1830s—private fraternal societies, usually at the élite level, were organized to supplement or provide municipal services such as water, light, fire, and library companies. But by the 1880s some organizations had relinquished charitable and service goals to provide entertainment and companionship for their members.

The Church

Catholicism   The mid-Victorian era was an absolutely crucial era for Roman Catholicism in Canada. Within French Canada the period witnessed the emergence of the Church as the leading voice of French Canada's nationalistic aspirations and the assumption of local leadership by the curé. It also saw the Church take on the ultramontane character that would remain with it for much of the ensuing century. English-speaking Catholics pretty well succeeded in separating themselves from their francophone compatriots within the administrative hierarchy. By 1840 the hierarchy had succeeded in firmly establishing its control over the laity, which had assumed considerable autonomy in the absence of local bishops and clergy. Nevertheless, anglophone bishops from the Maritime Provinces were among those who tried to prevent the issue of papal infallibility from being decided at the Vatican Council of 1869/70. Despite the relatively accommodating attitude of the anglophone members of the Church hierarchy, hostility between Catholics and Protestants existed just beneath the surface in most provinces, and could emerge at almost any point, as it did in the PEI Bible Question in the 1850s or in the New Brunswick School Act of 1871, which terminated public support for denominational (i.e., Catholic) schools in the province. Nevertheless, outside Quebec—and perhaps Newfoundland—the Church generally kept a low profile and tried to get along with other denominations.

In Quebec, one man symbolized the ultramontane Church in the mid-Victorian period. Bishop Ignace Bourget (1799-1885) was consecrated coadjutor to the bishop of Montreal in early 1837, on the very eve of the Rebellion, and succeeded to the see in 1840. He died in June 1885, on the eve of the second Riel uprising, although he had retired a few years earlier. Bourget was always an active defender of both the papacy and the position of the Church in Canada. He introduced the Roman liturgy and fervently opposed the principles of the European revolutions of 1848. Gradually he became the leading opponent of liberal thinking in the province, particularly as it was represented by the Institut Canadien, the Montreal centre for intellectual criticism of the Church. Bourget carried on a lengthy battle against the Institut and especially its library, which contained many prohibited books. Equally important was his expansion of the ecclesiastical administration of his diocese, so that nearly every parish had a priest and nearly half the priests an assistant. The clergy were now able to mobilize public opinion, as they did in 1868 when they helped raise 507 Zouaves in Quebec (and over $100,000 to support them) to serve in the papal army. Quebec bishops also strongly supported the doctrine of papal infallibility at the Vatican Council.

The Guibord Affair of 1869-74 was the culmination of Bourget's struggle with the Institut. Joseph Guibord (1809-1869) was a typographer and a member of the Institut. On his death-bed he refused to resign his membership in the Institut after receiving absolution and was denied burial in consecrated ground; he was buried in a Protestant cemetery. His widow took the Church to court, and he was ordered buried in the cemetary of Côte-des-Neiges by the Privy Council in 1874. The first attempt at interment failed in September 1875; the second successful attempt took place with an armed military escort. But Bourget declared the place of burial 'under an interdict and separate from the rest of the cemetary.'[24] Although not all of Bourget's fellow bishops were as willing as he to equate political liberalism with anti-clericalism, Archibishop Elzéar Taschereau (1820-99) was forced in 1875 to issue a pastoral letter denying that anyone in 'good conscience' could be 'permitted to remain a Catholic liberal'. The battle between ultramontanism and liberalism would continue in Quebec for another twenty years.

Protestantism   By 1840 Protestantism everywhere in British North America had largely cut itself free from its foreign origins, in either Great Britain or the United States. The major development of the mid-Victorian period, particularly in Ontario—where Protestantism emerged as a distinctive and all-embracing culture—was the construction of a broad alliance among the major denominations: Anglicans, Presbyterians, and Methodists. This alliance was made possible by the gradual elimination of the major points of public friction between the established churches and the dissenters, as the establishment ceased attempting to insist on exclusive state support and connection: once such matters as the clergy reserves and higher education were secularized, old hostilities melted away. Moreover, the Methodists became far more respectable and far less evangelical in their attitudes as the wilderness settled. Camp meetings and itinerancy were replaced by church buildings and settled ministers among the Methodists, and the denominations of main-line Protestantism found how much they shared.

The result was a Victorian Protestant value system that could be found everywhere in British North America/Canada, but was most pervasive in Canada West/Ontario. It emphasized the relationship between social stability and Protestant morality, which in turn was based on a firm belief in God and His millenium. It saw gradual social change as progressive, offering a way of understanding the events and changes that swirled around the individual in the Victorian era. It recognized the need for a moral code, but one that was chiefly voluntary and individualistic. Protestant morality began with the individual Christian.[25]

Clubs, Societies, and Charities

The Protestant churches were one of the keys to the growth of a vast pattern and network of clubs, societies, and charities. By the mid-nineteenth century male governance in the churches was being implicitly challenged by the increasing proportion of women members. Evangelically oriented churches frequently employed their ladies' aid or women's auxiliary groups to sponsor missionary activity. By 1885 there were over 120 Baptist Women's Missionary Aid Societies scattered across the Maritimes. Women usually supported their own religious organizations with their own money, kept separate from the larger funds of the church, and these missionary-aid societies offered many women their first opportunity at independent administration.

Technically independent of the churches, but closely connected in overlapping membership and social goals, were reform organizations like the Woman's Christian Temperance Union. The first Canadian local of the WCTU was founded in Picton, Ontario, in 1874 by Letitia Youmans (1827-96), a public-school teacher and Sunday School teacher in the Methodist Church. The WCTU spread rapidly across Canada in the 1880s, preaching that alcohol abuse was responsible for many of the social problems of contemporary Canada and campaigning for public prohibition of the sale of alcoholic beverages. Most of its members came from the middle class, and much of its literature was directed at demonstrating that poverty and family problems among the lower orders could be reduced, if not eliminated, by cutting off the availability of alcohol to the male breadwinner. In 1897 the Nova Scotia WCTU had become concerned about temperance for seamen:

> In view of the fact that sailors and fishermen, owing to long absences from land, are specially liable to be the victims of the saloon when on shore, and in view of the promised plebiscite in the near future, we suggest, that our provincial and local superintendents of this department pay marked attention to the distribution of suitable prohibition literature, as a means of improving the minds, and influencing the votes, of these classes.

Twelve reasons for temperance were cited, beginning with:

1. It is right;
2. It will reduce criminals;
3. It will exterminate pauperism;
4. It will cut down the cost of penitentiaries, jails, poor houses and asylums;[26]

The WCTU, despite its growing influence, measured its membership only in the thousands. That most characteristic Canadian society, the Orange Order, could count participation in the hundreds of thousands. It had been founded in Ulster in 1795 with the twin aims of defending Protestantism and maintaining loyalty to the British monarchy. Within a Protestant context its appeal was non-sectarian, but religion was important, and the final qualification for membership in the early Order called for 'the strictest attention to a religious observance of the Sabbath, and also of temperance sobriety.'[27] In Canada the Order added to its politico-religious aims a strong fraternal aspect, providing social activity and ritual for its local members. Although Orangism came to British North America with the Irish, and served to some extent as an instrument of Protestant Irish ethnicity, it became very popular with Scots in some provinces, and gradually took on an air of WASPishness rather than Irishness. At its height, the Orange Order probably never contained more than 50,000 actual members, scattered across the Dominion and across social classes, but that membership was highly volatile, and one estimate suggests that as many as one in three Protestant Canadians in the Victorian period had strong Orangist links. The Order had lodges every-where, but was most important and influential in Ontario.

Orangism has tended to be associated with public matters—organizing parades on July 12, opposing Roman Catholicism across a range of issues, responding to the 1870 execution of Thomas Scott*—and with the Irish. The Order's importance and influence, however, rested on the twin facts that its membership united British Protestants of all origins and that it served as a focal-point at the local level for social intercourse and conviviality. As a 'secret' society it had elaborate initiation rites and a ritual, most of it borrowed from the Freemasons, that appealed to men who spent most of their lives in mundane occupations. In the initiation ceremony for one of its graduated degrees:

> The door is then opened, and the Candidate (having the Bible in his hand) shall be introduced between his two Sponsors, each bearing an Orange Rod, decor-ated with Blue Ribbon, and one carrying, also, the Blue Book of the Lodge, with the Obligation thereon and open, and the other an Inkstand; he shall then be conducted to the side of the room, and then East, towards the Deputy-Master, before whom shall be burning one *bright* light; and before the Master there shall be placed eleven candles, in a semi-circle, and also one candle placed in the centre of the circle. The eleven candles are not to be lighted until the Candidate has reached the Deputy-Master; the one in the centre is not to be lighted.[28]

Lodges provided a variety of services for their members, including an elabo-rate funeral. But if local fraternity was the key to Orangism's success, its public influence was enormous, particularly in Ontario.

While the Orange Order was the most prominent of the fraternal organi-zations of the period, it was hardly the only one that grew and flourished in Canada. Because most of these organizations were semi-secret societies with rituals based on freemasonry, their appeal was for the most part to Protestants. The Masons expanded enormously during the mid-nineteenth century, and were joined by a number of other orders, such as the Independent Order of Odd-Fellows (founded in England in 1813 and brought to Canada by 1845), the Independent Order of Foresters (founded in the United States in 1874 and brought to Canada in 1881), and the Order of Knights of Pythias (founded in Washington, DC, in the early 1860s and brought to Canada in 1870). Fellowship and mutual support were the keys to the success of all these societies, most of which were deliberately non-denominational. Their suc-cess led to the formation in 1882 of the Knights of Columbus as a similar fraternal benefit society for Roman Catholic men, although the first chapters in Canada probably were not founded until the early 1890s. While few of

---

*This is discussed on pages 373-5.

these societies admitted women directly, most had adjunct or parallel organizations for women. By the 1880s many Canadians belonged to more than one of these organizations. The growth of fraternal benefit societies was a characteristic of this age of mobility. Membership provided a means of social introduction into a new community, offered status and entertainment to members, and increasingly provided assurance of assistance in time of economic or emotional need.

Family, religion, and fraternal organizations were so important in the later nineteenth century partly because most Canadians did not even consider that the state might ever come to their assistance in times of trouble. For some, politics and government were a source of employment or patronage. But for the average Canadian the government (whether local, provincial, or federal) existed mainly to act as an impartial and somewhat distant umpire, affecting mostly events outside their personal experience, rather than as a participant in, or influence on, their everyday life. In the autobiographies and correspondence of Wilson Benson, James Thomson, or Félix Albert, politics and political allegiances were simply not very important subjects.

Still, politics and government attracted a great many people (some with questionable motives, but many who were selfless and dedicated), who by 1885 had brought Canada to a point where not only its survival but its future growth could not be questioned. For better or worse, Canada was resolving many of the most pressing problems that Confederation had created. Its continued development as a nation '*a mari usque ad mare*' would increasingly involve the lives and affairs of its citizens.

chapter thirteen

The Completion of Confederation

In 1881 the chief clerk of the House of Commons, John Bourinot (1837-1902), published a book entitled *The Intellectual Development of the Canadian People: An Historical Review*, the first of his many books on history and Canadian government. Born in Sydney, Nova Scotia, he was educated at the University of Toronto and then founded the Halifax *Herald* in 1860, becoming chief reporter of the Nova Scotia Assembly in 1861. He had moved to Ottawa in 1868 to join the *Hansard* staff of the House of Commons, attracted—like many other intellectuals—by the economic opportunities and wider horizons that seemed to beckon there after Confederation. In his book Bourinot sought to correct the deprecation of the intellectual efforts of Canadians at home and abroad. Canada, he insisted, had moved 'beyond the state of mere colonial pupilage', and, he implied, the cultural products of the new nation were entitled to a better press to match its political achievements.

Bourinot argued chiefly from advances in education and literacy. He began by writing glowingly of the system of public education—free and accessible—available in most provinces, and of the country's twenty-one colleges and universities. He pointed out that $64,000,000 had been spent on public schools across the Dominion since 1867, adding that in 1839 about one in thirteen young British North Americans had been attending school, while in 1881 the proportion was one in four. Newspapers were another sign of intellectual development, increasing from 65 in all British North America in 1840 to 465—56 of them dailies—in 1880. Fond of arguing from sheer numbers, Bourinot wrote that in 1879, 4,085,454 pounds of newspapers at one cent per pound 'passed through the post offices of the Dominion', and over 30 million copies of newspapers were circulated annually in Canada through the mails.* He concluded with a chapter on literature, which catalogued a number of French-Canadian historians and poets—including Léon-Pamphile Lemay (1837-1918), Octave Crémazie (1827-79), Benjamin Sulte (1841-1923), and Louis Fréchette (1839-1908), whose elegy 'Les Morts' he compared favourably to Victor Hugo's work—and offered a handful of English-Canadian writers, chiefly from the Maritimes. The 'firm, broad basis of general education', Bourinot concluded, meant 'a future as full of promise for literature as for industry.'

Some of Bourinot's comments, especially about French Canada, sound extremely patronizing to the modern ear. He wrote of the 'greater impulsiveness and vivacity of the French Canadians', and was pleased to remind his readers that French Canadians were descendants of Normans and Bretons, 'whose people have much that is akin with the people of the British Islands.' Although such ideas were in common circulation in the Canada of his time, colouring many of the efforts to define the new Canadian identity after Confederation, Bourinot also insisted that in Quebec 'there exists a national French Canadian sentiment, which has produced no mean intellectual feats', and maintained that

> . . .in the essential elements of intellectual development, Canada is making not a rapid but certainly at least a steady and encouraging progress, which proves that her people have not lost, in consequence of the decided disadvantages of their colonial situation, any of the characteristics of the races to whom they owe their origin. [p. 3]

While the work was characterized by a strong underpinning of that great Victorian concept, progress, the very fact that someone in 1881 made an attempt to deal with such a subject as the intellectual development of the Canadian people indicates some of the changes that had been brought about in what the author himself saw as the movement from raw frontier colonies to civilized nation. That development, however, was hardly the simple progression that John Bourinot sought to document.

---

*The federal power that probably touched most Canadians immediately was control of the postal service. In 1867 the Dominion took over the running of 3,477 post offices, which became 13,811 by the Great War in 1914, and almost immediately lowered rates from 5.5 cents to 3 cents per half-ounce on letters; by 1899 the rate was 2 cents per ounce. Post-office patronage greased the wheels of party politics, and Canadians saved their money in the postal savings banks. Throughout the first fifty years of Confederation the Canadian post office made profits, while providing efficient public services that affected every inhabitant of the Dominion. The fact that the postal service was a major federal power in the nineteenth century suggests how much times could change by the twentieth.

❧ Completing the Union

Although 1 July 1867 was obviously a beginning in the development of a Canadian Confederation, in the larger sense it was only an interim point. The new union consisted of four provinces—Ontario, Quebec, Nova Scotia, and New Brunswick—carved from the three that had created it, and Macdonald's government was conscious that a lot of British territory on the continent had been excluded. The new government was also quite obviously the old Canadian coalition, with a few Maritime faces, organized into the old Canadian departments and using buildings erected in Ottawa for the old Union of the Canadas. If the new administration seemed familiar, so did its policies. The malcontents in Nova Scotia were bought off with 'better terms' that were entirely financial, and the Intercolonial Railway was set a-building along the eastern coast of New Brunswick. Much energy was devoted to rounding up the strays.

Manitoba

In 1868 a ministerial delegation was sent to London to arrange the transfer of the Northwest to Canada by the Hudson's Bay Company. While complex negotiations continued, the Canadian government began building a road from Fort Garry to Lake of the Woods—as part of the road and water system connecting Red River with Canada—and establishing informal connections with Dr John Christian Schultz (1840-96), a doctor, the owner of a general store, and the influential leader of the local faction in Red River that had for years been agitating for Canadian annexation. As had been the case with Lord Selkirk fifty years earlier, nobody paid any attention to the Métis, the mixed-bloods who constituted the bulk of the local population of Red River. The Canadian delegation in London finally worked out a deal for the transfer, with the British government receiving Rupert's Land from the Hudson's Bay Company (the Canadian government put up £300,000 and agreed to substantial land grants for the Company) and subsequently transferring it intact to Canada.

Since all of the arrangements for Rupert's Land were made without bothering to inform the Red River people of their import, it was hardly surprising that they were suspicious and easily roused to protest. The Métis were concerned on several counts. A Canadian roadbuilding party had been involved in a number of incidents that had racist overtones, and the transparent haste of the Canadian government to build a road and send in men to survey land suggested, quite reasonably, that Canadian settlement would inundate the colony with no regard for its Métis inhabitants. Furthermore, some of the road-builders were discovered buying land cheaply from the Indians—land the Métis thought was theirs. The Canadians were now seen as a threat not only to the land, but also to the language and religion of the Métis—perhaps to their very existence. The Canadian government was

warned in 1869 that trouble was brewing—by the Anglican archbishop of
Rupert's Land, Robert Machray (1831-1904); by the governor of the Hudson's Bay Company, William Mactavish (1815-70); and by Bishop Alexandre
Taché (1823-94), the Catholic Bishop of St Boniface—but it received all
reports with little or no interest.

At this point a leader of the Métis appeared in the person of Louis Riel
(1844-85), a member of a respected family in the community; his father, for
whom he was named, had successfully led a Métis protest in 1849 against the
Hudson's Bay Company over many grievances, including the right to trade
freely in furs. The young Riel spoke out publicly against the surveys. In
October 1869, while the surveyors were running their line south of Fort
Garry through the land of André Nault, his neighbours, led by Riel, rushed
to the farm. They stood on the surveyors' chain and told them to stop. This
act was Riel's first resistance to Canada's acquisition of the Northwest.

In the meantime William McDougall (1822-1905) was on his way from
Canada to assume office as lieutenant-governor of the Northwest. A newly
formed National Committee of the Métis resolved that McDougall should
not be allowed into the country. They drafted a message to McDougall, who
was approaching Pembina on the American border: 'The National Committee of the Métis orders William McDougall not to enter the Territory of the
North West without special permission of the above-mentioned committee.'

The town of Winnipeg as shown in the *Canadian Illustrated News*, 18 December 1869: 'To the right, and
the most prominent building in the picture, is the building occupied by Dr Schultz as a residence and
drug store. Adjoining that is the office of the *Nor'Wester* newspaper; while on the left is shown one of the
HB Company's stores.' Metropolitan Toronto Reference Library.

This warning was signed 'Louis Riel, Secretary'.[1] It was his second act of resistance to Canada.

The Council of Assiniboia—which had been appointed by the Hudson's Bay Company to govern the settlement—summoned Riel to explain his action. Riel made quite clear that the Métis were 'perfectly satisfied with the present Government and wanted no other'; that they 'objected to any Government coming from Canada without their being consulted in the matter'; that they 'would never admit any Governor no matter by whom he might be appointed, if not by the Hudson's Bay Company, unless Delegates were previously sent, with whom they might negotiate as to the terms and conditions under which they would acknowledge him'. Finally, Riel insisted that his compatriots were 'simply acting in defence of their own liberty' and 'did not anticipate any opposition from their English-speaking fellow countrymen, and only wished them to join and aid in securing their common rights.'[2]

In early November Riel and a large group of his men, accompanied by sympathizers, walked into Fort Garry, the Hudson's Bay Company fort, and took possession of it. On 7 December he and his men surrounded Dr Schultz's store, taking Schultz and forty-eight Canadians—including Thomas Scott (c.1841-70), one of the road-builders—to Fort Garry as prisoners. The next day Riel issued a 'Declaration of the People', announcing

Louis Riel and his councillors, 1869-70. National Archives of Canada, 12854.

a Provisional Government to replace the Council of Assiniboia. He, as President, offered to negotiate with Canada on the terms for Red River's entry into Confederation. Riel thus declared that what the Métis sought was to be allowed to become a part of the Confederation process. On 18 December McDougall left Pembina and returned to Canada.

On 27 December Donald A. Smith (1820-1914)—the head of the Hudson's Bay Company in Canada, who had been appointed by Sir John A. Macdonald to explain to the people of Red River how Canada intended to govern the country, and to report on the disturbances—arrived at the settlement and suggested a mass meeting.* Two were held, on 19 and 20 January 1870. Smith won the crowd's confidence, particularly among the anglophone mixed bloods, with his assurances that Canada would not interfere with the property, language or religion of the people of Red River. On the second day Riel proposed a convention of 40 representatives, equally divided between the two language groups, and at these meetings a 'List of Rights' was debated, Riel's Provisional Government was endorsed, the Canadian prisoners (many had already escaped) were released, and three delegates were appointed to go to Ottawa to negotiate provincial status within Confederation.

Meanwhile on 12 February 1870 a force of Canadian settlers, led by Major C.A. Boulton (1841-99), a surveyor—and including Charles Mair (1838-1927) and Thomas Scott, both of whom had escaped imprisonment in Fort Garry—left Portage la Prairie to join a party led by John Schultz (another escapee) at Kildonan, near Fort Garry. The plan was to overthrow the Provisional Government. But on 17 February a small force of Riel's men arrested and imprisoned most of these guerillas, except for Schultz, who managed to return to Ontario. Up to this point Riel's strategy and tactics were little short of brilliant. Although bordering on the illegal, the Provisional Government was arguably necessary to maintain order in the settlement, and despite some talk about negotiations with the Americans, Riel and the Métis clearly wanted Red River to be admitted to Confederation. But Riel permitted his men to vent their spleen on Thomas Scott, an Orangeman who hated 'halfbreeds' and was an unruly bully-boy. A Métis jury summarily sentenced Scott to death, and Riel accepted the sentence, commenting 'We must make Canada respect us.' On his way to his execution, just before noon on 4 March 1870, Scott said to the Methodist minister, Thomas Young, who accompanied him: 'This is horrible! This is cold-blooded murder! Be sure to make a true statement!'[3] Scott's eyes were bandaged and he was placed before a firing squad and shot; as his body moved, one man's revolver delivered the *coup de grâce*. Riel stood silently in the background throughout the execution,

---

*Smith later became the largest shareholder of the Company (he provided financial backing for the Canadian Pacific Railway) and in 1889 its chief executive officer. In 1897 he was elevated to the peerage as Lord Strathcona.

This illustration—which appeared in the *Canadian Illustrated News* on 23 April 1870 over the caption 'The Tragedy at Fort Garry'—suggests that Riel himself administered the *coup de grâce* to Thomas Scott, which was certainly not the case. Metropolitan Toronto Reference Library.

and apparently never thought much about it. But this treatment of Thomas Scott would have enormous repercussions in Orange Ontario, which was looking desperately for an excuse to condemn the Red River resistance.

Of the three-man delegation that went to Ottawa with the List of Rights, Abbé Ritchot (1825-1905) was the chief spokesman. A formidable negotiator, he gained concessions from the Canadian government that would guarantee some protection for the original inhabitants of Red River against the expected later influx of settlers and land speculators. At what the Canadian government of Macdonald always regarded as the point of a gun, the Métis extorted the Manitoba Act of 1870, which granted provincial status to Manitoba (a name favoured by Riel), a province of only 1,000 square miles, with 1,400,000 acres set aside for the Métis and bilingual services guaranteed.

In May 1870 the Canadian government sent a so-called peaceful military expedition to Red River, made up of imperial troops and militia units that included many Orangemen eager to kill Riel. A few hours before their arrival at Fort Garry, Riel and several of his associates fled across the American border—that favourite sanctuary for those who defied the Canadian government.

The Scott execution provided the Canadian government with the excuse to deny Riel and his lieutenants an official amnesty for all acts committed during the 'uprising', although those who negotiated with Canada always insisted that such an amnesty had been unofficially guaranteed. The result was that Louis Riel went into long-term exile instead of becoming premier of the province he had created.* Whether the government would keep better faith over its land guarantees to the Métis was another matter.

British Columbia

While the question of Rupert's Land dragged slowly to its conclusion, the Canadian government was presented with the unexpected (although not totally unsolicited) gift of a request from British Columbia—to which Vancouver Island had been annexed in 1866—for admission to the new union. The initiative from the Pacific colony had originated with the Nova Scotia-born journalist Amor De Cosmos (William Alexander Smith, 1825-97), who was a member of the colony's legislative council. In March 1867 he had introduced a motion that the British North America Act, then about to be passed by the British Parliament, allow for the eventual admission of British Columbia. Its entry into Confederation would bring about the introduction of responsible government, as well as resolving the colony's serious financial difficulties resulting partly from the interest on debts incurred for road-building during the gold rushes. One-third of British Columbia's annual revenue was required to service its debt, and office-holders had been forced to take salary reductions. Confederation with Canada received an additional impetus when—coterminously with the passage of the British North America Act but quite separate from it—the American government purchased Alaska from the Russians, touching off expected howls for the annexation of British Columbia. Officially the colony was notified in November 1867 that no action could be taken until Rupert's Land had been duly incorporated into Canada.

While union was put on hold, the colonists played hard to get, some of them even organizing a petition for annexation to the United States. But in early 1870 the British Columbia legislature passed a motion calling for union, providing satisfactory financial terms could be arranged. The legislature wanted to eliminate the debt and to undertake a vast program of public

---

*An amnesty was granted Riel in 1875, conditional on his being banished for five years.

improvements. It did not at first insist as a non-negotiable demand on the building of a transcontinental railroad, an undertaking that British business-men had long supported, although Governor Anthony Musgrave (1828-88) reported to Britain, 'If a Railway could be promised, scarcely any other question would be allowed to be a difficulty'.[4] However, the British Colum-bia delegates to Ottawa came equipped with maps and proposed routes.

The negotiations between British Columbia and Canada took place in the late spring of 1870, just as the Canadian government was sending a military expedition to Red River to occupy that territory. The Canadians were generous to a fault. Of course British Columbia could have responsible government. Of course the debt could be wiped out. Of course there would be subsidies and grants, as well as federal support for the naval station at Esquimalt. And of course British Columbia could have a rail link with Canada—which was begun within two years and completed within fifteen.

Governor Musgrave was astounded. The terms were so much better than expected, 'And then the Railway, Credat Judaeus! is *guaranteed* without a reservation! Sir George Cartier says they will do that, or "burst".'[5] The promise was certainly audacious, although hardly surprising. For a variety of reasons, some of them political and some economic, Canada needed a transcontinental railroad to match the lines rapidly being constructed across the United States. As predicted, the railway guarantee virtually wiped out hesitancy in British Columbia, which had to promise in the end that it would not insist on the terms to the letter. On 20 July 1871 British Columbia entered Confederation as the sixth province, and while at the last moment a few lamented the event, one official commenting, 'We are a conquered country & the Canucks take possession tomorrow', most of the Pacific colonists seemed satisfied with their bargain.

While in most respects the new province remained until after 1885 too isolated from Canada to be much influenced by the union, Confederation encouraged and facilitated the gradual development of a new land policy for British Columbia, which opened the lands of the province to massive pre-emption and free land grants.[6] The government of British Columbia would exceed the federal government in its generosity to new settlers.

Prince Edward Island

Prince Edward Island's acceptance of 'terms' in 1873—given the vehemence of its initial rejection of union in 1866—was anti-climactic. The tiny prov-ince had been warned by the British to expect little favour outside Confeder-ation, and it was actively wooed by both the Americans and the Canadians, who sent a series of formal proposals to the Island late in 1869. They were rejected on the grounds that they did not resolve the land question. But this was not the decisive factor in the end. In 1871 the Island entered on a profligate policy of railroad construction. Many saw the railway as a scheme to lure the Island into union, and between contracting overruns and the

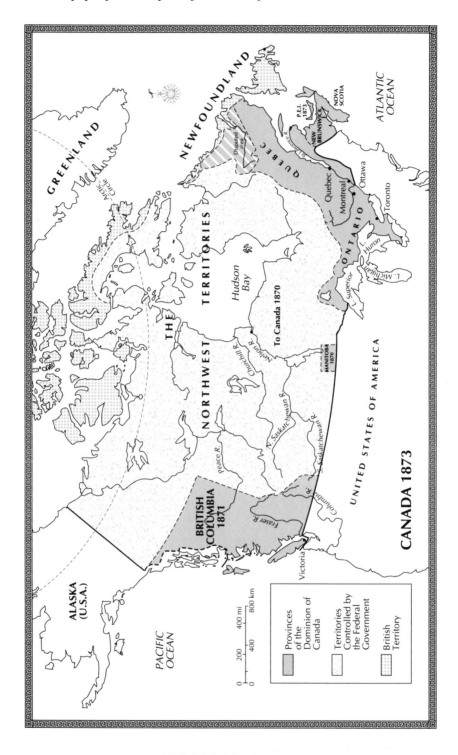

CANADA 1873

	Provinces of the Dominion of Canada
	Territories Controlled by the Federal Government
	British Territory

demands of every village for service, the province quickly found its debentures unacceptable on the London market. Union with Canada was the only way to maintain the public credit, and the Dominion quickly made an offer the Island could not refuse. As well as taking over the debt and the railway, Canada offered to guarantee continuous communication with the mainland and to help buy out the last of the old proprietors. As Sir Leonard Tilley disingenuously explained to the Canadian House of Commons: 'The great local works there having been now completed, there could never be any large local expenditure in the future, and it was in consideration of this fact that the Dominion Government had granted such liberal terms.'[7] Once admitted, the Island would come cheap. Only one Island MLA, the crusty farmer Cornelius Howatt, refused to vote for the Canadian offer.

Newfoundland

Canada was not always successful in convincing latecomers to join the union. Although Newfoundland had sent delegates to the Quebec Conference in 1864, their enthusiasm for union was never matched by two of the colony's major groups: the Protestant merchants and the Irish Roman Catholics. The former feared the economic consequences of intercontinental integration, the latter opposed political unions out of a historical sense that in Ireland they had represented 'a conquest, in which the relationship must always be that of master and slave' and involve the destruction 'of the Irish people as a nation'.[8] Deteriorating economic prospects for the colony in the late 1860s seemed to bode well for an election to be held on the issue of union with Canada in 1869, fulfilling an understanding of popular consultation agreed to in the Newfoundland legislature in 1865. The economy improved, however, while opponents of Confederation employed every argument in their rhetorical arsenal, including rumours that Newfoundland children would be used as wads for Canadian cannon. The 1869 election went decisively against the pro-Confederates. Both the British and Canadian governments acquiesced in Newfoundland's maintaining the automony that continued—despite occasional union discussions, as in 1887 and 1895—until 1949.

❧ The Quest for National Policies

As well as completing the take-over of the northern part of the continent, the Macdonald government gradually improvised some national policies with which to govern the new Dominion. Most of them were left over from the earlier Canadian system, occasionally writ larger to accommodate the other provinces. Sometimes, of course, the interests of the constituent parts had to be sacrificed to larger concerns—one of which was Anglo-American *détente*. The imperial government was most unhappy about efforts by both Nova Scotia and the new Canadian government to keep American fishermen outside a three-mile limit off Canadien shores after the abrogation of reciprocity, particularly given a number of other outstanding issues involving the Americans. These included the *Alabama* claims (the *Alabama* was a Confederate raider built by Britain for the Southern States; the Americans, half-seriously, demanded the cession of British American territory in compensation for the losses it inflicted on northern shipping) and the Fenian claims. In 1871 the British government made Macdonald a member of an international joint commission set up in 1870 to deal with the fisheries question. It advised the Canadians to cede its claims to a three-mile limit only 'in return for an adequate consideration'. Sir Charles Tupper, representing Nova Scotian interests, insisted that fishing rights could not be sold only for a 'money consideration', but the British were willing to surrender Canadian (really Maritime) interests, eager as they were to settle outstanding Anglo-American differences or have them brought to international arbitration. These views prevailed, and Macdonald signed the resulting Treaty of Washington, seeing his signature as some recognition of Canadian diplomatic autonomy and the treaty as a recognition by the United States of the Canadian presence on the continent.

On the domestic front, the banking system of the new nation grew rapidly after Confederation, from 123 chartered bank branches in 1868 to 279 in 1879 and 426 by 1890. There were two major pieces of national legislation: the Dominion Notes Act of 1870 and the Bank Act of 1871. The former allowed the government to issue circulating notes of small denominations, only partly backed by specie, while the latter exerted control over the banking system. The Bank Act specified capital requirements for banks, prohibited new foreign-owned banks, and supplied general regulation, including standards for bank-note issue. Canada was integrated into the international gold standard, but the government would share the issuance of currency (and control of the creation of money) with the banks well into the twentieth century.

Confederation suggested an economic future for Canada that was generally encouraging to foreign investment. From its inception, Canada was able to import large amounts of capital to help create its economic infrastructure, including $166,000,000 (or 7 per cent of the Gross National Product) in the years 1871-5.[9] Between 1865 and 1869 Canada raised $16.5 million in Great Britain, a figure that rose to $94.6 million in 1870-74, $74.7 million in 1875-9, and $69.8 in 1880-4.[10]

The opportunity for further railway expansion was one of the principal economic arguments for Confederation—and railroads were a prime target of foreign investors. Nevertheless, despite the beginning of the Intercolonial Railway through New Brunswick, the Macdonald government was slow to move on that greatest of all railroads, an intercontinental line, chiefly because of the enormous expense involved in building so much ahead of population needs. To some extent the offer to British Columbia was intended to cast the die, and was followed by the usual unseemly scuffling over a charter, which was awarded in 1873 by Parliament to Sir Hugh Allan's Canada Pacific

Railway Company.* Then the Pacific Scandal broke. Allan had provided the government with money—more than $350,000—for its 1872 election campaign, and Macdonald was unable to step clear of this patronage. In November 1873 the government resigned, and was replaced by a Liberal government headed by a former stonemason, Alexander Mackenzie (1822-92), who sought to build a transcontinental line more gradually, using public funds. He was also prepared to encourage private interests to hook up with American western lines, and trains began running from Minnesota to Winnipeg late in 1878. By that time Mackenzie's earnestness had worn thin with the voters, and the probity of his government was not sufficient to save it in the 1878 election.

On his return to power Macdonald recognized the temper of the times and worked very hard to restore in the public mind a sense of total identity between his party and the process of nation-building, in which a certain decisiveness and flamboyance were part of the image. Even before the election he had his platform, introducing into the House of Commons a resolution 'That this House is of the opinion that the welfare of Canada requires the adoption of a National Policy, which, by a judicious readjustment of the Tariff, will benefit and foster the agricultural, the mining, the manufacturing and other interests of this Dominion.'[11] Macdonald invented neither the policy nor the term used to describe it. Both went well back into the development of economic policy for the Province of Canada, which had begun using a tariff as an instrument of both protection and revenue in the late 1840s. Nor did John A. ever articulate a version of the National Policy as it was later described by economic historians and textbook writers, although they have often suggested that he did. He certainly recognized a relationship involving tariffs, manufacturing, employment, and 'national prosperity'. He also wanted a transcontinental railroad and the accompanying western settlement necessary to make it a reality. But all this was a traditional part of Canadian economic expansionism.

What Macdonald achieved was masterful, however. He succeeded in persuading a large number of Canadians that policies strongly driven by the economic self-interest of some of the people in some of its constituent parts were in the best interest of the nation as a whole, and in identifying the party he led with the successful building of that nation. The fact that the opposition party had a different version of the meaning of Confederation helped in this identification.

Seeking National Identity

Politicians were not alone in endeavouring to create a sense of nationality to accompany Confederation. No guarantees came with the British North America Act that political unification would inevitably create a nation,

---

*Allan had been knighted by Queen Victoria in 1871.

particularly given the competing interpretations of the meaning of Confederation. Intellectuals and artists played their part as well, both in terms of rhetorical flourishes and in the more mundane business of creating national institutions in which the arts could operate.

Act or Pact?

The development of nationhood in the years after 1867 should not obscure the fact that not all Canadians shared in the same vision (or version) of the meaning of the nation. Put most simply, was Canada an indissoluble new creation or was it the product of a compact among the provinces that they could either modify or even withdraw from? Since the time of the debate over Confederation in the 1860s, people had disagreed over the nature of the union. While most Canadians in 1867 saw Confederation as creating a strong central government, the legislatures of the provinces had certainly not been eliminated, and they would quickly reassert more than a mere 'local power'. An arch-critic of Confederation, Christopher Dunkin, had prophesied in 1865:

> In the times to come, when men shall begin to feel strongly on those questions that appeal to national preferences, prejudices and passions, all talk of your new nationality will sound but strangely. Some older nationality will then be found to hold the first place in most people's hearts.[12]

Even John A. Macdonald had admitted in Parliament in 1868: '. . . a conflict may, ere long, arise between the Dominion and the States Rights people.'[13]

The emergence of a states'-rights (or provincial-rights) interpretation of the new union was initially spearheaded by Ontario rather than by Quebec, although such a movement was inherent in the constitutional arrangements and could have begun anywhere. The arguments of Nova Scotia's repealers in and after the 1867 elections could have become part of such a position, but their failure and surrender seemed not to qualify. In any event, as early as 1869 Ontario became distressed at 'the assumption by the Parliament of Canada of the power to disturb the financial relations established by the British North America Act (1867), as between Canada and the several provinces.'[14] Not surprisingly, it was the old Reform party of Canada West, in the persons of George Brown, Edward Blake (1833-1912), and Oliver Mowat (1820-1903), that took the lead in demanding, in Blake's words of 1871, 'that each government [dominion and provincial] should be absolutely independent of the other in its management of its own affairs.'[15] The *Rouges* of Quebec soon joined in the same call, adding the identification of French-Canadian 'national' rights to Quebec's 'provincial' ones. Before long, Liberals in most provinces—many of whom had opposed Confederation or had been lukewarm about it—had embraced provincial rights.

Provincial rights often seemed interchangeable with Ottawa-bashing for local political advantage, lacking in any other principle than the desire to pressure Ottawa into fiscal concessions. In its early years, the movement was neither dominated by Quebec nor by arguments of a cultural deal between two distinct societies. In 1884, for example, the Honourable Honoré Mercier (1840-94) tabled resolutions in the Quebec legislature that insisted merely that 'the frequent enroachments of the Federal Parliament upon the prerogatives of the Provinces are a permanent menace to the latter.'[16] The ensuing debate did not involve any more cultural nationalism than one backbencher's assertion that '*le Québec n'est pas une province comme les autres.*'[17] Although the Riel business of 1885 (discussed later) pushed Quebec towards arguments of cultural distinctiveness, when Mercier—by this time premier of Quebec—invited the provinces to the Interprovincial Conference in 1887 to re-examine the federal compact, broad agreement could be reached on demands for better terms and constitutional change by the five provinces attending without the need for such clauses.

Canada First

The identification of emerging cultural nationalism in Canada, in the years immediately after 1867, with the movement that called itself 'Canada First' is an unfortunate one, for the Canada Firsters had neither a monopoly on national sentiment nor a very attractive version of it. The original Canada First movement was founded by a small group of intellectuals in Ottawa in 1868, to perpetuate the memory and sentiments of the late lamented D'Arcy McGee.* The founders were not a very prepossessing group of young men. Their ranks included Charles Mair (1838-1927), who had been publicly horsewhipped in Red River for his disparaging remarks about mixed-blood women; Robert G. Haliburton(1831-1901), the son of T.C. Haliburton and lobbyist for the Nova Scotia Coal Owners' Association; and George Denison (1839-1925) of Toronto, a militia officer who had long advocated military preparedness and would later boast of his part in arousing Ontario sentiment against Louis Riel over the 'murder' of Thomas Scott.

Indeed, turning the Canadian public against the Métis was Canada First's chief accomplishment. Its nationalism was in several senses racist. Haliburton was one of the earliest exponents of the notion of Canadians as the heirs of 'Aryan' northmen of the old world and their glorious destiny. 'We are the Northmen of the New World,' he trumpeted in an address to the Montreal Literary Club in March 1869—a new nationality comprising 'the Celtic, the Teutonic, and the Scandinavian elements' and embracing 'the Celt, the Norman French, the Saxon and the Swede'.[18] The group looked down their noses at Indians and Métis, seeing the French as the great 'bar to progress, and to the extension of a great Anglo-Saxon Dominion across the Continent' (the Toronto *Globe*, 4 August 1870). While these notions went together, to some extent, with Canadian westward expansion, they were fortunately not

---

*As a Member of Parliament, McGee had spoken out strongly against the Fenians and was assassinated by one (James Patrick Whelan) in Ottawa on 7 April 1868.

totally typical of the conscious development of Canadian nationalism. The French-Canadian poet Octave Crémazie, for example, lamented ironically that Canada's major literary languages were of European origin, arguing that '. . . if we spoke Huron or Iroquois, the works of our writers would attract the attention of the old world. . . One would be overwhelmed by a novel or a poem translated from the Iroquois, while one does not take the trouble to read a book written in French by a native of Quebec or Montreal.'[19]

The search for an essential 'Canadian-ness' went on in many corners of the new Dominion, but was nowhere so crowned with success as in that somewhat remote New Brunswick town, Fredericton, home of the University of New Brunswick. There the rectory of St Anne's Parish (Anglican) produced Charles G.D. Roberts (1860-1943), while not far down the road lived his cousin Bliss Carman (1861-1929). Along with Ottawa's Archibald Lampman (1861-99) and Duncan Campbell Scott (1862-1947), Roberts and Carman comprised the 'Confederation Poets', a designation invented by modern literary critics for the first school of Canadian poets who wrestled with Canadian themes, notably the local or regional landscape, with any degree of skill and sensitivity.

While many intellectuals and artists sought creative ways to express Canadian distinctiveness in their work, others took a more prosaic route in expressing a Canadian national identity. Curiously enough it was the painters who took the lead in organizing national groups to maintain professional standards and publicize Canadian art. The Ontario Society of Artists, formed in 1872 and incorporated in 1877, took the lead in this effort, becoming instrumental in the formation of the Royal Canadian Academy of Arts in 1880—in collaboration with the Governor General, Lord Lorne—and in the establishment that same year of the National Gallery of Canada. The Academy not only held an opening exhibition in Ottawa, but planned others in Toronto, Montreal, Halifax, and Saint John. As one of the founding academicians wrote, '*We are bound to try to civilize the Dominion a little*.'[20] The year 1880 was doubly important in art circles, for it was in that year that the Canadian Society of Graphic Art was also founded.

The Royal Society of Canada was founded in 1882 to promote research and learning in the arts and sciences. Lord Lorne again provided much of the impetus in replicating a British institution to establish the importance of cultural accomplishments in creating a sense of national pride and self-confidence. The first president, J.W. Dawson (1820-99), principal of McGill University—another Nova Scotian transported to central Canada—emphasized in his presidential address a sense of national purpose, especially 'the establishment of a bond of union between the scattered workers now widely separated in different parts of the Dominion.' Thomas Sterry Hunt (1826-92), a charter member and later president, observed that 'The occasion which brings us together is one which should mark a new departure in the intellectual history of Canada,' adding that 'the brightest glories and the most enduring honours of a country are those which come from its thinkers and its scholars.'[21] However romantic that statement may be, what is important is Hunt's emphasis on the country as a whole. Like the Royal Canadian Academy, the Royal Society had its headquarters in Ottawa.

The first president of the Royal Canadian Academy, the painter Lucius O'Brien (1832-99), was art director of an elaborate literary and artistic celebration of the young nation, *Picturesque Canada* (1882), which was based on the highly successful *Picturesque America* and *Picturesque Europe* and was the idea of two Americans, the Belden brothers, who had established themselves in Toronto. The editor of the project—George Monro Grant (1835-1902), Principal of Queen's University—stated in the Preface: 'I believed that

One of the illustrations in *Picturesque Canada*, this engraving shows the three Parliament Buildings in downtown Ottawa as they looked in the early 1880s. The East, West, and Centre Blocks (including the Library of Parliament), were erected in 1860-6. The Centre Block, except for the Library, was destroyed by fire on 3 February 1916, and was rebuilt in 1916-24 to designs by John A. Pearson, who also designed the soaring Peace Tower (1919-27) that stands in front of it today.

a work that would represent its characteristic scenery and the history and life of its people would not only make us better known to ourselves and to strangers, but would also stimulate national sentiment and contribute to the rightful development of the nation.' The two large volumes of *Picturesque Canada* contained some 540 illustrations—wood-engravings based on paintings and, for the West, photo-engravings of photographs—of serene vistas that fulfilled the promise of the title. The descriptive texts by Grant, Charles G.D. Roberts, and others presented an idealized, complacent view of the cities, towns, and regions of Canada, praising the present and pointing to their glorious future. *Picturesque Canada* was a monument to the optimism of the time.[22]

Education

As John Bourinot's comments at the beginning of this chapter indicate, Canadians of his time—if asked to comment on their cultural achievements—would have responded with pride about their school systems, particularly for their accessibility and universality. British North America's first Free Education Act, under which schools were fully financed by the state, was passed in Prince Edward Island in 1852, but the progress of Canadian education in the mid-Victorian age in all provinces observed a pattern of passage from private to public financial support at the same time that schooling became increasingly universal. The movement to public financing permitted the colonial governments and their provincial successors to provide centralized control over education, and small bureaucracies emerged after 1870 in all provinces. Attempts by these centralized agencies to regulate denominational schools in the same way that they controlled public ones would lead to much controversy.

Not all provinces moved at the same pace or in exactly the same way, of course. Education was left in the hands of the provinces by section 92 of the British North America Act, and it is almost impossible to talk about any integrated national movements. Indeed, education would become one of the most central and divisive issues in the new nation, and educational diversity was still the norm. Canada East had been somewhat slower than Canada West to move towards universality, and most of its schools continued to be—as they always had been—dominated by both clerical teachers and clerical values, although Protestants were able to establish their own institutions, particularly after education was reorganized in 1875. In Canada West, rudimentary common schools had always received some state support, but under Egerton Ryerson (1803-82), who served as chief superintendent of education from 1844 to 1876, a series of landmark School Acts gradually moved Ontario education towards state support and universality, at increasingly higher levels of educational attainment. Most western provinces would eventually emulate Ontario.

As early as 1868, a Canadian National Series of Readers was introduced into Ontario based on the Irish National Readers, but 'greatly improved and Canadianized'.[23] An emphasis on using material published in Canada and adapted to its uses was not the same thing as promulgation of a strident or even standard Canadian chauvinism in the schools. In the short run, English-Canadian educators tended to Canadianize by emphasizing 'the rich heritage of British history ... reflected in our national escutcheon.'[24]

Other Cultural Activities

Not all cultural activity in Canada after Confederation was greatly affected by the creation of a nation. Indeed, most culture in Canada existed quite apart from national considerations. Despite their self-consciousness about the need for cultural achievements to match their new political accomplishments, in documenting progress Canadians would probably have ignored some of the most interesting arenas for culture, such as the various elements of popular culture. Only a brief sampling of other cultural activity in Canada — focusing on music and organized sport — can be included here.

Music

Although the occasional trained musician existed in colonial British North America, the mid-Victorian era saw the development of a widespread musical life that transcended the singing of hymns and folk songs. Most of the skilled musicians were immigrants who had learned their musical skills abroad, and much of the early advance involved garrison bands and choral groups. The bands often provided the musicians, and choral singing was something that could be done with a minimum of musical knowledge and training.

In Montreal the band of the 23rd Regiment, considered one of the best in the country, was heard with enthusiasm by Charles Dickens in 1842. On the West Coast the band of the Royal Engineers brought new standards of musical performance when it arrived in the colony in 1859, and from that year until 1863 — when it was reposted to Britain — it entertained in various guises in New Westminister. It was in turns a militia band, a fire-brigade band, a brass band, and even a dance band. Some of its members remained in the province after it was reposted. In British Columbia, as elsewhere, brass bands were the most common and popular forms of instrumental ensembles throughout the nineteenth century. Bands were formed in Victoria in 1864, in Nanaimo in 1872, and in Kamloops in 1886. Moreover, a number of brass bands were organized in native communities and residential schools, at least 33 between 1864 (when the Oblates founded the St Mary's Mission Band near Mission City) and the end of the century. One famous community band made up of native musicians, 21 members strong, was established in 1875 by

William Duncan at Metlakatla, a major missionary station and school on Vancouver Island.[25]

By the time of Confederation, larger cities were producing substantial numbers of musical societies, chiefly choral in their orientation. In 1864, for example, the Montreal Oratorio Society was joined by the Mendelssohn Choir and the Société Musicale des Montagnards Canadiens and Les Orphéonistes de Montréal. The Philharmonic Society of Montreal, founded in 1877, performed many large-scale works, particularly under conductor Guillaume Couture (1851-1915), who had studied in Paris with Franck and Saint-Saens. Couture led a chorus of over 200 voices. Montreal also helped produce the first well-known Canadian composer, Calixa Lavallée (1842-91), who is best known today for the music to 'O Canada' (the words having been composed by a series of political committees). Lavallée made his début at the piano in Montreal at age 13, and spent much time in the United States until he was sent by supporters to Paris in 1873. He returned to settle in Quebec, writing a grand cantata for the reception of Governor General Lord Lorne and his royal wife, which concluded with a stirring contrapuntal intramixture of 'God Save the Queen' and 'Comin' thro' the Rye'. The cantata was acclaimed, but the composer lost money, complaining: '*Le gouvernement Joly [Joly de Lotbinière, premier of Quebec, 1878-9] a reçu la Princesse. Mais c'est moi qui ai payé le violon* [But it is I who paid the piper].'[26] Lavallée spent the last years of his life in exile in the United States.

Sports and Games

The mid-Victorian period saw a continued development of organized sports and games in British North America/Canada. Most were imported, although some—like lacrosse—had local origins. Lacrosse had begun life as a native game called variously 'baggataway' or 'tewaarathon', and was played by many tribes under different rules. In 1833 it was played by the First Nations near Montreal, and in 1856 the Montreal Lacrosse Club was organized, joined by two others before 1860. The game was codified in Montreal and was promoted across Canada by a Montreal dentist, William George Beers (1843-1900), who by October 1867 had brought to life 80 lacrosse clubs with 2,000 members across the new Dominion. The game flourished between 1868 and 1885, achieving great success as a spectator sport. Snowshoeing, which became very popular as an organized winter activity in the 1860s, often among the summer lacrosse crowd, was another obviously Canadian development. The Montreal Snow Shoe Club was organized in 1843, and in Winnipeg a snowshoe club, begun in 1878, was by the early 1880s the major winter diversion for members of the city's élite.

The formulation of rules for these and other sports occurred in most cases between 1840 and 1880, although precise dates are very contentious, with many communities advancing their own claims for 'firsts'. Certainly by 1880 most sports and games familiar to us today had reached a stage of rule development that a modern Canadian could understand. What is important about the development of sport is not simply the introduction of new rules, techniques, and equipment, but the sheer scope and ubiquity of sporting activity, on the part of both participants and spectators. The development of any of the major games followed roughly the same path. Baseball is perhaps one of the most important, for in this period it and lacrosse were probably the closest to a 'national' game in Canada, greatly exceeding in popularity ice-hockey, which required more equipment, special skills (skating), and indoor facilities (arenas) in order to become a true spectator sport.

A composite photograph of a baseball game in Tecumseh Park, London, Ontario, between the London Tecumsehs and Syracuse in 1871. The Middlesex County Court House can be seen in the background. National Archives of Canada, PA 31482.

Baseball was extremely popular in British North America, particularly in Upper Canada, and it spread rapidly both east and west after 1870. By the mid-1850s there were organized teams that gradually came to play American rules. There was an unofficial Canadian championship by the early 1860s, and in the year of Confederation a team from Ingersoll, Ontario, won the junior championship at an American 'world' tournament. By 1876 a Canadian league had been formed, with teams in Kingston, Toronto, Hamilton, Guelph, and London. Its players were for the most part amateurs or semi-professionals, although American players were imported and paid. During this era the Americans organized a professional league, and in 1886 a Toronto team joined one of the American feeder (or minor) leagues. Although initially Upper Canadian in origin, baseball became a major sport in the

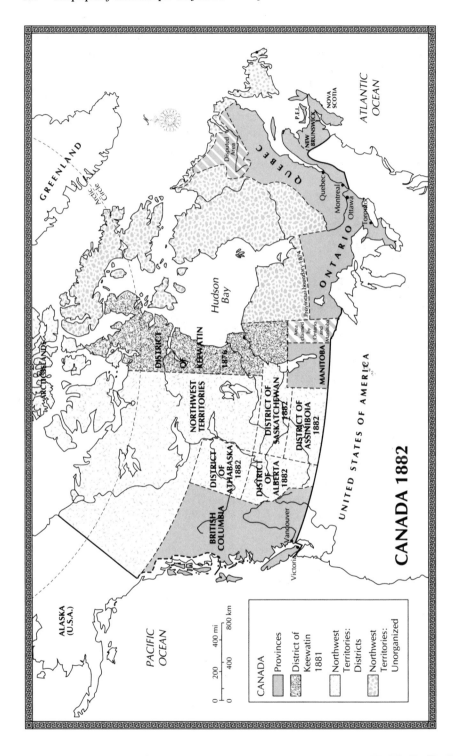

CANADA 1882

GREENLAND

ATLANTIC OCEAN

NOVA SCOTIA

P.E.I.

NEW BRUNSWICK

QUEBEC

Disputed Area

Quebec
Montreal
Ottawa
Toronto

ONTARIO

Provincial boundary 1874

Area claimed by Ontario and Manitoba

Hudson Bay

DISTRICT OF KEEWATIN 1876

MANITOBA

NORTHWEST TERRITORIES

DISTRICT OF SASKATCHEWAN 1882

DISTRICT OF ASSINIBOIA 1882

DISTRICT OF ATHABASKA 1882

DISTRICT OF ALBERTA 1882

ARCTIC ISLANDS

UNITED STATES OF AMERICA

BRITISH COLUMBIA

Vancouver

Victoria

ALASKA (U.S.A.)

PACIFIC OCEAN

0   200   400 mi
0   400   800 km

CANADA

Provinces

District of Keewatin 1881

Northwest Territories: Districts

Northwest Territories: Unorganized

Maritimes and in the West, where it was played by farmboys on fields across the Prairies. By the 1870s large crowds would assemble to watch a game between two local teams, and massive crowds paid admission fees to observe the finest semi-professional and professional teams. Hockey and football followed a similar organizational pattern, the latter sport in both Canada and the United States being particularly associated with university teams, which began playing each other in the 1870s.[27]

By 1885 two aspects of sport in Canada had evolved: participation and spectacle. It still had not achieved a political meaning, through the creation of either national leagues or national teams to play in international competitions. But its expansion, sophistication, and growing organization matched the development of the nation. The mobility of the population moved various sports and games around the country and made the interchange of rules possible. Both the development of 'official' rules and growing hierarchies of teams and players anticipated the future.

Confederation and the Less-Visible Minorities

Despite sincere efforts on the part of many in the new Dominion to encourage a sense of nationhood that transcended the linguistic differences between French and English, and the geographical barriers of the provinces and the regions, the fact remains that the new Canadian nationality remained fragile, more than a bit artificial, and very racist. In addition, at least outside French Canada it mainly expressed the prejudices and beliefs of British Ontario writ large. The crucible for the new Canadian nationality, many believed, was in that vast expanse of territory west of the Great Lakes. But here its limitations were most clearly evident.

The interests of the Canadian government in the Northwest, especially under Sir John A. Macdonald, were focused on agricultural settlement, both as an outlet for excess eastern population and as a means of encouraging the development of a truly transcontinental nation. In the process the native inhabitants of the region were pushed aside as quickly as possible. A series of treaties was negotiated with the Indians that extinguished native titles in exchange for reserves on the most marginal and least attractive land. In August 1876, for example, the Indians of central Saskatchewan foregathered at Fort Carlton to consider the terms of the government's Treaty no. 6. The Plains Cree chief Poundmaker (Pitikwahanapiwiyin, *c.*1842-86) objected, saying that the government should be prepared to train the Indians as farmers and assist them in other ways after the buffalo disappeared. This suggestion was not well received by the lieutenant-governor, who presented the terms. Nevertheless, Poundmaker signed the Treaty, and three years later accepted a reserve on the Battle River. Another important Plains Cree chief, Big Bear (Mistahimaskwa, *c.*1825-88), refused to sign for six years. On 8 December 1882, he signed when his people were starving and he wished to provide

Poundmaker. National Archives
of Canada, PA 28853.

Big Bear trading at Fort Pitt, a Hudson's Bay Company post on the North Saskatchewan River until
1884, when it was taken over by the North West Mounted Police. In April 1885 Big Bear and his band
attacked it; it was evacuated, and then burned by Big Bear's Cree followers. National Archives of
Canada, PA 118768.

them with food. The next July his small band was moved north to a reservation near Fort Pitt.

The North-West Mounted Police, based on the Irish constabulary, were established in 1873 to act as a quasi-military agent of the Canadian government in the West. Its officers, drawn from the élites of eastern Canada, were committed to the notion of public stability that associated crime and violence with the 'lower orders' and the native peoples. The 'Mounties' moved ahead of settlement and have always been seen as the chief instruments of a more peaceful western expansion than was true in the neighbouring United States. Certainly in Canada there was less individual violence, but this was often owing to the exertion of state intervention and control.

Like the First Nations, the Métis were systematically driven to the margins. Macdonald's government had created Manitoba as a province only under duress, and the Prime Minister regarded the mixed-bloods as a people to be 'kept down by a strong hand until they are swamped by the influx of settlers.'[28] And swamped they were. As thousands of new settlers, mainly from Ontario, arrived in the province, guarantees of land rights to the Métis were gradually whittled away, and the land itself—about 2 million of the two-and-a-half-million acres promised the Métis in 1870—ended up in the hands of speculators. By 1885 Ontario-born settlers outnumbered Métis 5-to-1 in Manitoba, and only seven per cent of the population of the province was of mixed-blood origin. Many Métis drifted further west, to the Saskatchewan Valley, forming several small mission settlements, including Qu'Appelle, Batoche, and Duck Lake. But the buffalo were becoming scarce. French, English, and Scottish mixed-bloods demanded grants similar to those given to the mixed-bloods of Manitoba under the Manitoba Act. Government surveyors caused uncertainty and fear, as they had done in Manitoba a decade earlier. In addition, the Indians were unable to provide for themselves. The winter of 1883-4 was particularly severe and many were starving. Indian agents complained to Ottawa, but nothing was done. In June 1884 Big Bear and his followers, with many other Indians, travelled to Poundmaker's reserve to hold a big meeting. They discussed the serious state of affairs, after which some 2,000 Indians put on a Thirst Dance, a religious ritual. The Métis, in despair, turned to their old leader Louis Riel.

Riel had apparently put his life back together after years of exile in the United States and hospitalization in 1876-8 for mental disturbance at Longue Pointe, Quebec. He had become an American citizen and was teaching in St Peter's, Montana (where he had married), when a delegation from the Saskatchewan country visited him on 4 June 1884. They told him of all the grievances that were burdening the peoples of the Saskatchewan region, explained that agitation was developing against the Canadian government, and pled with him to return to Canada to lead them. Why Riel agreed to do so is one of the many mysteries surrounding his life. But within a month he and his family were in Batoche.

By December 1884, Riel and W. H. Jackson (secretary of the Settler's Union) had finished drafting a long petition, with 25 sections, which they sent to Ottawa. It concluded by requesting that the petitioners 'be allowed as in [1870] to send Delegates to Ottawa with their Bill of rights; whereby an understanding may be arrived at as to their entry into confederation, with the constitution of a free province.'[29] The petition was acknowledged, but no other response was vouchsafed by Ottawa.

In March 1885 events took a menacing turn. On the 18th Riel and some of his men strode into the Walters and Baker store in Batoche. Riel announced: 'Well, gentlemen, it has commenced.' 'What has commenced?' asked Walters. 'Oh, this movement for the rights of the country,' was the reply.[30] The visitors then helped themselves to ammunition and provisions. On 21 March, Riel sent a letter to Superintendent Crozier of the North-West Mounted Police at Fort Carlton, which was manned by a force of Mounted Police and volunteers. The missive demanded Fort Carlton's surrender, or it would be attacked by Riel and his men. Crozier refused. On 26 March, Gabriel Dumont (1836-1906), Riel's military leader, intercepted a small detachment from Fort Carlton near Duck Lake. When Crozier heard of this action he left the fort with as many men as he could muster. This force met Riel and 300 Métis on horseback before it could reach Duke Lake. Startled, Crozier gave the order to fire. Thirty minutes of gunfire exchanges followed, during which lives were lost on both sides.

The Métis, who outnumbered Crozier's men, forced them to retreat. Gabriel Dumont later recalled this confrontation in vivid detail:

> They had to go through a clearing so I lay in wait for them, saying to my men: 'Courage, I'm going to make the red coats jump in their carts with some rifle shots.' And then I laughed, not because I took any pleasure in killing but to give courage to my men.
>
> Since I was eager to knock off some of the red coats, I never thought to keep under cover and a shot came and gashed the top of my head, where a deep scar can still be seen. I fell down on the ground and my horse, which was also wounded, went right over me as it tried to get away. . . . When Joseph Delorme saw me fall again, he cried out that I was killed. I said to him: 'Courage! As long as you haven't lost your head, you're not dead!'. . . .
>
> While we were fighting, Riel was on horseback, exposed to the gunfire, and with no weapon but the crucifix which he held in his hand.[31]

Riel wrote a letter to Crozier blaming him for the battle. 'A calamity has fallen upon the country yesterday,' he insisted. 'You are responsible for it before God and man. . . .'[32] He then appealed to the Indians to assist him. Poundmaker's Indians broke into buildings in Battleford, terrifying settlers, and the Cree warrior Wandering Spirit (Kapapamahchakwew, c.1845-85) led a band that attacked Frog Lake, killing nine.

Prime Minister Macdonald was determined to crush this rebellion quickly, sending a force under Major-General Frederick Middleton (1825-98) — by

These men of the Winnipeg Field Battery are having a snooze in a special railway car
taking Louis Riel from Swift Current to Regina to stand trial for treason, 22 May 1885.
Photographed by O.B. Buell. Saskatchewan Archives photograph, B2298.

way of the new Canadian Pacific Railway—to put it down. Lieutenant-
Colonel William Otter (1843-1929) relieved Battleford, but was fired on by
Indians at Cut Knife Hill and had to withdraw. Middleton battled with Métis
at Fish Creek, which delayed his march on Batoche, where he intended to
confront Riel. The Canadian force of 800 men arrived there on 9 May, and
quickly defeated Riel and about 200 Métis. The uprising was over by 12
May. Dumont fled to the United States and Riel was arrested.

A formal charge of high treason, carrying the death penalty, was laid
against Riel on 6 July.* The trial began on 28 July at Regina, where feelings
against him were heated. It was a political trial, infamously coloured in many
ways by Macdonald's determination to have Riel found guilty and executed.
Riel passionately denied a plea of insanity introduced by his lawyers, and the
jury recommended mercy. Ottawa dismissed two appeals, and Riel was
hanged on 16 November.**

This execution had a lasting impact on Canada, particularly in Quebec,
where French-Canadian nationalism was strengthened and voters were

---

*Despite the fact that Riel was an American citizen, the Canadian government held
with the British government that he was also a British subject—that British
citizenship could never be renounced.
**Poundmaker stood trial for treason and was sentenced to three years in prison.
Released after a year, he died four months later. Big Bear received a similar
sentence, but was released after a year and a half. Wandering Spirit was hanged.

Riel in the prisoner's box. He addressed the court twice during his trial, once after all the evidence had been presented, when he spoke for over an hour, and once before sentence was pronounced. National Archives of Canada, C-1879.

Wilfrid Laurier, *c.*1882. A member of Parliament in 1885, he became leader of the Liberal party in 1887 and the first French-Canadian prime minister in 1896. National Archives of Canada, PA 13133.

turned away from the Conservative party. On 22 November 1885, at a huge gathering in the public square in Montreal called the Champ de Mars, Honoré Mercier, the Liberal leader in Quebec, joined Wilfrid Laurier in denouncing the government action. Mercier insisted: 'In killing Riel, Sir John has not only struck at the heart of our race but especially at the cause of justice and humanity which ... demanded mercy for the prisoner of Regina, our poor friend of the North-West.'[33] Wilfrid Laurier added: 'Had I been born on the banks of the Saskatchewan. . .I would myself have shouldered a musket to fight against the neglect of governments and the shameless greed of speculators.' The two leaders disagreed over Mercier's proposal that French Canadians leave the two major parties and form one of their own. 'We are a new nation,' said Laurier, 'we are attempting to unite the different conflicting elements which we have into a nation. Shall we ever succeed if the bond of union is to be revenge?'[34] Laurier argued that Mercier's proposal would destroy Confederation.

The military defeat of the Métis and the public execution of Louis Riel in November 1885 for treason were only half the reason why that year (and that month) was so significant, not only in the history of the West but in the history of Canada. For in November 1885 the last spike was driven at Craigellachie in eastern British Columbia to mark the completion of the Canadian Pacific Railway. The CPR had been resurrected in 1881 as a hybrid corporation controlled by private capitalists and financed largely by the state—which, along with public subsidies, gave it about 25 million acres of land along its right-of-way, and other concessions. The question of build-ing in advance of settlement—what T.C. Keefer had called 'colonization lines'—was actively debated at the time, particularly given the inducements needed to convince hard-headed businessmen to proceed with construction; but the Macdonald government defended the railroad on the grounds of national interest. Since this concept is not measurable in quantitative terms, it is impossible to know whether the price was too high. What we can say with certainty is that the construction of the CPR was a spectacular feat of engineering, partly thanks to the managerial skills of William Van Horne (1843-1915). The CPR was executed, however, chiefly on the backs of 6,500 Chinese coolie labourers specially imported for the job. Many died, and those who survived were summarily discharged when the work was com-pleted. Macdonald had defended Chinese immigration in 1883, arguing that 'it will be all very well to exclude Chinese labour, when we can replace it with white labour, but until that is done, it is better to have Chinese labour than no labour at all.'[35] With the completion of the CPR, the Canadian government moved swiftly to limit Chinese immigration.

The West was to be an anglophone colony of Canada. Not only were Indians, Métis, and Chinese cast aside as quickly as possible, but French Canadians were not expected to move there in any substantial numbers. Most Québécois in the years after Confederation saw the West as important mainly

A CPR construction crew at Malakwa, BC. National Archives of Canada, C-1602.

Arrival of the first transcontinental passenger train at the foot of Howe Street, Vancouver, 23 May 1887. City of Vancouver Archives, CAN. P.78, N.52.

in commercial terms, or at best as a better destination for determined Quebec migrants than the United States. Certainly by 1879 the die appeared to have been cast. As *L'Opinion Publique* (Montreal) stated: 'For five years English emigration has flooded Manitoba, and French emigration has been pretty well nil...The North-West, founded and settled by the French, is destined, like the rest of North America, to be English.'[36] The French-Canadian response to the execution of Louis Riel, however, was hardly so fatalistic. By 1885 Quebec public opinion was prepared to believe in theories of anti-French conspiracies, and was convinced that Riel had died because he was French. Certainly a major factor in Riel's execution was the vehemence of Ontario opinion against him; Thomas Scott was still not forgotten. National consolidation was arguably completed in 1885, but much Canadian 'nationalism' still bore the distinctive sting of the Ontario WASP; and two cultures, French and English, were firmly set in opposition to each other. Trying to satisfy the country's two main components was the most challenging task facing the Canadian government.

Epilogue

Before 1763 the history of the northern part of the continent had been such as to guarantee not only cultural diversity but conflict among its inhabitants. The First Nations had been virtually overwhelmed by the European intruders—though neither their culture nor their claims to the land had been eliminated—and the French were very thoroughly established. This condition was aggravated in the years between the Conquest and Confederation, but especially after the end of the American Revolution in 1783, with the formation of British North America: a loose collection of disparate colonies that happened to be ruled by the same colonial authorities. One of the most striking features of the provinces of British North America was the relative lack of connection that existed, most of the time, between formal political/constitutional developments, as well as public policy, and the bulk of the population. Politics were the preserve of the few. Most people—many of them, outside French Canada, immigrants from the British Isles—were engaged in a struggle to adapt to North American conditions, to survive, and to establish themselves and their families. Within the context of what we see today as a patriarchal, racist, and élitist society, hundreds of thousands of people were simply attempting to improve their lot in life.

Economics were as fragmented as the politics, with the British Empire being the major unifying thread; but once imperial free trade and colonial manufacturing emerged after 1840, merchants and businessmen began thrusting for more integrated continental markets, as the economy in which they operated became more and more sophisticated. As it made the transition to industrialism, the economy influenced society, society influenced politics, and all influenced culture.

Using watershed dates to separate major periods of historical development is always problematic, but there is something compelling about 1885 as a symbolic year for dividing the formative from the modern period in Canadian history. Unlike the more traditional break-off year of 1867, which marks the beginning of confederated Canada, 1885 is significant for containing not just one event but several events of far-reaching importance. It marks the completion of Canada's first intercontinental transportation system, connecting the entire nation from sea to sea. Politically crucial, the Canadian Pacific Railway was also visible evidence of the establishment of an integrated Canadian economy that would experience further industrialization over the ensuing decades. The year 1885 also marks the firm establishment of Canada's control of the West, with the military defeat of the Métis and their native allies. The execution of Louis Riel provided Canada with a major political martyr, and the frenzied public debate surrounding his case brought to the surface a deep division between anglophone Canada (chiefly Ontario) and francophone Canada (chiefly Quebec). Moreover, Riel's execution in 1885, and that of his Indian ally Wandering Spirit, began to symbolize the attitude to its minorities of the Canadian government of the time, as did the decision of Ottawa that same year to impose a head-tax on every Chinese person entering the country.

Canada would change enormously after 1885. Indeed, the very rate of change would be speeded up. A British North American of 1785 could probably have functioned in the Canada of 1885, despite many changes. But that a Canadian of 1885 could easily adapt to the Canada of 1985 is most unlikely.

Notes

Chapter One: The People of Early North America

[1]H.P. Biggar, ed., *The Voyages of Jacques Cartier* (Ottawa, 1924), p. 65.

[2]For the ice sheets, see R. Cole Harris, ed., *Historical Atlas of Canada: Volume I: From the Beginning to 1800* (Toronto, 1987), plate 1.

[3]R.A. Bryson and W.M. Wendland, 'Tentative Climatic Patterns for Some Late Glacial and Post-Glacial Episodes in Central North America', in W.J. Mayer-Oaks, ed., *Life, Land and Water* (Winnipeg, 1967), pp. 271-98; see also V.K. Prest, 'The Late Wisconsin Glacial Complex,' in R.J. Fulton, ed., *A Canadian Contribution to IGCP Project 24*, pp. 21-36, Geological Survey of Canada, Paper 84-10 (1984).

[4]The classic work remains James P. Howley, *The Beothuks or Red Indians: The Aboriginal Inhabitants of Newfoundland* (Cambridge, 1915).

[5]Quoted in A.G. Bailey, *The Conflict of European and Eastern Algonkian Cultures, 1504-1700: A Study in Canadian Civilization* (2nd ed., Toronto, 1969), p. 13. See also W.D. and R.S. Wallis, *The Micmac Indians of Eastern Canada* (Minneapolis, 1955).

[6]Bruce Trigger, ed., *Handbook of North American Indians, Vol. 15, Northeast* (Washington, 1978).

[7]For the projectile points, see the *Historical Atlas of Canada*, op. cit., plates 2-10.

[8]Ibid., plate 12, plate 14.

[9]J.V. Wright, *The Ontario Iroquois Tradition* (Ottawa, 1966); Conrad Heidenreich, *Huronia: A History and Geography of the Huron Indians* (Toronto, 1971).

[10]See the *Historical Atlas of Canada*, op. cit., plates 2-8.

[11]Samuel Eliot Morrison, *European Discovery of America: The Northern Voyages A.D. 500-1600* (New York, 1971), p. 526.

[12]Timothy Foote, 'Where Columbus Was Coming From', *Smithsonian Magazine*, December 1991, p. 32.

[13]See Arthur Ray and Donald Freeman, *'Give Us Good Measure': An Economic Analysis of Relations between the Indians and the Hudson's Bay Company before 1763* (Toronto, 1978).

[14]Francis Jennings, *Ambiguous Empire: The Convenant Chain Confederation of Iroquois and Allied Tribes with English Colonies from its Beginnings to the Lancaster Treaty of 1744* (NY, 1984).

[15]James Axtell, 'The Scholastic Philosophy of the Wilderness', *William and Mary Quarterly*, 1973.

[16]Joyce Marshall, ed., *Word from New France: The Selected Letters of Marie de l'Incarnation* (Toronto, 1967), p. 341.

Chapter Two: The Explorers of the Sixteenth and Seventeenth Centuries

[1]Vilhjalmur Stefansson, ed., *The Three Voyages of Martin Frobisher in Search of a Passage to Cathay and India by the North-West, A.D. 1576-8* (2 vols., London, 1938).

[2]*The Vinland Sagas: The Norse Discovery of America*, translated by Magnus Magnusson and Hermann Palsson (London, 1965).

[3]T.J. Oleson, *Early Voyages and Northern Approaches 1000-1632* (Toronto, 1963).

[4]R.A. Skelton et al., *The Vinland Map and the Tartar Relation* (New Haven, 1965); Robert McGhee, 'The Vinland Map: Hoax or History?', *The Beaver*, 67:2 (April/May 1987), pp. 37-44.

[5]H.P. Biggar, *The Precursors of Jacques Cartier* (Ottawa, 1913); J. A. Williamson, ed., *The Cabot Voyages and Bristol Discovery Under Henry VIII* (Cambridge, 1962).

[6]See the *Dictionary of Canadian Biography* (*DCB*), I, pp. 234-6; H. P. Biggar, *The Voyages of the Cabots and of the Corte-Reals to North America and Greenland, 1497-1503* (Paris, 1903).

[7]Williamson, op. cit., p. 128.

[8]E.G.R. Taylor, 'Master Hore's Voyage of 1536', *Geographical Journal*, LXXVII (1933), 469-70; *DCB*, I, pp. 371-2.

[9]Quoted in Lawrence Wroth, *The Voyages of Giovanni da Verrazzano 1524-1528* (New Haven, 1970), p. 142.

[10]Quoted in the *DCB*, I, p. 165.

[11]H.P. Biggar, *The Voyages of Jacques Cartier* (Ottawa, 1924), pp. 106-7.

[12]Ibid., pp. 169-71.

[13]J.E. King, 'The Glorious Kingdom of Saguenay', *Canadian Historical Review*, 31 (1950), pp. 390-400.

[14]H.P. Biggar, ed., 'A Collection of Documents Relating to Jacques Cartier and the Sieur de Roberval', *Publications of the Public Archives of Canada*, no. 14 (193).

[15]Biggar, *Cartier's Voyages*, pp. 264-5.

[16]André Thevet, *Cosmographie Universelle* (Paris, 1558), cited in the *DCB*, I, p. 423.

[17]*DCB*, I, pp. 425-6; quotation from André Thevet, *Cosmographie universelle* (Paris, 1558). Translation.

[18]Michael Lok quoted in the *DCB*, I, p. 316.

[19]Quoted in the *DCB*, I, p. 317.

[20]Vilhjalmur Stefansson, ed., *The Three Voyages of Martin Frobisher in Search of a Passage to Cathay and India. . . .*(London, 1938), I, p. cvi.

[21]*DCB*, I, p. 317.

[22]Ibid.

[23]In general, see Daniel Francis, *Discovery of the North: The Exploration of Canada's Arctic* (Edmonton, 1986), and L. Neatby, *In Quest of the Northwest Passage* (New York, 1958).

[24]Quoted in the *DCB*, I, p. 131.

[25]Arthur T. Adams, ed., *The Explorations of Pierre Esprit Radisson: From the Original Manuscript in the Bodleian Library and the British Museum* (Minneapolis, 1961).

[26]Ibid., p. 39.

[27]Ibid., p. 75.

[28]*DCB*, I, pp. 81-4.

[29]*DCB*, I, p. 173.

[30]Ibid.

[31]Pierre Margory, ed. *Découvertes et Etablissements des Français dans l'Ouest et dans le Sud de L'Amérique Septentrionale* (Paris, 1879-1888), II, pp. 181-5.

[32]Quoted from the historian Charlevoix in *DCB*, I, p. 183.

[33]Francis Parkman, *La Salle and the Discovery of the Great West* (rev. ed., Boston, 1891).

Chapter Three: Colonizers and Settlers in the Early Seventeenth Century

[1]For Calvert, see the entry by Allan M. Fraser in the *DCB*, I, pp. 162-3; see also J. P. Kennedy, *Discourse on the Life and Character of Sir G. Calvert* (Baltimore, 1845).

[2]Calvert to Charles I, 19 August 1629, reprinted in Gillian Cell, ed., *Newfoundland Discovered: English Attempts at Colonisation, 1610-1630* (London, 1982), pp. 295-6.

[3]Ibid., p. 110.

[4]Ibid., p. 96.

[5]Quoted in D. B. Quinn, *England and the Discovery of America, 1481-1620* (New York, 1972), p. 347.

[6]See the *DCB*, I, pp. 390-2.

[7]Luca Codignola, *The Coldest Harbour of the Land: Simon Stock and Lord Baltimore's Colony in Newfoundland, 1621-49* (Kingston and Montreal, 1988).

[8]*DCB*, I, p. 421.

[9]Quoted in Christopher Hibbert, *The English: A Social History 1066-1945* (London, 1987), pp. 183-4.

[10]William Vaughan, *The Golden Fleece* (London, 1626), the third part, p. 14, p. 9.

[11]Gillian Cell, *English Enterprise in Newfoundland 1577-1660* (Toronto, 1969), pp. 83-5.

[12]G.P. Insh, *Scottish Colonial Schemes, 1620-1686* (Glasgow, 1922); John Reid, *Acadia, Maine, and New Scotland: Marginal Colonies in the Seventeenth Century* (Toronto, 1981), pp. 21-40.

[13]Quinn, op. cit., p. 317.

[14]Quoted in the *DCB*, I, p. 421.

[15]Ibid., I, pp. 87-88.

[16]Ibid., I, pp. 331-6.

[17]Ibid., I, p. 422.

[18]Marcel Trudel, *The Beginnings of New France, 1524-1663* (Toronto, 1973), p. 68.

[19]Marc Lescarbot, *Nova Francia: A Description of Acadia, 1606*, translated by P. Erondelle, 1609, with an introduction by H. P. Biggar (London, 1928), p. 90, p. 43. This is a contemporary translation of the Acadian part of Marc Lescarbot's *Histoire de la Nouvelle France* (Paris, 1609).

[20]Quoted in the *DCB*, I, p. 597.

[21]Nicolas Denys, *The Description and Natural History of the Coasts of North America* (Toronto, 1908), pp. 136-7—a translation of the second volume (*Histoire naturelle*

des peuples...de l'Amérique Septentrionale) of his two-volume account of Acadia published in 1672.

[22]*DCB*, I, p. 383; see also M. A. MacDonald, *Fortune and La Tour* (Toronto, 1982).

[23]*DCB*, I, p. 514.

[24]W. L. Grant, ed., *Voyages of Samuel De Champlain: 1604-1618* (Toronto, 1907), p. 131.

[25]Ibid., p. 136.

[26]Ibid., p. 165.

[27]*DCB*, I, pp. 367-8.

[28]Marcel Trudel, op. cit., pp. 118-81.

[29]Edna Kenton, ed., *The Jesuit Relations and Allied Documents: Travels and Explorations of the Jesuit Missionaries in North America (1610-1791)* (New York, 1954), p. 23.

[30]H.P. Biggar, ed., *The Works of Samuel de Champlain* (Champlain Society, Toronto, 1922-3), vol. VI, Appendix VII, pp. 378-9. Translation.

[31]*DCB*, I, p. 330.

[32]François Dollier de Casson, *A History of Montreal 1640-1672* (1928), translated and edited by Ralph Flenley, p. 99.

[33]Edna Kenton, op. cit., p. 181.

[34]Dollier de Casson, op. cit., p. 155.

[35]See Cornelius J. Jaenen, *Friend and Foe: Aspects of French-Amerindian Cultural Contact in the Sixteenth and Seventeenth Centuries* (Toronto, 1976); and Bruce Trigger, *The Children of Aataentsic: A History of the Huron People to 1660* (Montreal, 2 vols, 1976).

[36]Reuben Gold Thwaites, ed., *The Jesuit Relations and Allied Documents* (Cleveland, 1896-1901), X (1636), pp. 93-5.

[37]Quoted in *DCB*, I, p. 357.

[38]Joyce Marshall, ed., *Word from New France: The Selected Letters of Marie de l'Incarnation* (Toronto, 1967), p. 259.

[39]Ibid., p. 265.

[40]Ibid., pp. 288-9.

[41]Ibid., p. 297.

[42]Ibid., p. 314.

[43]Quoted in W. J. Eccles, *Canada Under Louis XIV 1663-1701* (Toronto, 1964), p. 4.

Chapter Four: New France: War, Trade, and Adaptation

[1]The English translation by J.R. Forster, *Travels into North America...* (3 vols., Warrington, Eng., and London, 1770-1) was republished with additional material as *The America of 1750: Peter Kalm's Travels in North America*, edited by Adolph B. Benson (2 vols, New York, 1927), which is still available in a reprint by Dover Publications (2 vols, New York, 1966).

[2]Benson, op. cit., II, p. 558.

[3]Ibid., I, p. 511.

[4]Ibid., I, p. 402.

[5]Yves Zoltvany, ed., *The Government of New France: Royal, Clerical, or Class Rule?* (Toronto, 1971); Terence Crowley, "Thunder Gusts': Popular Disturbances in Early French Canada', *Canadian Historical Association Historical Papers*, 1979, pp. 11-31.

[6]Order of the Bishop of Quebec, Ville Marie, 26 April 1719, National Archives of Canada, Robinson Collection, II, 34, translated and quoted by Cameron Nish and Pierre Harvey, eds, in *The Social Structures of New France* (Toronto, 1968), p. 16.

[7]Cornelius J. Jaenen, *The Role of the Church in New France* (Toronto, 1976); W. J.

Eccles, 'The Role of the Church in New France', in Eccles, *Essays on New France* (Toronto, 1987), pp. 26-37.

[8]Quoted in W. J. Eccles, 'The Social, Economic, and Political Significance of the Military Establishment in New France', in Eccles, *Essays on New France*, p. 111.

[9]Baron de Lahontan, *Mémoires de l'Amérique septentrionale* (1703), quoted in J.M. Bumsted, ed., *Documentary Problems in Canadian History*, I (Georgetown, 1969), p. 45.

[10]Ibid., p. 45.

[11]Ibid., p. 45.

[12]Quoted in Eccles, op. cit., p. 114.

[13]Quoted in Bumsted, op. cit., I, p. 47.

[14]*DCB*, II, p. 400.

[15]The best modern biographies are: Nellie Crouse, *Le Moyne d'Iberville: Soldier of New France* (Ithaca, NY, 1954) and Guy Frégault, *Iberville le conquérant* (Montreal, 1944).

[16]Quoted in H.A. Innis, *The Cod Fisheries: The History of an International Economy* (Toronto, 1940), pp. 136-7.

[17]R. C. Harris, 'The Extension of France into Rural Canada', in J. R. Gibson, ed., *European Settlement and Development in North America* (Toronto, 1978).

[18]E. B. Greene, *American Population Before the Federal Census of 1790* (New York, 1932).

[19]Quoted in W.J. Eccles, *The Canadian Frontier 1534-1760* (Revised Edition, Albuquerque, 1983), p. 104.

[20]Ibid., p. 105.

[21]R. Cole Harris, *The Seigneurial System in Early Canada: A Geographical Study* (Toronto, 1966); Marcel Trudel, *The Seigneurial Regime* (Ottawa, 1963); Morris Altman, 'Seigniorial Tenure in New France, 1688-1739: An Essay on Income Distribution and Retarded Economic Development', *Historical Reflections*, 10 (Fall 1983), pp. 334-75.

[22]A stimulating discussion of such matters is contained in Roberta Hamilton, 'Feudal Society and Colonization: A Critique and Reinterpretation of the Historiography of New France', in Donald Akenson, ed., *Canadian Papers in Rural History* (Gananoque, Ont., 1988), pp. 17-136.

[23]Cameron Nish, *Les Bourgeois-gentilshommes de la Nouvelle-France, 1729-1748* (Montreal, 1968).

[24]See the entries on Boucault and Charbly Saint-Ange in the *DCB*, III.

[25]J. F. Bosher, *The Canada Merchants, 1713-1763* (Oxford, 1987); Dale Miquelon, *New France, 1701-1744: A Supplement to Europe* (Toronto, 1987).

[26]Adam Shortt, *Canadian Currency and Exchange under French Rule* (Montreal, 1974).

[27]*DCB*, IV, pp. 471-3.

[28]Jacques Mathieu, *La Construction navale royale à Québec, 1739-1759* (Quebec, 1971); Albert Tessier, *Les Forges du Saint-Maurice, 1729-1883* (Trois Rivières, 1952).

[29]Hubert Charbonneau et al., 'Le Comportement démographique des voyageurs sous le régime français', *Histoire Sociale / Social History*, 21 (1978), pp. 120-33.

[30]Benson, op. cit., II, pp. 416-17.

[31]Louise Déchène, *Habitants et marchands de Montréal au xviie siècle* (Paris, 1974); 'The Growth of Montreal in the 18th Century', in J.M. Bumsted, ed., *Canadian History Before Confederation: Essays and Interpretations* (Toronto, 1979), pp. 154-67.

[32]Alison Prentice et al., *Canadian Women: A History* (Toronto, 1988), pp. 41-64.

[33]Jacques Henripin, *La Population canadienne au début de xviiie siècle* (Paris, 1954).

[34]"Mémoire on the Present State of Canada Attributed to Bougainville, 1757',

translated by Cameron Nish and P. Harvey in their *The Social Structures of New France* (Toronto, 1968), p. 76.

[35]Quoted by Nish and Harvey, op. cit., p. 75.

[36]Benson, op. cit., II, p. 554.

[37]R. Cole Harris, 'The French Background of Immigrants to Canada before 1700', in J.M. Bumsted, ed., *Interpreting Canada's Past* (Toronto, 1986), I, pp. 52-62.

[38]Phillippe Barbaud, 'Retour sur l'Enigme de la Francisation des Premiers Canadiens: Le Choc des patois en Nouvelle-France', in *APART: Papers from the 1984 Ottawa Conference on Language, Culture and Literary Identity in Canada*, in *Canadian Literature*, Supplement I (May 1987), pp. 51-7.

[39]I. K. Steele, *The English Atlantic, Sixteen Seventy Five to Seventeen Forty: An Explanation of Connection and Community* (New York, 1986).

[40]Quoted in Helmut Kallmann, *A History of Music in Canada 1534-1914* (Toronto, 1960; reprinted 1987), p. 12.

[41]Ibid., p. 84-5.

[42]Benson, op. cit., II, p. 460.

[43]Jean Palardy, *The Early Furniture of French Canada* (Toronto, 1965).

[44]Peter Moogk, ' "Thieving Buggers" and "Stupid Sluts": Insults and Popular Culture in New France', in J.M. Bumsted, ed., *Interpreting Canada's Past*, I, pp. 63-83.

Chapter Five: The Atlantic Region; The Cockpit of Empire 1670-1758

[1]Max Savelle, *The Origins of American Diplomacy: The International History of Anglo-America, 1492-1763* (NY, 1967), pp. 373-86.

[2]Most of the documents in the Acadian affair, including the minutes of this meeting, were published by Thomas B. Akins in *Selections from the Public Documents of the Province of Nova Scotia* (Halifax, 1869).

[3]John Winthrop to Fitz-John Winthrop, Boston 1707, *Collections of the Massachusetts Historical Society*, 6th ser., III (1889), pp. 387-8.

[4]N. Dièreville, *Relation of the Voyage to Port Royal in Acadia or New France*, translated by Alice Webster, ed. with notes by J.C. Webster (Champlain Society, Toronto, 1933), p. 95.

[5]Ibid., p. 166.

[6]Ibid., p. 183-4.

[7]Quoted in J. B. Brebner, *New England's Outpost: Acadia Before the Conquest of Canada* (New York, 1927), pp. 86 ff.

[8]Translated by Naomi Griffiths in her collection *The Acadian Deportation, Deliberate Perfidy or Cruel Necessity?* (Toronto, 1969), p. 25.

[9]Thomas Hutchinson, *History of the Province of Massachusetts Bay* (Boston, 1767), II, p. 408.

[10]Alan Greer, 'Mutiny at Louisbourg, December 1744', *Histoire Sociale/Social History*, 10 (1977), pp. 305-36.

[11]G. M. Wrong, ed., *Louisbourg in 1745: The Anonymous Lettre d'un Habitant de Louisbourg* (New York, 1897), p. 15.

[12]Louis Effingham de Forest, ed., *Louisbourg Journals 1745* (New York, 1932), p. 12.

[13]Quoted in John A. Schutz, *William Shirley* (Boston, 1961), p. 101.

[14]De Forest, op. cit., p. 715.

[15]The Duke of Bedford to Mr. Stone, 10 November 1746, British Library Additional Manuscripts 32713, pp. 426-7.

[16]*Boston Independent Advertiser*, 14 November 1748.

[17]Lord John Russell, ed., *Correspondence of John, Fourth Duke of Bedford* (London, 1842), Bedford to the Duke of Cumberland, 28 October 1748, I, pp. 572-3.

[18]Paul Mascarene, 'Description of Nova Scotia', 1720, Public Archives of Nova Scotia, A/11.

[19]'Representation of the State of His Majesty's Province of Nova Scotia', 8 November 1745, National Archives of Canada, A27.

[20]C. Grant Head, *Eighteenth-Century Newfoundland: A Geographer's Perspective* (Toronto, 1976), p. 73.

[21]Ibid., *passim*.

[22]Ibid., pp. 76-7.

[23]Quoted in Brebner, op. cit., p. 187.

[24]George T. Bates, 'The Great Exodus of 1749 or the Cornwallis Settlers Who Didn't', *Collections of the Nova Scotia Historical Society*, 38 (1973), pp. 27-62.

[25]Quoted in W. P. Bell, *The 'Foreign Protestants' and the Settlement of Nova Scotia: The History of a Piece of Arrested British Colonial Policy in the Eighteenth Century* (Toronto, 1961), p. 344n.

[26]Ibid., p. 109n.

[27]Ibid., pp. 436-7.

[28]Ibid., pp. 417-42, esp. p. 435.

[29]John Brenner, 'Canadian Policy Towards the Acadians in 1751', *Canadian Historical Review*, 12 (1931), pp. 284-7.

[30]Quoted in Brebner, op. cit., p. 220.

[31]Ibid., p. 221.

[32]'Journals of Colonel John Winslow', *Collections of Nova Scotia Historical Society*, IV (1883), pp. 113-246.

[33]Richard G. Lowe, 'Massachusetts and the Acadians', *William and Mary Quarterly*, 3rd ser., 25 (1968), pp. 212-29.

[34]Quoted in Brebner, op. cit., p. 230.

[35]Quoted in L.F.S. Upton, *Micmacs and Colonists: Indian-White Relations in the Maritimes, 1713-1867* (Vancouver, 1979), p. 52.

[36]Quoted in Brebner, op. cit., p. 135.

[37]Quoted in Brebner, op. cit., p. 257.

[38]Kimberly Maynard Smith, 'Divorce in Nova Scotia 1700-1890', in Jim Phillips and James Girard, eds, *Essays in the History of Canadian Law vol. III Nova Scotia* (Toronto, 1990), pp. 232-71.

Chapter Six:
1759-1781 The Expansion and Contraction of Britain's North American Empire

[1]Quoted in C.P. Stacey, *Quebec 1759: The Siege and the Battle* (Toronto, 1959), p. 134.

[2]Ibid., pp. 144-5.

[3]Ibid., pp. 64-5.

[4]George Townshend, quoted in Stacey, op. cit., p. 93.

[5]Quoted in Gordon Donaldson, *Battle for a Continent; Quebec 1759* (Toronto, 1973), p. 89.

[6]Quoted in Stacey, op. cit., p. 118.

[7]Ibid., pp. 97-8.

[8]Ibid., p. 101.

[9]Ibid., pp. 124-5.

[10]Verner W. Crane, ed., 'Hints Relative to the Division and Government of the Conquered and Newly Acquired Countries in America,' *Mississippi Valley Historical Review*, 8 (1922), p. 371.

[11]R.A. Humphreys, 'Lord Shelburne and the Proclamation of 1763,' *English Historical Review*, 41 (1934), pp. 258-64.

[12]John MacDonald to J.F.W. Desbarres, 8 November 1795, DesBarres Papers, National Archives of Canada.

[13]Quoted in Hilda Neatby, *The Quebec Act: Protest and Policy* (Toronto, 1972), pp. 38-9.

[14]Ibid., p. 40.

[15]C. P. Lucas, ed., *Lord Durham's Report on the Affairs of British North America* (Oxford, 1912), II, pp. 63-5.

[16]Quoted in George Stanley, *Canada Invaded*, 1775-1776 (Toronto, 1977), p. 27.

[17]Ibid., p. 29.

[18]Quoted in Robert Hatch, *Thrust for Canada* (New York, 1979), p. 60.

[19]Ibid., pp. 84, 85.

[20]Quoted in Stanley, op. cit., p. 103.

[21]Quoted in Gwynne Dyer and Tina Viljoen, *The Defence of Canada: In the Arms of the Empire 1760-1939* (Toronto, 1990), p. 49.

[22]Ibid., p. 50.

[23]Ibid., p. 48.

[24]Ernest A. Clark, 'Cumberland Planters and the Aftermath of the Attack on Fort Cumberland' in Margaret Conrad, ed., *They Planted Well: New England Planters in Maritime Canada* (Fredericton, 1988), p. 49.

[25]Ibid.

[26]C. Grant Head, *Eighteenth-Century Newfoundland: A Geographer's Perspective* (Toronto, 1976), p. 197.

[27]Ibid., p. 180.

[28]*DCB*, V, pp. 513-14.

[29]Quoted in Alan Everest, *Moses Hazen and the Canadian Refugees in the American Revolution* (Syracuse, 1976), p. 62.

[30]Harold A. Innis, ed., *The Diary of Simeon Perkins 1766-1780* (Champlain Society, Toronto, 1948), p. 134.

[31]Ibid., p. 145.

[32]J.M. Bumsted, *Henry Alline 1748-1784* (Toronto, 1971; reprinted Hantsport, 1984), p. 37.

[33]Ibid., p. 47.

[34]Captain John MacDonald to Lord George Germane, 30 October 1776, Public Record Office, C.O. 217/53.

Chapter Seven: The New Immigrants: Peopling British North America, 1783-1845

[1]James N. St. G. Walker, *The Black Loyalists: The Search for a Promised Land in Nova Scotia and Sierra Leone 1783-1870* (Halifax, 1976), pp. 1-18.

[2]Quoted in J.M. Bumsted, ed., *Understanding the Loyalists* (Sackville, 1986), p. 34.

[3]Quoted in J.J. Talman, ed., *Loyalist Narratives from Upper Canada* (Champlain Society, Toronto, 1946), p.xxiv.

[4]Ibid., pp. xxxi-xxxii.

[5]Ibid., p. xxxvi.

[6]Quoted in E.C. Wright, *The Loyalists of New Brunswick* (Fredericton, 1955), pp. 41-2.

[7]Neal MacKinnon, *This Unfriendly Soil: The Loyalist Experience in Nova Scotia 1783-1791* (Kingston & Montreal, 1986).

[8]Mary Beth Norton, 'Eighteenth-Century American Women in Peace and War: The Case of the Loyalists', in *William and Mary Quarterly*, Third Series, Volume 33, 1976, pp. 386-409.

[9]Quoted in Walker, op. cit., p. 1.

[10]Ibid., p. 2

[11]Ibid., p. 8.

[12]Ibid., p. 21.

[13]Quoted in Ann Condon, *The Envy of the American States* (Fredericton, 1984), p. 100.

[14]Quoted in David Bell, *Early Loyalist Saint John* (Fredericton, 1984), pp. 64-5.

[15]Ibid., p. 75.

[16]Population data from Volume IV of the 1871 Canadian census; immigration data from the appendices in Helen I. Cowan, *British Emigration to British North America; The First Hundred Years* (Toronto, 1961).

[17]J.M. Bumsted, *The People's Clearance* (Edinburgh and Winnipeg, 1982), pp. 129-154.

[18]See J.M. Bumsted, ed., *Collected Writings of Lord Selkirk, 1799-1809*, I (Winnipeg, 1984), pp. 101-241.

[19]See J.M. Bumsted, ed., *The Collected Writings of Lord Selkirk, 1810-1820*, II (Winnipeg, 1988), pp. 263, 262.

[20]Robert Lamond, *A Narrative of the Rise and Progress of Emigration from the Counties of Lanark and Renfrew to the New Settlements in Upper Canada* (Glasgow, 1821), pp. 103-4.

[21]Thomas Carlyle, *Chartism* in *Works*, 29, p. 203.

[22]Quoted in G. Palmer Patterson, *The Canadian Indian: Indian Peoples of Canada* (Toronto, 1982), pp. 86-7.

[23]Quoted in Helen I. Cowan, *British Immigration Before Confederation* (CHA, 1968), p. 79.

[24]Quoted in Peter Thomas, *Strangers from a Secret Land* (Toronto, 1986), p. 75.

[25]Ibid., p. 105.

[26]Ibid., p. 139.

[27]Wilson Benson, *Life and Adventures of Wilson Benson. Written by Himself* (Toronto, 1876), p. 18.

Chapter Eight: The Resource Economy and its Society, 1783-1840

[1]*DCB*, VIII, pp. 845-50.

[2]*DCB*, VIII, pp. 4-12.

[3]H. Clare Pentland, *Labour and Capital in Canada: 1650-1860* (Toronto, 1981), p.121.

[4]Ibid., p. 110.

[5]John Reeves, *History of the Government of the Island of Newfoundland*...(London, 1793), quoted in H.A. Innis, *The Cod Fisheries: The History of An International Economy* (Toronto, 1940), p. 289.

[6]Shannon Ryan, 'The Newfoundland Salt Cod Trade in the Nineteenth Century,' in James Hiller and Peter Neary, *Newfoundland in the Nineteenth and Twentieth Centuries: Essays in Interpretation* (Toronto, 1980), pp. 40-66.

[7]Quoted in E.T.D. Chambers, *The Fisheries of the Province of Quebec* (Quebec, 1912), p. 117.

[8]Quoted in Innis, op. cit., p. 281.

[9]Susan Fairlie, 'British Statistics of Grain Imports from Canada and the U.S.A., 1791-1900', in D. Alexander and R. Ommer, *Volumes not Values: Canadian Sailing Ships and World Trades* (St John's, 1979), pp. 187-8.

[10]*Quebec Gazette*, 22 April 1842, quoted in A. R. M. Lower, *Great Britain's Woodyard* (Montreal, 1973), p. 88.

[11]Graeme Wynn, *Timber Colony: A Historical Geography of Early 19th Century New Brunswick* (Toronto, 1980), *passim*.

[12]See particularly John McCallum, *Agriculture and Development in Quebec and Ontario until 1870* (Toronto, 1980).

[13]See Douglas McCalla, *The Upper Canada Trade 1834-1872: A Study of the Buchanans' Business* (Toronto, 1979).

[14]Lewis R. Fischer, ' "An Engine, Yet Moderate": James Peake, Entrepreneurial Behaviour and the Shipping Industry of Nineteenth Century Prince Edward Island', in Lewis R. Fischer and Eric Sager, eds, *The Enterprising Canadians: Entrepreneurs and Economic Development in Eastern Canada, 1820-1914* (St John's, 1979), pp. 97-118.

[15]Quoted in Wynn, op. cit., p. 153.

[16]Edith G. Firth, ed., *The Town of York: 1815-1834* (Champlain Society, Toronto, 1966), p. lxxxii.

[17]Anna Jameson, *Winter Studies and Summer Rambles in Canada* (London, 1838), p. 67.

[18]Ibid., p. 17.

[19]Edward Talbot, *Five Year's Residence in the Canadas* (London, 1824), I, p. 66.

[20]Quoted in Jean-Claude Marsan, *Montreal in Evolution: Historical Analysis of the Development of Montreal's Architecture and Urban Environment* (Montreal, 1981), p. 146.

[21]Ibid., p. 145.

[22]Quoted in Eric Arthur, *Toronto: No Mean City* (3rd ed., Toronto, 1986, revised by Stephen A. Otto), p. 44.

[23]Quoted in Patrick Brode, *Sir John Beverley Robinson* (Toronto, 1984), p. 175.

[24]Quoted in Arthur, op. cit., pp. 43-4.

[25]Watson Kirkconnell, ed., *The Diary of Deacon Elihu Woodworth* (Wolfville, 1972), p. 7.

[26]On regional élites, see J.K. Johnson, *Becoming Prominent: Regional Leadership in Upper Canada, 1791-1841* (Montreal and Kingston, 1989).

[27]Quoted in J. Fingard, 'The Winter's Tale', in J.M. Bumsted, ed., *Interpreting Canada's Past*, I (Toronto, 1986), p. 255.

[28]Quoted in Fingard, 'The Relief of the Unemployed Poor in Saint John, Halifax, and St. John's, 1815-1860' in David A. Frank and Phillip A. Buckner, eds., *The Acadiensis Reader*, I, (rev. ed., Fredericton, 1988), p. 197.

[29]Quoted in Allan Greer, *Peasant, Lord, and Merchant: Rural Society in Three Quebec Parishes 1740-1840* (Toronto, 1985), p. 186.

[30]Catharine Parr Traill, *The Backwoods of Canada* (London, 1836), p. 101.

[31]See Brian Lee Coffey, 'The Pioneer House in Southern Ontario, Canada: Construction Material Use and Resultant Forms to 1850', unpublished Ph.D. dissertation, University of Oregon, 1982.

[32]Traill, op. cit., pp. 98-101.

[33]Peter Ward, *Courtship, Love, and Marriage in Nineteenth-Century English Canada* (Montreal and Kingston, 1990), p. 158.

[34]Ibid., p. 158.

[35]Quoted in L.F.S. Upton, *Micmacs and Colonists: Indian-White Relations in the Maritimes, 1713-1867* (Vancouver, 1979), p. 84.

[36]Quoted in the *DCB*, VII, p. 685.

Chapter Nine: Politics and Culture, 1783–1840

[1]Quoted in J. Murray Beck, *Joseph Howe* (Montreal and Kingston, 1982), I, 134.

[2]Ibid., p. 140.

[3]*Quebec Gazette*, 5 July 1792, quoted in Jacques Monet, ed., 'Electoral Battles in French Canada, 1792-1848', in J.M. Bumsted, ed., *Documentary Problems in Canadian History* (Georgetown, 1969), I, p. 175.

[4]*DCB*, VII, p. 865.

[5]*DCB*, IX, pp. 330-6.

[6]*DCB*, V, pp. 347-57.

[7]J.M. Bumsted, 'The Loyal Electors,' *The Island Magazine*, 8 (1980), pp. 8-14.

[8]*DCB*, VI, pp. 41-9.

[9]*DCB*, VII, p. 40.

[10]Gerald M. Craig, *Upper Canada: The Formative Years 1784-1841* (Toronto, 1963), p. 205.

[11]Quoted in David Flint, *William Lyon Mackenzie: Rebel Against Authority*, Canadian Lives (Toronto, 1971), p. 78.

[12]Quoted in Craig, op. cit., p. 219.

[13]Quoted in the *DCB*, X, p. 573.

[14]Margaret Fairley, ed., *The Selected Writings of William Lyon Mackenzie* (Toronto, 1960), p. 217.

[15]Quoted in the *DCB*, X, p. 571.

[16]Fairley, op. cit., p. 223.

[17]*P.E.I. Assembly Journals*, 1832, Appendix A.

[18]*Brockville Recorder*, 14 March 1833.

[19]Quoted in P.A. Buckner, *The Transition to Responsible Government: British Policy in British North America 1815-1850* (Westport, Conn., 1985), pp. 232-3.

[20]Quoted in the *DCB*, X, p. 574.

[21]Quoted in Fernand Ouellet, 'The 1837/8 Rebellions in Lower Canada as a Social Phenomenon', in J.M. Bumsted, ed., *Interpreting Canada's Past* (Toronto, 1986), I, p. 211.

[22]Ibid., p. 214.

[23]Gerald M. Craig, ed., *Lord Durham's Report*, Carleton Library (Toronto, 1963), pp. 22-3.

[24]Quoted in David Flint, *John Strachan: Pastor and Politician*, Canadian Lives (Toronto, 1971), p. 85.

[25]Quoted in S.F. Wise, 'Sermon Literature and Canadian Intellectual History', in J.M. Bumsted, ed., *Canadian History Before Confederation: Essays and Interpretations* (Georgetown, 1972), p. 257.

[26]Ibid., p. 261.

[27]Quoted in Flint, *Strachan*, p. 89.

[28]Quoted in L.F.S. Upton, ed., 'The Quebec School Question, 1784-90', in J.M. Bumsted, ed., *Documentary Problems*, I, p. 104.

[29]Quoted in Fairley, op. cit., p. 84.

[30]Ibid.

[31]J. Donald Wilson, 'The Ryerson Years in Canada West' in J. Donald Wilson, et al., *Canadian Education: A History* (Toronto, 1970).

[32]*A Man of Sentiment: The Memoirs of Philippe-Joseph Aubert de Gaspé 1786-1871*, translated by Jane Brierley (Montreal, 1988).

[33]Quoted in William Sherwood Fox, 'School Readers in Early Canadian Education', in J.M. Bumsted, ed., *Canadian History Before Confederation*, p. 368.

[34]Introduction to Thomas McCulloch, *The Stepsure Letters*, New Canadian Library (Toronto, 1960), p. ix.

[35]Quoted in Margaret MacDonnell, *The Emigrant Experience: Songs of Highland Emigrants in North America* (Toronto, 1982), pp. 69-73.

[36]Don Morrow *et al.*, *A Concise History of Sport in Canada* (Toronto, 1989), p. 109 and *passim*.

[37]D.C. Harvey, ed., *The Heart of Howe: Selections from the Letters and Speeches of Joseph Howe* (Toronto, 1939), pp. 49-66.

Chapter Ten: Developing the Economy, 1840-1865

[1]Quoted in Elaine Mitchell, 'Edward Watkin and the Buying-Out of the Hudson's Bay Company,' *Canadian Historical Review*, vol 34 (1953), p. 242.

[2]Ibid., p. 224.

[3]Ibid., p. 235.

[4]Quoted in Bernard Semmel, *The Rise of Free Trade Imperialism* (Cambridge, 1970), pp. 23-4.

[5]Ibid., p. 132.

[6]Ibid., p. 145.

[7]Quoted in Donald Creighton, *The Empire of the St Lawrence* (Toronto, 1956). p. 369.

[8]Quoted in Gilbert Tucker, *The Canadian Commercial Revolution 1845-1851* (Ottawa, 1970), p. 131.

[9]Ibid., p. 135.

[10]Ibid., p. 136.

[11]Ibid., p. 139.

[12]Quoted in Donald C. Masters, *The Reciprocity Treaty of 1854*, (Ottawa, 1963), p. 5.

[13]Ibid., p. 9.

[14]Ibid., p. 10.

[15]Tucker, op. cit., p. 110.

[16]Quoted in Masters, op. cit., p. 42.

[17]Quoted in T.C. Keefer, *The Philosophy of Railroads* (Toronto, 1972), edited by V.C. Nelles, p. 6.

[18]Ibid., p. 27.

[19]Quoted in the *DCB*, IX, p. 526.

[20]Quoted in George P. de T. Glazebrook, *A History of Transportation in Canada* (Ottawa, 1964), I, p. 169.

[21]Quoted in Keefer, op. cit., p. 141.

[22]Ibid., p. 158-9.

[23]Ibid., p. 9.

[24]Quoted in Paul Craven and Tom Traves, 'Canadian Railways as Manufacturers, 1850-1880', *CHA Historical Papers*, 1983, pp. 254-81.

[25]Quoted in John McCallum, *Unequal Beginnings: Agriculture and Economic Development in Quebec and Ontario Until 1870* (Toronto, 1980), pp. 96-7.

[26]Peter Cook, *Massey at the Brink: The Story of Canada's Greatest Multinational, and Its Struggle to Survive* (Don Mills, 1981).

[27]Quoted in R. L. Jones, *History of Agriculture in Ontario, 1613-1880* (Toronto, 1946), p. xi.

[28]Quoted in McCallum, op. cit., p. 97.

[29]Quoted in Bryan D. Palmer, *Working-Class Experience: The Rise and Reconstitution of Canadian Labour 1800-1980* (Markham, 1983), pp. 33-4.

[30]Quoted in Stephen Langdon, 'The Emergence of the Canadian Working-Class Movement, 1845-1867', in J.M. Bumsted, ed., *Interpreting Canada's Past*, I, p. 352.

[31]James E. Fitzgerald, *An Examination of the Charter and Proceedings of the HBC* (London, 1849), *passim*.

[32]Quoted in Robin Fisher, *Contact and Conflict: Indian-European Relations in British Columbia 1734-1890* (Vancouver, 1979), p. 59.

[33]Quoted in J.M. Bumsted, ed., *Documentary Problems in Canadian History*, I (Georgetown, 1969), p. 220.

[34]John Palliser, *Journals, Detailed Reports, and Observations Relative to the Exploration, by Captain Palliser* (London, 1863), p. 18.

[35]Quoted in Douglas Owram, *Promise of Eden: The Canadian Expansionist Movement and the Idea of the West 1800-1900* (Toronto, 1980), p. 69.

[36]Dorothy Blakey Smith, *James Douglas: Father of British Columbia*, Canadian Lives (Toronto, 1971), p. 63.

[37]Quoted in Margaret A. Ormsby, *British Columbia: A History* (Toronto, 1958), p. 142.

[38]Ibid., p. 163.

[39]Ibid., p. 170.

[40]Quoted in Richard Preston, ed., *For Friends at Home: A Scottish Emigrant's Letters from Canada, California, and the Cariboo, 1844-64* (Montreal, 1974), p. 305.

[41]Quoted in Fisher, op. cit., p. 104.

[42]Ibid., p. 105.

Chapter Eleven: Political Reform and Unification 1840–1867

[1]J.M.S. Careless, *Brown of the Globe, Volume One: The Voice of Upper Canada, 1818-1859* (Toronto, 1959), p. 315.

[2]Ibid., p. 321.

[3]Quoted in P.A. Buckner, *The Transition to Responsible Government: British Policy in British North America 1815-1859* (Westport, Conn.), p. 301.

[4]Quoted in Gertrude E. Gunn, *The Political History of Newfoundland, 1832-1864* (Toronto, 1966), p. 113.

[5]Quoted in J.M.S. Careless, *The Union of the Canadas: 1841-1857* (Toronto, 1972), p. 169.

[6]Quoted in Ian Robertson, 'The Bible Question in P.E.I.', in Philip A. Buckner and David A. Frank, eds, *Atlantic Canada Before Confederation* (Fredericton, 1985), p. 282.

[7]Quoted in Careless, *Union of the Canadas*, p. 202.

[8]Quoted in G.F.G. Stanley, *A Short History of the Canadian Constitution* (Toronto, 1969), pp. 75-6.

[9]Quoted in Patrick Brode, *Sir John Beverley Robinson: Bone and Sinew of the Compact* (Toronto, 1984), pp. 90-1.

[10]Ibid., p. 91.

[11]Quoted in A.S. Raspovich, ed., 'National Awakening: Canada at Mid-Century', in J.M. Bumsted, ed., *Documentary Problems in Canadian History* (Georgetown, 1969), I, p. 250.

[12]Quoted in Robert Burns, 'D'Arcy McGee: A Father of Confederation', in J.M. Bumsted, ed., *Documentary Problems*, p. 273.

[13]Quoted in Peter B. Waite, *The Life and Times of Confederation, 1864-1867: Politics, Newspapers, Union of British North America* (Toronto, 1962), pp. 80-1.

[14]Ibid., p. 95.

[15]Ibid., p. 98.

[16]William Garvie (editor of the Halifax *Citizen*), *Barney Rooney's Letters on Confederation, Botheration and Political Transmogrification* (Halifax, 1865).

[17]Quoted in A.I. Silver, 'Confederation and Quebec', in J.M. Bumsted, ed., *Interpreting Canada's Past* (Toronto, 1986), II, p. 408.

[18]Ibid., p. 412.

[19]Quoted in Peter Neary and Patrick O'Flaherty, eds, *Part of the Main: An Illustrated History of Newfoundland and Labrador* (St John's, 1983), p.92.

[20]Quoted in Waite, op. cit., pp. 232-3, 240.

[21]Ibid., p. 268.

[22]Ibid., p. 194.

[23]Ibid., p. 207.

[24]Ibid., pp. 226-7.

[25]Ibid., p. 294.

Chapter Twelve: Mid-Victorian Society

[1]Quoted in V. Veronica Strong-Boag, ed., *A Woman with a Purpose: The Diaries of Elizabeth Smith 1872-1884* (Toronto, 1980), pp. 295-6.

[2]J.I. Little, *Nationalism, Capitalism, and Colonization in Nineteenth-Century Quebec* (Montreal and Kingston, 1989), p. 17.

[3]David Gagan, *Hopeful Travellers: Families, Lands and Social Change in Mid-Victorian Peel County, Canada North* (Toronto, 1981), p. 46.

[4]Ibid., pp. 44-5.

[5]Quoted in Cecil Houston and William Smyth, *Irish Emigration and Canadian Settlement* (Kingston and Montreal, 1990), p. 321.

[6]Wilson Benson, *Life and Adventures of Wilson Benson. Written by Himself* (Toronto, 1876).

[7]Frances H. Early, ed., *Immigrant Odyssey: a French-Canadian Habitant in New England* (Orono, 1991).

[8]Aline Gubbay and Sally Hooff, *Montreal's Little Mountain* (Montreal, 1979).

[9]Luc d'Iberville-Moreau, *Lost Montreal* (Toronto, 1975), pp. 87, 96, 92-4; Aline Gubbay, *Montreal: The Mountain and the River* (Montreal, 1981), pp. 78-80.

[10]Gilbert Stelter and Alan F.J. Artibise, *The Canadian City: Essays in Urban History* (Toronto, 1977) pp. 82-3.

[11] Quoted in Bettina Bradbury, 'The Family Economy and Work in an Industrializing City: Montreal in the 1870s', in J.M. Bumsted, ed., *Interpreting Canada's Past* (Toronto, 1986), II, p. 102.

[12] Ibid., p. 96.

[13] Ibid., p. 109.

[14] Ibid., p. 111.

[15] Joy L. Santink, *Timothy Eaton and the Rise of His Department Store* (Toronto, 1990), p. 122.

[16] Quoted in Alison Prentice et al., *Canadian Women: A History* (Toronto, 1988), p. 143.

[17] Claudette Lacellie, *Urban Domestic Servants in 19th-Century Canada* (Ottawa, 1987).

[18] Quoted in Peter S. Li, *The Chinese in Canada* (Toronto, 1988), p. 24.

[19] Ibid., p. 22.

[20] J.R. Miller, *Skyscrapers Hide the Heavens* (Toronto, 1989), pp. 99-117.

[21] Ibid., p. 153.

[22] Ibid., p. 162.

[23] Robin Fisher, *Contact and Conflict: Indian-European Relations in British Columbia, 1774-1890* (Vancouver, 1979), pp. 175-211.

[24] Lovell Clark, ed., *The Guibord Affair* (Toronto, 1971).

[25] William Westfall, *The Protestant Culture of Nineteenth Century Ontario* (Montreal and Kingston, 1989).

[26] Quoted in Ramsay Cook and Wendy Mitchinson, eds, *The Proper Sphere: Woman's Place in Canadian Society* (Toronto, 1976), p. 205.

[27] Houston and Smyth, op. cit., p. 4.

[28] Ibid., p. 122.

Chapter Thirteen: The Completion of Confederation

[1] Quoted in George F.G. Stanley, *Louis Riel* (Toronto, 1963), p. 63.

[2] Ibid.

[3] Quoted in Hartwell Bowsfield, *Louis Riel: The Rebel and the Hero*, Canadian Lives (Toronto, 1971), p. 35.

[4] Quoted in Margaret A. Ormsby, *British Columbia: A History* (Toronto, 1958), p. 245.

[5] Ibid., p. 248.

[6] Robert G. Cail, *Land, Man, and the Law: The Disposal of Crown Lands in British Columbia 1871-1913* (Vancouver, 1974).

[7] Quoted in Frank P. MacKinnon, *The Government of Prince Edward Island* (1951), p. 136.

[8] Quoted in James Hiller, 'Confederation Defeated: The Newfoundland Election of 1869', in James Hiller and Peter Neary, eds., *Newfoundland in the Nineteenth and Twentieth Centuries* (Toronto, 1980), pp. 70-1.

[9] A.I. Bloomfield, *Patterns of Infrastructure in International Investment Before 1914* (Princeton, 1968), pp. 42-4.

[10] M. Simon, 'New British Investments in Canada 1865-1914', *Canadian Journal of Economics*, 3 (1970), p. 241.

[11] Quoted in W.T. Easterbrook and M.H. Watkins, eds., *Approaches to Canadian Economic History* (Ottawa, 1962), p. 238.

[12] *Confederation Debates in the Province of Canada*, p. 511.

[13] Quoted in Ramsay Cook, *Provincial Autonomy, Minority Rights and the Compact Theory 1867-1921* (Ottawa, 1969), p. 10.

[14] Ibid., p. 11.

[15] Ibid., p. 13.

[16] Ibid., p. 31.

[17] Ibid., p. 33.

[18] Quoted in Carl Berger, 'The True North Strong and Free', in J.M. Bumsted, ed., *Interpreting Canada's Past*, II, (Toronto, 1986), pp. 154-60.

[19] Quoted in A.W. Rasporich, 'National Awakening: Canada at Mid-Century', in J.M. Bumsted, ed., *Documentary Problems in Canadian History* (Georgetown, 1969), I, p. 225.

[20] Quoted in Moncrieff Williamson, *Robert Harris 1849-1919: An Unconventional Biography* (Toronto, 1970), p. 64.

[21] The Royal Society of Canada, *Fifty Years' Retrospect 1882-1932* (Toronto, 1932), pp. 91-2.

[22] For further discussion, see Dennis Reid, *Our Own Country Canada: Being an Account of the National Aspirations of the Principal Landscape Artists in Montreal and Toronto 1860-1890* (National Gallery of Canada, Ottawa, 1979), pp. 298ff.

[23] Quoted in Neil McDonald, 'Canadianization and the Curriculum: Setting the Stage, 1867-1890', in E.B. Titley and Peter J. Miller, eds., *Education in Canada: An Interpretation* (Calgary, 1982), p. 97.

[24] Ibid., p. 100.

[25] Dale McIntosh, *History of Music in British Columbia 1850-1950* (Victoria, 1989).

[26] Quoted in Helmut Kallmann, *A History of Music in Canada* (Toronto, 1987), pp. 137-8.

[27] Don Morrow et al., *A Concise History of Sport in Canada* (Toronto, 1989), pp. 45 ff., 109 ff.

[28] Quoted in D.N. Sprague, 'The Manitoba Land Question, 1870-1882', in J.M. Bumsted, ed., *Interpreting Canada's Past*, II, p. 4.

[29] Quoted in the *DCB*, XI, p. 746.

[30] Quoted in Bowsfield, op. cit., p. 116.

[31] Ibid., p. 121.

[32] Ibid., p. 122.

[33] Ibid., p. 153.

[34] Quoted in Barbara Robertson, *Wilfrid Laurier: The Great Conciliator*, Canadian Lives (Toronto, 1971), pp. 50-1.

[35] Quoted in Peter Li, *The Chinese in Canada* (Toronto, 1988), p. 29.

[36] Quoted in A.I. Silver, *The French-Canadian Idea of Confederation, 1864-1900* (Toronto, 1982), p. 147.

Suggestions for Further Reading

These brief bibliographies attached to each chapter are not intended to be comprehensive: they provide merely an introduction to the complex literature. For general works covering more than one chapter, see the General Bibliography on pp. 428-9.

Chapter One:The People of Early North America
The history of Canada before the arrival of the first Europeans is, of course, that of the native peoples. It is a history in which there are no written records of the ancestors of people who have in recent years become extremely sensitive about the treatment of their past. This combination produces a very volatile literature with rapid shifts in terminology and conceptualization. The older term for this period— 'pre-history'—is no longer acceptable in many quarters, for example, because it suggests a European bias. The best discussion of these problems is in Bruce Trigger, *Natives and Newcomers: Canada's 'Heroic Age' Reconsidered* (Montreal and Kingston, 1985). See also J.V. Wright, 'The Development of Prehistory in Canada', *American Antiquity*, 50 (1985), pp. 421-33. The standard overview of Canadian native peoples remains Diamond Jenness, *The Indians of Canada* (7th ed., Toronto, 1977), although readers are warned that his Eurocentrism is considerable. A number of surveys of the pre-contact period are available, including: Knut R. Fladmark, *British Columbia Prehistory* (Ottawa, 1986); James A. Tuck, *Maritime Provinces Prehistory* (Ottawa, 1984) and *Newfoundland and Labrador Prehistory* (Ottawa, 1976); Bryan H.C. Gordon, *Of Men and Herds in Barrenland Prehistory* (Ottawa, 1975); Moreau S. Maxwell, *Prehistory of the Eastern Arctic* (Orlando, Florida, 1985); J.V. Wright, *Quebec Prehistory* (Toronto, 1979), *Ontario Prehistory* (Ottawa, 1972), *Six Chapters of Canada's Prehistory* (Ottawa, 1976); George C. Frison, *Prehistoric Hunters of the High Plains* (New York, 1978); Robert McGhee, *Canadian Arctic Prehistory* (Toronto, 1978). Climate is obviously an important consideration for this period. A useful introduction is in R.A. Bryson and F.K. Hare, 'The Climates of North America', in R.A. Bryson and F.K. Hare, eds, *World Survey of Climatology*, II (Amsterdam, 1974); see also F.K. Hare and M.K. Thomas, *Climate Canada* (Toronto, 1979). For vegetation, see J.S. Rowe, *Forest Regions of Canada* (Ottawa, 1972) and J.C. Ritche, *Past and Present Vegetation of*

the Far Northwest of Canada (Toronto, 1984). Plates 1 to 15 (and their bibliographies) of Volume I of *Historical Atlas of Canada*, edited by R. Cole Harris (Toronto, 1989) are extremely useful, and all serious students of Canadian history should possess their own copy of this invaluable work.

Chapter Two: The Explorers of the Sixteenth and Seventeenth Centuries

The European discovery and exploration of North America is not a popular topic for current research. Most of the scholarly literature is quite old, although new syntheses and overviews constantly appear, and much interesting work is being done on the native perspective. There are several reasons for the relative neglect of this topic. One is the lack of new documentary material uncovered since the nineteenth century. Another is the currently fashionable tendency to see studies of explorers as old-fashioned at best, and hopelessly Eurocentric at worst. The Columbus celebrations in 1492 may provoke some further re-evaluations, but on the whole it is likely to concentrate along existing lines of criticism. For the latest interpretations of Canadian explorers, consult the early volumes of the *Dictionary of Canadian Biography* (Toronto, 1967-), which contains current bibliographies. The *DCB*, as it is commonly known, is organized by death date, thus major figures in this chapter and those that follow are supplied with birth and death dates to help orient the reader and facilitate further research. Among general studies, the following Canadian-oriented works are particularly useful and stimulating: J.B. Brebner, *The Explorers of North America, 1492-1806* (New York, 1933, 1955); Tryggvi J. Oleson, *Early Voyages and Northern Approaches: 1000-1632* (Toronto, 1963), although this work is regarded as idiosyncratic rather than synthetic by most scholars; Daniel Francis, *Discovery of the North: The Exploration of Canada's Arctic* (Edmonton, 1985); and L. Neatby, *In Quest of the Northwest Passage* (New York, 1958). A number of non-Canadian syntheses are also invaluable: Samuel Eliot Morison, *The European Discovery of America: The Northern Voyages A.D. 500-1600* (New York, 1971); David B. Quinn, *England and the Discovery of America, 1481-1620* (New York, 1973), and *North America from Earliest Discovery to First Settlements: The Norse Voyages to 1612* (New York, 1977). An invaluable study of early maps is B.G. Hoffman, *Cabot to Cartier: Sources for a Historical Ethnography of Northeastern North America 1497-1550* (Toronto, 1960). For a native perspective, Alfred G. Bailey's classic *The Conflict of European and Eastern Algonkian Cultures, 1504-1700: A Study in Canadian Civilization* (Sackville, 1937), is still useful. French interior exploration may be generally followed in W.J. Eccles, *The Canadian Frontier 1534-1760* (Revised edition, Albuquerque, 1983). The Radisson journals are available in an edition by Arthur T. Adams, *The Explorations of Pierre Esprit Radisson* (Minneapolis, 1961). Two wonderful coffee-table books, full of up-to-date scholarship and many maps and illustrations (often in colour), are W.P. Cumming et al., eds, *The Exploration of North America 1630-1776* (Toronto, 1974), and Fernand Braudel et al., *Le Monde de Jacques Cartier* (Montreal and Paris, 1984).

Chapter Three: Colonizers and Settlers in the Early Seventeenth Century

There is no full-length modern study that covers all early settlement in what is now Canada. But see D.C. Harvey, *The Colonization of Canada* (Toronto, 1936). On Newfoundland, consult Gillian Cell, *English Enterprise in Newfoundland 1577-1660* (Toronto, 1969), and her edition of documents entitled *Newfoundland Discovered: English Attempts at Colonisation, 1610-1630* (London, 1982). An overview of the

Maritime region in the seventeenth century is provided by John Reid in *Acadia, Maine, and New Scotland: Marginal Colonies in the Seventeenth Century* (Toronto, 1981). For New Scotland, see G.P. Insh, *Scottish Colonial Schemes, 1620-1686* (Glasgow, 1922). For Acadia, Andrew Hill Clark, *Acadia: The Geography of Early Nova Scotia to 1760* (Madison, Wisconsin, 1968), and M.A. MacDonald, *Fortune and La Tour* (Toronto, 1982). On early New France, Marcel Trudel, *The Beginnings of New France, 1524-1663* (Toronto, 1973). Champlain has been the subject of a number of biographies, including: N.-E. Dionne, *Champlain* (Toronto, 1906); Samuel Eliot Morison, *Samuel de Champlain: Father of New France* (Boston, 1972); and Joe C.W. Armstrong, *Champlain* (Toronto, 1987). H.P. Biggar edited *The Works of Samuel de Champlain*, (6 vols, Champlain Society, Toronto, 1936). Joyce Marshall edited *Word from New France: The Selected Letters of Marie de l'Incarnation* (Toronto, 1967). R.G. Thwaites edited *The Jesuit Relations and Allied Documents* (73 vols, Cleveland, 1896-1901). For the interaction between natives and Europeans, see Cornelius J. Jaenen, *Friend and Foe: Aspects of French-Amerindian Cultural Contact in the Sixteenth and Seventeenth Centuries* (New York, 1976). For the Hurons, Conrad Heidenreich, *Huronia: A History and Geography of the Huron Indians, 1600-1650* (Toronto, 1971); Bruce Trigger, *The Huron Farmers of the North* (New York, 1969) and *The Children of Aataentsic: A History of the Huron People to 1660* (Montreal, 1976).

Chapter Four: New France: War, Trade, and Adaptation

The history of New France was once a testing ground for arguments about the subsequent development of Canada, especially Quebec. The arguments can be followed in Dale Miquelon, ed., *Society and Conquest: The Debate on the Bourgeoisie and Social Change in French Canada, 1700-1850* (Toronto, 1977). In recent years, however, French-Canadian historians have largely neglected New France, and much of the good work has been done by historians writing in English. The best introduction to the colony remains Marcel Trudel's *Introduction to New France* (Toronto, 1968). The period from the royal takeover is covered sequentially in three volumes of the Canadian Centenary series, all of which have lengthy bibliographies: W.J. Eccles, *Canada Under Louis IV, 1663-1701* (Toronto, 1964); Dale Miquelon, *New France, 1701-1744: A Supplement to Europe* (Toronto, 1987); and George F.C. Stanley, *New France: The Last Phase, 1744-1760* (Toronto, 1968). Other useful works by Eccles include *Frontenac: The Courtier Governor* (Toronto, 1968) and *Essays on New France* (Toronto, 1987). On government, see Yves Zoltvany, ed., *The Government of New France: Royal, Clerical, or Class Rule* (Toronto, 1971). On the Church see Cornelius J. Jaenen, *The Role of the Church in New France* (Toronto, 1976). For the seigneurial system, R. Cole Harris, *The Seigneurial System in Early Canada: A Geographical Study* (Toronto, 1966). For the merchants, J.F. Bosher, *The Canada Merchants, 1713-1763* (Oxford, 1987). On Montreal, Louise Dechene, *Habitants et marchands de Montréal au XVIIe siècle* (Paris, 1974). Rural society in the mid-eighteenth century is discussed in Allan Greer, *Peasant, Lord, and Merchant: Rural Society in Three Quebec Parishes 1740-1840* (Toronto, 1985). The élite are treated in Cameron Nish, *Les bourgeois-gentilshommes de la Nouvelle-France, 1729-1748* (Montreal, 1968). A fascinating account of artisans is Peter Moogk's *Building a House in New France: An Account of the Perplexities of Client and Craftsmen in Early Canada* (Toronto, 1977).

Chapter Five: The Atlantic Region: the Cockpit of Empire, 1670-1758
The best overview of the complex international situation in northeastern North America is Max Savelle's *The Origins of American Diplomacy: The International History of Anglo-America, 1492-1763* (New York, 1967), which is judicious despite its national-istic title; the book also contains detailed bibliographies. From the Canadian perspec-tive, a brief but fascinating outline is provided by Ian K. Steele, *Guerillas and Grenadiers: The Struggle for Canada, 1689-1760* (Toronto, 1969). The matter of the imperial conflict is covered by Lawrence Henry Gipson, whose magisterial *The British Empire Before the American Revolution* ran to fifteen volumes (Caldwell, Idaho, 1936-1970). On Acadia, see John Bartlett Brebner, *New England's Outpost: Acadia before the Conquest of Canada* (New York, 1973), and Naomi E.S. Griffiths, *The Acadians: Creation of a People* (Toronto, 1973) and *The Contexts of Acadian History 1586-1784* (Montreal, 1992). The controversy over the expulsion may be followed in Griffiths' collection entitled *The Acadian Deportation: Deliberate Perfidy or Cruel Necessity* (Toronto, 1969). For Louisbourg, Bona Arsenault, *Louisbourg, 1713-1758*, and the award-winning *Louisbourg Portraits: Life in an Eighteenth-Century Garrison Town* (Kingston, 1984) by Christopher Moore. The American campaign of 1745 is treated in George Rawlyk, *Yankees at Louisbourg* (Orono, Maine, 1967). On the foundation of Halifax, Winthrop Pickard Bell, *The 'Foreign Protestants' and the Settlement of Nova Scotia: The History of a Piece of Arrested British Colonial Policy in the Eighteenth Century* (Toronto, 1961), and George T. Bates, 'The Great Exodus of 1749; or, The Cornwallis Settlers Who Didn't', in Nova Scotia Historical Society, *Collections*, XXXVIII (1973), pp. 27-62. On early Prince Edward Island, D.C. Harvey, *The French Regime on Prince Edward Island* (New Haven, 1926). On Newfoundland, Graham Head, *Eighteenth-Century Newfoundland: A Geographer's Perspective* (Toronto, 1976), and W. Gordon Handcock, *Soe Long as There Comes Noe Women: Origins of English Settlement in Newfoundland* (St John's, 1989). The standard work on early British Nova Scotia remains John Bartlett Brebner, *The Neutral Yankees of Nova Scotia: A Marginal Colony during the Revolutionary Years* (New York, 1937). But see also Graeme Wynn, 'A Province Too Much Dependent on New England', *Canadian Geographer*, XXXI (1987), pp. 98-113, and George Rawlyk, *Nova Scotia's Massachusetts: A Study of Massachusetts-Nova Scotia Relations 1630 to 1784* (Montreal, 1973). Indian policy and treatment are considered in L.F.S. Upton, *Micmacs and Colonists: Indian-White Relations in the Maritimes, 1713-1867* (Vancouver, 1979).

Chapter Six:
1759-1781 The Expansion and Contraction of Britain's North American Empire
For the military aspects of the Conquest, see C.P. Stacey, *Quebec, 1759: The Siege and the Battle* (Toronto, 1959), and Gordon Donaldson, *Battle for a Continent: Quebec 1759* (Toronto, 1973). On constitutional matters after 1759, Adam Shortt and Arthur G. Doughty, eds., *Documents Relating to the Constitutional History of Canada, 1759-1791* (Ottawa, 1907), which reprints most of the major documents. For the British debate over the retention of colonies, see my 'The "Canada-Guadeloupe" Debate and the Origins of the Grenville Programme for America', in *Man and Nature/L'Homme et la Nature*, V (1986), pp. 51-62. For the New England Yankees in Nova Scotia, M. Conrad, ed., *They Planted Well: New England Planters in Maritime Canada* (Fredericton, 1988) and *Making Adjustments: Change and Continuity in Planter*

Nova Scotia (Fredericton, 1991). For Americans in Quebec, Allan S. Everest, *Moses Hazen and the Canadian Refugees in the American Revolution* (Syracuse, NY, 1976). The Island of St John is treated in my *Land, Settlement, and Politics in Eighteenth-Century Prince Edward Island* (Montreal and Kingston, 1987). Quebec politics are covered in Hilda Neatby, *Quebec: The Revolutionary Age, 1760-1791* (Toronto, 1966), and the revolutionary period in Gustave Lanctot, *Canada and the American Revolution* (Cambridge, Mass., 1967). The invasion of Quebec is discussed from the Canadian perspective in George Stanley, *Canada Invaded, 1775-1776* (Toronto, 1973), and from the American in Robert Hatch, *Thrust for Canada: The American Attempt on Quebec in 1775-1776* (Boston, 1979). For Nova Scotia, see the Champlain Society edition of *The Diary of Simeon Perkins* (3 vols, Toronto, 1948-61): the first volume (1766-80) was edited by H.A. Innis; the second volume (1780-9) by D.C. Harvey and C. Bruce Fergusson; and Fergusson edited the third volume. See also my *Henry Alline 1748-1784* (Toronto, 1971) and Gordon Stewart and George Rawlyk, *A People Highly Favoured of God: The Nova Scotia Yankees and the American Revolution* (Toronto, 1972). For the Iroquois, Barbara Graymont, *The Iroquois in the American Revolution* (Syracuse, 1972). The West is treated in E.E. Rich, *The Fur Trade and the Northwest to 1857* (Toronto, 1967), and in Richard Ruggles, *A Country So Interesting: The Hudson's Bay Company and Two Centuries of Mapping* (Montreal, 1991). For Captain Cook, J.C. Beaglehole, *The Life of Captain James Cook* (Stanford, 1974), and Robin Fisher and Hugh Johnston, eds, *Captain James Cook and His Times* (Vancouver, 1979).

Chapter Seven: The New Immigrants: Peopling British North America, 1783-1845
On the Loyalists in general, see my *Understanding the Loyalists* (Sackville, 1986). See also Wallace Brown and Hereward Senior, *Victorious in Defeat: The Loyalists in Canada* (Toronto, 1984); Christopher Moore, *The Loyalists: Revolution, Exile, and Settlement* (Toronto, 1984); Neil MacKinnon, *This Unfriendly Soil: The Loyalist Experience in Nova Scotia, 1783-1791* (Kingston, 1986); Esther Clark Wright, *The Loyalists of New Brunswick* (Sackville, 1955); Larry Turner, *Voyage of a Different Kind: The Associated Loyalists of Kingston and Adolphustown* (Belleville, Ont., 1984); and Ann Condon, *The Envy of the American States: The Loyalist Dream for New Brunswick* (Fredericton, 1984). On Loyalist women, Mary Beth Norton, 'Eighteenth-Century American Women in Peace and War: The Case of the Loyalists', *William and Mary Quarterly*, 3rd ser., 33 (1976), pp. 386-409. For Indian Loyalists, Isabel T. Kelsay, *Joseph Brant, 1743-1807, Man of Two Worlds* (Syracuse, 1984). For Black Loyalists, consult James W. St G. Walker, *The Black Loyalists: The Search for a Promised Land in Nova Scotia and Sierra Leone, 1783-1870* (Halifax, 1976). On Shelburne, Marion Robertson, *King's Bounty: A History of Early Shelburne, Nova Scotia* (Halifax, 1983). Saint John is treated in David Bell, *Early Loyalist Saint John: The Origin of New Brunswick Politics, 1783-1786* (Fredericton, 1983). Kingston is considered in Jane Errington, *The Lion, the Eagle and Upper Canada: A Developing Colonial Ideology* (Kingston, 1987). On immigration in general, Helen T. Cowan, *British Immigration to British North America: The First Hundred Years* (rev. ed., Toronto, 1961); Norman Macdonald, *Canada, 1763-1841* (London, 1939); H.J.M. Johnston, *British Emigration Policy 1815-1830: 'Shovelling Out Paupers'* (Oxford, 1972). On the 'four nations' approach to British history, Hugh Kearney, *The British Isles: A History of Four Nations* (Cambridge, 1989). For the Irish, Bruce S. Elliott, *Irish Migrants in the Canadas: A New Approach* (Kingston, 1988); Donald Akenson, *The Irish in Ontario: A Study in Rural History* (Kingston, 1984);

Cecil J. Houston and William Smith, *Irish Emigration and Canadian Settlement: Patterns, Links, and Letters* (Toronto, 1990). For the Scots, see my *The Peoples' Clearance: Highland Emigration to British North America, 1770-1815* (Edinburgh, 1982) and my editions of *The Collected Letters and Papers of Lord Selkirk, 1799-1820* (2 vols, Winnipeg, 1984, 1988); and D. Campbell and R.A. MacLean, *Beyond the Atlantic Roar: A Study of the Nova Scotia Scots* (Toronto, 1974). For the Welsh, Peter Thomas, *Strangers from a Secret Land: The Voyages of the Brig Albion and the Founding of the First Welsh Settlements in Canada* (Toronto, 1986). On the English language, Robert McCrum et al., *The Story of English* (New York, 1986); on the French language, consult Mark M. Orkin, *Speaking Canadian French: An Informal Account of the French Language in Canada* (rev. ed., Toronto, 1971).

Chapter Eight: The Resource Economy and its Society, 1783-1840
Most of the material in this chapter is based on a synthesis of recent journal articles too numerous to list. For accessible samplings of this literature, see J.K. Johnson and Bruce G. Wilson, eds, *Historical Essays on Upper Canada: New Perspectives* (Toronto, 1989), and P.A. Buckner and David Frank, eds, *The Acadiensis Reader: Volume One, Second Edition: Atlantic Canada Before Confederation* (Fredericton, 1990). On the fishery, Harold A. Innis, *The Cod Fisheries: The History of an International Economy* (Toronto, 1954); E.T.D. Chambers, *The Fisheries of the Province of Quebec* (Quebec, 1912); and Roch Samson, *Fishermen and Merchants in Nineteenth-century Gaspé: The Fisherman-Dealers of William Hyman and Sons* (Ottawa, 1984). For the West and the fur trade, Eric Ross, *Beyond the River and the Bay: Some Observations on the State of the Canadian Northwest in 1811* (Toronto, 1970); Marjorie Wilkins Campbell, *The North West Company* (rev. ed., Vancouver, 1983); A.J. Ray, *Indians in the Fur Trade: Their Role as Trappers, Hunters, and Middlemen in the Lands Southwest of Hudson Bay, 1660-1870* (Toronto, 1974); J.S. Galbraith, *The Hudson's Bay Company as an Imperial Factor, 1821-1869* (Toronto, 1957); James R. Gibson, *Farming the Frontier: The Agricultural Opening of the Oregon Country, 1786-1846* (Vancouver, 1985); and Michael Payne, *The Most Respectable Place in the Territory: Everyday Life in Hudson's Bay Company Service: York Factory, 1788 to 1870* (Ottawa, 1989). On the timber industry, Graeme Wynn, *Timber Colony: A Historical Geography of Early Nineteenth Century New Brunswick* (Toronto, 1981); A.R.M. Lower, *Great Britain's Woodyard: British America and the Timber Trade, 1763-1867* (Montreal, 1973). On the commercial system of the St Lawrence, Donald Creighton, *The Empire of the St. Lawrence* (Toronto, 1956). On the wheat economy, John McCallum, *Unequal Beginnings: Agriculture and Economic Development in Quebec and Ontario until 1870* (Toronto, 1980). On Quebec, the various writings by Fernand Ouellet, especially *Economic and Social History of Quebec, 1760-1850: Structures and Conjectures* (Toronto, 1980). On merchants, Douglas McCalla, *The Upper Canada Trade 1834-1872: A Study of the Buchanan's Business* (Toronto, 1979), and L.R. Fischer and Eric Sager, eds, *The Enterprising Canadians: Entrepreneurs and Economic Development in Eastern Canada, 1820-1914* (St John's, 1979). On shipbuilding, see Eric Sager and L.R. Fischer, *Shipping and Shipbuilding in Atlantic Canada, 1820-1914* (Ottawa, 1986). On cities, T.W. Acheson, *Saint John: The Making of a Colonial Urban Community* (Toronto, 1985); Jean-Claude Marsan, *Montreal in Evolution: Historical Analysis of Montreal's Architecture and Urban Environment* (Montreal, 1981). For women, Peter Ward, *Courtship, Love and Marriage in Nineteenth-Century English Canada* (Montreal, 1990); Jennifer Brown, *Strangers in Blood: Fur Trade Company*

Families in Indian Country (Vancouver, 1980); and Sylvia Van Kirk, *Many Tender Ties: Women in Fur-Trade Society in Western Canada 1670-1870* (Winnipeg, 1980). For native peoples, J.R. Miller, *Skyscrapers Hide the Heavens: A History of Indian-white Relations in Canada* (Toronto, 1989). For a snapshot of Upper and Lower Canada in 1841, Eric Ross, *Full of Hope and Promise: The Canadas in 1841* (Montreal, 1991).

Chapter Nine: Politics and Culture, 1783-1840

On British colonial government, see Helen Taft Manning, *British Colonial Government After the American Revolution, 1782-1820* (New Haven, 1933). On the interaction between the imperial government and colonial governments, John Manning Ward, *Colonial Self-Government: The British Experience, 1759-1856* (London, 1976); Peter Burroughs, ed., *The Colonial Reformers and Canada, 1830-1849* (Toronto, 1969), and his *The Canadian Crisis and British Colonial Policy, 1828-1841* (Toronto, 1972); and Philip A. Buckner, *The Transition to Responsible Government: British Policy in British North America, 1815-1850* (Westport, Ct, 1985). For colonial politics, Gordon T. Stewart, *The Origins of Canadian Politics: A Comparative Approach* (Vancouver, 1986); John Garner, *The Franchise and Politics in British North America, 1755-1867* (Toronto, 1969); and David Mills, *The Idea of Loyalty in Upper Canada, 1784-1850* (Kingston, 1988). For the leaders of the Upper Canadian Family Compact, J.L.H. Henderson, ed., *John Strachan: Documents and Opinions* (Toronto, 1969); Davis Flint, *John Strachan: Pastor and Politician*, Canadian Lives (Toronto, 1971); Patrick Brode, *Sir John Beverley Robinson: Bone and Sinew of the Compact* (Toronto, 1984); J.E. Rea, *Bishop Alexander Macdonell and the Politics of Upper Canada* (Toronto, 1974). For studies of leading political reformers, William Kilbourn, *The Firebrand: William Lyon Mackenzie and the Rebellion in Upper Canada* (Toronto, 1964); David Flint, *William Lyon Mackenzie: Rebel Against Authority*, Canadian Lives (Toronto, 1971); J.M. Beck, *Joseph Howe*, 2 vols (Kingston, 1982-3). For the writings of these reformers, J.M. Beck, ed., *Joseph Howe, Voice of Nova Scotia: A Selection* (Toronto, 1964), and Margaret Fairley, ed., *The Selected Writings of William Lyon Mackenzie: 1824-1837* (Toronto, 1960). For complex legal reasons there is no good modern study of Louis-Joseph Papineau; but see Fernand Ouellet, *Louis-Joseph Papineau: A Divided Soul* (Ottawa, 1964). Other political figures can be read about in the *DCB*. On the rebellions, Colin Read and Ronald Stagg, eds., *The Rebellion of 1837 in Upper Canada: A Collection of Documents* (Toronto, 1985); Colin Read, *The Rising in Western Upper Canada, 1837-8: The Duncombe Revolt and After* (Toronto, 1982); Helen Taft Manning, *The Revolt of French Canada, 1800-1835* (Toronto, 1962); Fernand Ouellet, *Lower Canada, 1791-1840: Social Change and Nationalism* (Toronto, 1980). On Lord Durham and his Report, Janet Ajzenstat, *The Political Thought of Lord Durham* (Kingston, 1988); Reginald Lucas, ed., *Lord Durham's Report on the Affairs of British North America* (Oxford, 1912, 3 vols). On religion, Judith Fingard, *The Anglican Design in Loyalist Nova Scotia, 1783-1816* (London, 1972); John Moir, ed., *Church and State in Canada, 1627-1867: Basic Documents* (Toronto, 1967); Goldwin S. French, *Parsons and Politics: The Role of Wesleyan Methodists in Upper Canada and the Maritimes from 1780 to 1855* (Toronto, 1962); Jean-Pierre Wallot, *Un Québec qui bougeait: trame socio-politique du Québec au tournant du XIXe siècle* (Quebec, 1973), esp. pp. 183-224. On education, C. Bruce Sissons, *Church and State in Canadian Education: An Historical Study* (Toronto, 1959); Claude Galarneau, *Les Collèges Classiques au Canada Français (1620-1970)* (Montreal, 1978); and J. Donald Wilson, *Canadian Education: A History* (Toronto,

1970). On early Canadian literature, Carl T. Klinck, ed., *Literary History of Canada: Canadian Literature in English* (Toronto, 1976); William Toye, ed., *The Oxford Companion to Canadian Literature* (Toronto, 1983); Maurice Gagnon, *The French Novel of Quebec* (Boston, 1986); Ben-Z. Shek, *French-Canadian and Québécois Novels*, Perspectives on Canadian Literature (Toronto, 1991); and Jeanne d'Arc Lortie, *La poèsie nationaliste au Canada français, 1606-1867* (Quebec, 1975). For Haliburton, V.L.O. Chittick, *Thomas Chandler Haliburton ('Sam Slick'):A Study in Provincial Toryism* (New York, 1924); and Richard A. Davies, ed., *The Letters of Thomas Chandler Haliburton* (Toronto, 1988). Thomas McCulloch's *Letters of Mephiboseth Stepsure* are available in a new edition edited by Gwendolyn Davies (Ottawa, 1991). On the bards, Margaret Macdonell, *The Emigrant Experience: Songs of Highland Emigrants in North America* (Toronto, 1982). For painting, J. Russell Harper, *Painting in Canada: A History* (Toronto, 1977); Dennis Reid, *A Concise History of Canadian Painting* (2nd ed., Toronto, 1988). For architecture, Alan Gowans, *Building Canada: An Architectural History of Canadian Life* (Toronto, 1966). On the early writing of history, M. Brook Taylor, *Promoters, Patriots, and Partisans: Historiography in Nineteenth-Century English Canada* (Toronto, 1989). A useful recent work analysing the relationship between politics and society is S.J. Noel, *Patrons, Clients, Brokers: Ontario Society and Politics, 1791-1896* (Toronto, 1990).

Chapter Ten: Developing the Economy, 1840-1865
On the Grand Trunk Railway, see A.W. Currie, *The Grand Trunk Railway of Canada* (Toronto, 1957). On transportation in general, G.P. de T. Glazebrook, *A History of Transportation in Canada* (Toronto, 1938). For imperial trade, Bernard Semmel, *The Rise of Free Trade Imperialism: Classical Political Economy, the Empire of Free Trade and Imperialism 1750-1850* (Cambridge, England, 1970). For the Canadian response, Gilbert Tucker's old but still useful *The Canadian Commercial Revolution, 1845-1851* (New Haven, 1936). For the Reciprocity Treaty, D.C. Masters, *The Reciprocity Treaty of 1854* (London, 1937). On shipping, L.R. Fischer and Eric W. Sager, *Merchant Shipping and Economic Development in Atlantic Canada* (St John's, 1982). For T.C. Keefer, see H.V. Nelles, ed., *The Philosophy of Railroads and Other Essays by Thomas Keefer* (Toronto, 1972). On railroad politics, Donald R. Beer, *Sir Allan Napier MacNab* (Hamilton, 1984); and Brian Young, *Promoters and Politicians:The North Shore Railways in the History of Quebec, 1854-1885* (Toronto, 1978). On industrialization (not well covered in the literature), Ben Forster, *A Conjunction of Interests: Business, Politics, and Tariffs, 1825-1879* (Toronto, 1986); Donald C. Masters, *The Rise of Toronto, 1850-1890* (Toronto, 1947, 1974); Gerald Tulchinsky, *The River Barons: Montreal Businessmen and the Growth of Industry and Transportation, 1837-1853* (Toronto, 1977); and Michael B. Katz, *The Social Organization of Early Industrial Capitalism* (Cambridge, Mass., 1982). Labour's response is considered in G. Kealey, *Toronto Workers Respond to Industrial Capitalism 1867-1892* (Toronto, 1980). For Palliser, Irene M. Spry, *The Palliser Expedition:An Account of John Palliser's British North American Exploring Expedition, 1857-1860* (Toronto, 1963, 1973). There is no good study of the British Columbia gold rush, but see David R. Williams, *The Man for a New Country: Sir Matthew Baillie Begbie* (Sidney, B.C., 1977); and Dorothy B. Smith, *James Douglas: Father of British Columbia*, Canadian Lives (Toronto, 1971).

Chapter Eleven: Political Reform and Unification 1840-1867
The relevant volumes in the Centenary Series are J.M.S. Careless, *The Union of the Canadas:The Growth of Canadian Institutions, 1841-1857* (Toronto, 1967), and W.L. Morton, *The Critical Years:The Union of British North America, 1857-1873* (Toronto, 1964). On Quebec (Canada East), see Jacques Monet, *The Last Cannon Shot:A Study of French-Canadian Nationalism, 1837-1850* (Toronto, 1969). For Canada West, Donald Creighton, *John A. Macdonald*, vol. 1 (Toronto, 1952); Donald Swainson, *Sir John A. Macdonald:The Man and the Politician* (Kingston, 1989); J.M.S. Careless, *Brown of the Globe*, 2 vols (Toronto, 1959, 1963); B. Hodgins, *John Sandfield Macdonald, 1812-1872* (Toronto, 1971). On Newfoundland, Gertrude Gunn, *The Political History of Newfoundland, 1832-1864* (Toronto, 1966). For New Brunswick, W.S. MacNutt, *New Brunswick:A History, 1784-1867* (Toronto, 1963). For Nova Scotia, J.M. Beck, *Politics of Nova Scotia*, vol. I (Tantallon, N.S., 1985). On Confederation, consult W.M. Whitelaw, *The Maritimes and Canada Before Confederation* (2nd ed., Toronto, 1966); Ged Martin, ed., *The Causes of Canadian Confederation* (Fredericton, 1990); Donald Creighton, *The Road to Confederation:The Emergence of Canada, 1863-1867* (Toronto, 1964); Peter B. Waite, *The Life and Times of Confederation, 1864-1867: Politics, Newspapers, and the Union of British North America* (Toronto, 1962); A.I. Silver, *The French-Canadian Idea of Confederation, 1864-1900* (Toronto, 1982). For the debates over Confederation in Canada, *Parliamentary Debates on the Subject of the Confederation of the British North American Provinces* (Ottawa, 1951), misleadingly titled since it includes only the debates in the Province of Canada. For the various provinces and Confederation, Francis W. Bolger, *Prince Edward Island and Confederation, 1863-1873* (Charlottetown, 1964); William M. Baker, *Timothy Warren Anglin, 1822-96: Irish Catholic Canadian* (Toronto, 1977); James Hiller and Peter Neary, eds, *Newfoundland in the Nineteenth and Twentieth Centuries: Essays in Interpretation* (Toronto, 1980); and Kenneth Pryke, *Nova Scotia and Confederation: 1864-1874* (Toronto, 1979).

Chapter Twelve: Mid-Victorian Society
For Elizabeth Smith, see Veronica Strong-Boag, ed., *A Woman with a Purpose: The Diaries of Elizabeth Smith 1872-1884* (Toronto, 1980). On emigration and migration, Bruce Elliott, *Irish Migrants in the Canadas:A New Approach* (Kingston, 1988); Cecil Houston and William Smyth, *Irish Emigration and Canadian Settlement: Patterns, Links, and Letters* (Toronto, 1990); Marjory Harper, *Emigration from North-East Scotland*, 2 vols (Aberdeen, 1988); Norman Macdonald, *Canada: Immigration and Colonization, 1841-1903* (Toronto, 1966); J.I. Little, *Nationalism, Capitalism and Colonization in Nineteenth-Century Quebec:The Upper St. Francis District* (Kingston, 1989); Yves Roby, *Les Franco-Américains de la Nouvelle-Angleterre, 1776-1930* (Sillery, 1990); Raymond Breton and Pierre Savard, eds, *The Quebec and Acadian Diaspora in North America* (Toronto, 1982); Frances H. Early, ed., *Immigrant Odyssey:A French-Canadian Habitant in New England* (Orono, Me., 1991); David Gagan, *Hopeful Travellers: Families, Land, and Social Change in Mid-Victorian Peel County, Canada West* (Toronto, 1981); Patricia A. Thornton, 'The Problem of Out-Migration from Atlantic Canada, 1871-1921: A New Look', in P.A. Buckner and David Frank, eds, *The Acadiensis Reader*, II (Fredericton, 1988), pp. 34-65; and Alan Brookes, 'The Golden Age and the Exodus: The Case of Canning, Kings County', *Acadiensis*, xi, 1 (Autumn 1982), pp. 57-82. For Quebec developments, Jean Hamelin and Yves Roby, *Histoire économique du*

Québec, 1851-1896 (Montreal, 1971); Gabriel Dussault, *Le Curé Labelle: Messianisme, utopie, et colonisation au Québec, 1850-1900* (Montreal, 1983); René Hardy and Normand Seguin, *Forêt et société en Maurice: La Formation de la région de Trois-Rivières, 1830-1930* (Montreal, 1984); and Serge Courville and Normand Seguin, *Rural Life in Nineteenth-Century Quebec* (Ottawa, 1989). For James Thomson, see Richard A. Preston, ed., *For Friends at Home: A Scottish Emigrant's Letters from Canada, California, and the Cariboo, 1844-1864* (Montreal, 1974). On businessmen, Aline Gubbay, *Montreal: The Mountain and the River* (Montreal, 1981); and Jo L. Santink, *Timothy Eaton and the Rise of His Department Store* (Toronto, 1990). On Victorian cities, Michael Katz, *The People of Hamilton, Canada West: Family and Class in a Mid-Nineteenth-Century City* (Cambridge, Mass., 1975); Peter Goheen, *Victorian Toronto, 1850-1900* (Chicago, 1970); Warwick T. Hatton, *A Feast of Gingerbread from Our Victorian Past* (Montreal, 1976). On the office revolution, Graham S. Lowe, *Women in the Administrative Revolution: The Feminization of Clerical Work* (Toronto, 1987). On Indians, Sarah Carter, *Lost Harvests: Prairie Indian Reserve Farmers and Government Policy* (Montreal, 1990). On blacks, Robin Winks, *The Blacks in Canada: A History* (Montreal, 1971). On the Chinese, Edgar Wickberg, ed., *From China to Canada: A History of the Chinese Communities in Canada* (Toronto, 1982). For women, Beth Light and Joy Parr, eds, *Canadian Women on the Move, 1867-1920* (Toronto, 1983); Susan Jackel, ed., *A Flannel Shirt and Liberty: British Emigrant Gentlewomen in the Canadian West, 1880-1914* (Vancouver, 1982); Joy Parr, *The Gender of Breadwinners: Women, Men, and Change in Two Industrial Towns, 1880-1950* (Toronto, 1990). For servants, Claudette Lacellie, *Urban Domestic Servants in 19th-Century Canada* (Ottawa, 1987). On the Orange Order, Cecil Houston and William Smyth, *The Sash Canada Wore: A Historical Geography of the Orange Order in Canada* (Toronto, 1980). On music, Dale McIntosh, *History of Music in British Columbia 1850-1950* (Victoria, 1989); Helmut Kallmann, *A History of Music in Canada, 1534-1914* (Toronto, 1987). For sports, Don Morrow et al., *A Concise History of Sport in Canada* (Toronto, 1989), and Alan Metcalfe, *Canada Learns to Play: The Emergence of Organized Sport 1807-1911* (Toronto, 1987).

Chapter Thirteen: The Completion of Confederation

For the first Riel rebellion, W.L. Morton, ed., *Alexander Begg's Red River Journal: and Other Papers Relative to the Red River Resistance of 1869-1870* (Toronto, 1956), and his edition of *Manitoba: the Birth of a Province* (reprinted Winnipeg, 1986); George F.G. Stanley, *Louis Riel* (Toronto, 1963); and Hartwell Bowsfield, *Louis Riel: The Rebel and the Hero*, Canadian Lives (Toronto, 1971). For British Columbia, Margaret A. Ormsby, *British Columbia: A History* (Toronto, 1958) and D.B. Smith, ed., *The Reminiscences of Doctor John Sebastian Helmcken* (Vancouver, 1975). For the Métis, D.N. Sprague, *Canada and the Métis, 1869-1885* (Waterloo, 1988), and Thomas Flanagan, *Métis Lands in Manitoba* (Calgary, 1991). On cultural nationalism, Dennis Reid, *'Our Own Country Canada': Being an Account of the National Aspirations of the Principal Landscape Artists in Montreal and Toronto 1860-1890* (Ottawa, 1979); and Suzanne Zeller, *Inventing Canada: Early Victorian Science and the Idea of a Transcontinental Nation* (Toronto, 1987). On racism, which was hardly confined to the west coast but was only most obvious to contemporaries there, see Patricia Roy, *A White Man's Province: British Columbia Politicians and Chinese and Japanese Immigrants, 1858-1914* (Vancouver, 1989).

General Bibliography

Among the works that do not fit into neat chronological pigeon-holes, readers should familiarize themselves with the riches of information in the multi-volumed *Dictionary of Canadian Biography* (Toronto, 1967-). They should also appreciate the magnificent new *Historical Atlas of Canada*, two volumes of which have been published: *Volume I, From the Beginning to 1800* (Toronto, 1987), edited by R. Cole Harris, and *Volume III, Addressing the Twentieth Century, 1891-1961* (Toronto, 1990), edited by Donald Kerr and Deryck W. Holdsworth. *The Encyclopedia of Canada: Second Edition* (Edmonton, 1988) is a useful guide. Middle-level synthesis (between the survey and the monograph) has never been one of Canadian historiography's strong suits, but there are a few good works. On Canada in the world, see R.T. Naylor, *Canada in the European Age, 1453-1919* (Vancouver, 1987). On Canadian business, Michael Bliss, *Northern Enterprise: Five Centuries of Canadian Business* (Toronto, 1987). An overall view of economic development is to be found in William L. Marr and Donald G. Paterson, *Canada: An Economic History* (Toronto, 1980), and in Kenneth Norrie and Douglas Owram, *A History of the Canadian Economy* (Toronto, 1991). For women, see Alison Prentice et al., *Canadian Women: A History* (Toronto, 1988). On the constitution, G.F.G. Stanley, *A Short History of the Canadian Constitution* (Toronto, 1969). On politics, David Bell and Lorne Tepperman, *The Roots of Disunity: A Look at Canadian Political Culture* (Toronto, 1979). For Indians, J.R. Miller, ed., *Sweet Promises: A Reader on Indian-White Relations in Canada* (Toronto, 1991). On Quebec thinking, Denis Monière, *Ideologies in Quebec: The Historical Development* (Toronto, 1981). For education, J. Donald Wilson et al., *Canadian Education: A History* (Scarborough, Ont., 1970). For Canadian-American relations, Edelgard E. Mahant and Graham Mount, *An Introduction to Canadian-American Relations* (Toronto, 1984), and J.L. Granatstein and Norman Hillmer, *For Better or Worse: Canada and the United States to the 1990s* (Toronto, 1991). Much good work has been done on provincial history. I particularly recommend John Chadwick, *Newfoundland: Island into Province* (Cambridge, 1967); F.W.P. Bolger, *Island into Province* (Charlottetown, 1973); W. Stewart MacNutt, *New Brunswick, a History: 1784-1867* (Toronto, 1984); Susan M. Trofimenkoff, *A Dream of Nation: A Social and Intellectual History of Quebec* (Toronto, 1983); Joseph Schull, *Ontario Since 1867*

(Toronto, 1978), and Robert Bothwell, *A Short History of Ontario* (Toronto, 1986); W.L. Morton, *Manitoba: A History* (Toronto, 1957); John Archer, *Saskatchewan: A History* (Saskatoon, 1980); Howard Palmer with Tamara Palmer, *Alberta: A New History* (Edmonton, 1990); Margaret Ormsby, *British Columbia: A History* (Toronto, 1958), and Jean Barman, *The West Beyond the West; A History of British Columbia* (Toronto, 1991).

Index